DMITRI DONSKOI

VASILI I
1389–1425

IURI

VASILI II
1425–62

VASILI   DMITRI

IVAN III, "The Great"   SOPHIA PALEOLOGA
1462–1505

IVAN
d. 1490

VASILI III
1505–33

D0282465

TSARS OF RUSSIA, 1547–1917

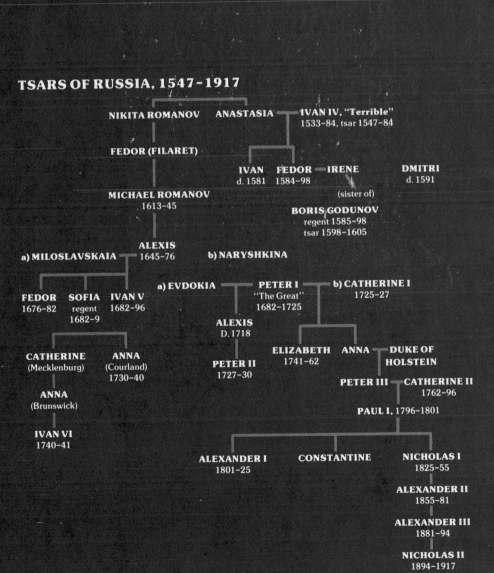

NIKITA ROMANOV   ANASTASIA   IVAN IV, "Terrible"
1533–84, tsar 1547–84

FEDOR (FILARET)

IVAN   FEDOR   IRENE   DMITRI
d. 1581   1584–98   d. 1591

MICHAEL ROMANOV   (sister of)
1613–45

BORIS GODUNOV
regent 1585–98
tsar 1598–1605

ALEXIS
a) MILOSLAVSKAIA   1645–76   b) NARYSHKINA

a) EVDOKIA   PETER I   b) CATHERINE I
"The Great"   1725–27
1682–1725

FEDOR   SOFIA   IVAN V
1676–82   regent   1682–96
1682–9

ALEXIS
D. 1718

CATHERINE   ANNA
(Mecklenburg)   (Courland)
1730–40

PETER II
1727–30

ELIZABETH   ANNA   DUKE OF
1741–62   HOLSTEIN

ANNA
(Brunswick)

PETER III   CATHERINE II
1762–96

IVAN VI
1740–41

PAUL I, 1796–1801

ALEXANDER I   CONSTANTINE   NICHOLAS I
1801–25   1825–55

ALEXANDER II
1855–81

ALEXANDER III
1881–94

NICHOLAS II
1894–1917

A History of Russia and the Soviet Union

The Dorsey Series in European History

Consulting Editor
GENE A. BRUCKER
University of California, Berkeley

A History of Russia and the Soviet Union

David MacKenzie
Department of History
The University of North Carolina
  at Greensboro

and

Michael W. Curran
Department of History
The Ohio State University

1977

THE DORSEY PRESS   Homewood, Illinois   60430
Irwin-Dorsey Limited   Georgetown, Ontario   L7G 4B3

© THE DORSEY PRESS, 1977

First Printing, March 1977

ISBN 0-256-01934-7
Library of Congress Catalog Card No. 76–47729
Printed in the United States of America

To Bruce, Bryan, and Brendan MacKenzie;
To Sara and Elizabeth Curran;
and
In memory of Peter F. Curran

Preface

To WRITE a one-volume history of Russia and the Soviet Union is difficult because of the length and complexity of that history. Should one
concentrate perhaps on the story of the Great Russian people around
Moscow or deal at length with other eastern Slavs (Ukrainians and
Belorussians) and non-Slavic peoples of the present USSR? We decided to emphasize the Great Russian core of tsarist and Soviet Russia
while seeking to trace the role of other peoples that contributed to Russian development. Instead of attempting a comprehensive study of the
various peoples and nationalities of the USSR, we have introduced them
as they affected the Russian core. Believing (unlike some Ukrainian
historians) that Kievan Russia was linked indissolubly with the subsequent history of Muscovy and the Russian Empire and comprised the
first major phase of Russian history, we do not deny that major historical and cultural influences differentiated Great Russians from
Ukrainians and Belorussians.

We find the Soviet scheme of periodization based on Marxism-Leninism challenging and sometimes illuminating. Marxism teaches that
mankind has passed through a series of well-defined socioeconomic
stages (primitive communism, slavery, feudalism, and capitalism) on
a road leading inevitably to communism, each stage representing a different and more advanced mode of production and conflict between a
ruling and a subject class. We reject the Marxist tendency to force facts
and trends of Russian history into rigid preconceived patterns and deny
that socioeconomic change must precede or determine political change.
To designate, as do Soviet historians, all of Russian history from 860
to 1861 as "feudalism" we find untenable, although undeniably the Russian economy and political system then contained feudal features. We
find more satisfying a periodization combining geographical and chrono-
logical factors, that is, Ancient, Kievan, Muscovite, Imperial, and Soviet
eras, though no single scheme of dividing Russian history into periods
seems wholly satisfactory.

We follow a middle course between the geographical determinism of
the Eurasian school and the organic, inner-oriented approach of Soviet
and many 19th century Russian historians. Much of earlier Russian
history may be viewed as interaction or conflict between forest and

steppe peoples, but the growth of mass urban industrial society has largely neutralized this factor. To view Russia, as the Eurasians do, as a continuous plain covering much of eastern Europe and northern Asia seems valid, but Siberia's role in Russian development was minimal until the 19th century. External influences upon Russia's evolution— Scandinavian, Byzantine, Asiatic, west European, and recently North American—have been important, but we agree with the organic school that such factors have not deflected Russia from her path nor determined her internal development. Russia is neither Europe nor Asia, though it has derived important values and institutions from each; like China, Russia remains essentially a world of its own, absorbing and integrating various external elements into a distinctive blend of the Oriental and the Western. Russia remains a bridge between East and West.

This book has been conceived out of love for Russia and its people and the desire to convey this to college students who often have little idea of Russia's sufferings and contributions to humanity. To introduce the student to major controversies and stimulate him or her to probe more deeply we have included ten problems that present contrasting views and interpretations of key events. Since Western textbooks on Russian history have often slighted Soviet research and viewpoints, we have included Soviet interpretations throughout. While sometimes rejecting our Soviet colleagues' theories and approaches, we recognize and respect their knowledge and contributions.

The authors have tried to present a balanced account: to do justice to often neglected Kiev and Muscovy as well as to the history of imperial Russia and the USSR. Social, economic, religious, and cultural developments—mostly described by Mr. Curran—have been included as well as more traditional political, diplomatic, and military history—written by Mr. MacKenzie. Seeking to write directly and straightforwardly for the present college generation and interested lay reader, we hope that they will suggest improvements.

February 1977   DAVID MACKENZIE
                                        MICHAEL W. CURRAN

Acknowledgments

To all those who taught me Russian history I owe a profound debt of gratitude and without their inspiration I could not have written this book. I wish to express heartfelt thanks to Boris Miller of Stuttgart, West Germany, my first teacher in the Russian language and history, who encouraged me to devote myself to study the Russian experience. At the Russian Institute of Columbia University I had the good fortune to study with Philip E. Mosely, G. T. Robinson, Henry L. Roberts, and John Hazard. Samuel Baron, David Griffiths, E. Willis Brooks, and John Keep contributed their expert advice and suggestions on individual chapters of this work. They, of course, are not responsible for the errors which it may contain. Extended visits to the USSR in 1958–59 and 1966 under the auspices of the Inter-University Committee on Travel Grants provided me with essential first-hand exposure to Russia and the opportunity to do research in Soviet libraries and archives. Finally, without the patience and self-sacrifice of my wife, Patricia, this volume could not have been written.—DAVID MACKENZIE

While it is not possible to acknowledge all those who have contributed to this endeavor, I do wish to recognize some of the most important. I owe a very special debt of gratitude to those who first introduced me to Russia and to Russian history: Michael B. Petrovich of the University of Wisconsin and Werner Philipp of the Free University of Berlin. Their knowledge of Russia and their scholarly enthusiasm have been a source of inspiration over many years. My brief association with the late George C. Soulis did much to shape my views of Russian history. Special thanks are due my colleagues at The Ohio State University: Arthur E. Adams, Charles Morley, and Myron W. Hedlin. Their criticisms, encouragement, and constant stimulation are reflected in this volume. I hasten to add that any shortcomings and errors contained in this study are entirely my own. I also wish to express my thanks to the Inter-University Committee on Travel Grants and to the Ministry of Higher and Specialized Secondary Education of the USSR which together provided me with two periods of extended study and research in the USSR in 1962–63 and in 1966. The contributions of my wife Marie-Luise Petersen Curran are too numerous to recount; suffice it to say that without her patience, understanding, and encouragement this work would never have been completed.—MICHAEL W. CURRAN

Finally, we wish to acknowledge the invaluable assistance of Gene Brucker, Daniel R. Brower, Joan Hall, Herbert H. Kaplan, James Long, Robert H. McNeal, Thomas S. Noonan, Walter M. Pintner, and Charles Timberlake, who read through and criticized all or parts of the manuscript while it was being prepared for publication. Their advice and comments improved the final product considerably, but naturally any mistakes or shortcomings which remain are ours, not theirs.

A Note on Russian Dates, Names, Measures, and Money

Dating Russian events has been complicated by the use in Russia until 1918 of "Old Style" dates of the Julian calendar which in the 18th century were 11 days behind those of the Gregorian calendar employed in the West. In the 19th century the lag was 12 days and in the 20th 13 days. Early in 1918 the Soviet regime adopted the "New Style" Gregorian calendar. Generally, here dates have been rendered according to the calendar utilized in Russia at the time, except that we have shifted to "New Style" dates beginning with 1917.

Transliterating Russian names into English likewise presents some peculiar problems. We have adhered largely to the Library of Congress system but have omitted diacritical marks for the sake of simplicity. Most Russian first names have been replaced with English equivalents, such as Peter, Nicholas, and Catherine, but not John and Basil instead of Ivan and Vasili.

Russian weights, measures, and distances have been rendered in their English equivalents for the convenience of English-speaking readers. However, Russian rubles have been retained with indications of their dollar value. The ruble, containing 100 kopeks, was worth about 50 cents in 1914. The official value of the Soviet ruble in 1975 was about $1.20.

Contents

part III
Modern Russia, 1855 to the Present

List of Maps

part I

Early Russia To 1689

THIS SECTION describes the origins of Russia from the dawn of recorded history to the accession of Peter the Great in the late 17th century. We begin with the migrations of peoples from Asia before the birth of Christ, the struggle between inhabitants of the steppe and the forest regions, and the formation of the Russian people. The controversial establishment of Kievan Russia and its institutions late in the 9th century is described, followed by a description of Russia's fragmentation that began c. 1139, and the devastating Mongol invasion in the 13th century. There follows the rise of Moscow in the 14th century, the unification of Great Russia in the 15th and 16th centuries, and the development of autocratic monarchy under Ivan III and Ivan IV. The end of this Muscovite dynasty in 1598 touches off a Time of Troubles; then during the 17th century the early Romanovs succeed in consolidating absolutism and serfdom and expanding Muscovy into a great empire spanning half the globe.

1

Introduction

To PLACE Russian history in proper context, one must comprehend the underlying geographical, climatic, and ethnic factors. The peoples of what is now the Union of Soviet Socialist Republics (USSR) commonly called the Soviet Union have been shaped by their natural environment and have responded in distinctive ways to its challenges. These responses have made Russia and the Soviet Union significantly different from the United States or the countries of western Europe.

GEOGRAPHY

The Soviet Union, of which Russia comprises about three-fourths the area and over half the population, is a huge country almost three times the size of the United States and about equal in area to all of North America. Spanning most of eastern Europe and northern Asia, it extends about 6,000 miles east to west and over 3,000 miles north to south to include about one sixth the land area of the globe. By its vastness and location the Soviet Union is in a position to dominate the combined land mass of Europe and Asia called Eurasia.

Most of the USSR is a huge plain extending eastward from Poland almost to the Pacific Ocean. Narrowing as one moves across Siberia, it runs out in the plateau and mountainous terrain of eastern Siberia. This expanse is barely interrupted by the low, worn Ural Mountains (maximum height 6,214 feet) which divide Europe from Asia only in part. Between the Urals and the Caspian Sea to the southwest is a gap some 800 miles wide through which successive waves of Asiatic invaders poured into Europe until the 13th century. Impressive mountain ranges are limited to the frontiers: the Carpathians in the southwest, the Caucasus to the south and the Pamir, Tien-Shan and Altai mountains on the borders of Afghanistan, India, and China. European Russia, where the main drama of Russian history has been played, is mostly flat and low. The Valdai Hills, a plateau in the northwest where the great European Russian rivers rise, reaches a maximum elevation of only 1,000 feet above sea level.

Flowing slowly through the European Russian plain, the rivers have served throughout history as arteries of communication and commerce. The Northern Dvina and Pechora flow northward into the Arctic basin; most of the others flow southward: the Dniester, Bug, Dnieper and Don into the Black Sea and the Sea of Azov, and the majestic "mother" Volga, comparable in breadth and importance to the Mississippi, into the Caspian Sea. These rivers and their tributaries form an excellent water communications system, greatly improved in modern times by connecting canals. In Siberia (the region east of the Urals and north of Central Asia) the Ob, Lena, Enisei and Kolyma rivers, moving northward into the frozen Arctic, are of limited commercial value. Only the Amur, part of the modern boundary with China, moves eastward into the Pacific.

The climate of the Soviet Union is continental, that is, marked by extremes of heat and cold. Most of Russia lies in the latitudes of Canada and Alaska. The Gulf Stream which moderates the climate of the east coast of the United States and the northwest coast of western Europe, affects only the western part of the north Russian coast from Murmansk to Archangel. Extremes of temperature generally increase as one moves eastward, but even in European Russia there are no internal mountain barriers to keep icy winds from sweeping to the Black Sea. Northeast Siberia is one of the world's coldest regions: temperatures as low as −90° F have been recorded in Verkhoiansk region. However, heat waves occur in European Russia and even Siberia during the summer. In the Central Asian deserts temperatures of 120° F are not uncommon. Precipitation in the USSR, partly because of the continental climate, is generally moderate or light and often greatest in summer.

There are five major soil and vegetation zones in the USSR, stretching generally northeast to southwest. About 15 percent of the country in the extreme north is level or undulating treeless plain, called tundra, and 47 percent of it has permanently frozen subsoil. The tundra, a virtually uninhabited wasteland, has many lakes and swamps, with moss and low shrubs the only vegetation. South of it lies the taiga, or coniferous forest in the north and mixed coniferous and deciduous forest further south. This vast forest belt, the largest in the world, extends clear across Russia and covers over half its territory. The poor ashy soils, called *podzol,* of the boggy coniferous forest with their low acid content are mostly unfit for crops. Agriculture is possible only in cleared portions of the southern forest region. The mixed forest zone to the south, the heart of Muscovite Russia, has richer gray and brown soils. Below this the forest shades into wooded steppe or meadow, mostly with very fertile black soil (*chernozem*), excellent for grains wherever there is sufficient rainfall. Still further south is mostly treeless prairie like the American Great Plains, extending monotonously for hundreds and hundreds of miles, also a fertile black soil region. East of the Caspian Sea this black soil shades into semidesert, then true desert to the south and east. In the Crimea and along the Caucasian shore of the Black Sea lies a small subtropical region, Russia's Riviera. Early frosts, a short growing season, and barren or frozen soil mean that only about ten percent of the Soviet Union is under cultivation, although one third is potentially arable. In some regions with rich soil rainfall is often insufficient for crops. Even the black soil region of the southern steppe has a shorter growing season than the American plains.

How has geography affected Russia's history? Until the late 19th century chiefly European Russia should be considered. Siberia remained sparsely populated, its great resources unexploited; Central Asia and the Caucasus were acquired only in the 19th century. European Russia's flat plains fostered colonization and expansion, persistent themes in Russian history for almost 1,000 years. Unworried by waste, Russians cleared forest glades and ploughed up virgin steppe lands. In the 19th century a continental colonialism developed as the Russians occupied areas next to their borders.

Geography has provided the USSR with natural ocean frontiers on the north and east and mountain boundaries in the south and southwest. These frontiers were attained after centuries of struggle with Asian invaders and by Russian outward expansion. In the west such natural barriers were lacking. In modern history foreign invasions of Russia have come from the west, and Russian efforts at expansion have focused there. Until recently Russia was largely landlocked without ready access to warm water ports or to foreign markets. Some historians, such as R. J. Kerner, have interpreted Russian expansion as a drive to secure such ports and unfettered access to the Pacific, Baltic, Black, and Mediterranean seas. Vast distances, while contributing to the eventual defeat or absorption of invaders, have complicated the achievement or maintenance of unity and perhaps have promoted highly centralized, authoritarian regimes. The severe climate of the north and Siberia contributed to easy Russian conquest of those regions.

THE PEOPLES

Within the USSR live almost 180 distinct nationalities and tribes speaking about 125 languages and dialects and practicing 40 different religions. Ninety-five groups number over 100,000 persons each; 54 have their own national territories. About three fourths of the Soviet population are eastern Slavs, divided into three major groups. Russians, or Great Russians, comprising about half the total population, inhabit chiefly northern and central European Russia and Siberia and major cities elsewhere. Great Russians, developing in the region around Moscow, are the dominant people who built the Russian Empire and the Soviet Union. Ukrainians, or Little Russians, numbering more than 40 million, live mainly in southern European Russia and speak a variant of Russian, now a separate Slav language. Belorussians, or White Russians, numbering more than 9 million, reside in the west adjacent to Poland and speak a dialect of Russian. These Eastern Slavs are mostly Greek Orthodox whereas the Poles, some of whom live in the extreme west, are Roman Catholic. The more than 20 million Turco-Tatars are chiefly descendants of Mongol and Turkic warriors who conquered Russia in the 13th century and were overrun in the subsequent Russian advance eastward. They include Crimean and Kazan Tatars, Bashkirs and Chuvash in the Volga basin, and Azerbaijani of the Caucasus. Most of them, including Uzbeks, Turkmens, Kazakhs, and Kirgizians, live in Central Asia. Most Turco-Tatars are Moslems, and Islam is the USSR's second most important religion. The Japhetic peoples of Transcaucasia (Armenians, Georgians, Abkhazians etc.) number some 8 million. Some 5 million Finno-Ugrians (Finns, Karelians, Estonians, Mordovians, and others), also believed to be of Asiatic origin, reside in western European Russia. The 4 million Balts (Latvians and Lithuanians) were incorporated involuntarily into the USSR together with the Estonians in 1940. Jews, still numbering more than 2 million, mostly inhabit cities of southern and western European Russia. In Siberia smaller peoples and tribes, many of Mongolian origin, live along rivers and coasts. Unlike the United States, a melting pot for diverse national and racial groups, the Soviet Union has preserved distinct national territories and languages.

CHALLENGE AND RESPONSE

Location, climate, and topography have confronted the Russian people with severe challenges during a difficult, turbulent history. Until recently Russia, and the USSR, was a poor country where most people extracted a precarious living from the soil. Poverty, vulnerability to attack, and poor interior communications helped produce responses distinguishing Russian history and culture in important ways from those of western Europe and the United States. The chief responses to peculiar Russian conditions and problems seem to have been autocracy, collectivism, and mysticism; these may provide keys to unlock the complex Russian past. The first two, especially, have persisted regardless of regime or ideology as vital elements of the Russian experience.

Autocracy, or statism, appeared first during the unification of Great Russia about 1500 and has persisted in the form of a monarchical or Communist state with a virtual monopoly of power, except for a few brief "times of trouble" (1598–1613 and 1917–21). Institutions which challenged its authority, such as town assemblies and noble councils, were gradually stripped of influence and disappeared. Principalities such as Novgorod and Pskov, which continued the political diversity and limited rule of the Kievan era, were conquered and absorbed by the expanding Muscovite state. Growing more powerful and pervasive with time, autocracy mobilized Russia's natural and human resources to resist external invasions, conquer contiguous areas, and, in the Soviet period, created formidable industrial and military power. Autocracy absorbed parts of the Byzantine and Mongol political traditions and used the principle of service to the state to subordinate to its dictates both the bodies and the minds of individuals.

Collectivism, which contrasts with the individualism prevalent in western Europe and the United States, has been another Russian response linked closely with autocracy. For centuries under tsars and commissars alike most land in Russia has been held and worked in common, and taxes were gathered and paid collectively by village communities. Collectivism aided Muscovy, the Russian Empire and finally Soviet Russia to mobilize resources to combat severe external challenges. The collectivism inherent in the Great Russian repartitional commune of the 18th century foreshadowed that of the Soviet collective and state farms in our own era. About 1600 autocracy helped subject a semifree Russian peasantry to the collective bondage of serfdom, a degrading but vital feature of Russian life until the 1860s.

Finally, the prevalent mysticism of the Russian Orthodox tradition and the relative lack of intellectual inquiry within the Orthodox Church differed greatly from the rationalism and questioning in western Catholic and Protestant faiths. In Muscovite Russia matters such as the spelling of the name of Jesus and elements of ritual and tradition acquired vast significance for a superstitious populace. The prevalent belief that Russia was the center of the only true faith tended to intensify suspicion of foreigners and their institutions. In a sense Soviet Communism, despite a theoretically antithetical ideology, continued this mystical tradition. Until World War II Soviet spokesmen reiterated that the USSR was the only land of socialism and center of the true Marxist faith. Xenophobia, extreme fear of foreigners, persisted and was reinforced deliberately by the Soviet regime.

To be sure, the roles and personalities of rulers, tsarist and Soviet, have been important in shaping Russian history and provide a convenient, if not always revealing method of dividing Russian history into periods. Such major figures as Ivan the Great, Ivan the Terrible, Peter the Great and Catherine the Great in the tsarist epoch and Lenin and Stalin in the Soviet period stand out above the flood of events. But unless one accepts the "great man" theory of history, to view an era through the career and character of the ruler exaggerates the importance of personal leadership and oversimplifies complex and continuing trends. Instead, the authors urge the student to trace major themes such as Autocracy, Collectivism and Mysticism through Russia's lengthy and colorful history.

Suggested Additional Reading

GEOGRAPHY

ADAMS, ARTHUR et al.   *An Atlas of Russian and East European History* (New York, 1967).

CHEW, ALLEN.   *An Atlas of Russian History* (New Haven, 1970).

GOODALL, GEORGE.   *The Soviet Union in Maps* (London, 1942) (Brief but excellent).

LYDOLPH, P. E.   *Geography of the USSR* (New York, 1964).

PARKER, W. H.   *An Historical Geography of Russia* (London, 1968).

GEOPOLITICAL FACTORS

Dow, ROGER.   "Prostor: A Geopolitical Study of Russia and the United States," in R. A. Goldwin, ed. *Readings in Russian Foreign Policy* (New York 1959).

HARCAVE, SIDNEY.   *Readings in Russian History.* 2 vols. (New York, 1962), I, nos. 1–3.

KERNER, R. J.   *The Urge to the Sea: The Course of Russian History* (Berkeley, 1942).

MORRISON, JOHN.   "Geographic Factors and Fancies in Russian and Soviet Expansion," in G. Hoffman, ed. *Recent Soviet Trends.*

MOSELY, PHILIP.   "Aspects of Russian Expansion," *ASEER*,[1] vol. 7, pp. 197–213.

SUMNER, B. H.   "The Frontier," in *A Short History of Russia* (New York, 1949).

TREADGOLD, DONALD.   "Russian Expansion in the Light of Turner's Study of the American Frontier," *Agricultural History*, vol. 26, pp. 147–52.

PEOPLES

BARTOLD, V. V.   "Slavs," in *Encyclopedia of Islam*, vol. 4.

BIDLO, J.   "The Slavs in Medieval History," *SEER*, vol. 9 (1930–31).

DVORNIK, FRANCIS.   *The Slavs in European History and Civilization* (New Brunswick, N.J., 1962).

———.   "The Significance of the Missions of Cyril and Methodius," *SR*, vol. 23, 1964, pp. 196–211.

HOOSON, DAVID.   *The Soviet Union: People and Regions* (London, 1966).

———.   "The Soviet People: Population Growth and Policy," *The Population Bulletin*, vol. 28, no. 5.

KOLARZ, WALTER.   *The Peoples of the Soviet Far East,* (Camden, Conn., 1969).

For abbreviations of periodical titles, see Bibliography in the Appendix, pp. 635.

2

Ancient Russia

THE VERY EARLIEST history of the great Eurasian plain, located north of the Black Sea, the region which later comprised the center of the first Russian or Kievan State, is shrouded in mystery because of an almost total lack of historical sources. In recent times, however, archeology has contributed significantly to our knowledge and understanding of the earliest known inhabitants of this region. That the area was inhabited for many thousands of years before the Christian era, and that the region served as the center of a whirlpool for many cross-currents of cultural influences coming from western Asia, the Black Sea, and the Caucasus Mountains cannot be disputed, but there is no hard evidence to suggest that the region was the aboriginal homeland of Slavic or proto-Slavic peoples. Indeed, very little is known of the origins of the Slavs, and apparently they did not settle in the Eurasian plain until several centuries after the beginning of the Christian era.

The great Eurasian plain, the cradle of Russian history, was inhabited by primitive man for tens and hundreds of thousands of years before the arrival of the Slavs. Archeological excavations have unearthed layer upon layer of evidence of human habitation beginning as far back as the Paleolithic Age (the Old Stone Age), dating back over 1,000,000 years and extending down to about 8000 B.C. Still clearer evidence of the existence of primitive man in the region has been uncovered from the Neolithic era (the New Stone Age), dating back to about 4000 B.C. Finally, beginning at least a thousand years before the birth of Christ, the Eurasian plain was inundated by wave after wave of migrating peoples moving westward out of Asia and the Middle East. These successive waves of people, each with its own distinctive civilization, left a mark on the region, and the most distant past of this important geographical area has been reconstructed in broad outline by archeologists rather than historians.

The first historically recorded people to enter the territory north of the Black Sea coastal region were the Cimmerians, who appeared about 1000 B.C. They were apparently of Thracian stock and entered the steppe region as conquerors, imposing their rule on the fragmented primitive peoples already occupying the great plain. Information about the Cimmerians is meagre, although archeological evidence suggests that they were skilled in the use of iron and may have introduced the advantages of iron as opposed to stone implements to the indigenous population. The widespread use of iron in the area, however, appears to date from about the seventh century B.C. when the Cimmerians were replaced as the dominant ruling element by the Scythians whose ethnic origin is a subject of continuing dispute. Some scholars have suggested that they were Iranian; others have argued that they were of Mongol origin; and some Russian scholars have even advanced the view that the Scythians were Slavic or proto-Slavic. As George Vernadsky suggests, all three elements may have existed within the broad Scythian group. Moreover, there was a considerable admixture of Scythian and Cimmerian elements because Scythian culture simply overlaid the older Cimmerian culture, and the survivors of the Cimmerians remained in their former territories as subjects of the Scythians.

At about the same time, the Greeks appeared in the Crimea (a name which may derive from Cimmeria) and spread out along the northern coast of the Black Sea. The Greeks established trading colonies and founded cities in the region. The Greek city, Olbia at the mouth of the Bug River was founded in 644 B.C. and the establishment of other centers followed shortly. By entering into trade with the Scythians and other peoples living to the north, these Greek colonies served to link the Eurasian plain with the Hellenistic world of the eastern Mediterranean. Greek sources have provided a wealth of information about the Scythians, although some of the material is not very reliable. Especially valuable is Herodotus' famous *History*, written in the fifth century B.C. Herodotus himself lived for a time in Olbia and collected many kinds of information about the Scythians. Herodotus used the name Scythia to denote not only a geographic area, but also in an ethnic sense to apply to all the diverse peoples living within the general territory of the Eurasian plain. This inaccurate use of the term Scythia has led to a certain confusion in precisely identifying the Scythians and tracing their origins. The historian Michael Rostovtzeff has suggested an Iranian origin for the Scythians, and it appears that at least the ruling group of the Scythians spoke an Iranian language. Most recently, the Soviet historian B. D. Grekov claimed that a genetic relationship existed between the Slavs and a portion of the Scythians, the so-called Scythian plowmen. The evidence for this view is tenuous, based on physical similarities of Scythian and early Slavic figures as portrayed in artifacts unearthed by archeologists. No incontrovertible evidence linking the Scythians with Slavic or proto-Slavic peoples has been turned up to date.

In general, during Scythian times three basic cultural areas may be differentiated within the Eurasian plain: (1) Scythia proper, composed of the lower reaches of the Bug and Dnieper rivers; (2) the Crimean steppe region somewhat to the east; and (3) the Azov steppe region located still further to the east. All these territories were occupied by a confederation of related tribes, partly settled agriculturalists (the Scythian plowmen referred to by Herodotus) and partly nomads. The

MAP 2–1a
Romans and Sarmatians, 200 B.C.–200 A.D.

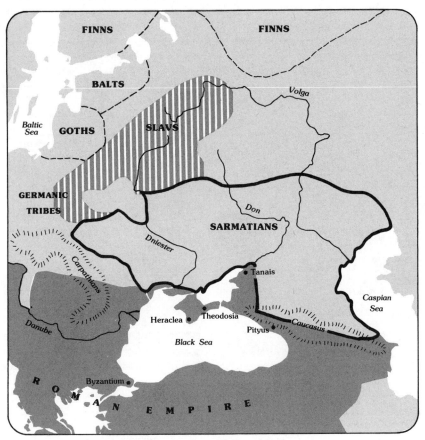

dominant group seems to have been a tribe called by Herodotus the Royal Scythians. These various tribes appear to have shared a common language and customs. Another group of tribes of different origin were settled to the west of Scythia proper and were engaged, according to archeological evidence, in agriculture and animal husbandry. Some Soviet historians have argued that a part of these nonScythian tribes consisted of proto-Slavic peoples, although no concrete evidence has been produced to support such a view. To the east of Scythia proper were still other groups of people not related to the Scythians but sharing certain common cultural features with the dominant Scythians. Indeed, there was a degree of cultural homogeneity in the whole region extending from the Caucasus Mountains in the east to the Danube River in the west, and this homogeneity may account for Herodotus' imprecision in identifying the various ethnic groups. The cultural unity of the region was vividly expressed in common weaponry, horse ornaments, and the famous animal style in art. The Scythians lived close to nature

MAP 2–1b
Slavs and Norsemen by 880

Slav settlement by 880 A.D.

"Kievan Russia" ruled by Norsemen

SERBS Principal Slav tribes

BALTS Other tribes

Adapted with permission of MacMillan Publishing Co., Inc. from *Russian History Atlas* by Martin Gilbert. Cartography by Martin Gilbert. Copyright © 1972 by Martin Gilbert.

as herdsmen, hunters, warriors, and agriculturalists, and in so doing they acquired a knowledge, understanding, and respect for the animal world. Thus animals played an important role in both the life and the art of the Scythians. The common cultural elements to be found in the whole region of southern Russia during the Scythian period testify to the existence of extensive trade and cultural contacts among the diverse peoples occupying the Eurasian plain in this early period.

Beginning in the third century B.C. a new group of warrior tribes, the Sarmatians, began to advance into the Eurasian plain, moving out of Central Asia. The Sarmatians were ethnically Iranian in origin, and by the mid-second century B.C. they had replaced the Scythians as the rulers of south Russia. The Sarmatians were nomadic cattle-breeders who lived in felt huts mounted on wheels to facilitate easy and rapid movement as they followed their wandering herds of cattle and horses. The Sarmatians adopted much of Scythian culture, infusing it wtih a primitive dynamism of their own. The Sarmatians continued the Scythian practice of maintaining trade with the Greek colonies on the northern shores of the Black Sea, and the Sarmatians too were drawn into the eastern Mediterranean cultural sphere. One of the main groups of Sarmatians, the last to enter the Eurasian plain, were the Alans, the ruling element of this confederation of nomadic tribes. One of the tribes of the Alans was the Rukhs-As (the fair-haired As), and an effort has been made to establish a link between the terms, Rukhs-As and Russian, the latter deriving from the former. According to this theory, the Rukhs-As emerge as the ancestors of the modern Russians. Still another tribe of the Sarmatians was known as the Roxolani, and Grekov has advanced the view that the term Rus derived from this tribal name. Arguing that the letters x and s are linguistically interchangeable, Grekov theorized that Roxolani became Rosolani, which in turn was shortened to Ros and then became Rus. Many such theories of the origin of the term Rus or Russian abound but none of them can be authoritatively substantiated at present.

Meanwhile, migration was erupting in another area, to the north of the Eurasian plain. During the first century A.D., the Goths began to move out of Scandinavia, migrating southward into the region of the lower Vistula River and from there further south into the Eurasian plain. As the Goths moved southward they conquered and plundered as they went, subduing and absorbing many tribes living in the Dnieper River basin and dislocating many others. Mention is made in the historical sources of several such tribes which were· overrun by the Goths: the Venedae, the Sclaveni, and the Antes. Jordanis, a Goth writing in the sixth century A.D., associated these tribes with the Slavs, or more accurately, he suggested that the descendants of these tribes served as the nucleus of the future Slavs. Like their predecessors, the Goths, a Germanic people whose way of life was conditioned by the forests they had traditionally occupied, were a confederation of tribes, but a confederation lacking any real unified state structure and so were able to impose only a superficial degree of unity on the diverse peoples then occupying the Eurasian plain. By the mid-fourth century A.D. the Goths had become divided into two powerful confederations, the Ostrogoths (East Goths) and the Visigoths (West Goths). The Goths in general probably had not achieved as high a level of culture as either the Scythians or Sarmatians, and therefore they tended to adopt the general culture of the Sarmatians. There is clear evidence of a general cultural continuity in the Eurasian plain extending roughly from 500 B.C. to 500 A.D.

David MacKenzie

Old Church in Mtskheta, Georgian SSR

During the second half of the fourth century A.D. a new and terrifying force swept out of Central Asia into the Eurasian plain and beyond. These were the fearsome Huns, a powerful and rapidly expanding people who were prevented from spilling over into China by the Great Wall which had been constructed as a barrier against this turbulent and aggressive tribe. The Huns, forced to migrate westward, eventually entered the eastern reaches of the Eurasian plain by about 370 A.D. They encountered and crushed the Alans living between the Don River and the Sea of Azov. Many Alans fled westward, pursued by the marauding Huns who now met the Goths. The momentum of the Huns could not be halted and what followed is known in historical literature as the Great Migration of Peoples (German: *Völkerwanderung*) in which the advance of the Huns caused tremendous dislocations further to the west. The Visigoths and Ostrogoths, together with the remainder of the Alans, were forced out of the Eurasian plain by the inexorable advance of the Huns. The Visigoths took refuge in southern Gaul and then moved on into Spain. The Ostrogoths fled first into Thrace and then seized Italy, destroying the western Roman Empire. A group of the Alans survived the Hunnish attack and moved into the Caucasus Mountains during these vast upheavals and their descendants survive today under the name Ossetians. Certainly the most well-known Ossetian or part Ossetian of modern times is Joseph Stalin, whose mother was an Ossetian.

The Huns reached their zenith under Attila, who menaced the eastern

Roman or Byzantine Empire in 447, invaded Frankish Gaul in 451, and moved against Italy in 452. All of western Europe shuddered before the advance of the Huns. But Attila died in 453 and thereafter his far-flung empire rapidly crumbled as a result of jealous rivalries and fratricidal warfare among his less talented successors. Many historians believe that it was during this period of the *Völkerwanderung* that the Slavs began to migrate out of central and eastern Europe in various directions—to the east, to the south, and to the west.

The Huns eventually had to give way to yet another wave of migration into the Eurasian plain, that of the Avars, a mixture of Turkish, Mongolian, and Chinese elements. The Avars conquered the region by the mid-sixth century and amalgamated the remaining Hunnish elements and other surviving groups into a powerful state extending from the Volga River in the east to the Elbe River in the west. So powerful were the Avars that they were able to pressure the Byzantine Empire into paying tribute in 581, and from Byzantine sources it is clear that Slavic groups participated in these Avar campaigns against the Byzantine Empire. The Slavs were identified as the Sclaveni in Byzantine sources. Thus, Slavic elements, having moved into the Eurasian plain, were now incorporated into the Avar state. The earliest written source of Russian history, *The Primary Russian Chronicle* (*Povest vremennykh let*) records how the Avars oppressed the Slavic tribes:

> And the Avars [called Obry] made war upon the Slavs and harassed the Dulebians who were Slavs. They [the Avars] did violence to the Dulebian women: when an Avar made a journey he did not cause either a horse or a steer to be harnessed, but gave command instead that three or four or five Dulebian women should be yoked to his cart and be made to draw him. Even thus did they harass the Dulebians.[1]

The Avars held sway in the Eurasian plain until the first quarter of the seventh century and then were decisively defeated by the Byzantines, at which point the Avar state entered upon a period of decay and decline.

Over this welter of diverse peoples, including remnants of the Huns, Avars, Antes, Altaic Turks, and Slavs, there arose, in the eighth century a new military power along the northern shores of the Black and the Caspian Seas, the Khazars, a people of Turkic origin. Although originally nomadic, the Khazars were quickly drawn into commercial relations with the Byzantine Empire and the rising Arab Empire to the east. A lively and lucrative trade developed with the Khazars serving as middlemen between the Greeks and the Arabs and the native tribes living to the north of the Khazar economic sphere. In an effort to maximize trade opportunities, the Khazars extended their control over numerous Slavic tribes living in the Dnieper River basin. Although many Slavs were compelled to pay tribute, the Khazars maintained a healthy respect for the military prowess of the Slavs. *The Primary Chronicle* relates the account of a Khazar expedition sent out to collect

---

[1] Samuel Cross, "The Russian Primary Chronicle," *Harvard Studies and Notes in Philology and Literature*, vol. 12 (Cambridge, Mass., 1930), pp. 140–41.

tribute among the Poliane, a Slavic tribe settled along the Dnieper River in the vicinity of the future center of Kiev. "Oh, Kagan [ruler]! This tribute bodes no good. We achieved it with sabres, our single-bladed sword, but their [the Slavs'] weapon is the sword, sharp on both sides. The time will come when they exact tribute from us Khazars, and from other peoples." This was to be a prophetic statement.

For the time being, however, the Khazars maintained at least nominal control over several of the Slavic tribes in the Dnieper River basin and gradually drew them into lucrative trade and commerce. Although the Khazars maintained extensive trade contacts with the Byzantine Empire and provided military assistance to the Byzantines, Greek culture and Greek Christianity made little headway among the Khazars and the peoples living under their control. To be sure, the Khazars had ample contact with representatives of the three great religions, Christian, Jewish, and Moslem. There is evidence that all three religions actively proselytized among the Khazars, each making moderate progress. Sometime during the late eighth or early ninth century, the Khazar kagan and members of his court were converted to Judaism. No effort was made, however, to make Judaism a state religion. What is important is that the Khazar state, with its extensive commercial contacts, served as a meeting ground or point of confluence for the great civilizations of the period, each of which left some imprint on the Khazars and by extension on those living within the Khazar sphere. The whole area of south Russia was, as a result, a relatively cosmopolitan region. The participation of the Slavs in the trade and commerce of the Khazars provided a bond of unity, but whether this unity expressed itself in any formal state structure is a subject of debate. By the eighth century Slavic tribes had settled permanently in the Dnieper River region and the nucleus of the future Kievan state had been established.

It is evident from the preceding account that numerous groups of peoples moved into and out of the Eurasian plain during the most ancient period of Russia's history. It is also evident that the Slavs were relative late-comers to the region. No definite evidence of their presence in the Eurasian plain is available until about the sixth century. By that time Slavic or proto-Slavic tribes had moved out of central Europe and spread out along the Dnieper River basin. These tribes formed the nucleus of the eastern Slavs, later subdivided into three groups: the Great Russians, the White Russians, and the Little Russians or Ukrainians. Other Slavic tribes moved in other directions; some to the south, into the Balkans, and these formed the nucleus of the South Slavs. The South Slavs also became subdivided into various groups: the Serbs, the Croats, the Slovenes, and the Bulgars. Still other Slavic tribes migrated westward, becoming the nucleus of the western Slavs, which later were divided into various ethnic groups: the Poles, the Czechs (or Bohemians), the Slovaks, the Moravians, the Kashubs, and the Wends.

The Primary Russian Chronicle, recording events in the ninth century, refers to 13 eastern Slavic tribes: (1) the Slovenes, located in the north around Novgorod; (2) the Krivichi, located slightly to the south of the Slovene; (3) the Polochane, in the region of Smolensk; (4) the

Viatichi, in the region around the future Moscow; (5) the Severiane, on the eastern bank of the Dnieper River in the region of Chernigov; (6) the Radimichi, on the upper reaches of the Dnieper, to the south of Smolensk; (7) the Drevliane, on the west side of the Dnieper, slightly north of Kiev; (8) the Ulichi, in the region of the Southern Bug River; (9) the Tivertsy, slightly to the west of the Ulichi; (10) the Khorvaty, on the upper reaches of the Dniester River; (11) the Poliane, on the east bank of the Dnieper River, in the region of Kiev; (12) the Dregovichi, on the lower reaches of the Niemen River, to the west of Smolensk; and (13) the Dulebians, located to the west of the Drevliane. Among these widely scattered tribes there was a degree of cultural and linguistic unity, but it is bitterly disputed whether these tribes, or at least some of them, enjoyed in the eighth and early ninth century a degree of political unity commensurate with a state structure.

The unification of these scattered tribes into a formal state will be the subject of the next chapter.

Suggested Additional Readings

BRUTZKUS, J. "The Khazar Origin of Ancient Kiev," *SEER*, vol. 22 (1944), pp. 108–24.

CZEKANOWSKI, J. "The Ancient Home of the Slavs," *SEER*, vol. 25 (1946–47), pp. 356–72.

DUNLOP, D. M. *The History of the Jewish Khazars* (Princeton, 1954).

HARMATTA, J. *Studies in the History of the Sarmatians* (Budapest, 1950).

JOHNSON, J. "The Scythian: His Rise and Fall," *JHI*, 20 (1959), pp. 250–57.

KAIMYKOW, A. D. "Iranians and Slavs in South Russia," *JAOS*, vol. 45 (1925), pp. 68–71.

MILLER, M. *Archeology in the USSR* (London, 1956).

MONGAIT, A. L. *Archeology in the USSR* (London, 1961).

PASZKIEWICZ, H. *The Making of the Russian Nation* (London, 1963).

ROSTOVTZEFF, M. *Iranians and Greeks in South Russia* (Oxford, 1922).

———. *The Animal Style in South Russia and China* (Princeton, 1929).

VERNADSKY, G. *Ancient Russia* (New Haven, 1943).

———. *The Origins of Russia* (Oxford, 1959).

WEINRYB, B. (comp.) "The Khazars: An Annotated Bibliography," *Studies in Bibliography and Booklore*, vol. 6 (1963), pp. 11–129.

WREN, M. *Ancient Russia* (London, 1965).

PROBLEM 1: THE FORMATION OF THE FIRST RUSSIAN STATE

How did Russia come into being? Did native Slavs or Scandinavians create the first Russian state? When and where did it originate? Was it the product mainly of external influences or internal socioeconomic change? These questions are part of a major historical controversy about Russia's beginnings, heightened by the scarcity and dubious nature of written records from that shadowy epoch. The debate among historians has centered on the Norman theory which affirmed that the first Russian state was established in the mid-ninth century by Scandinavian Vikings. The chief Normanists have been Scandinavian and German scholars, although some Russian historians accepted many of their arguments. Soviet historians, however, especially after a strong patriotic trend set in about 1935, have repudiated the Norman theory completely and argued that native Slavs created a Russian state long before the Vikings arrived.

The founders of the Norman theory were the eighteenth century German scholars, G. Bayer and A. Schlözer, working in the infant Russian Academy of Sciences. They relied chiefly upon the account of the formation of Russia in *The Primary Russian Chronicle*, which describes the period from 852 to 1110 A.D., portions of which were probably written in the 12th century by the Kievan monk Nestor. Although the *Chronicle* has come down to us only in later and revised copies, it remains an important, though controversial, source for early Russian history. It states that about 860 the Slavs of the Novgorod region, unable to govern themselves, invited the Scandinavian Vikings, or Varangians, to come and rule over them. The Norman theory, elaborated during the nineteenth century by V. Thomsen and E. Kunik, was accepted by most contemporary Russian historians.

During the past 50 years scholars working in Soviet Russia, utilizing much new archeological evidence, especially from burial mounds in northwestern Russia, have subjected the Norman theory to systematic criticism. Rejecting the Normanist emphasis on external Scandinavian influences on Russian development, they have stressed the socioeconomic changes which occurred within the eastern Slav tribes and have concluded that the first viable Russian political system, or state, emerged from the transition of the eastern Slavs during the sixth to the ninth centuries from primitive communism to feudalism. This process, assert Soviet historians, was little affected by Scandinavian incursions, and a Russian state existed before they arrived. A few western historians accept many of their arguments. The Soviet challenge forced the Normanists to reexamine their premises and make important concessions, but the Normanists still argue that the Varangians made a substantial contribution to the formation of Kievan Russia. The sections which follow present the main outlines of the controversy over the Norman theory.

THE PRIMARY RUSSIAN CHRONICLE

> In the year 852 . . . the land of Rus was first named . . .
> 859: The Varangians from beyond the sea imposed tribute upon the Chuds, the Slavs, the Merians, the Ves, and the Krivichians. But the Khazars imposed it upon the Polianians, the Severians, and the Viatichians, and collected a squirrel-skin and a beaver-skin from each hearth.
> 860–862: The tributaries of the Varangians drove them back beyond the sea and, refusing them further tribute, set out to govern themselves. There was no law among them, but tribe rose against tribe. Discord thus ensued among them, and they began to war one against

another. They said to themselves, "Let us seek a prince who may rule over us, and judge us according to the law." They accordingly went overseas to the Varangian Russes: these particular Varangians were known as Russes, just as some are called Swedes, and others Normans, Angles and Goths. . . . The Chuds, the Slavs and the Krivichians then said to the people of Rus: "Our whole land is great and rich, and there is no order in it. Come to rule and reign over us." They thus selected three brothers, with their kinsfolk, who took with them all the Russes and migrated. The oldest, Rurik, located himself in Novgorod; the second, Sineus, in Beloozero; and the third, Truvor, in Izborsk. On account of these Varangians, the district of Novgorod became known as the land of Rus. The present inhabitants of Novgorod are descended from the Varangian race, but aforetime they were Slavs.

After two years Sineus and his brother, Truvor, died, and Rurik assumed the sole authority. He assigned cities to his followers. . . . In these cities there are thus Varangian colonists, but the first settlers were, in Novgorod, Slavs. . . . Rurik had dominion over all these districts. With Rurik there were two men who did not belong to his kin, but were boyars [noblemen]. They obtained permission to go to Tsargrad [Constantinople] with their families. They thus sailed down the Dnieper, and in the course of their journey they saw a small city on a hill. Upon their inquiry as to whose town it was, they were informed that three brothers, Kii, Shchek, and Khoriv, had once built the city, but that since their deaths, their descendants were living there as tributaries of the Khazars. Oskold and Dir remained in this city, and after gathering together many Varangians, they established their dominion over the country of the Polianians at the same time that Rurik was ruling Novgorod.[1]

These excerpts from this semilegendary account suggest that in the mid-ninth century the tribes of Rus, some of them Slavic, were caught between the Varangians of Scandinavia and the Khazar Empire along the Volga River. The Russes, affirms the Chronicle, were Scandinavian Vikings who created a state for the tribes of northern Russia. Rus, it continues, was located originally around Novgorod and ruled by Riurik, founder of the first Russian dynasty; his vassals established Kiev as the capital of the Russian state. The Russians, it concludes, were descendants of the Varangians and native Slavs.

THE NORMAN THEORY

Contemporary Normanists differ somewhat among themselves, but most affirm that: (1) the words, *Rus*, and *Variag* (Varangian) are Scandinavian; (2) that the Rus and the Swedes were identical; and (3) that the latter founded the first Russian state in the Novgorod region. Some Normanists go far beyond this to claim that the Varangians conquered and colonized the east Slav lands, introduced feudal landholding and Christianity into Russia, and created the upper classes of Kievan Russia. Extreme Normanists have suggested that the primi-

---

[1] Cross, "The Russian Primary Chronicle," pp. 144–45.

tive and disorganized eastern Slavs were ushered into civilization and statehood by culturally superior Germanic Varangians.

A recent scholarly and moderate summary of the Normanist interpretation is that of Stender-Petersen from which the following excerpts are taken:

> That the Northmen or Normans from mid-Sweden, Östergotland, and Gotland Island played a part in the origin of the Russian state can scarcely any longer be denied seriously. But what this participation consisted of, its extent, and how it occurred must still be considered unresolved questions and over these questions rages the old quarrel between the so-called Normanists and Anti-Normanists. . . . The story of the invitation of the three brothers from across the Baltic, who with the entire Rus people emigrated to the Slav-Finnish frontier regions of northern Russia and settled in . . . Ladoga, Izborsk, and Beloozero is merely a variant of a passage common to many compositions in various places among the Swedish population in Finland and Estonia. . . . Ture J. Arne . . . after archeological investigation in Russia, proved that in an archeological sense Russia was a cultural passageway between the north, especially Sweden, and the East and Byzantium, and that in Russia there was undeniable material evidence of Swedish-Nordic settlements. . . .
>
> . . . In Soviet sources we get a rather confused and unclear picture of Slav-Russian prehistory, a mosaic of hypotheses which they turn into facts, bald assumptions, and false interpretations whose main purpose is to shatter the Norman theory by any means . . .
>
> The Russian state therefore owes its existence not to supposed Viking expeditions by the three legendary brothers who conquered the lands beyond the Baltic Sea and founded a state. . . . We must reckon with the interbreeding of two racial elements. One was the autonomous Slav tribes with their relatively developed agriculture . . . , but the second factor was the Nordic Rus people, originally a Swedish land-grabbing and colonist people who knew how to resist the expansion of the Khazar kaganate, release itself from dependence on the Swedish king, and so establish its own commercial kaganate around Lake Ladoga. The cooperation between the Slavs of the Dnieper valley and the Normans led to the founding of the Norman-Russian state.[2]

SOVIET ANTI-NORMANISM

Recent Soviet historians and a few Western colleagues have sought to refute part or all of the Norman theory. Their critique emphasizes: (1) the unreliable nature of *The Primary Chronicle;* (2) that the first Russian state arose as a result of socioeconomic changes among the eastern Slavs long before the Varangians arrived; and (3) that the Rus were a south Russian tribe living along the Ros River directing a large tribal league which gave its name to the Russian land. From the sixth to the ninth centuries, claim Soviet historians, occurred a gradual shift of the eastern Slavs from a primitive communal society in which

---

[2] Ad. Stender-Petersen, "Der älteste russische Staat," *Historische Zeitschrift,* vol. 191 (August–December 1960), pp. 1–17.

land was held in common to a feudal order in which land became the private property of powerful feudal landowners. By the ninth century feudal states had developed in both eastern and western Europe. Ninth-century Kievan Russia, they affirm, was a fully consolidated feudal state comparable to the Carolingian Empire in the West; the idea that the eastern Slavs lagged behind western Europe in their development is a myth. Archeological investigation, they conclude, has proved that Kiev and the Kievan state were founded before the Varangians came.

In the new detailed *History of the USSR*, the role of the Varangians in the early history of Russia is described as follows:

> The "Norman period" in Russian history has always been exaggerated by bourgeois [Western] scholarship which stretches it out to several centuries, intentionally identifies the Varangian-Normans with the Rus, and attributes to the Varangians the creation of the first Slav state. This has been achieved by selecting tendentious sources, making a tendentious interpretation of disputed passages, and ignoring evidence unfavorable to the "Normanists."
>
> What is the actual role of the Varangians in the history of our fatherland? In the mid-ninth century, when Kievan Russia had already been formed in the mid-Dnieper valley, on the far northern outskirts of the Slav world . . . , there began to appear detachments of Varangians from beyond the Baltic Sea. The Slavs and Chuds drove these detachments away. . . . In 862 or 874 . . . the Varangian konung, Riurik, appeared at Novgorod. From this adventurer, leading a small retinue, has been traced without any real basis the genealogy of all the early Russian princes. . . . The Varangian newcomers did not conquer Russian towns but set up fortified camps nearby. . . . Nowhere did the Varangians control Russian towns. Archeological findings reveal that the number of Varangian warriors, living permanently in Rus, was very small.
>
> In 882 one of the Varangian leaders, Oleg, penetrated from Novgorod southward . . . to Kiev where by deception and cleverness he succeeded in killing the Kievan prince, Oskold, and seizing power. With Oleg's name is connected several campaigns for tribute against nearby Slav tribes and the famous campaign of 911 by Russian troops against Tsargrad. Evidently, Oleg did not consider himself master of Rus. It is curious that after the successful campaign to Byzantium he and his Varangian retinue were not in the capital of Rus [Kiev], but far to the north in Ladoga, near their homeland, Sweden. It also seems strange that Oleg, to whom is ascribed wholly undeservedly the creation of the Russian state, disappeared from the Russian horizon without a trace. . . .
>
> The rule of the Varangian, Oleg, in Kiev was an insignificant and brief episode, excessively inflated by a few pro-Varangian chroniclers and subsequent Normanist historians. . . . The Varangians' historical role in Rus was insignificant. Appearing as "discoverers," the newcomers, attracted by the gleam of riches in the already renowned Kievan Russia, plundered northern regions in isolated raids but penetrated only once to the heart of Rus. As to the Varangians' cultural role, there is nothing to be said. . . . The Varangians had nothing to do with the creation of the [Kievan] state, construction of cities or

establishment of trade routes. They could neither speed up nor significantly retard the historical process in Rus. . . .[3]

A MIDDLE ROAD

The distinguished historian V. O. Kliuchevskii, whose *Course of Russian History* appeared in the decade before the Bolshevik Revolution, arrived at an interesting compromise between Normanism and its opponents about the origins of the first Russian state:

> From the beginning of the ninth century and the end of Charlemagne's reign armed bands of pirates from Scandinavia began to roam the coasts of western Europe. . . . About this time along the river routes through our plains began to appear sea rovers from the Baltic who were given the name, Varangians. During the tenth and eleventh centuries these Varangians were coming constantly to Russia either to trade or at the invitation of our princes who selected from them their military retinues. But . . . *The Primary Chronicle* records Varangian visits to Russian towns as early as the mid-ninth century. A Kievan legend of the 11th century exaggerated their numbers . . . [noting that] these Varangians swarmed into Russian commercial towns in such numbers that they formed a thick layer of their population and submerged the local inhabitants. Thus, according to the *Chronicle,* Novgorodians at first were Slavs and later became Varangians. . . . In the area of Kiev they became especially numerous. According to the *Chronicle,* Kiev was even founded by Varangians. . . . Thus the dim recollection of the *Chronicle* appears to move back the Varangians' arrival in Russia to the first half of the ninth century . . .
>
> These Baltic Varangians, as well as the Black Sea *Rus,* according to many signs, were Scandinavians, and not Slavs. . . . These Scandinavian Varangians entered the military-commercial class which arose in the ninth century in the large trading towns of Rus. . . . The Varangians came to us with different aims and appearance than the Danes brought to the West: there the Dane was a pirate, a coastal brigand; the Varangian was primarily an armed merchant coming to Rus in order to make his way onward to rich Byzantium, there to serve the Emperor with profit, to trade, and sometimes to plunder the rich Greeks if the opportunity arose. . . .
>
> The Varangians, settling in the larger commercial towns of Rus, met there a class of armed merchants, socially akin to them and needing them; they were gradually absorbed into it, entering into commercial association with the natives or hiring themselves out for a good price to protect Russian trade routes. . . .
>
> . . . The hazy Chronicle account designates the first political units formed in Rus about the mid-ninth century: the city state, a commercial district administered by a fortified town which served as the commercial center for that region. . . . When the Kievan principality was formed, incorporating the tribes of the eastern Slavs, these ancient city states—Kiev, Chernigov, Smolensk, and others, formerly independent, were absorbed as administrative districts and ready-made subdivisions. . . .

---

[3] *Istoriia SSSR s drevneishkh vremen do nashikh dnei* (Moscow 1966), vol. 1, pp. 488–91.

The evolution of this earliest Russian political formation was accompanied elsewhere by the development of a secondary local form: the Varangian principality. In commercial centers where the Varangian immigrants had arrived in especially large numbers, they readily abandoned their role in commercial associations or as hired guards over trade routes and became rulers. . . . The transformation of Varangians from allies into rulers was, under favorable circumstances, achieved rather easily. . . . Thus some fortified towns and their environs under certain circumstances fell into the hands of the overseas immigrants and became possessions of Varangian konungs. We find a few such Varangian principalities in Rus during the ninth and tenth centuries. . . . The rise of these Varangian principalities explains fully the tale in the *Chronicle* about the beginning of Rus after the invitation of princes from overseas.[4]

CONCLUSION

The Soviet challenge has blunted the force of, and demolished some of the bolder Normanist claims about, the Scandinavian origin of the Kievan state and culture, but it has not destroyed the Norman theory. This, in the modified form propounded by Stender-Petersen, remains a provocative interpretation of early Russian history. Meanwhile the controversy between Normanists and anti-Normanists has provoked intensive investigation of this distant period and has lifted part of the veil which obscured it previously.

Suggested Additional Reading

ARBMAN, H.   *The Vikings* (London 1962).

BRUTZKUS, J.   "The Khazar Origin on Ancient Kiev," *SEER*, vol. 22, no. 1, 1944, pp. 108–24.

CHUBATY, N. D.   "The Beginnings of Russian History," *Ukr. Quar.*, vol. 3, 1946–7, pp. 262 ff.

CROSS, SAMUEL H.   "The Scandinavian Infiltration into Early Russia," *Speculum*, vol. 21, 1946, pp. 505–14.

PASZKIEWICZ, H.   *The Origins of Russia* (New York, 1954).

POLONSKA-WASYLENKO, N.   "The Beginnings of the State of Ukraine-Rus," *Ukr. Quar.*, 1963, no. 2, pp. 33–58.

RIASANOVSKY, A. V.   "The Embassy of 838 Revisited," *Jahrb. Gesch. Osteuropas*, vol. 10, Heft 1, 1962, pp. 1–12.

RIASANOVSKY, N. V.   "The Norman Theory of the Origin of the Russian State," in S. Harcave, ed., *Readings in Russian History* (N.Y. 1962), vol. 1, 128–38.

RYBAKOV, B.   *Early Centuries of Russian History* (Moscow, 1965) (Soviet view).

SAWYER, P. H.   *The Age of the Vikings* (London, 1962).

SHASKOLSKII, I. P.   *Normanskaia teoriia v sovremennoi burzhuaznoi nauke* (Moscow, 1965).

STENDER-PETERSEN, AD.   *Russian Studies* (Copenhagen, 1956)

———.   *Varangica* (Aarhus, 1953).

---

[4] V. O. Kliuchevskii, *Kurs russkoi istorii* (Moscow, 1937), vol. 1, pp. 126–35.

3

Kievan Russia: Politics and Foreign Affairs

As VARANGIAN AND SLAV princes formed a Russian federation centering in Novgorod and Kiev during the ninth century, the Kievan Russian era began. Kievan princes, all from one dynasty, and their people soon adopted Greek Orthodoxy, and for over three centuries Kievan Russia, uniting the eastern Slavs, played a significant role in medieval civilization. Because the Kievan religion and cultural heritage came from Constantinople, some consider it as an offshoot of Greek Byzantine civilization. Indeed, Russia and South Slavs such as Serbs and Bulgars adopted the Cyrillic alphabet, designed in the 860s by two Orthodox monks from Macedonia. How profound and persistent were Byzantine and Scandinavian influences in Kievan Russia? Was Kiev a satellite of the Byzantine Empire or an independent, leading force in eastern Europe? Did a centralized Kievan state ever exist and, if so, when? Was Kievan Russia feudal in its characteristics?

POLITICAL HISTORY

Kievan Russia's history may be divided into nearly a century of imperial expansion (878–972); an era of internal consolidation, growth, and prosperity (972–1054); and disintegration after 1054 interrupted by a brief recovery (1093–1132). Soviet historians and the prerevolutionary scholar, Kliuchevskii, consider 1132, the year when the last effective Kievan prince died, the end of the Kievan era. As internal violence increased and unity dissolved, Kiev lost its leadership, and Russia divided into several disparate segments. A distinctive old Russian political, socioeconomic, and cultural order, however, lasted until the Mongol conquest in the 13th century.

Kievan history began with a century of bold adventure. Varangian and Slav rulers strove to create an empire from the Black Sea to the Baltic, from the Caspian Sea to the Carpathian Mountains. The Russian attack upon Constantinople in 860 was part of Viking exploration

24

and conquest in eastern and western Europe. At first Varangian princes such as Oleg led Russian expansion; later the Slav population absorbed the Vikings and produced its own princes and heroes. Kievan expansion, seeking mainly commercial advantages rather than conquest, aimed at Constantinople and the Transcaucasus. Repeated Russian assaults on Constantinople sought to compel Byzantium to open markets to Russian goods and merchants; for this purpose Tmutarakan in the Azov region had been since the eighth century an important Russian base of operations. Its communications with Kiev, however, were poor, and complications with Khazar and Bulgar states along the Volga River frequently distracted the Russians. Unable to fight successfully on two such widely separated fronts, the Kievan princes eventually abandoned their imperial designs.

Oleg (882?–913), a Varangian prince of Novgorod, not the legendary Riurik, united Kievan Russia by linking Novgorod with Kiev and fusing the Varangian aristocracy with the Slavs. About 878 he moved southward along the Dnieper River, seized Kiev, and thus secured a base for further advances. He defeated several east Slavic tribes and imposed tribute upon them. *The Primary Chronicle* depicts him as a successful warrior, shrewd diplomat, and a wise, farsighted ruler. Securing the river route of the Dnieper and its tributaries northward to the Baltic and southward to the Black Sea, in 907 he marched against Constantinople, combining an overland advance across Bulgaria with an assault by some 2,000 ships. After his forces plundered Constantinople's outskirts, Byzantium granted Oleg a favorable commercial treaty, paid a large indemnity, and admitted Russian merchants to the city. The Treaty of 911 authorized regular and equal commercial relations, an unthinkable concession had Byzantium not suffered defeats.

Oleg's successor, Igor (913?–945), fought constantly to control east Slav tribes and collect tribute from them. Kiev, noted the Byzantine emperor, Constantine Porphyrogenitus, comprised Russia's central core; peripheral Slav tribes paid it tribute in furs or money. Each major Russian town had its prince, but all deferred to the grand prince of Kiev. Igor married Olga. (Was she a Slav maiden from Pskov, as some claim, or of Scandinavian origin?) In 941 and 944 Igor's forces, swelled by Pecheneg and Varangian mercenaries, moved against Byzantium and in 945 obtained a new favorable commercial treaty. The Russians impressed the Arab chronicler, Ibn-Miskawaih as "a mighty nation with vast frames and great courage. They know not defeat, nor does any of them turn his back until he slay or be slain." For seeking excessive tribute, Igor was killed by the Drevlianians.

His wife, Olga, Russia's first female ruler (945–962), avenged Igor's death by burning Drevlianian delegates to death in a large bathhouse. To consolidate Kievan power and avoid the future murders of princes, Olga divided her realm into districts with a tax collector for each. The *Primary Chronicle* praised her as "the wisest of women," partly because while in Constantinople in 955 she became a Christian. Russia, however, still remained pagan.

Olga's venturesome son Sviatoslav (962–72), a typical Viking de-

MAP 3–1
Kievan Russia, 880–1054

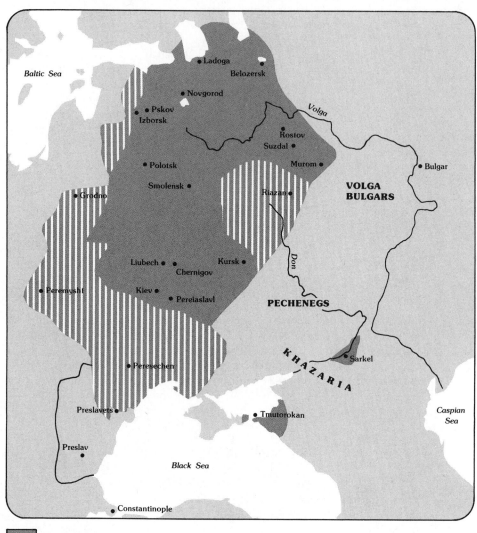

Kievan Russia

Territorial gains by 1054

spite his Slav name, concentrated on conquest. Some historians consider him a brilliant general; others a reckless adventurer. Relates the
Chronicle:

> Stepping light as a leopard, he undertook many campaigns. Upon
> his expeditions he carried with him neither wagons nor kettles, and
> boiled no meat, but cut off small strips of horseflesh, game, or beef,

and ate it after roasting it on the coals. Nor did he have a tent, but he spread out a garment under him, and set his saddle under his head; and all his retinue did likewise.[1]

In the campaigns of 964–65 Sviatoslav conquered the Viatichians and Volga Bulgars, who had established a flourishing commercial state, and smashed the Khazars near the Volga's mouth. He completed east Slavic unification around Kiev and inaugurated Russian trade with the east. Entering the Azov principality of Tmutarakan in triumph, Sviatoslav apparently became its ruler, temporarily uniting its forces with Kiev's. In 967 with a powerful army he assisted Byzantium against the Balkan Bulgars, conquered northern Bulgaria, and established his capital at Pereiaslavets (Little Preslav) on the lower Danube. Russia then had commercial and military outposts at both ends of the Black Sea. Had Sviatoslav's ambitious Balkan campaigns succeeded, Russia's expansion might have shifted westward. A Bulgar-Byzantine alliance defeated him, however, and he abandoned his Bulgarian claims. On his homeward journey Sviatoslav was ambushed and killed by Pecheneg nomads. Kiev's imperial pretensions in the Balkans ended, but its hold over the Don, Volga, and Azov regions was strengthened.

After an interlude of civil war, Vladimir, Sviatoslav's youngest son and of pure Scandinavian blood, ruled all Russia (c. 980–1015) as Vladimir I. A judicious and successful prince, Vladimir reasserted Kiev's authority over the Slav tribes, expanding Russia to the Baltic Sea and the eastern frontier deeper into the steppe. Early in his reign, related the monkish *Chronicle* writer, Vladimir gave his sexual impulses free rein:

> Now Vladimir was overcome by lust for women. His lawful wife was Rogned. . . . By her he had four sons . . . and two daughters. The Greek woman bore him Sviatopolk; by one Czech he had a son, Vysheslav; by another Sviatoslav and Mstislav; and by a Bulgarian woman, Boris and Gleb. He had 300 concubines at Vyshegorod, 300 at Belgorod and 200 at Berestovo. . . . He even seduced married women and violated young girls. . . . But Vladimir, though first deluded, eventually found salvation.[2]

The chronicler was alluding to a major event of his reign: the conversion of Vladimir and his people to Orthodox Christianity about 988.[3] This conscious and fateful choice helped set Russia apart from the Latin West and Moslem East and increased Byzantine political and cultural influences. Vladimir became renowned for practical Christianity and generous hospitality. Making peace with neighboring princes, he defended Kiev's southern and eastern borders against dangerous Pecheneg raids.[4] Along the banks of steppe rivers he built fortified lines and strongpoints. Late in his reign the rebellion of his ablest son, Iaroslav of Novgorod, demonstrated growing rivalry between Kiev and Novgorod, the leading towns of southern and northern Russia.

---

[1] Cross, "The Russian Primary Chronicle," p. 170–71.

[2] Ibid., p. 181.

[3] On the Christianization of Russia see below, pp. 47–51.

[4] On the steppe nomads see below, pp. 33–34.

Intermittent, bitter civil strife among Vladimir's sons threatened Kievan Russia's fragile political unity. One son, Sviatopolk, seized Kiev with Pecheneg aid. For murdering his trusting younger brothers, Boris and Gleb (later the first Russian saints), he was known as "the Damned." After Sviatopolk lost Pecheneg and Polish support, he was expelled from Kiev, which temporarily lost its political preeminence. In 1026 Iaroslav of Novgorod and Mstislav of Tmutarakan divided Russia between them, but when the latter died, Iaroslav became grand prince of all Russia.

Iaroslav the Wise (1036–54) restored Kiev's leadership and brought Kievan Russia to its peak of power and influence. He ruled from the Black Sea to the Baltic, from the Oka River in the east to the Carpathian Mountains. His defeat of the Pechenegs gave Kiev respite for a generation from nomadic attacks. Europe's royal houses sought marriage alliances with his family. Some contemporaries called him *kagan* (khan), others called him tsar like the Byzantine emperor. Under Iaroslav Kiev became a magnificent capital and center of learning rivalling Constantinople. Byzantine masters erected fine churches, including the great St. Sofia Cathedral. The metropolitan of Kiev headed a Russian church under the Patriarch of Constantinople. In 1051, seeking religious independence, Iaroslav convened a bishops' assembly which elected a Russian, Ilarion, as metropolitan. Once this quarrel was settled, Iaroslav's son, Vsevolod, married a Byzantine princess.

Iaroslav assigned major Russian towns to his sons' administration. His *Testament* bequeathed authority over Russia to his sons and urged them to live at peace:

> Love one another, since ye are brothers by one father and mother. If ye dwell in amity with one another, God will dwell among you, and will subject your enemies to you, and ye will live at peace. But if ye dwell in envy and dissension, quarreling with one another, then ye will perish yourselves and bring ruin to the land of your ancestors, which they won at the price of great effort.[5]

Iaroslav willed the Kievan throne to his eldest living son, Iziaslav, warning the others: "Heed him as ye have heeded me." He distributed leading towns to individual sons without dividing the country formally. Supposedly the prince of Kiev retained final authority over rulers of other principalities. Henceforth a town's rank in the *Testament*, a prince's seniority in the dynasty, and the fortunes of war determined succession to the grand princely throne. Theoretically a hierarchy of thrones existed: Kiev, Chernigov, Pereiaslavl, etc., but interprincely strife often prevented orderly rotation. Strong links were forged between local princes and their subjects and separatism grew.

After Iaroslav's death, Iziaslav ruled until in 1072 his brothers forced him to flee. Civil strife persisted under his ineffective successors. To end civil wars, an interprincely conference met at Liubech in 1097, representing all branches of Iaroslav's descendants. The princes, records the *Chronicle*, told one another: "Why do we ruin the Russian

---

[5] Ibid., p. 231.

land by our continued strife against one another? The Cumans [Polovtsy] harass our country in divers fashions and rejoice that war is waged among us. Let us hereafter be united in spirit and watch over the Russian land, and let each of us guard his own domain. . . ." The Liubech Conference assigned the keeping of domestic order and the organizing of external defense to the princes collectively. While the seniority principle was retained, each princely line ruled its own territory. Kievan Russia became a loose confederation of independent princes with increasingly tenuous family ties and a vague tradition of national unity.

The Cap of Monomakh, the crown of Vladimir Monomakh, the oldest Russian crown (Armory of Kremlin, Moscow)

A severe political and social crisis followed the death of Sviatopolk II in 1113. Popular disaffection in Kiev subsided only when Vladimir Monomakh assumed the throne as Vladimir II (1113–25). Renowned for his writings and numerous successful campaigns against the Polovtsy, Monomakh restored Kievan Russian unity temporarily and ruled firmly and wisely. Apparently he was a true Christian prince with a practical mind, unusual energy, military ability, and ambition. Soviet historians stress his lofty patriotism, leadership, and sensible, popular rule. Vladimir's *Testament* depicts his love for his fellow men and strong sense of responsibility. Well educated himself, he urged his sons: "Forget not what useful knowledge you possess, and acquire that with which you are not acquainted, even as my father, though he remained at home in his own country, still understood five languages. . . . Laziness is the mother of all evil. . . ."[6] His eldest son and successor, Mstislav I (1125–32), exercised strong authority; but his brother, Iaropolk II (1132–39), failed to preserve unity and Kiev's political leadership was undermined fatally.

During the final century of Kievan Russia, virtually sovereign principalities fought to control Kiev. At times their princes united to repel invasions from the steppe, and the church sought to preserve national

[6] Ibid., p. 279.

unity. After years of strife among Monomakh's descendants, Prince Andrei Bogoliubskii of Suzdal captured and sacked Kiev in 1169. Andrei controlled Suzdalia and Novgorod and placed a vassal on the Kievan throne but could not reunite Russia. After his death political fragmentation accelerated. Thus before the Mongol invasion Russia had split into several segments: a declining Kiev, the southwest (Galicia and Volhynia), a dynamic northeast (Suzdal and Vladimir), and the commercial republics of Novgorod and Pskov in the northwest.

GOVERNMENT

Was Kievan Russia "feudal" and what does this term mean?[7] As Marxist-Leninists, Soviet scholars consider feudalism a socioeconomic formation common to all medieval Europe. Wrote L. V. Cherepnin:

> The ancient Russian state with its center in Kiev . . . was feudal because it was the organ of the power of the feudal landowners dominating over and dependent upon the peasants. And in this respect, there was no principal difference between Kievan Rus and the medieval states which emerged in the Romano-Germanic countries. . . . Just as in other countries, the feudal property in land bore a partition character and medieval Rus had a ladder of privileged feudal lords of different ranks. Doubtless, contracts also existed among them.[8]

Soviet scholars contend that feudal relationships between landowners and dependent peasants arose in ninth century Russia and were fully established by the 12th century. Landowners comprised a unified hierarchy, or feudal state, resembling those of western Europe, to defend manorial privilege. Vassals performed military service for their overlords and prevented princely autocracy. Most Western scholars, on the other hand, view feudalism mainly as a method of government with a defined hierarchy of lords and vassals (lesser lords) and estates (fiefs) distributed in return for service to an overlord. Kievan Russia, asserts Vernadsky, possessed elements of feudalism: fusion of public and private law and decentralized political authority, but its foreign trade did not fit a feudal pattern. Even after 1054 a single Kievan dynasty, with all princes considered equal, exercised political power; lesser lords could freely shift overlords; the manor was not universal; and land was bought and sold without restrictions.[9] Western medievalists, stressing vassalage and the fief as feudalism's chief features, believe that neither institution existed fully in Kievan Russia. The controversy is partly semantic, partly whether one stresses feudalism's political or socioeconomic aspects. In any case feudal elements in Kievan Russia took forms markedly different than in western Europe.

Was Kievan Russia a "state" in the sense of a unified, centralized administration? In the late 19th century N. I. Kostomarov affirmed that

---

[7] See discussion of feudalism in the appanage period below, pp. 107–9.

[8] In T. Riha, ed., *Readings in Russian Civilization*, 2d ed. (Chicago, 1969), vol. 1, p. 83.

[9] G. Vernadsky, "Feudalism in Russia," in Riha, *Readings*, vol. 1, pp. 69–81.

old Russia with a single ruling family of princes was a federation based upon common origin, customs, language, and religion, but that each principality retained its peculiarities and own government. Soviet historians emphasize Kievan Russia's unity and strength down to 1132: the wars of Igor and Sviatoslav united eastern Slavs in a powerful feudal monarchy reaching its peak under Iaroslav. Interprincely wars, fought largely to control Kiev, resembled those within early medieval European monarchies. Soviet scholars stress national unity and patriotism. Even after 1139, when principalities had their own dynasties and foreign policies, the concept of the Russian land persisted. To Vernadsky the numerous old Russian terms for state or government suggested that Kievan Russia was heterogeneous, a number of city-states united under the prince of Kiev, some coinciding with ancient tribes. By the late 12th century ten such states existed, each with its capital and dynasty (except Kiev and Novgorod) and all virtually sovereign. The remaining eight were Chernigov, Suzdalia, Riazan, Pereiaslav, Smolensk, Polotsk, Volhynia, and Galicia.

Kievan government, combining princely power with the city-state form, contained monarchical, aristocratic, and democratic elements. Even the greatest princes such as Iaroslav and Vladimir II, though their model was the absolute Byzantine emperor, were limited rulers. In a sense these two stood above classes and reflected popular desires in striving for unity and order. But though they claimed to be God's representatives on earth, neither could achieve absolute authority. Princes were the chief executives, directing justice and defense and protecting the Orthodox Church. Early princes regarded Russia as their joint patrimony; after Iaroslav the dynasty's senior prince supposedly occupied Kiev, the next eldest Chernigov and so on, but the growth of the princely dynasty soon made this rotation system too complex to administer. By the late 12th century civil wars and elections by the Kiev town assembly apparently were as important as seniority in the elevation of princes.

Princes governed with noble councils (*boiarskaia duma*) without whose consent no important decisions were made. The boyar council developed from the princely retinue (*druzhina*), whose leading Varangian and Slav members became boyars with estates and commercial interests. Acquiring extensive hereditary lands, boyars grew more independent of the prince than warrior chieftains of his retinue had been. Boyar councils helped to make laws, approve treaties, and served as courts of appeal, but their functions and powers were ill defined and differed in various parts of Russia. An inner cabinet (*muzhi perednie*) apparently met daily. Major state affairs were often discussed in plenary council sessions with the prince presiding.

The town meeting (*veche*) included some democratic aspects. Prerevolutionary Russian and many Western historians, stressing the popular character and importance of the *veche*, note that the prince consulted it before reaching important decisions. Soviet historians claim that aristocratic elements dominated the *veche*. Notes a Soviet account, "The *veche*, one of the most archaic institutions of popular authority, was utilized by landowners and placed in the service of the state in the form of a peculiar feudal democracy."[10] Often powerful nobles and merchants bribed the *veche,* which existed in all Russian principalities. Only the *veche* of Kiev exercised genuine national influence, though people from outlying regions rarely attended it. All freemen might participate in *veche* meetings, but only male heads of households voted. Meetings were convened by ringing the town bell or by announcement in the marketplace. Usually the mayor or a leading churchman presided. Custom required unanimity, and small minorities usually yielded to the majority. If a *veche* were evenly divided, the two factions might fight it out or a decision could be deferred. In case of disputed succession, the *veche* might select a new ruler; occasionally it demanded removal of an unpopular prince. The wealthy often determined *veche* decisions, but other freemen participated to some degree in government. Relationships of prince, boyar council, and *veche* varied widely by period and region. Princely authority tended to predominate except in the northwest, where aristocratic and representative bodies gained in power.

Kievan Russia lacked a central administration or bureaucracy; each principality was administered by the prince's court. Until 1054 and from 1113 to 1132 the prince of Kiev exercised considerable power over other towns, appointing governors (*posadniki*), often a son or relative, to govern for them. After 1054 Kievan control almost disappeared. Each town had an elected or appointed chiliarch (literally leader of 1,000 men; *tysiatskii*), who commanded the town militia and sometimes acted as spokesman against an unpopular prince.

Kievan Russia's army was decentralized and comprised princely and militia forces. Princely retinues, originally Varangians and Slav warriors, later boyars, were relatively small but mobile and well armed. Militia forces, recruited from townspeople and usually supplied with horses and weapons by the prince, were mobilized for major campaigns or emergencies. Among the forces which confronted steppe nomads, cavalry predominated, sometimes supplemented with peasant infantry. The Kievan warrior wore armor and a helmet, carried a shield, and was armed like Western knights with spear and sword. Bows and arrows were also frequently used. Each prince had his private army, but such forces often cooperated during invasions from the steppe.

FOREIGN RELATIONS

Kievan Russia played a significant role in medieval international affairs, and until the 12th century its chief commercial and cultural relations were with the Byzantine Empire, the leading Christian power of this era. Kievan foreign policy was much influenced by the frequent incursions of fierce steppe nomads, but Russia also had important dealings with Scandinavia, other Slavs, western Europe, and traded with the Orient. Russia's international position was favorable in the

---

[10] V. T. Pashuto and L. V. Cherepnin (eds.). *Drevnerusskoe gosudarstvo i ego mezhdunarodnoe znachenie* (Moscow, 1965), pp. 33–34.

south, tolerable in the west, but unfavorable in the southeastern steppe. Its principal external mission, claim Soviet historians, was to defend eastern Europe from Asiatic barbarism. Even after a unified Kievan foreign policy yielded to complex, rival policies of individual princely states, Russia remained important in eastern Europe.

Byzantium was Kievan Russia's political, economic, and cultural focus until Constantinople's decline in the 12th century. Some Western historians regard Kiev as a Byzantine satellite, while one Russian historian affirmed: "All the laws of the Greco-Roman emperors were binding upon Russia from the moment of their publication in Constantinople."[11] Soviet scholars, vehemently denying this, assert Kievan Russia's dignity and equality. Early tenth century Russian attacks on Constantinople led to regular commercial and diplomatic relations on an equal basis. Russian merchants flocked to Constantinople, and in 957 Princess Olga was received with honors befitting an independent sovereign. Dynastic intermarriage made Russian princes feel at home in Constantinople and visit it frequently. Vladimir I married Princess Anna, the Byzantine emperor's sister, and his grandson and two grandsons of Iaroslav also had Greek brides; a number of prominent Byzantines picked Russian spouses. Russia's adoption of Orthodoxy promoted commercial, political, and cultural ties and a degree of dependence on Byzantium. A fresco showing Iaroslav the Wise with a model of Kiev's St. Sofia Cathedral approaching a figure with imperial robes appears to confirm his vassalage to Byzantium. During the tenth and eleventh centuries Byzantine rulers frequently hired Russian military detachments. Sometimes Kiev and Constantinople were allies; at other times Byzantium sought to weaken Russia by allying with its steppe rivals. Byzantine and west European rulers, but not Russian leaders, considered Kiev a satellite or vassal of Constantinople, especially in the 11th century. There was never, however, any clear Russian political subordination to Byzantium.

Kievan Russia faced great peril from nomadic pressure in the east and southeast. Its birth coincided with the apogee of the Khazar khanate, a federation of mostly Turkic tribes from the lower Volga and north Caucasus. Sviatoslav virtually destroyed the Khazars, but that victory exposed Russia to the Pechenegs, a fiercer and more dangerous Asian opponent. In the mid-tenth century eight nomadic Pecheneg tribes formed a military league and invaded Russian lands. At first Russia repelled them, maintaining links with Tmutarakan, Byzantium, and Oriental markets; at times it employed Pecheneg mercenaries in its civil wars. As Kievan unity weakened, the traumatic struggle with the Kipchak tribes whom the Russians called Polovtsy developed. In 1055 Polovtsy appeared on the Dnieper River and until the 13th century remained Russia's most dangerous foe. Organized into two major tribal leagues along the Don and Dnieper rivers, they cut Russia off from the Black Sea, severed its commercial lifeline to Con-

---

[11] V. Ikonnikov, quoted in A. Vasiliev, "Was Old Russia a Vassal State of Byzantium?", *Speculum*, vol. 6, no. 3, p. 350.

stantinople, and destroyed Tmutarakan. From 1061 to 1092, notes the *Chronicle*, continual Polovtsy raids devastated Russian frontier towns and took thousands of Russians captive. Polovtsy incursions into the fertile Black Soil region stimulated Russian colonization of the Oka-Volga forest region but undermined the Kievan economy. By fostering national Russian efforts to repel them, especially under Vladimir II, however, the Polovtsy may have delayed Kievan Russia's disintegration. In 1185 occurred a famous episode in the Russo-Polovtsian wars. The Polovtsy defeated Prince Igor of Novgorod-Seversk, took him prisoner, and devastated the Pereiaslavl region. The *Tale of Igor*, the best known old Russian epic, depicts an embryonic national consciousness:

> [Igor], imbued with fighting spirit
> Led his brave troops against the land of the Polovtsians
> For the sake of the Russian land . . .
> And Igor spoke to his troops:
> Brothers and soldiers!
> It would be better for us to perish than to surrender . . .
> "I wish," he said, "to break my spear
> With you, Russian people, at the frontier of the Polovtsian land!
> I want either to die or be able to drink a helmetful of the Don."[12]

After 1190 Polovtsian pressure against Russia lessened, but it had helped to define Russia's national territory and character. Russia's successful resistance, Soviet historians affirm, protected medieval Europe from conquest.

Kievan Russia developed significant ties also with the Latin West. Military and commercial contacts with Scandinavia persisted into the 11th century. Simultaneously Russia established relations with the Holy Roman Empire. In 955 Olga requested a bishop from Emperor Otto I; in 990 Vladimir I's marriage to Anna, a relative of Otto II, reinforced these ties. Later, Iaroslav, as a counter to Byzantium, allied with France. The Crusades revealed Byzantine decline (especially the crusaders' sack of Constantinople in 1204) and the rise of the Latin West. Byzantine eclipse and Polovtsy incursions shifted much of Russian commerce into west European markets, notably through the German town of Regensburg.

Russia had important dealings with other Slav peoples. About 800 the western boundary of Slav settlement ran from Hamburg on the Elbe southward to Trieste on the Adriatic. Gradually the Germans thrust eastward to the Oder River, and in the early 13th century the Poles invited German Teutonic knights into East Prussia. Soviet historians, emphasizing friendship between Russian and east European peoples, stress Russia's partnership with Czechs, Slovaks, and Poles against German "aggression" and "drive to the east." In 1017 and 1029, however, Iaroslav cooperated with German princes against the Poles. Among the South Slavs, the Bulgars, a slavicized Asian people, acted

---

[12] Quoted from Basil Dmytryshyn, *Medieval Russia: A Source Book, 900–1700*, 2d ed. (Hinsdale, Illinois, 1973), p. 82.

as intermediaries between Russia and Byzantium. They supplied Russia with church books in Slavic translation, sent priests and translators to Kiev, and were middlemen in Russo-Byzantine commerce. From the 11th century on Serbian influence on Russian church literature gradually replaced Bulgarian, and Russian missionaries were active in Serbia. With western Slavs, too, there were dynastic intermarriages despite the schism of the 11th century between the Catholic and Orthodox churches.

Early Russian relations with the Orient were sporadic and limited. In the tenth century the Russian conquest of the north Caucasus opened commercial contacts with Islamic areas to the south and southeast; numerous Russian merchants visited Baghdad. Russians also traded with the Volga Bulgars and Khorezm in Central Asia, but the Moslem faith inhibited close social contacts or intermarriage. After the fall of Tmutarakan in the 11th century, ties with the Orient weakened.

Kievan Russia was usually hospitable to foreigners and receptive to external influences. Its relationship with Byzantium at first greatly overshadowed those with other regions, but its contacts with the Latin West became increasingly numerous and fruitful before the Mongol invasion.

DECLINE AND FALL

Free, productive Kievan civilization, rich in artistic achievement, succumbed to the primitive Mongols for both internal and external reasons. Kievan Russia's evident political disunity and weakness after 1054 resembled that of the Greek city-states before their conquest by Rome. Only the ablest Kievan rulers preserved unity for relatively brief periods. After 1054 separatism and regionalism prevailed over national unity and cooperation. Fratricidal wars and princely disputes reflected Kiev's failure to create effective central institutions. The princes could not control increasingly assertive towns; boyar councils and town assemblies grew in power.

Geographical factors were also significant. Kiev's leadership had been based upon its location on the great water route "from the Varangians to the Greeks" (Baltic to the Black Sea). This advantage disappeared when the Dnieper lifeline was cut. Kievan Russia never really secured its eastern flank in the steppe where stable boundaries were lacking. Russia's size and inadequate internal communications contributed to its disunity.

Kiev's prosperity and strength, some historians argue, depended upon foreign trade with Constantinople. As Byzantium declined commercially and politically, Kiev's commercial importance waned. Much Kievan trade passed to the Baltic towns; the economic importance of centers such as Novgorod and Smolensk increased. Kiev's strength was drained in wars with steppe nomads and by their destructive raids.

Soviet historians stress rising social tensions connected with the growth of feudalism as a factor in tearing Kievan Russia asunder. Antagonism developed between feudal landowners and peasants who were gradually losing their freedom of movement. In the towns growing class conflict between the poor and the boyar-merchant ruling element produced serious social revolts.

Finally, external events contributed to Kiev's decline and destruction. The numerous Russo-Polovtsian wars, by exhausting both parties, eased the way for the Mongol triumph. Just before the Mongol conquest these conflicts lessened and political conditions in Russia seemed to be improving, but neither the Russians nor other settled peoples could withstand the tremendous Mongol impact.

Suggested Additional Reading

CROSS, S. H.   "The Russian Primary Chronicle," *Harvard Studies and Notes in Philology and Literature,* vol. 12, p. 77ff.

DVORNIK, F.   "Byzantine Political Ideas in Kievan Russia," *Dumbarton Oaks Papers,* Nos. 9–10, 1956, pp. 73–123.

GREKOV, B.   *Kiev Rus* (Moscow, 1959).

LANTZEFF, G.   "Russian Eastward Expansion before the Mongol Invasion," *ASEER,* vol. 6, 1947, pp. 1–10.

PHILIPP, W.   "Russia's Position in Medieval Europe," *Russia: Essays in History and Literature,* ed. L. Legters (Leiden, 1972).

POLANSKA-WASYLENKO, N.   *Russia and Western Europe 10–13 Centuries* (London, 1954).

RIASANOVSKY, A. V.   "Runaway Slavs and Swift Danes . . .", *Speculum,* vol. 39, no. 2, 1964, pp. 288–97.

RYBAKOV, B.   *Early Centuries of Russian History* (Moscow, 1965).

SHULGIN, B.   "Kiev: Mother of Russian Towns," *SEER,* vol. 19, 62–82.

STOKES, A.   "The Balkan Campaigns of Svyatoslav Igorevich," *SEER,* vol. 41, 1962, pp. 466–96.

TIKHOMIROV, M.   *The Towns of Ancient Rus* (Moscow, 1959).

VERNADSKY, G.   *Kievan Russia* (New Haven, 1948).

———.   *Medieval Russian Laws* (New York, 1947).

4

Kievan Russia: Society, Culture, Religion, and Economic Life

By the ninth century the society and culture of the eastern Slavs had undergone considerable development and had achieved relative organization and sophistication. The precise nature of many facets of this society and culture, however, is still subject to debate owing to incomplete and often contradictory sources. On the all-important question regarding the nature of Kievan economic life two historiographical camps may be distinguished. The leading representative of the older view was the eminent Russian historian, V. O. Kliuchevskii, who argued that foreign trade constituted the chief determining element in the evolution of the economic life of Kievan Russia, and this view conditioned his evaluation of Kievan social and political life as well. Kliuchevskii's interpretation has been challenged by the prominent Soviet authority on Kievan Russia, B. D. Grekov, who argued that agriculture rather than foreign trade was the chief occupation of the population and the mainstay of the economic life of Kievan Russia, and that this agricultural life provided the key to understanding Kievan society and culture.

Indeed, Kliuchevskii ignored agriculture almost completely, assigning to it only a minor role in Kievan life. Grekov, on the other hand, while acknowledging the existence of foreign trade in Kievan Russia, tended to minimize its importance. The essence of Kliuchevskii's view is contained in the following often cited passage:

> The history of our society would have been substantially different had not our economy been for eight or nine centuries at variance with the nature of our country. In the 11th century the bulk of the Russian population was concentrated in the black-earth region of the middle Dnieper, and by the mid-fifteenth century it had moved to the upper Volga region. It would seem that in the former area agriculture should have been the chief basis of the national economy, and in the latter foreign trade, forestry, and other industries should have predominated. But external circumstances were such that while the Russians remained

in the Dnieper black-earth region they traded in products of the forest and other industries and began vigorously to plow only when they moved to the clayey soil of the Upper Volga.[1]

Grekov countered with an entirely different view: "There is no evidence in our sources to substantiate the basic theses of Kliuchevskii, Rozhkov, and their followers. In Kievan, Novgorodian, and Suzdalian Rus agriculture was the main occupation of the people."[2]

It would appear from a careful reading of the sources that the truth lies somewhere between these two interpretations. The sources, both written and archeological, provide ample evidence of the existence in Kievan times of a lively and lucrative foreign trade, carried on primarily with the Byzantine Empire, and at the same time there is evidence of extensive local and regional commerce within the Kievan lands. Constantine Porphyrogenitus, ruler of Byzantium from 945 to 959, has left us an invaluable description of the commercial activities of the Slavs in his *De Administrando Imperio*. He recounted how Russian princes and their agents assembled great trade convoys which sailed down the Dnieper River across the Black Sea to Constantinople, arriving each summer laden down with slaves and products of the forest: honey, furs, and wax. According to Porphyrogenitus, the princes and their retinues gathered tribute from the Slavs during the winter; and then with the arrival of spring, huge trees were felled and hollowed out to form boats, which transported the collected products down the Dnieper. In Constantinople these products were exchanged for luxury items: silks, wines, fruits, and fine weapons.

However important foreign trade was to the princes and their retinues, the bulk of the population derived a livlihood from agriculture. Archeological evidence clearly attests that agriculture was the primary occupation of the majority of the population. Excavations have uncovered evidence of the widespread use of the iron plowshare in the south by the eighth century and evidence of the use of a wooden forked plow (*sokha*) in the north. Evidence of the extensive cultivation of wheat, buckwheat, rye, oats, and barley, along with a wide variety of primitive agricultural implements, have been unearthed by archeologists. In pre-Kievan times various systems of tillage were in use. In the northern forested regions the slash-burn method was employed, which involved the felling of trees in the spring, burning them in the autumn, leaving the ashes over the winter, and sowing the cleared land the following spring. The ashes served as fertilizer, and the seeds were broadcast randomly and covered over by means of rakes or tree branches. Such fields were cultivated for anywhere from two to eight growing seasons or until the fertility of the soil was exhausted; then a new plot would be cleared and prepared. The tremendous amount of time and labor involved in this method of farming made extensive cooperation and communal methods essential to success.

---

[1] Kliuchevskii, *Boiarskaia duma drevnei Rusi* (Moscow, 1902), p. 13.

[2] B. D. Grekov, *Kievskaia Rus* (Moscow-Leningrad, 1948), p. 35. See the English translation of this work, *Kiev Rus* (Moscow, 1959), p. 70.

In the unforested steppe region to the south, there was no need to clear land, and cultivation was easier. Land was cultivated until its productivity was exhausted and then new lands would be opened up for cultivation. There was no regular system of crop rotation until Kievan times. Initially, a two-field system prevailed in which a plot of land was cultivated for several years, then left fallow for a number of years, and then replanted. Gradually, as in Western Europe, a three-field system was introduced in which crops were systematically rotated and one third of the land was allowed to remain fallow each year.

The harsh climate and primitive methods of agriculture fostered the need for cooperation and combined effort which resulted in the early emergence of the commune, or *obshchina*, in which land, implements, and livestock were owned in common by groups of people; and the obligation to work was shared equally. Two types of communal organization existed in Kievan times: first, family communes made up of blood relatives or what might be called a patriarchal commune consisting of several related generations; and second, the rural or territorial communes made up of unrelated neighbors who banded together to share the burdens of labor and the meager fruits of the earth. Each commune was, to a large extent, self-sufficient, producing all that was needed by the individual members: food, clothing, shelter, and implements. In addition, hunting, fishing, beekeeping and other forest industries were important supplemental occupations practiced by the rural population.

SOCIAL STRUCTURE

Having established the importance of trade and commerce for the upper classes, the princes and their retinues, and the importance of agriculture for the bulk of the population, let us now turn to an analysis of the structure of Kievan society. The process of social stratification had begun among the eastern Slavs long before the establishment of the Kievan state. As early as the sixth century, three distinct social categories had emerged: an aristocracy, a class of freemen, and slaves. The social structure became more complex once a formal state framework had been created. The basic judicial sources for the Kievan period are the *Russkaia pravda* (Russian Justice) of the first half of the 11th century, a collection of laws known as the *Pravda* of Iaroslav's sons of the second half of the 11th century, and the *Russkaia pravda* (expanded Russian Law) of the 12th century.[3] These law codes delineate several distinct social categories within Kievan society. The relative social status of individual social groups was reflected in the respective *wergeld*, or monetary value, placed on an individual's life in cases of unavenged murder.

At the very pinnacle of society in Kievan Russia stood the rapidly proliferating princely family, the House of Riurik. Directly beneath the princely class on the Kievan social ladder were the *muzhi*, or upper-

---

[3] For an annotated translation of these important documents see George Vernadsky, tr., *Medieval Russian Laws* (New York, 1969).

class freemen, who were assigned a wergeld of 80 *grivna* (there is no general consensus among historians as to the value or precise meaning of this monetary unit; its value must have fluctuated widely during Kievan times). The *muzhi* made up the *druzhina*, or military retinue, of the princes. Initially, the composition of the *druzhina* was Scandinavian, but by the 11th century Slavic elements freely entered this important social and economic group. These servitors of the prince derived their wealth and social prestige from participation in trade, from war booty, from grants of land, and from other rewards and favors bestowed upon them by the prince. The members of the *druzhina* were the closest associates of the prince, serving as his advisers in both military and commercial affairs, and acting as his administrative agents in local affairs.

In addition, there was a nonservice aristocracy, which was made up of the descendants of the old Slavic tribal aristocracy and some others who had succeeded in amassing great wealth from lucrative foreign trade or other enterprises. The wergeld for this nonservice aristocracy was fixed at 40 *grivna*, half that of a member of the *druzhina*. Gradually, these two aristocracies, the aristocracy of service, and the aristocracy of social origin and wealth, merged into the boyar class. The origin of the term "boyar" is obscure, but it was clearly in widespread use by the mid-tenth century and was used to denote the upper class. As time passed, the House of Riurik increased in size and became divided into groups of senior and lesser princes. The lesser princes often became almost indistinguishable from the boyars. During Kievan times the boyar class was not a closed, corporate class; movement into and out of the ranks of the boyars was possible, and boyars maintained the right of departure, that is, they were free to leave the service of one prince and take up service with another prince without jeopardizing their hereditary rights, privileged social position, or economic power. They enjoyed, however, no special legal rights and were on an equal footing with other freemen in terms of their right to own land and participate in trade and commerce.

In a category below the *muzhi* were the *liudi*, or middle-class freemen. The wergeld for *liudi* was fixed by *Russkaia pravda* at 40 *grivna*, the same as for a member of the nonservice aristocracy. Sources are vague when it comes to a precise definition of the *liudi*. Many were apparently urban citizens who owned such industrial enterprises as smithies, carpentry shops, and tanneries, while others were middle-class merchants involved in both local and regional trade as well as foreign trade. Still other *liudi* derived their wealth from property owned outside the city, and finally, some members of this group lived in rural areas as moderately well-to-do landowners. The *liudi* enjoyed no special legal privileges aside from those enjoyed by all freemen.

The lower classes in Kievan society were made up of diverse elements both rural and urban. The wergeld for lower-class freemen was fixed at 5 *grivna*, indicating a substantial gulf separating the upper classes from the lower classes. In the towns and cities the lower classes were known collectively as the *molodshie liudi* (younger men). These were the artisans of various types: tanners, potters, armorers, goldsmiths, glaziers, carpenters, masons. They generally were employed by the shop-owners or merchants, and they were often organized into associations or guilds and lived in designated sections of the city: the potters' section, the carpenters' section, the tanners' section, etc.

In the rural areas lower-class people were known collectively as *smerdy* ("stinkers"). This term has been subject to long and still unresolved controversy. Kliuchevskii believed that *smerdy* were free peasants living on princely land and referred to them as state peasants. Other historians have advanced the view that two types of *smerdy* existed in Kievan times: village *smerdy* living on communally held land not yet assimilated by the boyar class, and *smerdy* dependent on princes and boyars. The prerevolutionary historian, A. S. Presniakov, argued that the term *smerdy* was used to denote the entire undifferentiated rural population. Grekov has argued in favor of two types of *smerdy*: the free and the dependent. The free *smerdy* were, in his opinion, organized into free communes and enjoyed all the rights and privileges of any freemen in Kievan society. The dependent *smerdy* were those living on princely land or boyar land and were required to perform corvée (labor service) for the landlord or to pay him rent in kind. Dependent *smerdy* were subject to the special jurisdiction of the prince and could not be arrested or prosecuted without the prince's authorization. If a dependent *smerd* died without male heirs, his property reverted to the prince. From the sources, it would appear that *smerdy* were clearly divided into two groups, the free and the dependent, but it would be a mistake to call dependent *smerdy* serfs as Soviet accounts often do.

It is difficult to estimate the number of *smerdy* in Kievan Russia, but they clearly constituted the bulk of the rural population, with the free vastly outnumbering the dependent, although the latter probably increased significantly in number during the later Kievan period when the upper classes turned more and more to landowning as a source of income. Little is known about the way of life, habits, attitudes, and customs of the *smerdy* because the sources invariably concentrate on the upper classes and urban population.

Two more social categories require mention: the half-free and the slaves. It should be emphasized that serfdom as a legal institution was unknown in Kievan times, but there were social groups whose rights were proscribed by law. These are known in the sources as *zakupy*, whom Vernadsky refers to as the half-free, and a second group known as *cheliad*, or slaves.

As with other aspects of the Kievan social structure, there has been little agreement among historians about a precise definition of the *zakupy*. The *zakup* was not a serf. The relationship between him and his lord was one of debtor to creditor. The debt incurred was, by agreement, to be repaid by specified labor service rather than money, although money, if available, could be used to pay it off. The debtor was usually a *smerd* who borrowed money for some specific purpose and agreed to repay it by his own labor. The debtor might also be a hired laborer who contracted to receive his wages in advance, thus acquiring a legal debt calling for repayment with interest over a period of time. In this manner, the *smerd* became a *zakup,* or indentured laborer, until his debt was repaid. Soviet historians, especially Grekov, argue that the existence of *zakupy* indicates the growth of feudalism in Kievan times. "The *zakup,* then, is by origin generally a *smerd,* deprived of the means of production and forced by economic circumstances to seek a source of subsistence from the large landowners. This is a symptom of the degradation of the village community under the impact of feudal relationships."[4] This interpretation is tantamount to calling the *zakup* a serf, but clearly his social and economic status was envisaged as being temporary because once his debt was repaid he immediately became a freeman again with all the rights associated with that category. Still, at certain times, *zakupy* must have been numerous because the sources credit them with staging a serious rebellion in Kiev in 1113. Afterwards, the legal rights and status of *zakupy* were more clearly defined.

Kievan judicial sources make a clear distinction between the *zakup* and the slave—the *cheliad,* or *kholop.* Indeed, the Expanded *Pravda* provides that if a *zakup* attempted to flee to evade his legal obligation, he *became* a slave. The existence of slavery in Kievan times has been amply documented, and it is clear that slaves were a major element in trade between Kiev and Constantinople. There were two essential types of slavery: temporary and permanent. The former category was made up of war prisoners, both military and civilian. Usually, with the conclusion of peace such captives were returned on payment of ransom. Otherwise, the captives remained slaves and became part of the war booty. Permanent slavery, according to the Expanded *Pravda,* resulted from several specific factors. A man became a permanent slave if he sold himself into slavery voluntarily or married a female slave without first making an agreement with her lord about his own free status. A person became a slave if he attempted to flee his master in order to evade a legal obligation. From the considerable number of articles on slavery in the Expanded *Pravda,* it must have been widespread in Kievan Russia.

In summary, Kievan social structure was complex and stratified with diverse, clearly delineated social groups. The princely class expanded greatly in Kievan times and occupied the pinnacle of the social structure. Beneath it was the boyar class, followed by middle-class freemen, comprising the bulk of the urban population. Lower still were the "younger men" (*molodshie liudi*) in towns, and *smerdy,* or "stinkers," as the bulk of the semiobligated rural population. At the bottom of the social ladder were the half-free and the slaves. Kievan Russia's social structure remained fluid. There were no built in barriers to social mobility, and movement from one segment of society to another was determined by chance, opportunity, and skill. Except for the princely class, heredity counted for little in determining one's status.

---

[4] B. D. Grekov, *Kiev Rus* (Moscow, 1959), p. 275.

URBAN LIFE

The land of Rus was known in Scandinavian sources as Gardariki, the land of towns. The Soviet historian, Tikhomirov, the leading authority on old Russian towns, has combed the sources and arrived at a figure of 271 towns recorded in Rus in the Kievan era. He admitted that this was a modest estimate.[5] Many towns were founded between the 11th and 13th centuries, but the oldest date back to the eighth and ninth centuries and perhaps even earlier. Many early towns developed around the sites of earlier fortified settlements (*gorodishche*), located usually on elevated, easily defended ground situated at strategic points. Kiev, on the hills overlooking the Dnieper River, must have been originally an early *gorodishche*. *The Primary Chronicle* records that long before the emergence of the Kievan state three brothers, Kii, Shchek, and Khoriv, "built a town in honor of their eldest brother and named it Kiev. Around the town lay a wood and a great pine forest in which they used to trap wild beasts."[6] Around this small fortified settlement the city of Kiev, "the mother of Russian cities," grew and developed. *The Primary Chronicle* offers two versions of Novgorod's origin: One ascribes its foundation to the Slavic tribe, the Slovene; the other attributes its origin to Riurik and his retinue. The important point is that Novgorod is at least as old as Kiev, if not older. These two urban centers, one at either end of the great waterway, have been extensively excavated by archeologists, and a great quantity of information has been unearthed which reveals much detail about the nature of urban life during Kievan times.

The extensive development of urban centers in Kievan Russia, like so many other aspects of Kievan history, has been subject to ongoing controversy. Kliuchevskii, in conformity with his view on the central importance of trade in Kievan society, observed that the earliest Russian towns were located along the great waterway "from the Varangians to the Greeks," and along the upper Volga River. He noted several exceptions, but nevertheless connected the emergence of urban centers with the development of trade and commerce. "These towns emerged as gathering places for Rus trade," Kliuchevskii suggested, "depots where Rus exports were stored and prepared for shipment. Each one of them was a center of some industrial area and [served as] an intermediary between the latter and the maritime markets. But very quickly events turned these trading centers into political centers and their industrial areas into their dependent regions."[7] The Soviet authority, S. V. Iushkov, reversed Kliuchevskii's interpretation by arguing that the prince and his retinue settled, with the elders of Slavic tribes, in tribal towns owing to the protection they offered, transforming these places of refuge into political and administrative centers. Later, craftsmen and traders were attracted to these towns, and trade and commerce were

---

[5] M. N. Tikhomirov, *The Towns of Ancient Rus* (Moscow, 1959), p. 43.

[6] S. H. Cross, "The Russian Primary Chronicle" *Harvard Studies and Notes in Philology and Literature,* vol. 12, p. 54.

[7] Kliuchevskii, *Boiarskaia duma drevnei Rusi,* p. 22.

fostered and developed.[8] Tikhomirov offered still another alternative: "In my opinion, towns arose primarily where agriculture developed, where craftsmen and merchants made their appearance and urban districts took shape around their centers."[9] In this view, developing agriculture and handicrafts in a given region led to the appearance of towns which in turn led to the development of trade and commerce. Tikhomirov rejected the view that the waterways were vital to the emergence of towns, noting the many urban centers which sprang up at some distance from waterways, but he did not deny that commerce contributed significantly to the growth of towns and helped to expand their wealth.

The medieval town of Kievan Russia was first of all a walled enclosure, perhaps stemming from the old fortified citadel. Gradually craftsmen and merchants gathered in the immediate vicinity of the citadel, which offered protection in times of danger. These settlements of craftsmen and merchants became known as *posady,* or suburbs. These centers of trade and industry divided, as they grew, into sections, or *kontsy,* connected with the practice of a given handicraft or skill, e.g. the potters' section, the carpenters' section, the smithies' section, etc. Central marketplaces gradually emerged in which trade was conducted on a broad scale. Although handicrafts and trade dominated the town economy, close contact with surrounding agricultural areas was maintained because the towns needed their products.

The productive capacities of the larger towns were extremely diverse, and many skills became highly developed. The leading Soviet authority on medieval handicrafts is B. A. Rybakov, whose comprehensive research has led him to single out the practice of no less than 64 specific trades in Kievan Russia. Tikhomirov provides a list of thirty-four trades, which although incomplete demonstrate the diversity of Russian skills in Kievan times.[10] Archeological excavations have turned up many examples of these crafts and testify to the high level of craftsmanship in Kievan times.

Most artisans and craftsmen were freemen in business for themselves or employed by merchants or members of the upper classes, although there were significant numbers of craftsmen who were slaves of princes and boyars. There were also *zakup* craftsmen. The numerous crafts pursued in Kievan times indicate that these towns, at least major ones, were highly developed centers of production, engaging in local, regional, and foreign trade. Such major centers as Kiev, Novgorod, Smolensk, Rostov, Suzdal, and Riazan must have been very large, although we do not know their precise population during Kievan times. Still, their populations must have numbered in the tens of thousands. The populations of other towns rarely exceeded 1,000.

Russian towns in this period were built chiefly of wood. Thus we know little about how these early towns looked because wood is so

[8] S. V. Iushkov, *Obshchestvenno-politicheskii stroi i pravo Kievskogo gosudarstva* (Moscow, 1949), 257–67.

[9] M. N. Tikhomirov, *The Towns of Ancient Rus,* p. 60.

[10] Tikhomirov, *The Towns of Ancient Rus,* pp. 91–92.

perishable. One of the greatest ravages of medieval times was fire, and the chronicles record frequent and terrible fires, which wiped out entire towns. Despite its impermanence, wood had obvious advantages because it was plentiful, especially in the northern forest region, and offered better protection than other materials from the cold, damp climate. Wooden structures were easier to heat and provided better insulation than stone or brick buildings, and wood was easier to work with, more flexible than stone or brick, and thus wooden buildings could be constructed quickly with few tools, of which axes were the most important.

In Kievan times, most Russian towns had wooden fortifications which, in the absence of firearms and heavy siege equipment, offered sufficient protection from external attack. The citadel, or kremlin, of medieval Russian cities was usually constructed on elevated ground, often where two rivers met or on heights overlooking a river bank. The citadel was surrounded by timber walls much like stockades around American western forts. The walls were fortified by towers, sometimes constructed on stone foundations for stability and permanence. The number of gates in the wooden stockade depended on the size of the

Michael Curran

Wooden church in the Suzdal principality

town. Kiev had at least four gates. In major towns one gate was designated the main entrance and it was often of stone. The remains of the famous Golden Gate of Kiev, modeled after those of Constantinople, still exist, and Vladimir's Golden Gate has survived intact. By the 12th century, stone walls began to replace the wooden stockades in the major centers.

As towns grew and expanded, the territory of the citadel became too confined to accommodate the entire population and this led to the establishment of suburbs (*posady*), new sections built up around the walls of the citadel. They were in turn surrounded by new walls serving as an outer belt of fortifications. As the town developed outside the citadel, recognizable streets emerged and finally whole sections became defined. In larger towns streets were paved with logs. The method of paving streets was uniform in Kievan Russia. Three or four thin wooden poles were laid out longitudinally along the axis of the street. Split half-logs, usually of pine, were notched on the rounded bottom side and laid transversely, side by side, on the thin poles. Thus a stable roadway was constructed, immune to frequent freezing and thawing and accompanying thick mud. Summer and winter sleds were used on these paved streets, the runners moving easily over the flat, uniform surface of the log streets.

There were several types of buildings in the typical medieval Rus-

David MacKenzie

Golden Gate of Vladimir (about 1160)

sian town: houses, workshops, warehouses, official buildings, and churches. Most buildings were of wood, although stone churches appeared as early as the 11th century in major cities. Most wooden dwellings were of the box-frame type with logs notched at the end and fitted together much like log cabins of early America. The living quarters (the *izba*) were square or rectangular, a single large room with a stove in one corner for heating and cooking. The living quarters were often connected to an unheated storeroom or outhouse (*klet*) by a lobby or entry way. Wooden buildings were often decorated with beautiful and elaborate wood carvings on the gables and around the windows. The towns must have had a rather picturesque appearance.

RELIGION AND CULTURE

A major turning point in the history of Kievan Russia and in all of Russian history was the conversion to Christianity, ascribed by tradition to the year 988. Before discussing this momentous event in the development of Russia, we must first sketch briefly the nature of Kievan religion before conversion.

The religion of the early eastern Slavs was a diverse paganism with no single pantheon of gods accepted by all. Each Slavic tribe worshipped its own group of pagan gods in accordance with its own customs. Nonetheless, there were several common features of Slavic pagan practice. For example, ancestor worship and the worship of nature and of various wood, river, and household spirits were widely practiced among the Slavic tribes. Sacrifices of animals and occasionally of human beings were made to appease and placate these spirits.

Several pagan gods were widely venerated by the ancient Slavs. The *Chronicles* make frequent reference to efforts by the Christian clergy to stamp out pagan practices after the conversion, especially the cult of Rod and Rozhanitsa. These gods represented the concept of fertility, so essential to an agricultural people. The term, *rod,* means clan or family, and in the broad sense Rod and Rozhanitsa represented the forces of reproduction essential to renew the clan. They may also have represented the forces of fertility inherent in the soil upon which the clan's livlihood and prosperity depended. As late as the 13th century, the clergy felt compelled to attack continuing sacrificial rites to these pagan gods.

Vernadsky has suggested that the Russian word for God—*Bog*—may have had an earlier meaning of simply "light," it is also the root of the Russian word for wealth—*bogatstvo*. The Slavic pagan gods Svarog and Dazhbog often mentioned in the sources, were associated with the heavens and the sun, respectively, and represented the givers of life, the providers of wealth. Stribog, another frequently mentioned deity, was associated with the air and represented forces controlling the winds. Finally, there was Perun, the god of thunder and lightning, often associated with the Scandinavian god Thor. Deeply rooted in the Slavic mentality, the cult of Perun was later transformed into a cult of the Prophet Elijah, the Christian counterpart to the pagan thunder-god.

In spite of these common features, Slavic paganism did not involve a hierarchical priesthood nor the use of elaborate temples. Statues of pagan idols were erected by the early Slavs and several examples of stone idols have survived, but the diversity of pagan cults and the absence of a formal priesthood meant that organized resistance to the new Christian religion never became unified or consistent, though pagan practices persisted in Russia into modern times.

Christianity was known to the Slavs before 988. Christian influences entered Rus during the early tenth century from a variety of sources, from Byzantium, Scandinavia, and Central Europe. We know, for example, from the treaty signed between Prince Igor and the Byzantines in 945 that some members of his military retinue were already Christians. The treaty announced,

> If any inhabitant of the land of Rus, thinks to violate this amity, may such of these transgressors as have adopted the Christian faith incur . . . punishment from Almighty God in the shape of damnation and destruction forevermore. If any of these transgressors be not baptized, may they receive help neither from God nor from Perun. . . .[11]

There was a Christian church in Kiev, the Church of St. Elias, where the baptized Russes swore to observe the conditions of the treaty of 945. We also know that Princess Olga, the wife of Prince Igor, was converted to Christianity and baptized in Constantinople in 955. Yet Christianity did not strike permanent roots at that time, and paganism persisted as the official religion. Nevertheless, these significant early Christian influences helped prepare the way for Russia's subsequent conversion.

Paganism was also being swept aside in many areas bordering on Kievan Russia. By the 980s, Kiev was surrounded by peoples who had at least nominally given up paganism in favor of one of the great world religions. The Khazars (at least the ruling class) had embraced Judaism around 865, and the Volga Bulgars had become Moslem by 920. Christianity was also making rapid progress among Kiev's western neighbors: the Baltic Slavs, the Poles, the Hungarians, the Bulgars, the Danes, and the Norwegians. Kievan Russia, the last great pagan stronghold in the region, found herself increasingly isolated.

About 980, Prince Vladimir, once firmly established on the throne of Kiev, recognized the need to overcome this cultural and religious isolation. A common and unified religion, he realized, would help consolidate his precarious control over eastern Slav lands. Vladimir's extensive foreign contacts offered him various choices of religion. According to *The Primary Chronicle,* Vladimir called together his military retinue and city elders to discuss the religious situation and to investigate the Moslem, Jewish, and Christian faiths.

Vladimir first investigated the Moslem religion, being informed by the Volga Bulgars that "they believed in God, and that Mahomet instructed them to practice circumcision, to eat no pork, to drink no wine,

---

[11] Cross, "The Russian Primary Chronicle," p. 160.

and, after death, promised them complete fulfillment of their carnal desires." Vladimir, although impressed by the latter promise, rejected Islam, saying, "Drinking is the joy of the Russes. We cannot exist without that pleasure." Likewise, he rejected the views of the Pope's agents, and the Judaism of the Khazars. The chroniclers then recorded the visit of learned Greek scholars from Byzantium, and, as one might have expected, Vladimir was reputedly deeply impressed with their presentation of Orthodoxy.

> Vladimir summoned together his boyars and city elders, and said to them, "Behold, the Bulgars came before me urging me to accept their religion. Then came the Germans and praised their own faith; and after them came the Jews. Finally, the Greeks appeared, criticizing all other faiths but commending their own, and they spoke at length, telling the history of the world from its beginning. Their words were artful, and it was wondrous to listen and pleasant to hear them. They preach the existence of another world. Whoever adopts our religion and then dies shall arise and live forever. But whoever embraces another faith, shall be consumed by fire in the next world." What is your opinion on this subject and what do you answer?[12]

Vladimir was advised to send out his own emissaries to investigate the various faiths at first hand. And it was done. His emissaries reported to Vladimir that they were overwhelmed with Greek Christianity. "Then we went to Greece, and the Greeks led us to the edifices where they worship their God, and we knew not whether we were in heaven or on earth. For on earth there is no such splendor or such beauty, and we are at a loss to describe it." Note that it was the splendor of the church services and the beauty of the churches of Constantinople that so impressed the emissaries, not the spiritual content of Greek Christianity. This preoccupation with external form over internal content was to remain a hallmark of Russian Christianity. After listening to the emissaries, the boyars reminded Vladimir, "If the Greek faith were evil, it would not have been adopted by your grandmother Olga who was wiser than all other men."[13] Vladimir decided to adopt the Orthodox faith of Byzantium.

The *Chronicle* version is essentially a myth, but it contains an underlying kernel of truth. Vladimir certainly had opportunities to hear the merits of various religions debated in Kiev from Arabs, Jews, Bulgars and Greeks who visited the city for trade and from Russian travellers. The advantages of accepting Greek Orthodoxy were compelling owing to the extensive commercial contacts already existing between Kiev and Constantinople. The example of Olga and other Kievan converts to Christianity also influenced him. So his decision appears to have been preordained. What remained was how to arrange the actual conversion.

In this Vladimir was aided by fortuitous events. The Byzantine emperors, the brothers Basil II and Constantine VIII, threatened by

---

[12] Ibid., pp. 197–98.
[13] Ibid., p. 199.

internal and external enemies, desperately needed Kievan military aid. Appealing to Kievan Russia, they offered their sister Anna in marriage to Vladimir in return for his military support. In January 988 Vladimir agreed and promptly dispatched 6,000 troops, with whose help the Byzantine emperors defeated their enemies. Once the immediate threats to the Byzantine Empire had been removed, Basil and Constantine hesitated to send their sister to barbaric Kiev. After all, marriage into the Byzantine imperial family was an honor reserved for the most illustrious ruling families in the Christian world. Vladimir could hardly have been considered worthy of such an honor.

This situation offered Vladimir a great opportunity, for he could now adopt Orthodoxy on his own terms, preventing Kiev from becoming a dependency of Byzantium. Because the Byzantine emperors refused to honor their promise, Vladimir marched against Greek held territories in the Crimea. In July 988 he captured the Greek city of Kherson, forcing the Byzantines to sue for peace. As a condition of peace Basil and Constantine agreed to send their sister to Kherson, where, after Vladimir's baptism, the wedding took place.

Shortly thereafter Vladimir returned to Kiev with his new wife and many Greek priests and monks authorized to help him establish Orthodoxy in the Kievan realm. Vladimir "directed that the [pagan] idols should be overthrown, and that some should be cut to pieces and others burned with fire. . . . Thereafter Vladimir sent heralds throughout the whole city to proclaim that if any inhabitant, rich or poor, did not betake himself to the river, he would risk the Prince's displeasure."[14] By Vladimir's order, Kiev's entire population was baptized in the Dnieper River. Similar orders were sent out to all cities and territories of Kievan Rus.

Thus Kievan Russia became a civilized Christian nation. This conversion in itself was important, but even more significant was that Russia's Christianity came from Byzantium. Byzantine influences would shape the development of Russian thought and culture for centuries to come. At the time of Russia's conversion Christianity was still one, although deep rifts had appeared between the western Latin Church and the eastern Greek Church. These broadened into an open break in 1054, and after that Kievan Russia nurtured herself on the Byzantine forms and patterns which became all pervasive, influencing Russian art, architecture, literature, law, philosophy, and religion.

Byzantine Christianity, while raising Kievan Russia to a new and higher level of civilization, introduced a degree of rigidity and formalism into her cultural tradition, which would inhibit future Russian cultural development. Orthodoxy was accepted with the uncritical enthusiasm of the new convert, and Byzantium became the model for Kievan culture as the Russians tried to duplicate the minutest details of the Byzantine Christian tradition. The seductive cultural heritage of the Byzantine Empire remained unquestioned; thus Russia accepted "the Byzantine achievement . . . without the Byzantine inquisitive-

---

[14] Ibid., p. 204.

ness."[15] The Russians were never able or even inclined to develop or expand on the Byzantine heritage; instead they tenaciously defended the acquired habits of thought.

Nevertheless, the impact of the conversion cannot be overestimated even though Soviet historians tend to minimize it. The Soviet scholar Rybakov has summarized the current view: "Christianity cannot be counterposed to paganism, since they are but two forms, two variations of the one and the same primitive ideology, differing only in their outward manifestations." Rybakov admitted, however, that the Russian Church played an important role in consolidating the Kievan state, and bringing Russian culture closer to the cultural treasures of Byzantium by spreading education and creating enduring literary and artistic traditions. But, in sum, he argued,

> it must be remembered that the Russian people paid dearly for that positive contribution of the Church: the poison of religious ideology penetrated (deeper than in pagan times) into all the pores of the people's life, it dulled the class struggle, revived primitive notions in a new form, and for long centuries fastened in the consciousness of the people the ideas of a world beyond, of the divine origin of rulers, and providentialism, i.e., the concept that the fates of people are always governed by God's will.[16]

At first the conversion was only nominal; pagan practices persisted for many years, especially among the lower classes to whom the spiritual substance of the new religion was alien. This situation led to a cultural dualism in postconversion Russian culture, fostered by the existence of a small, highly cultivated, Byzantinized upper class which struggled to assimilate a sophisticated religion and culture, while the primitive Slavic masses adhered to the old culture and traditions. At first Christianity overlaid the older culture; then it gradually absorbed and enveloped it.

Almost all aspects of Russian life felt the impact of the conversion. When a written language was introduced to make Greek Christian beliefs accessible to Russians, it was Old Church Slavonic, based on forms devised in the ninth century by the apostles of the Slavs, Cyril and Methodius, for Moravian converts to Christianity. Church Slavonic, along with Greek and Latin, emerged as one of Christianity's three great languages. Kievan Russia was flooded with religious tracts and sermons, which along with Church service books, all translated into Church Slavonic, formed the backbone of the Russian literary language until the 17th century. In old Russia written literature was almost exclusively religious, and the chronicles too were composed by learned monks and written in religious language. Although painstakingly copied by hand, books must have been produced in considerable numbers because more than 500 written works from the 11th to the 14th centuries

---

[15] G. Florovsky, "The Problem of Old Russian Culture," *SR*, March, 1962, p. 14.

[16] B. A. Rybakov, *The Early Centuries of Russian History* (Moscow, 1965), pp. 51, 67.

have survived. Since the level of literacy in Russia was extremely low, these written works were accessible only to a few.

The common people, whose illiteracy prevented direct access to Church literature, had their own highly developed oral literary tradition, enough of which has survived to allow us insight into popular folklore. Its basic element was song, in which all life was celebrated from everyday occurrences to great historic events. Especially important were the old sagas (*byliny*) which depicted activities of epic warriors (*bogatyri*), the popular heroes of the Kievan period. The most famous *bogatyri*, members of Prince Vladimir's retinue, were always prepared to defend their prince and native land against all enemies. Each had an individual, fully developed personality and identifiable character traits. Among them was Ilia Muromets, a huge man of peasant stock, a Slavic Paul Bunyan, able to bend nature to his will. Also there was Aliosha Popovich, son of a priest, who accomplished great feats by cunning and cleverness and invariably outsmarted his enemies. Dobrynia Nikitich was a boyar exemplifying loyalty and reliability, a man of action available to perform any task. Finally, there was the humorous and charming Churilo Plenkovich, a true Don Juan, who always had time to charm beautiful women despite terrible danger. Such tales of the exploits of the *bogatyri* were recited by bards and preserved orally from generation to generation. There were also whole cycles of fairy tales replete with magic, mystery, and extraordinary events. Such folktales contrasted sharply with the somber, abstract Byzantine religious works.

Perhaps the most remarkable example of the folk genre is *The Tale of Igor*, written in the late 12th century, to record the actual struggle of a minor prince and his retinue against the steppe nomads. Skillfully combining Christian and popular pagan traditions, the author produced a highly sophisticated literary work which sounded a call for unity and common action among the princes. The author laments the lack of political unity and cooperation among Russian princes whose selfishness and pursuit of personal glory would doom Kievan Russia.

In art and architecture Byzantine influences were most palpable. The ornate splendor of Byzantine art and architecture, more than an abstract theology, overawed the Russians and persuaded them to accept Orthodoxy. Church art became the focus of faith for the Russians: the great stone churches, icons, frescoes, and mosaics assaulted the senses and lifted people toward heaven, transporting them from the mundane world. These outward manifestations of religion were extremely important in spreading the new beliefs, as Kiev's rulers recognized. Vladimir undertook an extensive building program after his conversion, and his son, Iaroslav the Wise, resolved to give Kiev some of Constantinople's imperial splendor. The climax of Iaroslav's massive building program was the great St. Sofia Cathedral in Kiev. Completed in 1036, it was the most impressive religious structure in Russia and served as the prototype for later stone churches throughout the land. Not only the massive external form of St. Sophia impressed the laity but also its luxurious internal decorations, frescoes and mosaics which are among the finest examples of Byzantine art. St. Sophia's interior supplied the basic iconographic models followed in Russia for almost a thousand years.

Smaller in scale but no less impressive was the St. Sofia Cathedral in Novgorod, completed in 1062. It reveals the adaptation of Byzantine forms to northern conditions and tastes. Much external ornamentation typical of the Kiev St. Sophia was eliminated in Novgorod, reflecting the northern desire for uniformity and simplicity. The characteristic Russian onion domes, flared sides, and elongated spires developed early in Novgorod.

Iconography was vital to the Russian religious tradition, and here Byzantine tradition was paramount. Found primarily in the Eastern Orthodox tradition, icons are religiously inspired pictures painted on specially prepared panels of wood. Icons were produced in Russia in great numbers, both for churches and for homes of the faithful. Just as the Church was to reflect God's kingdom on earth, so icons served to convey a sense of spirituality and provide an entry into that mystical world lying beyond sense experience. The iconographer, rather than portray worldly objects and situations, sought to create a link with the boundless eternity of God and to evoke a spiritual reality. Icons were created to foster reverence and aid in worship. They helped instruct an illiterate population by attempting to bring Heaven down to earth.

Russian iconographers were especially remarkable for their use of color, and this distinguishes Russian icons from other types. This characteristic reflected the Russians' lively concern with nature. A leading Soviet expert on iconography wrote about a famous Russian icon painter, Andrei Rublev:

> He takes the colors for his palette not from the traditional canons of color, but from the Russian nature around him, the beauty of which he keenly sensed. His magnificent deep blue is suggested by the blue spring sky; his whites recall the birches so dear to a Russian; his green is close to the color of unripe rye; his golden ochre summons up memories of fallen autumn leaves; in his dark green colors there is something of the twilight shadows of the dense pine forests. He translated the colors of Russian nature into the lofty language of art.[17]

Indissolubly linked with the ritual and tradition of the Orthodox faith, icons have remained an important element of Russian religious expression.

Administratively, the Russian Church was organized like the Byzantine Church and headed by a metropolitan appointed by the Patriarch of Constantinople. For the first two centuries all but two of its metropolitans were Greek. Larger towns had bishops, often native Russians, nominated by the princes and confirmed by the metropolitan. At first the clergy were Greek priests and monks, but a native clergy developed rapidly, organized on Byzantine patterns and divided into two general categories: the "black clergy," monks who had taken vows renouncing the earthly world, and "white clergy," parish priests and deacons whose

---

[17] V. Lazarev, *Andrei Rublev* (Moscow, 1960), p. 19.

mission was to minister to the needs of the faithful. Ecclesiastical officials—bishops, abbots and others—were drawn from the celibate monastic clergy. Parish priests, in contrast to regulations of the Western Church, had to be married.

Monasteries were among the most important of Church institutions. Many devout Orthodox believed that the Christian ideal could best be achieved in monastic life, and significant numbers chose this ascetic approach. The chief monastery of this era was Kiev's Monastery of the Caves, established in the mid-11th century. Monasteries served to spread Christianity, learning, and the arts. The first Russian libraries were established in monasteries, and it was monks who kept records, composed chronicles, copied books and manuscripts, and engaged in charitable activities, providing care for the sick and the destitute. Monasteries therefore played a key social and cultural, as well as a vital religious, role in Kievan Russia.

Kievan culture was dominated by the Church and its most lasting achievements—in art and architecture—originated there. Kievan Russia, however, despite some remarkable contributions, was culturally isolated from Latin Christendom and western Europe by the accident of adopting Byzantine Christianity when the two halves of the Christian world were diverging. Although Kievan Russia was the religious offshoot of Byzantium, Russians found Greek civilization largely inaccessible because of the Church Slavonic idiom and the narrow religious preoccupations of the Christian elite. Cultural and spiritual isolation were reinforced by political turmoil and internecine strife which opened the way to Kiev's external enemies, the Tatars and the Teutonic Knights. In spite of its decline and eventual disappearance, Kievan Russia provided a rich legacy of culture, language, and institutions upon which future generations would build.

Suggested Additional Reading

BLUM, J. "The Smerd in Kievan Russia," *ASEER*, vol. 12 (1953), pp. 122–30.

CROSS, S. H. (trans. and ed.) *The Russian Primary Chronicle* (Cambridge, Mass., 1953). (Page references in text are to 1930 edition.)

GREKOV, B. D. *Kiev Rus* (Moscow, 1959). A standard Soviet interpretation.

TIKHOMIROV, M. N. *The Towns of Ancient Rus* (Moscow, 1959).

VASILIEV, A. A. "Economic Relations Between Byzantium and Old Russia," *JEBH*, vol. 4 (1932), pp. 314–34.

VERNADSKY, G. *Kievan Russia* (New Haven, 1948).

———. *Medieval Russian Laws* (New York, 1947 and 1969).

———. "Notes on the Social History of Kievan Russia," *ASEER*, vol. 3, pp. 81–92.

ZGUTA, R. "Kievan Coinage," *SEER*, vol. 53 (1975), pp. 483–92.

5

The Southwest and the Northeast

THE UNITY of the Kievan state, fragile and tenuous even in the best of times, broke down completely following the death of Grand Prince Iaropolk II in 1139. In the ensuing years the various branches of the House of Riurik vied with one another for supremacy, but none was strong or farsighted enough to exert significant national leadership. Occasional inter-princely alliances created to oppose the threat of the steppe nomads rapidly gave way to jealous conflicts, and consequently the Kievan state disintegrated into a series of virtually independent principalities, each pursuing its own interests and goals. This period is known in Soviet historiography as "the period of feudal fragmentation," and is viewed as the culmination of a process which had begun in the ninth century with the founding of the Kievan state. This schematic view is perhaps oversimplified, but it is true that separatist tendencies triumphed at least temporarily with the decline of Kiev. Still, it would be an error to ignore completely persisting elements of unity, fostered in part by the common culture and religion shared by all eastern Slavs, and also maintained by vaguely defined familial ties among the various ruling houses, all tracing their ancestry back to Riurik.

With the decline of trade and commerce centered in the Dnieper region, Kiev ceased to function as the center of a unified state, and the Kievan principality itself descended rapidly to relative insignificance. The decline of Kiev was paralleled, however, by the rise to importance of other regions, most notably the southwestern territories of Volhynia and Galicia, and the northeastern territory variously known as Rostov-Suzdal or Vladimir-Suzdal. It is to these two politically important regions that we now turn.

THE SOUTHWEST

Volhynia and Galicia had formed an integral part of the Kievan state, participating fully in the political, cultural, and religious life of the country. Volhynia, the larger of the two territories, extended westward from Kiev, encompassing the broad fertile plain which stretches from

55

the foothills of the Carpathian Mountains northward into what is present day Belorussia. Galicia, situated along the northern slopes of the Carpathian Mountains, controls the headwaters of the important rivers Pruth and Dniester. Bordering on both Hungary and Poland, Galicia represented the furthest westward expansion of the Kievan state. From earliest times these two territories enjoyed great prosperity resulting both from the fertile soil of the region and from the extensive trade carried on with the West via Hungary and Poland. Both Volhynia and Galicia were relatively secure from the devastating raids of steppe nomads because of their western location. This fact enhanced the region's economic prosperity, and the result was a rapid growth of population and the extensive development of urban centers. From as early as the 11th century the economic prosperity of the southwest, coinciding with the gradual decline of Kiev, was translated into a desire by the Volhynian and Galician princes to act independently of Kiev.

These political ambitions were not to be fully realized until the late 12th century when Kiev's decline accelerated. The growing political importance of the southwest was converted into virtual independence by one of the most powerful and successful Russian princes of the second half of the 12th century, Iaroslav Osmomysl of Galicia (1153–87), whose name is thought to mean eight-minded, or exceedingly wise. He succeeded in transforming Galicia into a powerful force in south Russia. His interests were not restricted to the Galician lands; he was concerned with broader issues as well, something clearly attested to by the famous author of the *Tale of Igor*, who left a memorable and vivid portrait of this remarkable and highly respected prince.

> O Iaroslav Osmomysl of Galicia, "You sit high on your gold-forged throne; you have braced the Hungarian [Carpathian] mountains with your iron troops; you have closed the Danube's gates, hurling mighty missiles over the clouds, spreading your courts [laws] to the Danube. Your thunders range over lands; you open Kiev's gates to avenge the Russian land, and the wounds of Igor, turbulent son of Sviatoslav.[1]

Iaroslav was not merely a local prince, but one of the greatest and most powerful princes of the time, one whose power and might were such that he not only guarded the western borders of the Kievan land, but could protect Kiev itself and administer crushing defeats to the steppe nomads, thus avenging Igor's defeat. The wise and enlightened rule of Iaroslav Osmomysl raised immeasurably the power and prestige of Galicia, and the whole of south Russia reflected his glory. Galicia at this time was quite independent of Kiev, forming an important center in its own right.

But without strong rule Galicia was vulnerable to outside interference and harassment. Following Iaroslav's death in 1187, Galicia experienced weak rule, which led to constant intervention by the Hungarian king, who even managed briefly to establish his son on the Galician throne. Only in 1197 were the fortunes of Galicia restored.

---

[1] V. Rzhiga et al. (eds.), *Slovo o polku Igoreve* (Moscow, 1961), p. 26.

Strong rule was provided by Galicia's neighbor, Volhynia, in the person of Prince Roman of Volhynia (1197–1205), who united the two territories into a powerful state. For a time, Roman even occupied the increasingly insignificant throne of Kiev, from which he mounted several successful campaigns against the steppe nomads, temporarily relieving pressure on Kiev. He was even more successful in opposing the imperialist ambitions of the Hungarians, the Poles, and the Lithuanians, all of whom were intent on controlling southwest Russia. While on campaign against the Poles in 1205 Roman was killed (at the age of 36), leaving two minor sons. As a result of this unfortunate event Volhynia and Galicia entered upon a period of internal strife, civil war, and Polish and Hungarian intervention.

The lack of continued strong leadership was one factor which prevented the southwest from assuming the mantle of leadership in the Russian lands. Another deterrent to political stability in the southwest was the intense social conflicts there. The fertile soil of Volhynia and Galicia encouraged the boyar class to carve out great landed estates and bring the local population under increasing control. Furthermore, the success of these ventures encouraged the boyars to seek to dominate the princely authority as well, to translate their economic power into political power. The result was frequent clashes between boyars and the ruling princes. The boyars were never above appealing to the Poles and the Hungarians for help in achieving their political ambitions. Without strong princely rule capable of curbing the ambitions of the boyar class, political stability was impossible. These tensions broke into the open after 1205. Roman's son and successor, Daniel, was only four years old when he ascended the throne of Volhynia and throughout his youth he lived amidst bitter and protracted political turmoil which eroded the wealth and power of the territory.

Not until 1221 did Daniel establish himself firmly on the throne of Volhynia and assert his authority, bringing the boyars under his control. It appeared that the fortunes of the southwest were once more on the rise, but in 1223 Daniel was faced with a new and even more potent threat, the Tatars. In his first fateful Russian encounter with a Tatar expeditionary force at the Battle of the Kalka River, he escaped with minor wounds and returned to Volhynia; but the portent for the future was foreboding. Between Daniel's first encounter with the Tatars and the full-scale Tartar invasion beginning in 1237, Daniel administered Volhynia wisely, developing trade and commerce, building new cities, and working to restore the unity of Volhynia and Galicia. He accomplished their union in 1238, but had little time to consolidate his power because in 1241 the Tatars swept westward out of Kiev, conquering and pillaging Volhynia and Galicia, thus ending independent existence for these rich territories.

Without the Tatar conquest, Volhynia and Galicia might have provided the basis for a resurgence of south Russia and the beginnings of a genuine rapprochement with the West. As it was, however, Volhynia and Galicia rapidly declined after the initial Tatar conquest and during the 14th century were absorbed by their rapacious neighbors; Galicia was incorporated into the Polish state, and Volhynia became part of the expanding Lithuanian state. Both internal conditions and foreign intervention prevented Galicia and Volhynia from inheriting Kiev's political mantle. That honor would be reserved for the northeast; first the territory of Vladimir-Suzdal, later Moscow.

THE NORTHEAST

The future of Russia was to be determined not in the southwest, but in the northeast, in the plains and forests situated in the region of the Kliazma and Moskva rivers, between the Oka and the Volga. When the eastern Slavs arrived, this northeastern region was occupied by Finnish tribes, which in the ensuing centuries peacefully intermingled with the Slavs. Out of this slow and partial amalgamation emerged the Great Russian nationality. But during the latter part of the ninth century, when the Kievan state was being organized, the northeast was only sparsely settled and certainly did not constitute one of the more important regions of old Russia.

From the 11th century on, however, the history of the northeast becomes extremely complex and important, far more so than that of the southwest. The northeast has occupied the attention of historians to a greater degree because of the subsequent emergence of a new unified Russian state around Moscow which is located in the forest zone of the northeast. Historians have long debated the rise of the northeast as a prelude to the emergence of Moscow, and have tried to ascertain the precise relationship between the northeast and the central Dnieper region of Kiev in an effort to establish the historical continuity, or lack of such, between Kiev and Moscow.

Two basic positions have been taken on this question. The older view, advanced by such historians as Soloviev and Kliuchevskii, drew a sharp line between Kievan Russia and Muscovite Russia. It was argued that with the transition of the political center from Kiev to the northeast, to a new geographic region, Russian development moved off in an entirely new direction. These historians denied any continuity and implied that there was a decisive rupture between the traditions of Kievan Russia and those of northeastern Russia. Other historians, beginning with Presniakov in the early 20th century and continuing with Soviet historians, have advanced the view that there was a direct link, a profound historical continuity extending from Kiev through Vladimir-Suzdal to Moscow. The weight of the evidence seems to support the latter view.

All historians of the northeast agree that during the 12th century there was a massive population shift or migration away from Kiev in the south to the northeast. The northeast was a remote and relatively inhospitable region, less productive agriculturally than the more fertile south. What then caused this significant population shift? Precisely the remoteness of the region coupled with the added security afforded by the forest zone attracted large numbers of settlers from the south who were intent on escaping the constant disruptions and growing insecurity fostered by feuding princes and the ever present threat of devastating raids by the steppe nomads.

The basic question dividing the two historiographical camps centered on the nature of the Rostov-Suzdal land when this migration was beginning. Kliuchevskii and Soloviev argued that northeastern Russia in the 11th and 12th centuries was a harsh and savage land, quite removed from the traditions of the south. Consequently, a new order of relationships emerged on new and virgin soil. Soloviev cited as evidence for this view the fact that the sources refer to the region as a great and empty land, "where only one town is mentioned as having arisen before the coming of the Varangians—Rostov the Great from which the whole region received the name the Rostov land."[2] Kliuchevskii, likewise, characterized the Rostov land as more alien to Russia than any of her frontier lands. A new nationality (the Great Russians) and a new political system (the *udel*, or appanage, system) were, in his opinion, formed under the influence of northeastern geographical and ethnological conditions, both of which were in sharp contrast to all previous conditions. Kliuchevskii concluded that the consequences of the Russian colonization of the upper Volga were to establish "the earliest and deepest roots of a form of state which will appear in a later period," that is, the Muscovite period.[3]

Other historians, most notably Presniakov, have argued that the Rostov land was far from being hostile, savage, or primitive. A firmly established way of life built upon complex internal relationships was growing out of the same conditions that had prevailed at the time in Kiev, Volhynia, Galicia, and Chernigov. Even before the influx of settlers from the south reached important dimensions in the 12th century, the Rostov land had achieved a high level of culture. Presniakov pointed to the extensive program of building undertaken by the first Suzdal princes. There was a striking increase in the construction of stone churches, and an original and highly sophisticated artistic style had already been elaborated. Such developments, he argued, were possible only in a land with a highly developed urban civilization, a strong tradition of local trades and crafts, and a high overall level of culture. To be sure, the migration contributed much to raising the material resources of the land and helped to transform the Rostov land into the rich and powerful principality of Vladimir-Suzdal, but there was not movement in an entirely new direction as suggested by Soloviev and Kliuchevskii. Strong ties were maintained all along between the northeast and the south.

In reviewing the history of the northeast, we find that in 1054, at the death of Iaroslav the Wise, the northeast territory passed to one of the younger sons, Vsevolod, as a supplement to the territory of Pereiaslavl. Within less than a century Rostov land had emerged as an independent principality in the possession of Prince Iuri Dolgoruki

---

[2] S. M. Soloviev, *Ob otnosheniiakh Novgoroda k velikim kniaziam* (Moscow, 1846), p. 17.

[3] V. O. Kliuchevskii, *Sochineniia* (Moscow, 1956–59), vol. 1, p. 316.

(Long-Arm) (1149–57), a younger son of the last great ruler of Kiev, Vladimir II Monomach. Iuri became one of the most important and powerful princes in Russia, so powerful that he aspired to the supremacy traditionally attached to Kiev's golden throne. For almost a decade (1146–55), he waged a bitter and tenacious struggle with his nephew Iziaslav for control of Kiev. Only with the death of Iziaslav in 1155 was Iuri finally able to realize his ambition of occupying the throne of Kiev, a position he held for only two years until his own death in 1157.

Iuri Dolgoruki was definitely a prince in the Kievan mold. Encouraged by the growth of the power and prestige of the Rostov land, Iuri, in the best Kievan tradition, sought to gain supremacy over his "brother" princes by establishing himself in Kiev. These aspirations fit perfectly into Kiev's political traditions. It should be pointed out, however, that Iuri's desire to occupy the throne of Kiev did not imply an abandonment of his northeastern possessions. He merely wished to claim genealogical seniority for the Rostov dynasty. Iuri tried to preserve and strengthen his power in south Russia in order to better pursue his local Suzdal interests. He was motivated in this by a desire to control the territorial center, or what was thought to be the territorial center, of the entire system of inter-princely relationships. In other words, his was a policy designed to prevent rival princes from gaining influence that could potentially threaten Suzdal interests, particularly Suzdal's relations with Novgorod, Smolensk, and Chernigov, as well as with other territories. Only by controlling Kiev could Iuri actively pursue Suzdal interests without fear of external intervention by other princes.

In addition, there were also commercial and cultural interests of great importance which caught Iuri's attention. The commercial and cultural relations existing between Suzdal and other parts of Russia were extensive and of vital importance if Suzdal were to play a dominant role. A flourishing trade existed between the northeast and the south. Moreover, large quantities of important and valuable products flowed into Suzdal from the west. Iuri was determined to maintain and expand these commercial relations, especially those dependent on the waterway from Novgorod down the Volga, a commercial route which passed through Suzdal. In order to pursue this policy effectively, Iuri had to control Novgorod, or at a minimum assure Novgorod's cooperation. In an effort to assure good relations, Iuri tried to place his sons or nephews on the throne of Novgorod. On occasion he was even forced to apply pressure on Novgorod to adopt a pro-Suzdal policy by cutting off its trade routes to the north and the west, thereby crippling Novgorod's economy. It was, in fact, this pressure on Novgorod that brought Iuri into conflict with his nephew, Iziaslav, a struggle which eventually centered on control of Kiev. Iuri's success in this struggle in 1155 seriously weakened the hostile forces concentrated in the south, giving him a relatively free hand in the north.

During this same period Iuri embarked on a program designed to strengthen the princely administration in the Rostov land in order to consolidate his position. The result was the consolidation of the territory into a *votchina*, or hereditary holding. That is, he endeavored to make the Rostov land the personal possession of his family. This desire to increase his princely power was reflected in a vigorous building program and extensive colonization. New towns were built and settled by Iuri and these "younger towns" were considered his private, personal property. To Soloviev this circumstance introduced a new element, one in which "property stood above family relationships, each prince seeing himself as the sole owner of a particular domain, and no longer as a member of a given family, a particular dynasty."[4] Thus emerged the concept of the *udel*, or appanage, a form of property which could be disposed of at will by the owner. Although Soloviev saw this as a sharp break between Kievan political traditions and those of the northeast, there is evidence that the same process was occurring in the south, particularly in Volhynia and Galicia.

These efforts to enhance princely power did not go unchallenged. A powerful boyar class in the Rostov land opposed the growth of princely power which often adversely affected local boyar interests. Adventuresome and costly foreign policy schemes were particularly resented by the boyars, who felt that the interests of the princely dynasty did not always coincide with their own. The first Rostov princes were frequently challenged by the boyar class. Iuri Dolgoruki moved his capital from Rostov to Suzdal in an effort to get away from the troublesome boyars and avoid open clashes with them. The opposition continued, however, and Andrei Bogoliubskii, Iuri's son and successor, in turn moved from Suzdal to Vladimir for the same reason.

Andrei Bogoliubskii (1157–74) continued and expanded the policies worked out by his father, concentrating on enhancing his own political power and controlling Novgorod. He too resorted to force to place obedient princes on the throne of Novgorod, sometimes installing his sons, sometimes his nephews. He brought pressure to bear on Novgorod by effectively controlling the vital transport of grain into the city from the Volga region. Andrei also campaigned successfully against the Volga Bulgars to insure Suzdal control of the important Volga trade routes. Eventually Andrei was also drawn into a struggle for Kiev as a result of his efforts to control Novgorod. In 1169 Andrei mounted a huge campaign against Kiev, held by Iziaslav's son Mstislav. Andrei captured and sacked Kiev, administering the fatal blow to Kiev's claim to a central position. Andrei seized the grand princely title, but he was even less interested in Kiev itself than his father had been. Having no desire to remain in Kiev, Andrei installed a friendly prince on the throne and established himself in Vladimir, which became a flourishing city and the center of Russian political life. Andrei refused to live in the city of Vladimir and instead built for himself a magnificent palace at nearby Bogoliubovo from which his surname derives. These moves clearly reflected Andrei's conviction that the fortunes of Russia were tied to the northeast rather than the south.

---

[4] Soloviev, *Ob otnosheniiakh Novgoroda*, pp. 19–20.

Andrei's efforts to create a monarchy, to establish the absolute power of the prince, involved him in a conflict with the firmly established boyar class of Vladimir-Suzdal. The tense situation was further aggravated by his ambitious foreign policy, which involved Vladimir-Suzdal in costly wars with the Volga Bulgars, Novgorod, and Kiev. In 1174 the boyars were galvanized into action in the wake of a new and unsuccessful campaign against Kiev which had been ordered by Andrei, in the words of the chronicler, "out of overweening pride and arrogance." The boyars organized a conspiracy against Andrei, who was assassinated in his palace at Bogoliubovo. This action touched off a bloody rebellion of the local population against the harsh princely administration. Anarchy and strife continued for several years until Andrei's younger brother Vsevolod managed to bring the situation under control. In 1177 Vsevolod assumed the title of grand prince and restored the princely power to the unchallenged position inaugurated by his brother.

Vsevolod's long reign (1177–1212) marked the zenith of the power of the northeast, a time when Vladimir-Suzdal controlled the thrones of Novgorod and Kiev, reduced many lesser princes to vassal status, and even forced powerful and independent Galicia and Volhynia to reckon with its power. Andrei and Vsevolod tried to justify their authority by appeals to the principle of seniority among the princes. Seniority was now firmly attached to the principality of Vladimir-Suzdal, but in

Michael Curran

Church of the Virgin of the Intercession, at Bogoliubovo on the River Nerl (1165)

Michael Curran

Cathedral of the Assumption, Vladimir (1185–89)

the hands of Andrei and Vsevolod, had undergone a significant change. Presniakov argued:

> The earlier Kievan seniority was justified and sustained by the common interests of all elements of Kievan Russia, above all by the task of opposing the steppe nomads. In contrast, the seniority of the Suzdal prince became a force compelling the brotherhood of Russian princes to serve goals and pursue policies that were either unrelated to or indeed opposed to their own interests.[5]

---

[5] A. E. Presoniakov, *Obrazovanie velikorusskogo gosudarstva* (Petrograd, 1918), p. 38.

Thus the Suzdal princes were no longer "the first among equals," but stood significantly higher than any others and could impose their wills on the brotherhood of princes to an unprecedented extent. Still, the Suzdal princes lacked a well-defined national policy. Their interests were dictated by a concern to advance the fortunes of their own territory, Vladimir-Suzdal. The result was bitter hatred, jealousy, and antagonism among the Russian princes. The author of the *Tale of Igor* perhaps expressed the situation best: "O, great Prince Vsevolod! Do you not think of flying here from afar to safeguard the paternal golden throne? For you can splash out the waters of the Volga with your oars, and empty the Don with your helmets!"[6] He implied that Vsevolod should abandon his narrow regional interests, take an interest in the all-Russian problem of invasion by the steppe nomads, and defend the national interest. His participation in the struggle against the steppe nomads could mean victory for Russia.

In spite of the power and prestige won by the Suzdal princes, the forces of disintegration were at work in the northeast as well and the region's unity and stability broke down following the death of Vsevolod in 1212. His numerous offspring, who won him the appellation "Big Nest," quarreled bitterly over the inheritance. The principle of patrimonial succession, however, remained intact. This principle, not unique to the northeast, provided that a single princely family was associated with a particular territory, and the right of all male descendants to share in the inheritance was guaranteed. The rivalry between Vsevolod's two eldest sons, Constantine and Iuri, was finally settled by compromise in 1217 when it was agreed that Constantine would occupy the throne of Vladimir and Iuri the throne of Suzdal, with the former enjoying the title of grand prince. The two elder brothers then determined the positions to be occupied by the younger brothers. The result was that the Rostov-Suzdal land was divided up into a number of quasi-independent territories, all nominally under the authority of the "senior" prince, the Grand Prince of Vladimir. Thus the common interests of the whole Rostov-Suzdal land contributed to slow down the disintegration of the land into many separate *votchina* holdings. One element contributing to unity, curiously enough, was provided by the boyar class. The boyars resented the growth of princely power, but they also generally opposed any change in the ruling dynasty of the region because a new prince would be accompanied by new boyars who could diminish or curtail the influence of the old boyar class. Often such developments led to civil war, which did not serve the boyars' interests. The boyar class, therefore, was intent on supporting the dynastic ambitions of the local princely family as it sought to retain control over the territory.

The principles of unity and consolidation, although strained somewhat after 1212, were maintained and even after the terrible Mongol invasion they were not lost. They were revived and refined by the principality of Moscow in the 14th century. Nevertheless, the existing

---

[6] Rzhiga et al., *Slovo*, p. 26.

political divisions and the rather narrowly defined policies of the Rostov princes made the task of the Tatars easier than it might otherwise have been if the senior Russian princes had had a broader political conception.

Suggested Additional Reading

There are no satisfactory studies of Volhynia-Galicia or Vladimir-Suzdal in English or other Western languages. Soviet scholars have recently begun an intensive study of the sources for the history of Vladimir-Suzdal (see I. A. Limonov, *Letopisanie Vladimiro-Suzdalskoi Rusi* (Leningrad, 1967).

Two short articles in English are:

ANDRUSIAK, M.   "Kings of Kiev and Galicia," *SEER*, vol. 33, pp. 342–50.

ZDAN, M. B.   "The Dependence of Halych-Volyn Rus on the Golden Horde," *SEER*, vol. 35, 505–23.

For the northeast see:

PRESNIAKOV, A. E.   *The Formation of the Great Russian State* (trans. from Russian), New York, 1971.

See also general histories of the Ukraine:

ALLEN, W.   *The Ukraine: A History* (New York, 1940, 1963).

DOROSHENKO, D.   *History of the Ukraine* (Edmonton, Canada, 1939).

HRUSHEVSKY, M.   *A History of the Ukraine* (New Haven, 1941).

6

The Mongol Conquest

BETWEEN 1237 and 1241 the Mongols, a nomadic east Asian people and their Turkish allies, conquered all of Russia except the commercial republics of the northwest. Overcoming ill-coordinated resistance by the Russian princes, they stormed or occupied the leading cities, killed some ten percent of the population, and deported thousands to slavery in Asia. Their onslaught shattered Kievan civilization and accelerated the political fragmentation of Russia. For over two centuries Mongol khans ruled much of Russia indirectly from their capital at Sarai on the Volga, and northeastern Russia was effectively isolated from western Europe. The results of Mongol rule remain debatable, but in any case this great Asian assault had major effects upon Russian development.

The 13th century Mongol invasion of eastern Europe is comparable to the fifth century assault by Germanic barbarians on the Roman Empire. Before advancing into Russia the Mongols had conquered large parts of China, Persia, and Central Asia, causing great destruction and slaughtering all who opposed them. From Russia they moved westward into Poland and Hungary as far as the Adriatic Sea before turning back toward their native steppes. Western Europe, whose rulers trembled at the news of their advance, was spared since the Mongols found European mountains and forests inhospitable and the great khan of Mongolia died opportunely. Mongol expansion produced a vast though shortlived Mongol empire over the Eurasian plain from the Pacific to the Adriatic.

The Mongols, so dynamic and successful in war, comprised nomadic tribes and clans which had wandered with their flocks over broad areas of the Mongolian steppes in search of water and pasturage. Before the time of Chingis-khan, these primitive sky-worshipers played no significant role in steppe politics and lacked unity and organization. Temuchin (1167?–1227), later known as Chingis-khan (great ruler or "Prince of the Ocean"), was the son of a tribal chieftain in Mongolia who had been poisoned by his rivals. Surviving by his shrewdness and courage, Temuchin defeated his tribal enemies in a series of bloody victories and finally brought all of the Mongolian tribes under his control. In 1206 Mongolia's unification was completed and Temuchin's power was legitimized by a great council (*kuriltai*) of clan chieftains, which named him supreme ruler as Chingis-khan. Henceforth Chingis regarded himself as a divine ruler; his slogan became: "*One* sole sun in the sky; *one* sole sovereign on earth." With the aid of the *kuriltai*, which included his chief advisers, Chingis within a few years constructed a centralized and absolute monarchy, an administration, and a strictly disciplined army based upon the decimal system with detachments of tens, hundreds, thousands, and myriads (ten thousands). Chingis selected personally the commanders of the larger units from among his boyhood friends. After consolidating his power, Chingis undertook a series of military expeditions which led to the creation of the Mongol Empire.

The conquest of Eurasia by a Mongol people numbering slightly more than 1 million persons was an amazing triumph of discipline, organization, and leadership. Mongol horsemen and their mounts possessed great endurance, outmaneuvered their sedentary opponents, and made able use of Chinese military techniques and weapons. The Mongols usually struck by surprise and with terrifying fury and were accompanied by large numbers of Turkish auxiliary troops. Chingis himself, notes Vladimirtsov, was "a savage of genius" convinced of his divine mission to conquer the world and bring it unity and peace. Declared Chingis: "Man's highest joy is in victory: to conquer one's enemies, to pursue them, to deprive them of their possessions, to make their beloved weep, and to embrace their wives and daughters."[1] To the end of his life he remained an illiterate sky-worshiper, though not without appreciation of culture. Besides conquest, his principal delights were hunting and gathering numerous concubines.

At Chingis' death in 1227, each of his four sons was awarded a portion (*ulus*) of the empire and part of the army. The great council elected unanimously as the new great khan Ugedei, who shared his father's concept of universal empire. Juchi, to whom was assigned the western ulus, had died before his father, and it passed to his son, Chingis' grandson, Batu, who obtained Ugedei's support for a westward advance.

The campaign of 1237 against Russia was carefully prepared. Fifteen years earlier a Mongol army had defeated a force of Russians and Polovtsy at the Battle of Kalka, then had retreated into the steppe. This warning went unheeded by the Russians, and in 1237 the Mongols came to stay. Batu's army had a Mongol core of some 50,000 horsemen, but with its Turkish auxiliaries probably numbered about 120,000 men. Sudubei, the chief Mongol commander, struck initially at the Volga Bulgars and conquered them. The Russian princes, still not realizing how serious was their plight, proved unable to unite their efforts for defense. In December 1237 Batu stormed the town of Riazan,

---

[1] V. Ia. Vladimirtsov, *Chingis-Khan* (Berlin, 1922), p. 166, quoted in G. Vernadsky, *The Mongols and Russia* (New Haven, 1953), p. 43.

MAP 6–1
Mongol Conquest, 1237–1300

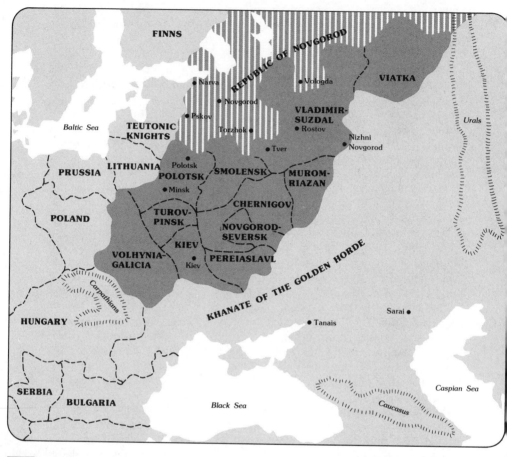

Russian principalities conquered by Mongols

Novgorod, tributary states

Adapted with permission of Macmillan Publishing Co., Inc. from *Russian History Atlas* by Martin Gilbert. Cartography by Martin Gilbert. Copyright © 1972 by Martin Gilbert.

then advanced to Moscow, then a minor but strategic town, and burned it to the ground. Dividing the army of the Russian grand prince, Batu defeated both parts of it and conquered Vladimir, the chief city of northeast Russia. In 1240 Kiev fell after a heroic resistance along with the other main Dnieper River towns. Wherever the Russians resisted, the Mongols slaughtered the populace without mercy. Many Russian princes fled into Poland and Hungary; the rest submitted to Batu. Novgorod was spared direct conquest because of its protective forests and swamps, but later it submitted to the Mongols.

The death in 1241 of Khan Ugedei in Mongolia precipitated a political crisis within the far-flung Mongol empire. Suspending his operations in Hungary, Batu returned to southern Russia whence he could influence the selection of a new khan. Guyuk, who was chosen, never exercised actual control over the western *ulus*. This permitted Batu to construct his own autonomous state.

In 1242 began to emerge the outlines of this state, generally known as the Golden Horde. Formed from the western *ulus*, it comprised Russia and the neighboring steppes. Only a small minority of the Horde's population was Mongol; the rest was mostly Turkic and the Mongols who remained there speedily became Turkified. Batu and his fellow Mongol commanders established firm authority and an administration centering in Old Sarai on the east bank of the Akhtiuba River, some 65 miles north of the present city of Astrakhan. From this vast city of tents Batu sought to insure the obedience and cooperation of the various Russian princes and to collect tribute and army recruits from them on a regular basis. The west Russian regions of Kiev, Chernigov, and Podolia were subjected to direct Mongol rule and soon were supplying recruits for their army. East Russian princes likewise hastened to pledge their allegiance. In 1242 Grand Prince Iaroslav I of Vladimir was confirmed in office at Batu's camp, and his son Constantine made the long journey to Karakorum in Mongolia to confirm his father's allegiance to the great khan. In 1251 when Mongka was elected Mongol emperor, all Russian princes had to obtain new patents (*yarlyki*) of authority by traveling to Sarai. This action confirmed the growing decentralization of the Mongol Empire, and the Golden Horde became the true authority for Russia. Late in the 13th century the Horde became Muslim but continued to tolerate Orthodoxy. Its economy was diversified, including nomadic herdsmen, settled agriculturalists, and a sizable urban population of merchants and handicraftsmen.

In the years after 1242 the Golden Horde, crushing sporadic resistance, consolidated its hold over nearly all Russia. The grave threat to northwest Russia posed by invading Swedes, German crusading knights, and Lithuanians aided Mongol success. This Western menace caused Prince Alexander Iaroslavich, the last effective Russian grand prince of the 13th century, to pledge utter loyalty to the Mongol khan and undertake repeated humiliating journeys to his capital at Sarai. Simultaneously, however, he defended the Russian land valiantly against invasions from the west. In July 1240 a Swedish armada under Karl Birger proceeded up the Neva River from the Gulf of Finland toward Novgorod and Pskov. As Prince of Novgorod, Alexander with his retinue of warriors and the Novgorod militia in July 1240 surprised the Swedes while they were disembarking and forced them to flee in panic. For this exploit he acquired the nickname Nevskii. In 1241, aided by the forces of Vladimir, he expelled the German knights from the area of Pskov, Russia's gateway to the west. The following April Alexander Nevskii lured the heavily armed German Teutonic knights onto the treacherous ice of Lake Chud and through a bold attack encompassed their destruction, delivering Pskov from threatened German conquest. Three years later he defeated the Lithuanians, thus preserving a corner of Russia from direct foreign rule. Soviet historians have lauded Nevskii's successful struggle against Germanic invaders while underplaying his unquestioned subservience to the Mongols. Alexander Nevskii became the hero of a classic Soviet film of the 1930s by Serge Eisenstein and inspired a cantata composed in his honor by the great Soviet composer Serge Prokoviev. Nevskii's great victories blunted the German drive to the east and prevented western Russia's subjugation by Swedish and German forces.

In the 1250s the Mongols, defeating the rebellious Prince Andrei of Vladimir, gave its throne to Alexander Nevskii. In the west King Daniel of Volhynia, who briefly asserted his independence and defied the Mongols, was forced to flee. Later he too became a loyal vassal of the khan of the Golden Horde. In 1262, town assemblies (*veche*) organized an uprising in Suzdalia in northeast Russia, but it was quickly crushed. The Russian princes, seeking confirmation of their titles from the khan, worked to consolidate their authority within their own appanages. To promote stability the Horde encouraged this and supported obedient, trustworthy princes against the town assemblies. The Mongols in this period maintained firm control by superior military strength, periodic raids and expeditions, and Russian awe at their power and administrative efficiency.

The twin aims of Mongol administration in Russia were tax collection to support their state apparatus and to secure army recruits to replace their losses. Tatar (Mongol) policies differed in various parts of Russia. In the southwest the Tatars displaced Russian princely administration and ruled directly. In most other areas Mongol administration coexisted with that of the Russian princes who usually were allowed to rule their domains as vassals of the Horde and under the vague suzerainty of the great khan of Mongolia. Each prince had to obtain a patent and be installed by an envoy of the Horde, retaining his post during good behavior. The khan, however, could revoke his patent at any time. In the period after 1242 the Mongols conducted a series of censuses in Russia to determine the population and its tax paying capabilities and appointed Tatar officials to supervise recruitment and tax collection.

Such an administrative set-up lasted in most of Russia for at least a century. In Galicia it was terminated in 1349 when that region was annexed to Poland. By 1363 most other west Russian areas had been absorbed by Lithuania. In east Russia the "Tatar yoke" lasted almost another century. From the early 14th century the four Russian grand princes were obligated to collect tribute and taxes and turn them over to a special Mongol official. About 1360 internal troubles began within the Horde, initially taking the form of a family feud among the sons of Khan Janibeg. This situation encouraged the Russian princes to play off one Mongol claimant against another and assert an increasing degree of independence. The internal crisis within the Horde, coinciding as it did with the growing strength of Lithuania and Moscow, gradually undermined the authority of the khan and his hold over the subject peoples. Toward the mid-15th century the Golden Horde disintegrated: separate khanates were formed in Kazan, the Crimea, and

Icon of Alexander Nevskii, Prince of Novgorod

Astrakhan. The remnant of the Golden Horde, known now as the Great Horde, competed with these khanates. This division and internecine strife among the Tatar states prepared the way for Russia's emancipation from tribute payment and Mongol control.

PROBLEM 2: THE MONGOL IMPACT

The Mongols undertook to gather and organize Russia as they did their own state in order to introduce into the country law, order, and prosperity. . . . As a result of this policy the Mongols gave the conquered country the basic elements of future Muscovite statehood: autocracy, centralism, and serfdom. (E. Khara-Davan, *Chingiz-khan kak polkovodets i ego nasledie*, p. 200.)

The bloody business begun by Chingiz-khan and continued by his descendants cost the Russians and other peoples of our country dearly. . . . The liberation struggle of peoples against the despotism of Chingis-khan and his successors was a supreme act of progress. (*Istoriia SSSR*, 1962, no. 5, p. 119.)

As these quotations suggest, historians differ greatly in assessing the effects of the Mongol invasion and the "Tatar yoke" upon Russia. Contemporary and later Muscovite chronicles, depicting the invasion as a terrible misfortune for Russia, emphasized the terrible slaughter, disorder, and civil strife. Prerevolutionary Russian historians divided sharply over the effects of Mongol rule. N. M. Karamzin, an early 19th century nationalist historian, blamed the Tatars for Russian backwardness, but he added that they had "restored autocracy" and strengthened Moscow which "owed its greatness to the khans."[2] On the other hand, S. M. Soloviev, the leading scholar of the so-called "organic school," regarded the Mongols as merely the more powerful successors of the Polovtsy. "We have no reason to assume," he wrote, "any great influence [of the Mongols] on [Russia's] internal administration as we do not see any traces of it."[3]

Since the Bolshevik Revolution two sharply contrasting views of the Mongol impact have emerged. Soviet historians, repudiating the balanced approach of the 1920s presented by V. V. Bartold, have stressed the negative, destructive aspects of the Mongol conquest and argued that Tatar rule delayed the development of a unified Russian culture, economy, and national state. On the other hand, the Eurasian school of Russian emigres, depicting the Mongol unification of Eurasia as historically progressive, have viewed Russia's unification under Moscow as the direct outgrowth of Mongol rule: "The Russian state was the heir, successor, and continuer of Chingis-khan's historic work."[4] Derived from the Eurasian view is the approach of Professor George Vernadsky, a Russian emigre living in the United States, which assessed Mongol influence by analyzing differences between Kievan and Muscovite Russia. Here is a summary of these three approaches to the problem of the Tatar yoke in Russia.

THE SOVIET VIEW

The Mongol invasion, Soviet historians agree, brought terrible physical destruction to Russian towns and villages and dealt severe blows to agriculture, trade and handicrafts. During the balance of the 13th century occurred repeated Tatar raids which devastated new regions

---

[2] N. M. Karamzin, *Istoriia gosudarstva Rossiiskago* (St. Petersburg, 1842, vol. 2, part 5, pp. 215 ff.

[3] S. M. Soloviev, *Istoriia Rossii s drevneishikh vremen* (St. Petersburg, n.d.,), vol. 4, p. 179.

[4] I. R., *Nasledie Chingis-khana* (Berlin, 1925), pp. 9, 21.

and prevented economic recovery. The Russians and other peoples within the territory of the present USSR fought bitterly against the Mongols:

> The heroic defense of their native land and cities by the Russian people was the decisive factor which wrecked the plan of the Tatar-Mongol aggressors to conquer all Europe. The great worldwide significance of the exploit of the Russian people was that it undermined the strength of the Mongol army. The Russian people defended the peoples of western Europe from the approaching avalanche of the Tatar-Mongol hordes and thus secured for them the possibility of normal economic and social development.[5]

Only Russia's feudal division, claims another Soviet historian, prevented able Russian princes such as Alexander Nevskii from coordinating massive resistance by peasants and townsmen against the invader. Feudal princes, boyars, and merchants for selfish reasons often collaborated with the enemy. Nonetheless, Russia's vigorous resistance to the Mongols gave her greater autonomy than other regions subject to Mongol rule. Instead of administering Russia directly, the Tatars, as Karl Marx noted, "oppressed from a distance."

The invasion and subsequent Mongol yoke, contend Soviet historians, greatly delayed Russia's economic development. Plunder and tribute payments drained silver and other precious metals from the country. The destruction of commercial centers delayed the growth of a money economy: "Russian town handicrafts were completely destroyed. Russia was thrown back by several centuries, and during those centuries when the guild industry of the west shifted to a period of original accumulation, Russian handicraft industry again had to pass through part of that historic path which was traversed before Batu."[6] Likewise, the Mongols undermined Russian agriculture, a basis for towns which might have counterbalanced the influence of feudal lords.

The invasion worsened Russia's international and commercial position, especially toward the West. Weakened by Tatar attacks, the Russian states lost control of the important Dvina River trade route and territory in the west to Lithuania, Sweden, and the German knights. Russia's links with Byzantium were mostly cut. Not until the 14th century came some revival of commerce with Russia's southern and western neighbors. In the Mongol era much of Russian trade shifted eastward, although Novgorod remained an important gateway to the west. The net effect of the Tatar yoke on the Russian economy, emphasize most Soviet historians, was overwhelmingly negative. Destroying, looting, and burning, the Mongols gave nothing to the Russian people in return.

Politically, affirm these historians, the conquest interrupted the gradual consolidation of the Russian lands and deepened feudal divisions. The Mongols shattered the grand princely administration in the

---

[5] V. T. Pashuto, *Geroicheskaia borba russkogo naroda za nezavisimost XIII vek* (Moscow, 1956), p. 159.

[6] B. Rybakov, *Remeslo Drevnei Rusi* (Moscow, 1948), pp. 780–81.

northeast and weakened the towns, the supporters of centralization. The centralized Muscovite state of the 15th century emerged not with the aid of the Tatars, but "contrary to their interests and despite their will." Mongol policy in Russia "was not aimed at creating a unified state out of a divided society, but in every way to hinder consolidation, support mutual dissension of individual political groups and principalities."[7]

THE EURASIAN VIEW

Emphasizing the necessity to treat the history of the Eurasian land mass as a unit, these emigre Russian scholars regard the Mongol invasion as the chief turning point in Russian history. Kievan Russia, they affirm, had merely been "a group of principalities run by Varangian princes" which became historically obsolete. "The political unification of Eurasia was a historic necessity from the beginning, and the people who took this on—the Mongols—were performing a historically progressive and necessary task." What they did for Russia was most significant: "The Mongol yoke summoned the Russian people from a provincial historical existence in small separated tribal and town principalities of the so-called appanage period onto the broad road of statehood." Russia, at first only a province of the Mongol Empire, adopted the Mongols' concept of the state and later took their place. "The Russian state was the heir, successor, and continuer of Chingiskhan's historic work. . . . The unification of the Russian lands under the power of Moscow was the direct result of the Tatar yoke."

The Mongol impact, assert the Eurasian historians, proved highly beneficial to the Russians. "The Tatars defended Russia from Europe," sparing it from conquest by the West. After the conquest Mongols and Russians coexisted in harmony and peace. From their conquerors the Russians adopted typical Turanian character traits: steadiness, conviction, strength, and religiosity, all of which promoted the development of the Muscovite state. The Mongols assured to Russia secure commercial and cultural relations with the Orient; they enhanced the position of the Orthodox Church. In the mid-13th century Alexander Nevskii, prince of Novgorod, faced with a fateful choice, wisely chose the East over the West: "Alexander saw in the Mongols a friendly force in a cultural sense which could assist him to preserve and consolidate Russian cultural identity from the Latin West."

Thus the Eurasian school, largely overlooking the destruction and disruption caused by the Mongol invasion, stressed the Mongols' positive contributions to all aspects of Russian development. It ascribed to them a role similar to that which the Normanists attributed to the Varangians. Both of these schools affirm that external influences outweighed domestic socioeconomic change as a factor in Russia's growth.[8]

---

[7] A. N. Nasonov, *Mongoly i Rus* (Moscow, 1940), p. 5.

[8] See I. R. *Nasledie* (Berlin, 1925); N. S. Trubetskoi, "O turanskom elemente v Russkoi kulture," *Evraziiskii vremennik*, vol. 4 (1925); and E. Khara-Davan, *Chingiz-khan kak polkovodets i ego nasledie* (Belgrade, 1929).

VERNADSKY'S APPROACH

The problem of Mongol influence, affirms Vernadsky, is many-sided: it involves the immediate effects of the invasion, the direct impact of Mongol rule, and unintended contributions of the Tatars through delayed action. One can gauge the extent of Mongol influence, he believes, by contrasting the institutions and spirit of Kievan Russia with those of Muscovy, by comparing the preMongol with the postMongol era.

Kievan political life had been free and diversified with monarchic, aristocratic, and democratic elements roughly in balance, but under the Mongols this pattern changed drastically. In place of the Kievan pan-Russian federation, sharp rifts developed between east and west Russia. In the east, the region most exposed to Mongol influences, monarchical power became highly developed. After visiting Muscovy in 1517, Baron von Herberstein affirmed that the grand prince's authority over his subjects surpassed that of any European monarch. Under Mongol rule Russian political life was curbed and deformed and its traditional balance upset. The Mongols crushed town assemblies because of their defiant independence; landed estates, rather than cities, became the bases of political life. Princely power grew as checks on their authority crumbled. When the prince of Moscow prevailed over the rest, he became the sovereign of east Russia, clothed with awesome power.

Tatar influence upon Muscovite administrative and military affairs, asserts Vernadsky, was also profound. "It was on the basis of the Mongol patterns that the grand ducal system of taxation and army organization was developed [in Muscovy] in the late 14th to the 16th centuries." For more than 50 years the khans of the Golden Horde had exercised full and direct power over taxation and conscription in east Russia. When the Russian princes recovered authority over them, they continued the Mongol systems. The Turkic origin of the Russian words for treasury (*kazna*) and treasurer (*kaznachei*) suggest that the Muscovite treasury followed a Mongol pattern. The division of the Muscovite army into five large units resembled Mongol practice. The Russians adopted Tatar tactics of envelopment and their system of universal conscription.

In the social realm, the foundations of the relatively free and mobile Kievan society were chipped away during the Mongol period. Tatar rule helped subordinate the boyars to the ruler and prepared the way for enserfment of the peasantry. When Ivan III announced Russia's emancipation from the Tatar yoke in 1480, the framework of a new service-bound society was virtually complete.

Economic results of the Mongol conquest were mixed. Devastated major cities, especially Kiev, Chernigov, and Suzdal, lost their importance for centuries. Mongol conscription of craftsmen almost exhausted Russia's reservoir of skilled manpower; industry was crippled. In Novgorod the economic depression lasted for 50 years, in east Russia for a full century. Revival only followed the relaxation of Tatar control. Agriculture, affirmed Vernadsky, suffered less and became the leading branch of the Russian economy, especially in the northeast. Mongol regional governors and khans, however, encouraged the development of Russian trade with both east and west.

Mongol rule affected the Orthodox Church mostly indirectly but significantly. The devastation and decline of Kiev soon induced the Church to shift its center of operations to the northeast. The khans of the Golden Horde issued a series of charters permitting the church to build up its material wealth and influence without fear of state interference or persecution. In many ways it emerged from the Mongol era stronger and richer than before.

The Mongol cultural impact, he believes, was considerable. By a process of osmosis Turkish, Persian, and Arabic words entered the Russian language as late as the 17th century (e.g., *dengi, tamozhnia, bazar, balagan,* and *bakaleia*). Some of the descendants of Tatars who settled in Russia, such as Karamzin and Chaadaev, became outstanding intellectual leaders. Russia adopted the stiff, formal diplomatic ritual of the Orient from the Mongols. In a sense, concluded Vernadsky, Russia itself was a successor state of the Golden Horde.[9]

CONCLUSION

Today one can no longer deny the important and profound effects of Mongol rule upon Russian development. The contrasting Soviet and Eurasian approaches, while often extreme and one-sided, have deepened our perspective and understanding of this epoch. The linguistic and cultural influences of the Mongol conquest, like the Scandinavian ones earlier, seem to have been minor; but the influence upon the political and military institutions and concepts of Muscovy, as Vernadsky suggests, was important. The economic effects of the Mongol conquest and rule remain rather obscure and debatable, but some recent studies suggest that Russia did not suffer any significant economic decline in this period. If true, this conclusion would tend to refute Soviet assertions that Russia's economic lag behind the west was due in large measure to the "Tatar yoke."

Suggested Additional Reading

BOOKS

HOWORTH, H. H. *History of the Mongols from the Ninth to the Nineteenth Century,* 4 vol. (London, 1876–1927).
ISHBOLDIN, B. *Essays on Tatar History* (New Delhi, 1963).
PRAWDIN, M. *The Mongol Empire: Its Rise and Legacy,* 2d ed. (New York, 1967).
SPULER, BERTOLD. *Die Goldene Horde* (Wiesbaden, 1965).
———. *The Mongols in History* (New York, 1971).
VERNADSKY, GEORGE. *The Mongols and Russia* (New Haven, 1953).
WITTFOGEL, KARL. *Oriental Despotism* (New Haven, 1957).
YAN, VALENTIN. *Batu Khan: A Tale of the Thirteenth Century.* Soviet novel.

---

[9] George Vernadsky, *The Mongols and Russia* (New Haven, 1953), pp. 333–90.

ARTICLES

CHERNIAVSKY, M. "Khan or Basileus . . . , *Journal of Hist. of Ideas*, vol. 20, pp. 459–76.

KARGALOV, V. V. "Osvoboditel'naia bor'ba Rusi protiv mongolo-tatarskogo iga," *Voprosy istorii*, no. 2, 1969.

KRADER, L. "Feudalism and the Tartar Polity of the Middle Ages," *Comparative Studies in Society and History*, vol. 1, pp. 76–99.

SAKHAROV, A. "Les Mongols et la Civilisation russe," in *Contributions à l'histoire russe* (Neuchâtel, Switz., 1958), pp. 77–97. Soviet account.

SZCZESNIAK, B. "A Note on the Character of the Tartar Impact upon the Russian State and Church," *SEESt.*, vol. 17, 1972, pp. 92–98.

TREADGOLD, D. "Russia and the East," in *The Development of the USSR* (Seattle, 1964).

VOEGELN, E. "The Mongol Orders of Submission to European Powers, 1245–1255," *Byzantion*, vol. 15, 1940–41, pp. 378–413.

7

Lord Novgorod the Great

IN NORTHWEST RUSSIA, where several major trade routes intersected, lay the self-governing commercial republic of Novgorod, known as Lord Novgorod the Great, one of medieval Europe's largest cities. Maintaining intimate contacts with the west through trade with the Baltic cities of the Hanseatic League, Novgorod served for several centuries as Russia's chief window to Europe. Until Moscow conquered it in the 1470s, Novgorod had never been captured or devastated. Until the mid-15th century Novgorod, escaping direct Mongol invasion or rule, kept alive the Kievan traditions of diversity and political freedom. Was Novgorod a haven of freedom like west European towns? Was it a democratic republic or a boyar oligarchy? Was its *veche* (assembly) truly sovereign? And if Novgorod was free and democratic, why did it fall before Muscovite expansion?

Traditional accounts describe Novgorod as one of the earliest military-commercial centers of Varangian and Slav princes. It was Novgorod's inhabitants, states the *Primary Chronicle,* who in 860 invited Riurik to come and rule over them. At first, the *Chronicle* continues, Novgorod enjoyed primacy; but after Oleg moved to Kiev about 880, Novgorod was relegated to second place among Russian towns and its citizens resented Kiev's preeminence.

Recent Soviet archeological excavations and writings have altered considerably this older, *Chronicle*-based view.[1] Novgorod was founded, affirm recent Soviet accounts, as an administrative center for a federation of three tribes. It was not heavily settled before the mid-tenth century and therefore was indeed a "new city" much younger than Pskov to the west. The excavations uncovered 28 layers dating from 953 to 1462. At intervals from seven to 30 years the log streets of the town were relaid to keep pace with the rising levels of adjoining yards. A peculiarly favorable climate preserved this five hundred years of wooden Novgorod. Post-World War II excavations have uncovered thousands of sheets of well preserved birch bark, some of whose inscriptions

[1] *Novgorod the Great: Excavations of the Medieval City directed by A. Artsik-hovsky and B. A. Kolchin,* ed. M. Thompson (New York, 1967).

MAP 7–1
Novgorod

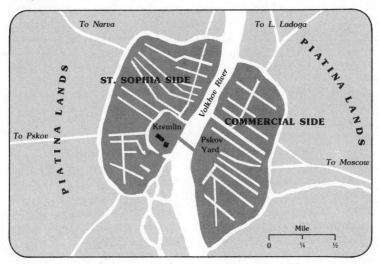

have been deciphered. The number and variety of these inscriptions suggest that literacy in Novgorod was much more widespread than had hitherto been assumed.[2]

During the 12th and 13th centuries Novgorod's chief source of wealth was probably its workshops rather than its trade with the south; what ruined the city was not isolation from Byzantium and the Arab world but conquest by Moscow. The findings in the excavation reveal that Novgorod's society resisted innovation, partly perhaps because the city was not conquered by the Mongols. Numerous foreign coins were in circulation there from the 10th century, but not until the 15th century were there native coins. In most aspects of its life Novgorod in 1450 had advanced little beyond its status in 950, whereas western Europe during that period had experienced rapid change and development. This contrast suggests that Russia's backwardness in relation to the West, often attributed by Russian and Soviet historians to the "Tatar yoke," may have been partly the result of lack of innovation. The discovery by Soviet archeologists of numerous workshops and their products prove that Novgorod was a major center of crafts, especially between the 11th and 14th centuries. The Soviet conclusion that "Novgorod was not a mercantile republic . . . , but a feudal state ruled by a few score aristocratic families . . . ," however, is most disputable.

Geographical position helped determine Novgorod's unusual history and unique role among the Russian states. The city is situated on both sides of the Volkhov River some two miles north of Lake Ilmen. Screened on the east by treacherous bogs and dense forests, it escaped devastation by the Pechenegs, Polovtsy, and Mongols. Its location on

[2] V. Yanine, "The Dig at Novgorod" in Riha, *Readings,* vol. 1, pp. 47–59.

water routes leading northward to the Baltic, eastward to the Volga, and southward to Kiev and Byzantium enhanced its commercial importance in the Kievan period and afterwards. As the logical Russian outlet for trade with the west, it was little affected by Byzantine decline and the shifting patterns of trade. Yet Novgorod's position in a food-deficit region made it vulnerable to pressure from Suzdalia and Muscovy in the northeast and dependent in famine years on grain from there or the south.

During the early period of its history—the 10th and 11th centuries —Novgorod was a political dependency of Kiev, which appointed its prince. The Kievan princes watched Novgorod carefully and generally sent their eldest sons as governors or princes to maintain control over this strategic commercial center. In 1095, however, following a dispute, Novgorod expelled its prince and invited another in his place. Seven years later when the grand prince of Kiev announced his intention to install his son as prince of Novgorod, the latter's emissaries declared: "We were sent to you, oh Prince, with positive instructions that our city does not want either you or your son. If your son has two heads, you might send him."[3] In 1136 the Novgorod *veche* asserted the city's sovereign rights by forbidding the prince and his non-Novgorod followers to own estates within its territory. Novgorod now became a republic and Kiev ceased to interfere in its internal affairs. From this time onward the power of the prince in Novgorod steadily waned. Whereas elsewhere in Russia local dynasties established firm roots, none existed in Novgorod, which elected a ruler. With the eclipse of Kiev, Novgorod about 1200 shifted its allegiance to Vladimir and later to Moscow. The princes of Vladimir-Suzdal sought to control the city to insure their supremacy, but sometimes Novgorod invited in an outside prince. Novgorod's prince, acting as its military leader to ward off external threats, was also chief magistrate and administrative head. Compelled to swear to preserve Novgorod's institutions, he could be deposed for violating his contract or infringing its liberties. Residing in the *Gorodishche* outside the city, the prince could act only while in Novgorod. Other officials could operate without his consent and the *veche* could issue laws without his approval. Elected officials even audited his revenues. Careful to prevent its prince from becoming autocratic, Novgorod treated him as an outsider with limited and specified powers. By the 1290s Novgorod had asserted its independent urban rule. After the early 14th century it had no prince of its own but recognized the vague suzerainty of Tver or Moscow.

The church of Novgorod likewise asserted its independence and chose its archbishop by lot from among local candidates. At times the archbishop, especially in later years, became the real ruler of the Novgorod republic. He lived within the kremlin, and sometimes mediated disputes within the city *veche*.

The all-Novgorod *veche*, or popular assembly, at least in theory was sovereign. By the late 12th century it elected the *posadnik* (mayor),

[3] Cross, *The Russian Primary Chronicle*, p. 291.

tysiatskii (chiliarch), and other high officials. After 1354 the number of *posadniki* gradually increased and during the early 15th century reached 24. Thus Novgorod's government became oligarchical. All free male citizens from Novgorod and the outlying regions could attend meetings of the *veche*, which were convened by the prince or a top official by ringing the *veche* bell, symbol of Novgorod's freedom. Meetings were held in the square in front of the prince's residence or before the St. Sofia Cathedral. Unanimous decisions were required. If the minority refused to yield, the issue might be resolved by a free-for-all and the losers dumped from the main bridge into the Volkhov River, which bisected the city. The *veche* supposedly dealt with all legislative questions, with foreign relations, and tried serious crimes. This large, unwieldy body, however, never developed regular rules of procedure. Novgorod was divided into five boroughs (*kontsy*), in turn subdivided into hundreds (*sotni*) and streets (*ulitsy*). Each borough had its own local *veche* and elder, and smaller subdivisions also had some rights of self-government. When the borough assemblies agreed on a measure, the all-Novgorod *veche* would readily enact it. When they disagreed, a decision would often be delayed. To the end of its existence the Novgorod *veche* retained its vitality and its frequent role as spokesman for the interests of the ordinary citizen.

The size and disorderly nature of the *veche* suggest that it was not the effective ruler of the city. By the 15th century a 50 member Council of Notables (*Soviet Gospod*), acting as the special committee of the *veche*, exercised much of its authority. Consisting of higher elected officials, borough elders, and influential boyars, the committee prepared measures in the archbishop's palace for presentation to the *veche*. This aristocratic organ often determined *veche* policy and deprived Novgorod's democracy of some of its substance. In the boroughs, too, the boyars came to exercise preponderant influence.

From the 12th century onward, Novgorod gradually acquired control of vast territories in northern European Russia stretching eastward to the Ural Mountains and north to the Arctic Ocean. Boyars and other well-to-do citizens of Novgorod took the leadership in organizing the colonization of these areas, providing resources to outfit and arm expeditions of settlers and to hew routes through the wilderness. Novgorod's settlers subdued scattered natives and established strongpoints; later they were joined by monks. By the 15th century the entire White Sea coast was studded with a settler population dependent on boyars or monasteries in Novgorod. Their chief purpose was to supply the Novgorod market with furs, fish, and forest products. In the more southerly regions of the Northern Dvina and Onega rivers, the peasant commune with its democratic flavor prevailed. These colonial regions, which Novgorod defended stubbornly and successfully against Muscovite incursions until the mid-15th century, were divided into five provinces, each subject to one of the boroughs and subdivided into districts (*volosti*) with their own capitals. Novgorod appointed officials to administer this empire and collected tribute from it, especially furs. The dependencies made frequent attempts to escape central administrative control, but except for Pskov, which secured broad autonomy, their revolts were suppressed.

Foreign trade accounted in considerable measure for Novgorod's wealth and prosperity. Since the time of the Varangians it had traded with the Baltic, and from the late 12th century its merchants concluded agreements with traders of Visby on Gotland Island and later with other German merchants of the Hanseatic League. Novgorod sent out merchants to other parts of Russia but rarely maintained them abroad and lacked a commercial fleet. Its trade was handled largely by German merchants living in a separate settlement, the Peterhof, where they were exempt from arrest and constituted a closed corporation. Novgorod merchants organized trade guilds the earliest and most powerful of which was the Ivanskoe *sto* (hundred). Novgorod exported furs, wax, and lumber and imported grains, woolens, wine, metals, and sweets. It served as intermediary between other Russian territories and the German world. After 1300 it gradually lost its trade monopoly with the Hanse as German merchants began using the western Dvina route and set up warehouses in Smolensk and Polotsk. After that Novgorod traded increasingly with the rising centers of the northeast, Tver and Moscow. The Novgorod empire retained its commercial prosperity, based partly on its workshops and extensive domains, until the end of its independent existence. In the 15th century it included 18 towns. None of these rivalled Novgorod itself, which attracted agricultural and handicraft products from all parts of its empire. In many ways Novgorod's economy and institutions were comparable to those of the oligarchical commercial republics of Venice and Florence.

Novgorod society, like that of Kiev, remained diversified and relatively mobile. The boyar upper class derived its wealth from trade and ownership of large estates, which provided articles of export, and it controlled credit, banking, and higher political offices. Soviet historians emphasize the "feudal" nature of this class, but it would seem to have been concerned mainly with commerce rather than manorial landholding. The higher clergy was wealthy and influential, and numerous monasteries possessed large landholdings and enterprises. The clergy remained an open estate: any citizen of Novgorod could be ordained and any clergyman might become a layman. Lesser landowners or business men not belonging to the ruling aristocracy were known as *zhitye liudi* (well-off people). Merchants were counted as boyars or *zhitye liudi* depending on their wealth and land holdings. Lower-class urban dwellers, known as rye-bread eaters in contrast to wealthier wheat-bread eaters, included artisans, petty tradesmen, and laborers and were designated collectively as *molodshie* or *chernye liudi*. In rural areas there were free peasants, tenant farmers, and sharecroppers. Slaves (*kholopy*), owned by boyars and wealthy merchants, were more numerous in Novgorod than in Moscow. Equality before the law, proclaimed by the statutes, existed mostly on paper. The Novgorod Charter of 1471, like the *Russkaia Pravda* of Kiev, contained a scale of fines for injuring officials which revealed the extent of social inequality. The wealthy dominated the courts and the poor often suffered injustice. Sometimes, however, the *veche* defended the legal rights of ordinary citizens.

Soviet accounts stress the intense class struggle in Novgorod, fueled by the growth of feudal landownership and increasing exploitation of the peasantry and urban lower classes by the boyar-merchant aristocracy. Periodic interruptions of grain imports caused hunger among the city poor and contributed to several urban revolts in the 14th and 15th centuries. Toward the mid-15th century, claim Soviet historians, these social contradictions sharpened, undermined Novgorod's unity, and contributed to its fall. A western scholar, Joel Raba, notes that in the late 14th century the boyars, who formerly had often fought among themselves, closed ranks to form an efficient oligarchy while the *veche* continued to provide a forum for cooperation between the ruling elements.[4]

Externally, Novgorod before the 13th century remained relatively secure from invasion. After repelling western attacks by Swedes and German knights in the 13th century, it relied upon skilful diplomacy to balance itself between Lithuania and Moscow. Novgorod's political aim continued to be independence and perhaps, as Vernadsky suggests, to revive a Russian federation. By 1450, however, Moscow and Lithuania had absorbed most of the formerly independent Russian principalities. Early in the 15th century Novgorod had demonstrated its continuing viability by crushing efforts of its dependencies to break away with Moscow's support. Novgorod, however, clearly had less to fear from Lithuania than from Moscow and thus sought friendly ties with lesser princes of the Lithuanian House of Gedymin. During the civil war in Muscovy between Vasili II and Dmitri Shemiaka,[5] Novgorod supported Vasili's boyar opponents. But Novgorod was more dependent economically upon Moscow than upon Lithuania. Periodic conflicts with the Muscovites, besides costing Novgorod the areas of Torzhok, Vologda, and Volok-Lamskii, brought suspensions of grain deliveries and of Oriental trade. Also Novgorod had important political links with Moscow: since about 1300 it generally had selected the Muscovite grand prince as its overlord because he could provide the most protection.

Vasili II's victory in the Muscovite civil war doomed the Novgorod republic. Resentful of its support for his enemies and for granting asylum to their leader, Dmitri Shemiaka in 1452, Vasili acted to restrict Novgorod's freedom. In 1456 he led a successful military expedition against it and forced Novgorod to sign a humiliating peace. Novgorod preserved its formal independence but had to allow Vasili to collect a special tax (*chernyi bor*) and allow Moscow to control its foreign policy. Oblivious of impending disaster, Novgorod's aristocratic factions struggled for power. An influential boyar group headed by the energetic *posadnitsa* (mayor) Marfa Boretskii looked to Lithuania for salvation and arranged for Michael Olelkovich, a lesser

---

[4] Joel Raba, "Novgorod in the Fifteenth Century: A Re-examination," *Canadian Slavic Studies*, vol. 1, No. 3 (Fall 1967), pp. 348–64.

[5] See below, p. 96.

Gedymin prince, to become Novgorod's ruler. The Novgorod *veche* in a riotous session approved Boretskii's proposal of a formal alliance with Lithuania against Moscow. Ivan III of Moscow asserted promptly that such a treaty with Catholic Lithuania endangered the Orthodox faith, violated tradition, and constituted treason to Russia. With a strenuous propaganda campaign, Ivan secured the support of Tver and Novgorod's own dependencies, Pskov and Viatka. When Lithuania failed to send troops to assist her, Novgorod lay isolated and helpless.

The city-republic's internal disunity, though exaggerated by Soviet historians, contributed to its fall. The boyars, anxious to retain their lands, directed the opposition to Moscow and sought Lithuanian support. On the other hand, the Orthodox clergy feared that Catholic Lithuanians would subvert their church. Archbishop-elect Feofil refused to send his cavalry against Orthodox Muscovites. Many commoners wavered, confused by the religious issue. To the lower classes good relations with Moscow meant cheap bread and more impartial justice. Consequently the morale of the large citizen militia was low when it opposed Moscow. Novgorod's troops were untrained and inferior in quality to the smaller Muscovite forces. In 1470 a series of skirmishes culminated in the Battle of Shelon. The Novgorodians were badly beaten and had to accept permanent dependence on Moscow. In 1478, when the boyar party revolted against Muscovite domination, Ivan III sent a massive expedition aganist the city. Novgorod and its dominions were incorporated into Muscovy, almost doubling the latter's territory, and the *veche* bell was carried off to Moscow. During the 1480s thousands of boyars and merchants were deported and their lands distributed to Muscovite gentry. In 1494 foreign merchants in Novgorod were seized and the Peterhof closed. The window to Europe had been slammed shut.

Pskov, Novgorod's so-called "younger brother" and former dependency, suffered a similar fate. Pskov had developed as early as the eighth century along the Velikaia River trade route and by the tenth century was involved in commerce with east and west. Governed in the earlier years by a mayor sent from Novgorod, Pskov after 1260 was ruled at times by Lithuanian princes and came under strong Lithuanian influence. The Lithuanian prince, Dovmont, serving in Pskov (1265–99), however, led its forces against Lithuania and the Germans. In its political and social institutions Pskov resembled Novgorod, but it possessed no colonies. As it flourished from the transit trade with the Baltic, it emancipated itself gradually from direct Novgorodian control. A treaty of 1348 recognized its independence though Novgorod retained a shadowy suzerainty. When Novgorod proved unable to protect it from the German knights, Pskov turned once again to Lithuania. Pskov had a sovereign *veche*, a prince with limited powers, a council of notables, and two elected mayors. Though suffering from sharp social tensions, it acted consistently as Russia's chief defensive bastion on the west. During Ivan III's reign, Pskov recognized Moscow's supremacy and was formally incorporated into Muscovy in 1510.

The conquest of these flourishing and politically vital northwest Russian commercial republics by Moscow resulted from the consolidation of Muscovite absolutism.[6] Under Ivan III Moscow united the power and resources of east Russia against city-states which were more advanced culturally and economically than their conqueror. One can surely question assertions by Soviet historians that their fall was "progressive" and "historically inevitable." Their destruction and absorption by Muscovy, which some historians consider a tragedy, reduced the chances for the development of representative institutions in Russia.

Suggested Additional Reading

BARON, S. H.   "The Town in Feudal Russia," *SR*, vol. 28, 1969, pp. 116–22.

BEAZLEY, R.   "The Russian Expansion towards Asia . . . to 1500," *AHR*, 13,

FLORINSKY, M.   *Russia: A History* . . . , vol. 1, 110–25.

KLUCHEVSKY, V. O.   *Course of Russian History* (N.Y., 1911), vol. 1, pp. 319–68.

LANGER, L.   "V. L. Ianin and the History of Novgorod," *SR*, vol. 33, 1974, pp. 114–19.

MITCHELL, R. and N. FORBES, eds., *The Chronicles of Novgorod (1016–1471)* (London, 1914) (excerpts in Riha, *Readings*, vol. 1, pp. 29–46).

RABA, JOEL.   "The Fate of the Novgorodian Republic," *SEER*, July 1967, pp. 307–23.

———.   "Novgorod in the Fifteenth Century," *CanSISt.*, Fall 1967, p. 48–64.

SMITH, R. E.   "Some Recent Discoveries in Novgorod," *Past and Present*, no. 5, 1954, pp. 1–10.

THOMPSON, W. W., ed. *Novgorod the Great: Excavations of the Medieval City* . . . (New York, 1967).

VERNADSKY, G.   *Russia at the Dawn of the Modern Age*, "Novgorod," pp. 27–66.

YANINE, V. L.   "The Dig at Novgorod," in Riha, *Readings*, vol. 1, pp. 47–59.

---

[6] See below, pp. 96 ff.

8

The Rise of Moscow

WHILE THE Mongols of the Golden Horde ruled Russia, the obscure principality of Moscow on the southern fringe of Vladimir-Suzdal rose to prominence and power. During the 14th century Moscow emerged as successor to Vladimir and became the center of grand princely authority. Gradually overshadowing Tver, another new principality, Moscow became the focal point of religious, political, and economic life in northeast Russia. Prince Dmitrii Donskoi's victory of 1380 over the Mongols shattered the myth of Tatar invincibility and confirmed Moscow's leadership. How and why did Moscow achieve such striking successes? Did its rise correspond to the artistic and beautiful pattern woven by the prerevolutionary Russian historian Kliuchevskii, or to the disorderly, complex process of ebb and flow described later by A. E. Presniakov and M. T. Florinsky? Did Moscow triumph from superior internal economic and political strength or because of its relationship with the Golden Horde?

Many Western scholars still accept much of Kliuchevskii's imaginative and majestic theory about the rise of Moscow.[1] Politically he divided the Russian middle ages into two sharply distinct periods: an era of feudal division and disintegration following Kiev's decline when Russia was split into hereditary princely appanages; then a period when the princes of Moscow gathered these territories inexorably into what became the Muscovite autocratic state.

The chronicles first mentioned Moscow under the year 1147 as a frontier town of Vladimir-Suzdal. In that year Prince Iuri Dolgoruki of Suzdal invited a distant prince to a meeting with the words: "Come to me, brother, in Moscow." Whether Moscow was already a town or merely a princely estate is unknown. In 1156 Iuri supposedly founded Moscow as a fortified town at the mouth of the Neglinnaia River, surrounding it with a wooden palisade on the hill where the Kremlin stands today. This settlement seems to have been part of Iuri's policy of creating strategic and commercial centers in the south and west of

---

[1] Kliuchevskii, *Kurs russkoi istorii* (Moscow, 1937), vol. 2, pp. 3–27.

his domains. Far from the main centers of Suzdalia, this new town, developing on the crossroads between the Dnieper and Volga waterways, went to a junior prince. Moscow arose, claims a ·"schismatic chronicle," near the residence of Kuchko, a wealthy boyar who in 1147 suddenly left the service of Iuri Dolgoruki after a personal quarrel. Supposedly Iuri rode there, killed Kuchko on the spot, then, admiring the location of his fine estate, decided to found a town there. He called ·it Moskva (Moscow) after the river of that name.[2] On the other hand, the Soviet scholar, Rabinovich, on the basis of excavations in the Zariadie area of Kitai-gorod hill, concludes that Moscow already possessed a commercial district (*posad*) in the 10th and 11th centuries stretching in a narrow band along the Moscow River and traded with Europe and the Orient. Other Soviet historians have disputed this. In 1237, when Moscow fell to the Mongols, the *Chronicle* described it as already a sizable, densely populated town. The Mongols set fire to the town and its wooden churches and departed with much loot.[3] In 1263, when Moscow was granted to Daniel, youngest son of Prince Alexander Nevskii, it became the capital of a separate principality.

Turbulent events in northern Russia provided the background for Moscow's rise. From the late 12th century to the Mongol invasion, first Suzdal, then Vladimir assumed from Kiev the mantle of all-Russian leadership. Under Vsevolod III Suzdalia installed obedient princes, preferably relatives, in Novgorod and led resistance to German and Lithuanian incursions from the west. Simultaneously, Vsevolod attacked the Volga Bulgars in the east and pursued vigorous colonization of the Volga region. Employing the old principle of seniority, the grand princes of Vladimir-Suzdal sought to subordinate other princes to their authority.

But the Mongol conquest changed conditions in the north fundamentally. Suzdalia's trade was wrecked, its colonization halted, and its power undermined. As Novgorod and Pskov gradually assumed the burden of defending Russia against western invaders, the centralizing role of the grand prince weakened. Toward the end of the 13th century the authority of the grand prince of Vladimir declined grievously as he became wholly dependent on the Golden Horde. Among some other northern princes developed the notion of acquiring power rather than lands or seniority. After 1300 emerged "new towns," especially Tver and Moscow, as independent political entities contending for the succession to declining Vladimir.[4]

Favorable geographical location promoted the rise of Moscow. Lying on the Moskva River in the area between the Volga and Oka river basins, it developed where several major trade routes intersected. To the east, Moscow was guarded by dense forests; on the west, more forests and marshes west of Mozhaisk provided protection. Uprooted

---

[2] H. Dewey, "Tales of Moscow's Founding," *Canadian-American Slavic Studies*, vol. 6, pp. 595–96.

[3] M. Tikhomirov, *The Towns of Ancient Russia*, p. 434.

[4] A. E. Presniakov, *The Formation of the Great Russian State* (Chicago, 1970), p. 45 ff.

by Mongol raids, migrants flocked to the Moscow region from the north, west, and south. Settling at first along the rivers, the newcomers later penetrated their interior tributaries. Even before Moscow became important, titled servitors came there from many parts of Russia. The town's commerce expanded rapidly, providing Moscow's princes with customs revenues and helping them outpace their rivals economically.

Moscow, affirms Kliuchevskii, became the ethnographic center of Great Russia. During the 13th and 14th centuries, while Mongols and Lithuanians blocked colonization outside the Volga-Oka region, Moscow's central position and forests protected its growing population from their depredations. Before 1368 Moscow suffered little from Mongol raids, which laid waste more exposed Riazan, Iaroslavl, and Smolensk. Generally, Kliuchevskii underestimates external factors such as the Mongol invasion and Lithuanian pressure in explaining Moscow's rise. The Moscow princes' position within the House of Riurik, he argued, fostered their untraditional and defiant course. At first they could not aspire to the grand princely throne in Vladimir because of their junior status. They had to provide for their security by bold, untraditional policies. Externally the Moscow princes were aggressive, the sworn enemies of the grand prince of Vladimir; at home they won a reputation as careful administrators and proprietors.

In the 14th century Moscow gained rapidly in area and power. In 1300 it had been an insignificant principality smaller than the present Moscow province. From this central core it expanded in all directions, much as did the French monarchy from the Île de France around Paris. Just after 1300 the conquest of strategic Mozhaisk on the west and Kolomna to the south almost tripled Moscow's territory, gave it full control of the Moskva River, and allowed it to exploit its strategic situation at the intersection of trade routes from the east, south, and west. Moscow's southern borders were extended far enough along the Oka River to afford it additional protection against Mongol raids and bring it close to the borders of Riazan principality. Moscow grew by conquest, by settlement of the Volga region, by purchase of territory from others princes, by Mongol military aid, and by treaties with neighboring princes.

In the early 14th century Moscow's most dangerous rival was Tver principality. Lying at the confluence of the Volga and Tvertsa rivers about a hundred miles northwest of Moscow, Tver (now Kalinin) had a superb location for trade but with fewer natural defenses than its rival, being open to attack from all sides. Tver, first mentioned in the chronicles under the year 1209, was apparently settled during the tenth century. At first regarded by Novgorod as an outpost on its border with Suzdalia, Tver for a time was ruled by the princes of Pereiaslavl. After the Mongol conquest, its strategic position dominating the best route from Suzdalia to Novgorod and its relative security brought it numerous inhabitants. In 1304, when the contest of Moscow and Tver for supremacy in the northeast began, there was little to choose between them economically or politically; Tver was the stronger militarily. Probably for that reason, the Golden Horde in order to maintain a

MAP 8–1
Lithuanian-Russian state in 14th Century

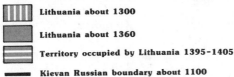

	Lithuania about 1300
	Lithuania about 1360
	Territory occupied by Lithuania 1395–1405
	Kievan Russian boundary about 1100

Adapted from *A History of Russia, Second Edition* by Nicholas V. Riasanovsky. Copyright
© 1969 by Oxford University Press, Inc. Used by permission.

balance of power in the east aided Moscow repeatedly against Tver and against Lithuanian efforts to expand eastward.

Tver and Moscow fought over control of the grand princely throne in Vladimir and over control of Novgorod. During their contest Prince Michael of Tver (1304–18) sought unwisely to depose Metropolitan Peter, leader of the Orthodox Church, who henceforth backed Moscow with increasing effectiveness. In 1317 at Bortenovo Michael badly defeated a larger Muscovite army, but the following year the Horde intervened and granted the grand princely title to Prince Iuri Danilovich of Moscow. Michael of Tver was condemned and executed in Sarai, capital of the Horde. The Mongols carefully supervised Iuri Danilovich's actions as grand prince. Then in 1327 Tver revolted against local Mongol merchants and troops, an action which the Tatars may have provoked deliberately. Prince Ivan I of Moscow received support from a powerful Mongol punitive force which captured Tver and sacked it mercilessly. Tver's pretensions to supremacy were shattered; it took the city almost 40 years to recover from this blow. Moscow's success in competition with Tver owed more to initial military weakness than to strength. The Golden Horde and the Orthodox Church had proved to be indispensable allies.

Ivan I ("Kalita"—moneybags; 1328–40) exploited Tver's misfortune to become grand prince of Moscow and Vladimir. Lithuanian pressure on western Russia helped solidify relations between Moscow and the Horde. In 1328, by shrewd diplomacy and perhaps bribery, Ivan obtained the khan's patent as grand prince of Vladimir. Mongol attacks virtually ceased in northern Russia. As collector of tribute money for the Horde from all the Russian princes, Ivan began cautiously to lead Great Russia out of apathy and disunity. Simultaneously, Moscow became Russia's chief religious center. After Kiev's fall, the metropolitan of the Orthodox Church had transferred his headquarters to Vladimir, but on visits to the south he sometimes stayed in Moscow. A close friendship developed between Ivan I and Metropolitan Peter, who died and was buried in Moscow in 1326. His successor, Theognostus, took up residence in Moscow, became its zealous supporter, and intervened in Novgorod and Pskov in behalf of the Moscow prince. Great material contributions began to flow into Moscow church coffers and the first stone churches were built there between 1326 and 1333. After two severe fires, Moscow was largely rebuilt; the Kremlin and its walls were built of stout oak. The Church, centering in Moscow, provided a spiritual basis for unification of Great Russia. Ivan Kalita, however, maintained supremacy over other princes of east Russia by complete subservience to the Golden Horde.

Ivan Kalita's successors continued his consolidation of Moscow's strength and sought with shifting fortune to maintain its preeminence among the Russian states. Gradually they built up their power and grand princely authority. Under Dmitri "Donskoi" (1359–89), a large measure of unity was forged among Russian princes in the struggle against Lithuanian invasion. Metropolitan Alexis played a key role, ably seconding the Grand Prince's policies. In these years bases for

Great Russian unity were laid and strengthened while serious discord within the Golden Horde caused it temporarily to lose control over Moscow.

As factions contended within the Horde, Tatar bands plundered some Great Russian territories. Dmitri of Moscow, to defend his lands and the grand princely power, appealed to other princes to aid him against the forces of Khan Mamai, which had devastated the lands of Riazan and Nizhegorod. When Dmitri refused to pay additional tribute money, Mamai backed by Lithuania resolved to crush Moscow. As Dmitri mobilized an army to resist the Mongols militarily, noted later chronicles with exaggeration, the mood in Russia resembled that of Greece before the Battle of Marathon. Few Russians believed that Dmitri could defeat the supposedly invincible Mongols, and Novgorod, Pskov, Nizhnii-Novgorod, and Tver declined to supply troops for his campaign. Oleg of Riazan, seeking to save his principality, sought to bargain with both sides. Here are excerpts from the *Chronicle* account of the famous Battle of Kulikovo of 1380:

> That Year Prince Mamai of the Horde, accompanied by other princes and all the Tartar and Polovtsi forces . . . , and supported by Iagello of Lithuania and Oleg of Riazan, advanced against Grand Prince Dmitri and on September 1 made a camp on the bank of the Oka River. . . . The Grand Prince went to the Church of the Mother of God, where he prayed for a long time; . . . [then] he sent for all the Russian princes, voevodas, and all the people . . . There never was such a mighty Russian army, for all forces combined numbered some 200,000. . . . Mamai's camp was in a meadow not far from the Don where, with all his forces he awaited for about three weeks the arrival of Iagello. . . .
>
> When Mamai learned of the arrival of the Grand Prince at the Don . . . he said, "Let us move toward the Don before Iagello arrives there. . . ." At six in the morning the godless Tartars appeared in the field and faced the Christians. There was a great multitude of both; and when these two great forces met they covered an area 13 versts long. And there was a great massacre and bitter warfare and great noise, such as there never had been in the Russian principalities; and they fought from six to nine, and blood flowed like a heavy rain and there were many killed on both sides . . . Shortly thereafter, the godless fled and the Christians pursued them . . .[5]

The Battle of Kulikovo, dramatized by priestly chroniclers as a crusade against Moslem tyranny, shattered the legend of Mongol invincibility but changed little in Russo-Tatar relations. Because the Russian princes failed to preserve unity, only two years later Dmitri had to abandon Moscow to the avenging army of Khan Toktamysh. Once again Moscow and northern Russia had to submit to Mongol overlordship.

Historical theories about Moscow's rise have undergone a considerable evolution since Kliuchevskii's famous pre-World War I interpretation.

---

[5] B. Dmytryshyn, *Medieval Russia: A Source Book, 900–1700* (Hinsdale, Illinois, 1972), pp. 165–67.

Kliuchevskii summarized his view of the rise of Moscow as follows:

> . . . During the 14th century the north Russian population with the Moscow principality and its prince: . . . (1) came to regard the Moscow grand prince as a model ruler-administrator, creator of civil peace and order, and his principality as the point of departure for a new system of political relationships whose first result was the creation of greater internal peace and external security. (2) They became accustomed to regard the senior Muscovite prince as Russia's national leader in the struggle with external enemies, and Moscow as responsible for the first national victories over pagan Lithuania. . . . (3) Finally, northern Russia became accustomed to regard the Moscow prince as the eldest son of the Russian church . . . with whom were bound up the religious and moral interests of the Orthodox Russian people.[6]

Recently M. T. Florinsky has questioned the "logical perfection and consistency" of this Kliuchevskii scheme:

> . . . History can seldom be fitted into a well-rounded scheme without suffering grievous distortions. Less romantically minded historians would hesitate to use such a metaphysical concept as that of a new ethnographical formation—in this case Great Russia—"waiting for a leader" and when the leader was somewhat suddenly discovered, carrying him "to the exalted heights of the sovereign of Great Russia."[7]

Presniakov has written the most comprehensive pre-Soviet Russian account of Moscow's rise.[8] Unlike Kliuchevskii, who treated Muscovite and Kievan Russia as wholly distinct and different chapters in the country's history, Presniakov stressed their close connection and held that Great Russia represented a union between the Novgorod and Suzdalian regions. Whereas Kliuchevskii described successive and sharply contrasting eras of feudal division and unification, Presniakov argued that they had existed simultaneously, and that the formation of Muscovy involved a process of ebb and flow. Kliuchevskii emphasized the gathering of lands by Moscow's rulers, but Presniakov depicted the unification of Great Russia as a gradual accumulation of authority and sovereignty by the grand prince of Moscow, achieved by the destruction in fact and denial in principle of customary law in favor of autocracy.

Early Soviet historians stressed economic factors in Moscow's rise virtually to the exclusion of political ones. Thus M. N. Pokrovskii viewed the 15th century Muscovite state as "a huge association of feudal landowners" which swallowed its rivals because of Moscow's exceptionally favorable location for trade. The feudal, appanage order was being destroyed by the shift from a natural to a commercial economy and the creation of a broader market. These developments, concluded Pokrovskii, preceded political unification. As early as the 13th century, Moscow had been a populous commercial center with financial resources providing a sound basis for unification. Once the

---

[6] Kliuchevskii, *Kurs*, vol. 2, pp. 26–27.

[7] Florinsky, vol. 1, p. 77.

[8] Presniakov, *The Formation* (originally published in Petrograd [now Leningrad], 1918).

Moscow prince became grand prince of Vladimir, a Novgorod-Moscow alliance became an economic necessity for both parties.[9]

After World War II, Soviet historians, rejecting Pokrovskii's commercial theory, emphasized instead radical changes in agricultural technology as paving the way for unification around Moscow. The introduction of the three-field system and better plows and better economic conditions attracted landowners, peasants, and artisans to Muscovy. What enriched Moscow was less its location for trade than "the plow, the scythe, and manure on the peasant's fields." Other scholars, such as V. V. Mavrodin, objected that such an agricultural emphasis denied the significant role of towns and awakening national consciousness. "All progressive elements of the old Russian society [peasants, gentry, merchants etc.] . . . gravitated toward the grand prince who personified the unity of Russia."[10]

In the post-Stalin era, Soviet historians have adopted a relatively balanced, multicausational interpretation of Moscow's rise. After 1300, notes *Istoriia SSSR*, when Russia began to recover from the Mongol invasion, agriculture grew, towns revived, and their commercial districts expanded. The existing feudal political division of Russia then hampered its socioeconomic development. External attacks by Mongols, Lithuanians, and Swedes hastened a process of unification supported by all progressive classes. Moscow's power, growing under Ivan Kalita, was enhanced by Dmitri's victory at Kulikovo, which helped liquidate feudal division. The growth of productive forces and culture established conditions for the creation of the Great Russian people and language.[11] The Moscow region, affirms Cherepnin, was one of developed agriculture, handicrafts, and industries. Convenient river and land routes favored colonization outward from Moscow and facilitated an exchange of goods and economic contacts with border regions. Moscow's rise stemmed indeed from popular participation, the labor of peasants and artisans, but it would be wrong to overlook the positive role of the Moscow princes. Allying themselves with the townspeople in the 14th century, they promoted the rise of the Moscow state.[12] Recent Soviet historians, while continuing to emphasize economic and social factors, include also the political aspects of the rise of Moscow.

Clearly Kliuchevskii's traditional theory of the rise of Moscow now needs considerable revision. Presniakov's work in particular has shown convincingly the linkage between the Kievan and Muscovite eras, dispelling the consistency and purposefulness which Kliuchevskii read into the bloody, chaotic events of 13th and 14th century Russia. Likewise, Presniakov has demonstrated the vital importance of external

---

[9] M. N. Pokrovskii, "Obrazovanie Moskovskogo gosudarstva." *Russkaia istoriia s drevneishikh vremen* (Moscow, 1933), vol. 1, pp. 119–57.

[10] P. P. Smirnov, "Obrazovanie russkogo tsentralizovannogo gosudarstva v XIV–XV vv.," *Voprosy istorii*, 1946, nos. 2–3, p. 89; ibid., no. 4, p. 52; V. V. Mavrodin, *Obrazovanie edinogo russkogo gosudarstva* (Leningrad, 1951), p. 310.

[11] *Istoriia SSSR* (Moscow, 1966), vol. 2, p. 65.

[12] L. V. Cherepnin, *Obrazovanie russkogo tsentralizovannogo gosudarstva v XIV–XV vekakh* (Moscow, 1960), pp. 455–59.

factors, such as the policies of the Horde, in Moscow's rise. Soviet historians have deepened our understanding by using archaeological findings and by making intensive study of economic and social factors. Nonetheless, the Kliuchevskii thesis remains valuable and contains suggestive insights when it is revised to take account of later scholarship.

Suggested Additional Reading

ALMEDINGEN, E. M.   *The Land of Muscovy: The History of Early Russia* (New York, 1972).

BIRKETT, G. A.   "Slavonic Cities, 4: Moscow 1147–1947," *SEER*, vol. 25, pp. 336–55.

DEWEY, H.   "Tales of Moscow's Founding," *CanAmSlSt.*, vol. 6, pp. 595–605.

FENNELL, J. L.   *The Emergence of Moscow, 1305–1359* (Berkeley, 1968).

———.   "The Tver Uprising of 1327. . . ," *Jahr. Gesch. Ost.*, vol. 15, pp. 161–79.

HOWES, R. C., ed.,   *The Testaments of the Grand Princes of Moscow* (Ithaca, 1967).

NOWAK, FRANK.   *Medieval Slavdom and the Rise of Russia* (New York, 1970, reprint).

PRESNIAKOV, A. E.   *The Formation of the Great Russian State* (Chicago, 1970, translation).

VOYCE, ARTHUR.   *Moscow and the Roots of Russian Culture* (Norman, Oklahoma, 1964).

9

Unification of Great Russia

UNDER Dmitri Donskoi's successors, the rise of Moscow continued by a process of ebb and flow with both successes and failures. Vasili II's reign (1425–62) proved crucial: after civil wars came internal consolidation and heightened power. At Ivan III's accession in 1462, the unification of Great Russia was well begun. When his son, Vasili III, died in 1533 it was complete. Great Russian patriotism and consciousness of a need for unity grew markedly. Grand princely power increased considerably while the Golden Horde splintered into several feuding khanates. Assisting an emerging and expanding Muscovite state were a strong national Orthodox Church and a national judicial system. Soviet historians also stress the importance of improving agricultural techniques and gradual formation of a Great Russian market and assert that Muscovite autocracy forcibly destroyed the Tatar yoke. Were Vasili and Ivan III true autocrats? Was the destruction of Novgorod and unification of Great Russia a blessing or disaster for the Russian people?

EXPANSION AND THE GROWTH OF GRAND PRINCELY POWER

After the short-lived Kulikovo victory of 1380, Moscow gyrated feebly between Lithuania and the Golden Horde. During Vasili I's bloody, chaotic, and obscure reign (1389–1425) repeated Tatar incursions and internal princely strife devastated the land. Division of Great Russia among the grand principalities of Moscow, Tver, and Riazan insured continued Mongol domination. Though the Horde permitted Moscow to absorb the Nizhnii-Novgorod principality, it exploited Moscow's continuing rivalry with Tver to rule a tormented Russia. Lithuania under the able Vitovt expanded almost to Moscow, and only a Mongol victory on the Vorskla River (1399) denied to Lithuania rule over all western Russia. The Lithuanian danger temporarily united Great Russians and induced them to seek Tatar aid.

Early in the reign of Vasili II (1425–62), Moscow suffered a severe political eclipse. His uncle Iuri and three of his sons, Vasili Kosoi,

Dmitri Shemiaka, and Dmitri Krasnyi, representing the feudal appanage principle, warred against Vasili II, sometimes seizing Moscow.
Meanwhile to the west Grand Duke Casimir of Lithuania reunited his
lands, then in 1447 became king of Poland. Lithuania and Poland retained their own governments but henceforth had the same ruler. For
the next two centuries Poland-Lithuania was Moscow's chief eastern
European rival. East of Moscow the weakened Golden Horde fragmented: separate khanates formed in Kazan, Astrakhan, and the
Crimea, enabling Moscow gradually, without glorious victories, to free
Russia from Mongol rule.

As Muscovite princes contended in civil war, Ulu-Muhammed, a
Tatar chieftain, founded Kazan khanate and captured Vasili II. In
Moscow, panic and dismay were dispelled by his release. Traditional
accounts mention payment of a ransom while Keenan affirms that
Vasili's release followed conclusion of an alliance which contributed
much to Vasili's subsequent victory in the civil war.[1] When Vasili returned to Moscow with Tatar troops, Dmitri Shemiaka, his chief rival,
exploited Vasili's friendship with Ulu to attract boyar and merchant
support, captured Moscow, blinded Vasili, and deported him to Uglich.
The victors planned to split Muscovy into independent appanages and
destroy grand princely authority altogether, but their selfishness provoked a sharp reaction. The clergy and leading Muscovites compelled
Shemiaka to release Vasili who, supported by Tver principality and
Tatar allies, seized Moscow, resumed power, and compelled his enemies
to make peace.

In the final 15 years of his reign Vasili II, though no great ruler,
consolidated his position at home and moved to unify and strengthen
Great Russia. Friendship with Lithuania freed Moscow from western
threats, and Riazan principality to the southeast became its vassal.
Shemiaka's appanage was confiscated and the Moscow metropolitan excommunicated him. His flight to Novgorod gave Vasili a pretext for a
campaign against Novgorod in 1456, which prepared for its subsequent
incorporation into Muscovy.[2] Shemiaka's defeat ended Muscovy's civil
strife and smashed Great Russia's traditional appanage system irreparably. Emergence of the Moscow-dominated Tatar khanate of
Kasimov in 1452 heightened Moscow's prestige in the Moslem world
and encouraged many Tatars to enter its service. That same year Moscow ceased paying regular tribute to the disintegrating Horde. Some
historians affirm that this date marked Great Russia's de facto independence; others date removal of the "Tatar yoke" from the abortive
Mongol campaign against Moscow in 1480. In any event, Moscow at
Vasili II's death was far stronger than before. His gains, prepared by
the work of his predecessors and fostered by support from the Church,
servitor princes, and gentry, constituted a major turning point in Russian political history.

The Russian Church became narrowly Muscovite as it achieved inde-

---

[1] Edward Keenan, "Muscovy and Kazan; Some Introductory Remarks on Steppe
Diplomacy," *SR*, vol. 26, p. 554.

[2] See above, p. 83.

MAP 9–1
Rise of Moscow to 1533

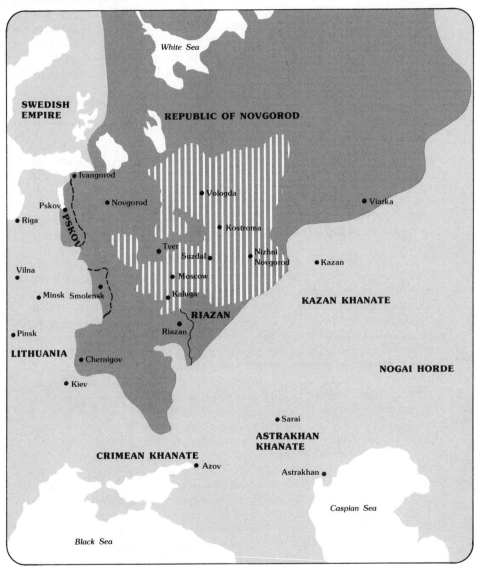

	Principality of Moscow by 1462
	Acquired by Moscow, 1462-1533

Adapted with permission of Macmillan Publishing Co., Inc. from *Russian History Atlas* by Martin Gilbert. Cartography by Martin Gilbert. Copyright © 1972 by Martin Gilbert.

pendence from crumbling Byzantium. Byzantine leaders, desperately seeking western aid against the oncoming Turks and yielding to Papal pressure, agreed at the Council of Florence (1439) to rejoin the Roman Catholic Church. The violently anti-Catholic Muscovites, however, rejected this union and deposed Metropolitan Isidor, their chief delegate to the Council. A council of Russian bishops chose Iona, bishop of Riazan, as metropolitan and he became Vasili's chief adviser. They sought reconciliation with Byzantium, but in 1453 the Turks captured Constantinople and ended the Byzantine Empire. The Russian Church became virtually independent, enhancing Moscow's international significance. After Iona, the Moscow ruler confirmed metropolitans in office, and closer church-state cooperation developed in Muscovy. After 1458 when West Russia formed a separate Uniate Church, the Muscovite church asserted its superiority over the Greek church, claiming to lead the Orthodox world and that Moscow's prince was destined to replace the Byzantine emperor. The basis had been laid for the Third Rome theory (that with the apostasy of Rome and the fall of Byzantium, Moscow would replace them) and the later "Greek Project" of Catherine the Great."[3]

Ivan III, "the Great" (1462–1505), like his contemporaries Henry VII of England and Louis XI of France, achieved national unification and centralization and is often called "gatherer of the Russian lands." Aiding his father against Shemiaka and serving as co-ruler, Ivan was well prepared for power. His father's testament, insuring Ivan's territorial, fiscal and political supremacy over four younger brothers, exhorted them to "respect and obey [their] older brother in place of their father." Preferring diplomacy and intrigue to war, Ivan achieved ambitious aims with a minimum of bloodshed. He sought to unite Russia around Moscow and rule it autocratically, and his campaigns, reforms, and marriages occurred as if by divine plan. Better than other Muscovite rulers, he knew his resources, his goals, and how to attain them. This tall, awe-inspiring Machiavellian prince—dedicated, hardheaded, and cautious—was feared not loved.

At his accession Great Russia remained fragmented, and the Kievan tradition of a confederation of equal sovereign princes persisted. Tver to the northwest and the republic of Viatka to the northeast preserved a fragile independence, while Novgorod and Riazan, independent in name, were actually Moscow dependencies. Autonomous Iaroslavl and Rostov, virtually encircled by Muscovite lands, were annexed in 1463 and 1474 respectively. Throughout his reign Ivan faced his brothers' claims to compensation and powerful, jealous neighbors: Lithuania and the Khanate of Crimea. In handling this complex situation successfully, Ivan proved a master tactician and diplomat. The campaigns during the 1460s against Kazan secured Moscow's eastern flank, and during the 1470s Ivan exploited Novgorod's internal dissension, vulnerability, and military weakness to add its broad domains to Muscovy.[4]

---

[3] See below, p. 238.

[4] See above, p. 84.

Emblem of the Russian State under Ivan III

Novgorod's fall compelled the grand prince of Tver to face Moscow alone. The expulsion of Ivan's envoy and Tver's conclusion of an alliance with Lithuania gave Ivan pretexts to act decisively. In 1485 his army invaded Tver, its boyars defected to him, and its prince fled to Lithuania. Four years later Viatka was incorporated; its populace was largely deported to Moscow and replaced with Muscovites. Except for autonomous Pskov and Riazan, Great Russia had been unified by force.

Kremlin of Tver, 15th century (from an icon)

Ivan III's second marriage was political and controversial. Maria of Tver, his first wife, died in 1467, leaving but one son, Ivan Ivanovitch. The Papacy, anxious to convert Muscovy to Catholicism and enlist its support against the Turks, arranged Ivan's betrothal to Zoë Paleologus, niece of the last Byzantine emperor. Raised in Rome as a Catholic under Papal guardianship, Zoë came to Moscow in 1472 to marry Ivan. Disregarding Papal wishes, she became Orthodox and assumed the name Sofia. This "Byzantine marriage," claimed some earlier Russian historians, by allowing Ivan to claim the vacant Byzantine throne, influenced him to espouse the Third Rome theory and cast off the "Mongol yoke." Recent scholarship, however, minimizes Sofia's direct political influence and affirms that before she came to Moscow Ivan III had set his basic national policies.

In 1480 Khan Akhmat of the Great Horde, allied with Poland-Lithuania, invaded Muscovy in order to reassert Tatar control. On the Ugra River Mongol and Muscovite armies faced each other. Ivan III's eldest son, commanding the Russians, displayed more courage than his father. Some contemporary chroniclers and later historians portrayed Ivan's sudden departure for Moscow as cowardice, though probably he left to reach agreement with his rebellious brothers and assure united resistance to the Tatars. A chronicle account relates:

> Akhmad arrived at the Ugra with all of his forces, with the intent of crossing the river. When the Tartars came they began to shoot at our [forces] and our [forces] shot at them. Some Tartars advanced against Prince Andrei; others against the Grand Prince. . . . Our forces, using arrows and harquebusses, killed many Tartars; their arrows were falling among our forces but did not hurt anyone. They pushed the Tartars away from the river, though they tried to advance for many days; as they could not cross the river they stopped and waited until it should freeze.[5]

Akhmat's army, however, withdrew without forcing a showdown with the Muscovites. Troubles within the Horde and the Polish king's failure to send troops justified this withdrawal, but Akhmad's retreat ended Moscow's subservience to the Mongol khans beyond any doubt.

Great Russia's unification and independence enabled Ivan to inaugurate regular diplomatic relations with foreign powers. In 1486 after he had established ties with the Holy Roman Empire, its envoy, Nikolaus Poppel, hinted that the German emperor might grant Ivan a royal title. Ivan rejected the offer haughtily: "By God's grace we have been sovereigns in our land since the beginning; . . . and as beforehand we did not desire to be appointed by anyone, so now too we do not desire it."[6] Muscovy refused to be anyone's vassal.

In the Baltic region Ivan scored notable successes. In 1492 in order to break the monopoly of Baltic trade held by the German Hanseatic League, he established the port of Ivangorod opposite German controlled Narva, closed Novgorod's foreign settlement, and ended German mer-

---

[5] Quoted in Dmytryshyn, *Medieval Russia*, p. 192.

[6] Cited in Fennell, *Ivan the Great of Moscow* (London, 1961), p. 121.

chants' special privileges there. As a natural outgrowth of Novgorod's annexation, he sought for Russian merchants the right to trade freely in the Baltic.

Lithuania, whose holdings extended perilously close to Moscow, was Ivan's principal opponent. In undeclared border warfare in the 1480s, the Muscovites softened Lithuanian resistance and induced many west Russian princes to shift their allegiance and lands to Moscow. After intensive fighting, Viazma province was added to Muscovy by the truce of 1494. Demanding all Lithuanian territory to the Berezina River, Ivan claimed all Kievan Russian lands and entitled himself sovereign of all Russia. Alleged Lithuanian persecution of Orthodox Russians served Ivan as a pretext for further warfare. Ivan allied with the Crimean khan, Mengli-Girei, who wished to plunder Lithuania and Poland. Muscovy and the Crimea had defeated the Great Horde in 1491; a decade later the Crimeans destroyed it completely. The Muscovites defeated the Lithuanians on the Vedrosha River in 1500 but could not capture Smolensk. In the uneasy truce which followed, Ivan's title and claims to Smolensk remained disputed, but he had achieved a significant expansion westward into Belorussia.

INTERNAL CHANGES AND CONFLICTS

Within a much enlarged Muscovy, Ivan III consolidated control over disparate and newly annexed territories, built a national administration, and established himself as sovereign rather than first among equal princes. Deporting leading families from annexed regions and replacing them with Muscovite service people and boyars gained him support from an expanding class of loyal gentry servitors and freed him from dependence on older boyar and princely elements. Gradually, lesser princes, their appanages absorbed, lost their former independence and became boyars.

In his centralizing policies Ivan overcame strong resistance from appanage princes led by his own brothers who had at first exercised sovereign authority over considerable territories. As Muscovy expanded, he moved against separatism cautiously but effectively with a minimum of violence, defying tradition by refusing to increase his brothers' appanages. When Iuri of Dmitrov died without heirs, Ivan III seized his appanage and compensated his remaining brothers, Andrei and Boris, minimally. To win their support during Akhmat's invasion of 1480 he made minor concessions; then he took the lands of Novgorod and Tver as they watched helplessly. In a treaty of 1486 his brothers recognized Ivan as sovereign of all Russia, and later when Andrei refused to supply troops, Ivan arrested him and appropriated his domains. Eventually Ivan controlled all his brothers' territories, effectively undermining separatism and feudal division.

The dynastic crisis of 1497 threatened this newly found unity briefly. Ivan Ivanovitch, Ivan III's eldest son, died in 1490 leaving his son, Dmitri, and Ivan III's second son, Vasili, as heirs to the throne. Since in Muscovy an eldest son with a male heir had never predeceased his father, the choice lay with the grand prince. Behind the candidates stood their mothers, Sofia Paleologus and Elena Stepanov. In 1498 Ivan had Dmitri crowned grand prince of all Russia, but four years later Dmitri and his mother were arrested and his title passed to Vasili. Dmitri's defeated faction, some historians claim, represented boyars opposed to centralization.

Muscovite administration developed significantly with territorial expansion. At first Ivan permitted newly annexed territories some autonomy under Moscow-appointed governors (*namestniki*) and district chiefs (*volosteli*). These officials were supported by the "feeding" system (*kormlenie*) in which a portion of local tax revenues provided for their maintenance. Because greedy governors often extorted excessive *kormlenie,* regional charters sometimes specified the amounts and sought to allay local discontent. The White Lake Charter of 1488, furthermore, set rules for apprehending and trying criminals to prevent abuses by local officials. Such regional charters were a first step in unifying Great Russia's administration and legal procedures. Later, to limit the powers of governors, their authority and functions were described more clearly, and Ivan III appointed agents, usually gentry, to restrict their power.

The first Muscovite national law code, the *Sudebnik of 1497*, required by the transformation of Moscow principality into the extensive Muscovite state, derived largely from *Russkaia Pravda*[7] and charters of Pskov. Boyar courts handled ordinary cases; important ones were heard by a supreme court under the chairman of the Boyar Duma, the supreme legislative and administrative body, and a few cases went to the grand prince for final decision. In the provinces justice was left to officials under the *kormlenie* system. The prescription of the *Sudebnik* of capital punishment for major political crimes, especially armed rebellion, strengthened grand princely authority. Its stipulation that peasants settling accounts with their landlord might move from one estate to another only during St. George's Day in November[8] confirmed the rising influence of service gentry and state secretaries as governing elements.

Muscovy's territorial expansion necessitated a rapid growth of the grand prince's court, which became an unplanned, rather chaotic and inefficient national bureaucracy. Previously administration had been territorial and decentralized, and as late as 1533 regional princely courts still existed in Novgorod, Tver, Riazan, and Uglich, though their functions were gradually assumed by Moscow-appointed officials. The grand princely court in Moscow had an elaborate hierarchy of officials to handle finances, princely banquets, horses, and weapons. These positions were determined by *mestnichestvo,* a system based upon noble birth and posts occupied by relatives, which limited the grand prince's power of appointment. The embryo of the new central administration was the state treasury whose secretaries (*diaki*) became more specialized, competent, and numerous and assumed the tasks of

---

[7] See above, pp. 39–40.
[8] See below, pp. 139, 173–75.

handling state administration, finance, and foreign affairs. These agencies grew eventually into separate administrative boards (*prikazy*) subject to the Boyar Duma.

A more effective, centralized army developed under Ivan III. Dmitri Donskoi, lacking a national army, had relied in emergencies on voluntary cooperation by princes and boyars. As the grand princely court expanded under Vasili II, some servitors were assigned to military service, often receiving estates from the government in return. From this practice emerged the service gentry with landholdings (*pomestie*) conditional upon service to the state. Under Ivan III service gentry and boyar children associated with his court comprised the core of Muscovy's cavalry and fostered centralization and grand princely control within the army. The expansion of the gentry militia cavalry, which became the core of the army, reduced Ivan's dependence on the haphazard forces provided by his brothers and boyars. Auxiliary infantry were recruited sporadically from townsmen.

Ivan III urgently needed lands with which to reward his service gentry. In Muscovy the principal categories of land were state (*chernye*), grand princely (*dvortsovye*), church, and patrimonial estates (*votchiny*) of princes and boyars. Most state and grand princely lands were virgin forest or already cultivated by peasants paying state taxes. Ivan could seize lands of individual boyars who defected or resisted his rule, but he dared not challenge the boyar class, which ran his administration. In conquered territories, however, such as Novgorod, Tver, and others, he was bound by no traditions or restrictions; and by confiscating boyar and church properties there, he obtained by 1500 almost 3 million acres for distribution to loyal servitors.

Nonetheless, the boyars with large estates still exercised much political influence through the Boyar Duma, the supreme legislative and administrative body, which made important decisions together with the ruler. The grand prince appointed its members and presided when he wished, but *mestnichestvo* tradition required him to select representatives of senior princely and boyar families. Before the Novgorod campaign of 1471, Ivan also consulted the service gentry, but boyar power prevented a repetition of this until Ivan IV's reign. Ivan III limited boyar influence somewhat in the Duma by relying more on the *diaki*, usually educated commoners, whom he could appoint and dismiss without consulting it and who were now recognized as Duma members.

Reformers and heretics challenged the conservative leadership of the Orthodox Church as Ivan pondered the fate of church lands. In late 14th century Novgorod, the Strigolniki had affirmed that the individual could achieve salvation without the church hierarchy. A century later the Judaizers denied some Christian doctrines and refused to venerate icons or the Virgin Mary. Subscribing to the law of Moses, the Judaizers celebrated the sabbath on Saturday and repudiated church ownership of property. Led by able theologians, they won highly placed converts (Ivan himself sympathized) and threatened the established church seriously. Another threat was posed by the Trans-Volga Elders led by Nil Maikov (Nil Sorskii) of Sora Hermitage who denounced church wealth and corruption and espoused an ascetic life in remote monasteries as 13th century European friars had done. At a church council in 1503 Nil Sorskii with Ivan's support urged monasteries to renounce their landed estates, but Vasili, heir to the throne, backed conservative circles led by Father Joseph.

Joseph Sanin (1439?–1515) had founded Volokolamsk Monastery near Moscow as a bulwark against heresy and reform. Though prosperous, its strict rules stressed ritual, obedience, and submission. The Church, argued Joseph, must own property in order to fulfill its functions and attract able clerics. Monks should concentrate on religious matters without having to perform manual labor. Joseph's writings strongly advocated divine right absolutism. The ruler with authority derived directly from God should be the guardian of his people, supreme judge and defender of Orthodoxy and set a Christian example:

> The sun has its task—to shine on the people of this earth; the king has his task too—to take care of those under him. You [rulers] received the sceptre of kingship from God, see to it that you satisfy Him who has given it to you. . . . For in body the king is like unto all men, but in power he is like unto God Almighty.[9]

Against an unworthy ruler the subject's only recourse would be passive disobedience. Joseph provided full justification for tsarist absolutism and subordination of church to state.

Ivan faced a difficult, perplexing choice. On the one hand, the Trans-Volga Elders and Judaizers backed his desire to seize church lands but were political conservatives who supported boyar power. The Josephists, espousing Ivan's claims to absolutism, insisted that the Church retain its lands and wealth. In 1504 Ivan finally yielded to Vasili, and a church council condemned leading Judaizers to death. Ivan won loyal backing from church conservatives, but the Church lost vital, reforming elements.

His last years brought Ivan III disappointment and frustration. His wife and son, whose political views he distrusted, had triumphed; and attempts to control Kazan with Moscow-trained puppet rulers had failed. Worst of all, the Lithuanian war ended indecisively with Smolensk in enemy hands. Although Ivan died unmourned and unloved in October 1505, he fully deserved his title, the Great. Building on sound foundations, he "gathered" the Great Russian lands, undermined separatism, and achieved centralization. He paralyzed the Tatar threat and began reconquering Belorussia and the Ukraine from Lithuania. Ivan acquired glory and prestige abroad without ruining Muscovy financially. The price of unity, however, was temporary cultural stagnation and spiritual decline because his suppression of political and religious dissent raised barriers against cultural contacts with the West.

---

[9] M. Raeff, "An Early Theorist of Absolutism: Joseph of Volokolamsk," in S. Harcave, *Readings* (New York, 1962), vol. 1, p. 181.

VASILI III (1505–1533)

Ivan III's son Vasili III ably continued most of his policies. The more brilliant reigns of his father and in turn of Vasili's son, Ivan IV, have obscured Vasili's considerable achievements. Though lively and physically active, he displayed a Byzantine subtlety. Like his father, Vasili resorted to force only when it was necessary and coerced without cruelty. Baron von Herberstein, who visited his court, asserted with exaggeration: "In the control which he exercises over his people [Vasili] easily surpasses all the rulers of the entire world."[10] Though able to act more authoritatively than Ivan, he was still not a true autocrat. Careful not to offend the boyars as a group, Vasili consulted often with the Boyar Duma, which remained in permanent session. He treated individual boyars disdainfully but neither removed prominent grandees from office nor interfered with their manorial rights. Boyar support remained indispensable to the crown.

Backed by the Josephists, Vasili III continued Ivan's work of centralization. His father's testament granted him 66 towns against 30 for his four brothers combined, and if a brother died intestate, his portion would revert to the crown. Appanage rights were reduced: Vasili's brothers could no longer coin money or deal with foreign powers. Centripetal forces attracted remaining Great Russian lands and princes irresistibly to Moscow. Semi-independent Pskov was annexed in 1510 and Riazan principality was incorporated in 1517. Deportation of their leading families consolidated Moscow's control and allowed Vasili to reward loyal servitors. Muscovite officials were instructed to suppress any opposition.

Joseph Sanin's disciple, Daniel, continued his policies at Volokolamsk and became metropolitan in 1522. Over objections from traditionalists, he solemnized Vasili's divorce from a barren first wife and his marriage to Elena Glinskii. When this marriage produced a male heir, Ivan, Vasili repudiated the faction led by the learned Maxim the Greek. Josephism triumphed fully at the church council of 1531, which sentenced the monk Vassian, leader of the Trans-Volga Elders, and Daniel's chief opponent, to life imprisonment.

Muscovite expansion helped produce an imperial ideology under Vasili III. Like Ivan III, he used the title, "Sovereign of All Russia" and occasionally tsar, that is Caesar or emperor. Religious writers elaborated theories to explain his divine authority. According to Spiridon of Tver, Riurik was a descendant of the Roman emperor, Augustus; the grand prince of Kiev, Vladimir II, had obtained his crown and regalia from the Byzantine ruler, Constantine Monomachus. In 1510 Abbot Filofei of Pskov in a letter to Vasili formulated the famous Third Rome theory: 'Two Romes fell down, the third [Moscow] is standing, and there will be no fourth." After Rome's fall, he explained, the center of true Christianity had moved to Constantinople, and after

---

[10] Cited in Vernadsky, *Russia at the Dawn of the Modern Age* (New Haven, 1959), p. 134.

the Byzantine union with Rome of 1439 to Moscow. Filofei did not urge, as some historians assert, Moscow to rule the world but rather emphasized Vasili's duties and responsibilities as Orthodoxy's leading ruler. The sincerely religious Vasili accepted such theories and laid ideological bases for the tsardom of his son, Ivan IV.

Abroad, the defection of Moscow's former ally, the Crimean khanate, complicated Vasili's tasks. Between them began a difficult and protracted struggle. Khan Mohammed Girei's troops reached Moscow's outskirts in 1521 and caused widespread devastation while the Crimea and Lithuania combated Muscovite influence in Kazan. Trouble with this eastern neighbor induced Moscow to strengthen defenses along the Oka River and settle Cossack frontiersmen in border regions to the south. Vasili also resumed the struggle with Lithuania, and in 1514 the key fortress city of Smolensk was captured and retained. Attempts by Vasili's brothers to use the war to intrigue against him failed. Vasili divided Muscovy between his two sons, but Iuri's death without issue eventually consolidated the entire country under Ivan the Terrible. The unification of Great Russia under Ivan and Vasili III and the development of grand princely power and a Muscovite administrative system laid sound bases for the autocracy of Ivan IV.

Suggested Additional Reading

BOOKS

BACKUS, OSWALD. *Motives of West Russian Nobles in Deserting Lithuania for Moscow, 1377–1514* (Lawrence, Kansas, 1957).

FENNELL, J. L. *Ivan the Great of Moscow* (London, 1961).

GREY, IAN. *Ivan III and the Unification of Russia* (New York, 1964).

HALECKI, O. *From Florence to Brest, 1439–1596* (New York, 1959).

MEDLIN, W. K. *Moscow and East Rome . . .* (Geneva, Switz., 1952).

VERNADSKY, GEORGE. *Russia at the Dawn of the Modern Age* (New Haven, 1959).

ARTICLES

ALEF, G. "Muscovy and the Council of Florence," *SR*, vol. 20, no. 3, 1961, pp. 389–401.

———. "Reflections on the Boyar Duma under Ivan III," *SEER*, vol. 45, 1967, pp. 67–123.

BACKUS, O. "Muscovite History in Recent Soviet Publications," *SR*, vol. 20, pp. 517–22.

BILL, V. "The Circular Frontier of Muscovy," *RusR.*, vol. 9, 1950, pp. 45–52.

DEWEY, H. "The 1497 Sudebnik . . .", *ASEER*, vol. 39, 1951, pp. 325–38.

ESPER, T. "Russia and the Baltic, 1494–1558," *SR*, vol. 14, 1966, pp. 458–74.

FENNELL, J. L. "The Attitude of the Josephians . . . ," *SEER*, vol. 29, pp. 486–509.

———. "Russia, 1462–1583," *Camb. Mod. Hist.*, vol. 2, 1958, pp. 534–61.

RAEFF, M. "An Early Theorist of Absolutism: Joseph of Volokolamsk," *ASEER*, vol. 8, 1949, pp. 79–89.

YARESH, LEO (pseud), "The Formation of the Great Russian State," in C. E. Black, *Rewriting Russian History*, pp. 198–223.

10

Society, Religion, and Culture in Appanage Russia

THE SO-CALLED APPANAGE ERA—that is the period of feudal division and political fragmentation of Russia from the mid-12th to the mid-15th centuries—served as a transitional stage in the evolution from Kievan to Muscovite Russia. Social relationships and religious and cultural traditions all developed from the Kievan period without any sharp break or abrupt change in direction. On the other hand, the Mongol invasion and the subsequent Tatar hegemony in Russia caused colossal disruptions and hardships for the Russian people. Life became difficult and uncertain, but social and economic relations evolved generally along lines well established during the Kievan era.

The Mongol conquest with its destruction of urban centers, depopulation, and destruction of life and property altered profoundly the material level of Russian life. Destruction of so many cities was a calamitous blow because they had been centers of handicraft industry, trade, and centers of culture. Long established patterns of life and production were disrupted or disappeared altogether. The Mongol system of political dependence and reduction of the country's wealth by imposition of heavy tribute, taxes, and conscription created an inhospitable atmosphere for cultural growth and contributed to economic and cultural stagnation, which made Russia lag significantly behind Western Europe.

An analysis of Russian society and economic life in the appanage period must be preceded by a discussion of the problem of feudalism. Efforts to compare Russian institutions of the appanage era with those of feudal Western Europe have provoked long and still unresolved historical controversy. Was appanage Russia "feudal"? Largely ignored by 19th century historians, this issue has become a major point of contention between Western and Soviet historians of Russia.

Feudalism in the Marxist scheme of history is a socioeconomic stage through which every society must pass. Thus Soviet historians argue that Russia experienced a feudal stage, although they have found it difficult to set precise dates for Russian feudalism. In broad terms, they have designated the entire period from Kievan times to 1861 as a feudal era. Western historians have affirmed, however, that Russian historical development differed markedly from that of western European countries, pointing to the absence of a well developed feudal order as reflecting that difference.

Both sides of the argument have weaknesses. Soviet and Western scholars have tried to fit Russian development into preconceived schemes, into abstract historical models. The former construct a shadowy model based on the concept, "feudal productive relations," involving a socioeconomic system where privileged "feudal lords" dominated socially underprivileged masses by concentrating in their own hands rights of landownership and other political and judicial rights. Within this broad definition of feudalism, appanage Russia did exhibit feudal characteristics.

In contrast, many Western historians, notably George Vernadsky, rejected the Soviet claim that Kievan and appanage Russia were feudal. Vernadsky argued that a truly feudal regime included political feudalism, involving mediatization of supreme political authority and producing a hierarchy of greater and lesser rulers (suzerain, vassals, subvassals) bound by personal contract. Also inherent in feudal society, Vernadsky stated, was economic feudalism involving the existence of a manorial system, which restricted the peasant's legal status, and a distinction between right of ownership and the right to use the land. Finally, he referred to a feudal nexus or connection between military service and landholding. These elements, claimed Vernadsky, characterized Western feudal societies. Absence of one or more of them disqualified a society from being classed as feudal. Vernadsky stressed the political, economic, and judicial powers combined in the hands of suzerain princes and delegation of some or all of these powers to vassals and subvassals by reciprocal contracts as bases of a genuinely feudal society. Kievan and appanage Russia, he concluded, were not feudal societies.

Soviet historians criticize Vernadsky for creating an "ideal type" of feudalism and measuring Russian society against it to determine whether it was feudal or not. The Soviet historian Cherepnin argued:

> Feudalism is not an ideally typical construction, not a scheme of development to which the concrete historical paths of separate peoples either correspond or from which they deviate. Feudalism is a socioeconomic formation which represents a natural stage in its own specific way, and not according to a standard pattern.[1]

Cherepnin suggested that Russian feudalism was unique and need not have conformed to Western feudalism. There are strong arguments favoring both points of view. Whether appanage Russia was feudal or not depends largely on one's choice of definitions.

Appanage Russia of the 13th to 15th centuries, however, clearly displayed more feudal characteristics than did Kievan Russia. Many fea-

---

[1] L. V. Cherepnin et al., *Kritika burzhuaznykh kontsepsii istorii Rossii perioda feodalizma* (Moscow, 1962), p. 84.

tures of appanage Russia's economy conformed to traditionally accepted forms of Western feudalism. Appanage Russia was essentially an agrarian society passing through a lengthy political and economic decline. Increasingly, military service was being performed by boyars and other princely servitors. Landholding had become the main source of political power and economic wealth, providing the landowner with extensive control over those living on his land. A manorial system was developing, and along with it a new form of land tenure was emerging, which contrasted with *votchina,* or patrimonial landholding: the *pomestie* system involving the temporary grant of land to a servitor in return for service.

There were important dissimilarities as well. For example, social relations were not determined by contracts of mutual fealty between prince and servitor. Boyars and other princely servitors, not vassals in the strict sense, were free to shift from one prince and take up service with another without jeopardizing their patrimonial rights. No feudal law books or contracts spelling out relationships between lords and their servitors are known to have existed in medieval Russia. No clearcut standards of rights and obligations governed mutual relations of prince and servitor. The *votchina* holder was not obliged to perform service for his suzerain, although he often did. Finally, the peasantry's legal status did not begin to deteriorate seriously until the end of the 15th century.

Clearly, the socioeconomic systems of appanage Russia and Western Europe reveal differences and similarities. To label one feudal and the other nonfeudal contributes little to explain and understand their differences. Whatever labels are applied to appanage Russia's socioeconomic structure, one should understand that this structure was weak when the Mongol invasion struck, so weak that it could offer little resistance to the invaders or, subsequently, to the rising ambitions of the grand princes of Moscow. A better understanding of the complex Russian society of the appanage period may be gained by analyzing changes occurring in Russian society at this time.

Russia was beset with problems of such vast magnitude in this period that it is surprising that it survived at all. The Mongol invasion, as we have seen, brought death, destruction, and depopulation of enormous dimensions. Continual Tatar exactions—heavy annual tribute, escalating tolls, and many destructive raids by armed detachments —deepened and prolonged the tragedy. How much the Russians actually paid annually to the Mongols is unclear from the extant sources, but in a period of economic depression the sums were large and strained Russia's capacity to pay. Also, Mongol rule was not the sole burden upon the Russian people. Lithuanians, Poles, German crusaders, Swedes, and others pressured Russia from the west, causing further destruction and frequent warfare, which drained Russia's remaining material and human resources.

Other calamities afflicted Russia in these years, including constant princely feuding and competition, epidemics of the Black Death, fires, famine and drought. These produced further depopulation, migration, and death. The sources describe at great length the extent of abandoned land, fallow fields, and depopulation of towns and whole regions. All this affected disastrously the level of Russian productivity in the 13th century especially. The number of towns fell by one half, and remaining urban centers lost much of their population. Urban handicrafts virtually disappeared as the Tatars continued to conscript the most talented artisans and craftsmen. The art of stonecutting declined and most building in stone halted; glassmaking and enamel work ceased altogether. As trade and commerce declined, the populace retreated into local self-sufficiency, further undermining the economy. Soviet historians quite correctly stress how seriously these developments inhibited the rise of an urban merchant class. These factors also enhanced the importance of landowning as the major source of wealth and increased the pressure on the rights of free peasants.

Encouraged by the Tatars in order to fragment Russia politically, the *votchina* principle of inheritance spread during the appanage era. Princely families proliferated, and with each generation territories were split into smaller parcels so as to provide an inheritance for each surviving son. Where there had been one large principality before, there emerged over the years tiny princedoms, often only manorial estates, scarcely able to support a princely family. The inhabitants of these lands became subjects of the local prince or boyar. As long as the peasantry remained free, the right to leave the land and reside elsewhere was guaranteed. Uncertain times, economic insecurity, and Tatar taxation, however, fostered migration as people sought security and better economic conditions. This situation brought growing competition for settlers and agricultural laborers on estates of princes, boyars, and the Church. Gradually this competition led to efforts to curb freedom of movement for the rural population, culminating in 1497 when a peasant's right to leave an estate and take up residence elsewhere was restricted to a two week period around St. George's Day (November 26). The process of peasant enserfment thus began in the appanage period.[2]

As the princely class multiplied, so did the boyars because each prince had a retinue of servitors who themselves became major landowners. They received immunities and virtually sovereign powers to govern their estates, administer justice, collect taxes, and control their subjects without princely interference. Such immunities granted to the boyars further undermined peasant rights and freedoms. In addition, landowners appropriated large amounts of hitherto free land to the detriment of the peasantry. As many peasants were transformed from free landowners into renters, their economic status deteriorated markedly.

Landholdings of the Church also expanded greatly during the Tatar era. The Church, even in Kievan times, had been a landowner on a vast scale, receiving grants of land from the princes and bequests from private individuals seeking God's blessing and salvation of their souls. During the period of the Tatar yoke the privileged status of

---

[2] On the establishment of serfdom, see below, pp. 173–75.

the Church, enjoying exemption from Tatar taxation and tribute, permitted the monasteries in particular to amass great wealth. Freedom from taxation gave monasteries great advantages over secular landowners because peasants could live on Church property without having to pay Tatar tribute. Monasteries received immunities from princes, who provided them with the same rights and privileges as secular landowners. Monasteries also expanded their holdings by outright purchase and by colonizing frontier regions where land was simply appropriated to support the monks. By 1500 the Church owned an estimated 25 to 30 percent of all cultivated land. Later, the Church's vested economic interests would create serious political problems for the Muscovite state.

Since its establishment in the 10th century, the Orthodox Church had played a major role in Russian life, but never was it more important than in the Mongol era. When the Tatars first appeared, the Church had exerted moral leadership by trying to rally Russian princes in a unified resistance to the invaders. When this failed, the Church had to accept the Tatar conquest, rationalizing it as God's retribution for Russia's sins.

The Church, like all Russian institutions, suffered terribly at first from the conquest. Large numbers of priests and monks, and even the metropolitan, were killed, and many churches and monasteries suffered devastation; but the Church's spirit was not broken. Within a short time it revived, and thanks to the Tatar policy of religious toleration, worked out a *modus vivendi* with the Golden Horde. In return for public prayer for Tatar khans, the Church received a guaranteed privileged status by a formal accord of 1266 and concessions even earlier. Besides economic privileges the Tatars guaranteed the Church protection from insults and persecution, and infringement of Church rights was punishable by death. The Tatars assured the Church's cultural functions and its economic wealth and power, thus allowing it to become paramount in Russian life.

Some historians have suggested that the accord between the Church and the Tatars altered relations between the Church and Russian princes by prohibiting the latter from interfering in its affairs. This, however, was not the case. The princes continued to select bishops (subject to Tatar approval) and often encroached on Church property as they had done before 1240. In short, despite Tatar mediation, the Church remained largely dependent on princely power. The Byzantine tradition of a close church-state relationship was too ingrained to permit any significant alteration of political relations. The Church and princes were mutually dependent, each sharing similar interests and long-range goals, and both were dependent on the Tatars. These conditions demanded maximum church-princely cooperation if Russia were to emerge from Mongol domination.

Migrations of the Metropolitan See of the Russian Church in the appanage era reveal the close identification of religious and secular power. Kiev's political power had long been in decline, confirmed by its destruction by the Tatars in 1240. The metropolitanate, bound by the inertia of tradition, remained attached to Kiev, although Vladimir-Suzdal had become the chief political center before the Tatars arrived. Nonetheless, there was increasing recognition of the need to relocate the center of Church power, especially after the devastating Tatar raid on Kiev in 1299. Kiev's inhabitants, including Metropolitan Maxim, had to flee the city, and in 1300 Maxim, for security and because it was the grand princely center, took up residence in Vladimir. Like his immediate predecessors, Maxim traveled extensively throughout the Russian lands, hoping to keep alive the spirit of national unity in a demoralized country split into many rival principalities, all suffering under the Tatar's heel. In 1303 Maxim died and in a departure from ancient tradition, he was buried in Vladimir, confirming the permanent transfer of religious authority to the northeast.

This action shattered the political aspirations of the southwestern princes, who now had to recognize that they had lost the struggle for all-Russian hegemony to the northeast. To prevent a potential religious dependence on the northeast from becoming a political one as well, the southwestern princes, especially Prince Iuri of Galicia, broke from the jurisdiction of the Metropolitan of Kiev (established now in Vladimir) and petitioned the Greek patriarch and the emperor to create a separate southwestern metropolitanate. In 1302 or 1303 the patriarch named the Galician bishop, Nifont, metropolitan of southwestern Russia.

Soon Nifont died, leaving both Russian metropolitan thrones vacant. The Grand Prince of Vladimir, Michael of Tver, hoped to restore the unity of the Russian metropolitanate, and to secure the elevation of another native Russian bishop to the metropolitan throne. Prince Michael proposed Abbot Geronti of Kiev, but at the same time Prince Iuri of Galicia supported the candidacy of the Galician bishop, Peter. The Greek patriarch and emperor decided to confirm Peter as Metropolitan of Kiev and All Russia in 1308. Although Peter was Iuri of Galicia's candidate, he was appointed to the metropolitan throne of Kiev, located now in Vladimir. The unity of the metropolitanate had been restored, but the new metropolitan was from the southwest.

In 1309 Peter arrived in Vladimir, an unwelcome guest of Prince Michael of Tver, whose own candidate had been rejected. Proceedings were immediately initiated by Prince Michael to remove Peter. Trumped-up charges against Peter were dismissed by an ecclesiastical court, however, and the new metropolitan was confirmed in office. This struggle caused a permanent breach between Metropolitan Peter and Prince Michael. Because Michael was now involved in a political struggle with Moscow principality, Peter became Moscow's staunch ally. He endorsed the Moscow princes' political ambitions with the full power and prestige of the Orthodox Church. Close relations were established between Peter and Prince Iuri of Moscow, and after 1324 the metropolitan spent much time at the court of Prince Ivan I ("Kalita") of Moscow. They embarked on an extensive building program within the Kremlin walls, and in 1326 the first stone church there was begun. It became the famous Cathedral of the Assumption. In December 1326 Peter died and, as he had requested, was interred in the still uncom-

Michael Curran

Moscow—Church of the Ascension in Kolomenskoe,
1530–1532

pleted cathedral. In retrospect, many historians have concluded that
Peter shifted the metropolitan see to Moscow and imparted to Moscow
a religious prominence foreshadowing its future political successes as
the "gatherer of the Russian lands." Some, like the Church historian,
N. Zernov, suggested that "the presence in Moscow of the tomb of one
so highly revered, by all the people, elevated the city to a place of
prominence and helped Peter's successors . . . overcome the opposition of other princes to make Moscow his permanent residence."[3]
Peter's burial in Moscow may have been important symbolically, but it
had little immediate practical significance because Moscow was not

---

[3] Nicolas Zernov, *The Russians and Their Church* (London, 1964), p. 35.

then the capital of a grand principality and could not, therefore, aspire to house the metropolitan see of the Orthodox Church.

What is significant about Metropolitan Peter is that he established a precedent by lending Church support to Moscow in its struggle with Tver, helping to create a framework for the Muscovite national mission. Prince Ivan 'I of Moscow, after Peter's death, submitted his own candidate for the metropolitan throne, Archimandrite Feodor. The Greeks, however, refused to acknowledge Feodor as a legitimate candidate, claiming that only the grand prince could recommend a candidate. Finally, the Greeks selected one of their own bishops, Theognostus, in 1328. That same year Prince Ivan I of Moscow secured from the Tatars the right to use the grand princely title which implied genealogical seniority. When Theognostus arrived in Vladimir to take up his duties as metropolitan, he recognized that power had shifted towards Moscow and promptly moved there. Though Theognostus was of foreign origin, he followed Peter's precedent and supported firmly the process of unification under Moscow's aegis. The metropolitan thus employed the moral authority of the Church to support Moscow's political ambitions. The religious authority of Moscow, from Theognostus onward, contributed substantially to its success in uniting Great Russia.[4]

Not only in the political sphere was the Church destined to play an important role in Moscow's rise. The Church became also a vital, visible symbol of the continuity of Russian history, the embodiment of national unity and strength, remaining the sole national institution to which the Russian people could turn for guidance and inspiration. The spiritual revival fostered by the Church during the Tatar yoke was among its chief contributions. Monasteries played a major role in stimulating the development of Russian civilization. The monastic revival, beginning in the 1330s, left its deepest imprint on the northeast where the cultural renaissance and stimulus to colonization were most profoundly expressed.

St. Sergius of Radonezh (1322–92) typified the Church's role in society. His life and activity constitute one of the brightest chapters in the history of Russia in the bleak Mongol period. Born into a noble family, Sergius at an early age responded to the call of Christ and entered God's service. Determined to lead an ascetic life of isolation and solitude, unencumbered by the cares of this world—impossible in an urban Moscow monastery—he took refuge in the impenetrable forest outside. His undeviating devotion to the strictest principles of monastic life: simplicity, contemplation, discipline of the flesh, and hard physical labor, won him a reputation as a true disciple of Christ. People from all walks of life sought him out for guidance, advice, and understanding, hoping to find some of the spiritual tranquillity he so clearly personified. Gradually, a few devout and fervent souls decided to remain with Sergius and follow his example. A small brotherhood developed around his isolated retreat, and by 1340 the nucleus of the famous Trinity Monastery had formed. Establishment of a monastery

---

[4] For unification of Great Russia, see above Chapters 8 and 9, pp. 86–106.

attracted to the remote region settlers who began to carve villages and homesteads, fields and pastures from the forest, making the monastery the center of a thriving agricultural district.

Sergius' reputation as an ascetic and devoted disciple of Christ spread rapidly in the sombre atmosphere of Tatar-dominated Russia. The Trinity Monastery became a place of pilgrimage for the faithful who sought a clearer understanding of themselves and the Christian spirit. All who sought his advice and guidance, whether princes or peasants, boyars or merchants, were graciously received and counseled. Sergius' message, grounded in Christ's teachings, was disarmingly simple. He preached the need for toleration fortified by love, repentence rooted in humility and self-sacrifice, and kindness and patience born of love and

Michael Curran

New Convent of the Virgin, Cathedral of the Icon of Our Lady of Smolensk, Moscow—(1524–1525)

self-effacement. He was always prepared to serve as mediator of the quarrels which undermined Russian princely cooperation, to promote mutual understanding and national unity.

Sergius shared credit with Dmitri Donskoi and his army for the victory over the Tatars at Kulikovo in 1380. Dmitri appealed to Sergius for advice. Should he negotiate with the Tatars or fight them? Sergius was torn by a crisis of conscience. The devout Christian struggled against the Russian national patriot. His Christian conscience urged him to advise reconciliation, nonresistance to evil; his national feeling impelled him to grant his blessing to a bloody battle. Initially he cautioned against confrontation and urged negotiation, but after further prayer and meditation, he recognized a great national crusade in the making. God's will made struggle against the infidel Tatars a just and sacred responsibility. Sergius advised Dmitri: "Go forth to do battle against the infidels without fear or hesitation, and you shall triumph." Sergius opened the monastic coffers to support the cause and sent two of his monks with the army. The blessing of so highly venerated a monk endowed the cause with a sense of religious mission and righteousness, which greatly raised the morale of Dmitri's troops.

The Russian victory at Kulikovo stimulated a growing sense of national mission in Moscow. St. Sergius of Radonezh contributed profoundly to its growth and the spiritual revival. Wrote Kliuchevskii:

> There are historical names which escape the barriers of time and whose work profoundly influences subsequent generations, because the figure of a personality is transformed into an idea. Such is the case with St. Sergius; in invoking him the people today still affirm that political strength is well founded only when it is based on moral strength.[5]

The activity of another monk, Andrei Rublev, exemplified another dimension of Russia's spiritual revival. Perhaps the greatest master of Russian iconography, Rublev was one of the few creative geniuses of the age. Under influence of his remarkable skill, an indigenous tradition of Russian icon painting emerged. Born in the 1370s, Rublev grew up in the atmosphere of religious and national revival stimulated by St. Sergius. As a young man Rublev may have spent time at the Trinity Monastery and was influenced by the spiritual intensity of Sergius' followers. The earliest example of his work dates from about 1405 when he began decorating the Cathedral of the Annunciation in the Moscow Kremlin. Rublev's teacher, Theophanes the Greek, had been trained in Byzantium and had moved to Moscow shortly after 1400. Theophanes influenced Rublev profoundly, acquainting him with a freer iconographic expression in the use of color and brush strokes. Rublev, responding to the rebirth of national feeling and Theophanes' influence, developed a unique style which influenced Russian painters for generations.

In 1422 Rublev was invited back to the Trinity Monastery to redecorate the Cathedral of the Trinity. He also produced then perhaps the most famous Russian icon, the Old Testament Trinity. This work,

---

[5] V. O. Kliuchevskii, *Ocherki i rechi* (Moscow, n. d.), pp. 201, 214.

Old Testament Trinity by Andrei Rublev

inspired by Sergius' memory, was an artistic achievement, which testified to his expressive and subtle manner, and his mastery of composition and color. The Old Testament Trinity was considered so perfect in conception and execution that a Church Council of 1551 declared it the obligatory model for all future icons dealing with that subject. Rublev, with extraordinary vitality, depicted the supreme mystery of Christian belief—the Trinity—in symbolic yet human form, readily comprehensible to the religious faithful. Striving for simplicity and directness, Rublev reduced his portrayal to the bare essentials. The three angels who appeared to Sarah and Abraham in the account of the Old Testament, were portrayed as symbolically representing the Trinitarian nature of God. The serenity and deeply felt religiosity of the three figures was marvelously and subtly expressed. They flow harmoniously together, creating a single impression, yet each remains distinct and unique, the essence of the Trinitarian mystery. The central figure, representing God the Father, stretches his hand over a cup containing the sacrificial lamb as though beckoning the figure to his left representing Christ to accept the summons to the supreme sacrifice for the redemption of fallen man. The figure representing Christ is a profoundly moving portrait of resigned acceptance, the Son accepting the Father's will. Rublev was a master of expressing psychological insight. In all his works there is a sense of great dignity and calmness, an impression of eternal verity and tenderness. Using human forms he penetrated the deepest religious mysteries. Nothing reflected more graphically the successful mission of the Church in guiding Russia through the hardest period of the Tatar yoke than Rublev's works.

Russian culture, after experiencing a period of decline and stagnation, was powerfully stimulated in the late 14th and early 15th centuries by the religious revival and growth of national feeling after the Kulikovo victory. The main vehicle of cultural development remained the Orthodox Church, which became the focus of the spiritual and secular aspirations of the Russian people.

Suggested Additional Reading

FEDOTOV, G. "Religious Background of Russian Culture," *CH,* vol. 12 (1943), pp. 35–51.

———. *The Russian Religious Mind: The Middle Ages: The Thirteenth to the Fifteenth Centuries* (Cambridge, Mass., 1966).

———. *A Treasury of Russian Spirituality* (New York, 1948).

FLOROVSKY, G. "The Problem of Old Russian Culture," *SR,* vol. 21 (1962), pp. 1–15.

KLIUCHEVSKII, V. "St. Sergius . . . , in Harcave, *Readings* . . . , vol. 1, pp. 153–64.

LAZAREV, V. N. *Russian Icons, From the Twelfth to the Fifteenth Century* (New York, 1962).

OBOLENSKY, D. "Byzantium, Kiev and Moscow: A Study in Ecclesiastical Relations," *DOP,* vol. 11 (1957), pp. 21–78.

ONASCH, K. *Icons* (New York and Leipzig, 1963).

ŠEVČENKO, I. Intellectual Repercussions of the Council of Florence," *CH,* vol. 24 (1955), pp. 291–323.

VOYCE, A. *The Art and Architecture of Medieval Russia* (Norman, Okla., 1964).

II

Ivan the Terrible (1533–1584)

THE REIGN of Ivan IV (the Terrible)[1] was vital to the development of the autocratic, Russian national state. This epoch and Ivan himself remain rather obscure and disputed partly for lack of reliable documentary materials. For many Westerners Ivan's cruelty typifies the barbaric, self-destructive, Asiatic qualities of old Russia. A modern tyrant, Joseph Stalin, ordered Ivan rehabilitated, intensifying debate whether his reign was a constructive era of state building or one of senseless destruction and bloodshed. Recent Soviet historians, filling in many factual gaps, generally portray the reign as the triumph of autocratic monarchy over feudal anarchy and Ivan as a farsighted statesman crushing the opposition of a reactionary titled aristocracy. They praise him for building a centralized state and fostering Russia's international greatness. To what extent can a powerful ruler determine a country's course and shape its institutions? Did Ivan's violent and highhanded policies really smash feudal opposition and construct a centralized monarchy or did they cause disorder and threaten the Russian state with destruction? The Oprichnina, Ivan's most controversial measure in this regard, is discussed in the problem at the end of this chapter.

MINORITY AND RULE WITH THE CHOSEN COUNCIL

Ivan IV's minority was a period of feudal disorder, violence, and intrigue which threatened to destroy Muscovite central institutions. When Vasili III died in 1533, his heir, Ivan IV, was only three. At first his mother, Elena Glinskii, directed a regency which resisted the appanage princes and undertook town construction, notably the Kitai-gorod section of Moscow. But after her death in 1538, powerful boyar families—Shuiskii, Belskii and Glinskii—contended for power and wealth. They seized state lands, looted the treasury, and enhanced the power of the Boyar Duma. Unlimited application of the principle of

---

[1] The Russian term *groznyi* is sometimes translated "The Dread" or "The Awe-Inspiring."

mestnichestvo, which stressed noble birth and relatives' position, under-mined the army's effectiveness. As they exiled, executed, and poisoned one another, the boyars, like the French nobility of the Fronde, dis-credited themselves as a ruling group while support grew among gentry and merchants for strong central rule.

Ivan IV's character and unhappy childhood inclined him to assert full autocratic power. Information about his youth is fragmentary and disputed, but by the age of nine he had lost both parents and his favorite governess. The boyars, though according him outward respect, scorned and abused him in private. Later Ivan supposedly wrote Prince Andrei Kurbskii:

> What sufferings did I not endure through lack of clothing and from hunger! For in all things my will was not my own. . . . While we [Ivan and his younger brother] were playing childish games in our in-fancy, Prince Ivan Vasilevich Shuiskii was sitting on a bench, leaning with his elbows on our father's bed with his leg up on a chair. . . . And who can endure such arrogance?[2]

Sudden gyrations between grandeur and neglect, adding to Ivan's emo-tional instability, stimulated his intense hatred and suspicion of the old boyar aristocracy. At the age of 13 he first asserted himself by having a chief tormentor, Prince Andrei Shuiskii, executed. Kurbskii relates that young Ivan often hurled pet animals into the palace court-yard and watched their convulsions. With boon companions Ivan en-gaged in orgies and rode through Moscow trampling people underfoot. According to some sources, Ivan read religious and historical texts avidly, becoming Russia's most literate ruler before Catherine the Great. Recently Edward Keenan cast some doubt on the authorship of many works formerly attributed to Ivan and even questioned his literacy.[3]

Metropolitan Macarius, a trusted adviser, urged the youthful Ivan to rule as autocrat. His formal coronation in the Kremlin in January 1547 as Muscovy's first tsar enhanced his authority at home and his prestige abroad. In February Ivan married Anastasia Zakharin-Koshkin, from an ancient boyar family which supported centralization, but disorders per-sisted. In June a mysterious fire burned most of Moscow and killed over 2,700 persons. A rebellious mob seized control of Moscow, broke into Ivan's quarters and left only when convinced he was not shielding the Glinskiis who were believed to be responsible. Uprisings in Moscow and other towns and peasant revolts revealed grave social tensions and unrest.

Frightened by these events and influenced by Archpriest Silvester who warned him that God was punishing him for his sins, Ivan ap-parently placed the government in the hands of a Chosen Council of leading aristocrats and churchmen. Including Silvester, Macarius and

---

[2] Fennell, *The Correspondence between Ivan IV and Kurbsky* (Cambridge, Eng., 1955), p. 75.

[3] E. Keenan, *The Kurbskii-Groznyi Apocrypha* (Cambridge, Mass., 1971), pp. 53 ff.

Alexis Adashev, a courtier of gentry background, this oligarchy made important decisions and directed the young tsar. Wrote Kurbskii, an advocate of such limited monarchy:

> There gathered around him [Ivan IV] advisers, men of understanding and perfection . . . and all of these are wholly skilled in military and the land's affairs . . . and they drew close to him in amity and friendship so that without their advice nothing is planned or undertaken . . . and at that time those counsellors of his were called the Chosen Council.[4]

To win public support the government apparently convened an assembly of the land (*zemskii sobor*) composed of members of the clergy, titled aristocracy, and gentry. Ivan S. Peresvetov, a leader of the ordinary west Russian gentry, petitioned Ivan to use men of service like himself to build a reliable army and a centralized monarchy. Greeting Ivan as "a sovereign terrible and wise," Peresvetov denounced boyar limitations on the ruler and proposed royal courts to protect commoners against magnates and governors. For favoring autocracy over feudalism and denouncing slavery, Peresvetov is considered a progressive by Soviet historians.

Governmental and military reforms heralding oncoming absolutism had begun even under boyar rule. In the Boyar Duma princely families, supplying top political and military figures, were challenged by state secretaries and upper gentry (*dumnye dvoriane*), supporters of central authority. In the provinces the *kormlenie* (tax feeding) system and its officials had become obsolete and corrupt,[5] and frequent rotations of princely provincial governors reduced their judicial and political power. To prevent princes and boyars from defecting to a foreign suzerain, the grand prince had begun to demand loyalty oaths from them.

The cautious Chosen Council could not reverse this tide of centralization and was caught between demands of the gentry favoring strong monarchy and a still powerful titled aristocracy which opposed it. In the army *mestnichestvo* was restricted and sometimes set aside for individual campaigns by the ruler but not abolished. An official stud book (*Rodoslovets*) of noble families was compiled and the government tried to adjudicate service disputes. Establishment of central command enhanced the effectiveness of gentry forces, and newly formed detachments of royal musketeers (*streltsy*) comprised a regularly paid infantry loyal to the crown. The tsar's control of the army was thus increased without any direct attack on the prerogatives of the feudal lords. Some central administrative departments (*izby*) were reformed on a functional basis, including the Petitions Board, which heard gentry appeals against boyars, and what became the Foreign Office.[6] The growing central secretarial bureaucracy prevailed increasingly over regional

---

[4] Fennell, ed., *Kurbsky's History of Ivan IV* (Cambridge, Eng. 1965), p. 21. Some historians question the existence of the Chosen Council.

[5] See above, p. 102.

[6] At first the latter was called the Board of State Secretary I. M. Viskovaty, the able official who developed it as a separate institution.

courts and officials. An optional *zemstvo* (local self-government) reform gradually replaced governors with local organs having police, judicial, and financial powers and chosen by free peasants and townspeople, not for genuine self-government but to insure more efficient tax collection. The *Sudebnik* (law code) of 1550, like that of 1497,[7] aimed to improve judicial procedure and protect gentry interests by making governors responsible for their subordinates' misdeeds and facilitating alienation of hereditary landholdings. The Council even sought to assuage the gentry's land hunger but found little free land and dared not confiscate boyar estates.

In the later 1550s, indeed until its fall in 1560, the Chosen Council extended these reforms and further curtailed boyar power.[8] The *kormlenie* (tax feeding) system was abolished except in frontier regions, and in the central provinces governors were largely superseded by military men (*voevody*). Freed from their tax collection duties, the gentry became more effective army officers. A law of 1556 regularized and standardized military service, which for noblemen was to last from age 15 to death or incapacitation. Regular salaries were prescribed for army service depending on birth and the size of one's estate. This decree produced a more efficient, loyal army of some 150,000 men, about half gentry cavalry supplemented with *streltsy* (musketeers), Cossacks, Tatar auxiliaries, and foreign troops. Because army service and the possession of landed estates were made hereditary, the distinction between *votchina* (patrimonial) and *pomestie* (service) lands dwindled.

In March 1553 Ivan IV's grave illness provoked a brief political crisis which threatened central authority and confirmed his suspicions of princes and boyars. With death seemingly near, Ivan drew up a testament which directed his courtiers to swear allegiance to his infant son, Dmitri. Almost half the Boyar Duma, however, some perhaps to avoid another chaotic regency, supported his cousin, Prince Vladimir Staritskii, the candidate of the appanage princes. Ivan's sudden recovery ended the crisis, but this episode reaffirmed boyar hostility toward Ivan's policies of autocracy and centralization. When Dmitri died, the tsar's newborn son, Ivan Ivanovich, became heir and Prince Staritskii's influence waned.

Compromise prevailed in church reform. To glorify Russian Orthodoxy and outdo the Catholic Church, Metropolitan Macarius had church councils canonize 39 saints, more than in the previous 500 years. In 1551 Ivan convened the Hundred Chapters Council (*Stoglav*), named from 100 questions submitted in Ivan's name, to reform the Church and dramatize its independence from foreign control. Reaffirmed was the Byzantine principle of the symphony of church and state: "Mankind has two great gifts from God. . . . : the priesthood and the tsardom. The former directs the spiritual needs; the latter governs and

---

[7] See above, p. 102.

[8] A. N. Grobovsky in *The "Chosen Council" of Ivan IV: A Reinterpretation* (New York, 1969) has argued that the Council never existed as an institution but was merely a group of well intentioned individuals.

Russian cavalryman, 16th century

takes care of the human things. Both derive from the same origin."[9] The church hierarchy was scolded for incomplete services, charging excessive fees, and tolerating corrupt and drunken priests. Though pledging to remedy such abuses, the conclave balked at more drastic reform. Church landholding and tax privileges were restricted (henceforth new land could be acquired only with the tsar's consent), but Ivan's wish to secularize clerical lands was disregarded. Displeased at this half-measure, Ivan soon removed from office leading opponents of secularization. In decisions which later became significant, the Council approved crossing oneself with two fingers (symbolizing the dual nature of Christ) and the double alleluia.[10]

Generally speaking, the reforms of the Chosen Council consolidated central authority while compromising on key political and social issues. During the 1550s the policies of Ivan IV as ruler and those of the Council largely coincided and produced constructive though only partial reforms.

EXTERNAL AFFAIRS

Ivan IV's principal external success—the conquest of Kazan—enhanced his prestige, whereas the subsequent Livonian War in the Baltic left the autocracy gravely weakened. Since the creation of the Kazan khanate in 1445,[11] Moscow had sought to insure its friendship or vassaldom. Until the 1520s peaceful relations, vital to Moscow's eastern trade, were generally preserved, and Muscovite campaigns to Kazan aimed to end internal strife there, not to conquer it. Under Vasili III, Kazan, recognizing Moscow's suzerainty, pledged not to select

[9] Quoted by G. Vernadsky, *The Tsardom of Muscovy* (New Haven, 1969), Part I, p. 47.
[10] See below, pp. 168–71.
[11] See above, pp. 70, 96.

MAP 11–1
Expansion of Russia, 1533–1598

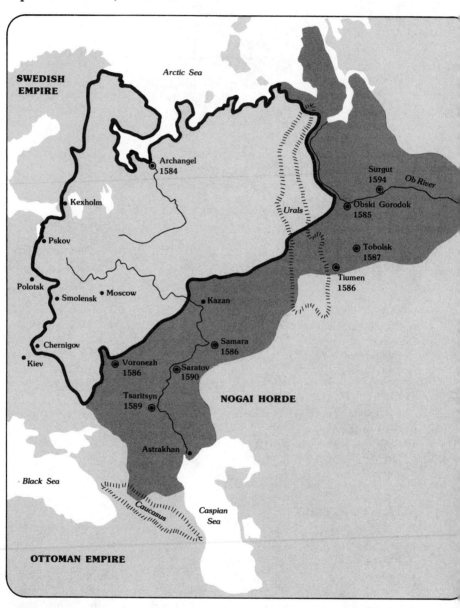

■■■   **Russia in 1533**

▮   **Russian gains 1533–1598**

⦿   **Towns founded 1584–1594**

Adapted with permission of Macmillan Publishing Co., Inc. from *Russian History Atlas* by Martin Gilbert. C
tography by Martin Gilbert. Copyright © 1972 by Martin Gilbert.

a khan without Russian approval. After 1535, however, frequent raids from Kazan struck Muscovy, and numerous Muscovite captives were sold into slavery: in 1551 some sources reported that over 100,000 Muscovites were held prisoner in Kazan. Muscovite reconnaissance expeditions after 1547 revealed Kazan's growing military strength. For religious reasons the Orthodox Church had long advocated the annexation of Moslem Kazan; for the gentry, Peresvetov stressed profits and lands to be won. After Safa-Girei's death in 1549, some Kazan magnates backed the Muscovite candidate as khan, but Muscovy's territorial demands encouraged anti-Moscow elements to seize control, invite Iadigar of Astrakhan to take Kazan's throne, and to prepare for war. Moscow faced a possible Tatar coalition.

In April 1552 Ivan and his advisers decided to attack Kazan. Metropolitan Macarius exhorted the army to fight the infidels who were shedding Christian blood and to free Russian captives. Ivan's large army, besieging the city, shut off its water supply. After breaching the walls with artillery, a major technological innovation, the Muscovites stormed Kazan, killed many of its defenders, and annexed the khanate. In 1554 Ivan's troops moved south to conquer the weaker Astrakhan khanate and opened the entire Volga valley to Russian colonization and the Caspian Sea to its trade. The Volga Tatar region was Muscovy's first major nonSlavic annexation. Neighboring steppe peoples, impressed by Moscow's power, submitted voluntarily to the Russian tsar, successor to the khan of the Golden Horde. Later, as Muscovites moved eastward to the Ural Mountains and beyond, rulers of nomadic west Siberian tribes pledged vague allegiance to Moscow. In 1581 a small private army of Cossacks and steppe fugitives, hired by the wealthy Stroganov merchant family to protect its huge salt and fur empire, moved across the Urals under Ermak Timofeevich, a bold Cossack freebooter. By 1583 it had conquered the west Siberian domain of Khan Kuchum. Overcoming initial displeasure at this distant involvement, Ivan IV welcomed Ermak's Cossacks as heroes. Eastward expansion under Ivan IV laid the basis for a Eurasian Russian empire.[12]

A fortunate accident established direct relations between Russia and England. In 1553 Richard Chancellor's ship, *Edward Bonaventure*, part of an English expedition seeking an Arctic sea route to China, landed on the shores of the White Sea. For England this amounted to the discovery of Muscovy, which had been virtually unknown to the best educated Englishmen. Ivan welcomed Chancellor warmly in Moscow and granted the English Muscovy Company a monopoly of duty free trade with Russia. Carried in English ships, it profited both sides: Russia exchanged forest products and furs for English manufactures and luxuries. Anglo-Russian trade stimulated the development of the White Sea port of Archangel, which when Muscovy lost its Baltic ports in the Livonian War, remained its only direct sea link with western Europe. The English tie aided Ivan to overcome a blockade by his western neighbors. Livonia and Poland, fearful of Russia's potential

---

[12] See below, pp. 157–58.

Ermak (sculpture of M. M. Antokolskii)

strength, were barring technicians and merchants from reaching Muscovy. In 1547 when Hans Schlitte, a German adventurer, recruited specialists for Ivan, the Hanseatic League had them arrested.

The Baltic region therefore became for Ivan IV, as later for Peter the Great,[13] his chief foreign involvement. In the late 1550s the government debated priorities in foreign policy. Adashev and Viskovaty, who had been directing foreign relations, favored caution in the west. Believing that the Crimean Tatars were a direct threat to Muscovy, Adashev and Prince Kurbskii of the Chosen Council urged Ivan to lead the army in person to conquer the Crimea. Ivan and gentry leaders, however, favored attacking Livonia because of its military weakness, the availability of land there, and the importance of the Baltic Sea for Russian commerce. To conquer the Crimea, they argued, would require Polish aid. Soviet historians affirm that the Livonian War (1558–82), which would benefit the rising gentry and merchant classes, was progressive, whereas a southward advance, favored by the feudal aristocracy in order to seize new lands, was not. Vernadsky, however, points out that petty gentry and Cossacks then populated the southern borderlands and that Crimean raids into Muscovy affected the entire population. Instead of turning against the Crimea, Ivan became involved in war on two fronts and eventually suffered defeat.

By itself, Livonia, declining and split internally between the Livonian Order, the Archbishop of Riga, and autonomous cities, was no match

[13] See below, pp. 186–91.

Russian merchant of the 16th century

for Muscovy. In 1558 Ivan invaded it using the pretext of Livonia's alliance with Lithuania. Eastern Estonia was conquered and troops reached Riga's outskirts. Adashev advised peace provided Ivan could obtain eastern Estonia with the Baltic ports of Narva and Derpt. Ivan reluctantly authorized an armistice, but the Livonian Order used it to secure Lithuania's assistance. In 1560, against Adashev's advice, Ivan renewed the war in order to conquer all of Livonia. His territorial greed brought Lithuania, Sweden, and Poland together against him and overstrained Muscovy's resources in a war it could not win. Even Wipper, a Soviet historian who praised Ivan highly, admitted that the Livonian War became his obsession and ruined Russia.[14]

THE OPRICHNINA AND AFTER

Ivan broke with moderates of the Chosen Council to pursue a risky foreign policy and brutal terror at home. The breach occurred before the death of Anastasia, cited by traditional historians as its cause. As military reverses mounted in Livonia, Ivan punished boyar commanders whom he held responsible and promoted ordinary gentry servitors. Contrary to Russian law, Adashev and Silvester were convicted of treason

---

[14] R. Wipper, *Ivan Grozny* (Moscow, 1947), p. 73.

in absentia. The intervention of Metropolitan Macarius prevented their execution, but his death (December 1563) removed the last restraint upon Ivan's punishment of real or imagined enemies. Repression spread fear and confusion among Muscovite commanders and administrators. Lithuania exploited this, promising estates and high positions to Muscovite boyars if they would defect. In 1564 Prince Kurbskii, a top boyar commander and leader of the Chosen Council, tempted by promised rewards, fled to Lithuania.[15] Other boyar defections grew. The Crimean khan attacked Riazan and carried off numerous captives. Ivan confronted growing opposition to his war policy. Without vindicating Adashev he could not make peace with Lithuania and fight the Crimea as the metropolitan and loyal boyars advised. Instead Ivan established the Oprichnina to crush his opponents and enforce his personal rule.

In December 1564 Ivan left Moscow with his family, valuables, and some top officials. After prayers at the Trinity Monastery, he proceeded to nearby Alexandrovsk settlement and dispatched two messages to Moscow. The first, accusing the boyars of treason, announced his abdication as tsar. The second to the commoners absolved them of blame and sought their support for a new regime. Receiving a Moscow delegation headed by the metropolitan, Ivan agreed to cancel his "abdication" provided he received a free hand to punish "traitors." In January 1565 he announced formation of the Oprichnina, or a separate domain over which he would exercise full control. Ivan celebrated his return to Moscow by executing some leading boyars.

The Oprichnina produced a territorial division of Muscovy, a new royal court, and a security police.[16] Centering in Alexandrovsk settlement, a temporary second capital, it included scattered portions of Moscow, commercial areas of the northeast, and strategic western frontier towns; eventually it included about half the country. The rest —the *zemshchina*—remained under the regular administration of the Boyar Duma. In Alexandrovsk, Ivan acted as abbot of a "Satan's band" which combined monastic asceticism with violence and debauchery. His *oprichnik* corps, initially 1,000 strong, grew to 6,000 men from all social groups. Massive land transfers which accompanied the Oprichnina dislocated agriculture and army organization. At least 9,000 boyar sons and gentry were evicted from Oprichnina regions.

Having to choose between a compromise peace and continuing the Livonian War, in 1566 Ivan sought public support by convening an assembly of the lands, which contained many gentry and merchants. The assembly approved continuing the war until all Livonia and Riga had been won, but neither it nor Ivan foresaw the war's disastrous outcome.

The Church soon felt Ivan's wrath. After Macarius' death he barred top churchmen from his administration. After appointing Philip metropolitan (1566), Ivan discovered his strong opposition to Oprichnina

---

[15] The traditional explanation that Kurbsky's flight resulted from fear of punishment after a defeat is now disputed.

[16] See the problem below, pp. 132–36.

terror because Philip interceded repeatedly for its victims. Having ties with Prince Staritskii and Novgorod, the proponents of separatism, Philip opposed Ivan's centralizing policies. In 1568, after Philip denounced the Oprichnina openly, he was deposed, exiled to a distant monastery, and finally strangled. The predominance of the state over the church was confirmed.

A reign of terror prevailed during the Oprichnina as thousands of innocent people from all classes were killed. The mass executions in Moscow in 1570 were unprecedented in their sadism. State Secretary Viskovaty was dismembered publicly as the members of Ivan's entourage each hacked off a part of his body. Ivan himself killed a few with pike and sabre. Others had their skin torn off, and for each victim a different painful death was devised. The terror of 1570 also struck at *zemshchina* officialdom because Ivan wished to subject it wholly to his rule.

In the provinces Ivan crushed remnants of separatism and particularism. Receiving anonymous reports of supposed treason in Novgorod, in 1569 he prepared a massive punitive expedition by his private army of *oprichniki* and gave them lists of potentially dangerous persons to be killed or arrested. En route, other suspect towns were punished cruelly: in Tver alone some 9,000 persons from all social classes were murdered. In Novgorod Ivan confiscated monastic wealth to replenish his treasury, had some 40,000 persons killed, and turned Novgorod into a virtual ghost town. Ivan, seeing treason everywhere, eliminated most former advisers, then executed their executioners.

Excesses by debauched *oprichnik* troops, pervasive fear and suspicion, and splitting the army into *oprichnik* and *zemshchina* detachments complicated Muscovy's defense. During the Crimean invasion of 1571, Ivan's decision to execute the army's commander-in-chief wrecked morale. The tsar fled to Beloozero and the army retreated into Moscow while the Crimeans burned its suburbs and carried off some 100,000 captives. The following year Prince M. I. Vorotynskii defeated the Crimean khan decisively, but Ivan, jealous of his popularity, removed and executed him.

The Livonian War finally turned against Russia. The Union of Lublin (1569), joining the Polish and Lithuanian crowns, created a large and powerful state. In 1572 Stephen Batory, an able military leader, became king and defeated the Russians repeatedly. Militant Polish leaders dreamed of converting Russia to Catholicism. Finally Ivan appealed to Pope Gregory XIII to mediate: with infidel Turks threatening Europe, he wrote, it was no time for Christians to fight one another. The Pope, hoping to bring Muscovy into the fold, dispatched Antonio Possevino, a Jesuit, to settle the Polish-Russian conflict, and by the armistice of 1582 Ivan ceded Polotsk and Livonia to Poland-Lithuania. Meanwhile Sweden, by the armistice of 1583, secured Narva, Ivangorod, and most of the Baltic coastline. Ivan IV's Baltic ambitions lay shattered, and Muscovy was impoverished and had to wait for an outlet to the western seas.

Ivan's attempts at alliance with England also failed. Rejecting politi-

Muscovite envoys about to be received by the German emperor in 1576

cal ties, Queen Elizabeth sought more commercial privileges for the Muscovy Company. Writing Ivan in 1570 she spoke vaguely of an alliance and offered Ivan asylum in case he required it. In 1582 Ivan sought the hand of Mary Hastings, the Queen's lady-in-waiting, intimating that he would discard his wife, Maria Nagoi. When she bore him a son, however, the ill-fated Dmitri,[17] Ivan's marital and political overtures to England came to naught.

Ivan's final years produced little that was lasting or constructive. The Oprichnina, ineffective and divisive at home, gained a bad reputation abroad. In 1572 Ivan, after executing most of its leaders, abolished it; *oprichniki* lost their privileges, and their organization merged with the *zemshchina*. To deflect public indignation at continuing executions, Ivan proclaimed Simeon Bekbulatovich, a baptized descendant of Chingis-khan, grand prince of all Russia. Assuming the humbler title of prince of Moscow, Ivan pretended to defer to him while sending him secret orders. Bekbulatovich became his scapegoat for unpopular policies. When the year ended without the catastrophes predicted by soothsayers, Ivan reassumed his titles and named Bekbulatovich grand prince of Tver. One of Ivan's final acts was to kill his heir, Ivan Ivanovich, in a fit of rage. In 1584 Ivan died a disillusioned and broken man.

ASSESSMENT

Recent Soviet research has helped produce more favorable estimates of the reign of Ivan IV. He was a Renaissance prince whose methods resembled other "terrible" rulers of his time such as Henry VIII and Cesare Borgia[18] and who believed firmly in autocracy. In the first letter to Prince Kurbskii, Ivan (or was it S. F. Shakhovskoi?)[19] set forth a theory of divine right monarchy based on the views of Macarius and

---

[17] See below, p. 141.

[18] See Michael Cherniavsky, "Ivan the Terrible as Renaissance Prince," *Slavic Review*, vol. 27, no. 2 (March 1968), pp. 195–211.

[19] Edward Keenan in *The Kurbskii-Groznyi Apocrypha* (Cambridge, Mass., 1971) challenges the authenticity of the entire *Correspondence*, attributes much of it to Shakhovskoi in the 1620s, and questions the authorship of other writings hitherto attributed to Kurbskii and Ivan IV. His conclusions, however, have not been generally accepted.

Joseph of Volokolamsk. God has bestowed his crown, Ivan believed, and he was responsible to Him alone. The letter traced autocracy in Russia (incorrectly!) to Vladimir I (a limited monarch) and asserted that Ivan belonged to the oldest, most illustrious dynasty in Europe as a direct descendant of the Roman emperor, Augustus Caesar. The fall of Byzantium was cited as proof that autocratic rule was necessary in Russia. These views were unoriginal, but the Third Rome thesis combined with assorted Biblical texts constituted the most complete Muscovite theory of autocracy. Ivan admonished his sons to learn their trade carefully before becoming tsar:

> You should become familiar with all kinds of affairs: the divine, the priestly, the monastic, the military, and the judicial; with the patterns of life in Moscow and elsewhere; . . . how the administrative institutions function here and in other states. All this you must know yourselves. Then you will not depend on others' advice, you yourselves will give directions to them.[20]

On the other hand, Prince Kurbskii (if it was indeed he) from safe Lithuanian exile advocated limited monarchy and defended ancient boyar rights and the Duma's essential role in government. In letters to Tsar Ivan he justified his defection by the boyars' ancient right to shift suzerains at will. Kurbskii dreamed of a past when boyars were the ruler's equals, not his subjects. Ivan IV, he claimed, had ruled wisely with the Chosen Council. Unfortunately "such a fine tsar" had later resorted to unnatural personal autocracy to suppress boyar freedom.

Even with recent evidence supplied by Soviet historians it is difficult to draw up a fair balance sheet for Ivan IV's reign. Negative aspects, stressed by Kliuchevskii and Florinsky, are evident: the vengeful cruelty of Ivan which snuffed out so many lives, and external failures in the south and west, especially loss of the Baltic seacoast. It can be claimed that the Oprichnina undermined the state, demoralized the army, and disrupted land relationships, thus contributing powerfully to the coming Time of Troubles. The great cost of the unsuccessful Livonian War helped fasten serfdom upon the Russian peasantry. Ivan failed to crush the boyars politically, and they remained entrenched in state positions and the Duma. Concludes Vernadsky: "Ivan's policies—both external and domestic—ended in failure."[21]

Soviet historians stress the brighter side. During Ivan's reign, they note, political and military centralization triumphed in Muscovy, the antiquated appanage principle was virtually destroyed, and "progressive" gentry and merchant elements rose. The reforms of the 1550s, though compromises, built firm foundations for a powerful monarchy able to protect Russia's security. In foreign affairs Ivan ended the Livonian War without crippling losses, and his eastern conquests began Muscovy's transformation into a Eurasian empire. Chancellor's arrival broke the Western blockade, brought in vitally needed technicians, and began mutually profitable Anglo-Russian trade.

Farsighted in some ways, nearsighted in others, Ivan and his reign

---

[20] Cited in Vernadsky, *Tsardom*, vol. 1, p. 170.

[21] Vernadsky, *Tsardom*, vol. 1, p. 175.

should neither be glorified nor totally condemned. A Soviet apologist for Ivan writes: "The fate of Ivan IV was the tragedy of a warrior who was beaten by circumstances over which he had no control. He threw all his possessions into the scales of fortune, and not only did he lose his newly acquired territories, but the state, which he had only just built up, was shaken to its foundations."[22]

PROBLEM 3: THE OPRICHNINA

Historians have differed sharply over this major but obscure measure of Ivan IV. Some ascribed it to Ivan's "change of soul" after the death of Anastasia, his beloved first wife; others to his quest for security from boyar plots; or to a conscious plan to build a centralized autocratic state. The Oprichnina has also been depicted as Russia's first security police, an instrument to destroy the boyar class, and as a weapon of personal terror. A historian's view of the Oprichnina usually reveals his assessment of the entire reign: as constructive and statesmanlike, or as bloody and despotic. The following selections give divergent interpretations of the Oprichnina's causes, social composition, and significance.

The outstanding prerevolutionary Russian historian V. O. Kliuchevskii asserted that the Oprichnina failed to solve the major political question of the time: conflicts between the ruler and the boyars, and that it was essentially aimless:

> The Oprichnina at first glance . . . represents an institution lacking all political purpose. Actually, while declaring in his message [to Moscow in January 1565] that all boyars were traitors and despoilers of the land, the tsar left its administration in the hands of these same traitors and plunderers. . . . The word, *oprichnina* in the 16th century was already an antiquated term which the contemporary Muscovite chronicle translated as separate court . . . [and] was borrowed from the ancient appanage language. . . . The Oprichnina of Tsar Ivan was a court economic-administrative institution managing lands set aside to support the tsarist court. . . . The difference was merely that the Oprichnina with later acquisitions comprised almost half the entire country. . . . But one asks why this restoration or parody of the appanage idea? The tsar indicated an unprecedented task for an institution with such an archaic name: oprichnina acquired the significance of a political refuge. . . . The idea that he must flee from his boyars gradually took possession of his mind, became an obsession. In his testament written about 1572 the tsar in all seriousness represented himself as an exile, a wanderer. There he writes: "for my numerous sins the wrath of God has been imposed upon me, the boyars have banished me from my property because of their wilfulness. . . ." Thus the Oprichnina was an institution to protect the tsar's personal security. It was given a political goal for which there was no special institution in the existing Muscovite state structure: . . . to wipe out sedition, nesting in Russia primarily among the boyars.

---

[22] Wipper, *Ivan Grozny,* p. 188.

The Oprichnina received the assignment as the highest police in matters of state treason. . . . As a separate police detachment, the Oprichnina obtained a special uniform. The oprichnik had attached to his saddle a dog's head and a broom; these were his insignia of office and his tasks were to track down, smell out, and sweep away treason and destroy state scoundrels. The oprichnik rode clad in black from head to toe on a black horse with black harness. . . . This was a type of hermit order . . . surrounded with monastic and conspiratorial solemnity. . . .

The boyars could not bring order into the state structure without the ruler's authority, nor could the tsar rule his kingdom in its new boundaries without the boyars' cooperation. . . . Unable to get along or part from one another, they sought to separate, live side by side but not together. The Oprichnina was such an -exit from their difficulty. . . . Unable to destroy a governmental system inconvenient for him, he wiped out individuals who were suspicious or hateful to him. In this consisted the political aimlessness of the Oprichnina: . . . it was directed against persons and not an order. . . . It was to a significant degree the fruit of the tsar's excessively fearful imagination. Ivan directed it against the terrible sedition supposedly persisting in boyar circles which threatened to destroy the entire tsarist family. But was the danger really so terrible? The boyars' political strength was undermined, aside from the Oprichnina, by conditions created directly or indirectly by the gathering of Russia around Moscow. . . .

Contemporaries understood that the Oprichnina, removing sedition, introduced anarchy; protecting the sovereign, it shook the bases of the state. Directed against imagined sedition, it prepared the real thing. . . . Colliding with the boyars . . . after his illness of 1553 and especially after Kurbskii's flight, the tsar exaggerated the danger and became frightened. . . . He began to strike left and right without distinguishing friends from foes. Thus for the direction the tsar gave to the political conflict, his personal character was much to blame. . . .[23]

On the other hand, S. V. Bakhrushin, a leading Soviet specialist in Muscovite history during the Stalin era, considered the Oprichnina an effective attack on feudalism and a conscious step toward centralization and autocracy.

The Oprichnina was directed against those layers of feudal society hindering the development of strong state authority: powerful feudal lords—titled and nontitled—and vassals who supported their resistance to autocracy. The Oprichnina was to tear out by the roots all survivals of feudal division, make even a partial return to it impossible and thereby guarantee the military defense of the country. . . .

Thus the tsar set as the Oprichnina's main task to prevent a repetition of the boyar-princely reaction of 1538–47, whose continuation Ivan discerned . . . in attempts of boyars close to Adashev to limit tsarist power. The second task was to strengthen the state defenses which suffered from inadequate military centralization. . . . The reform of 1565 first of all was to ruin large boyar land ownership, the basis for the feudal aristocracy's political power . . . by taking a significant

---

[23] V. O. Kliuchevskii, *Kurs russkoi istorii,* vol. 2, pp. 188–98.

part of the country's territory into the Oprichnina. . . . All lands in the Oprichnina belonging to the boyars were confiscated, and small *pomestiia* were distributed to nontitled oprichniks. Boyars from whom land was taken had the right to receive compensation elsewhere, but in practice this was not always fulfilled, and lands they received in exchange were far from equal in value to those forfeited. Torn from their long occupied nests, titled and nontitled magnates in their new holdings lacked the firm ties which they had had in hereditary *votchinas* where the populace had regarded them as sovereign lords. By this measure the tsar gained two aims at once: first, he weakened economically and deprived of political significance the powerful feudal lords, and second, created cadres of small landowners wholly dependent upon him, devoted to him, and ready to support his policies in every way.

Ivan Grozny recruited into the Oprichnina ordinary folk . . . , primarily lesser provincial gentry. . . . Obviously, both the tsar and the small provincial noblemen realized perfectly the mutual benefit of their alliance against the big feudal lords. The tsar also found support for his undertakings among the townspeople interested in increased centralization, which guaranteed them protection against arbitrary "strongmen" . . . and broad prospects to develop their trades and businesses. . . .

The Oprichnina naturally encountered strong opposition from big feudal lords. Among the boyars arose several dangerous conspiracies. To overthrow the tsar they established ties with foreign states at war with Russia. Prince Vladimir A. Staritskii again sought to lead the dissatisfied feudal lords. Some clerical magnates allied with the lay lords. In 1567 were exposed connections of an important group of boyars with Sigismund Augustus [King of Poland] aiming through treason to free themselves from Grozny's tyranny . . . [and] involving Prince Vladimir Andreevich [Staritskii] and Novgorod's upper crust. . . .

Militarily, the Oprichnina was far from satisfactory as the raids of the Crimean khan, Devlet-Girei, in 1571 and 1573 revealed. . . . Besides, the Oprichnina's main task had been achieved: large landholding had been destroyed and the most powerful feudal families wiped out or made impotent. This strengthened the centralized state. . . . The weakening of the feudal aristocracy's political power was a necessary precondition for creating an absolute monarchy, and in this at that historical stage lay the Oprichnina's progressive significance. . . .[24]

In the introduction to a recent monograph on the beginnings of the Oprichnina, a younger Soviet scholar presents this judicious and balanced analysis:

In the historiography of the Russian Middle Ages it is difficult to find a subject which has provoked as many differences and quarrels as the history of the Oprichnina. Some have seen the Oprichnina as the fruit of Tsar Ivan Vasilevich's sick imagination and considered it an historical accident. For others the Oprichnina was a planned, well-thought-out reform, a model of state wisdom, and the expression of objective necessity. Most recently have appeared major monographic studies on the Oprichnina's history, but even now the disputes it has caused are far from over. Generally, there is no objection to the fact that the stormy events of the Oprichnina were but a brief episode in

---

[24] S. V. Bakhrushin, *Nauchnye trudy*, II (Moscow, 1954), 300–304.

Russia's lengthy transition from feudal division to absolutism. In the final analysis the Oprichnina was brought into existence by the conflict between a powerful feudal aristocracy and a rising autocratic monarchy. This conflict of itself, strictly speaking, contains no riddles. The enigma is: under what circumstances such an ordinary conflict could produce the bloody drama of the Oprichnina, unprecedented Oprichnina terror, which quickly outgrew the original narrow bounds of conflict.

Contrary to a very widespread view, the policy of the Oprichnina was never consistent with unified principles unchanged during its entire existence. The Oprichnina's development was marked by many contradictions and shifts. In its first stage Oprichnina policy bears a basically anti-princely direction as is shown by the decree of the Kazan exile and the massive confiscation of princely *votchinas*. The return of the disgraced princes from exile, the calling of the *zemskii sobor* of 1566, and other measures connected with the period of compromise . . . mark the end of the first stage. The chief political event of the Oprichnina's second stage from the political standpoint was the grandiose case of the Staritskii plot, ending with the execution of leaders of the Oprichnina, Boyar Duma, and Novgorod's destruction. The chief victims of Oprichnina mass terror in that period were old Muscovite boyars, church leaders, upper bureaucratic administration, and in part gentry—the very layers of the ruling class which constituted the monarchy's most solid, traditional support. The Oprichnina's last victims were its own creators and inspirers. In a political sense the Oprichnina ended up by strengthening the power apparatus of the Russian centralized state. In the socioeconomic sphere its main results were the growth of feudal oppression, intensification of tendencies toward serfdom, and also deepening the economic crisis which reached its peak after the Oprichnina in the 1580s.[25]

George Vernadsky, a prominent American historian of Russian birth, presents a balanced recent interpretation of Ivan IV's reign. He discusses the origins of the Oprichnina against a background of Lithuanian attacks, boyar defections, and the growing breach between Ivan IV and Muscovy's ruling institution, the Boyar Duma.

He [Ivan IV] was not only angered; he was frightened. The alternative facing him was either to resign or to enforce his dictatorship by extraordinary measures. . . . The tsar attempted to split the people of Moscow by inciting the commoners against the officials and upper classes. . . . The oprichnina gave the tsar the means to effect his dictatorship and for a time assured his personal safety. . . . In the districts originally taken into the oprichnina, there were few boyar patrimonial estates (*votchiny*). The eviction thus affected mostly the gentry, the *dvoriane,* and boyars sons. . . .

. . . Many an historian expresses the opinion that in spite of all its horrors, the oprichnina performed an important social and political task . . . shattering the power of the princely and boyar aristocracy in order to clear the way for the rise of the gentry. . . . This policy could have been continued in an orderly way without recourse to such revolutionary measures as the oprichnina. . . . The hasty mobilization of

[25] R. G. Skrynnikov, *Nachalo Oprichniny* (Leningrad, 1966), pp. 3–4.

land caused by the oprichnina and the poor management of landhold-ings granted to the oprichniki resulted in a general decline of agri-cultural production. There was under the oprichnina no systematic confiscation of the princely and boyar latifundia. . . .

To sum up the historical results of the oprichnina, the havoc it caused added new burdens to Muscovite economics. . . . Hardly less disastrous were the undermining of public morale and the psychological depression of the nation. Perhaps the most tragic result of the oprichnina terror . . . was the destruction of so many gifted person-alities. The elite of Russian society had been decimated.[26]

CONCLUSION

Important differences persist in Soviet and Western interpretations of the Oprichnina and of Ivan IV's reign, although this divergence has narrowed considerably. Recent Soviet works, abandoning worshipful praise of Ivan current in the Stalin period, nonetheless still contend that the Oprichnina and his other major reforms were basically positive and progressive steps necessary to undermine political feudalism and promote absolutism and political centralization. Western historians emphasize somewhat more the Oprichnina's, and Ivan's, senseless vio-lence. The Oprichnina, they argue, was largely counterproductive and contributed to oncoming serfdom, dissolution of the Muscovite state, and the chaos of the Time of Troubles. This interpretation parallels negative Western reactions to Stalin's collectivization of agriculture in the 1930s and the violence of the Great Purges.[27]

Suggested Additional Reading

BOOKS

ANDERSON, M. S. *Britain's Discovery of Russia, 1553–1815* (London, 1958).
BERRY, L. and R. CRUMMEY, eds. *Rude and Barbarous Kingdom . . .* (Madison, 1958).
FENNELL, J. F., ed. *The Correspondence between Prince Kurbsky and Tsar Ivan IV of Russia, 1564–1579* (Cambridge, Eng., 1955)
———, ed. *Prince A. M. Kurbsky's History of Ivan IV* (Cambridge, Eng. 1965).
GREY, IAN. *Ivan the Terrible* (London, 1964).
KEENAN, EDWARD. *The Kurbskii-Groznyi Apocrypha* (Cambridge, Mass., 1971).
NORRETRANDERS, B. *The Shaping of Tsardom under Ivan Grozny* (Copen-hagen, 1964).
STADEN, HEINRICH. *The Land and Government of Muscovy* (Stanford, 1967).
TOLSTOY, GEORGE, compiler. *First Forty Years of Intercourse between Eng-land and Russia,* (New York, n.d.).
VERNADSKY, GEORGE. *The Tsardom of Muscovy, 1547–1682,* Part I (New Haven, 1969).

---

[26] George Vernadsky, *The Tsardom of Muscovy 1547–1682* (New Haven, 1969) Part I, 107–09, 138–39.

[27] See below, pp. 490–93, 500–506.

WILLAN, THOMAS.   *Early History of the Russia Company, 1553–1603* (Manchester, Eng., 1956).
WIPPER, ROBERT.   *Ivan Grozny* (Moscow, 1947).

ARTICLES

BOLSOVER, G. H.   "Ivan the Terrible in Russian Historiography," *Trans. of the Royal Hist. Society,* Series 5, vol. 7 (1957), pp. 71–89.
CHERNIAVSKY, M.   "Ivan the Terrible as Renaissance Prince," *SR,* vol. 27, no. 2, pp. 195–211.
KEENAN, E.   "Muscovy and Kazan," *SR,* vol. 26, Dec. 1967, pp. 548–58.
LUBIMENKO, I.   "The Correspondence of Queen Elizabeth with the Russian Tsars," *AHR,* vol. 19 (1914), 525–42.

12

The Time of Troubles

SHORTLY AFTER the death of Ivan IV in 1584, the old Muscovite dynasty died out, beginning a period of disorder and strife known as the Time of Troubles (*Smuta*). Starting as a struggle for the throne, the Troubles deepened into social revolution complicated by foreign intervention. Muscovy was threatened with dissolution and alien rule. Eventually a national movement which expelled foreign invaders and in 1613 enthroned the Romanov dynasty resolved the crisis. Interpretations of the Troubles vary. Kliuchevskii's traditional approach emphasized the dynastic issue as their chief cause and concluded that only election of a "legitimate" ruler ended the turmoil. Soviet historians view the Troubles primarily as an abortive revolution by peasants, slaves, and Cossacks against the boyars, their state, and oncoming serfdom. A secondary Soviet theme is the struggle by lower and middle class elements for national liberation. Historians agree that the development of the Russian autocratic state was interrupted: central authority, lacking legitimacy, was gravely, though temporarily, weakened. What were the major causes of the Troubles? Why did the Muscovite state virtually dissolve for a time? Which elements led the national resurgence of 1611–12? Why did the revolt of the borderlands against the center fail? How did the Troubles affect Muscovite society and institutions?

BACKGROUND AND CAUSES

The causes of the Troubles are complex and reach deep into Muscovite history. The unification process of the 15th and early 16th centuries, exacting a heavy toll from every social group, left numerous grievances and antagonisms. Ivan IV's political and social policies shattered the traditional order and sowed widespread discontent. His constant wars exhausted the country's resources while shifts of landowners and peasants during the Oprichnina created near chaos. In 1581 Ivan's senseless act of killing Ivan Ivanovich, his only capable son, presaged the end of the old dynasty. Perceptive contemporary witnesses such as the Englishman, Giles Fletcher, foresaw a grave crisis should the dynasty die out.

In 1584 every Muscovite class felt insecure and nurtured grievances, which needed only a spark to be expressed violently. Titled magnates had suffered grievously. Expelled from ancestral estates, often in winter, deprived of political influence and hereditary privileges, they had been harnessed forcibly into state service. During the Oprichnina most illustrious families, suffering execution or banishment, had lost much wealth. Growing depopulation of the central provinces threatened many with ruin. The service aristocracy, which had been drawn from virtually every social group except the great lords and under Ivan had become the main bulwark of army and state, also faced difficult problems. Even some former slaves and priests' sons received *pomestie* (tsar-granted) land. Thus *dvoriane* (gentry) could be army generals with vast estates or humble gentry with plots supporting but a single peasant household. In the south poor *dvoriane* often farmed their own land. Only compulsory army service and possession of *pomestie* lands bound together this disparate class. Because state lands were inadequate to supply the expanding servitor element, the *pomestie* system was extended aggressively into the Volga valley and the southern borderlands.

The gravest problem confronting the *dvoriane* was a shortage of peasant labor. Rising tax burdens and loss of personal freedom had provoked a massive peasant exodus, often by illegal flight, to the frontiers. In the center many lands and villages were abandoned. By 1585 in Moscow region only 60 percent of formerly cultivated land was tilled; in the Novgorod area less than ten percent. Intensive competition for peasant labor gave wealthier lay and clerical magnates manifold advantages over lesser gentry. Big lords secured tax exemptions allowing them to offer tenants better economic conditions and more security. Wealthy landlords and especially monasteries exploited their financial advantages unscrupulously and bought the services of tenant farmers from the *dvoriane*. This "exportation" (*vyvoz*) of peasants threatened the service gentry's very existence because without peasant labor its estates became almost worthless.

Noblemen and the state sought to halt peasant departures, which were ruining military servitors and removing taxpayers from state rolls. The government and private owners acted to bind to the land tenant farmers who had been in residence for a specified number of years. Defined as longtime residents (*starozhiltsy*), they lost their traditional right to depart on St. George's Day. Rising peasant indebtedness further curtailed that right. Customarily a peasant had to settle up with the landowner before leaving, but as taxes mounted, many peasants had to borrow from landlords at exorbitant interest rates. Unable to repay their noble creditors, some peasants became slaves (*kholopy*), or entered temporary bondage (*kabala*). As the *pomestie* system spread, tenant farmers often became completely dependent upon landlords. Often village communities, divided among a number of *dvoriane*, lost rights of self-government. Whereas *dvoriane* obtained state support and protection against magnates, the peasant's only recourses were submission or flight.

Urban dwellers were also affected negatively by dislocations of Ivan

IV's time. State efforts to simplify tax collection by concentrating trade in a few centers impaired urban growth and fostered class rivalries. Wealthy merchants (*gosty*) became government agents responsible for tax gathering; in return they were exempted from taxes and the jurisdiction of regular courts. Because other townspeople assumed their financial burdens, social conflict arose between privileged and non-privileged elements. Urban tradesmen had to compete with tax-exempt commercial settlements (*slobody*) established nearby by boyars and monasteries. Townsmen sought better conditions on the frontiers, thus leaving towns in the center depopulated. Between 1546 and 1582 Novgorod's population shrank from 5,000 to 1,000 households. Only the north escaped grave social and economic problems. Untouched by war, their commerce stimulated by contacts with England, towns flourished from the northern Volga to the White Sea.

DYNASTIC STRUGGLE: FEDOR I AND BORIS GODUNOV (1584–1605)

Ivan IV's death brought to the throne Fedor, his saintly but feeble-minded son. His brother-in-law, Boris Godunov, descendant of a Tatar family which had served in Moscow since the 14th century, became the actual ruler. Boris, a shrewd and determined boyar, had served in the Oprichnina and married the daughter of a leading *oprichnik*. Through his sister, Irina, wife of Tsar Fedor, he was linked closely with the throne. Early in Fedor's reign Boris Godunov and other boyars associated with the Oprichnina defeated attempts by the princely aristocracy to regain power and reassert their ancient rights. With a minimum of bloodshed Boris exiled the Shuiskiis, his principal antagonists, and in 1587 became regent (the English styled him aptly: lord protector). Authorized by the Boyar Duma to direct foreign relations, Boris set up his own court, received foreign envoys, and reigned in style. While the incapable Fedor visited monasteries and rang Moscow church bells, Boris won great power and wealth from landed estates and outdistanced his boyar rivals.

As regent, Boris Godunov achieved substantial successes. Contemporaries generally agreed that he was unusually able, had restored order after Ivan's death, was practical, firm, tactful and a superb organizer. His government gave generously to the needy, protected the weak, and won gentry support. Boris ended the terror of Ivan IV's time, restored public confidence, and promoted Muscovite foreign trade by securing transit rights for its merchants through Swedish territory. Taxes and service burdens were reduced. In 1589 Boris arranged creation of a separate Russian patriarchate. Through skillful negotiation and pressure, Boris induced Jeremiah II, visiting patriarch of Constantinople, to ordain Boris' supporter, Iov (Job), as Russian patriarch. The Russian Church ranked last among Orthodox patriarchates, but because the Turks controlled the rest, Muscovy's position was enhanced at home and abroad. Boris acted to restore Muscovite prestige, which had been badly shaken by Ivan IV's defeats. Ably assisted by state secretaries Andrei and Vasili Shchelkalov, he avoided war with Poland and recovered the Baltic territories of Ivangorod and Koporie from Sweden. His excessive caution perhaps prevented further gains. As head of the Kazan Board, Boris fostered Russia's Eurasian empire: forts erected at Tiumen and Tobolsk consolidated Russian control in western Siberia.

Boris, however, could not solve crucial internal problems of depopulation, peasant flight, and gentry impoverishment intensified by Ivan IV's draconian policies; he merely alleviated deep Muscovite social antagonisms temporarily. In the state's interest he backed the *dvoriane* against the magnates, sought to bind the peasantry to the land, and prohibited peasant transfers from small to large estates. The princely aristocracy, seeking revenge, exploited the mysterious death in 1591 of the boy, Dmitri, son of Ivan IV and his uncanonical seventh wife, Maria Nagoi. The dubious legality of his parents' marriage weakened Dmitri's claims to the throne. Some historians support the official version of Dmitri's death: that he fell on a knife during an epileptic fit at Uglich. Boris' enemies circulated rumors that his agent, Bitiagovskii, had murdered the boy to remove an obstacle to Boris assuming the throne. This unsubstantiated charge, depicting Boris as a conscience-stricken murderer, was accepted by a 19th century historian, N. M. Karamzin, and was incorporated in A. S. Pushkin's play and Musorgskii's great opera, *Boris Godunov*. A recent Soviet account affirms that Boris was probably involved in Dmitri's demise.

Tsar Fedor's death in 1598 without heirs ended the old Muscovite dynasty. The legitimate hereditary ruler, so important to conservative Muscovites, was no more, and Boris Godunov's best efforts failed to fill the vacuum. Fedor had bequeathed power to his wife, Irina, but she refused the crown. With her consent Patriarch Iov, a Godunov partisan, became regent and convened a *zemskii sobor,* an assembly, which besides clergy and boyars, contained some 300 gentry and 36 merchants. Boris' opponents and many other contemporaries believed that Boris engineered his own election. He probably did not pack the *sobor,* however, and remained in a monk's cell until it chose him. The other leading contender, Fedor N. Romanov, lacked Boris' advantages of long experience, proven ability as ruler, and broad popular support. Over boyar opposition the *sobor* elected Boris tsar overwhelmingly, and Muscovites expressed warm support by a great procession to the Novodevichii monastery.

As tsar (1598–1605) Boris Godunov became more isolated and vulnerable. No longer could he control from within the Boyar Duma, which contained his leading opponents. Ruling autocratically, he did not try to develop the *zemskii sobor* as a counterpoise to the Duma. To raise his dynasty's prestige he sought to marry his children to foreign royalty. Recognizing Muscovy's need for Western technology, he hired European doctors, engineers, and military men for state service. Conservative churchmen blocked his plans to have German scholars found a university in Moscow, but in 1602 Boris sent 18 youths to study in Europe. To counteract rising dissatisfaction, Boris reverted to a regime of fear. Frontiers were carefully guarded; deportations and confiscations of

David MacKenzie

Novodevichii Monastery (Moscow)

property resumed. The severe famine of 1601–03, caused by successive bad harvests, created widespread suffering and unemployment. Boris intensified a public works program and had fortresses, churches, offices, and storehouses built throughout Muscovy. The government distributed grain from its reserves, but general distress and continuing peasant flights promoted brigandage. Late in 1603 Boris had to suppress a major peasant-Cossack revolt led by Khlopko, a Cossack chieftain.

SOCIAL REVOLT AND FOREIGN INVASION (1605–1610)

Profound social tensions and discontent undermined and finally destroyed the Godunovs. Boris' boyar foes continued to hatch plots, while rumors spread that Tsarevich Dmitri had escaped death miraculously in Uglich and that Boris was a usurper. Other accounts labeled him Dmitri's murderer. In 1603 came news that "Dmitri" was in Poland, recognized as the true tsarevich. He was probably a native Muscovite prepared for his pretender's role by boyars hostile to Boris. Iuri Mniszech, a Polish magnate of extravagant tastes, viewed Dmitri as his opportunity to regain wealth and power and used his daughter as bait. Dmitri became infatuated with Marina who dreamed of becoming tsaritsa of Muscovy. Early in 1604 Dmitri converted secretly to Catholicism and requested Papal protection. He was to marry Marina only when he had become tsar and had to promise her father a million zlotys and to make Marina proprietress of Novgorod and Pskov. Boris declared him to be Grigori Otrepiev, a fugitive monk from Moscow's Chudov Monastery. Evidently Dmitri's Polish supporters did not believe he was Ivan IV's son, but he was a convenient tool to subjugate Muscovy and convert it to Catholicism. Dmitri himself apparently believed in his mission.

In the summer of 1604 Dmitri invaded Muscovy with about 2,000 Poles and Ukrainians. Before he reached Kiev 2,000 Don Cossacks joined him, and soon Russians greatly outnumbered Poles in his army. His strength derived more from the prestige of his name and the social disorder in Muscovy than from the size of his forces. The populace of the southern and western borderlands, the so-called "Wild Field," consisting largely of Cossack freebooters, poor gentry, and peasants who had fled from central Muscovy, was volatile, discontented with Moscow, and easily misled. The remnants of the army of the brigand Khlopko had taken refuge there. Some believed Dmitri was authentic, a "fine tsar" who would satisfy their grievances; others joined him to oppose Boris, autocracy, and serfdom. The Pretender and his agents roused this potentially rebellious borderland against the Godunovs. In January 1605, however, Boris' army inflicted a crushing defeat on Dmitri who barely escaped capture. Retiring to Putivl, he was rescued by some Don Cossacks and soon headed a new army of malcontents.

Moscow's weakness enabled Dmitri to triumph. The sudden death of Boris Godunov in April 1605 removed its only experienced leader. Fedor Godunov, his well educated 16-year-old son, reigned only six weeks; his army defected to Dmitri near Kromy. In June Dmitri entered Moscow, Fedor and his mother were brutally murdered, and the Pretender became tsar.

The rule of Dmitri I (1605–06) was brief and troubled. The anti-Godunov princely aristocracy neither believed in nor supported him. Surrounding himself with Polish favorites and Muscovite adventurers, Dmitri alienated conservative Muscovites by his poorly disguised hostility toward Orthodoxy, financial exactions from the Church, and disregard for court etiquette. By lavish gifts and allowing gentry officers to return to their estates, he won some gentry support, but Dmitri, though intelligent, proved venal and sensual, haughty and dissolute. The boyars, opposing his efforts to rule independently, exploited rapidly growing popular dissatisfaction with his reign. The wily Prince Vasili Shuiskii, who had confirmed the real Dmitri's death at Uglich and later recognized the Pretender as legitimate ruler, now told Muscovites that he was an impostor. In the spring of 1606 the elaborate Catholic wedding of Dmitri and Marina, attended by thousands of Poles, further alienated Muscovites and encouraged Shuiskii to instigate a popular uprising. While a mob massacred hundreds of Poles and Lithuanians, boyars invaded the Kremlin and murdered Dmitri. Marini and her father escaped and went into exile.

Moscow boyars then convened a fake *zemskii sobor,* which enthroned Shuiskii as Vasili IV, who was of distinguished lineage but modest abilities. His arbitrary elevation provoked social dissension, then civil war. The entire borderland, which had backed Dmitri, rose against the "boyars' tsar." The dynastic issue slipped into the background as the Troubles became mainly a social revolt. Installing Germogen, the metropolitan of Kazan, as patriarch, Vasili IV secured support from conservative churchmen but alienated the influential Romanovs whose leader, Filaret, coveted that post. Germogen had the remains of Ivan IV's son Dmitri brought from Uglich to Moscow and canonized him as a saint. Even this action could not destroy a feeling for the pretender rooted deep in popular antipathy to an oppressive regime in Moscow.

The rebellion against Tsar Vasili, which became a great peasant insurrection against serfdom, began in Putivl in the name of Ivan IV's son Dmitri. The ablest and most popular figure in the movement was Ivan Bolotnikov, glorified by Soviet historians as a popular hero and great general. Bolotnikov, a former Don Cossack, had been captured by the Tatars and served for years as a galley slave in Turkey before managing to return to Muscovy. A talented and dynamic leader, he became commander of a great revolutionary army of peasants, Cossacks, and runaway slaves. Bolotnikov attacked serfdom, the landowning nobility, and the city rich. Crude propaganda leaflets urged boyar serfs and city poor to "kill the boyars . . . , merchants and all commercial people" and seize their goods. Bolotnikov considered himself "the great chieftain" serving "the fine tsar, Dmitri Ivanovich" who wished to free the masses. His motley forces defeated Vasili's armies and for three months besieged Moscow. Dissension in Bolotnikov's army between Cossacks who favored freeing the peasants and gentry who opposed it permitted Vasili to drive off the rebels. Throughout 1607 this bitter social struggle raged. Vasili's army finally captured Bolotnikov's base at Tula and seized the rebel leaders. Inadequate organization, social antagonisms within insurgent ranks, and lack of a clear positive program doomed this great popular upheaval.

Vasili IV's government responded to the challenge with familiar Muscovite police tactics. The borderlands were plundered and devastated; thousands of prisoners were brutally tortured to death, many by slow drowning. Fugitive slaves and serfs were returned forcibly to their lords' control. The right of peasant departure, still sometimes allowed under Boris Godunov, was abrogated completely. The boyar regime took major steps toward establishing serfdom in Russia.

No sooner had Bolotnikov's movement subsided than a second Pretender Dmitri challenged Vasili's shaky regime. Polish and Lithuanian lords and adventurers used this vulgar man of unknown origin to

MAP 12–1
Time of Troubles, 1598–1618

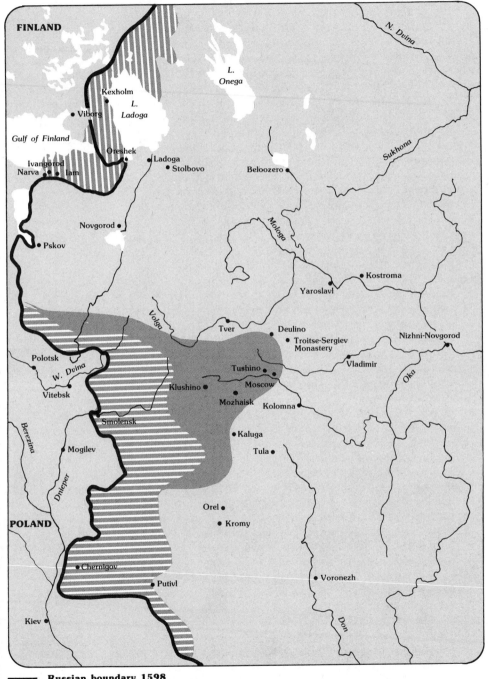

FINLAND

N. Dvina

L. Onega

Kexholm

Viborg

L. Ladoga

Sukhona

Gulf of Finland

Oreshek

Ladoga

Ivangorod

Narva • • Iam

Stolbovo

Beloozero

Novgorod

Mologa

Pskov

Kostroma

Yaroslavl

Volga

Tver

Deulino

Nizhni-Novgorod

Polotsk

Troitse-Sergiev
Monastery

W. Dvina

Tushino

Vladimir

Oka

Vitebsk

Klushino

Moscow

Berezina

Smolensk

Mozhaisk

Kolomna

Mogilev

Kaluga

Dnieper

Tula

POLAND

Orel

Kromy

Chernigov

Voronezh

Putivl

Kiev

Don

Russian boundary 1598

Area occupied by Poles, 1612–13

Ceded to Poles 1618

**Ceded to Sweden by Peace of
Stolbovo 1617**

attack and plunder Muscovy. King Sigismund of Poland, indignant at the recent massacre of Poles in Moscow, supported them. The Second Pretender proclaimed himself Tsar Dmitri Ivanovich, and by the spring of 1608 a sizable Polish-Lithuanian force had crossed the frontier and was swelled by military servitors, commoners from the Seversk borderland, and survivors from Bolotnikov's army. The Second Pretender, known to Muscovites as "The Brigand" (*Vor*), met little resistance. Looting as he advanced, he set up headquarters at Tushino, just outside Moscow, but could not capture the capital. Iuri Mniszech brought his daughter there, and Marina accepted the loathsome Brigand as her husband. Two years of civil war ensued. Nobles and rich merchants generally supported Vasili; commoners and some boyars backed the Brigand. A number of illustrious boyars, including Filaret Romanov, defected from Vasili's court to Tushino. Known derisively as "migratory birds," they changed sides as the tide of battle shifted. The Brigand's forces tried to encircle Moscow but were foiled by a heroic defense of the fortified Trinity Monastery. The Tushinites next sought to conquer the north, but its sturdy peasantry and merchants distrusted the Brigand even more than they did Tsar Vasili.

Vasili IV, seeking relief and reinforcement, dispatched his young nephew, Prince M. Skopin-Shuiskii, to the northwest. By an agreement of February 1609, Sweden agreed to supply mercenary troops in return for Muscovy's renunciation of claims to Livonia and Karela. Skopin's reinforced army defeated the Poles before Moscow and drove the Brigand south to Kaluga. The migratory boyars of Tushino, led by Filaret Romanov whom the Brigand had named patriarch, negotiated with King Sigismund of Poland, who was besieging Smolensk. Their agreement of February 1610 provided that Wladyslaw, the King's young son, should become Orthodox tsar of Muscovy. Before the agreement could be implemented, the Tushino government dissolved.

Vasili IV's worst troubles seemed over. But Skopin-Shuiskii died suddenly—some said he was poisoned—depriving his camp of its ablest figure and of popular support. In June 1610 the Poles under Zolkiewski defeated Vasili's poorly led army at Klushino. Vasili's regime and the old Muscovite state collapsed. Seven boyars from the Duma formed a provisional government in Moscow, but it was not widely obeyed. With Poles and the Brigand's Cossacks approaching the city, the Moscow boyars chose the Poles as the lesser evil. By a treaty of August 1610, a more conservative version of the February agreement, Wladyslaw was to become tsar if he accepted Orthodoxy and ruled with the Boyar Duma. A 1,200-man "grand embassy" went to Smolensk to make final arrangements.

A period of direct Polish rule in Moscow followed. General Zolkiewski occupied the city, consolidated Polish control, and helped defeat the Brigand. At Smolensk the delegates discovered, however, that King Sigismund coveted the Russian throne himself. Instead of sending his son, he had General Alexander Gosiewski, who replaced the disgusted Zolkiewski, arrest the seven boyars and set up a Polish military dictatorship. When the Muscovite delegates refused to recognize him as tsar, Sigismund had Filaret Romanov and other leaders imprisoned in Po-

David MacKenzie

Trinity Monastery at Zagorsk, near Moscow (16th Century)

land. At the end of 1610 there was no legal Muscovite government nor tsar.

NATIONAL REVIVAL AND THE ROMANOVS' ELECTION (1610–1613)

Polish and Swedish intervention triggered a national movement to liberate the country and restore a legitimate Orthodox Russian tsar. It blended religious and national elements in a way which appealed to all Russian social groups. Soviet accounts stress that it was inspired by the patriotism of ordinary townsmen and peasants. The traditional state had disintegrated, but the Church as before remained a focus of unity. Late in 1610 Patriarch Germogen, rejecting the Catholic Sigismund, advised Muscovites to accept Wladyslaw as tsar only if he became Orthodox and exhorted other towns to unite against Poles and Lithuanians. The ancient patriarch, affirm non-Soviet historians, became spiritual head of a movement to save the country from enslavement.

Towns of the still undevastated north and Volga valley responded. After the Brigand's murder (December 1610), his remaining Cossacks became the core of a militia led by Prokopy Liapunov of Riazan, Ivan Zarutskii of Tula, and the boyar, Prince Dmitri Trubetskoi, which moved on Moscow. Grave social antagonisms, however, wracked this national militia: Cossacks aimed to free the serfs while the gentry and merchants sought to restore the old social order. In June 1611 the Cossacks, fearing betrayal to the landlords, murdered Liapunov. Gentry contingents withdrew and the Cossacks restored their camp at Tushino.

A second attempt by middle elements of society to end the Troubles had failed. Meanwhile King Sigismund had conquered Smolensk and the Swedes seized Novgorod. Muscovy's complete dissolution seemed near.

Patriotic Russians made new efforts at unity. In August 1611 Patriarch Germogen from his captivity in the Kremlin appealed to Nizhnii-Novgorod, the leading north Volga commercial town, not to submit to Cossacks under the "Baby Brigand," son of Marina and the deceased Brigand. In September Kuzma Minin, an energetic butcher of Nizhnii-Novgorod, exhorted city elders to form a militia financed by voluntary contributions. Minin became the inspirational and financial leader of a movement of Volga towns, which soon involved all northern and central Russia, led by gentry and merchants against Cossack rule and Polish domination. Prince Dmitri Pozharskii, an experienced commander, assumed control of a sizable militia. Early in 1612 Pozharskii drove the Cossacks from the key Volga city of Iaroslavl, organized his army, and set up a provisional government. Messages went out to other towns to send delegates to a *zemskii sobor*. In August, learning that the Poles were seeking to reinforce and provision their garrison in Moscow, Pozhzharskii moved toward the city. Cossack forces in his path disintegrated: those under Prince Trubetskoi joined Pozharskii; the rest withdrew southward to seek their ideal of land and liberty. The Polish relief force was defeated and a provisional regime formed in October led by Minin, Pozharskii and, Trubetskoi. Soviet historians emphasize the significant role of peasant partisan detachments in liberating Muscovy. Pozharskii's army stormed Moscow's inner city, and in October 1612 the starving Polish garrison in the Kremlin capitulated. King Sigismund's attempt to retake the city failed, and Polish dominion in Moscow had ended.

It remained to prevent new social strife between Cossacks and gentry and to choose a permanent government. Because most of the gentry militia was soon demobilized, Trubetskoi's Cossacks exerted strong pressure upon the *zemskii sobor* which in January 1613 convened in Moscow to elect a new dynasty. Its membership exceeded 800, estimates Vernadsky, including about 500 provincial delegates. All classes were represented except peasants on private estates, but the assembly was dominated by gentry and merchant elements which had freed Moscow. One faction of boyars, court officials, and north Russian gentry prepared to back the Swedish prince, Charles Philip, if he turned Orthodox. Clergy, southern gentry, townspeople, and Cossacks favored a native candidate. The people of Moscow and vicinity strongly backed Michael Romanov, the sickly 16-year-old son of the imprisoned Filaret. Michael, the only figure round whom Cossacks and gentry could unite, was acceptable to the older aristocracy and traditionalists because he was weak and related to the old Muscovite dynasty: his great aunt, Anastasia Romanov, had been Ivan IV's beloved first wife. After the *sobor* had rejected foreign candidates, support grew for Michael. "It was the Cossacks who made your son the sovereign of Muscovy," Filaret learned the following year.[1]

---

[1] S. M. Soloviev, *Istoriia Rossii*, vol. 9, p. 38, cited in Vernadsky, *Tsardom*, vol. 1, p. 275.

During the interregnum the *zemskii sobor* ruled exhausted, devastated Muscovy as bands of Poles, Swedes, and marauding Cossacks roamed about. While young Michael was at the Romanov estate in remote Kostroma, a band of Poles, seeking to abduct him, asked a local peasant, Ivan Susanin, to lead them to the tsar-elect. To save the tsar, Susanin deliberately led them deep into the forest where he and they perished. This episode, the basis for Michael Glinka's 19th century opera, *A Life for the Tsar,* revealed the patriotism which had begun to inspire ordinary Russians. Soon afterward, delegates from the *zemskii sobor* arrived to talk with Michael Romanov, who at first refused the throne. (The fate of his immediate predecessors was scarcely encouraging.) After the delegates assured him that "the whole land" was demanding him, he yielded, and in July 1613 he was crowned solemnly in the Kremlin as Michael I. His coronation inaugurated the Romanovs' 300 year rule and ended the political aspect of the Troubles, but not until 1618 was the fighting ended by treaty with Poland and Sweden.

The Troubles, affirms Florinsky, represented an "abortive social revolution" leaving the structure of Muscovy apparently little changed. But the positions and relationships of the main social groups had altered substantially. The old titled aristocracy, shaken by the Oprichnina, never recovered fully from blows suffered during the years of disorder. The new dynasty would rely more upon state secretaries, military chieftains, and merchants from the middle layers of society, which would provide most of the new bureaucratic aristocracy. The national movement which ended the Troubles drew together and enhanced the influence of gentry, boyar sons, and merchants. On the other hand, lower social groups: Cossacks, peasants, and slaves, which had revolted repeatedly against the center and the traditional order, were defeated and subjugated more firmly to the landlords and the state.

Muscovite autocracy survived the Troubles little altered, but political attitudes had changed. Old traditions had been undermined and the new concept of "all the land" emerged. In the 16th century, Kliuchevskii notes, Muscovites had considered the ruler as possessor of the land (*votchinnik*) and themselves as tenants subject to his whims; his personal will had been the sole basis for political life. But during the Troubles representative assemblies had elected tsars repeatedly. Regimes and rulers lacking popular support had been overthrown (Dmitri I and Vasili IV), and from 1610 to 1612 there was no ruler at all, yet the Muscovite state survived. Evidently, the *zemskii sobor*, embodying the popular will, constituted an adequate basis for supreme legal authority and could solve fundamental questions such as dynastic change or major foreign war. Hitherto sporadic contacts between Muscovites and foreigners had intensified. Thousands of Poles, Lithuanians, and west Europeans, flocking to Moscow and Tushino, helped convince the Muscovite elite that European ways and technology must be mastered. The upper classes began to imitate Western dress, to be influenced by Western culture, and to question long established institutions and values.

The significance of the Troubles remains debatable. Some historians conclude that they produced little that was new and that the Romanovs restored previous social and political institutions. Soviet accounts emphasize class struggle: that the Bolotnikov movement revealed the tremendous latent force of a discontented peasantry. Muscovy's liberation from foreign domination, they assert, strengthened national unity although it was many years before the economy recovered from damage inflicted by foreign interventionists. Recent Soviet works make implicit comparisons between foreign intervention during the Troubles and in the Civil War of 1918–20.[2] Finally, the Troubles can be viewed as a contest between the borderlands ("Wild Field") and the center. Ultimately the center prevailed: the year 1613 marked the triumph of noble landowners and state power opening the way for the development during the seventeenth century of a bureaucratic, autocratic monarchy and serfdom, which were gradually extended to the borderlands. For a generation the Troubles left Muscovy severely weakened economically and militarily with unfavorable frontiers in the west.

Suggested Additional Reading

BOOKS

BARBOUR, PHILIP.   *Dmitry Called the Pretender, 1605–06* (Boston, 1966).
BARON, S. H., ed.   *The Travels of Olearius in Seventeenth Century Russia* Stanford, 1967).
FLETCHER, GILES.   *Of the Russe Commonwealth*, ed. R. Pipes (Cambridge, Mass., 1966).
HOWE, SONIA E., ed.   *The False Dmitri . . . Described by British Eye Witnesses, 1604–1612* (London, 1916) (Valuable).
PLATONOV, S.   *Boris Godunov*, trans. F. Pyles (Gulf Breeze, Florida, 1973).
———.   *The Time of Troubles*, trans. J. Alexander (Lawrence, Kansas, 1970). (The best brief account in English).
SMIRNOV, I. I.   *Vosstanie Bolotnikova 1606–1607* (Moscow, 1951).
VERNADSKY, GEORGE.   *The Tsardom of Muscovy*, Part I.
ZOLKIEWSKI, STANISLAS.   *Expedition to Moscow: A Memoir* (London, 1959) (Reprint of a contemporary Polish account).

ARTICLES

AFANASYEV, G.   "Boris Godunov and the First Pretender," *Rus. Rev.* (Liverpool), vol. 2, no. 4, 1913, pp. 31–53.
CRUMMEY, R.   "Crown and Boyars under Fedor Ivanovich and Michael Romanov," *Can. Am. Sl. Studies*, vol. 6 (1972), pp. 549–74.
NIKOLAIEFF, A. M.   "Boris Godunov and the Ouglich Tragedy," *RusR.*, vol. 20, 1950, pp. 275–85.
ORCHARD, G.   "The Frontier Policy of Boris Godunov," *EEur. Hist. Essays*, pp. 113–23.
VERNADSKY, G.   "The Death of the Tsarevich Dimitry . . ." *Oxf. Sl. Papers*, vol. 5, 1954, pp. 1–19.

---

[2] See below, pp. 470–77.

13

The Early Romanovs: Politics
and Foreign Affairs

SEVENTEENTH CENTURY Muscovy experienced an agonizing transition from a parochial, religious-oriented society to a secular, partially Westernized, multinational one. Traditional ways were being replaced by disturbing new patterns. Frequent wars and domestic violence imposed onerous burdens upon peasants and townsmen. For decades after their formal end in 1613 the Troubles persisted in the form of disorder and brigandage, economic and military weakness. Grievous external challenges promoted development of autocracy, a bureaucratic state, and a virtual caste system. While ordinary Muscovites were subjected to stricter state controls over religion, residence, and occupation, the elite explored alternatives to traditional policies and institutions. The new Romanov rulers faced monumental tasks, which they could not solve fully, and Russian leaders divided over policy as they faced a western Europe militarily and economically superior and culturally more advanced. Spurning European ways and values, conservatives strove unsuccessfully to preserve self-contained, religious traditions. To protect Russia and bring her out of backwardness, reformers urged the adoption of Western institutions and the employment of European military and economic experts. Russia survived this difficult and perplexing era and expanded eastward and southward despite its mediocre leadership. Soviet historians emphasize the growth of a unified Russian market as a basis for bureaucratic monarchy, a Russian nation, and a national culture. How did autocracy flourish under often ineffective tsars? Why did representative institutions wither and die? How did Muscovy cope with more advanced neighbors and, despite a blockade, establish closer commercial and political ties with western Europe?

THE RULERS AND THE ZEMSKII SOBOR

The early Romanov era presents an apparent paradox of weak tsars, with relatives or favorites exercising much actual state authority, and the growth of autocratic power. Contemporaries believed that Michael I (1613–45), who was frail, gentle, and incompetent to govern, had

151

agreed to consult with the Boyar Duma before making decisions. Probably his power was not limited formally, but his government depended at first on leading boyar families, which often treated him scornfully and feathered their nests. In 1619 Filaret Romanov, Michael's ambitious and imperious father, returned from Polish captivity. Named patriarch and co-ruler, he dominated his passive son and directed church and state effectively until his death in 1633. Alexis (1645–76), Michael's son, became tsar at 16. Humane, religious and endowed with a keen aesthetic sense, Alexis was more autocratic than Michael and achieved greater success at home and abroad. Fedor II (1676–82), a weakling manipulated by favorites, was succeeded by two young boys: Ivan V who was mentally deficient, and ten-year-old Peter I who later became the first masterful Romanov ruler, while Alexis' ambitious daughter, Sofia, acted as regent.

Such weak and ineffective rulers seemed to provide the *zemskii sobor* with opportunities to become a genuine national parliament. Like other east European assemblies, it flowered briefly in the 17th century before declining and disappearing. The selection of the Romanovs had ended the political crisis of the Troubles and enhanced the *sobor's* prestige; until Michael assumed the throne, it acted as a provisional government. Containing state peasants, provincial merchants, and other elements not included in 16th century assemblies, until 1615 the *sobor* met continually, and it functioned regularly until 1622. After Filaret consolidated his power, however, the *sobor* declined and convened irregularly. Its final resurgence came in 1648–49 when it helped draft the new law code.[1] In the early 1650s it met to discuss the annexation of the Ukraine but thereafter there were no more full meetings.

Among the *zemskii sobor's* numerous weaknesses was that it was never a well defined body with regular composition, representation, or procedure. The infrequent 16th century *sobors* had comprised government officials and representatives added to the Boyar Duma and Holy Council of church leaders. In the 17th century, at least in theory, it represented "men of all ranks." Elected representatives were mainly service gentry, merchants, and other townsmen, though in 1613 state peasants were included. Although government decrees prescribed that men of property and substance be selected, literacy was not required and about half the deputies in 1648 were illiterate. Delegates were supposed to represent their constituents by presenting petitions at the *sobor*, and the elected petitioner tended to replace the government agent of earlier *sobors*. At the assemblies with the largest provincial representation, criticism of government measures was loudest.

The *sobor's* competence remained unclear. Unable to initiate legislation or bind the tsar by its decisions, it usually merely confirmed previously made government decisions and provided popular sanction for expensive wars or controversial domestic measures. Except in 1613 when the *sobor* ran the administration and afterwards advised the young tsar, its sessions were brief and its delegates conferred little

---

[1] See below, pp. 155–56.

Reception of a foreign delegation by Tsar Alexis

beforehand. *Sobors* of the 1640s, unlike earlier ones, voiced merchant and gentry grievances against the ruling boyars, and the resulting petitions became the basis for many articles of the Law Code of 1649. The Great Sobor of 1648–49, notes J. H. Keep, tended to divide into an upper house of clergy and boyars and a lower house of elected middle-class representatives. Because the Duma and tsar retained full legislative power, however, Kliuchevskii regards this division as merely a separation of functions. The *sobor*'s dual nature: legislative when tsar and Duma were present, and consultative otherwise, revealed its institutional immaturity. With its legislative authority based neither on law nor popular will, the *sobor* remained throughout an instrument of the regime. Deputies of various social groups might be questioned separately and their replies compiled into written statements, but there was no regular voting procedure. At times *sobors* criticized government officials and measures, but the regime then usually would dissolve them quickly.

The *zemskii sobor* resembled the French Estates-General, which also withered in the 17th century, more than the English Parliament. State finances were usually discussed at its sessions, but unlike Parliament the *sobor* never asserted power over taxation. It lacked features such as gentry-merchant cooperation in bargaining with the crown, which accounted for the House of Commons' peculiar strength. Like the Estates-General the *sobor* was torn by antagonism between greater and lesser lords and between noblemen and townsmen. Influential Russian classes, instead of bargaining with the tsar, became subservient to his authority. Nineteenth century Slavophiles idealized the *sobor* as a unique representative body which cooperated with the ruler for the common good,[2] but Keep concludes that it basically resembled Western parliaments.[3]

The *zemskii sobor*, the peak of influence of which coincided with an insecure government in a confused country, developed not to limit but to reinforce central authority. Once political centralization was well advanced, it was no longer needed. The central bureaucracy, consolidated under Alexis, distrusted the representative principle and doubted the *sobor*'s usefulness. Meeting only when the government convened it and with inadequate organization and procedure, the *sobor* was helpless and dispensable. Social change undermined its representation: serfdom removed the peasantry, whereas gentry and merchants, becoming dependent on state favor, could no longer voice critical views. The development of autocracy, serfdom, and the caste system doomed representative institutions.

ADMINISTRATION

Centralization became the keynote in central and provincial government, and only a strong tsar was required to establish a true autocracy. The boyars' political decline and growing church subservience to the state eliminated gradually most restrictions on autocratic power. The *zemskii sobor* elected or confirmed the first Romanovs, but Russia had no clear law of succession or defined administrative structure. Especially in the later 17th century frequent coup d'états occurred, along with much court intrigue and abuse of power by ambitious favorites, the "accidental men." Muscovite leaders of this time, often lacking self-confidence, looked to the past for solutions. Because the Troubles had destroyed much of the political structure, however, even restoring the old was innovative. Some measures, derived from Muscovite experience, were cautious and lacking in new principles; others traced new paths which led to the reforms of Peter I.

As central government grew more complex and bureaucratic, administrative boards (*prikazy*)[4] increased in number under Michael to about 50. Created without definite plan, they often changed functions, and their jurisdictions were unclear and often overlapping. A cumbersome governmental machine developed with numerous departments and commissions. Seeking cohesion, the government grouped related departments under one official or merged smaller departments with larger ones. Two new agencies were created: a Department of Accounts to handle all state finance, and the Department of Secret Affairs, which became the tsar's personal chancellery and supervised other agencies. Reviving the unfortunate tradition of the Oprichnina, it enabled Tsar Alexis to act arbitrarily but failed to promote honesty or efficiency in administration.

---

[2] See below, pp. 306–7.

[3] J. H. Keep, "The Decline of the Zemsky Sobor," *SEER*, vol. 36, pp. 100–22.

[4] See above, p. 103.

Centralizing tendencies also prevailed in provincial and local government. In each district a governor (*voevoda*) became responsible for finance, law, police, and the army in town and countryside. Unlike the former governors (*namestniki*),[5] *voevody* were supposed to rule for the tsar's benefit. "Feeding" and bribes, though forbidden, persisted nonetheless, and often new governors were descendants of old *namestniki*. Their ill defined authority encouraged abuse of power and imposed heavy burdens on localities. Provincial representatives to the *zemskii sobor* of 1642 complained: "Your Majesty's governors have reduced the people of all stations to beggary and have stripped them to the bone."[6] Moscow, however, preferred to deal with one appointed governor than with many elected officials.

The *zemstvo* system of local self-government, remaining vital in the north, withered elsewhere. Elected officials in town offices still collected taxes for local needs but would seldom disobey the governor to aid their communities. As boards of justice and assessors were disbanded, judicial authority shifted to the governor. Elected mayors executed unpopular policies which the governor and his staff were loath to perform, and *zemstvo* institutions were deprived of initiative but not of onerous responsibility.

LAW

Bureaucratic Muscovy urgently needed a new law code. Since 1550 the Boyar Duma and other agencies had issued numerous uncoordinated decrees which made the Code of 1550 obsolescent. Tsar Alexis and his boyar advisers provided the initiative: terrified by the Moscow Revolt of 1648, they convened a Great Sobor to help compose a new code from the Acts of the Apostles, the Holy Fathers, decrees of previous tsars, and old charters. Legal sources for the Code of 1649 (*Ulozhenie*) included the *Sudebnik* of 1550, Byzantine codes and the Lithuanian Statute of 1588. A codification commission of two boyars, a courtier, and two secretaries, urged on by urban revolts, hastily drafted a body of law which often had to cover new situations. The Sobor's elected members suggested changes, gave advice, and presented petitions to the Boyar Duma. The result was superficial and inconsistent; its survival until 1833 meant that Russia had to do without a clear or precise collection of laws.

The *Ulozhenie*, Russia's first printed law code, had a preamble, 25 chapters, and 967 articles. The preamble proclaimed that justice would become equal for "men of all ranks," but the Code subjected most Muscovites to state bondage. Social relationships were defined by establishing a highly stratified class (*soslovie*) system, which prescribed each group's duties and obligations rather rigidly. Almost half its provisions dealt with the service gentry, whose social and political dominance was confirmed. The *dvoriane* received a virtual monopoly

---

[5] See above, p. 102.
[6] Florinsky, vol. 1, p. 270.

of landed estates farmed by serfs, complete authority over its peasants, and unlimited time to recover escapees. Restrictions were relaxed on *pomestie* estates, which now tended to become hereditary, but all noblemen now had to serve the state. The church retained lands obtained illegally since 1580, but it was forbidden to acquire new ones. Burghers received a monopoly of commerce and industry but were bound to their places of residence. Leading merchants became state wards protected from foreign competition but subservient to detailed government regulations. The *Ulozhenie*, a desperate expedient to protect loyal state servants and the Treasury against impoverishment, bound nearly everyone to his class, occupation, and residence.

THE ARMY

War, as Hellie notes, was the chief preoccupation of the Muscovite state. Until the mid-17th century the backbone of the army remained a gentry cavalry designed to combat steppe Tatars. Armed mainly with sabres and bows as late as 1600, it was poorly organized and lacked discipline and staying power. *Streltsy*, service Cossacks, and small contingents of artillerymen and foreign mercenaries comprised in 1630 the remainder of an army of about 90,000 men. Except for *streltsy* who had regular regional organizations, this motley army disbanded after each campaign. In 1630 impending war with Poland caused Filaret's government to improve this system by offering huge salaries and large estates to foreign officers and specialists, mainly from Protestant European countries. Colonel Alexander Leslie, a Scot in Russian service, was sent abroad to recruit officers and mercenaries and buy cannon and muskets. Foreign officers were placed in command of infantry and dragoon regiments, organized and drilled on a European pattern, which threatened the predominance of the gentry cavalry. Between 1630 and 1634 ten such regiments, totalling 17,400 men, were organized—almost half the army sent to capture Smolensk in 1632. After that campaign failed (primarily because of excessive interference from Moscow) and Filaret died, however, the regiments were disbanded and most mercenaries expelled from Muscovy.

Major reform in military organzation and weaponry was forced upon a reluctant regime by the need to combat the more technologically advanced and better organized armies of Sweden and Poland. In the mid-1640s Tsar Alexis' tutor and favorite, B. I. Morozov, an enthusiastic "Westernizer," revived foreign-style infantry regiments and established in Moscow new military chancelleries, which imposed changes to the last detail. The government, insisting that officers possess knowledge, ability, and experience, disregarded *mestnichestvo* (influence of noble birth and relatives) and traditional boyar privileges. At first most top posts went to foreigners, especially in new infantry and dragoon units. During the Thirteen Year War with Poland, as gentry cavalry and *streltsy* revealed their incapacity, the number of infantry armed with new flintlock muskets increased sharply. That war saw the definitive triumph in Muscovy of the "gunpowder revolution," which had swept Europe earlier, and the irreversible decline of the gentry cavalry. By 1681, with 81,000 infantry and only 45,000 cavalry on its roles, the army had increased greatly in size and was by far the largest force in Europe (more than 200,000 effectives). Even in peacetime the army consumed almost half the state budget. Most of the threefold increase in cost between 1630 and 1680 went to maintain regiments of foreign type and to pay their officers.

Anxious to make Muscovy self-sufficient in weapons, Michael's government modernized the Moscow Cannon Yard, the chief center for artillery manufacture. In 1632 Andrew Vinnius, a Dutch merchant, secured permission to construct and operate a major arms manufacturing plant at Tula, a pioneering effort in the development of Russian industry. By mid-century Russian artillery, now mainly of bronze, was becoming more standardized and accurate. The primitive Russian metallurgical industry, however, still could not supply fully the needs of a rapidly expanding army, and large imports of firearms from European lands were still required.

In the south Moscow created for the first time an effective system of border defenses against Crimean Tatar raids. In 1638 Prince Cherkasskii, governor of Tula, greatly reinforced its defenses. Soon afterwards a French Huguenot engineer designed the Belgorod Line, a formidable fortified network which secured central Muscovy and provided a base for penetration and colonization of the southern steppe. The obsolescent service gentry cavalry was left with little to do.

Such improvements in military organization, discipline, and weaponry prefigured the work of Peter I; though incomplete, they proved highly successful against Poland and the Crimean Tatars. In 1680, however, Muscovy still lacked a regular standing army (in peacetime only *streltsy* and officers cadres remained), and during campaigns "poor" gentry of uncertain skill and morale were still conscripted. Regiments of foreign type were filled by volunteers and by conscription from the peasantry, usually one recruit per 20 households, for infantry and dragoons. The large and costly Muscovite army remained inefficient and overcentralized compared to the Swedish army, and its commanders could not exercise much initiative.

EXPANSION

Major expansion to the east and south during the 17th century converted Muscovy into a multinational empire with vast resources. Whereas the conquest of Siberia had to overcome only negligible resistance, the struggle with Poland over the Ukraine strained the country's resources to the utmost and cost heavy casualties.

While the Time of Troubles temporarily reversed Muscovy's advance westward, the Russians surged east to build a huge Eurasian empire. Following up Ermak's conquests,[7] Muscovites by 1605 controlled the Ob basin with Tomsk as their outpost facing the Mongol-Kalmyk world.

---

[7] See above, p. 125.

The Troubles failed to slow an advance combining private enterprise and government action. Furs and adventure lured the Russians onward as their snares and traps, more sophisticated than native ones, depleted the numbers of fur-bearing animals in western Siberia. Hunters and Cossacks, following Siberia's interconnecting river systems, continually sought new territories. Private entrepreneurs, organizing primitive joint-stock companies with all members sharing in the returns, moved along the rivers in small armed bands. Forts built at strategic points subsequently grew into towns, and centralized administration and superior firepower crushed small-scale native revolts against extortion by Russian trappers and adventurers. In 1631 a Cossack force reached Lake Baikal; in 1638 an expedition arrived at the Pacific Ocean; and by 1650 Russia controlled nearly all of Siberia. In eastern Siberia the Russians encountered only scattered tribes: Tungus, Buriats, Mongols, Iakuts, and Paleo-Asiatic tribes engaged mainly in hunting, breeding reindeer, and raising cattle. Together they far outnumbered the invaders, but disunited and lacking firearms, most submitted voluntarily to Russian rule.

While losing some western provinces temporarily to Poland and Sweden, Russia was strengthened economically by its eastern acquisitions. In 1613 the Stroganovs, wealthy from Siberian furs, made a large loan to the Moscow treasury, and furs enriched the state and individual entrepreneurs. The government fostered mining and agriculture, and by 1645 some 8,000 peasant families had settled in western Siberia. Though criminals and war prisoners were employed in agriculture, the permanent Russian population was mostly peasants seeking free land who eventually produced a grain surplus in western Siberia. Iron mining began in the Tomsk and Kuznetsk areas, but no major efforts were made to develop Siberia's immense mineral resources until the late 19th century.

With a growing financial stake in Siberia, Moscow devoted attention to its administration, handled earlier by the Kazan Board. An independent Siberian Board, set up in 1637 and lasting until 1763, collected tribute systematically and improved communications. *Voevody* (governors) directly responsible to Moscow controlled Siberian towns, and the *voevoda* of Tobolsk coordinated their affairs and conducted relations with native peoples.

Russia's southward advance in Siberia caused friction with the new Manchu dynasty of China. Erofei Khabarov's expedition penetrated the Amur valley about 1650, yet few Russian settlers followed. Although Russian merchants and envoys visited China in the 1660s and 1670s, no regular relations resulted. After border clashes in the 1680s, Russia and China negotiated the Treaty of Nerchinsk (1689) (China's first treaty with a European power), confirming Russia's hold over Siberia but leaving the Amur region to China. For almost two centuries this frontier remained quite stable.

Until mid-century Moscovy remained mostly on the defensive in the west toward Sweden and Poland. By the Peace of Stolbovo (1617)

MAP 13–1
Russia's Eastward Expansion, 1598–1762

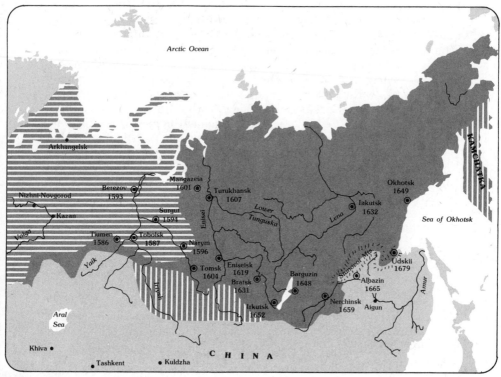

Russian territory 1598

Expansion in Asia 1598–1689

Expansion in Asia 1689–1762

Principal towns founded by
Russian settlers

Moscow recovered Novgorod but ceded towns on the Finnish Gulf to
Sweden, postponing indefinitely Russia's emergence as a Baltic power.
Wladyslaw of Poland failed to capture Moscow, but Russia by the
Truce of Deulino (1618) had to renounce strategic Smolensk. This poor
beginning reflected Russian weakness in the wake of the Troubles, but
provided a much needed breathing spell. When the truce expired in
1632, Muscovy attacked Smolensk, but the campaign ended disastrously. Surrounded by the Poles, Moscow's army surrendered and
its commander was executed. The "eternal peace" of 1634 confirmed
the Truce of Deulino though Wladyslaw finally renounced claims to the
throne of Muscovy.

Developments in the Ukraine—meaning the borderland—confronted Muscovy with perplexing and dangerous problems. The Ukraine, with Kiev as its political and cultural center, extended from southern Muscovy to the Black Sea, from the Carpathians eastward to the Don, and was divided among Poland-Lithuania, Muscovy, and the Crimean Tatars. Besides Ukrainians, descended from inhabitants of Kievan Russia, the region contained smaller groups of Poles, Belorussians, Great Russians, and Tatars. The Ukrainian Cossacks were its most volatile and warlike element. Cossack, a term probably of Turkic origin, meant free warriors or freebooters who first fought the Tatars in the steppe. Many Cossacks lacked permanent homes or occupations; others settled along south Russian rivers: the Dnieper, Don, and Volga. Impoverished boyar sons and peasants left Muscovy to join their ranks. The original Cossack country lay south of Moscow, around Tula and Riazan, until Muscovite and Polish colonization forced it further south. In 1570 the Don Cossacks, still virtually independent, agreed to serve Ivan IV. Poland secured a shadowy hold over the Dnieper Cossacks, and Polish and Lithuanian magnates enlisted them periodically in their service. Later the Cossack elite (*starshina*), becoming a regular paid frontier guard for Poland-Lithuania, received important privileges.

The Lublin Union of 1569, which led eventually to the Ukrainian revolt of 1648, joined Poland and Lithuania politically in an elective monarchy dominated by the Polish aristocracy (*szlachta*). Each portion had its own administration, army and laws, but in the western Ukraine Polish *szlachta* seized the richest lands and reduced the peasantry to serfdom. Within Poland-Lithuania, especially in the Ukraine, persecution of the Orthodox intensified. In 1596 the West Russian church split into an Orthodox organization and a Uniate church which accepted union with Rome; the two factions excommunicated each other. The Uniates, backed by Rome and Poland, persecuted the Orthodox and even desecrated their graves.

In the late 16th century militant Dnieper Cossacks created their own power center. On Khortitsa Island in the Dnieper, beyond the cataracts (*Zaporozhe*), they erected a fortified camp—the Sech—guarded by wooden ramparts studded with captured cannon, which became a refuge for Cossacks fleeing advancing Polish control. The "knighthood of the *Zaporozhe* Host," an exclusively male military-trading community, comprised marauders ready to plunder anyone for "Cossack bread." Ukrainian accounts idealize Sech democracy and patriotism, but early uprisings of these primitive Cossacks had few religious or national features.

Growing Polish pressure and Catholic-Uniate persecution helped unite Orthodox Ukrainians after 1596. As clergy and merchants sought Cossack and peasant support, an Orthodox hierarchy was restored in the Ukraine in 1620. Four years later Metropolitan Iov of Kiev, failing to secure rights for Orthodox from the Polish parliament (*seim*), requested Muscovite protection for the Ukraine. Because Moscow was then too weak and preoccupied to respond, Iov appealed to the *Zaporozhe* Cossacks to rally to a threatened Orthodoxy. These stateless ad-

MAP 13–2
Russian Expansion in Europe, 1618–1689

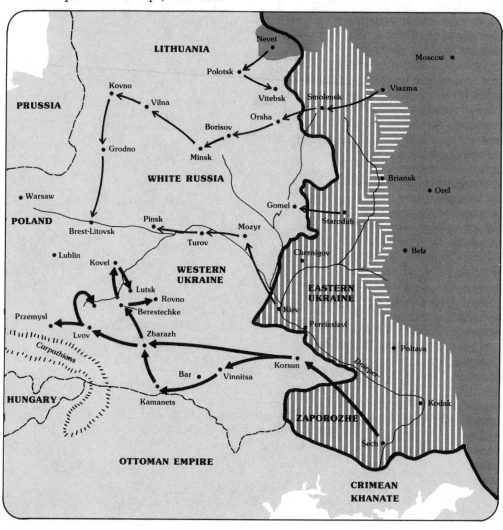

European Russia in 1618

Ceded to Russia by Peace of 1634

Ceded to Russia by Armistice of Andrusovo

Western boundary of Russia in 1689

Cossack revolt of 1648 led by Bogdan Khmelnitsky

Russo-Ukrainian advances against the Poles 1654–55

Adapted with permission of Macmillan Publishing Co., Inc. from *Russian History Atlas* by Martin Gilbert. Cartography by Martin Gilbert. Copyright © 1972 by Martin Gilbert.

venturers, becoming guardians of Orthodoxy and of Russian institutions in the Ukraine, sought to expel the Polish lords. As their authority increased along the mid-Dnieper, the Poles constructed Kodak fortress, which posed a threat to the nearby Sech's independence. In 1637–38 the *Zaporozhe* and most Cossacks in Polish service revolted unsuccessfully. The Poles virtually ended Sech autonomy, took registered Cossack lands, and forced unregistered Cossacks and Ukrainian peasants to choose between serfdom and rebellion.

The Poles sparked the great Ukrainian revolt of 1648. King Wladyslaw, seeking Cossack support against the Turks, promised to increase the number of registered Cossacks, but the Polish parliament refused to ratify this. Bogdan Khmelnitsky, a graduate of a Jesuit college and secretary of the Cossack army, was a delegate to the *seim* who favored expanding the Cossack forces and rights. Fleeing to the Sech, he was elected its leader (*hetman*) and, aided by the Crimean Tatars, led a massive Cossack revolt in 1648. Supported by the Ukrainian peasantry, his army defeated the Poles and entered Kiev in triumph. His Cossacks massacred hundreds of Jews in Ukrainian towns. Khmelnitsky had visions of ruling a greater Ukraine from the Don to the Vistula, but rising antagonism between peasants and ordinary Cossacks on the one side and registered Cossacks (*starshina*) on the other checked his soaring ambitions. The *starshina*, guarding their privileges against the lower classes, restricted the number of registered Cossacks. In 1649 Khmelnitsky made a peace with Poland which restored Cossack self-government and raised the number of registered Cossacks to 60,000; but when hostilities resumed, the Crimeans abandoned him and the Poles defeated him. Forced to accept a treaty which reduced Cossack territory and the number of registered Cossacks, he sought the protection of Moscow.

Tsar Alexis and his advisers hesitated, then negotiated cautiously with Khmelnitsky. To accept a protectorate of the Ukraine, they knew, would mean war with Poland. Among Ukrainians, ordinary Cossacks and peasants favored Muscovy; the *starshina*, having more in common with the Polish *szlachta*, opposed it. Moscow desired Cossack troops and its church needed Kiev's scholars and clergy. Nikon's selection as Russian patriarch[8] strengthened the unionist faction in Moscow, and in 1653 a *zemskii sobor* advised Alexis to become protector of the Ukraine.

At Pereiaslavl the Cossacks and a Muscovite grand embassy made final arrangements. Khmelnitsky told a Cossack assembly there: "We see that we can no longer live without a tsar." The Pereiaslavl Union placed the eastern Ukraine under Moscow's protection and confirmed the autonomy of the Sech, whose elected *hetman* could conduct foreign relations except with Poland and Turkey. Cossacks and Ukrainians swore allegiance to the tsar, but historians still debate whether this meant incorporation, vassaldom, or just military alliance for the Ukraine. Seeking to remain independent, Khmelnitsky continued to

---

[8] See below, p. 168.

Hetman Bogdan Khmelnitsky

wheel and deal in typical Cossack fashion with Sweden, Poland, and Transylvania. The Pereiaslavl Union produced the Thirteen Years War (1654–67) between Muscovy and Poland. Aided by Cossack forces and Sweden's invasion of Poland, the Russians captured Smolensk and much of Belorussia and the Ukraine. Alexis, seeking to unite all eastern Slavs, assumed the grandiose title: "Tsar of Great, Little, and White Russia." Then, to Khmelnitsky's dismay, Moscow made a truce with Poland and fought unsuccessfully against Sweden.

Khmelnitsky's death in 1657 plunged the Ukraine into chaos and civil war. A brave Cossack with a heroic capacity for vodka, he scarcely deserved subsequent accolades from nationalist Ukrainian historians, although he managed to preserve Ukrainian unity and some balance between the *starshina* and the rank and file. After his death they split irrevocably as his self-appointed successor, Ivan Vygovsky, representing the *starshina,* repudiated the accord with Moscow and reached agreement with Poland and the Crimea. Vygovsky defeated the Muscovites in 1659 only to be unseated by a revolt of ordinary Cossacks. The Ukraine divided: the "right bank," west of the Dnieper under Khmelnitsky's epileptic son, remained Polish; the "left bank" returned to Moscow's control. The Thirteen Years War dragged on at enormous cost to Russia and Poland and producing terrible devastation in the Ukraine until the Turco-Tatar threat induced them to stop fighting.

A farsighted boyar statesman, Afanasi Ordin-Nashchokin, engineered the Andrusovo armistice of 1667 and briefly altered Muscovite foreign policy. He favored peace and alliance with disintegrating Poland to break Sweden's stranglehold over the Baltic. At Andrusovo Russia gained Smolensk and Seversk provinces and the eastern Ukraine and occupied Kiev. After more warfare the "eternal peace" of 1686 confirmed these provisions. Because Belorussia reverted to Poland-Lithuania and the Ukraine was partitioned, Alexis failed to unite the eastern Slavs. Twenty-five years of bloody war gave Muscovy the eastern Ukraine and Kiev, but unable to penetrate the Swedish barrier, it remained blocked from the Baltic and Black seas. Muscovy joined a European coalition of Poland, the Holy Roman Empire, and Venice against the Turks and the Crimean khan, but Prince V. V. Golitsyn's ill managed Muscovite campaigns against the Crimea in the 1680s were dismal failures.

Muscovy's strength, prestige, and role in European affairs increased considerably under the early Romanovs. Its foreign relations grew more complex, and Moscow exchanged envoys with all important European states. Closer acquaintance with Europe caused imaginative Muscovite statesmen like Ordin-Nashchokin to question traditional methods and institutions and to use foreign models to overcome persisting Russian backwardness.

Suggested Additional Reading

BOOKS

DONNELLY, ALTON.   *The Russian Conquest of Bashkiria, 1552–1740* (New Haven, 1968).

FISHER, R. H.   *The Russian Fur Trade, 1550–1700* (Berkeley, 1943).

HELLIE, R.   *Enserfment and Military Change in Muscovy* (Chicago, 1971).

HERBERSTEIN, S. VON.   *Description of Moscow and Muscovy* (London, 1969, reprint).

KERNER, R. J.   *The Urge to the Sea* . . . (Berkeley, 1942).

KLYUCHEVSKY, V. O.   *A Course in Russian History: the Seventeenth Century,* transl. N. Duddington (Chicago, 1968).

LANTZEFF, GEORGE.   *Siberia in the Seventeenth Century* (Berkeley, 1943).

LANTZEFF, MARK.   *Russia and China* . . . *to 1728* (Cambridge, Mass., 1971).

O'BRIEN, C. B.   *Muscovy and the Ukraine* . . . *1654–1687* (Berkeley, 1963).

TREADGOLD, DONALD.   *The Great Siberian Migration* (Princeton, 1957).

ARTICLES

KEEP, J. H.   "The Decline of the Zemsky Sobor," *SEER,* vol. 36 Dec. 1957, pp. 100–22.

———.   "The Regime of Filaret, "1619–1633," *SEER,* vol. 38, 1959–60, pp. 334–60.

LOEWENSON, L.   "The Moscow Rising of 1648," *SEER,* vol. 27, 1948–49, pp. 146–56.

MAZOUR, A. G.   "Curtains in the Past," *JMH,* vol. 20, 1948, pp. 212–22.

PHILLIP, W.   "Russia: The Beginning of Westernization," *New Cambr. Modern History,* vol. 5 ch. 25, pp. 571–91.

14

The Early Romanovs: Society Culture, and Religion

THE 17TH CENTURY was an age of momentous social, cultural, and religious change in Muscovite Russia. It was a period of transition in which traditional values and attitudes were challenged and tested by foreign influences, which increased throughout the century, marking a gradual rapprochement between Muscovy and the West. The shock of the Time of Troubles had seriously undermined the state's material well-being and shaken popular confidence in historic traditions and customs. The resulting breakdown of old modes of thought created uncertainty and tension but also a more receptive atmosphere for the spread of foreign influences. Muscovite Russia's confrontation with the West was destined to be neither peaceful nor tranquil. Spreading foreign influences and growing consciousness of the world beyond the borders of Muscovy affected directly or indirectly almost every facet of Muscovite life.

During the Troubles foreigners had entered Russia in unprecedented numbers. Russians had regular and extensive contact with Poles, Swedes, Germans, and many others. Although remaining suspicious of foreigners, Russians were impressed by superior Western technology and captivated by the diverse and spontaneous Western culture. Perceptive Russians realized that if Muscovy were to recover and progress, it must learn from more knowledgeable, skilled, and sophisticated Europeans, especially in the vital field of military technology.

Similarly, after the Troubles the impoverished Russian economy allowed foreign capital and entrepreneurs to gain a firm foothold. Along with much needed capital came many foreign merchants— English, Dutch, and German—who rapidly acquired control of a substantial portion of Russian business activity. The influx of foreigners, both merchants and officers, elicited opposition from native Russians who found it difficult to compete with them. Russian merchants grumbled that English merchants with superior organization, knowledge, and experience were becoming too rich, powerful, and influential; that Russian merchants were losing out in commercial transactions. In a formal petition of 1627 Russian merchants begged the government

165

to prohibit foreigners from engaging in Russian internal trade and to monitor foreigners' activities more closely so as to control widespread bribery, deception, and fraud against their Russian counterparts. Official efforts to regulate foreign merchants had little effect because the foreigners were already firmly entrenched, and, more important, the government and the economy depended on their commercial and industrial skills. Most of the few manufactories of 17th century Muscovy were established directly by foreigners or with their capital, advice, and skill.

The merchants sought aid from other social groups to combat European influences. The service gentry, dissatisfied with the dominant role of foreign officers in Russian military affairs, resented being commanded by European officers. At the *zemskii sobor* of 1648–49, merchants and service gentry persuaded the government to recognize the problem of foreign influences.

In 1652 the government, using a plan initiated by Ivan IV in the 1570s, set up a foreign settlement outside of Moscow where foreigners were required to reside and do business in isolation from the Russian population. This foreign ghetto (*nemetskaia sloboda*) was to influence Russian development more profoundly than if foreigners had been allowed to operate and live freely in diverse parts of Russia. It became, noted Kliuchevskii, "a corner of Western Europe sheltering in an eastern suburb of Moscow," a full and tangible example of the diversity of European life. This foreign settlement housed a school, several Protestant churches, practical, well laid-out European houses and streets, and an aura of bustle and activity. From this "corner" Western culture and customs were transmitted to the Russians.

The spread of foreign influences captivated the imagination of certain enlightened Russians but raised disturbing doubts in the minds of more conservative, traditional segments of society, particularly among clergymen, who feared that Protestant and Catholic influences might undermine the purity of the Orthodox faith and popular morality. These fears, coupled with a nagging disquietude about Russian religious traditions, caused complex and explosive religious controversies within the Orthodox Church and among the laity, culminating in a great church schism.

The 17th century religious problem involved interconnected issues which reflected Russia's changing social, political, and cultural values. On the religious level, controversy developed over proposed changes in church liturgy and ritual. On the political side a great clash occurred between church and state, tsar and patriarch, which altered traditional relationships. The religious issue also reflected growing social tensions, as the lower classes particularly protested the growing expansion and secularization of state power and focused their anger and frustration on the question of church reform. The religious controversy reflected a deeper fear that the unique Russian civilization might be destroyed by subtly advancing foreign influences. To many, traditional ways, customs, and attitudes had to be preserved even at the cost of open resistance to the state.

For centuries controversies and heresies, such as the *strigolniki* (shorn heads) and Judaizers in Novgorod, had challenged the spiritual authority of the official Church. These heresies apparently were stimulated by Western ideas filtering into Western-oriented Novgorod. While combating these movements, the Church became suspicious and intolerant of deviations from established practice, however minor, and professed a missionary zeal in defending Orthodox purity. The elaboration of the Third Rome theory expressed the messianic mission of the Russian Church to maintain Orthodox purity throughout the world. Because, according to the theory, there would be no fourth Rome, Moscow became the last bastion of true Christianity.

Besides, the controversy between the followers of Joseph of Volokolamsk and Nil Sorskii[1] developed awareness of the need to increase the number of religious works available in Church Slavonic translation in Muscovy. To this end the government sought knowledgeable translators abroad. A learned monk from Mt. Athos in Greece, the center of Orthodox monasticism, who responded to this call was Maxim the Greek. Arriving in Moscow in 1518, he was drawn immediately into the religious controversies centering on political and economic questions. Drawing on the spiritual intensity of the monastic traditions of Mt. Athos, Maxim joined the ascetic followers of Nil Sorskii and argued for a spiritually revitalized clergy and a Church unencumbered by political and economic concerns. While translating from Greek into Church Slavonic, Maxim discovered numerous errors · which had crept into Russian church books over the centuries. His findings raised disturbing doubts about the Third Rome's Orthodox purity, doubts which were deepened during the 16th century by visiting Greek prelates who criticized Russian practices deviating from Byzantine custom. Despite growing awareness of divergence between Russian and Greek practice, even cautious and tentative efforts at reform met bitter criticism and denunciation. The atmosphere in early 17th century Muscovy was uneasy, uncertain, and tense, hardly a time to begin difficult and dangerous church reform. Later, new impetus for reform came from an unexpected source: Kiev.

The Grand Duchy of Lithuania under the Lublin Union of 1569 relinquished to Poland control of the Dnieper River basin, an area populated by peasants and Cossacks who were at least nominally Orthodox but were separated politically and ecclesiastically from Orthodox Muscovy. Thus the patriarch of Constantinople consecrated a metropolitan for this West Russian Orthodox Church to provide the faithful with spiritual guidance and strengthen the administrative structure of the Church. The years after the Lublin Union were difficult ones for the Orthodox population in Polish territory. In the mid-16th century the religious ferment of the Reformation had penetrated Poland and stimulated a strong Jesuit effort to suppress Protestantism in Poland. The Jesuits, after achieving this with support from the Polish government, pressured the Orthodox under Polish rule to acknowledge Papal

---

[1] See above, p. 104.

authority. Their proselytizing activity was so intense that some Orthodox bishops, fearing the destruction of the West Russian Orthodox
Church, consented to union with Rome provided the Eastern ritual and
use of Church Slavonic in the services were preserved. These bishops,
winning support from the Orthodox metropolitan in Kiev, dispatched a
delegation to Rome to negotiate an agreement which split the West
Russian Orthodox Church.

Once part of the West Russian Orthodox Church had united with
Rome, the Poles increased pressure on the Orthodox remaining under
their rule. The Orthodox clergy tried to counter this new offensive but
were ill prepared to oppose the incomparably more learned and dynamic
Jesuits. Realizing the notorious educational shortcomings of the clergy,
the Orthodox metropolitan of Kiev, Peter Mogila, in 1631 established
a Kievan Academy "for the teaching of free sciences in the Greek,
Slavonic, and Latin languages." Theology, philosophy, natural science,
and scriptural criticism together with foreign languages were the main
courses taught at this unprecedented educational institution. A new
generation of broadly educated and sophisticated monks was produced,
many of whom eventually went to Moscow and the patriarchal printing
office where their scholarly skills and spiritual intensity contributed to
growing religious disquietude in the Russian capital. During their
studies and activity as translators, these scholarly monks noted once
again the numerous errors in the Russian service books and ritual. By
mid-century the pressure for reform was mounting, but the rapid change
and widespread social unrest of this period made it unlikely that any
reform movement would succeed. The Russian Patriarch Nikon, however,
would take up the reform of ritual and church books with great vigor
beginning in 1654.

The extremely volatile religious issue became further complicated by
the introduction of political questions. During Michael Romanov's
reign the traditional pattern of church-state relations with the secular
ruler ascendant had been disrupted. In 1619 Michael's father, Filaret,
became Russian patriarch. A diarchy was established with patriarch
and tsar, father and son, as equals in rank, dignity, and power, marking a significant departure from the traditional Byzantine pattern.
This relationship ceased with Filaret's death in 1633, but a precedent
had been created which would contribute much to a direct collision
between church and state under Tsar Alexis.

To growing religious and political tensions were added deep social
frictions, outgrowths of the rigid social structure embodied in the Law
Code of 1649 (*Ulozhenie*) and the formalization of serfdom. Reflecting
growing secularization and bureaucratization of life, these frictions
contributed to growing restlessness, confusion, hatred and violence
which culminated in local rebellions affecting much of Muscovy.[2]
Church reform was the catalyst which ignited this tension into
flames of conflict.

In Russian Christianity from its inception, form had been more important than content, ritual had taken precedence over theological

---

[2] See below, pp. 175–76.

content or substance. For most of the Orthodox faithful *how* one performed the ritual and liturgy was far more important than the ideas behind them. Even minor changes in ritual could therefore become matters of life and death, salvation and damnation.

In 1652 Patriarch Joseph died and Tsar Alexis chose as his successor the metropolitan of Novgorod, Nikon, one of the most remarkable religious figures of the 17th century. Born a humble peasant, in 1605 admidst the turmoil of the Time of Troubles, Nikita Minov was intelligent and ambitious, and chose the only upwardly mobile path for one of low social origin, the priesthood. Soon, however, he felt that as a parish priest his talents were being wasted. Persuading his wife to enter a convent, he took monastic vows under the name Nikon.

Nikon was well suited for the rigors of monastic life because he accepted the ascetic views of the Trans-Volga Elders. His spiritual intensity, imposing physical stature (reputedly he was six feet six), and hypnotic personality brought him to his superiors' attention and promoted his rapid rise in monastic ranks. Named archimandrite of a small monastery in the far north in 1643, he visited Moscow in 1646, and as a visiting prelate was presented to Tsar Alexis. The young, devout tsar succumbed to the spell of Nikon's personality and insisted that he remain in Moscow as archimandrite of Novospasskii Monastery, which housed the Romanov family burial vault. Gradually, Alexis became dependent on Nikon's spiritual guidance. In 1648 Alexis appointed Nikon metropolitan of Novgorod, the second highest post in the Church hierarchy. As a member of the devout circle of young clergymen gathering around Alexis, Nikon had acquired a reputation as a reformer. These young clergymen, the Zealots of Piety, including Stefan Vonifatiev (the tsar's confessor), Ivan Neronov, and Simeon Avvakum, sought to revive the Orthodox Church spiritually, to enliven dead forms of Orthodox observance, to deepen communication between the clergy and the laity, and to make more tangible the teachings of Christ. Seeking to maintain the national peculiarities of Russian Orthodoxy, these reformers rejected the arguments of Kievan scholars. Russian practice differed from the Greek, they claimed, because Moscow was the Third Rome, the last center of true Orthodox Christianity. Nikon preached this doctrine in Novgorod and became wholly committed to the need for a religious revival.

While still in Novgorod, Nikon, recognizing that if reform were to be successful, the Church needed strong leadership, state support, and internal cohesion, sought to enhance its power and prestige. He persuaded Alexis to transfer the relics of Metropolitan Philip, murdered by order of Ivan IV, to Moscow. Philip was a symbol of the Church's moral authority and a folk hero to the people. Nikon prepared to assert Church authority, if need be, even over the state. He imposed rigid ecclesiastical discipline in Novgorod region as a pattern for the entire Church.

Nikon's autocratic methods in Novgorod and close relationship with Greek prelates worried his friends among the Zealots of Piety. Nikon was also urging reform in order to make Russian practices conform to Greek ones. His new views may have stemmed from ambition and the desire to win support from influential Greek prelates. Alexis, still enchanted by Nikon, ignored the protests of the Zealots and offered Nikon the patriarchal throne.

Aware of opposition to his candidacy and clerical antagonism toward him, Nikon demurred until a public demonstration of support was engineered on his behalf. Before agreeing to become patriarch, he insisted upon a free hand to organize and administer the Church. He observed:

> Now if you promise to keep the evangelical dogmas, and to observe the canons of the holy apostles and the holy fathers, and the laws of the pious emperors and tsars; if you allow me to organize the Church, then I shall no longer refuse the supreme archbishopric according to your wish.[3]

He was demanding total subservience of the tsar and the entire population to his will. Nikon's intention was to make Russian Church practices conform with Greek ones. "I am Russian and the son of a Russian," he declared, "but my faith and convictions are Greek."

To implement such a controversial and potentially disruptive reform program required the authority of the earlier diarchy of Michael Romanov and Filaret. Alexis, inexperienced and spiritually dependent, granted Nikon many powers which Filaret had exercised. Immediately Nikon asserted Church independence from secular control and ignored legal provisions of the *Ulozhenie* of 1649 which limited the Church's economic and juridical powers. He increased patriarchal land holdings, which had unlimited power over 120,000 peasant households. At first Alexis did not challenge Nikon's inroads on secular power.

Nikon threw himself eagerly into Church reform. He ordered changes in the service books, in the spelling of certain key words, ordered the sign of the cross to be made with three instead of two fingers, and other minor changes not involving basic questions of dogma. According to N. Kapterev, leading historian of the Church schism, Nikon instituted in Russia "the Greek ambos (pulpit), the Greek episcopal cross, Greek capes and cowls, and Greek plainchant melodies. He welcomed Greek painters and goldsmiths; he began to build monasteries on the Greek model; he had Greek friends whose advice he heeded." The national Russian Church was being reByzantized. As the Third Rome bowed to the fallen Second Rome (Constantinople), Nikon's actions were bitterly criticized by defenders of the national Russian religious tradition. His former friend, Ivan Neronov, admonished him:

> You approve foreigners' laws and accept their doctrines, and yet it was you who used to tell us constantly that the Greeks and Little Russians had lost their faith and their strength and that their ways were evil. Now they are for you saints and masters of religion.[4]

Opposition developed among the clergy and the faithful who considered Nikon's actions arbitrary and needless.

Challenges to his spiritual authority as patriarch caused Nikon,

---

[3] Quoted in W. K. Medlin, *Moscow and East Rome* (Geneva, Switz., 1952), p. 169.

[4] Quoted in P. N. Miliukov, *Ocherki po istorii russkoi kultury* (Paris, 1931), vol. 2, part 1, p. 45.

during Alexis' absence on campaign, to assert strong claims to secular power in order to force through his reforms. Initially supporting him on Church reform, Alexis grew apprehensive about Nikon's arrogance and appropriation of secular powers. As the patriarch sought omnipotence in both religious and secular spheres, he threatened the integrity of the secular state. In July 1658 Tsar Alexis, finally asserting his traditional autocratic powers, informed Nikon that the diarchy had ended. This action of Alexis shattered Nikon's ambition to lift the Church above the state. Believing he could negotiate from a position of power, Nikon left Moscow and renounced the patriarchal title, hoping like Ivan IV to be invited back on his own terms. Alexis, however, now more independent, refused to request his return. Nikon then claimed he had not resigned but had merely ceased to be patriarch "in Moscow." From self-imposed exile he asserted openly that ecclesiastical authority was superior to secular authority. For eight years this conflict remained unresolved because Alexis took no action.

Nikon's reforms were enforced against growing opposition centering around the Zealots of Piety, Avvakum and his friends. The Old Ritualists or Old Believers as they were called, argued that if Moscow were the Third Rome, reform was unnecessary. The Second Rome had fallen into heresy by adhering to the Florentine Union, and its religious

Patriarch Nikon

inheritance had passed to Moscow. Why, Avvakum asked, should Russian practices conform with those of a church which had rejected pure Orthodoxy? If reforms were necessary, then the Muscovite Church had fallen into error and no longer was the true center of Orthodoxy. Because there could be no fourth Rome, the end of the world must be near and salvation was no longer possible. Acceptance or rejection of the reforms became literally a matter of life and death.

A church council convened in 1666 with Alexis' blessing ending the impasse. Nikon was formally deprived of his title, demoted to simple monk, and banished to a remote northern monastery. The struggle between church and state was settled in favor of the state. The council rejected Nikon's extreme claims of church superiority and endorsed the traditional Byzantine formula of the symphony of church and state. Subsequently the Church would fall increasingly under state control.

The Council of 1666, while rejecting Nikon's political claims, accepted and endorsed his reforms, making failure to conform a civil and an ecclesiastical offense. This formalized the Church schism because many Russians rejected the reforms, minor as they may appear, and clung tenaciously to the old ways. Few upper-class Russians became Old Believers; the Schism drew its chief support from the peasantry, parish priests (themselves of lower class origin), and some merchants. Thus the Schism acquired a distinctive social quality. To defend themselves and their principles, Old Believers resorted to flight, passive resistance, and sometimes self-immolation.

The Old Believers remained a disruptive element, often refusing to pay taxes or serve in the army. Continuing to struggle against foreign influences, they came to believe that the sovereign, particularly Peter the Great, was Antichrist. Meanwhile the official Church fell more and more under state control. The result was a breakdown of the Byzantine cultural tradition as the conservative, inner-directed Muscovite ideology succumbed to external influences. To become a modern European nation, Russia first had to be released from the rigid Byzantine cultural tradition. The greatest legacy of the Schism was to open the way for the successful program of Westernization and modernization of Peter I.[5]

Because of the Schism and the accompanying bitter sectarian controversy, the Russian Church, as Billington points out, lost its spiritual vitality and moral authority. The Byzantine tradition could not withstand the pressures of rapid social, cultural and political change. The task of creating a new, more modern and viable secular culture, begun before Peter, fell to the state. Peter's program of sustained modernization would have been inconceivable without prior weakening of the Byzantine heritage.

Soviet historians explain the Schism mainly by citing the sharpening social contradictions of the 17th century and by emphasizing the rigid social structure and extension of state power into most aspects of Russian life under the Law Code of 1649. They conclude that lower-class elements used the issue of Church reform to express discontent

---

[5] See below, pp. 185, 192 ff.

Armed Russian peasants, 17th century

with an oppressive Muscovite bureaucratic system. The issues of Church reform and the formalization of serfdom undoubtedly became blurred for many who saw their spiritual and personal freedoms circumscribed by arbitrary government action. Old Believers, refusing to integrate themselves into the new secularized state, would remain a disruptive dissident group.

For all classes, particularly the lower classes, life was becoming more difficult and restricted. Service gentry, peasants, and townsmen all found their obligations to the state carefully elaborated in the Law Code of 1649. This code confirmed the completion of the long process of the enserfment of the peasantry. Hardly any other institution of pre-revolutionary Russia has been studied as thoroughly and elicited as much controversy as serfdom. Just how did this institution arise? What made it necessary?

Historians disagree on precisely how serfdom was imposed on the Russian peasantry and especially on the government's role in this enserfment. In the 18th century such historians as Tatishchev argued that government, by a series of decrees, gradually enserfed the rural population. Other historians argued that the state's role was minor, and that environmental factors such as long-term residency and rapid growth of peasant indebtedness produced serfdom. Until recently Soviet historians have contended that the Russian peasant had been a serf from the start of the Kievan era.

We have seen that during Kievan times a certain group of peasants, the *zakupy*, had their rights limited, but only temporarily.[6] The *zakupy*

---

[6] See above, pp. 41–42.

cannot be considered serfs in the technical sense. Gradually, however, the peasantry's social and economic status deteriorated and the basically free institutions of Kiev yielded to social and economic restrictions. In Kievan times peasants lived in free communes, working land owned by the commune cooperatively. In the Mongol era these communes had to pay tribute, which was collected by the Russian princes acting as the khan's agents. Responsibility for tax collection gave local princes certain administrative and judicial powers over the communes. As a centralized state formed under Moscow, the prince of Moscow made large land grants to noblemen and church officials in return for their support of centralization. More and more land formerly owned by free peasant communes passed into the hands of private individuals or church institutions, thus transforming peasants from free owners of land into renters. These communes had to pay taxes to the prince of Moscow and rent to the landlord, usually a nobleman.

Peasant obligations to landlords consisted of either cash payments or payments in kind (*obrok*) or labor service (*barshchina*). Despite the growing weight of these obligations, the individual peasant was free to move about as he wished, being bound neither to the land, the person of the landlord, nor even to the peasantry as a class. The individual could leave the countryside altogether and take up residence in a town. This very freedom of movement, however, began to work against the long-term interests of the peasant class. Princes and landlords were dependent on peasant labor, which produced much of the revenue vital to upper class political power and economic well-being. Informal princely-landlord agreements prevented peasants from being lured from one estate to another by more favorable terms.

By about 1500 it was clear that informal agreements were inadequate to curb peasant mobility and compensate for insufficient labor. Ivan III's *Sudebnik* (law code) of 1497 reduced the freedom of peasant movement to a brief period each year—the two weeks around St. George's Day, November 26—a major step toward serfdom. The peasant who chose to leave then had to fulfill all his legal obligations to the landlord and pay a sizable exit fee. Furthermore, dues and services demanded from peasants increased significantly during the 16th century. Peasant indebtedness rose sharply until it became virtually impossible for peasants to leave their landowners, even in the allowable period around St. George's Day.

Another factor detrimental to the peasant was the rapid growth of *pomestie* land tenure in the late 15th and 16th centuries. As the Muscovite state expanded, so did the need for administrators and army officers. Unable to pay these servitors, the government rewarded them with temporary grants of land (*pomestie*) to be held and exploited during the term of service. Such land grants were valuable only if there were peasants available to work the land. The service gentry, whose economic well-being and state service depended on successful management of their estates, clamored for rigid restrictions on peasant mobility. Despite growing economic burdens and legal restrictions, peasants could still be transferred to the estates of wealthy magnates by "exportation" (*vyvoz*), which deprived the service gentry of labor power on their lands. Many peasants also escaped by flight, and many fled during the economic and political chaos during the reign of Ivan IV.

Massive peasant flight and "exportation" threatened the entire *pomestie* system and the army. Ivan IV had to restrict further the peasants' right of departure by tying them permanently to the land. In 1570 Ivan began experimenting with a plan to prevent peasant movement. Peasants in designated regions of Novgorod were prohibited from moving for any reason during 1570. A decade later the concept of the "prohibited year" was applied on a national scale, and almost every year thereafter was "prohibited." Occasionally, a "free year" would be decreed, but not after 1602. Though certain refinements were required, peasants had virtually lost the right to move and serfdom was a fact. Initially, the law decreed a five-year recovery period for a fugitive peasant: he could be tracked down and forcibly returned to the estate within five years from his flight. Later, the recovery period was extended to ten, then 15 years, and finally abolished altogether, making a fugitive peasant subject to forcible return any time.

The *Ulozhenie* of 1649 confirmed and codified these measures. All peasants' names were to be included in government registers, which legally attached peasants to the estate where they resided when the registers were compiled. To be sure, the peasant serf was not a slave, and slavery continued to coexist with serfdom. The landowner's power over the peasant's person increased until the distinction between slave and serf virtually disappeared. The serf had no legal means to protect himself against arbitrary actions by his master; his only recourse was flight or violence. The serf owner could make a field serf into a domestic or household serf; eventually the serf could be sold without land, families were separated, and serfs were subjected to corporal punishment and physical abuse.

Thus the overwhelming majority of the Russian population was finally enserfed. Peasants made up about 90 percent of the total population, and at least three quarters of them were affected directly by the *Ulozhenie's* provisions. Serfdom was imposed from above by government decree to answer the needs of the state and the service class, which comprised the backbone of the Muscovite army, the government's chief support in times of crisis.

Enserfment of the peasantry and growing restrictions on other classes contributed to great social turmoil in 17th century Muscovy. Around mid-century occurred a series of scattered urban revolts. In 1648 in Moscow the populace rose against the onerous salt tax and rule by unpopular, tyrannical favorites. An angry mob besieged Tsar Alexis in the Kremlin until he dismissed his chief favorite, Boris Morozov, and yielded two others to popular vengeance. Subsequent revolts in Pskov and Novgorod expressed similar lower class grievances against local boyars and Muscovite tyranny. After the government debased the coinage by substituting copper for silver (1656), numerous disorders broke out in 1662, especially in Moscow. The Muscovite autocracy repressed all these lower class movements ruthlessly.

Stepan Razin

The culmination of this general mood of discontent was a massive insurrection in the Don and Volga regions under Stepan (Stenka) Razin between 1667 and 1671. Like the Bolotnikov rising earlier,[7] this was a movement of the turbulent frontier—the "Wild Field"—against the center, led by a Don Cossack of outstanding military ability, Stepan Razin, from an established Cossack family near Cherkassk. He had served the Cossack Host loyally in diplomacy and war before becoming a leader of the downtrodden. The historian N. Kostomarov noted that Razin was a man of "enormous will and impulsive activity, . . . now stern and gloomy, now working himself into a fury, now given up to drunken carousing, now ready to suffer any hardship with superhuman endurance."[8] The upheaval began, as had Bolotnikov's, in frontier urban settlements (*posady*), crowded with drifters, thieves, and laborers, impoverished and resentful of government impositions. Escaped peasants who had pressed into Don Cossack settlements resisted Moscow's efforts to recover them for their gentry masters. Initially, Razin's army, destroying local government forces, sought booty along the Volga River and the shores of the Caspian Sea. After seizing Astrakhan in 1669, Razin appealed to the poor to join him in a war against the rich, boyars, and officialdom to achieve freedom for the common man. As he advanced up the Volga, thousands of peasants flocked to his banners and numerous manor houses were burned. Finally, Razin's motley forces were defeated at Simbirsk by government troops, and he was turned over to the authorities by Cossack elders. He was tortured horribly, quartered, and his body was thrown to the dogs. Again the Muscovite regime wiped out popular revolt brutally, but the indomitable Razin remained a legend, a Robin Hood, to the oppressed lower classes of Russia.

[7] See above, p. 144.

[8] P. Avrich, *Russian Rebels, 1600–1800* (New York, 1972), p. 69.

The reign of Tsar Alexis witnessed the rejection of Muscovy's old religious ideology, the Byzantine tradition, and the imposition on society of a straitjacket by the state. These were crucial prerequisites for the full-scale program of modernization and secularization of Peter the Great. The existence of serfdom would mean, however, that modernization of the state would create a psychological schism between the upper classes and the mass of the people. Under the impact of Westernization a great cultural cleavage would open up in Russian society that would make understanding and communication between educated society and the masses well nigh impossible until the latter 19th century. This was the legacy of the momentous social, cultural, and religious developments of the seventeenth century.

Suggested Additional Reading

ANDREYEV, N.   *Studies in Muscovy* (London, 1970).

AVVAKUM, S.   *The Life of the Archpriest Avvakum by Himself* (London, 1924, 1968).

BOLSHAKOFF, S.   *Russian Nonconformity* . . . (Philadelphia, 1950).

CHERNIAVSKY, M.   "The Old Believers and the New Religion," *SR*, vol. 25 (1966), pp. 1–39.

CONYBEARE, F.   *Russian Dissenters* (Cambridge, Mass., 1921).

CRUMMEY, R. O.   *The Old Believers and the World of AntiChrist* (Madison, Wisc. 1970).

HELLIE, R.   *Enserfment and Military Change in Muscovy* (Chicago, 1971).

KEEP, J. H.   "The Regime of Filaret (1619–1633)," *SEER*, vol. 38 (1960), pp. 334–60.

LOEWENSON, L.   "The Moscow Rising of 1648," *SEER*, vol. 27 (1948), pp. 146–56.

MEDLIN, W. K.   *Moscow and East Rome* . . . (Geneva, 1952).

———.   *Renaissance Influences and Religious Reforms in Russia* (Geneva, 1971).

O'BRIEN, C. B.   "Agriculture in Russian War Economy in the Later Seventeenth Century," *ASEER*, vol. 8 (1949), pp. 167–74.

PALMER, W.   *The Patriarch and the Tsar.* 6 vols. (London, 1871–76).

SPINKA, M.   "Nikon and the Subjugation of the Russian Church to the State," *Church History*, vol. 10 (1941), pp. 347–66.

WOODCOCK, G. and I. AVAKUMOVIC.   *The Doukhobors* (New York, 1968).

ZENKOVSKY, S.   "The Old Believer Avvakum . . . ," *ISS*, vol. 1 (1956), pp. 1–51.

———.   "The Russian Church Schism . . . , *Rus. Rev.*, vol. 16 (1957), pp. 37–58.

part II

Early Imperial Russia, 1689–1855

THE HISTORY of early imperial Russia begins with the country's partial Westernization by the reforms of Peter the Great, a dynamic ruler building upon the work of early Romanov predecessors. The Russian Empire is forged in wars which impose a staggering burden upon a peasantry shackled in serfdom more oppressive than any in Europe. A small, Westernized elite of noblemen centering in the new capital, St. Petersburg, on the shores of the Baltic is set apart increasingly from the illiterate, impoverished masses. In the late 18th century Catherine the Great, ruling with a privileged nobility, fosters the emergence of a small intelligentsia imbued with Western ideals of humanitarian reform while her victorious armies partition Poland and humiliate the Ottoman Empire. Under Alexander I, Russia plays an ultimately decisive part in the Napoleonic Wars and finally encompasses the French emperor's defeat and downfall. In 1815 Imperial Russia reaches the peak of its power and prestige, which conceals grievous economic backwardness and unsolved social problems. Ten years later the Decembrists inaugurate the organized Russian revolutionary movement, but their failure brings to power the "Iron Tsar," Nicholas I, whose regime epitomizes the full development of autocracy and police power. Russia's defeat in the Crimean War, however, confirms her economic underdevelopment and sounds the death knell of serfdom.

15

Peter the Great—Politics, War, and Diplomacy

THE REIGN of Peter the Great (1689–1725) marked the culmination of a century of developing autocratic power, deepening serfdom and secularization of Russian life. War, centralization, and relations with Europe remained the focal points of Russian foreign and domestic policies, the basic guidelines of which had been set during the 17th century. Peter I's education, interests, and approach, however, differed radically from those of his predecessors. Unlike them, he exercised fully the absolute power they had constructed. Under his dynamic leadership, the significance of which historians dispute,[1] Russia acquired a well organized, powerful army, which enabled her to become a great European power, and a better integrated administration and diplomatic corps. The Church was wholly subordinated to the state, eliminating the last restriction on the ruler's authority. The shift of the capital northward to St. Petersburg symbolized the great changes which overtook Russia under Peter. In order to support the lengthy war against Sweden, the entire financial and political structure had to be overhauled, not according to any blueprint, but usually by trial and error. Were the reforms of Peter I mainly the work of a uniquely talented, unusually energetic ruler or the result of long historical development? Did war requirements trigger the changes and determine their form? Were the reforms so drastic as to make this a revolutionary era? Were they original and Russian or mainly borrowings from more advanced western Europe? Finally, did they set Russia onto the path of greatness and material progress or bring suffering and ruin to the Russian people? To attempt answers, we must examine Peter's education and character, his wars and diplomacy, and the military and administrative changes of his regime.

PETER'S YOUTH AND TRIP TO THE WEST

Peter I grew up in a confused, transitional epoch of violence and intrigue resembling in some ways the minority of Ivan IV. Innovative

---

[1] See Problem 4 below, pp. 196–200.

Western ideas and institutions clashed with traditional Muscovite ones. In the Kremlin's myriad apartments, court factions centering on the two wives of Tsar Alexis contended. The first was Maria Miloslavskii whose children included Fedor, the weak-witted Ivan, and six daughters of whom Sofia was the eldest. After Maria's death, Alexis married Natalia Naryshkin from an obscure country family, who in 1672 gave birth to Peter. Temporarily the Naryshkins displaced the Miloslavskiis, but for two decades these royal clans waged a bitter struggle for power which made court life turbulent and bloody. Tsar Alexis died when Peter was only four, and Maria Miloslavskii's weak, ineffective eldest son became tsar as Fedor II (1676–82). Until he was ten Peter was brought up in a traditional way in the Kremlin, tutored by Nikita Zotov, a gentle clerk who loved vodka, instructed him none too well in reading and writing, and introduced him to Russian history.

Tsar Fedor's death in April 1682 caused a succession crisis complicated by the Naryshkin-Miloslavskii feud. An improvised *zemskii sobor* (assembly) dominated by the Patriarch and the Naryshkins, proclaimed Peter tsar and his mother regent. Conservative *streltsy* (musketeers) loyal to the Miloslavskiis reacted with fury. There was no regular law of succession, but according to Muscovite tradition, Ivan, a Miloslavskii, as the elder brother, should have been named tsar. In May, amidst rumors that Ivan had been murdered, angry *streltsy*, numbering over 20,000 in Moscow; revolted, some burst into the Kremlin, and in Peter's presence murdered some Naryshkin adherents. After three days of rioting and bloodshed, they departed leaving the Miloslavskii faction in power. Ivan V and Peter I were proclaimed joint tsars with their elder sister, Sofia, as regent. Henceforth Peter loathed the Kremlin for its intrigue, court factionalism, and traditionalism.

Between 1682 and 1689, Sofia acted as Russia's first female sovereign since Princess Olga. A bulky, unattractive, sensual woman, Sofia was also intelligent, well educated (most unusual in those times), strong-willed, and insatiably ambitious. Gaining control of the unruly *streltsy*, she had their principal commander, Prince Ivan Khovanskii, apprehended and executed. She ruled with her cultivated, pro-Western but indecisive lover, Prince V. V. Golitsyn. Their regime announced ambitious plans of reform but soon turned conservative.

After the coup of May 1682, ten-year-old Peter divided his time between the court and living with his mother at nearby Preobrazhenskoe. On ceremonial occasions he and his half-brother Ivan sat together on a dual throne of ivory. Foreign observers remarked that Peter was energetic, strong, and alert; Ivan was apathetic and dull witted. Peter's formal education was neglected, and while his brothers and sisters learned Latin, Polish, and poetry, he was left largely to his own devices away from court influences. At first he played with toy soldiers; then he began to recruit and drill live ones. Peter filled his play regiments with hundreds of unemployed courtiers and commoners, equipping them from the Kremlin arsenal. Soon he had formed two well trained battalions of about 300 men each, named Preobrazhenskii and Semenovskii after nearby villages, the nucleus for his subsequent imperial guards. Dressed in full uniform, he would bombard his fake fortress of Pressburg. Some who joined his forces, such as Alexander Menshikov, son of a court equerry, and Prince Michael Golitsyn, the future field marshal, became intimate and trusted colleagues. Seeking knowledge of technical and military matters, Peter frequented the German Settlement near Preobrazhenskoe, a separate European town of diplomats, merchants, officers, and artisans, and joined readily in its gay and bawdy life. A Dutchman, Franz Timmermann, taught him rudimentary geometry, the art of fortification, geography, and cabinet making. From Brandt, another Dutchman, Peter learned the essentials of ship design and construction. After discovering an abandoned English sailboat, he developed a passion for seafaring. Visits to the White Sea in 1693 and 1694 deepened this interest, and he returned to Moscow determined to create a Russian navy. At the age of 16 Peter was absorbed in three lifelong concerns: soldiers, ships, and European technology. His mother, worried by his unrestrained life at the German Settlement, married him off to Evdokia Lopukhin, daughter of a conservative nobleman. Soon bored with his dull, conservative spouse, Peter escaped to the Settlement to drink and carouse.

Princess Sofia sought to achieve full power and remove the growing threat of young Peter. Hoping that victory over the Crimean Tatars would bring glory to her regime, she authorized campaigns under V. V. Golitsyn in 1687 and 1689, but his timidity and poor generalship and problems of supply led to failure. In August 1689, aided by a new lover, Fedor Shaklovity, she organized a new *streltsy* conspiracy against the Naryshkins. Warned of the plot, Peter fled to nearby Trinity Monastery where, joined by his family and personal troops, he appealed to loyal Muscovites and foreign officers to rally to the rightful tsar. Sofia's support crumbled, she was confined in a convent, and Peter's mother ruled as regent until her death in 1694. Most influential at court became Patrick Gordon, a Scottish mercenary and Peter's chief military adviser, and François Lefort, soldier of fortune and boon companion. He introduced Peter to Anna Mons, daughter of a Westphalian merchant, who became his mistress for ten years.

Peter was a most unconventional man and ruler. Almost seven feet tall and weighing 240 pounds, he nonetheless retained qualities of a small boy who revelled in noise, buffoonery, and horseplay and combined tenderness and devotion with vicious cruelty. He was curious, a keen observer, and possessed an excellent memory; obstacles and reverses left him undiscouraged. Like his contemporary, Frederick William I of Prussia, he embodied the concept of the ruler as first servant of the state. In everything he insisted on "going through the ranks" and doing things himself. He learned many manual skills and a dozen trades, setting an example for the gentry of firsthand knowledge and hard work. Peter hated ceremony, luxury, and artificiality; he disliked subterfuge and expected honesty from his subordinates. Although sincerely religious, he scorned and even made fun of the hidebound Orthodox clergy. Unlike his predecessors, who generally had remained ensconced in the Kremlin, he wandered restlessly around Russia, open

Emperor Peter I

to new ideas and ready to experiment. These qualities helped determine his iconoclastic, innovative policies as tsar.

The Azov campaigns matured Peter as man and ruler. Azov, a Turkish fortress dominating the Sea of Azov, blocked Russian access to the southern seas. The initial campaign of 1695 failed for want of a fleet, able commanders, and skilled engineers. Undismayed, Peter had a fleet built at Voronezh on the Don, severed Turkish communications, and in July 1696 forced Azov to surrender. Entering Moscow to frenzied cheers, Peter became sole tsar and autocrat. The capture of Azov began the struggle with the Turks over the Black Sea, but Peter realized that to win it he required allies.

In 1697 Peter decided to visit western Europe in order to forge an anti-Turkish alliance, study ship construction and European technology, and recruit foreign specialists for Russian service. His experience at the German Settlement had convinced Peter that Russians must study European techniques, and he had already sent some Russian youths abroad to do so. Hoping that traveling incognito would provide him freedom of movement, he joined the Grand Embassy as simple Peter Mikhailov with about 150 other persons. His 14-month journey, unprecedented for a Russian ruler, marked a turning point in his career. In Holland he worked as a laborer in a Zaandam shipyard and spent four weeks in Amsterdam. In England he learned much at the Deptford shipyards and Woolwich arsenal, but he had no use for debates in Parliament or Western constitutional theories. European contemporaries marvelled at Peter's outlandish behavior and table manners (He would seize and devour an entire roast!), but they were impressed by his frankness, intelligence, and hunger to learn. Wrote Sophie, electress of Brandenburg: "He is a ruler both very good and very evil at the same time. His character is exactly the character of his country." Wholly convinced now of Europe's technological and economic superiority, Peter recruited more than 750 specialists, mostly Dutch, for Russian service so they could instruct his countrymen. During his reign Russians streamed westward to study, but Europe's preoccupation with the Spanish succession doomed Peter's hopes for an anti-Turkish coalition.

Learning in Vienna of a new *streltsy* revolt, Peter immediately left for home. The *streltsy*, aiming to restore Sofia, exterminate the boyars, and protect Old Believers, had moved on Moscow, but General Gordon had repelled their uncoordinated attacks. Peter promptly disbanded the disorderly *streltsy* regiments in Moscow, forced Sofia to become a nun, and had several *streltsy* hung outside her window. He also implicated his wife, Evdokia, divorced her, and forced her to take the veil. Some 800 streltsy were executed in Moscow alone, and their corpses left hanging for months. Apparently Peter tortured some of the victims himself, and the numerous executions, revealing his implacable will, convinced Europeans that he was an Oriental despot and Muscovy a backward and barbarous land.

To civilize the Russian upper classes, Peter forcibly altered their appearance. Upon his return he shaved off some of his courtiers' beards. Shaving had been introduced gradually at court, but traditionalists believed that beards symbolized Orthodoxy and were essential for salvation. Patriarch Adrian thundered: "God did not create men beardless, only cats and dogs. . . . The shaving of beards is not only foolishness and a dishonor, it is a mortal sin." Nevertheless, except for clergy and peasants, Russians either had to shave or pay a beard tax (this helped the Treasury since many wealthy Muscovites chose to pay). Peter also disliked the loose-fitting Russian national clothing, with broad sleeves and long coats that hindered movement. For the court and officialdom he prescribed German or Hungarian dress so that Muscovites would not be considered barbarous. This sumptuary rule, however, affected only a tiny minority at court and in towns and marked off the upper class from the peasantry; in their villages peasants still wore beards and national dress. Conservatives, associating Peter with the "godless" West, strongly opposed these and other reforms.

The opposition gathered around Peter's eldest son, Alexis, and his mother, Evdokia. In childhood Alexis, who rarely saw his father, had learned Latin, French, and German, but he remained passive and pleasure-loving. Evading tasks assigned by his father, he drank heavily. In 1715 his German-born wife, Charlotte, bore a son, Peter, then died. Only weeks later, Catherine, Peter I's second wife, also had a son named Peter. As the succession issue further alienated father and son, Alexis renounced his and his son's rights to the throne and fled to Austria.

Streltsy at the walls of the Kremlin,
Moscow, c. 1600

Peter demanded his extradition but promised forgiveness if he returned home promptly. Alexis consented and recognized Peter Petrovich, his father's infant son, as heir. But with strong conservative backing, Alexis represented an intolerable political threat, and in 1718 Peter accused him of conspiring to destroy St. Petersburg and the fleet and to restore traditional ways. Alexis was interrogated, imprisoned, and apparently murdered in Peter and Paul fortress, not for overt opposition but as a symbol of resistance to Peter's reforms and tyranny. His death failed to settle the succession: Peter Petrovich soon died leaving Peter's daughters, Anna and Elizabeth, and Alexis' son, Peter, as possible heirs. In 1722 Peter the Great decreed that he would designate his heir personally. His wife, Catherine, was crowned empress in 1724 but not designated heir to the throne, and Peter died the next year without naming a successor.

WAR AND DIPLOMACY

In the almost continuous wars of Peter's reign, Muscovite institutions were tested severely, and many were found wanting and discarded. During the grueling conflict with Sweden known as the Great Northern War, Russia became a fully autocratic, military monarchy in which every social group was harnessed into onerous, lifelong state service. Severe early defeats in that war dispersed and discredited traditional military forces and compelled the state to organize a new regular army of conscripts.

Wars were fought to break Russia's bonds of isolation imposed by geography and hostile neighbors, to acquire seaports and direct commercial and cultural contacts with western Europe. For Peter, as for his great contemporary, Louis XIV, war and expansion became his chief aims. Winning access to the seas, however, was a long standing Muscovite objective. For a century Sweden had dominated the eastern Baltic, periodically blockading Russia, and Gustavus Adolphus had boasted: "Now this enemy [Russia] without our permission cannot sail a single ship into the Baltic Sea."[2] After his western trip Peter concluded that with European allies and technology Russia could and must break through to that sea.

During the Grand Embassy he had sounded out leaders of Saxony and Brandenburg who also wished to destroy Sweden's Baltic hegemony. The time seemed ripe because Charles XII, only sixteen and reputedly weak and foolish, had just mounted the Swedish throne; his bloated kingdom invited partition. Johan Patkul, a Livonian nobleman whom the Swedes had sentenced to death, organized an anti-Swedish coalition, winning over Denmark and Augustus II of Saxony, who became king of Poland, to his scheme. At Rawa Peter and Augustus decided to attack Sweden and to allow Russia to regain Ingria and Karelia. Peter pledged to fight after making peace with Turkey, meanwhile assuring the Swedes that Russia desired peace.

Protracted Russian negotiations with the Turks endangered Peter's northern plans. His envoy sought title to the lower Dnieper forts and the Azov region which Russia had conquered. Peter also demanded regular diplomatic and commercial relations with Turkey, free navigation of the Black Sea, and guarantees to protect Orthodox Christians in the Ottoman Empire. The Turks, however, refused to yield the forts or allow Russian ships in the Black Sea, and Russia had to renounce these claims in order to secure representation in Constantinople. In August 1700 peace was concluded, and the day after the news reached Moscow, Russia declared war on Sweden.

Plunging into a major war before building an effective army, Peter admitted later, was a serious blunder. The motley Russian militia had been recruited hastily and was mostly under foreign officers. The very day Russia entered the war Denmark made a separate peace with Sweden. Almost 40,000 poorly armed Russians besieged the Baltic port of Narva, and Charles XII with 8,000 Swedes rushed to its relief. As a pitched battle loomed between the Swedish professionals and his raw levies, Peter prudently (some say in fright) departed for Moscow. On November 30, 1700, Charles attacked in a blinding snowstorm. Except for the guards regiments which fought bravely, the Russians fled in panic, abandoning their artillery. The army was shattered and Russia exposed to invasion, but severe weather and illness among his troops dissuaded Charles from a move on Moscow. To Peter's profound relief, he turned westward into Poland to pursue Augustus II giving Russia a much needed respite.

---

[2] M. A. Alpatov, *Russkaia istoricheskaia mysl i zapadnaia Evropa XII–XVII vv.* (Moscow, 1973), p. 314.

In the aftermath of Narva Peter revealed his greatness. The prestige won at Azov was lost and Europe laughed, but Peter by incredible efforts raised, trained, and equipped a new and better army. Recruitment and training were regularized and over the next decade about 200,000 men, mostly peasants and townsmen, were conscripted. Soldiers served usually for life, receiving training at muster points and depots. Initially, peasant soldiers were freed from serfdom until noble protests grew too loud. Officers, mostly noblemen, likewise served for life. Inscribed in regiments at an early age, most received some education and served several years in the ranks, often in guards regiments, before receiving their commissions. Special schools prepared artillery and engineer cadres. Wartime need induced the government sometimes to promote able commoners to officer rank. The army's weapons, many produced in Russia, were improved until they equalled European ones. The bayonet was introduced, at first defensively, later in assaults, inaugurating a Russian tradition of cold steel. To replace lost artillery, many church bells in northern Russia were melted down. The new light and heavy artillery became renowned for its accuracy and effectiveness. Peter's tremendous energy, optimism, and organizing skill developed at huge cost a well equipped, amply supplied standing army. Under pressure of war this regular force, which numbered some 200,000 men by 1725, took shape with strict regulations, based on European models, unified recruitment, and standard uniforms.

Augustus II was kept in the field with subsidies and auxiliary detachments while the Russians conducted a counteroffensive. With Charles tied down in Poland, Russian forces led by Peter himself or by Menshikov, his intimate friend, seized Ingria from relatively weak Swedish garrisons. In 1703 at the mouth of the Neva River near the Gulf of Finland, Peter founded the city of St. Petersburg. At great expense in lives and resources, the future capital was laid out geometrically on swampy, barren land. The next year the capture of Narva and Derpt climaxed the Ingrian campaign, secured Livonia, and eased direct contacts with the West.

Charles XII, after finally compelling Augustus to make peace, invaded Russia in July 1708 with a veteran army of 46,000 men. Counting on a popular Russian uprising and aid from Hetman Mazepa's dissident Ukrainian Cossacks, Charles planned to advance to Moscow and partition Russia, but finding scorched earth and an elusive, retreating foe, he turned southward into the Ukraine to join Mazepa. General Lewenhaupt with reinforcements and supplies sought to join him, but Menshikov badly defeated him at Lesnaia in September and captured his supplies. Peter exulted: "We have never had a similar victory over regular [Swedish] troops, and then with numbers inferior to those of the enemy." Menshikov crushed Mazepa, seized his artillery, and forced the Ukraine to submit. Without needed supplies Charles' army suffered severely during the winter. The following spring, as Charles besieged Poltava in the Ukraine, Peter's main army came to its relief. In June 1709 some 40,000 Russians fought a decisive battle with the depleted Swedish army of 22,000. The Swedes were dispirited and Charles, al-

MAP 15–1
Russian Expansion under Peter the Great, 1695–1725

Russian frontiers in 1695

Areas of revolt against Tsarist rule 1705–1711

Swedish towns attacked by Russia 1710–1721

Territory annexed from Sweden in 1721 by the Treaty of Nystadt, and from Persia in 1723; Persian annexations restored in 1725

* Battle sites

Adapted with permission of Macmillan Publishing Co., Inc. from *Russian History Atlas* by Martin Gilbert. Cartography by Martin Gilbert. Copyright © 1972 by Martin Gilbert.

ready wounded, had to be carried on a litter. Peter exhorted his men: "The hour has come in which the destinies of our country will be decided. It is of her that you must think, it is for her that you must fight . . . and as for Peter, know that he does not cling to his own life provided Russia lives in her glory and prosperity."[3] The Swedish army was mostly destroyed and captured; only Charles, Mazepa, and a few followers escaped into Turkey. The great victory at Poltava ended the Swedish invasion, vindicated Peter's military reforms, and confirmed Russia's rise as a great European power.

The Northern War continued because Charles, backed by French diplomacy, persuaded the Turks to declare war on Russia in 1710. Peter overconfidently invaded the Balkans, calling on its Christians to rise against Turkish rule. Only tiny Montenegro responded, and its revolt failed to divert many Turkish troops. Advancing down the Pruth River, Peter's force was surrounded by a huge Turkish army. To save himself and St. Petersburg, Peter was prepared to yield his other northern conquests and even Novgorod and Pskov, but the Turks merely demanded the Azov region. For two more years Russia faced possible Turkish invasion until Charles overplayed his hand and was expelled.

In the north the war dragged on and on. A coalition of Brandenburg, Saxony, Denmark, and Poland gave Russia ineffective support while dynastic marriages involved the country deeply in German politics and roused suspicion among its princes. Anna, daughter of Peter's deceased half-brother, married the Duke of Courland and later became empress of Russia;[4] her sister, Catherine, married the Duke of Mecklenburg. Peter's support of German princelings complicated the conflict with Sweden. Russia's allies, he wrote, were "too many gods; what we want, they don't allow; what they advise, cannot be put into practice."[5] But Russian naval and land forces scored many victories. In 1713 all southern Finland was conquered. A year later Peter's new Baltic fleet, built from scratch during the war, defeated the Swedish galleys at Hangö. Peter's navy, eventually boasting 48 ships of the line, many galleys, and 28,000 seamen, made Russia master of the eastern Baltic and contributed greatly to ultimate victory.[6] The Russians captured the last Swedish fortresses on the southern Baltic shores and raided the Swedish coast, but Charles refused to yield. Even his death in Norway in 1718 did little to hasten peace because British support kept the Swedes fighting.

Finally in 1721, after a Russian landing near Stockholm, the Swedes yielded. By the Treaty of Nystadt, Russia, though evacuating Finland, paying an indemnity, and pledging not to interfere in Sweden's internal affairs, secured the provinces of Livonia, Estonia, Ingria, part of Karelia including Viborg, and Oesel and the Dagoe Islands, a far larger window

---

[3] Cited in Grunwald, *Peter the Great*, p. 112.

[4] See below, p. 215.

[5] Cited in B. Sumner, *Peter the Great and the Emergence of Russia* (London, 1951), p. 85.

[6] A few years after Peter's death, however, only a handful of vessels remained seaworthy. For the navy his personal interest was indispensable.

on the West than Peter had envisioned. The new Baltic provinces were western, Lutheran, and more advanced than Russia proper. They retained separate status and autonomy, and their German nobility continued to rule a Lettish and Estonian populace. Baltic German nobles, entering Russian military and civil service in large numbers, provided able and educated officials which Russia needed badly.

At the urging of the Senate, which Peter had instituted as the supreme organ of the state after abolishing the Boyar Duma in 1711, Peter now accepted the titles of emperor and the great. Russia's vast territory and diverse subjects entitled him to the former; his Baltic conquests led prominent contemporaries to accord him the latter. Prussia and Holland immediately recognized his imperial title; other countries followed after bargaining and delay. Russia's international status rose significantly after Poltava, and its voice was heard in all important affairs. "By our deeds in war we have emerged from darkness into the light of the world," noted Peter, "and those whom we did not know in the light now respect us."[7]

Russia showed sporadic interest in the Orient and Central Asia. Peter attempted with little success to increase trade with China. In the northern Pacific Russia annexed Kamchatka Peninsula and the Kurile Islands, and later Captain Vitus Bering, a Dane in Russian service, explored the waters separating Siberia from Alaska, which were named after him. Peter viewed Central Asia as the gateway to India and a potential source of gold. In 1700 he granted the request of the Khan of Khiva, faced with rebellion and foreign foes, for Russian citizenship. Later, he sought to build a Caspian fleet, and hearing that gold had been discovered along the Amu Darya River, Peter in 1717 sent Prince Bekovich-Cherkasskii with 3,500 men to Khiva. He defeated the Khivans, then lulled by their peaceful assurances, divided his forces. The Khivans overwhelmed them and killed the Russians or sold them into slavery. A more successful expedition under Captain Bukholts moved up the Irtysh River and in 1716 established a fort at Omsk, later the capital of western Siberia. Fortified posts at Semipalatinsk and Ust-Kamenogorsk (1718) became bases for subsequent Russian expansion into the Kazakh steppe.

Coveting Persia's Caspian shores, Peter in 1715 sent a cavalry officer, Artemi Volynskii, as envoy to the Shah's court. He concluded a commercial treaty before being expelled. As governor of nearby Astrakhan, Volynskii urged Russia to seize Persia's silk provinces along the Caspian. To foster Persia's collapse, Russia aided native rebels. After Dagestani mountaineers nominally subject to the Shah attacked some Russian merchants, Peter's army moved in to "restore order" and occupied the Caspian's western shores, including the key port of Baku, in 1722–23. In Transcaucasia Georgian and Armenian Christians appealed for aid against the Turks, but remembering the Pruth, Peter wisely avoided offending the Sultan.

After Poltava Russia played a major diplomatic role in Europe. In-

---

[7] Sumner, *Peter the Great*, p. 121.

sisting on making foreign policy himself, Peter carefully supervised its formulation and engaged periodically in frank personal diplomacy. During a state visit to France in 1717 he proposed an alliance in order to end French machinations in the Ottoman Empire and Sweden. The French would agree merely to a treaty of friendship but recognized Russia as a major diplomatic force.

Peter's ambitious and complex diplomacy forced a reorganization of the Foreign Office along western lines and a great increase in its personnel. In 1720 the College of Foreign Affairs, personally supervised by Peter, replaced the Posolskii Prikaz. Permanent diplomatic missions were established in leading European capitals, and consuls protected Russian commercial interests. Russian diplomats gradually discarded Oriental etiquette and adopted European methods and dress, but they could decide nothing without consulting Moscow. Peter protected them well: when A. A. Matveev, his ambassador to England, was arrested for debt in 1708, Peter backed him until he was released. An emerging group of skilled diplomats, aided by growing Russian power and a better organized foreign office, proved their ability in concluding the Treaty of Nystadt.

Petrine Russia had a mixed record in foreign affairs. Military and diplomatic successes, prepared by Peter's predecessors, altered Russia's relations with Europe fundamentally, but Russian nationalist and some Soviet historians have glorified the results unduly. Whether Petrine victories were worth their huge cost and militarization of the Russian state remains debatable. The Northern War reduced Sweden to a second-class power and made Russia dominant in the eastern Baltic. Poland was rendered helpless and the way prepared for its subsequent partition, but that scarcely benefited Poland or Russia. Against the Turks nothing was achieved: Peter had underestimated Turkish strength and had counted too much on the Balkan Christians. His marriage alliances with German princes drew Russia into the German quagmire and complicated the succession to the Russian throne. Failing to deflect France from support of Sweden and the Ottoman Empire, Russia began two centuries of alternating cooperation and rivalry with Austria over the Balkans. Peter's war against Persia was unnecessary and those against the Turks ended in failure; but Russia clearly needed the direct links with western Europe secured from Sweden. Peter's window on the Baltic and moving the capital to St. Petersburg were solid achievements.

ADMINISTRATION

Petrine administrative reforms stemmed largely from the requirements of war. Introduced piecemeal, they were coordinated only late in the reign. The atrophy or near collapse of the cumbersome Muscovite bureaucracy finally necessitated extensive reorganization after attempts to patch it up failed, but the new institutions at first often existed mainly on paper and some failed to take proper root.

The early Romanovs, having developed a highly centralized government over which the ruler exercised supreme legislative, executive, and judicial authority, prepared the way for Petrine administration. Seventeenth century tsars, however, had maintained a lavish court in Moscow, costing large sums, sums which Peter later exceeded at Peterhof. The Boyar Duma, no longer based wholly on birth, had become during the 17th century the chief governmental institution, a royal council handling many aspects of national life. It had directed the bureaucracy, drafted legislation, acted as a supreme court, and conducted foreign relations. Under the Duma were 40 to 50 administratve boards (*prikazy*) with overlapping and duplicating jurisdictions. The Duma and *prikazy*, though centralized and located in Moscow, were disorderly and unstable, and Peter's predecessors entrusted key tasks to favorites who bypassed this structure. Governors, appointed by and responsible to the *prikazy*, ruled the regional administration and possessed both civil and military authority. As central authority over towns and rural districts grew, self-government withered.

Until 1708 this central administration stumbled along without major structural change. Peter assumed personal charge of foreign and military affairs while the shrunken Boyar Duma implemented his hastily drafted decrees on internal matters. Peter urged the Duma to act independently in his absence but ordered it to keep detailed minutes signed by all members "so that the stupidity of each [member] shall be evident." Meanwhile new *prikazy* were being created, amalgamated, divided, or renamed. The Admiralty Board administered the new fleet, and the much feared Preobrazhenskii Board ran the secret police, the guards, and recruitment; unlike other *prikazy*, it exercised authority over the entire country. In 1699 creation of a Board of Accounts (*Ratusha*) to handle state finance heralded coming structural reform. Other *prikazy* had to submit frequent reports to it, and Peter hoped that it could gather enough revenue to support the army. By 1708 the Ratusha collected about two thirds of state revenues, but since the Treasury and Big Court boards still functioned, financial centralization was incomplete. The Ratusha and Preobrazhenskii Board revealed the obsolescence and inefficiency of the *prikaz* system.

In order to raise more money locally for the war, the government in 1699 offered towns relief from greedy governors by allowing them to elect mayors if they would pay double taxation to the state. When only a few towns agreed to this, the authorities dropped double assessment and made elected mayors compulsory. Peter hoped that wealthy merchants would improve the quality of local institutions and raise war revenues, but apathy and shortage of qualified personnel prevented substantial results. Elected gentry boards, set up in 1702 to assist governors, likewise proved ineffective.

The Ratusha's failure to raise adequate war revenues induced Peter to try decentralization to support the army. In December 1707 Russia was divided into eight huge regions (*gubernii*) under governors whom Peter appointed in 1711. Residing in regional capitals, they were expected to be more efficient and accessible than Moscow bureaucrats. Swedish style provincial boards (*landraty*) of eight to 12 members were created to assist the governors. Later, board members assumed charge of new units called *dolia* and were empowered to supervise the governor's work. As *dolia* chiefs, board members were the governor's subordinates; as supervisors they were theoretically his equals!

Peter experimented with various provincial subdivisions. Beginning in 1711 *guberniia* were divided into provinces (*provintsii*) and subdivided into districts (*uezdy*). Before these could take root, Peter created *dolia*, each supposedly comprising 5,536 taxable households, to support local army units. Some *dolia* coincided with districts, others comprised several districts. This array of political units established for different purposes caused confusion and waste. Petrine provincial legislation, concluded Kliuchevskii, revealed neither forethought nor wisdom. Abrupt institutional changes lowered civil service morale and failed to extract maximum revenue.

The creation of *guberniia* and wartime pressures deepened confusion at the center. Moscow ceased to function as the capital, yet St. Petersburg was still under construction, and so government centered wherever Peter happened to be. To fill the void during his absence on the Pruth campaign, Peter replaced the moribund Boyar Duma with a Senate, initially to control the *guberniia*, courts, government expenditures, and trade. Persons and institutions were supposed to obey it as they would the tsar. Theoretically, the Senate became, like the Duma before it, the supreme administrative body, top judicial authority, and a quasi-legislature, which formulated and interpreted Peter's rough decrees; actually Senate authority was undermined and often disregarded by Peter's favorites. Originally Peter selected nine senators whose decisions were to be unanimous; but despite their extensive, ill defined powers, senators lacked independence and were mostly second-rate men requiring constant supervision.

Senate structure and procedure later grew more complex. An *ober-fiskal*, or secret supervisor, was appointed to gather information about unfair court decisions and misappropriations of public funds. Assisted by a growing network of informers (*fiskaly*), he was supposed to indict offenders before the Senate, and for convictions he received half the fine imposed by the court. In 1715 Peter named an inspector general to enforce Senate decrees, punish negligent senators, and insure that the Senate performed its duties. Such measures proved inadequate, and Peter had to rebuke and fine senators who brawled, shouted, and rolled on the Senate floor! In 1722 he appointed a procurator general, as "our eye and mandatory in the affairs of state," to head the Senate's secretariat and mediate between the Emperor, Senate, and its subordinate departments. The procurator was to watch over the Senate, regulate *fiskaly*, preserve order, and report Senate opinions to Peter. Though not a Senate member and without a vote, he became its de facto president and the mainspring of the administration. Next to the Emperor, the procurator became the most powerful man in Russia.

After careful study of foreign models, Peter in 1717 replaced the *prikazy* with administrative colleges, then fashionable in Europe. The German philosopher, Leibniz, had written Peter: "Their mechanism is like that of watches whose wheels mutually keep each other in movement." Peter believed that the collegial (collective) principle would promote regularity, avoid arbitrary one-man rule, and end corruption in departments of state. Foreign experts organized the colleges and adapted them to Russian conditions. Peter staffed them initially with Swedish war-prisoner volunteers and foreign Slavs and sent young Russians abroad to study their operations. Vice presidents of the new colleges, except foreign affairs, were foreigners, but only three foreigners per college were permitted, and their presidents were mostly Russian. Not until 1720 did the administrative colleges actually begin to function in foreign affairs, army, admiralty, state revenue, commerce, mining and manufactures, state expenditure, justice, and state control. Later, new presidents were selected, the procurator general coordinated them with the Senate, and most foreigners were discharged. Administrative colleges soon resembled former *prikazy* because their boards became tools of the president. They relieved the Senate of many administrative tasks, however, and the judicial college assumed many legal functions. Since the colleges had clear jurisdiction over the entire empire, the central government became more orderly and efficient.

Such changes at the center necessitated further provincial reorganization. In 1718 on the Senate's recommendation Peter adopted local institutions modeled on Swedish ones. The *guberniia*, increased to 11 and later 12, were subdivided into 45, later 50 counties, each under an *oberkommandant*, responsible to.the governor. *Dolia* were abolished and the counties, except for military and judicial affairs, became largely self-governing. They were subdivided into districts of about 2,000 households with local commissars to collect taxes, supervise police, the economy, education, and even public morals. Regimental districts, set up to raise money for local army units, cut across county boundaries and complicated this neat pattern.

Beginning in 1720 Russian towns adopted institutions like those of the Baltic cities of Reval and Riga. Townspeople were divided by wealth into three guilds, but only first guild members could hold public office. Town councils, headed by a chief magistracy in St. Petersburg, were supposed to collect taxes and run city affairs. Actually they did little, and this reform failed to take root. A minority of wealthy merchants, protected by the government, dominated the towns. In 1727 the chief magistracy was abolished and town councils were subordinated to provincial governors. Here foreign models proved inapplicable to more primitive Russian conditions.

Petrine administrative reforms succeeded only in part. A coherent central administration clearly demarcated from local government emerged and lasted with little change for almost a century, but shortcomings were numerous. Judicial, administrative, and executive functions were not clearly separated, and the new agencies were expensive and sometimes superfluous (some colleges were later abolished as unnecessary). Some imported institutions did not work, and trained officials were lacking to run them efficiently. The perennial Russian problem of corruption persisted. "We all steal," declared Peter's favorite, Paul Iaguzhinskii. "The sole difference is that some do it on a bigger scale and in a more conspicuous manner than others." Peter could not afford to pay officials adequately, virtually compelling them to steal, and while he crusaded against peculation and encouraged *fiskaly* to uncover abuses, he protected or forgave corrupt favorites. His contempt for regular administrative agencies and reliance on military men hampered efforts to establish the rule of law. Abyssmally low standards of public morality rose little.

The administration, like that of Peter's contemporary Frederick William I of Prussia, depended greatly upon his personal direction. One of Europe's hardest working rulers, Peter drafted decrees on every subject and made all important and many minor decisions. Such personal government tended to break down when Peter was absent and deteriorated under weak successors. With Peter away, favorites more powerful than the Senate violated the law flagrantly and undermined the government's prestige. Guards officers with sweeping powers were given special missions, especially to punish high-ranking wrongdoers. The numerous administrative spies looking over one another's shoulders confirmed that corruption and malfeasance remained rife, although the system functioned well enough to achieve Peter's main objectives.

PROBLEM 4: HISTORIANS AND THE PETRINE REFORMS

The Petrine reforms, their origin, and their significance in Russia's evolution have been debated ever since by tsarist, Soviet, and Western scholars. As a true autocrat, Peter, like his contemporary, Louis XIV, believed that the state must reform administration and society according to reason, but that in backward Russia barbarous methods would often be required. Like subsequent European enlightened despots, Peter considered it his duty to uplift and improve his subjects by force if necessary. His ceaseless activity, inexhaustible energy, and authoritarian methods put a strong personal imprint on the changes which were made. Were the reforms original or borrowed, successful or disastrous?

Let us look at how leading tsarist and Soviet Russian historians have viewed these issues. Most of Peter's contemporaries considered his epoch one of transformation and Peter as the "great reformer." Eighteenth century Russian writers, impressed by Peter's work, described it as sweeping and desirable, accepted Europe as a valid model, and praised him for putting Russia on a progressive path. Prince M. M. Shcherbatov (1733–90), the leading noble historian and spokesman for his class, however, was of two minds: Peter's policies had brought Russia to a level which otherwise would have required a century or two to attain but had damaged Russian mores and reduced the role of the titled nobility unduly. At the end of the century the liberal noble, Alexander Radishchev, praised Peter for founding St. Petersburg and expanding Russian territory and power but denounced his despotism.

In the early 19th century the Petrine reforms were central in the debate between Slavophiles—glorifiers of all things Russian—and Westernizers over Russia's past and her future destiny.[8] For both he was the great—a genius, a thundercloud. Slavophiles, starting with N. M. Karamzin, blamed Peter for introducing western materialism and subordinating the Orthodox Church to the state. Lauding Peter's military victories and army reforms, Karamzin deplored his love of foreign customs and his disregard for national Russian traditions and attributed the deep rift between the upper and lower classes to Peter's reforms of dress. Founding St. Petersburg, Karamzin argued, had been a blunder because of its foul climate and the vast sacrifices required for its construction. The prominent Slavophile, Konstantin Aksakov, in a memorandum, "On the Internal State of Russia" (1855), called Peter "that greatest of all great men." But Peter's revolution, "despite all its outward brilliance, shows what immense spiritual evil can be done by the greatest genius as soon as he acts alone, draws away from the people." Peter's predecessors had built strongly and thrown off foreign domination without imitating outside models. Then "the state in the person of Peter encroached upon the people, invaded their lives and customs, and forcibly changed their manners and traditions and even their dress." In St. Petersburg he had surrounded himself with immigrants divorced from traditional values. "That is how the breach between tsar and people occurred."

Westernizers, on the other hand, praised Peter for founding the modern, enlightened, secular Russian state. This greatest Russian ruler, wrote Peter Chaadaev, had swept away all of Russia's traditions. "On one occasion a great man sought to civilize us; and in order to give us a foretaste of enlightenment, he flung us the mantle of civilization; we picked up the mantle but we did not touch civilization itself." Peter freed Russia from the dead weight of previous history: he "found only a blank page when he came to power and . . . wrote on it *Europe* and *Occident.*" Peter was a most enlightened despot, agreed the radical Westernizer, Vissarion Belinskii. He "opened the door for his people to the light of God and little by little dispersed the darkness of ignorance."

From the 1860s Russian historians challenged the older view that Peter's achievement was revolutionary and wholly novel. Reforms in seven essential fields, S. M. Soloviev pointed out, had begun a generation or more before Peter: foreign policy, army reorganization, administration, taxation, employment of foreigners, compulsory service, and education. Only four Petrine reforms were truly innovative: educating Russians abroad, abolishing the Patriarchate, creating a navy, and moving the capital to St. Petersburg. Nonetheless, Peter's personality and leadership, affirmed Soloviev, were decisive in launching Russia's modernization. A stern teacher of civic obligations, Peter explained at each step what he was doing and why. Popular sacrifices under his leadership made Russia a powerful nation. "The man who led the people in this feat can justly be called the greatest leader in

---

[8] See also below, pp. 305–9.

history." Knowing his duty to civilize Russia, Peter led the way by personal example:

> . . . We must stand astonished before the moral and physical powers of the Reformer. . . . We know of no historical figure whose sphere of activity was as broad as Peter's. . . . He developed entirely on his own, unguided and undeterred by anyone, yet stimulated by a society which was already at a turning point, which wavered between two directions. . . . Peter was endowed with the nature of an ancient Russian epic hero. . . .[9]

V. O. Kliuchevskii, Soloviev's greatest pupil, writing shortly before World War I, agreed that 17th century statesmen had outlined most of the Petrine reforms and that Peter had become a reformer more by accident than design. War provided the main impetus for changes, at first modest and limited, later becoming a great internal struggle which aroused all social groups. The reforms were revolutionary not in goals or results but in methods and the impression they made on contemporary minds and nerves. Kliuchevskii stressed Peter's contradictory nature: tyranny and cruelty combined with patriotism, unshakable devotion to his work, and bold plans conceived and executed with boundless energy. By despotism and threats Peter sought to inspire free, independent activity in an enslaved society.

Peter's personal role, wrote the early 20th century liberal historian, P. N. Miliukov, affected the reforms significantly. Peter had performed incredibly varied tasks, had served the state with a deep sense of responsibility, and had supplied momentum to a regime working by fits and starts. Not an independent thinker or student of political theory, Peter was nonetheless strongly influenced by European institutions. Had he lived longer he might have Russified state reforms which later required adaptation to Russian conditions. Though copied from the West, the changes, nevertheless, were profoundly national in what they destroyed or created. "Russia," added Miliukov, "received nothing but the reforms for which she was fitted."

After the 1917 Revolution, Soviet historians, developing their interpretations of the Petrine period, found little in Marx or Lenin to guide them. George Plekhanov, father of Russian Marxism, ascribing to Peter an important role in executing the reforms, affirmed that the Petrine regime was an Asiatic despotism in which an absolute ruler and bureaucracy controlled the means of production and disposed at will of their subjects' property. "In Europeanizing Russia Peter carried to its extreme logical consequence the population's lack of rights vis-à-vis the state that is characteristic of Oriental despotism." Peter's implementation of the reforms, however, suggested enlightened despotism. M. N. Pokrovskii, the true pioneer in Soviet Marxist interpretation and a leading Soviet historian of the 1920s, calling Peter's reign an era of merchant capitalism, criticized the reforms for creating economic havoc and concentrating power in the hands of the bourgeoisie. Pokrovskii

---

[9] S. M. Soloviev, *Istoriia Rossii s drevneishikh vremen* (St. Petersburg, n.d.), vol. 18, pp. 848–49.

portrayed Peter as the dissolute tool of merchant capital whose personal actions had little influence. Later, Pokrovskii toned down his emphasis on merchant capitalism, but the final edition of his *Russian History in Briefest Outline* (1933) sought to discredit the tsar reformer in a four sentence biographical sketch dealing wholly with Peter's lusts, tortures, and syphilis!

N. A. Rozhkov, the other major Marxist historian of the 1920s, disagreed with Pokrovskii and described the Petrine era as the final phase of "the revolution of the court nobility." Foreign wars, he argued, helped precipitate reform and forced Russia to adopt European standards. Peter was treated respectfully but not as a powerful or colorful figure. "In the time of Peter the Great the court nobility was to make the final, definitive and most strenuous effort . . . to master the situation and become in effect the ruling class."

In the mid-1930s during Stalin's dictatorship, Soviet interpretations of Peter's reign became strongly nationalistic. Pokrovskii was repudiated and accused of disregarding Peter's strengthening of the state and Russia's international position. Stalinist historians, carefully using their master's stray remarks, rehabilitated Peter and many of his reforms, and compared his constructive efforts with Stalin's Five Year Plans. They depicted Peter as a progressive leader whose Russian-inspired reforms had strengthened Russia at home and abroad. Declared a post-World War II Stalinist account:

> Under the reign of Peter I, Russia made great progress. Nevertheless it remained a country in which serf oppression and the tyranny of the tsar reigned supreme. The Russian Empire was enlarged and strengthened at the cost of the lives of hundreds of thousands of toilers and the impoverishment of the people. Peter I did a great deal to create and strengthen the state of the landlords and the merchants.[10]

A. M. Pankratova's textbook of the same period called Peter "a good organizer and an outstanding statesman." In sharp contrast to Pokrovskii's negative assessment, she stressed his positive qualities:

> Peter hated cowardice, falsehood, hypocrisy and dishonesty. Above all he hated attachment to old usage which interfered with the country's regeneration. He strove to eliminate all backwardness. . . . Strong-willed, resolute, and persistent, Peter swept aside all obstacles that stood in the way of his reforms. He was irreconcilable in his fight against backwardness and barbarity.[11]

Here once again we see Peter as hero.

Recent post-Stalinist views of Peter and his reforms are better balanced. According to a 1966 text the nobility allied with a rising bourgeoisie were dominant under Peter. Both classes helped absolutism combat the old aristocracy as Russia completed the transition from a class-representative to an absolute monarchy. In the center of the reforms stood Tsar Peter, "a truly great man." Declares a recent Soviet history:

---

[10] Shestakov, *Short History of the USSR*, p. 81.

[11] A. M. Pankratova, *History of the USSR* (Moscow, 1966), vol. 2, p. 43.

Peter was the representative of the ruling class and the exponent of its interests, and understood the need for reform and for the development of noble Russia. He persisted to achieve the reconstruction of the state apparatus in order to adapt it to the needs of his time. In this Peter did not restrict himself to his country's historical experience, but . . . selected from [abroad] whatever corresponded to Russian conditions. The chief features of his character, containing much that was contradictory, along with exceptional mental ability, were his will and inexhaustible energy. He knew how to select assistants of ability and initiative. . . . He destroyed traditions and introduced new forms of organization and reconstructed the state apparatus, army, and fleet utilizing the most decisive, even barbarous methods.[12]

Soviet historians today, like most earlier ones, agree that Peter I was an outstanding ruler who used Russian experience and pertinent foreign models to develop Russia as a power. Extreme praise of Peter, associated earlier with the great man theory of history and resurrected under Stalin to build that dictator's image, has yielded to a sober appraisal of strengths and weaknesses and to a recognition of the limits of an individual ruler's influence. Controversy persists nonetheless over the degree of Peter's personal influence and how successful and positive his reforms were.

Suggested Additional Reading

BLACK, CYRIL. "The Reforms of Peter the Great," in *Rewriting Russian History* (New York, 1962), pp. 233–59.

BRUCE, PETER H. *Memoirs* . . . (New York, 1970, reprint).

DMYTRYSHYN, BASIL, ed. *Modernization of Russia under Peter I and Catherine II* (New York, 1974).

GRUNWALD, C. DE. *Peter the Great* (London, 1956).

JACKSON, W. G. *Seven Roads to Moscow* (London, 1957). (On Poltava.)

KLYUCHEVSKY, V. O. *Peter the Great* (New York, 1961).

MARSDEN, CHRISTOPHER. *Palmyra of the North* (London, 1942). (Early St. Petersburg.)

O'BRIEN, C. B. *Russia under Two Tsars, 1682–1689* (Berkeley, 1952).

PUTNAM, PETER B. *Peter, the Revolutionary Tsar* (New York, 1973).

RAEFF, MARC, ed., *Peter the Great: Reformer or Revolutionary?* (Boston, 1974).

SUMNER, B. H. *Peter the Great and the Emergence of Russia* (London, 1951).

————. *Peter the Great and the Ottoman Empire* (Oxford, 1949).

TOLSTOI, ALEXIS. *Peter the First.* (New York, 1959). (Soviet historical novel.)

---

[12] *Istoriia SSSR* (Moscow, 1967), vol. 3, p. 249.

16

Peter the Great: Social, Economic, and Religious Policies

PETER THE GREAT's reforming activity touched almost every facet of human activity. Social and economic relations were affected by his relentless search for efficiency and productivity. Cultural affairs and Church matters were of less immediate practical concern to Peter, but the swift pace of change would not allow these areas to escape attention. Kliuchevskii aptly suggested: "The government's most important and terrible weapon was Peter's pen."

The military and administrative reforms initiated by Peter could be properly implemented only by an adequately trained and sizable corps of military and civil servants. The chief administrators of the Muscovite state had been members of the capital nobility (*stolichnoe dvorianstvo*), composed of the most prominent and distinguished families and long associated with court service. These old families possessed *votchina* (patrimonial) land holdings on a large scale. In addition, many noble families owning *pomestie* (service) estates around Moscow had been brought to Moscow by earlier tsars to protect the capital. The capital nobility were simply too few and too conservative in spirit to staff the new military and administrative institutions created by Peter's reforming policies.

Peter turned to the provincial nobility living in provincial urban centers and in remote rural areas. Provincial noblemen were notoriously negligent in fulfilling their service obligations. Many sought to hide in dark and distant recesses of remote provinces, so that the central government was often ignorant of their numbers, location, and service obligations. To ascertain these facts, Peter's decree of 1700 ordered all noble landowners to register themselves and all male family members over the age of ten. As soon as their names were registered, noblemen were assigned to specific regiments or civil administrative posts. The number of registered noble families increased dramatically from 3,000 recorded in 1670 to 15,041 in 1700, the extraordinary increase stemming from better record keeping. Of these registered only about 535 noblemen owned more than 100 peasant households, 13 had between 1,000 and 2,000, and only five owned more than 2,000 peasant households. The figures confirm that noble status implied wide divergencies in economic wealth and political power. The 535 families with over 100 peasant households comprised the noble elite of Russia and would mostly remain such during Peter's reign.

Peter's social program contributed to the gradual amalgamation of the old capital and provincial nobility. The official adoption of the term, *shliakhetstvo* (from the Polish) to designate the entire nobility, indicated this leveling process. On the surface this new name signified a shift away from the paramountcy of family standing in determining state service to the elusive quality of suitability for service. The change did not mean, as so often suggested, that family status ceased to count. On the contrary, Peter continued to expect the leading families to play prominent roles in state affairs by virtue of their traditional proximity to the centers of state power.

Meritorious service could only be expected from well-educated noblemen, and so Peter ordered all nobles between the ages of ten and 15 taught "mathematics," which to him meant all types of useful information. Though perhaps haphazard, this innovation was a first halting step toward a totally secular educational system designed to serve state interests. Following his preparatory "education," the young noble was expected at the age of fifteen to enter state service at the lowest rank regardless of his family's social position. Those assigned to military ranks—by far the majority—were expected to serve two years in the ranks before receiving officers' commissions. One could avoid this demeaning and difficult form of "conditioning" only if he were selected to serve in an elite Guards regiment, whose members were drawn exclusively from the nobility. Peter used appointment to the Guards to foster loyalty, cooperation, and devotion. For the provincial nobility,

Michael Curran

17th century rural estate dwelling

service in the Guards regiments afforded an opportunity to enter the power center around the throne which for so long had been the capital nobility's exclusive prerogative.

The nobleman was expected to serve the state for life or until incapacitated. His estate was left in the hands of his wife, relatives, or a steward or overseer, and consequently most estates were badly managed and unproductive, and the nobility suffered severe economic distress. The success of Peter's new service organization was determined largely by the servitor's economic well-being. To compensate servitors, Peter resorted to the traditional method of land grants, extending both the granting of estates and the ownership of serfs. So that all land would carry service obligations, Peter in 1714 abolished all distinctions between *votchina* and *pomestie* tenure and decreed that henceforth all land was inheritable and carried precise service obligations. Each estate owner now had an incentive to maintain and develop his estate and maximize its productivity; all were bound to perform specific service to the state in return for the right to exploit their landholdings.

To improve further the nobility's economic status and foster a competitive service atmosphere, Peter decreed new regulations governing inheritance. The aim was to prevent families from so diluting their resources that their continued service became unsatisfactory or impossible. It had long been customary to divide an estate into equal shares for distribution among all remaining heirs. Over centuries this practice had undermined the nobility's economic well-being. Peter proclaimed the law of entail, which provided that land be passed intact from father to a single designated heir, not necessarily the eldest surviving son. This new law was designed to maintain landholdings as economically viable units capable of supporting the state servitor and to encourage sons not receiving land to carve out for themselves a career in state service, commerce, or industry. These measures, like so many of Peter's plans, were not entirely successful but clearly reflected his desire to introduce order, uniformity, and efficiency into the service structure.

The establishment of the Table of Ranks in 1722 capped Peter's efforts to create a dependable and capable class of state servitors. The Table of Ranks recognized three parallel categories of state service: military, civil, and court, each divided into 14 grades. This new hierarchical system formalized the earlier decision that name alone did not assure one of an honorable position in the state. Rank had to be earned and was granted only as a reward for meritorious service. Although the Table of Ranks provided that a commoner could acquire hereditary noble status upon achieving the lowest (14th) officer rank or the eighth rank in the civil hierarchy, family status remained significant because Peter continued to expect state leaders to belong to the traditional nobility. Did the Table of Ranks, as many historians contend, have a democratizing influence on the Russian social structure by making noble status accessible to men of talent and ability? In theory, perhaps, and some non-nobles did enter service, but in practice it was generally assumed that an individual was of noble origin before he entered the competitive sphere of the Table of Ranks.

The service structure and the Table of Ranks demanded at least a rudimentary education and began a process which would gradually break down the cultural homogeneity of the Russian people. The upper classes with their Western-oriented education were effectively deprived of traditional Russian culture, and a tremendous chasm opened up in Russian society. The upper and lower classes were separated not only by social position and wealth, but also by education and cultural values. In short, the upper classes became increasingly Westernized while the lower classes remained attached to the traditional culture of their ancestors.

The landowners of Russia were then consolidated into a single class of *dvorianstvo* (gentry), which controlled the state apparatus and fostered the spread of Western culture. The nobility's political and economic position was strengthened and consolidated by the establishment of the formal bureaucratic structure of the Table of Ranks.

While the nobility was subjected to regularized, compulsory, and permanent state service, the peasantry bore the major financial burden of transforming Russia into a modern, militarily powerful state. The peasantry endured a rising burden of taxation and provided labor for state and private industry and for the landowning nobility. Under Peter, serfdom, now firmly entrenched, produced the worst forms of exploitation and abuse. The peasantry was affected by Peter's reforms only in the negative sense of suffering greater hardships and heavier burdens.

The tremendous costs of Peter's wars required a reexamination of the tax structure. In old Muscovy, state taxes, paid exclusively by peasants and some townspeople, had been assessed according to the number of households. The census of 1678 enumerated some 800,000 taxable households, while that ordered by Peter in 1710 listed only 640,000, a disastrous decline in the tax base in face of growing demands for revenue to pay for the Great Northern War. Many factors explain this decline: inaccurate information, inefficient collection of data, peasant desires to avoid taxes by amalgamating households, conscription of peasants into the army, and their flight to outlying areas to escape oppression. The solution to this potentially grave fiscal situation was to substitute a capitation tax, or tax on individuals, for the former household tax. A decree of 1718 made every nonprivileged male subject to a uniform tax determined by computing the costs of war and administration and dividing by the number of males subject to taxation. The resulting figure was assessed against each male that year. This simple method depended on accurate census information. "Revisions" of the census of 1719 were made several times until the number of males subject to the capitation or poll tax reached about 5,600,000. This new method represented an immense new financial burden for the already overburdened peasantry. The amount of tax revenue thus squeezed from the peasantry increased more than fivefold by 1724. Nevertheless, in the first year almost 27 percent of these new taxes remained unpaid.

Besides higher state taxes, heavier dues and obligations were imposed on privately owned serfs and state peasants. As the amount of rent in cash and/or kind (*obrok*) and labor service (*barshchina*) steadily increased during the early 18th century, it became more and more difficult for the serfs to keep body and soul together. For those private serfs unable to pay, their owners were responsible for paying the capitation tax, giving them even greater control over the lives of their serfs. The capitation tax had the effect of abolishing slavery, which had existed side by side with serfdom. Slaves, since they were not considered persons legally, paid no taxes, but the new capitation tax provided that *all* male "souls" (*dushi*) pay the tax. Actually, as the landowner's powers increased, serfs became virtual slaves.

The landlord's legal powers over his serfs were almost unlimited, and he could interfere in their private affairs at will.[1] He did as he pleased about land allotments for peasant use. He could increase or decrease the amount of payment in grain, money, or labor the peasants had to provide. He could confiscate any or all of the serfs' meagre possessions. Corporal punishment for the smallest infractions was commonly meted out by landowners. As before, the only recourse was flight to the frontier or bloody rebellion. The government acted to return and punish fugitive peasants, but it acknowledged more than 200,000 cases of illegal peasant flight from 1719 to 1726 alone.

State peasants were slightly better off than privately owned serfs. The two groups were roughly equal in numbers, had comparable ways of life, and both bore crushing burdens of taxation and dues, but state peasants occupied state lands where their obligations were more precisely defined. State peasants paid the capitation tax, a fixed amount of *obrok* to the state, and performed some labor service to maintain roads, canals, and bridges. They were legally bound to their villages and could not leave without proper authorization by state officials. Subject to increasing taxation and dues and growing obligations, state peasants also faced the danger of being transformed arbitrarily into private serfs or conscripted into government labor gangs to construct new cities, fortifications and roads, or as laborers in state-owned mines and industries. During the early 18th century many state peasants were given away by Russian rulers to private individuals or were sold, loaned, or granted outright to owners of private mines and factories as a form of government subsidy. Often these factory serfs were viciously mistreated and exploited, chained to their machines, beaten at whipping posts, poorly housed, and badly fed and clothed. Whole villages of state peasants were haunted by the fear of becoming factory serfs. So terrifying was this prospect that many joined their privately owned brethren in illegal flight.

Escaping serfs fleeing to the south and southeast fed the ranks of the discontented: Cossacks, *streltsy*, army deserters, ethnic minorities, and Old Believers, all of whom awaited an opportunity to revolt. In the fortress city of Astrakhan, government efforts to enforce Petrine reforms of dress and to prohibit beards caused general indignation. In

---

[1] For more on the landlord's powers see below, pp. 253–54.

Michael Curran

Stone family dwelling, 17th century

July 1705 soldiers and *streltsy* surprised and destroyed the garrison, killed foreigners whom they associated with the hated reforms, the military governor, and more than 300 noblemen. The insurgents, seizing the property of the rich, formed a rebel government under a merchant, Iakov Nosov. The revolt, supported by Terek Cossacks, soon spread over much of southeast Russia. Peter had to send Field Marshal Sheremetiev with an army to quell the uprising. Insurgents who did not succumb to his troops or to torture by the feared Preobrazhenskii Board were executed in Red Square in 1707.

No sooner had that movement been crushed than a Don Cossack leader appeared to lead the disgruntled against the Petrine regime. Kondraty Bulavin was old enough to recall the revolt of Stenka Razin,[2] who like him came from a leading Cossack family. In October 1707 with a few followers he ambushed a government detachment sent into the Don region to round up escaped peasants. Bulavin revived Razin's dream of joining Cossacks of the Don and Dnieper into a united Ukraine to halt Muscovite expansion and encroachments on Cossack freedom. His army of "the insulted and the injured," estimated at 100,000, included Cossacks, peasants, priests, deserters, barge haulers and raftsmen. Bulavin fought against serfdom, but his movement, less widespread than Razin's, was chiefly a Cossack rising. In the summer of 1708 he briefly threatened Peter's new and still fragile state structure, which also faced Swedish invasion. Bulavin managed to occupy

---

[2] See above, p. 176.

Cherkassk and become Cossack *ataman* (chieftain) before his undisciplined levies were defeated by a well trained Muscovite army aided by the Cossack oligarchy. Afterwards some 2,000 Cossacks fled to the Kuban and later across into refuge in Turkey.

Peter's economic policies were neither new nor innovative. He used the existing economic structure but with a new urgency from the needs of his new state organization and the necessity to equip his nascent army and navy. Reduced to simple terms, Peter's economic views were based on a clear recognition of the connection between economic prosperity and national power. Practical considerations combined with the mercantilist doctrine, prevalent in Europe, provided the "theoretical framework" for his economic policies. He sought to maximize exports in order to secure a favorable balance of trade, decreed high protective tariffs, sought self-sufficiency, and to acquire and preserve hard currency. These were the commonly accepted mercantilist goals of most of contemporary Europe.

Observing the drain on Russia's meagre supply of hard currency, depleted by expensive imports of military supplies, Peter was determined to make Russia more self-sufficient by encouraging the development of native industry and commerce. The outbreak of the Great Northern War stimulated rapid growth of foundries and armament enterprises organized to supply the army and navy. These industries, initiated by the government, were rather quickly turned over to private individuals. The government embarked on a program to survey the country's natural resources, the result of which convinced Peter that Russia was superior to other countries in natural resources. He recognized, however, that the state must take the lead in developing them.

Russians were often reluctant to venture into new economic endeavors, forcing the government to encourage private individuals to become involved in economic development. The state offered a variety of fiscal and legal inducements, including monopoly rights, large standing government orders, outright subsidies, tax exemptions, free supply of labor (state peasants), and high tariffs or the complete exclusion of foreign competition. Even with such generous concessions, the government found it difficult to persuade individuals to embark on industrial ventures. Failure or inefficient management of industry brought harsh official reprisals, including heavy fines and even imprisonment. Most of the industrialists came from the merchant class, which was often better prepared and more ambitious than noblemen. Because merchants lacked sufficient wealth, the state provided much of the capital for industry. Shortage of capital severely limited Peter's program of industrialization.

Another problem facing the government was an inadequate labor force for new industries. The state used the numerous state peasants at its disposal in both government and privately financed enterprises. In the latter cases, peasants were sold, loaned, or given outright to factory owners. Peter also tried to solve a distressing social problem by impressing beggars, prostitutes, criminals, and illegitimate children into the industrial work force. Even fugitive serfs who had found employment in factories were protected against forcible return to their

MAP 16–1
Industry and Agriculture, 18th Century

▬▬▬ **Russian frontier in 1800**	**G Glassmaking**
▬▬▬ **Russian frontier in 1700**	
⟶ **Principle trade routes, with commodities**	**T Textile products**
★ **Main trade fairs**	**S Silk products**
◉ **Shipbuilding centres**	**L Leather products**

▨ **Iron mining, smelting, and processing**

▥ **Copper smelting and processing**

Furs etc. **Agricultural and farming centres**

Adapted with permission of Macmillan Publishing Co., Inc. from *Russian History Atlas* by Martin Gilbert. Cartography by Martin Gilbert. Copyright © 1972 by Martin Gilbert.

assigned villages. Labor, however, was less of a problem than chronic lack of capital, foreign competition, and the poor quality of products. Still, some 200 large industrial enterprises were established in Russia during Peter's reign. In absolute terms success in industrialization was modest, but relatively it was enormous, even though some of the enterprises did not long survive Peter. Mining and metallurgy received powerful stimuli, as did textiles and armaments, essential industries for a powerful state destined to play a prominent international role.

The Orthodox Church, weakened during the traumatic controversies of the 17th century, was affected deeply by Peter's reforming activity. Peter merely completed, however, the subordination of the Church to the state begun by his father, Alexis. Following the death of Joachim, patriarch between 1674 and 1690, Peter the Great suffered a setback when his candidate for the patriarchal throne was ignored and Metropolitan Adrian of Kazan was selected. Like his predecessor, Adrian was extremely suspicious of foreigners and foreign influences in Russia, a fact which did not bode well for the future. Peter's candidate, Markell, Metropolitan of Pskov, was unlike Adrian, openminded, well-read and well-disposed toward foreigners. Markell was hated by the boyars and the clergy, noted one observer, "because of his learning and other good qualities"; Adrian had been chosen because of his "ignorance and simplicity." While Adrian served in undistinguished fashion for the next decade, Peter and his cronies formed the "Most Drunken Council," an insulting mockery of the most Holy Council of Church hierarchs. Some historians have tried to connect the drunken parodies of ecclesiastical rites practiced with such delight by Peter and his cohorts with his bitterness over the defeat of his candidate or with his decision to reform the Church. Neither explanation seems to provide an adequate answer because the revelries continued until the end of the reign.

Whatever the explanation, Peter was determined never again to see the Church fall into the hands of a person he disapproved of as he did of Adrian. In 1700, when the patriarchal throne fell vacant, Peter refused to sanction election of a new patriarch. Instead he turned over the patriarch's secular duties to the appropriate organs of state administration and referred his ecclesiastical duties to Stefan Iavorskii, Metropolitan of Riazan, who served as caretaker of the patriarchate for the next two decades. Peter, however, lacked at this point any long-range plan to abolish the patriarchate as an institution. Indeed, his initial purpose in refusing to allow a new patriarch to be elected was to win time to appropriate for the state some of the revenues and to abolish some of the economic privileges of the Church. The time was, after all, one of crisis: the Russians had just been thoroughly beaten by the Swedes at Narva, and Peter needed revenues and even church bells to melt down to reequip his armies. The absence of a patriarch would facilitate his appropriation of patriarchal and monastic revenues and allow him to have church bells turned into cannon with a minimum of opposition. Iavorskii remained metropolitan of Riazan, although as temporary head of the Church, he administered its affairs and was one of Peter's chief advisors on ecclesiastical questions.

Iavorskii's relations with Peter were often stormy and embittered, but the patriarchal "caretaker" never attempted to use the Church as a political weapon against Peter. Despite frequent discord, Iavorskii served as head of the Church (1700–21) longer than any previous primate in Muscovite history. The first indication that Peter was embarking on reforms that would alter the Church structure and administration came in November 1718 when he announced his intention to establish an Ecclesiastical College to manage Church affairs. This was a logical step given Peter's familiarity with the organization of the Church of England and other Protestant churches. In an absolute monarchy, he believed, the state is served by three orders—military, civil, and ecclesiastical—over which he, as supreme ruler, had complete authority. Furthermore, revelations about the clergy's role in the conspiracy which led to the death of Alexis, Peter's only son (June 1718), must have convinced him that state control should be imposed on the clergy. Finally, Peter had just proclaimed his decision to establish administrative colleges, and an ecclesiastical college would have occurred to him quite naturally.

Peter entrusted the delicate task of drafting the regulations governing the proposed Ecclesiastical College to the Bishop of Pskov, Feofan Prokopovich, the chief clerical ideologist of the absolute monarchy. Prokopovich's completed draft of the *Ecclesiastical Regulation,* submitted to Peter early in 1720, was promulgated in January 1721 after careful scrutiny and revision. The patriarchate had been abolished, noted the *Regulation,* because the administration of the Church is "too great a burden for a single man whose power is not hereditary," and seeing no better means to reform the ecclesiastical order, "we hereby establish an Ecclesiastical College." Thus the patriarch was replaced by a consistory of bishops or clerical leaders appointed by the tsar for an indefinite term of office. The *Regulation* suggested 12 as an appropriate and perhaps symbolic number of members for the college, but Peter actually selected only 11 clergymen to serve. The Ecclesiastical College consisted of a president, two vice presidents, four councillors, and four assessors, each of whom could vote on all issues brought before the college. Iavorskii was appointed president, Prokopovich became second vice president, and the other appointees were all at least nominal supporters of Peter's regime and among the most enlightened and well-educated clergymen in Russia. Nonetheless, these clerics did not enjoy Peter's complete confidence. In May 1722 he issued a decree providing for selection of a well-informed and experienced person versed in ecclesiastical affairs, "from among the [army] officers and [to be] made Chief Procurator [of the Holy Synod]." The following month Colonel I. V. Boltin was appointed to that post. The Chief Procurator was to serve as Peter's "eyes and ears" and act as a watchdog to insure that the Synod conducted its business properly and with regard for state interests.

Peter's church reform was clearly the most radical of his innovations because it broke most sharply and decisively with the past. The Russian patriarchate was only about a century old, but throughout its brief his-

David MacKenzie

Bishop's Palace in Rostov, near Vladimir

tory it had been a powerful institution which had guarded the autonomy of the Church. Precisely this autonomy was incompatible with Peter's conception of absolute monarchy. Prokopovich enunciated this view unequivocally in the *Ecclesiastical Regulation:* "From an administrative organ embodying the collegial principle there is no reason to fear rebellions and confusions that grow out of the control of the Church by a single individual." No longer could there be two institutions competing for popular loyalty and allegiance; emperor and state could no longer be rivalled by patriarch and Church. The autonomy of the Church was swallowed up by the state bureaucracy; secular power triumphed over ecclesiastical authority. Declared the oath required of all members of the Holy Synod: "I confess with an oath that the final judge of this ecclesiastical college is the Monarch of all Russia Himself, Our Most Gracious Sovereign."

Suggested Additional Reading

BISSONNETTE, G.   "Peter the Great and the Church as an Educational Institution," in J. Curtiss (Ed.), *Essays . . .* (Leiden, 1963), pp. 3–19.

CRACRAFT, J.   *The Church Reform of Peter the Great* (Stanford, 1971).

———.   "Feofan Prokopovich" in J. Garrard, ed., *The Eighteenth Century in Russia* (Oxford, 1973), pp. 75–105.

GRAHAM, H. F.   "Theophan Prokopovich and the Ecclesiastical Ordinance," *Church History*, vol. 25 (1956), pp. 127–35.

KAHAN, A.   "Continuity in Economic Activity and Policy during the Post-Petrine Period in Russia," *JEH*, vol. 25 (1965), pp. 61–85.

————. "The Costs of Westernization in Russia . . . ," *SR*, vol. 25 (1966), pp. 40–66.

KIRCHNER, W. *Commercial Relations Between Russia and Europe, 1400–1800* (Bloomington, 1966).

MULLER, A. (Trans. and Ed.) *The Spiritual Regulation* . . . (Seattle, 1972).

SEGEL, H. *The Literature of 18th Century Russia* . . . , 2 vols. (New York, 1967).

SERECH, J. "Stefan Yavorsky and the Conflict of Ideologies . . . ," *SEER*, vol. 30, (1951–52), pp. 40–62.

WITTRAM, R. *Peter I, Czar und Kaiser* . . . 2 vols. (Göttingen, 1964).

ZERNOV, N. "Peter the Great and the Establishment of the Russian Church," *CQR*, vol. 125 (1937–38), pp. 265–93.

ZGUTA, R. "Peter I's 'Most Drunken Synod of Fools and Jesters,' " *JfGO*, vol. 21 (1973), pp. 18–28.

17

The Era of Palace Revolutions, 1725–1762

THE PERIOD BETWEEN Peter and Catherine the Great, though full of complex and important events, has been rather neglected by scholars. Nationalist historians called it a second time of troubles during which weak rulers dominated by greedy favorites caused disorder at home and impotence abroad. Admirers of Peter I, architect of reform, Westernization, and Russian power, lamented his successors' indecision and ineffectiveness. Some Russian and Western scholars, however, view this period much more positively. The Russian people, noted Soloviev, no longer driven by the state, could deal with its own problems. With autocracy somewhat relaxed, the nobility became better adapted to Western values, a shift which made it possible to end its compulsory state service in 1762. As cultural growth continued, bases were laid for intellectual development and greater freedom of expression. The early Soviet historian Pokrovskii affirmed that western European capital dominated Russian internal and foreign policy under Anna Ivanovna, and that then followed a "new feudalism" and gentry rule. Recent Soviet accounts, repudiating Pokrovskii's stress on commercial capital, stress heightened contradictions within the ruling feudal landowning class and an intensified mass struggle against it. Should this era be called *the* period of palace revolutions, though there were similar coups before and afterwards? Did Peter I's successors reverse or continue his reforms? Was the political crisis of 1730 a struggle of individuals, feudal factions, or a movement for constitutional monarchy? What were the chief social and economic trends? Was it an era of rising commercial capitalism or continuing feudalism?

POLITICS

Coups d'états brought several of the seven rulers between Peter and Catherine to the throne. Peter's decision of 1722 to name his successor arbitrarily and abrogate traditional rules of succession, claimed Kliuchevskii, produced chronic political instability. Peter's failure to name an heir split the Romanov dynasty into an imperial line of his descendants and a royal line from his half brother, Ivan V. Never in Russia nor in any major country did supreme power pass by a line so broken and exposed to chance, intrigue, and foreign influence. In recurrent succession crises, the two (later three) regiments of the Imperial Guard containing the elite of the Russian nobility and behind which stood titled aristocrats, gentry, and the bureaucracy, played the key role. Despite these palace coups, most of the period was taken up by the reigns of Anna and Elizabeth, both unchallenged once they were firmly in power.

In no case could Peter's successors have exercised his tremendous absolute authority. In one sense the years 1725–30, sometimes designated the "era of collective leadership," resemble the post-Stalin period of 1953–57.[1] Conservatives and titled aristocrats led by the highly educated Prince D. M. Golitsyn and the Dolgoruki family, favoring a traditional succession, backed Alexis' son, Peter, the only surviving male Romanov. Top Petrine bureaucrats such as Prince Menshikov, fearing loss of their posts, supported Peter I's widow, Catherine, and promised the Guards lighter service and more privileges. With Guards' backing, the Senate named the former servant girl autocratic empress. Coarse and ill-educated, Catherine I left most state business to Menshikov and his cronies.

In February 1726 top Russian leaders formed a six member Supreme Privy Council, all except Golitsyn being Petrine bureaucrats. The other original members were Menshikov, Apraksin, Golovkin, Tolstoi, and Ostermann. For four years this oligarchy, *de facto* rulers of Russia, supervised the Senate and administrative colleges. The problems of this difficult transition period needed an able ruler's full attention; instead the Council members intrigued and played petty politics. Mainly out of apathy they preserved most of Peter's central institutions while discussing futilely how to remedy administrative disorder. Supporting Peter's reforms, Catherine executed his decrees. Council members, though close collaborators of the Reformer, regarded his work negatively:

> After a discussion of the present condition of the all-Russian state, it appears that almost all affairs . . . are in bad shape and require immediate rectification. Despite the tireless diligence with which [Peter] labored to establish good order in all affairs . . . and to institute suitable regulations in the hope that appropriate order would follow, the results are not yet evident.[2]

Attracted by Muscovite administrative practices, the oligarchs condemned the Petrine provincial government for burdening state and people with superfluous officials. They abrogated most Petrine regional institutions and restored a single official, the *voevoda*, subject to the provincial governor. Instead of adapting Peter's work to Russian conditions, the Supreme Privy Council rejected innovation, reduced the

---

[1] See below, pp. 575–77.

[2] N. P. Pavlov-Silvanskii, "Ocherki po russkoi istorii . . . ," in *Sochineniia* (St. Petersburg, 1910), vol. 2, pp. 378–79.

staffs of the Senate and colleges, and abolished unpopular procurators and fiscal overseers.

Catherine's death in 1727 brought the boy emperor, Peter II (1727–30) to the throne. Soon thereafter Menshikov was arrested, and the Dolgoruki family with its anti-Petrine policies dominated the Supreme Privy Council, which continued to dissolve Petrine institutions though later they had to be restored. Early in 1728 the court and some central agencies moved to Moscow for the coronation of Peter II, who became a plaything of the Dolgorukis.

Peter's sudden death (January 1730) without a designated successor sparked a dramatic political crisis. Prince D. M. Golitsyn, the Council's outstanding leader, persuaded his fellow oligarchs to offer the throne to a widow believed to be docile, Anna of Courland, second daughter of Ivan V. Aiming at limited monarchy, Golitsyn induced the Council to adopt "Conditions" obligating the new ruler to act only with the Council's consent:

1. Not to start war with anyone.
2. Not to conclude peace.
3. Not to burden our loyal subjects with new taxes.
4. Not to promote to high ranks . . . above those of colonel, and not to appoint to high office, and to have the Guard and other regiments under the authority of the Supreme Privy Council.
5. Not to deprive [members of] the nobility of life, property, and honor without trial.
6. Not to grant estates and villages.
7. . . . not to promote either Russians or foreigners to court offices.
8. Not to spend state revenues.[3]

Anna must either observe these "Conditions" or be deprived of the crown.

Apparently Golitsyn considered the "Conditions" a type of bill of rights and an initial step toward a constitutional monarchy dominated by the top aristocracy. "It would be highly expedient to limit the supreme authority by salutary laws," he explained. To top leaders assembled in the Kremlin palace, he declared that Russia had suffered grievously from Peter's despotism and from foreigners imported to operate it, and the Council concurred. Three emissaries notified Anna Ivanovna of her selection, explained the "Conditions," and secured her signature. Leading Petrine bureaucrats Iaguzhinskii and Prokopovich, however, opposing limited monarchy and Council rule, encouraged her secretly to disregard the "Conditions" and make herself an autocrat. As opposition to the "Conditions" and the Council mounted among the assembled gentry, the Council invited them to submit plans for political change. Variously estimated from seven to 12, these proposals were mostly drafted hastily and included mainly specific gentry demands to ease state service and relax training requirements and inheritance laws. The Supreme Privy Council, however, became their chief target. Rule

---

[3] Marc Raeff, *Plans for Political Reform in Imperial Russia, 1730–1905* (Englewood Cliffs, N.J., 1966), pp. 45–46.

by a narrow noble oligarchy, they feared, might take Russia the way of disintegrating aristocratic Poland. Recalling court cliques under the early Romanovs, with sovereignty divided among princely families and that periods without autocracy had produced turmoil and bloodshed, rank and file gentry opposed the "Conditions" strongly. V. N. Tatishchev's complete, well argued proposal warned that aristocratic rule might bring Russia to ruin. Using Western political theory, notably that of Thomas Hobbes, he urged restoration of the autocracy. Encouraged by overwhelming gentry support for autocracy (and, some claim, popular backing as well) and aided by her powerful favorite, Biron, Anna convened the Senate and Council of State. In a dramatic scene she tore up the "Conditions," proclaimed herself autocratic empress, and ended an abortive attempt at limited monarchy for which tradition and popular support were lacking.

Anna Ivanovna's reign (1730–40) remains controversial. Nationalist Russian historians have depicted it as a dark page in Russian history with selfish German favorites exploiting the state, wasting its resources, and betraying national interests. But foreign predominance, notes A. Lipski, a Western historian, was not so great as earlier believed. Germans dominated the Cabinet, but the Senate remained Russian, and the administrative colleges had no more foreigners than under Peter the Great. Furthermore, Germans such as Field Marshal Münnich and Count Ostermann, proved able, honest and loyal to Russia. Under Münnich, president of the War College, "the Russian army was put upon the respectable footing it has since maintained, and a discipline till then unknown was introduced into the troops, thus finishing the work begun by Peter I."[4] In official policies of the 1730s few antinational tendencies are evident. Anna began her reign with a traditional coronation in the Moscow Kremlin, and in 1732 the court returned to St. Petersburg after four years in Moscow.

Anna, explains a contemporary, "was naturally gentle and compassionate, . . . but she had the fault of weak princes: allowing evil to be done in her name. . . ." Nationalists call her rule the Bironovshchina because of the dominant role of Biron (Bühren). This haughty, cruel man established the sinister Secret Chancellery, which arrested many highly placed dignitaries. In his reign of terror many were executed and more than 20,000 sent to Siberia, often without trial or the empress' knowledge. This practice, however, represented a restoration of Peter I's secret police, the Preobrazhenskii Board.[5] Executions, favoritism and abuse of power had existed previously and would recur often. Terror against noblemen was designed partly to silence opponents of autocracy. In 1731 the Supreme Privy Council was abolished and replaced by a Cabinet of Ministers (Prince Cherkasskii, Ostermann, and Golovkin) without whose consent nothing important could be done. At first Anna attended it and signed all decrees. When her interest flagged, the Cabinet and Biron ruled Russia.

---

[4] C. H. von Manstein, *Contemporary Memoirs of Russia* (reprint New York, 1968), p. 54.

[5] See above, pp. 193, 206.

Anna Ivanovna's death (October 1740) brought a baby, Ivan VI, grandson of her sister, Catherine, to the throne with the unpopular Biron as regent. Only three weeks later Biron was toppled by a palace coup led by Field Marshal Münnich and sent to Siberia. During the regency of Anna, mother of Ivan VI, German favorites contended for power and wealth, aided by foreign ambassadors seeking Russia's international support. This disgraceful interlude ended with another coup in behalf of Elizabeth, the daughter of Peter the Great. Urged on by Lestocq, her doctor, and La Chétardie, the French ambassador, she led the Guards in a torchlight procession to the imperial palace and arrested the baby emperor and his ministers. Elizabeth I (1741–61), beautiful, charming, and popular with the Guards, lacked inconvenient moral scruples. Generously rewarding the Guards, she promised to deliver Russia from foreign rule. In M. Lomonosov's panegyric: "Like Moses Elizabeth had come to release Russia from the night of Egyptian servitude; like Noah she had saved Russia from an alien flood."

Elizabeth's return to Petrine policies was very superficial. Like her father she was impatient, fond of fast travel, and was oriented toward Europe, but she was pious, fearful, and indolent. Immersed in court balls and intrigue, Elizabeth neglected government and the populace. Foreign diplomats testified to her inability to reach decisions; documents remained piled on her desk for weeks. Her learning was slight, and she believed that reading was unhealthy! To the joy of nationalists, Münnich and Ostermann were removed and top administrative posts went to native Russians, but she promptly named as her heir the German, Peter of Holstein (later Peter III), whose mother was Anna, daughter of Peter the Great. Some administrative colleges eliminated under Anna were restored and the Cabinet abolished. At first Elizabeth presided over a restored Senate, but soon wearying of personal rule, she turned matters over to her ministers and favorites. Her personal popularity enabled her to abolish the death penalty and release many political prisoners. Elizabeth's chief legacies were more than 15,000 dresses and immense debts (her courtiers followed her dubious example assiduously), but autocracy survived despite the vagaries and inattention of the autocrat.

SOCIETY AND ECONOMY

Under Peter's successors the *dvorianstvo* (gentry) achieved many cherished objectives and subjected a wretched peasantry to its complete authority. Seeking to satisfy grievances of noblemen in their petitions of 1730, Anna that very year created a third regiment of imperial guards, the Izmailovskii; but unwisely she named as its officers mostly Baltic Germans and Swedes. Biron's rule promoted the nobility's moral unity as remaining titled noblemen became gentrified. In the relatively peaceful post-Petrine era, the state needed fewer noble officers and became more concerned with the economic status of the *dvorianstvo*. Legislation of Anna's reign reinforced the noble's position as landowner and serfowner and eased the burdens of compulsory service, but failed to satisfy *dvoriane*, who wished to escape state service altogether. In 1727 many noble officers obtained long leaves without pay to put their estates in order. A decree of 1736, reducing compulsory state service to 25 years and allowing one son to remain to manage the estate, created a nonserving *dvoriane* element. Other noblemen, beginning service at the age of 20, could retire at 45 and administer their estates while still vigorous. After the Turkish War (1739) so many noble officers requested retirement that the government restricted the decree's application in order to prevent depletion of the officers corps.

The Cadet Corps, founded by Münnich and beginning to function in 1732, had mollified the gentry because it enabled them to become officers without first serving in the ranks. At first only 200, its student body was soon increased to 360 but still only enrolled some prospective officer candidates. Its broad curriculum prepared noblemen for civil as well as military service. In 1732 Russian officer pay was made equivalent to that of foreigners. The state, however, retained tight control over noble education: by a decree of 1737 young nobles had to register for schooling at the age of seven and take examinations in basic subjects at the ages of 12, 16, and 20. Those failing the tests could be enrolled as ordinary seamen, which Russian nobles considered a terrible fate.

Noble and state economic interests meshed closely. In 1731 the Senate revoked Peter's unpopular inheritance law of 1714,[6] which the gentry had evaded. Henceforth, immovable property could be divided equally among all heirs, and noblemen again fragmented their estates. *Pomestie* land came under full private ownership, which stimulated noble interest in managing their estates. To encourage noblemen short on capital to revive neglected estates, the government opened a Noble Bank (1754), which loaned up to 10,000 rubles to an individual at low interest rates.

The state also extended the gentry's authority over private serfs. Responsible for their poll taxes since 1722, noblemen in 1731 became government agents to collect them. No longer could serfs obtain freedom by enlisting in the army, and landowners could order their serfs to marry and prevent marriages outside the estate which cost them labor power. A serf needed his lord's consent to work off the estate or to purchase land. From 1734 landowners were supposed to provide food and seed to serfs in hard times but rarely did so, and the state seldom intervened. The government granted hereditary *dvoriane* a virtual monopoly of estates farmed by serfs by prohibiting other classes from owning them, thus separating the hereditary nobility juridically from other social groups.

As the peasants' social status deteriorated, their poverty deepened. The Supreme Privy Council considered alleviating the peasant's lot not from humanitarian concern but because peasant flight deprived the state of taxpayers and army recruits and the gentry of revenues from rents. Entire villages fled to Poland, to the Don, and to Siberia, and when forcibly returned to an estate, they would often flee again with

---

[6] See above, p. 203.

new companions. The threat of such flights prevented the landowners from raising money rents. The government was also plagued by numerous small-scale peasant uprisings, especially on monastic estates where conditions were particularly bad. Peasant bands, at times numbering thousands, fought pitched battles with government punitive detachments. The state's resort to military action and brutal punishments instead of seeking causes of peasant discontent brought grievous depopulation of many rural areas. Landowners competed feverishly for peasants, who were then forced to pay the taxes of those who had fled. Less autocracy in St. Petersburg brought no respite to Russia's impoverished and unfortunate peasantry.

Russian towns continued a slow but steady growth. Especially in the more developed central provinces, there was a peasant influx into urban areas. In 1750, however, the town population was still only about three percent of the total, and the development of the merchant class, hampered by increasing state favoritism for gentry interests, by no means kept pace with the rapid growth of mercantile elements in western Europe.

The government, though caught between competing merchant and gentry commercial interests, sought with some success to foster Russia's domestic and foreign commerce. Bills of exchange were introduced for merchants in 1729, and a Commercial Bank opened in St. Petersburg in 1754. During the 1740s gentry entrepreneurship had begun on a significant scale, and in the 1750s the government turned over many state-owned metallurgical works to noblemen. They, however, proved unable to run them successfully. The gentry did set up flourishing alcohol distilling enterprises, mostly on their estates, as they sought extra income to pay for Western luxuries and travel abroad. As conflict between gentry and merchant entrepreneurs increased, the state granted the nobility a virtual monopoly of alcohol distilling and curtailed the merchants' trading rights. The state, however, stimulated domestic commerce by abolishing internal tolls and charges on the movement of goods (1753), creating virtually free domestic trade. Customs duties on imports made up the lost revenue in a return to Petrine protectionism. Few Russian merchants ventured abroad, and Russia's foreign commerce remained mostly in English hands.

The Anglo-Russian Treaty of 1734 was the era's most significant commercial agreement. England and Russia, though natural trading partners, had been at political odds for years, mainly over Russian naval power in the Baltic Sea. After Peter's death, deterioration of the Russian fleet and Russia's conciliatory approach reduced friction. When normal diplomatic relations were resumed by the two countries in 1731, the Russia Company, a private English concern, actively sought a commercial accord. Throughout the negotiations the English, anxious for markets, raw materials, and naval stores, took the initiative. The Treaty helped Russia's balance of payments considerably because Britain normally bought as many Russian goods as any two other countries and paid more cash to Russia than all other European nations combined. The English received most-favored-nation treatment and the right to sell some woolens cheaper than their competitors. Russian consumption of English cloth increased markedly, and by 1760 average annual English exports to Russia were double the pre-Treaty level.

This was an era of recurrent budget deficits and incompetent state financial management. The government could not raise poll taxes without swelling peasant arrears, increasing their flight, and drawing gentry opposition. Instead poll-tax rates were reduced repeatedly, but arrears remained high. To recover revenue lost from direct taxes, Senator P. I. Shuvalov, an enthusiastic amateur financier and project-maker, suggested raising the price of salt and spirits (state monopolies) and devaluating the coinage. Large state sums could not be discovered or accounted for: in 1749 the Senate, seeking back accounts from the College of State Revenue, threatened to lock up its members under guard until they submitted a report! State finances were further burdened by lavish court expenditures and large grants to favorites.

CULTURE AND WESTERNIZATION

In the considerable cultural gains of the post-Petrine epoch, the Imperial Court and emerging educational institutions in the capitals were the chief sowers of European ideas and values. In Russia court life had greater relative impact than courts did in the West. Most well-to-do persons were received there, and it alternated between Moscow and St. Petersburg, transmitting its influence also to regional centers and noble residences.

Under Anna, prominent, well educated Germans in her administration, such as Ostermann and Münnich, and reform-minded Russians, such as Feofan Prokopovich and Prince Kantemir, fostered Westernization. The Academy of Sciences (1725), aided by Anna's government, promoted geographical exploration, mapped Russia, and issued the first Russian atlas (1745). Attached to the Academy was Russia's first university (opened 1748); its secondary school gave a European education to some future Russian leaders. Under Academy auspices was published the *St. Petersburg News*, the second oldest Russian newspaper, with material drawn from European sources.

Educational progress under Elizabeth was promoted chiefly by her favorite, Ivan Shuvalov. At his proposal the Senate authorized the opening in 1755 of Moscow University with Shuvalov as its rector. At first lectures were mostly in Latin and its students were few, but public debates were soon held there. Only in the next century did it become a leading center of higher learning. Shuvalov's plan to establish secondary schools in provincial capitals and primary schools in larger towns was shelved, but two secondary schools opened in Moscow and one in Kazan. Hitherto educational institutions and the few printing presses had been fully state controlled, but in the 1750s the Academy of Sciences acted as its own censor and the number of printing presses doubled. French cultural influences increased and prominent Russians corresponded with philosophes such as Voltaire and Diderot. French influences spread beyond court circles as the nobility's educational level rose. Official attitudes toward free expression remained negative and professors were carefully supervised, but cultural secularization nonetheless caused some erosion of old attitudes and restrictions.

After 1730 a national Russian literature began to develop, fostered by writers who had lived and studied in the West. They adopted prevalent Western classicism but introduced Russian themes and improved the Russian literary language. Prince Antiokh Kantemir, a poet and diplomat, wrote satires which were published posthumously. Russia's first professional men of letters were Vasili Trediakovskii, a prolific translator and writer, and Alexander Sumarokov, playwright and director of St. Petersburg's first Russian theater (1756). Michael Lomonosov (1711–65), a peasant's son who became professor of chemistry at the Academy of Sciences, is praised extravagantly by Soviet scholars as a genius and universal man who transformed literature, science and history. Wrote Alexander Pushkin, the great 19th century Russian poet:

> Combining unusual strength of will with unusual power of understanding, Lomonosov embraced all branches of knowledge. . . . Historian, rhetorician, mechanic, chemist, minerologist, artist, and poet, he tried everything and penetrated everything.[7]

Less worthy were Lomonosov's odes praising Peter I and his successors and his role in suppressing his rivals' writings. Political and ideological factors, he declared, must prevail over scholarly objectivity. Nonetheless, Lomonosov contributed much to public enlightenment and was Russia's outstanding mid-century intellectual figure.

Sound foundations were laid for the study of Russian history. Especially notable was V. N. Tatishchev's monumental *Russian History* based on chronicles and other primary materials. At the Academy of Sciences G. F. Müller, a German scholar, who wrote the first thorough study of Siberia, promoted the Norman theory provoking a heated controversy with the patriotic Lomonosov.[8]

In the arts, progress was modest. In 1736 an Italian opera company performed at Court; under Elizabeth opera performances occurred regularly. An Italian architect, Bartholomo Rastrelli, designed the magnificent Winter Palace and Smolny Convent, two of St. Petersburg's architectural gems. The National Academy of Arts, founded by Ivan Shuvalov (1757), stimulated development of the fine arts.

FOREIGN RELATIONS

Peter the Great's successors sought sporadically to continue his policies abroad which had made Russia a great European power. Frequent changes of ruler and political instability, however, encouraged foreign intrigue, bribery of Russian officials, and open interference in Russian affairs. Russian armies scored some major victories, but inept commanders and sudden shifts in state policy prevented significant gains in territory or prestige. Russia's attention focused on the Polish and

---

[7] Cited in A. Morozov, *Lomonosov* (Moscow, 1965), pp. 7–8.

[8] For Norman theory see above, pp. 17 ff.

Turkish questions with weakened Sweden a secondary concern. Nationalist historians such as Kliuchevskii blame German influence in St. Petersburg and unpatriotic diplomacy by German ministers such as Andrew Ostermann for Russia's lack of success abroad. Soviet historians, however, regard this as an era of preparation for solving the Polish question and praise Ostermann and A. P. Bestuzhev-Riumin as outstanding diplomats loyal to Russian national interests. Recent Western accounts tend to agree with them.

From 1725 to 1740 Ostermann, a German from Westphalia, formulated and directed Russian foreign policy. Taken into Russian service by Peter the Great and made his private secretary, Ostermann became vice chancellor of the College of Foreign Affairs in 1727. In the crisis of 1730 he feigned illness to avoid compromising himself. Schooled in intrigue, he emerged as Anna Ivanovna's leading diplomat. His contemporary, C. H. von Manstein, regarded Ostermann as an able minister who knew foreign interests and intentions, was quick of mind, hardworking, "and so incorruptible that he never accepted the least present from any foreign court."

> He had so strange a way of talking that very few persons could ever boast that they had succeeded in comprehending him. Very often foreign ministers, after a conversation of two hours with him, found on leaving his room that they knew nothing more than when they entered. All that he said and all that he wrote could be taken two ways. A master in subtlety and dissimulation, he had perfect command over his passions and could even shed tears when the occasion required. . . .[9]

Ostermann's system was close alliance with Austria and opposition to France, which sought to restrict Russia's influence by supporting Sweden, Poland, and the Ottoman Empire against it. To counter France Ostermann promoted peace and rapprochement with other European states and England.

In the early 1730s the Polish succession engrossed Ostermann's attention. The wholly dominant Polish aristocracy (*szlachta*) had reduced the elective monarchy to impotence, which encouraged foreign intervention in Polish affairs. The death of the Polish king Augustus II in 1733 provoked a power struggle between Stanislas Leszczynski, sponsored by France and Sweden, and Frederick Augustus, elector of Saxony, backed by Russia and Austria. Regarding Leszczynski's election as a threat to its position in eastern Europe, Russia sent in a powerful army. Leszczynski fled to Danzig, but the Russians besieged and captured it, and a "confederation" of Polish nobles, obedient to Russia and Austria, elected Augustus III king of Poland. Russia's primacy in Polish affairs was confirmed and France suffered a major diplomatic defeat.

Anna Ivanovna's ambitious and overconfident advisers led by Field Marshal Münnich provoked war with the Turks. Ill-defined frontiers and periodic raids into Russia by the Crimean Tatars, vassals of the Sultan, provided pretexts for conflict. The Turks, opposing growing

---

[9] C. H. von Manstein, *Contemporary Memoirs* (New York, 1968), pp. 334–35.

Russian influence in Poland and recalling the Pruth campaign of 1711,[10] had contempt for the Russian army. The Russian ambassador in Constantinople, however, reported that Turkish forces were weak and that the Balkan Christians would rise at Russia's signal. Allied with Austria, Russian armies under Münnich gained repeated victories: they invaded the Crimea, captured Azov, Ochakov, and Jassy, and occupied Moldavia. But Russian commanders quarreled, victories went unexploited, and the army's supply system collapsed. Austria made a separate peace, and Russian heroism was largely nullified by inept handling of peace negotiations with the Porte. The Treaty of Belgrade (1739), extravagantly celebrated in St. Petersburg, brought Russia little compensation for her 100,000 casualties and millions of expended rubles. Azov was recovered but minus its fortifications. Russian warships and merchant vessels were barred from the Turkish-dominated Black Sea, and the Sultan even denied Anna's imperial title.

French mediation in arranging the Treaty of Belgrade improved Franco-Russian relations briefly. Marquis de la Chétardie, the new French ambassador in St. Petersburg, sought to wreck the Austro-Russian alliance and oust Ostermann. He helped overthrow Ivan VI, enthrone Elizabeth, and remove Ostermann who died in Siberian exile. A. P. Bestuzhev-Riumin, his successor as head of the Foreign Affairs College, had to contend with La Chétardie, Dr. Lestocq and a pro-Prussian clique around Peter of Holstein, heir to the throne. The French encouraged Sweden to attack Russia, but the Swedes were defeated at Vilmanstrand in Finland. The Treaty of Åbo (1743) reconfirmed the Treaty of Nystadt[11] and added more Finnish territory to Russia.

During the War of Austrian Succession (1740–48) Bestuzhev-Riumin resumed Ostermann's pro-Austrian course after overcoming pro-French and pro-Prussian groups. These conflicting Court factions, however, helped make Russian policy indecisive and ineffective. La Chétardie, discredited by his intrigues, was expelled and Bestuzhev became chancellor. In 1746 he renewed the Austrian alliance and secured an English subsidy for Russian forces protecting England's possessions in Hannover. Russia's role in the war was minor and it was excluded from the Austro-Prussian settlement of 1748. Bestuzhev, having overcome the pro-Prussian faction at Court, reached his peak of influence.

In 1756 the Westminister Convention produced an Anglo-Prussian alliance and a fundamental realignment of European powers. In this "Diplomatic Revolution" Prussia and England opposed France and Austria, which ended centuries of rivalry to combat growing Prussian power. In St. Petersburg pro-French and pro-British factions strove to win over Empress Elizabeth and bribe her ministers. Chancellor Bestuzhev, noted Sir Charles Hanbury-Williams, the British ambassador, remarking that his salary would not allow him to live in his accustomed style, requested a large English pension. To his amazement Hanbury-Williams promised him 12,000 rubles annually for life. Bestuzhev was

---

[10] See above, p. 190.

[11] See above, pp. 190–91.

also taking money from other foreign governments without altering his policy. Elizabeth and her ministers decided to join with France and Austria. Three strong-willed women, Elizabeth of Russia, Maria Theresa of Austria, and Madame Pompadour of France, allied to destroy or weaken Frederick II of Prussia.

During the subsequent Seven Years War (1756–63), the 300,000 man Russian army fought bravely, only to be stymied by an incompetent command and St. Petersburg politics. Repeatedly the Russians defeated the great Frederick or fought him to a standstill; they invaded east Prussia, occupied Berlin, and were in a position to dominate central Europe. Contemplating suicide, Frederick was saved by Elizabeth's death (January 1762), which ended abruptly Russia's participation in the war. Peter of Holstein, now Tsar Peter III, reversed Russian policy overnight and threw away Russia's hard-won wartime gains. An admirer of Frederick and the Prussian army, Peter immediately recalled Russian troops, allied with Prussia, and prepared to attack Denmark.

The lavish expenditure of Russian lives and treasure in mideighteenth century wars produced few lasting results. Under Empress Elizabeth Russia continued to play an important role in European power politics and increased its influence in Poland but could not exploit its advantages in manpower and resources. Ostermann's and Bestuzhev-Riumin's pro-Austrian orientation, though hampered by Court intrigue and coups d'états, proved sound because Austria was Russia's natural ally against the Ottoman Empire, its most dangerous neighbor.

.CONCLUSION

Nationalist critiques of this era of palace revolutions appear exaggerated, but western attempts to rehabilitate its second-rate, frivolous, and lazy rulers have not succeeded well either. Petrine administrative reforms, at times reversed, at others continued, could not be pursued systematically by governments which, though often tyrannical and brutal, were impotent to tackle fundamental problems. Autocracy was preserved, often by unworthy, undignified rulers, and selfish favorites. The atmosphere of fear, suspicion, and gloom, noted by so many contemporaries, marked little improvement over the Petrine period. Noble ascendancy was growing and with it the deplorable degradation of the peasant masses with the state unable and unwilling to intervene. More positively, Westernization and secularization continued, there were cultural and economic advances, national consciousness developed, and some respite was gained from Peter the Great's incessant wars.

Suggested Additional Reading

BOOKS

DANIELS, R. V.   V. N. Tatishchev . . . (Philadelphia, 1973).
KUDRYAVTSEV, B. B.   *The Life and Work of Mikhail V. Lomonosov* (Moscow, 1954).

MANSTEIN, C. H. VON. *Contemporary Memoirs of Russia* . . . *1727–1744* (N.Y. 1968).

PAPMEHL, K. A. *Freedom of Expression in 18th Century Russia* (The Hague, 1971).

RAEFF, Marc. ed. *Plans for Political Reform in Imperial Russia, 1730–1905* (Englewood Cliffs, N.J., 1966).

READING, D. K. *The Anglo-Russian Commercial Treaty of 1734* (New Haven, 1938).

ROGGER, HANS. *National Consciousness in 18th Century Russia* (Cambridge, Mass, 1960).

ARTICLES

BELOFF, MAX. "Russia," in Harcave, *Readings,* vol. 1, pp. 265–77.

DANIELS, R. L. "V. N. Tatishchev and the Succession Crisis of 1730," *SEER,* vol. 49, 1971, pp. 550–59.

DASHWOOD, F. "Sir Francis Dashwood's Diary . . . ," *SEER,* vol. 38, pp. 194–222.

DVOICHENKO-MARKOV, D. "Demetrius Kantemir and Russia," *BS,* vol. 12, ii, pp. 383–99.

HASSELL, JAMES. "Implementation of the Russian Table of Ranks . . . ," *SR,* vol. 29, 1970, pp. 283–95.

HUNT, N. C. "The Russia Company and the Government, 1730–42," *OSPP,* vol. 7, pp. 27–65.

HUNTINGTON, W. C. "Michael Lomonosov and Benjamin Franklin . . ." *RR,* vol. 18, pp. 294–306.

KAHAN, A. "Continuity in Economic Activity and Policy during the Post-Petrine Period in Russia," *JEH,* vol. 25, 1965, pp. 61–85.

———. "The Costs of Westernization in Russia . . ." *SR,* vol. 25, 1966, pp. 40–66.

LIPSKI, A. "The 'Dark Era' of Anna Ioannova," *ASEER,* vol. XV, pp. 477–88.

LODGE, R. "Russia, Prussia and Great Britain, 1742–44," *EHR,* vol. 45, pp. 579–611.

18

Peter III and Catherine II: Politics and Foreign Affairs

BETWEEN 1762 and 1796 a part-German prince, and then his German wife ruled Russia. The prince, Peter III, after reigning six months, was overthrown by his wife who as Catherine II, ruled for a generation. The entire period is often called the era of Catherine the Great after the remarkable woman who so impressed contemporaries and posterity. Soviet historians regard this as an age of enlightened absolutism, which sought to strengthen the nobility's social and political dominance against the rising bourgeoisie.[1] Catherine's reign, they claim, was a great show from start to finish, testimony to effective use of propaganda. Slogans of the Enlightenment, they affirm, were used to defend serfdom, autocracy, and expansion. Most Western scholars, on the other hand, tend to accept Catherine's pretensions of liberalism for the first part of her reign but conclude that the Pugachov Revolt and French Revolution caused her government to adopt a reactionary, repressive course. Was Catherine II a true autocrat or a tool of the nobility and dominated by favorites? How genuine and significant were her political reforms? Did Russia benefit by partitioning Poland and allowing the German powers to reach her frontiers?

PETER III AND THE COUP OF JUNE 28, 1762

Peter of Holstein mounted the throne after Empress Elizabeth's death in January 1762 without opposition. At the age of 13, this grandson of Peter the Great had been summoned to Russia by his aunt, Empress Elizabeth, to become heir to the throne. Peter, notwithstanding recent efforts to rehabilitate him,[2] was a poorly prepared, narrow-minded Holsteiner, who scorned Russian ways. Orphaned in childhood, he remained an adolescent mentally and acted childishly. Peter worshipped Frederick II of Prussia and the army but never went much beyond playing with soldiers. He learned Russian and the Orthodox catechism

---

[1] See Problem No. 5 below.
[2] See Florinsky, vol. 1, pp. 496–99.

226

but remained at heart a German Lutheran. Surrounded with Holsteiners, he sought to build a little world divorced from things Russian.

During his brief reign some important decrees were issued attributable more to his advisers' efforts to strengthen their position than to Peter's desire for change. Many political prisoners were freed, and the security police was abolished. Old Believers, allowed to return from exile, were given freedom of worship, and the salt tax was reduced to win lower class support. Most important, Peter's Manifesto of February 18, 1762 freed the nobility from compulsory state service in peacetime and allowed nobles to travel freely abroad and to enter the service of friendly foreign powers.

Other actions, which alienated leading social elements, suggest that Peter neither sought personal popularity nor realized the significance of his acts. Church estates were secularized and placed under an Economic College. The clergy complained bitterly, but Peter, wanting to Lutheranize the Church, treated it with contempt. Peter alienated top noblemen by a direct attack on the Senate's powers. Equally foolish was his open admiration for Frederick of Prussia. Dressing himself in Prussian uniforms and decorations, he insisted that the Guards do likewise. He imposed strict discipline upon them and required Guards officers to march in parades. Giving his Holsteiners preference over Russians for military and civil posts, Peter alienated elements vital to his power.

Peter's abrupt reversal of Russian foreign policy hastened his removal. Ending Russia's participation in the Seven Years War against Prussia, he yielded all the Russian armies' costly gains. The war had been unpopular and many Russians admired Frederick, but Peter's Holstein patriotism, which led him into war against Denmark, triggered his fall. Peter's blatant insults to Russian national feeling and orthodoxy, his irregular private life, and his capricious, irresponsible behavior contributed to his unpopularity. He antagonized leading individuals and groups as if deliberately seeking to destroy himself. The public was prepared to welcome another ruler.

Catherine, Peter's wife, exploited disaffection by the Guards, nobility, and clergy to seize power. To her former lover, Stanislas Poniatowski, she wrote: "Peter III had lost the little wit he had. He ran his head against everything. He wanted to break up the Guards . . . He wanted to change his religion, marry Elizabeth Vorontsov and shut me up." The ambitious Catherine catered to Russian Orthodoxy and tradition and dissociated herself from Peter's unpopular policies. When he proposed to lead the Guards against Denmark, her opportunity came. After one of their number (Passek) was arrested, the conspirators moved swiftly.

Early on the morning of June 28, Alexis Orlov, brother of Catherine's lover, Gregory, awakened her at Peterhof palace: "It is time to get up; all is ready for your proclamation." At the Izmailovskii Regiment's barracks, recalled Catherine, "the soldiers came running out, kissing me . . . and calling me their deliverer. They began swearing allegiance to me." The other regiments joined her readily. In nearby St. Petersburg the Senate and Synod proclaimed Peter's dethronement and

Catherine was named autocratic empress in Kazan Cathedral. Leading many troops as a colonel of the Preobrazhenskii Regiment, Catherine marched toward Peterhof. Peter sought support at Kronstadt naval base but was not permitted to land. He returned despondently to Oranienbaum and abdicated meekly. Taken to a nearby estate by Alexis Orlov, he soon died under suspicious circumstances. Catherine's highly colored account reads:

> Fear had given him a diarrhoea which lasted three days, . . . on the fourth he drank excessively. . . . The only things he asked me for were his mistress, his dog, his Negro, and his violin; but for fear of scandal. . . , I only sent him the last three things. . . . The hemorrhoidal colic . . . affected his brain. . . . Despite all the assistance of the doctors, he expired whilst demanding a Lutheran priest. I feared that the officers might have poisoned him, so I had him opened. . . . Inflammation of the bowels and a stroke of apoplexy had carried him off. His heart was extraordinarily small and quite decayed.[3]

Catherine denied rumors of foul play, but it is generally accepted that Alexis Orlov strangled Peter either on his own initiative or at Catherine's orders.

CATHERINE II—WOMAN AND RULER

Catherine was born as Sophie in 1729 to the ruling family of Anhalt-Zerbst, a small German state on the Baltic. Her education was undistinguished and her financial and marital prospects slender. Then in 1744 Empress Elizabeth invited her and her mother to the Russian court. Elizabeth had been engaged to a brother of Sophie's mother, and her elder sister had married the Duke of Holstein; so the Empress regarded them as part of her family. To stabilize Russia's political future, Elizabeth wanted Grand Duke Peter safely married. En route to Russia, mother and daughter conferred in Berlin with Frederick II, who recruited the mother and charged her to get Elizabeth to ally with Prussia. At the Russian frontier, discarding their disguise, they were greeted as honored guests of the Empress. Rumors spread that Sophie was destined to marry Peter, heir to the throne. Young Sophie, casting her spell over Elizabeth, resolved to remain in Russia though her mother, soon unmasked as a Prussian spy, was expelled.

Sophie paid court to Peter who, by her account, was ugly, immature, and boastful. She studied Russian assiduously and won goodwill at the imperial court. Converted to Orthodoxy "without any effort," she was christened Catherine (Ekaterina Alekseevna) and in 1745 married Peter. Her 17-year cohabitation with that perpetual adolescent tested her patience and ambition fully. Catherine described one of Peter's pastimes: in his apartment she saw a large rat hanging from the ceiling. Peter explained that for eating two wax sentries it had been court-martialed, executed, and would remain in public view for three days. Soon Paul was born, son of Catherine and probably the courtier, Serge

---

[3] W. Walsh, ed. *Readings in Russian History* (Syracuse, N.Y., 1959), pp. 186–87.

Catherine II

Saltykov. Catherine busied herself with amorous adventures, extensive reading, and the study of court politics. She came to the throne as the best educated, most literate ruler in Russian history. Ambition, vitality, and political shrewdness were her outstanding traits. "I will rule or I shall die," she told the English ambassador in 1757. Frederick II wrote in 1778: "The empress of Russia is very proud, very ambitious, and very vain." Her actions as ruler confirmed the truth of his remarks.

The dubious means by which she achieved power at first helped determine how she ruled. In initial manifestoes she posed as a national ruler brought to the throne by public demand and denounced Peter III as a foreigner. "All true sons of Russia have clearly seen the great danger to which the whole Russian Empire has actually been exposed." The foundations of Orthodoxy had been threatened with destruction, and "the glory Russia has acquired at the expense of so much blood . . . has been trampled under foot by the peace lately concluded with [Prussia]." Catherine depicted herself as defender of Russia's faith and institutions to get the public to forget that she was a German usurper without legitimate claim to the throne and to foster loyalty of key groups to her regime.

Insecurity induced Catherine at first to act like an official who feared imminent dismissal and to compare herself with a hare being chased in all directions. In state matters she relied principally upon Nikita

Panin, the only experienced statesman among the conspirators, who acted as *de facto* chancellor. His proposal for a small, permanent Imperial Council to advise the ruler on legislation, however, was blocked by rival court groups and shelved by Catherine. New youthful courtiers like the Orlovs and Princess Dashkov, who rode into power with her, at first treated her as their creature and swarmed around seeking rewards of money, estates, and offices. Catherine was saved from becoming a figurehead by the greed and contention of court factions. At times she heeded the Orlovs' advice and showered favors upon them, but she played them against the Panin group, balancing astutely between these rival elements while building her own power. Early in her reign, to overcome her inadequate knowledge of Russian conditions and the court's isolation from the populace, Catherine undertook excursions to the northeast, the Volga region and Baltic provinces, accompanied by a huge suite and the entire diplomatic corps.

For years Catherine's right to the throne was questioned, and abroad many believed that her reign would be brief. She worried about the claims of Ivan VI, imprisoned at Schlüsselberg fortress since infancy, until in 1764 this human derelict died by her orders during a rescue attempt by a disgruntled army officer. Even his death failed to dispel the pretenderism produced by Catherine's usurpation and by popular discontent. Three pretenders emerged in 1764 alone and ten in the next decade who claimed to be Peter III resurrected, of whom Emelian Pugachov was the most famous.[4] Unlike Catherine, her son Paul possessed a legitimate, hereditary claim to the throne. The Panin faction wished Paul to obtain some power when he came of age in 1772, but Catherine opposed this and blocked its efforts. She proclaimed invariably that she was empress by divine plan and popular demand.

Insecurity at home made foreign support and approbation the more crucial. In Catherine's correspondence with the philosophes, she fostered her reputation as an enlightened monarch. Montesquieu's *Spirit of the Laws*, she boasted, stood by her bedside; she urged Diderot to complete the *Encyclopédie* in St. Petersburg. Catherine subsidized the philosophes generously and sought their advice on how to administer Russia. In return, praising her enlightened absolutism, they called her the "Semiramis of the North."

Catherine employed a series of favorites who shared her bed but rarely her power. Ten official favorites in turn occupied quarters next to hers and were loaded with decorations, money, and estates. Gregory Potemkin was by far the most powerful, and only he remained an important statesman after ceasing to be her lover. In old age Catherine chose 22-year-old Platon Zubov. She loved them passionately, especially Gregory Orlov and Potemkin, and treated discarded lovers generously, but she alone decided when they must leave the imperial presence. This system let her preserve autocratic power while indulging a sentimental, amorous nature.

---

4 See below, pp. 255–57.

The Empress, the government's motive force, showed a Germanic devotion to hard, regular labor. Rising regularly at 5 A.M., she worked long hours as the true first servant of the state. In 1769 she established the Imperial Council as the chief central political institution. Containing the empire's seven most powerful men, with Catherine presiding, it discussed frankly and secretly vital national issues, especially foreign policy, but it remained purely advisory and in no way limited Catherine's authority. Working closely with her were four or five state secretaries and a few clerks who constituted a type of imperial chancery.

THE LEGISLATIVE COMMISSION

Typical of Catherine's enlightened absolutism was the Legislative Commission and her *Instruction* (*Nakaz*) to it.[5] Her travels about Russia in the early 1760s convinced her of the urgent need to replace the antiquated Law Code of 1649 and recast Russian institutions. She set out to become Russia's Justinian and for two years labored over her *Instruction* to the Commission, which would provide the government with information about public grievances and desires as a basis for action.

Her manifesto of December 1766 summoned into being a Legislative Commission, reminiscent of the *zemskii sobor* of 1648–49, to draw up a new law code with the aid of the *Instruction*. The clergy were excluded from the Commission as too oppositionist, whereas the nobility (139 deputies) elected one delegate per district. Property-holding townspeople chose 216 delegates, state peasants 24, single householders 43, Cossacks 43, and non-Russians 51. Deputies from central state institutions (the colleges, Senate and Synod) brought the total to some 568, too many to compose articles of a law code. The deputies arrived with instructions (*nakazy*) from their constituents somewhat resembling *cahiers* to the French Estates-General of 1789. Noble *nakazy* complained about the problems of purchasing and selling estates because of red tape and about competition from merchants; they requested corporate organization for their class. Townsmen countered with demands for a monopoly of commerce, the right to own serfs, and urban self-government, while the state peasantry complained of inadequate land.

When the Commission convened in July 1767, Metropolitan Dmitri, the Church's sole representative, proposed that Catherine be offered the title, "the great, wise mother of her country." This proposal was approved, received the force of law, and was the only decision the Commission ever reached! Using the assembly to legitimize her power, Catherine advertised it to Europe through the philosophes. Once it began discussing a law code and preparing it in 19 committees, official interest in it waned, and government deputies rarely attended. Although

---

[5] See excerpts below, p. 242.

203 sessions of the Commission were held, not a single article was drafted. It could only discuss and reflect public opinion, not legislate. Confused by Catherine's highly theoretical, vague *Instruction,* the deputies, many of whom were illiterate and unprepared for their work, wrangled among themselves. The old aristocracy urged abolition of the Table of Ranks for admitting persons of non-noble origin, but the service gentry defeated that proposal. Courageous statements by a few deputies urging limitations of serfdom alarmed the government. A noble deputy, Gregory Korobin, advocated breaking the lord's unlimited power over his serfs, giving property rights to the peasantry, and limiting their obligations by law.

While Catherine used the Commission to strengthen her autocracy, she refused to let it limit her power. The philosophe, Denis Diderot, hoped it would become permanent, but after the Russo-Turkish War began in 1768, she prorogued the Commission, though some of its committees worked until 1774. Their proposals for reforming provincial and urban government were used in subsequent imperial legislation. Diderot commented sadly: "The Russian empress is doubtless a despot."

ADMINISTRATIVE CHANGES

At her accession, Catherine recalled later, the government was near collapse and unable to perform its functions. State credit was poor, the deficit was large, and governmental institutions lay in disorder, run by incompetent and corrupt officials. The Senate, supposed to supervise the administration, could handle little business and was, in Catherine's words, "apathetic and deaf." She ignored Professor Desnitskii's proposal to transform the Senate into an elected legislature of 600 to 800 members. Instead, in 1763 it was divided into six specialized departments and its staff considerably enlarged. Though the Senate's political importance declined further, it could handle much more business promptly and efficiently. Rather than consult directly with the Senate, Catherine enhanced the powers of the procurator general, a post held for many years by the industrious and loyal Prince A. A. Viazemskii. By 1768 Catherine could point already to major achievements in central administration: considerable surplus revenues, former debts paid, and state credit restored. The state's capacity to govern improved dramatically. During the 1780s several administrative colleges, superfluous because of provincial reform, were closed. In the chief colleges, Army, Admiralty, and Foreign Affairs, one-man administration had by then largely replaced former collective decision-making. Finally, the Table of Ranks was reorganized, the number of officials increased considerably, and their salaries raised. Corruption, while not eliminated, was reduced to more tolerable levels.

In local government the Empress could act as an enlightened despot without imperiling autocracy. In the 1760s salaries of most provincial officials were raised and their jurisdiction clarified. Appointed procurators supervised all levels of provincial administration, and governors were encouraged to exercise real authority and initiative. Such bureaucratic absolutism failed to prevent the Pugachov Revolt of 1773–74,[6] but the Revolt brought the state and nobility into closer harmony and cooperation and revealed the incapacity of the old local administration. Afterwards, concern for internal security stimulated Catherine to carry out far-reaching reform, a move which was also prompted by the vastness of the old provinces, territorial and population increases, and the nobility's expressed desire to participate in local government. Using materials from the Legislative Commission and private petitions to the Senate, Catherine drafted most of the Fundamental Law of 1775. She boasted to Voltaire: "This is the fruit of five months work carried out by me alone."

The Fundamental Law became the basis of Catherine's domestic policy for the rest of her reign, and its institutions lasted until 1861. By now she was a complete and experienced autocrat served by able and loyal officials, and the reforms owed much to the advice of Jakob Sievers, the able and industrious governor of Novgorod. Provincial administration was rationalized and simplified. The former *gubernii* and *provintsii* were replaced with 41 new *gubernii*. By the end of the reign territorial expansion had increased this number to 50, a number which changed little to the end of the empire. Each *guberniia*, with 300,000 to 400,000 male "souls," was divided into districts (*uezdy*) with 20,000 to 30,000 "souls." The top regional official was a viceroy (*namestnik*), who administered two to four *gubernii* along the frontiers with semiregal authority. The Tula governor generalship was inaugurated with an elaborate ceremony in a great hall as from the steps of a throne beneath the Empress's portrait, the new viceroy addressed the assembled nobility. A governor (*gubernator*) headed each *guberniia*, which received a uniform administrative structure. As Montesquieu had advised, administrative, judicial, and financial functions (but not powers) were carefully separated. State decrees were transmitted to the *gubernii* through a provincial board with the governor presiding. A subsidiary board supervised tax collection, expenditures, and economic affairs, and a Board of Public Charity ran schools and hospitals. A police official (*kapitan-ispravnik*), elected by the nobility, administered each *uezd*. Except for Moscow and St. Petersburg, which had the status of provinces, towns were run by lower ranking state-appointed officials.

The provincial court system reflected mainly noble desires and Montesquieu's principles. In each *guberniia* capital were criminal and civil courts, while at the district and local levels were separate courts for nobility, townspeople, and peasantry, perpetuating old estate-distinctions. Catherine introduced English-style courts to reconcile complainants and plaintiffs and to free those arrested without due cause, but they decided only minor cases.

In 1785 Catherine's Charter to the Towns (and Charter to the Nobility)[7] completed the recasting of regional administration. The growth

---

[6] See below, pp. 255–57.

[7] See below, p. 252.

of commercial and monetary relationships in towns and urban petitions preceded changes in town government. The urban population was divided into six categories based on property and wealth, including all urban property holders of whatever estate, and commercial and industrial elements were divided into guilds by wealth. A complex system of town self-government emerged which guaranteed control to men of wealth. A town assembly (*duma*) would select a six member board to run urban services. These elective institutions were supervised by the provincial governor.

In frontier regions and newly incorporated territories, Catherine pursued vigorous centralization and Russification. Favoring a single system of imperial administration, she disregarded national differences and destroyed remnants of autonomy. In 1764 she confided to Prince Viazemskii that perhaps Ukrainian and Baltic rights could not be abolished immediately, but "to call them foreign and treat them as such would be more than a mistake; it would be, indeed, plain stupidity."[8]

The full weight of this repressive policy struck the Ukraine, where the autonomous tradition of the Cossacks still threatened Russian control. In 1768 Russian troops crushed an uprising by ordinary Cossacks against the *starshina,* and seven years later the Sech itself was suddenly attacked and destroyed. *Starshina* aristocrats cooperating with Russia were rewarded with officer rank and estates. Some rank and file Cossacks, rather than submit, fled to the Ottoman Empire. Volga, Ural, and Don Cossacks also lost their freedom, and the Russian army absorbed their regiments. In 1781 the last remnants of Ukrainian autonomy were snuffed out: the left-bank Ukraine became a governor-generalship of three provinces ruled by Russians. The Baltic provinces' special status also ended: after a census had been conducted, the poll tax was introduced, and in 1783 the region became a governor-generalship.

Prince Potemkin, Catherine's powerful favorite and empire builder, ruled newly acquired areas in south Russia and the north Caucasus effectively. With his military background, administrative skill, and physical attractiveness to Catherine, he rose rapidly until he headed the War College and all administration in "New Russia." In the 1780s with unremitting energy he settled colonists and built towns, notably Sevastopol naval base in the Crimea and Ekaterinoslav on the Dnieper. Potemkin's work in the south strengthened Russia economically and enhanced its power in the Black Sea. In 1784 he was given large state funds to organize a triumphal visit of Catherine and Joseph II of Austria to "New Russia." From St. Petersburg to Kiev, stations were built and supplied with horses taken from the populace, triumphal arches constructed, and villages erected. Foreign observers, perhaps jealous of these successes, asserted that his villages were made of cardboard, originating the expression, "Potemkin village," but Potemkin's achievements in bringing order and prosperity to a vast region were undeniable. He died theatrically in 1791 on an Oriental rug in the midst of the steppe.

---

[8] Florinsky, *Russia* (New York, 1953), vol. 1, p. 555.

EXTERNAL AFFAIRS

Catherine II has been called "the Great" partly for her diplomatic and military successes. At home she faced peasant revolts, pretenders, and noble opposition; abroad she could exhibit her flair for diplomacy and satisfy her ambition. In her reign, Russia's power, prestige, and international importance increased markedly, though at heavy cost. The success of her diplomacy remains debatable, especially the alliance with Prussia and the partitions of Poland. Perhaps Russia should instead have incorporated only Belorussian and Ukrainian regions and created a friendly Polish client-state.

At Catherine's accession, Russia's chief external concerns were Poland and the Ottoman Empire. Immediate Russian objectives were to advance southward to the Black Sea, to cultivate rich grain lands of the southern Ukraine, and to develop foreign trade, but all this was impossible while the Crimean Tatars, Turkish vassals, controlled the northern Black Sea coast. Russia's goals in Poland were, for national and religious reasons, to annex largely Orthodox Belorussia and the western Ukraine and gain security from a potential Western invasion. The international situation seemed favorable: in the Seven Years War (1756–63), Prussia had been weakened, Sweden was no longer a major threat, the Ottoman Empire had begun to decline, and Austria had suffered heavy losses. Only Russia emerged from it with unimpaired resources.

Catherine, like Peter I, directed Russian foreign policy personally. She told Potemkin: "I wish to rule for myself and let Europe know it!" Schooled in intrigue since childhood, she soon mastered contemporary diplomatic techniques. Russia's greatness, she realized, would exalt her own and lessen her dependence on the nobility. By hard work, knowledge of Europe, patience, and courage, she surmounted all external crises with great aplomb. To restore Russia's prestige, shaken by Peter III's policies, she broke his alliance with Prussia and announced: "Time will show everyone that we won't follow anyone's tail." Toward Europe, Catherine's tone was confident, though she realized that Russia needed five years of peace to restore its finances and guarantee domestic order.

For almost 20 years her chief assistant in foreign affairs was Count N. I. Panin, senior member of the Foreign Affairs College and architect of the Northern System. Catherine supported this capable nobleman until his pro-Prussian policy became outdated. His Northern System aimed to align satisfied powers (Russia and Prussia) against attempts at revenge by disgruntled Austria and to remove hostile French influence from Russia's borders. The nucleus of the System was the Russo-Prussian Alliance of 1764, which sought to preserve a status quo in Poland and Sweden which guaranteed their impotence. Panin secured an alliance also with Denmark, and Britain in 1766 signed a commercial treaty. Until 1768, though opposed by some influential Russians, the Northern System appeared to achieve its aims.

Events in Poland had inclined Catherine to adopt Panin's concept. When King Augustus III died in 1763, Russia and Prussia backed

Stanislas Poniatowski, Catherine's former lover and member of the pro-Russian faction, as his successor. Catherine confided that "he had less right [to the throne] than the others and thus should be all the more grateful to Russia." Refusing to marry him, Catherine urged Poniatowski to wed a Catholic Pole before the Diet convened. The other major candidate, the elector of Saxony, was supported by Austria, France, and most Poles. To insure a "free" election, Russia bribed members of the Diet and surrounded its chamber with troops. Poniatowski's election gave Panin his first success over the Catholic powers.

In their controversial alliance of 1764, Russia and Prussia agreed to maintain Polish institutions unaltered and seek equal rights for Orthodox and Protestant minorities. The alliance, claimed a Soviet account,[9] allowed Russia to dominate Poland, play a major European role at slight cost, and restrain the Sultan. Kliuchevskii, however, viewed it as a blunder because exhausted Prussia needed Russia, not vice versa. Earlier Catherine had called Prussia Russia's worst enemy; so now she had to change her tune.[10]

At first Russia used the Prussian alliance to consolidate its position in Poland. Poniatowski, supported by patriotic elements, planned major reforms, but he could not implement them because Prussia and Russia insisted that Poland retain its archaic elective monarchy and *liberum veto*.[11] Catherine's support of Polish Orthodox dissidents in their efforts to recover lost political freedoms induced their spokesman in Russia, Gregory Konisskii, to state that the dissidents were her loyal subjects. Russian public sympathy for them encouraged Catherine to demand political equality for them, and when the Diet of 1766 refused, she ringed Warsaw with Russian troops until it complied. Wishing to retain the religious issue as a pretext for later intervention, she refused to support Orthodox demands for equality. When conservative Polish patriots of the Confederation of Bar sought Austro-French support against Russia, Catherine brought Poland under complete Russian military domination.

The Polish issue now became linked with the Turkish problem. To prevent Russia from absorbing Poland, Austria and France bribed Turkish officials who used an accidental Russian border crossing as a pretext to declare war on Russia. Though Russia was unprepared, Catherine was confident of victory. Her forces, superior in training, equipment, and command, invaded the Danubian Principalities (Moldavia and Wallachia) and largely freed them from Turkish rule. Using Balkan Christians against the Turks, Catherine urged them to revolt. A Russian fleet, advised by British officers, defeated the Turks at Chesme and Scio, but Balkan Christian risings failed. The Russians captured Azov and Taganrog and occupied the Crimea, revealing their rising power. Soon both sides wanted peace. Russian finances were strained, and plague raged in Moscow. Austria sought to halt the war in order

---

[9] V. P. Potemkin, ed., *Istoriia diplomatii*, 1st edition (Moscow, 1941), vol. 1, p. 287.

[10] Kliuchevskii, *Kurs*, vol. 5, p. 37.

[11] A free veto held by all members of the Diet which could block legislation or election of a king.

MAP 18–1
Expansion and Partitions of Poland 1772–1775

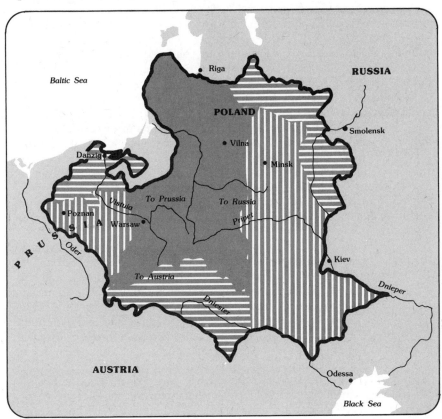

■ 1772

▥ 1793

■ 1795

to prevent Ottoman dismemberment, and Frederick II of Prussia urged Poland's partition, threatening otherwise to cancel his alliance with Russia. Catherine agreed reluctantly to a partition to avoid conflict with the German powers. Over Poniatowski's objections the three eastern powers each occupied part of Poland. Russia acquired eastern Belorussia and part of Latvia, while Prussia and Austria took mainly lands inhabited by Poles. Russian gains may have been justified on national grounds, but they undermined Polish independence.

When the Russo-Turkish War resumed, Austria withdrew support from the Porte, but France urged the Turks to continue fighting. Though Russia's efforts were complicated by the Pugachov Revolt,[12]

---

[12] See below, pp. 255–57.

during 1773–74 General P. A. Rumiantsev and the brilliant new general, A. S. Suvorov, won repeated victories, crossed the Danube and Balkan Mountains, and forced the Turks to yield.

The Treaty of Kuchuk-Kainarji (July 1774) ceded Azov, Enikale, and Kerch Straits to Russia, secured her access to the Black Sea, and enabled her to build a fleet there and send merchant ships into the Mediterranean. The Crimea secured political "independence" from the Porte. Russia expanded westward to the Bug River and acquired part of the northern Caucasus. Freed finally from Tatar threats, Russia now could develop its agriculture and trade in the southern Ukraine. For a Turkish indemnity, Catherine evacuated the Danubian Principalities, but they remained *de facto* a Russian protectorate. The Sultan recognized a vague Russian right to protect rights of Orthodox Christians in Constantinople, providing a pretext for subsequent Russian intervention in the Balkans. Confirming Russian emergence as a Black Sea power, Kuchuk-Kainarji was an important turning point in her relations with a declining Porte, although Catherine had not expelled the Turks from Europe.

Russia soon exploited its advantage by incorporating the Crimea. Crimean "independence" provoked fierce Russo-Turkish competition. In 1775, Devlet-Girei, a Turkish tool, seized the Crimean throne, and the Porte again appointed its judges and customs officials. The next fall Russian troops backed the pro-Russian pretender, Shagin-Girei, and named him khan. In 1783 Catherine, citing alleged Turkish violations of Kuchuk-Kainarji, annexed the Crimea, which enhanced Russia's security in the south, gave her Black Sea ports, and strengthened her position in the Caucasus.

By the late 1770s Russia was drifting away from Prussia toward Austria. Catherine mediated the German powers' conflict over the Bavarian succession, and as a guarantor of their peace became a protector of the moribund Holy Roman Empire. In 1780 Catherine and Joseph II, the new Austrian emperor, discussed an alliance against the Porte and their spheres of interest. Catherine offered Austria northern Italy and even Rome; not to be outdone, Joseph suggested Russia might occupy Constantinople. Their alliance of 1781, which confirmed the status quo in Poland, stipulated that if the Turks violated Kuchuk-Kainarji or attacked Russia, Austria would join Russia in war. The pro-Prussian Panin and his followers were ousted, and Russian foreign policy under Potemkin and A. A. Bezborodko grew more aggressive.

The Austrian alliance promoted Potemkin's and Catherine's grandiose "Greek Project" to chase the Turks from Europe, partition the Balkans, and, as Catherine put it, restore "the ancient Greek monarchy on the ruins of . . . barbaric rule." This neo-Byzantine empire was to be ruled by Catherine's grandson, appropriately named Constantine, but the Russian and Greek crowns were not to be combined. To Joseph II Catherine suggested creating a buffer state of Dacia, formed from Bessarabia, Moldavia, and Wallachia. Austria concurred with the Greek Project, and Britain viewed it as a way to foment a Russo-Turkish war. The British had been alienated by Catherine's Declaration of

Armed Neutrality of 1780, which was directed at Britain and Spain. It supported neutral countries' efforts to protect their merchant shipping and revealed Catherine's ambition to play a leading international role.

A Russo-Turkish war broke out in 1787 after Catherine and Joseph had inspected Russia's new domains in the south Ukraine and the Crimea. Accusing Russia of violating Kuchuk-Kainarji, the Turks demanded return of the Crimea, then suddenly attacked southern Russia. General Suvorov, however, repelled the Turks, and Austria joined Russia. Then Sweden, egged on by France, attacked Russia (June 1788), forcing Catherine to fight on two widely separated fronts. The Swedes, however, were defeated at sea and made little progress on land, and the Treaty of Verela of 1790 restored prewar boundaries.

Although Austria made a separate peace, Russia eventually defeated the Porte. The great Suvorov won major victories at Fokshany, Rymnik, and Ismail as other Russian forces captured Akkerman and founded the port city of Odessa. The Black Sea fleet under Admiral F. F. Ushakov defeated the Turks repeatedly. Reaching the Danube, a Russian army opened the way into the Balkans with its bayonets. Britain sought vainly to organize a European coalition against Russia and even planned a naval demonstration in the Baltic. Finally, the Sultan yielded, and by the Treaty of Jassy (1791) renounced all claims to the Crimea and Georgia. Russia obtained Ochakov and advanced its southern frontier to the Dniester River. Catherine hailed Jassy as a great triumph, though it fell far short of her aims and compensated Russian sacrifices poorly, but she never abandoned the Greek Project. A secret Austro-Russian agreement of 1795 planned to dismember the Ottoman Empire, and only Catherine's death blocked a Russian effort to seize Constantinople. Russian victories encouraged the Balkan Christians to seek to throw off the Turkish yoke.

During the Turkish war, Polish patriots, with Prussian backing, secured major reforms at the Four Years Diet (1787–91) and got Russian troops withdrawn. By the May Constitution of 1791 the liberum veto and right of confederation were abolished, and Poland became briefly an hereditary monarchy. Austria and Prussia approved, but Catherine called this constitution "revolutionary." She helped organize a confederation to "restore ancient Polish liberties," which appealed to Russia for aid. When 100,000 Russian troops invaded Poland, Poniatowski revoked the May Constitution and its supporters fled abroad. In 1792 Russia and Prussia in a second partition sliced up over half of Poland. Russia obtained the rest of Belorussia and the western Ukraine and the remainder of Poland became a Russian protectorate. British and French protests were ineffective, and a mortal blow was struck at Polish statehood.

Within Poland, national feeling boiled over: in 1794 the bourgeoisie, intelligentsia, city poor, and even some serfs rallied behind Thaddeus Kosciuszko in a desperate anti-Russian movement. To win mass support, Kosciuszko proclaimed the serfs free, but the nobility blocked this. The insurgents massacred Russian garrisons in Warsaw and Vilna, defeated Prussian and Russian units in the field, and forced the Prussians to withdraw. Suvorov, however, led a massive Russian invasion, defeated Kosciuszko at Maciejowice, and captured him.

Early in the uprising, Bezborodko, Catherine's chief adviser, had delimited shares of the eastern powers for a final partition. Russia reached agreement with Austria, and then imposed its terms on Prussia. In this third partition of 1795, Russia obtained Lithuania, Courland, and parts of Podolia and Volhynia. Soviet historians affirm that these former Kievan lands were Russia's by right and that incorporation benefited their people. Actually, Russia, Prussia, and Austria shared responsibility fairly equally for Poland's destruction.

The French Revolution preoccupied Catherine in her last years. At first, expecting the Bourbons to crush the revolt, she underestimated its scope. After the French royal family was arrested in 1791, she became the first European sovereign to recognize a French regime in exile. After considering joining in the Austro-Prussian military intervention of 1792 against France, Catherine commented: "I'll break my neck in order to involve the Vienna and Berlin courts. . . . I want to entangle them in the affair in order to have free hands . . . I have many unfinished enterprises . . ."[13] Once the radical Jacobins lost power in July 1794, she concluded: "They [the French] will do that work more surely than all the allies put together." Only Catherine's death, however, prevented a Russian expeditionary force from joining Britain and Austria in fighting the Directory.

Catherine's foreign policy has been variously interpreted. Traditional nationalist historians hailed Russia's westward expansion, and recent Soviet scholars, without praising Catherine or condoning tsarist methods, applaud the results. Acquiring the Crimea and southern Ukraine, they note, fostered development of Russia's productive forces. Solving the Polish question was "historically progressive" because it united the eastern Slavs and rejoined Ukrainian and Belorussian lands with the motherland. Catherine's foreign policy, though promoting noble interests, often corresponded to the incorporated peoples' interests.[14] On the other hand, Florinsky deplored the expense in lives and treasure to conquer territory inhabited partly by Tatars, Poles, and Lithuanians, who detested Russian rule. Two major blunders, argued Kliuchevskii, denied Catherine greater success abroad: ending the traditional alliance with Austria and adopting the Northern System embroiled Russia with Austria and France, whose support she needed against the Porte. The Russo-Prussian Alliance, he argued, prevented separate solution of the Polish and Turkish issues, reduced Russian gains against the Porte, and forced Russian acceptance of Frederick's plan of Polish partition. Instead of annexing just west Russia where Orthodox eastern Slavs predominated, Catherine antagonized the Slav Poles with squalid partitions. These benefited mainly the German states, while Russia in the 19th century would thrice have to fight Polish nationalism. In the

---

[13] A. V. Khrapovitskii, *Dnevnik* (Moscow, 1901), p. 226.
[14] *Istoriia SSSR* (Moscow, 1967), vol. 3, pp. 550–51.

south, Catherine, dreaming of driving the Turks from Europe, sought prematurely to rouse the Balkan Christians to revolt. The partitions of Poland and the Greek Project created fears in Europe that an insatiable Russia menaced its political independence. The coquette, argued Kliuchevskii, fell victim to the clever Prussian soldier, Frederick.[15]

Despite such persuasive arguments, it is undeniable that Russia under Catherine II achieved a major expansion of territory and population in the west and south. Firmly established on the Black and Baltic seas and controlling much of Poland, Russia could develop more freely its commercial, political, and cultural links with Europe. Some of Catherine's victories later rang hollow, but in her time few denied her great ability and achievements in foreign affairs.

PROBLEM 5: WAS CATHERINE II AN ENLIGHTENED DESPOT?

The generation before the French Revolution is often called the Age of Enlightened Absolutism. A number of European rulers—Catherine II, Frederick II of Prussia, Joseph II of Austria, to name the most prominent—are usually considered enlightened despots. Imbued with the concept of natural law and programs of the French philosophes, they attempted to rule by new progressive principles. To a greater or lesser extent they aimed to improve the peasant's well-being, at least on Crown lands, develop trade and industry and eliminate economic restrictions, rule in a just and orderly way under the law, and abrogate cruel and unusual punishments. Frederick II summed up one of their ideals: "I am the first servant of the state." Elsewhere he explained: "The prince is to the nation he governs what the head is to the man— it is his duty to see, think and act for the whole community. . . ."[16] The enlightened despots shared this attitude of benevolent patriarchal absolutism.

Did Catherine live up to the ideals of enlightened despotism or did she merely pay them lip service? Did she truly believe and seek to implement her professed intentions? Below are pertinent sections of her *Instruction* and analyses of her actions.

NAKAZ (1766)

More than three fourths of the 22 chapters and the 655 articles of "The Instructions to the Commissioners for composing a new Code of Laws" were borrowed verbatim from Montesquieu, the German cameralists, Beccaria, Quesnay, and the French Encyclopedists and comprised the most complete statement of Catherine's theories of government and society. It stressed typical Enlightenment concepts of

---

[15] Kliuchevskii, *Kurs*, vol. 5, pp. 44–46.
[16] Quoted in R. P. Stearns, *Pageant of Europe* (New York, 1961), p. 290.

natural law, freedom, and humanitarianism. When she submitted it to her advisers, they insisted on deleting the boldest sections, especially those on serfdom. Soviet and some western historians have affirmed that the *Nakaz* was only circulated abroad for propaganda purposes and forbidden at home; actually it went through eight editions in Catherine's lifetime and was sold publicly in Russia but was banned in France and in Russia under her son, Paul I.

1. The Christian Law teaches us to do mutual Good to one another as much as possibly we can.
3. . . . Every individual citizen in particular must wish to see himself protected by Laws, which . . . should defend him from all attempts of others that are repugnant to this fundamental rule.
6. Russia is a European State.
9. The sovereign is absolute, for there is no other authority but that which centers in his single person that can act with a vigor proportionate to the extent of such a vast dominion.
12. . . . It is better to be subject to the Laws under one Master than to be subservient to many.
13. What is the true end of Monarchy? Not to deprive people of their natural Liberty; but to correct their Actions in order to attain the *Supreme Good.*
15. The Intention and the End of Monarchy is the Glory of the Citizens, of the State, and of the Sovereign.
33. The Laws ought to be so framed as to secure the Safety of every Citizen as much as possible.
34. The Equality of the Citizens is . . . that they should all be subject to the same Laws.
35. This Equality requires Institutions . . . to prevent the rich from oppressing those who are not so wealthy as themselves.
38. *Liberty is the Right of doing whatsoever the Laws allow.*
96. . . . All Punishments, by which the human Body might be maimed, ought to be abolished.
123. The Usage of Torture is contrary to all the Dictates of Nature and Reason; even Mankind itself cries out against it. . . .
194. *The Innocent ought not to be tortured;* and in the Eye of Law, every Person is innocent whose crime is not yet *Proved.*
313. Agriculture is the first and principal Labour which ought to be encouraged in the People; the next is the Manufacturing of our own produce.[17]

CATHERINE AS RULER

The liberal prerevolutionary Russian historian Alexander Kizevetter presents an interpretation of Catherine's political methods and successes which stresses her personal role:

> It fell to Catherine's lot to give final legal form to the newly developed system of state and social relationships. . . . Catherine and her assistants . . . had to *gather the crop* from a field which had been

---

[17] *Documents of Catherine the Great* (Cambridge, Eng., 1931), p. 215 ff.

plowed, sown and cultivated by their predecessors. This was an important task; failure to complete it would have nullified all previous efforts and achievements. . . . The brilliant success of Catherine's efforts and the halo that surrounds her name are due primarily to the fact that the basic task of the period happened to suit the distinctive features of her personality. . . . By nature, she was not a plower or a sower. . . .

There was no lack of complicated and dangerous obstacles in Catherine's path, but she surmounted them all, and not so much by direct resistance as by great flexibility and resourcefulness. To challenge inimical elements in open battle and meet them in frontal attack, one must be a genius. But one need not be a genius to advance toward one's goal along the path of least resistance, not overthrowing one's enemies but taming them, not outstripping the surroundings, but keeping in step with them; for this it is sufficient to have talent.

. . . In her statesmanship she followed people and circumstances rather than led them. . . . What then was the source of Catherine's success? . . . It lay in her extraordinary personality, with its rare combination of two ordinarily mutually exclusive traits—impassioned desires and calculating self-control in the selection of ways and means to gain those desires. . . . Catherine never lost this ability to play on people's heartstrings and it was her principal tool of government. She let those around her feel her power, . . . but she could adopt a tone of trustfulness and relaxed humor with anyone she happened to be talking to, or even suddenly flash a ray of royal favor upon him. But in the "craft of ruling" Catherine attached even greater importance to *advertisement,* and she was infinitely skillful at this. She was equally adept at self-promotion and at using others to advance her. . . . Her numerous manifestos and edicts of the first months of her reign . . . repeated nearly every day the completely unsubstantiated claim that Catherine had seized the throne from her husband in fulfillment of the unanimous desire of all her subjects. . . .

In weaving the verbal wreath of her political glory, . . . she considered it necessary to influence western Europe too. She greatly valued her reputation as a liberal and enlightened monarch and was herself most energetic in spreading that reputation in Europe. In some cases the official statements she addressed to high state institutions concerning government actions were in fact intended chiefly for European consumption. . . . Catherine had no difficulty in obtaining all the foreign hired pens she wanted to write laudatory pamphlets. . . , but she achieved much more. The best-known luminaries of West European philosophical thought, headed by Voltaire himself, placed their literary talents and prestigious names at her feet and sang praises to the "northern Minerva. . . ."

Her correspondence served not only to camouflage her moods but also to touch up facts she did not want revealed as they really were. At the height of a crop failure and famine, she wrote Voltaire a self-satisfied description of the well-being of the well-fed Russian peasants. . . . Such information was obviously not intended for Voltaire alone, but for European public opinion. . . . Her first concern was for a respectable appearance; the substance of the matter was secondary, for it is the appearance that gives rise to rumors and affects the opinions and mood of the mob. . . .

Catherine's deliberate self-advertisement of her achievements, successes, and virtues gradually led her to believe that nothing but good could emanate from her, that everybody around her and under her wing was bound to prosper and bloom with happiness. . . . Catherine saw everything that emanated from her through the rose-tinted glasses of that optimism. . . . Errors and failures had no place in her record. . . .[18]

THE NATURE OF RUSSIAN ENLIGHTENED DESPOTISM

A recent Soviet work, *History of the USSR*, gives this highly critical view of Catherine's role, emphasizing its socioeconomic foundations:

The policy of "enlightened absolutism" was a general European manifestation. . . . To revolutionary-democratic reforms the theoreticians of "enlightened absolutism" proposed a peaceful means of eliminating obsolete feudal institutions. Such a path of development, retaining the key positions in society for the nobility, suited the monarchs. As a result was formed an "alliance of philosophers and kings." Monarchs invited into their service ideologists of "enlightenment," were in correspondence with them, called them their teachers, and themselves worked on the composition of political tracts. State decrees spoke of "the general good," "national benefit," of the concern of the state for the needs of "all loyal subjects." These words never conflicted as sharply with actuality as during the rule of "enlightened rulers." During the reign of Catherine II the slogans of the Enlightenment were utilized for the defense of serfdom and to forestall the approaching economic decline of the nobility. By old methods alone the working people of the country could not be held in obedience. . . .

Step by step the government satisfied the aspirations of the "noble" class, created conditions to adapt the *votchina* economy to commercial relationships. In many instances the expectations of the nobility, especially elements of it which renouncing aristocratic snobbery engaged in trade and industrial enterprise, coincided with the hopes of merchants and industrialists. If, however, the interests of these two classes came into conflict, absolutism satisfied the demands of the nobility at the expense of the merchants and industrialists. . . .

In the "enlightened age" of Catherine II trade in peasants reached broad proportions. Serfs, like slaves, were sold at markets, exchanged for horses and dogs, and lost at cards. . . . To a question of Denis Diderot about the relationship between masters and serfs in Russia the Empress gave the following cynical reply: "No definite conditions exist between master and serf, but each master, possessing common sense, seeks to treat his cow carefully, not exhaust her and not demand from her too much milk." Naturally, all "masters" sought to insure that this "milk" should constantly increase. . . .

. . . The convening of the Legislative Commission and all its activity bore a demonstrative, sham character, clearly illustrating the aspirations of "enlightened absolutism," without changing anything in the social or political structure but achieving "quiet and calm" in the country. . . . By creating this representative organ Catherine intended to strengthen her position on the throne. . . . [The *Instruction*] pre-

---

[18] Reprinted with the permission of Farrar, Straus & Giroux, Inc. from *Catherine the Great: A Profile* edited by Marc Raeff. Copyright © 1972 by Marc Raeff. Pp. 4, 5, 7, 10, 12, 14–17.

pared minds for the transition from feudalism to bourgeois society. . . . The Legislative Commission fulfilled . . . the task of strengthening absolutism in the interests of the nobility. . . .[19]

CATHERINE THE REPUBLICAN EMPRESS

David Griffiths has provided a balanced, judicious reinterpretation of Catherine's reign, disagreeing with many traditional views of western and Soviet scholars.

The conventional Soviet analysis is unconvincing from the point of view of personality theory, since it assumes that the empress passed her entire adult life in a state of tension between her liberal utterances and her conservative policies. Politically, it explains nothing: a "liberal" image abroad would hardly help secure her hold on the throne. And such a reputation within Russia could only serve to undermine her position: for the literate elements in society—the nobility and the merchantry—would react with suspicion to alien political tenets. Both analyses, Western and Soviet, suffer from a more fundamental shortcoming: the use Soviet as well as non-Soviet historians make of terms such as republican, liberal, and conservative displays a lack of historical perspective. . . . The terms liberal and conservative were not, and could not be, applied by contemporaries to Catherine II. . . . Catherine, on the other hand, was referred to, and referred to herself, as a republican; but the connotation was far from that envisioned by those who would equate republicanism with liberalism. Only with the advent of the French Revolution did these three labels acquire the specific modern designations with which we associate them today. Hence the utilization of post-revolutionary terminology to describe pre-revolutionary political activity is inappropriate. . . .

Social ordering via constituted bodies is frequently condemned as a form of class rule by modern scholars, who imply that Catherine II violated her own public pronouncements—consciously, as Soviet scholars assert—by granting a disproportionate share of the privileges to the nobility while further oppressing the peasantry. This interpretation fails to make the necessary distinction between estates in feudal societies and classes in capitalist societies. . . . To sustain this misinterpretation Soviet and non-Soviet scholars alike have distorted the content and hence the intent of Catherine's legislative activity. . . .

The 1785 Charter to the Nobility will serve as a first case in point. A close examination of the Charter, commonly misrepresented as a major concession to the nobility, reveals that it consolidated existing privileges rather than bestowing new privileges and that their enjoyment was still contingent upon successful performance of service obligations.

. . . It should now be apparent that Catherine II was hardly an early version of a modern public relations expert, conducting her own lavish campaigns to improve her image at home and abroad by deluding public opinion. The gap between her words and actions was no greater than that of any other ruler of the time, and where it existed it often signified nothing more than the limitations inherent in 18th century absolutism. Close examination of her reign reveals a clear correlation between the tenets of Montesquieu's *De l'esprit des lois*, the principles

[19] *Istoriia SSSR* . . . (Moscow, 1967), vol. 3, pp. 428, 433, 435, 445–47.

professed in the *Nakaz*, the equally advanced practices recorded in the Complete Collection of Russian Laws, and their evaluation by enlightened contemporaries. Her policies, in sum, were very much in harmony with the ideas of the age. . . .[20]

Catherine II may have been empress of the nobility; but by building an orderly bureaucratic monarchy, she subordinated them gently but effectively to the state. Though brought to power by the Guards, she soon escaped their tutelage and selected her statesmen for ability and loyalty to the Crown. Her seeming concessions to the nobility were a means to achieve full autocratic power and personal rule. Catherine built support for herself with bonds of self-interest, not terror. Her model was Le Mercier's "legal despotism," not Montesquieu's separation of powers. Her governmental reforms, making the nobility her administrative agents, gave them the shadow of authority but the substance to the Crown. The self-government she granted dramatically to nobles and towns proved largely conditional. Her greatness, notes Gershoy,[21] lay in flouting the logic she so admired in the philosophes and in uniting contradictions through patience, courage, and realistic flexibility. Like Peter I she made royal absolutism a cement of state. Securing the old regime by essential concessions, she reconsolidated its central and local institutions, enhanced absolutism, and made Russia safe for aristocracy and unlimited monarchy for another century.

Suggested Additional Reading

BOOKS

CATHERINE II. *Documents of Catherine the Great* . . . (Cambridge, Eng., 1934).

————. *The Memoirs of Catherine the Great* (New York, 1957).

DASHKOVA, E. *The Memoirs of Princess Dashkov* (London, 1958).

FISHER, ALAN. *The Russian Annexation of the Crimea* . . . (Cambridge, Eng., 1970).

FOUST, C. *Muscovite and Mandarin: Russia's Trade with China* . . . *1727–1805* (Chapel Hill, 1969).

KAPLAN, H. *The First Partition of Poland* (New York, 1962).

LONGWORTH, P. *The Art of Victory: The Life* . . . *of Suvorov* (London, 1965).

OLDENBOURG, ZOE. *Catherine the Great* (New York, 1965).

RANSEL, D. L. *The Politics of Catherinian Russia* (New Haven, 1975).

THOMSON, G. S. *Catherine the Great and the Expansion of Russia* (London, 1947).

ARTICLES

ANDERSON, M. "Great Britain and the Russo-Turkish War of 1768–74," *EHR*, vol. 79, pp. 39–58.

---

[20] D. Griffiths, "Catherine II: the Republican Empress," *Jahrbücher für Geschichte Osteuropas*, vol. 21 (1973), pp. 324, 327–28, 343–44.

[21] Leo Gershoy, *From Despotism to Revolution* (New York, 1944), pp. 106–26.

GRIFFITHS, DAVID. "Catherine II: the Republican Empress," *JfGO*, vol. 21 (1973), pp. 323–44.

————. "Nikita Panin, Russian Diplomacy and the American Revolution," *SR*, vol. 28, 1969, pp. 1–24.

HALECKI, O. "Why was Poland Partitioned?" *SR*, vol. 22, 1963, pp. 432–41.

JONES, R. E. "Catherine II and the Provincial Reform of 1775 . . ." *CSS*, vol. 4, 1970, pp. 497–512.

LORD, R. H. "The Third Partition of Poland," *SEER*, vol. 3, 1924–25, pp. 481–98.

RAEFF, M. "The Domestic Policies of Peter III . . . ," *AHR*, vol. 75, pp. 1289–1310.

19

Catherine II: Economic, Social, and Cultural Policies

IN THE LATE 18th century Russia experienced some economic and intellectual development, but its social patterns stagnated. The slow growth of commerce and money relationships prepared future industrialization, but agriculture, still weighted down by serfdom, remained backward. While the upper and middle nobility reached their peak of economic influence and dominated regional administration, the peasantry plumbed new depths of poverty and degradation. An intelligentsia began to emerge and criticized abuses hesitantly. Soviet historians emphasize the development of capitalist forms despite the predominance of feudal-serf relationships and dramatize the scope of the Pugachov Revolt, which they call "the Peasant War." How much economic growth occurred under Catherine? Was serfdom already declining economically? Did the regime ameliorate or worsen peasant conditions? What were the causes and significance of the Pugachov Revolt? What relationship existed between Catherine's government and the intellectuals?

ECONOMY

Under Catherine the serf-based economy reached its apogee. Russia remained basically an agrarian country low in productivity, though not notably backward by contemporary European standards, in which methods and systems of cultivation changed little. In the central region the three-field system prevailed; in the Black Soil area, becoming Russia's breadbasket, the fallow system developed. New lands north of the Black Sea and in the Crimea, Don, and north Caucasus added significantly to Russian grain production, and in the south arose some plantation-type estates. Changes in landownership and rents presaged serfdom's decline as merchants and wealthy peasants, especially in the north, challenged noble predominance in landholding. In non-Black Soil areas rising commercial activity accelerated a shift to money *obrok* (annual rent); in Black Soil regions *barshchina* (labor service) prevailed. Nomadic peoples from the Volga to the Pacific, spurred by

Russian settlers and state legislation, were shifting to settled agriculture. By 1800 Russians far outnumbered native peoples in Siberia.

Recent Soviet and western accounts challenge the older view that negative state policies slowed Russia's economic development after Peter I. To be sure, state policy became less vigorous, but it fostered industry through supervision, subsidies, and tax exemptions. The regime permitted more economic freedom, abolished some state monopolies, lowered tariffs, and stimulated private industries. Between 1725 and 1800, claims Blackwell,[1] the economy grew considerably as foundations were laid for the metallurgical and textile industries and peasant handicrafts expanded.

Imprecise statistics make the evaluation of industrial progress difficult. Soviet historians affirm that in the late 18th century the number of factories doubled to about 1,200. However "factory" (*fabrika*) was a vague term; the great increase in industrial concerns included tiny shops with only a few employees. Most industry was conducted in these or in peasant cottages, and estimates of industrial workers in 1800 vary from less than 200,000 (Blackwell) to 500,000. Large-scale enterprise grew slowly, but by 1800 Russia had hundreds of factories and mines, thousands of small plants and shops, and was a leading iron producer. Industrial goods lacked wide markets in Russia; the state and nobility purchased most military and luxury products. Light industry, notably that producing linen, cloth, and silk, showed marked gains. Russia underwent superficial military industrialization while remaining, like all countries of the 18th century except England, basically agrarian.

Noble entrepreneurs, seeking additional revenues, engaged in liquor distilling, woolens, and metallurgy. Distilling, a noble monopoly, required little technology, had a ready market, abundant raw materials, and serf labor. In the Urals the state, to foster private enterprise and rid itself of responsibility, granted factories and serf workers to noblemen, generals, and bureaucrats, but many noble enterprises soon failed or changed hands.

The labor force was changing in character. Hired workers (often still serfs on *obrok*) were used widely in light industry of towns or rural areas of non-Black Soil areas. Recruited from Russian, Chuvash, and Mordovian villages, they were paid substantial wages initially, but industrial wages generally were so low that many workers were hopelessly indebted to factory owners. Metallurgical plants, especially in the Urals, employed mainly serf labor. Incentives to introduce machinery were lacking, and inventions were little used or forgotten: a steam engine constructed by I. Polzunov at an Altai factory remained idle. Late 18th century Russian industry, despite significant growth, retained primitive methods and crude output.

Though Russia's domestic and foreign trade expanded considerably, aided by population increases, imperial expansion, improved internal security, and official encouragement, the early Soviet view (Pokrovskii)

---

[1] William Blackwell, *The Beginnings of Russian Industrialization 1800–1860* (Princeton, 1968), pp. 27–28.

that this was an era of commercial capitalism is much exaggerated. For a time Catherine continued efforts to liberalize domestic trade and provide merchants with easier credit. Responding to requests in the Legislative Commission for greater economic freedom, in 1775 she eliminated most monopolies and allowed anyone to operate an industrial enterprise, but noble landlords, not merchants, benefited most. Russia under Catherine, noted a foreign observer, had fewer restrictions on domestic trade than most European countries, and relatively liberal tariff policies stimulated Russian foreign trade. In 1782, rates increased somewhat over those of 1766 (20 to 30 percent of value) but still afforded Russian industry only modest protection. Only in the 1790s for political and fiscal reasons did the state adopt protectionist measures and prohibit trade with revolutionary France.

Exports still reflected Russia's largely agrarian economy. After the mid-1780s, exports of iron, the chief industrial product, declined because of high tariffs and the technological backwardness of the iron industry. Other leading exports were hemp, flax, linen cloth, timber, hides, and furs. Grain shipments were encouraged, but major growth in the grain trade came later. Leading Russian imports were luxury articles for noblemen and top merchants and woolen cloth for uniforms. Russia's foreign trade almost trebled in value from 1775 to 1795, but the quantitative increase was much less because of the ruble's depreciation. In 1794 the Commerce Department admitted that the balance of trade, depicted officially as favorable, may have been adverse.

Russia's best customer was Britain, notably for naval supplies, and most Russian exports were carried by English ships. England remained a coveted trading partner because it bought much more than it sold to Russia, and political frictions failed to disrupt the relationship. The Anglo-Russian commercial agreement of 1734,[2] highly favorable to England, was reaffirmed by a convention of 1766, renewed in 1793. Russian commercial accords with Denmark, Portugal, and France reduced somewhat British preeminence in the Russian market.

By 1800 St. Petersburg handled over 60 percent of Russian maritime commerce, and other Baltic ports (Riga, Narva, and Tallinn) conducted most of the rest. What remained went chiefly through White Sea ports because southern seaports (Taganrog, Kherson, Odessa and Sevastopol) had just begun to develop. The Treaty of Kuchuk-Kainarji allowed Russian merchantmen to use the Turkish Straits, but Russian ships were few and the Turks rarely permitted passage of other foreign merchant vessels; Black Sea commerce remained mostly in Turkish hands. Through Astrakhan, Russia supplied European products and its own industrial goods to Asia and traded European goods to Asians at trade fairs in Orenburg, Semipalatinsk, and Petropavlovsk. Economically backward compared to leading European states, to Asian neighbors Russia was an advanced country.

Catherine's financial policies were only a partial success. A sharp increase in national wealth (state revenues swelled from 17 million

---

[2] See above, pp. 219–20.

rubles in 1762 to 78 millions in 1796) must be viewed against depreciation of the ruble and a fourfold increase in expenditures. Income came mostly from the poll tax (33%), spirits (25%), salt (7–10%), customs levies (10%), and conquered territories, but embezzlement by tax collectors probably exceeded the amount reaching the treasury. Even in peacetime the army took over one third of the budget. Lavish state expenditures, inept financial administration, and frequent wars induced the treasury in 1768 to issue paper banknotes (assignats); by 1796 they had depreciated about one third. Extensive foreign borrowing weakened the ruble's value abroad. By 1796 state indebtedness totalled 215 million rubles and annual interest payments of almost 6 million. Under Catherine taxes rose some two and one half times, including inflation, with the heaviest burden falling on the unfortunate peasantry.

What the state of the economy was under Catherine remains in dispute. Chechulin asserted that economic advances in the 18th century were negligible,[3] but industrial and commercial expansion belies this negative verdict. Developing money relationships, notes a Soviet source with apparent justice,[4] preparing the way for capitalist development and the decline of serfdom, forced changes in the landlord economy. Russia was progressing economically, though not as rapidly as advanced western European countries.

SOCIETY

The Russian Empire, like most other regions of Europe, experienced rapid population growth in the 18th century. The population grew, claim official statistics, from about 15 million in 1719 to 37.2 million in 1795 (including about 7 million Poles incorporated during partitions of Poland). Table 1 provides raw data on population growth, distribution and general social composition.[5]

18th Century Demographic Developments

	1719	*Percent*	*1795*	*Percent*
Peasants............................	13,100,000	90	32,600,000	90
Urban dwellers......................	600,000	4	1,600,000	4
Total (taxed population).............	13,700,000	94	34,200,000	
Nobility, bureaucrats military, clergy...	1,300,000	6	3,000,000	6
Total......................	15,000,000	100	37,200,000	100

Catherine's reign has been called justifiably the golden age of the Russian nobility. The *dvorianstvo* reached its peak of wealth, influence, and power. But noble unity and esprit de corps should not be exag-

---

[3] N. D. Chechulin, *Ocherki po istorii russkikh finansov v tsarstvovanii Ekateriny II* (St. Petersburg, 1906).

[4] *Istoriia SSSR* (Moscow, 1967), vol. 3, p. 395 ff.

[5] Ia. E. Vodarskii, *Naselenie Rossii za 400 let* (Moscow, 1973), p. 56.

gerated: within its ranks persisted great differences in status and political interests. As a minister of Nicholas I noted later, it was an estate
extending "all the way from the steps of the throne almost to the
peasantry."[6] Books of nobility, held by the government until 1785, then
by noble provincial corporations, described gradations important to its
members. Old noble families (e.g. Dolgoruki, Golitsyn) still claimed
superiority; next came titled nobles (barons, counts). These top categories compared to the French nobility of the sword. Most noblemen,
however, had acquired their status since 1700 from civil or military
service or through patent like French nobles of the robe. Ennoblement
through state service prevented the *dvorianstvo* from becoming a closed
caste, and service rank (*chin*) largely determined a noble's power and
prestige. The upper nobility flaunted elegant manners, Parisian French,
and Western dress and attended special schools. Shallow imitation of
European customs made some noblemen virtual foreigners, conspicuous
by their laziness, vanity, and contempt for Russian ways. Nonetheless,
after 1725 the *dvorianstvo* had a sense of corporate unity and sought
to confirm their rights. From the state they won important concessions
culminating in emancipation from compulsory state service (1762).
Noblemen wanted these privileges confirmed in writing, and at the
Legislative Commission they requested a major role in local government.

Catherine, sympathetic to their aspirations, declared in French
shortly after her accession: "*Je suis aristocrate* [I am an aristocrat]."
Without noble support she could neither remain in power nor govern
her empire. Thus the early Soviet view of Pokrovskii that Catherine's
policies were pro-bourgeois does not stand up. In a recent study Blum
shows that most of her legislation was in noble interests.[7] Later,
Catherine became less dependent upon the nobility by granting its main
desires while restoring Crown control over its activities.

The Charter of Nobility (1785), marking the *dvorianstvo* ascendancy, aimed to regularize noble affairs. Noble status, defined as good
birth or superior rank gained through state service and previously
acquired privileges, was expressly reaffirmed. In each province noblemen organized as a corporate group; a noble assembly met triennially
to elect officials in the province and its districts. All noblemen could
attend, but only propertyholders over the age of 25 who had risen in
state service could vote and hold office. Noble desires for a political
role were satisfied while the state retained control over assemblies
which lacked real power of initiative or the ability to block government
measures. The *dvorianstvo* received apparent self-government while
the state retained the substance of power. Nonetheless, the Charter
promoted the rule of law because at least one group had defined rights
and some freedom.

A noble's economic and social status depended upon the number of
his serfs, not the amount of his land. At first Catherine gave away

---

[6] Florinsky, *Russia*, vol. 2, p. 802 note.

[7] Jerome Blum, *Lord and Peasant in Russia* . . . (Princeton, 1961), p. 352
note.

lands with state peasants (But not nearly so many as is commonly asserted!), mostly to about 100 families. Top noblemen owned far more serfs than plantation owners did slaves in the United States. A few great magnates with tens of thousands imitated standards of the imperial Court. Count P. B. Sheremetiev, the richest, owned 2,500,000 acres and 185,000 serfs. He had palaces in Moscow and Petersburg and a lavish country estate at Kuskovo known as "little Versailles." Well-to-do nobles possessed 500 serfs or more, but in 1777 only 16 percent owned more than 100 serfs and almost one third had less than ten apiece. These pauper nobles, unless they entered state service, often lived with their serfs under a single humble roof and ate at a common table. Insistence on subdividing their estates among all heirs and high living produced pauperization. The government curbed their luxurious tastes by forbidding expensive carriages and clothing, but nobles still incurred huge debts.

Under Catherine serfdom reached its maximum extent and development. In 1796 the peasantry—private serfs and state peasants—comprised more than 90 percent of the population. As their taxes increased, their personal and economic status deteriorated. Secularization of church lands brought some 1,000,000 privately owned serfs under state administration, undoubtedly improving their lot. At her accession, Catherine announced that "natural law" commanded her to promote the well-being of all her people, and she considered applying Enlightenment concepts of law and justice to the peasantry, but noble opposition helped dissuade her. In the Baltic provinces she suggested restrictions on serfdom, but they were not widely applied. Later, she limited serfdom's scope somewhat by prohibiting enserfment of orphans, war prisoners, illegitimate children, and other free persons, or re-enserfment, but such measures affected relatively few. Serfs were still forbidden to petition the Crown for redress of their grievances, and by abandoning the serfs to their lords' untender mercies, Catherine deepened serfdom. Her agents were merely to "curb excesses, dissipation, extravagance, tyranny, and cruelty" by the lords, but rarely were such matters investigated. Serfdom spread to the Ukraine and Belorussia. After 1765 when the administration of court and imperial peasants was combined with state peasants, two major categories remained: private serfs (53.2%) and state peasants (45%).

The peasant's position depended on his work and obligations. In the north and center, where most state lands were located, the system of *obrok* prevailed, a tax in kind (e.g. grain), money, or both, for use of the land and, on a peasant's side earnings, vital in the north with its short growing season. In Tver province in 1783 peasants derived less than half their cash income from agriculture; the rest came from handicrafts and labor in state or private enterprises. Between 1722 and 1787 *obrok* payments for state peasants rose five to seven times. In the forest region, where most peasants still lived, dues per acre in the 1780s were roughly double those of the early 20th century.[8] In

---

[8] G. T. Robinson, *Rural Russia* (New York, 1932), pp. 27–28.

southern Black Soil areas forced labor service (*barshchina*) prevailed, unlimited by law until 1797. Traditionally, a *barshchina* peasant worked three days per week for the landowner, three days for himself, and rested on Sunday, but lords often required four or five days *barshchina* per week and continuous labor while his harvest was gathered. *Barshchina* peasants generally were more dependent on the lord than those under *obrok*. Sometimes the two types of obligation were combined. In the late 18th century, noted V. I. Semevskii, 44 percent of Great Russian peasants were under *obrok*, 56 percent under *barshchina*.

On sizable estates numerous courtyard people (*dvorovye*) performed tasks in the lord's household. Generally landless, they were indistinguishable from slaves except for paying state taxes and being subject to conscription. As noble ostentation grew, hundreds of them were employed, especially to impress visitors. Lords could punish them brutally with little fear of state action.

Russian landlords were miniature monarchs and viceroys of the state to keep the serfs in obedience and labor. "Except for imposing the death penalty," declared Catherine, "the landlord can do anything that enters his head on his estate." The lord's whim determined serf obligations; the lord's legal responsibilities were minimal and rarely enforced. After 1765 lords could deport serfs to forced labor in Siberia or send them into the army as recruits. Included in the estate's inventory from 1792, serfs could be sold individually or in families, with or without land; they were commonly exchanged for dogs and horses and gambled away at cards. Lords could beat them almost to death (even deaths were seldom investigated) but were dissuaded from killing them by moral and economic considerations. Masters could decide serf marriages—permission to marry outside the estate usually involved a large fee—and sometimes insisted upon the first night with a new peasant bride.

How could one escape serfdom? A serf soldier who served his time or became a war prisoner was emancipated when released. A few lords voluntarily freed their serfs, and some wealthy serfs purchased their freedom. By 1796 there was a sizable group of freedmen who had to join the army or another estate within a year or revert to serfdom. For most the only way out was flight to areas without landlords. As state authority tightened over frontier areas, this escape became ever more difficult. Serfs who had migrated to Siberia became state peasants because Siberia had neither landlords nor serfdom.

Urban growth remained slow, and so Russia's bourgeoisie lacked the size and influence of those in western Europe. Even after a fourfold increase under Catherine, townsmen comprised only about four percent of the population. Catherine apparently wished to build up an urban middle class as a counterpoise to the nobility, but she had only modest success. A sparse urban population distinguished Russia socially from western Europe.

The clergy declined greatly under Catherine as secularization of its lands increased church dependence on the state. The government reduced the number of clergy by closing many monasteries, and Catherine made the Church wholly subservient to the state. The Holy Synod punished Arseni Matseevich, archbishop of Rostov, her chief clerical critic and opponent of secularization, as an example to others by reducing him to a simple monk and imprisoning him for life in a remote monastery. Catherine, however, granted toleration to Old Believers and revoked their double taxation. To attract colonists and foster her liberal image, she allowed Protestants and Catholics freedom of worship. Her secular emphasis and tolerance accorded fully with the Age of Reason.

THE PUGACHOV REVOLT, 1773–1774

During the early 1770s a great Cossack, tribal, and peasant revolt raged from the Urals to the Volga region, threatening to engulf the landlords and Catherine's regime. Called the Peasant War by Soviet historians, the Pugachov Revolt was the greatest rural upheaval of Russian history down to 1905. "The entire populace was for Pugachov . . . ," wrote the poet Alexander Pushkin. "Only the nobility openly supported the government." Since 1930, Soviet historians have glorified and often exaggerated what they consider the last spontaneous peasant rebellion against feudalism. They reject the thesis of Semevskii, a 19th century Populist historian, that the Ural Cossacks directed the revolt, as they do early Soviet assertions that it was a worker-peasant revolution. Western scholars stress the revolt's traditional elements: the demand for legitimate rule and Old Believer rights. A recent American historian calls it a "frontier jacquerie."[9]

The revolt's causes were many and deep-rooted. The spread of serfdom to the Ukraine and Don region and heavier taxation produced much peasant discontent. Forced serf laborers in Ural mines and factories worked under frightful conditions. Bashkirs and other national minorities were alienated by Russian seizure of much of their land, and the state had been depriving Cossacks of autonomy and forcing onerous service upon them. Among the Volga and trans-Volga peasantry were many Old Believers who opposed church and state. The mysterious death of an emperor who had permitted Old Believers to return to Russia and a foreign woman's usurpation of power gave Peter III undeserved popularity. Rumors spread that he had intended to emancipate the serfs, and believing deeply in the tsar's benevolence, many peasants concluded that their "fine tsar" still lived. Support for pretenderism was one means of expressing their grievances.

Shaky state control over southeastern Russia facilitated revolt. Orenburg was the center of a huge, remote province where Tatars outnumbered Russians and the latter were mainly Cossacks and factory serfs hostile to the regime. Government troops were few and dispersed among many forts. Insurrection now, as earlier,[10] began among Ural

---

[9] John Alexander, "Recent Soviet Historiography on the Pugachov Revolt," *CSS*, vol. 4, p. 617.

[10] See above, p. 176.

Cossacks whose autonomy had been whittled away and who were being conscripted to fight the Turks. Early in 1772 brutal actions by a government commission investigating Cossack complaints provoked open revolt. Its stern repression and the indemnity imposed on the Ural region created an explosive situation.

Early in 1773 a Don Cossack, Emelian Pugachov, came to the Urals and fanned tinder into flame. Born in the same settlement as Stenka Razin, he had participated in the first Turkish War, then refused to return to the army, and wandered around the southeastern frontier. He realized how deep was popular dissatisfaction and resolved to exploit it. Like Razin he was a bold, determined leader with military experience. Proclaiming himself "Peter III," he appeared on the Ural River as the "fine tsar" of peasant dreams. The inhabitants of Iletskii Gorodok led by the clergy greeted him with bread and salt as "Emperor Peter Fedorovich," a scene repeated in towns and villages throughout the Ural region. Peasants, Ural workers, lower townsmen, and non-Russians joined his Cossacks. Pugachov's forces captured many Ural forts, seized their artillery, and besieged Orenburg. Most of his followers merely wished to capture Orenburg and seize some property, but Pugachov believed that if Orenburg fell, the road to Petersburg would lie open and Catherine's regime would fall. General A. I. Bibikov's forces, however, defeated him and lifted the siege.

With his remaining followers, Pugachov moved westward to the Volga region where thousands of peasants flocked to his banner. As his undisciplined levies captured Saratov and most of Kazan, panic gripped noblemen and some government leaders. Pugachov's manifesto of late July 1774 pledged to free the peasantry from serfdom, recruitment, and the poll tax:

> . . . We order by this our personal ukase: whosoever were hitherto gentry in their estates and domains, these opponents of our rule and perturbators of the empire and despoilers of the peasant shall be caught, punished, and hanged, and treated just as they . . . have treated you peasants.[11]

The insurgents killed some 3,000 landowners and local officials, mostly that summer. But untrained peasants were no match for government regulars. After a catastrophic defeat near Tsaritsyn (now Volgograd), Pugachov fled into the steppe, where some followers betrayed him to the authorities. Chained hand and foot, Pugachov was taken to Moscow in an iron cage, was interrogated, executed and his body burned, and his chief followers and thousands of peasants were executed.

The Pugachov Revolt had far-reaching significance. By revealing a chasm of popular disaffection, it drew nobility and state together, tightening further the bonds of serfdom. Curiously, the revolt demonstrated the strength of the ideals of legitimate monarchy and the Old Belief among the peasantry—in a sense it was a revolution fought for reactionary goals. Whereas Semevskii and many Western scholars

---

[11] Quoted in John Alexander, *Autocratic Politics* . . . *1773–1775* (Bloomington, Indiana, 1969), p. 151.

conclude that the revolt failed and discouraged mass peasant upheaval for over a century, Soviet accounts assert that it shook the feudal system, heightened peasant class consciousness, and inspired abolitionists such as A. N. Radishchev. The revolt apparently induced Catherine to reform provincial and local government, and by crushing Pugachov and restoring order, her regime revealed its effectiveness and power.

EDUCATION AND CULTURE

Peter I's military-educational institutions had languished after his death, but Catherine II developed education for the elite considerably. After Peter, so anxious were noblemen to avoid service at sea that the Naval Academy's complement went unfilled. Moscow University, founded in 1755 to train specialists for the state, began with 100 students but had only 82 in 1782, and professors often did not deliver their lectures or gave them in French or Latin. The Cadet Corps, established in 1731 for gentry sons, however, flourished. Private boarding schools, stressing French, dancing, and other subjects desired by the nobility, had more success than state schools, and noble families employed many well qualified and often radical French tutors.

Catherine's educational policy reflected her personal enlightenment though less was achieved than she had hoped. Her first educational adviser was Ivan Betskoi, inspired by Locke, Rousseau, and the Encyclopedists, who urged Catherine to raise a breed of superior Russians in special state boarding schools. As director of the Cadet Corps, Betskoi stressed general education over military subjects and abolished corporal punishment. Women's education was begun: in 1764 Smolny Convent in St. Petersburg became a school for noble girls and flourished under court patronage and direction, and in 1765 a school for nonprivileged girls (except serfs) opened. Originally Catherine intended that boys' and girls' schools have identical curricula but later abandoned this advanced concept. Announced a government commission: "The intent and goal of the rearing of girls consist most of all in making good homemakers, faithful wives, and caring mothers."

When lack of teachers and public interest wrecked Catherine's dream of creating new men and women, she adopted the narrower goal of giving some Russians a general education. She employed Janković de Mirjevo, a Serbian graduate of Vienna University recommended by Joseph II, to set up Russia's first general educational schools. A statute of 1786 authorized a network of elementary, intermediate, and high schools of Austrian type, and high schools opened in 26 provincial capitals. The intermediate schools were dropped, but elementary schools open to children of all estates were set up in many different centers. Most pupils were sons of merchants, artisans, and minor officials. Many were enrolled forcibly, and some existing schools had to be closed to secure sufficient attendance in new institutions. A central teachers college supplied instructors, and de Mirjevo translated many Austrian texts for their use. In 1796 despite faltering official and public support, more than 22,000 students were enrolled in the new public schools, a substantial achievement for its time. Despite Catherine's encouragement, only some seven percent were females, mostly from St. Petersburg province. Catherine's reign marked a turning point in the development of Russian education.

In culture it was an era of laying foundations and absorbing lessons from the West. The modern Russian language, spurred by Petrine reforms of the alphabet, developed gradually. Foreign words and expressions, incorporated at first at random, later were included more systematically. The resulting literary language, richer and more flexible than Church Slavonic, was almost equally removed from popular speech and old Church Slavonic but resembled the colloquial language of the broader literate public emerging from new state schools. Michael Lomonosov contributed the first true Russian grammar (1755) and leading writers compiled a complete dictionary (1789–94).

In literature there were clashing styles, imitation of foreign authors, secularization, and sentimentalism, and abundant foreign works were available to noblemen schooled in French. Miliukov notes that two cultural strata developed and grew apart: the educated elite and the merely literate. The former adopted every new Western literary trend whereas the broader public with its simpler tastes helped vivify the elite's artificial style. Foundations were laid for a creative national Russian literature.

Catherine's reign revealed signs of independent Russian literary achievement. The leaders—Derzhavin, Fonvizin, and Karamzin—built upon such earlier pioneers as A. Kantemir. Lomonosov, Russia's universal man, was noted in literature chiefly for his odes. Alexander Sumarokov composed tragedies and comedies and directed the first permanent Russian theater. Toward the end of the century, public demand for love literature finally provoked a response: the ode gradually yielded to tragedy, tragedy to high comedy and finally to emotional light comedy. Sumarokov's classical tragedies, inspired by Racine, were succeeded by the plays of Iakov Kniazhnin, which were devoted more to adventure and emotion. Denis Fonvizin, noted for his plays, *The Adolescent* and *Brigadir*, satirized Frenchified noblemen and portrayed realistically behavior of the provincial gentry. Nicholas Karamzin, author of the first nationalistic Russian history, catered to ordinary tastes with his sentimental *Poor Liz*. In architecture and painting native achievement was slight, and many leading architects and artists were foreigners. Catherine and wealthy noblemen erected luxurious palaces in the prevalent, neoclassical style, and imposing public buildings were erected in "Russian imperial" style. Outstanding Russian architects included V. I. Bazhenev, known for a plan to reconstruct the Moscow Kremlin; M. F. Kazakov, designer of Moscow University and the Kremlin's Administration Building; and I. E. Starov, builder of Alexander Nevskii Cathedral and the lavish Tauride Palace of Prince Potemkin in St. Petersburg. The works of these architects and writers, though based on foreign models, created a sound basis for the more brilliant achievements of the 19th century.

THE RUSSIAN ENLIGHTENMENT

Westernization and increased noble leisure contributed to a significant development of Russian thought. A Populist historian, Ivanov-Razumnik, called the small group of educated noblemen deeply interested in ideas that emerged under Catherine "the intelligentsia." It was, he affirmed, a hereditary group outside of estate or class seeking the physical, mental, social, and personal emancipation of the individual. Soviet historians, emphasizing the originality of Russian thought, argue that a multiclass intelligentsia had begun earlier around Lomonosov. Some Western scholars, considering figures in Catherine's reign isolated individuals, believe the intelligentsia began in the 1820s.

Prince M. M. Shcherbatov was the old aristocracy's leading ideologist and writer. He defended serfdom as necessary and desirable: most serfs, he pontificated, were "satisfied with their lords who cared for them like children." In *Journey to the Land of Ophir* (1787), he described an ideal state where most people were slaves dependent on a nobility with a monopoly of land. The monarch, supervised constantly by a powerful elite, could do nothing without his council of lords. In *Petition of the City of Moscow on being Relegated to Oblivion* (1787), he recalled Moscow's ancient glory and called shifting the capital to St. Petersburg unnatural. Shcherbatov prefigured the Slavophiles' subsequent depiction of Petersburg as an alien, harmful element in Russian life. *On the Deterioration of Russian Morals* indicted the autocratic system and denounced Catherine's court for luxury, corruption, and arbitrariness. In his sophisticated defense of aristocracy, Shcherbatov used fully the terminology and works of the philosophes.

Between 1750 and 1770, affirms a recent Soviet work,[12] there developed a multiclass intelligentsia fostered by new higher educational institutions such as the Academic University (1748), Moscow University, and the Academy of Arts (1758). These *raznochintsy*[13] criticized prevalent noble ideology in a rationalist manner, and Lomonosov's followers especially advocated a middle-class ideology based on reason and natural law. Lomonosov, who embodied the supposed diversity and originality of Russian scholarship, believed that history should glorify the fatherland and its people, not princes, and that Russia must overcome its backwardness and dependence on the West. American scholars, however, note that Shtrange's *raznochintsy* were actually mostly noblemen.

Many members of the educated upper classes found Freemasonry the principal outlet for their growing frustration and deepening sense of alienation. Introduced into Russia as early as the 1730s, it became a significant movement only under Catherine II. A Christian movement existing outside the formally established churches, masonry provided the Russian nobleman with an opportunity to serve his fellow man through educational and philanthropic activities and created a frame-

---

[12] M. M. Shtrange, *Demokraticheskaia intelligentsiia Rossii v XVIII veke* (Moscow, 1965).

[13] Literally "men of various ranks," i.e., different social groups.

work for the development of profound religious feelings and aspirations no longer offered by the Orthodox Church. In secret or semisecret lodges, the Russian nobleman identified with the higher calling of Christian service in an atmosphere of brotherhood and common purpose.

Nicholas Novikov (1744–1818)—Freemason, journalist, and philanthropist—was the key figure in developing Russian humanitarian liberalism. Viewing individual moral development as the basis for happiness and material progress, Novikov popularized enlightenment, brought culture to remote areas, and instructed a generation of Russian noblemen. He saw masonry as a potential counterbalance to the rationalism, hedonism, and frivolous atmosphere of St. Petersburg. Disillusioned with the casual social dilettantism of Masons in the capital, Novikov organized his own more serious lodge. In Moscow after 1779, he and his followers organized an independent program of educational and philanthropic activities to alleviate human misery— aid to the sick, starving, and homeless—and spread enlightenment through lending libraries, publishing houses, and translation programs. These activities helped reestablish Moscow as a thriving intellectual center. Novikov favored free expression but not transformation of the political or economic order. He wished to "be useful to men of good sense," inculcate virtue, well-being, happiness, and self-knowledge. "Let us endeavor above all to love man" and "attack vice, wickedness, and inhumanity," he wrote in *On Man's High Estate* (1787). His journals, to which many progressives contributed, propagated liberal, humane social thought. In *The Drone* he satirized reactionary noblemen: Squire Nedum (Thoughtless) submits a plan to the government: "No creatures are to exist in the whole world except members of the gentry; the common people should be wholly exterminated." Later, in *The Painter* Novikov described excesses of serfdom and how it demoralized lords and peasants. His indirect satiric critique of abuses was most effective, and in the 1780s Novikov developed the largest private publishing enterprise in Russia. Beginning in 1786, the government curbed his activities and later arrested and imprisoned him for subversive activity. He fell victim to Catherine's fear of the French Revolution.

Alexander N. Radishchev (1749–1802) attacked serfdom and autocracy directly. The son of a well-to-do landowner of Saratov province, he attended the Corps de Pages in St. Petersburg, then studied five years at Leipzig University in Saxony. As protocolist for the Russian Senate after 1771, Radishchev read many documents relating to the peasantry; in the office of an army division, he studied the Pugachov Revolt. In 1780 he joined the customs service in St. Petersburg, becoming its director in 1790.

Radishchev's conventional bureaucratic career shielded daring literary activity. As Russia's first "repentant nobleman," he could not reconcile his progressive ideas with tyranny and exploitation in Russia. To him autocracy was "the state of affairs most repugnant to human nature." The ruler should be "the first citizen of the national society."

Alexander N. Radishchev (1749–1802)

In 1789 he submitted unsigned *A Journey from St. Petersburg to Moscow* to the censors who approved it for publication with some deletions. Radishchev's serfs ran it off on his private press, excisions and all! Catherine read it with rising fury, finding his rejection of autocracy and serfdom, and personal attacks on Potemkin, intolerable: he was "a rebel worse than Pugachov." In *A Journey* the traveler learns of the horrible nature of serfdom en route to Moscow: it is "a hundred-headed monster" repugnant to human nature, natural law, and the social contract, which must be gradually but completely abolished. (Later Russian abolitionists could add little.) Landowners in the name of reason, morality, and self-interest should end voluntarily a system economically and morally disastrous for all. The alternative was a mass revolution, which he seemed to welcome: "Oh, would that the slaves burdened with heavy shackles should rise in their despair and with the irons that deprive them of freedom crush our heads!" Actually, he sought to persuade the lords and state to forestall revolution with timely reform.

Radishchev and Novikov were Russian philosophes whose ideas

were largely of foreign origin. Rousseau's *Social Contract* influenced Radishchev deeply, and the American Revolution inspired his "Ode to Liberty" (1783), which demanded freedom and an end to censorship. Soviet historians, stressing his debt to Lomonosov's materialist philosophy and the Pugachov Revolt, portray him as a pioneer of the Russian revolutionary tradition, who prepared people to accept revolution as the sole means to a better order. Western and prerevolutionary Russian scholars generally view Radishchev as a liberal reformer and *A Journey* as the first program for political democracy and equality in Russia. His purpose, they argue, was to persuade the old regime to change before it was too late.

The French Revolution illuminated Radishchev's message with falling fortresses and burning manorhouses. Finding the book "quite flagrantly insurrectionary," Catherine had Radishchev imprisoned in Peter and Paul Fortress where he was interrogated by the torturer of Pugachov. He was condemned to death, but Catherine commuted his sentence to ten years exile in Siberia. She ordered *A Journey* seized and burned, but some copies escaped, circulating from hand to hand in Moscow and St. Petersburg. At first the French Revolution had found widespread approval in Russia until the nobility and regime became alarmed by its violence. With the execution of Louis XVI, Catherine retreated into open reaction and sought to isolate Russia from revolutionary thought. Belated repression, however, could not undo Russia's participation in the Enlightenment. The ideas of Radishchev, spreading among the educated public, prepared the way a generation later for the Decembrist movement.

Suggested Additional Reading

BOOKS

ALEXANDER, JOHN T.   *Emperor of the Cossacks: Pugachov and the Frontier Jacquerie of 1773–1775* (Lawrence, Kansas, 1973).
————.   *Autocratic Politics in a National Crisis: The Imperial Government and Pugachov's Revolt, 1773–1775* (Bloomington, Ind., 1969).
GARRARD, J. G., ed.   *The Eighteenth Century in Russia* (Oxford, 1973).
LANG, DAVID M.   *The First Russian Radical: Alexander Radishchev 1749–1802* (London, 1959).
McCONNELL, ALLEN.   *A Russian Philosophe: Alexander Radishchev* (The Hague, 1964).
RADISHCHEV, A. N.   *A Journey from St. Petersburg to Moscow* (Cambridge, Mass., 1958), trans. by L. Wiener, ed. by R. Thaler.
RAEFF, MARC.   *The Origins of the Russian Intelligentsia: The Eighteenth Century Nobility* (New York, 1966).
ROGGER, HANS.   *National Consciousness in Eighteenth Century Russia* (Cambridge, Mass., 1960).
SHCHERBATOV, M. M.   *On the Corruption of Morals in Russia* (ed. A. Lentin New York, 1969).

ARTICLES

BECKER, C.   "Raznochintsy: The Development of the Word and the Concept," *ASEER*, vol. 8, 1959, pp. 63–74.

KAHAN, A.   "The Costs of Westernization in Russia: The Gentry and the Economy in the Eighteenth Century," *SR*, vol. 25, 1966, pp. 40–66.

LANG, DAVID.   "Some Western Sources of Radishchev's Political Thought," *Revue des Etudes Slaves*, vol. 25, 1949, pp. 73–86.

McCONNELL, A.   "The Origin of the Russian Intelligentsia," *SEEJ*, vol. 8, 1964, pp. 1–16.

PETROVICH, M.   "Catherine II and a False Peter III in Montenegro," *ASEER*, vol. 14, 1955, pp. 169–94.

RAEFF, MARC.   "Pugachov's Revolt," in *Preconditions of Revolution in Early Modern Europe*, ed. R. Forster and J. Green (Baltimore, 1970), pp. 161–202.

———.   "State and Nobility in the Ideology of M. M. Shcherbatov," *ASEER*, vol 19, 1960, pp. 363–79.

SUMNER, B. H.   "New Material on the Revolt of Pugachov," *SEER*, vol. 7, 1928–29, pp. 113–27 and 338–48.

20

The Bureaucratic Monarchy of Paul and Alexander I

PAUL AND his son, Alexander I, both believers in enlightened absolute monarchy, ruled Russia between 1796 and 1825. In peaceful periods between the wars of the Napoleonic era, they sought by different means to strengthen and centralize the administration. The collegial principle, predominant at least in theory since Peter the Great, was discarded in favor of monocratic ministries organized on military, hierarchical principles. Holding jealously to their autocratic powers, both sovereigns believed that in Russia a powerful ruler was the only proper instrument of progress and popular well-being. They began hesitantly to restrict and alleviate the evils of serfdom, but they refused to contemplate its abolition seriously. After heroic sacrifices in the struggle with Napoleon, many Russians hoped for political and social reform from the enlightened Alexander, only to be rudely disillusioned by his increasingly reactionary and repressive policies. A few Russians turned unsuccessfully to revolutionary conspiracy to achieve the changes of which they dreamed.

The brief reign of Paul I (1796–1801) remains controversial and disputed. According to traditional accounts, it was a failure at home and abroad for lack of a consistent program and because Paul I was psychotic. Some recent historians, questioning this thesis, provide a more sympathetic picture and credit Paul with constructive domestic policies and considerable achievements despite his undeniable arbitrariness and volatility. They deny that Paul was mentally unbalanced.

Paul's personal life as heir had a profound impact on his conduct of affairs as emperor. He was afflicted with mental problems stemming from events in early life. Born in 1754, he was uncertain whether his father was Peter III (Catherine's husband) or one of her lovers. Empress Elizabeth soon removed Paul from his mother Catherine and placed him in the hands of nurses whose inept care weakened his health. His mother had little time for Paul and less interest in him. At six he began his formal education under his chief tutor, the watchful Nikita Panin, Catherine's close adviser. When Paul was only eight, his supposed father, Peter III, was deposed and murdered. Whatever Paul's feelings toward him, this violent death contributed to psychological stress, which was soon reflected in erratic behavior. Paul became quick-tempered, impulsive, inconsistent, and generally high strung. A tutor described his young student's behavior: "Paul has an intelligent mind in which there is a kind of machine that hangs by a mere thread; if the thread breaks, the machine begins to spin, and then farewell to reason and intelligence."[1]

Court gossips persuaded Paul that his mother would share power with him when he reached maturity. Catherine II, of course, had no such intention, and when Paul turned 18 she refuted such rumors. Paul felt wrongfully deprived of his inherent right to rule while Catherine was wary, regarding Paul more than ever as a potential threat to her rule. Deepening mutual suspicion and mistrust produced mutual alienation. Paul developed a morbid hatred of his mother and all that she stood for.

To keep Paul isolated from state affairs, Catherine tried to divert him by arranging his marriage to Princess Wilhelmina of Darmstadt in 1773. Paul refused to be diverted: he was heir to the throne and his views on important questions merited consideration. He submitted a detailed proposal for reorganization of the army which Catherine ignored completely, thus throwing him into a frenzy of anger and bitterness.

Soon after his first wife died in 1776, Paul married Princess Sophie of Württemberg. The births of his first two sons—Alexander in 1777 and Constantine in 1779,—further alienated Paul from his mother. Since Catherine considering bypassing her son in favor of one of her grandsons, she immediately removed them from their parents' care in order to supervise personally their upbringing and education.

In 1782 Paul retired despondently to his estate at Gatchina outside St. Petersburg to begin a long, frustrating wait for his mother's death. Lacking contact with the St. Petersburg court, he retreated into his own little military world. Paul gathered a small personal army, organized, equipped, and drilled in the Prussian style which he so admired. Military exercises became an outlet for his pent-up emotions. Woe to the man who had a button out of place or an unpolished weapon! For 14 years Paul awaited power, vowing to destroy everything his mother had done. Catherine's hatred for her son festered to such an extent that she decided to make her grandson, Alexander, her successor, but she died unexpectedly in 1796 before she could formalize this decision.

Once he had assumed power, Paul issued a series of decrees designed to subvert everything his mother had done. He filled the capital with his Gatchina "army" and exiled hundreds who had served Catherine. Paul also emptied the prisons, releasing such victims of Catherine as Radishchev and Novikov. Where Catherine had tried decentralization, Paul fostered centralization. Dismissals, transfers, and appointments proceeded at a dizzying pace. Wallowing in the pomp and circumstance of power, Paul insisted that high and low grovel before him

---

[1] P. Miliukov *et al.*, *History of Russia*, 3 vols. (New York, 1968), vol. 2, p. 140.

in recognition of his august authority. The army was reorganized and reequipped on the Prussian model, dressed in Prussian-style uniforms, and subjected to draconian discipline. Paul established a watch parade (*Wachtparade*) on the Prussian model to instruct soldiers and their officers. In a cocked hat, huge jack boots, and frock coat, holding a stick in his hands, the Emperor would yell out: "One, two, three!" even in sub-zero cold. The watch parade became a semiofficial institution at which Paul would issue decrees, receive reports, and set audiences. No one dared set foot on the parade ground without money in his pocket and a change of clothes in his knapsack because the Emperor might order any unit not "up to snuff" directly to Siberia! The discipline, orderliness, and conventions of the parade ground had always been Paul's overriding concern and remained so during his imperial rule.

Pursuing his avowed aim of reversing his mother's policies, Paul sought to curb the nobility and subordinate it more completely to the state. Catherine had cultivated noble support by granting concessions culminating in the Charter of the Nobility; Paul was unconcerned with noble privileges. His attitude toward noblemen was summed up by a comment he made to the Swedish ambassador: "Only he is great in Russia to whom I am speaking, and only as long as I speak [to him]."[2] Paul was acutely aware that during the 18th century the nobility had acquired great political power based on its ability to influence the succession to the throne by staging palace coups. Peter the Great's vague law of succession of 1722, allowing each sovereign to select his or her own successor, accounted for successful noble intervention on several occasions. Anxious to limit this power and determined to prevent future legitimate rulers from being deprived of the right to exercise power, Paul issued a new law of succession the day of his coronation in April 1797. Henceforth, succession would follow the principle of primogeniture: descent in the direct male line. Paul abolished provincial noble corporations stemming from Catherine's efforts to decentralize the administration, and instead appointed bureaucrats to perform their duties. To regulate relations between noble landowners and their serfs, he issued a decree forbidding landowners to force serfs to work their lands on Sundays and holidays and suggested a maximum of three days a week of *barshchina* as in the best interests of lords and serfs. These measures, directed primarily against the nobility, did not represent a well conceived plan of social reform but rather a desire to annul some privileges which Catherine had granted to nobles in return for their support of her usurpation of power. Paul restored the right of individual peasants to petition the crown, prohibited the sale of serfs without land in the Ukraine, and ordered some measures to improve the well-being of state and court peasants. He extended serfdom, however, by transferring in his short reign more than half a million state and crown peasants to private landowners' control.

---

[2] V. Kliuchevskii, *Kurs russkoi istorii*, vol. 5, p. 220.

Paul favored enlightened absolutism and held a high view of the sovereign's role as the guardian of his subjects and promoter of their well-being. He sought to establish a more rational, centralized, and efficient bureaucratic system. Restoring some government departments abolished by Catherine, his regime laid the bases of the ministerial reform implemented by his son. Lacking experience and often poorly advised, however, Paul pursued no definite plan, and his legislation lacked guiding principles. Toward the end of his reign a deepening mood of uncertainty and fear paralyzed the emerging bureaucratic structure, cowed the nobility, and weakened the economy. The populace from top to bottom lived in increasing fear of an arbitrary, capricious emperor, fond of dismissing a general in disgrace one day and recalling him with praise and honor the next. A police straitjacket tightened upon Russian society, arbitrary arrests multiplied, and insecurity rose among the elite. Decrees prohibited everything smacking of revolutionary France, which Paul feared as much as Catherine had. Many feared that the Empire could not long survive under Paul's high-handed and inconsistent rule. The familiar idea of a palace coup won support among high officials and army officers, who explored cautiously the idea of removing Paul and elevating his son Alexander to the throne. Among the leaders of the conspiracy was Nikita Panin (nephew of Paul's tutor), who had been Paul's foreign minister, Count Peter von der Pahlen, military governor of St. Petersburg, and the Zubov brothers.

For a long time Alexander refused to countenance any action against his father, but months of artful persuasion and Paul's arbitrariness won Alexander over to the conspiracy on condition that Paul's life be spared. Pahlen pledged that no harm would befall Paul, though he knew full well such a promise could not be kept. There is no concrete evidence to suggest that Alexander knew in advance of plans to murder Paul or accepted this as the price of gaining power. Alexander's grudging approval of a coup stemmed from Paul's dangerous foreign policy (see Chapter 21) and his resolve to exclude all his sons from the succession in violation of his own decree. Alexander thus participated in final preparations and selected the date: March 23, 1801. To his dismay, the conspirators beat and strangled Paul, which brought Alexander to the brink of collapse. Guilt and remorse never left him. Meanwhile there was general rejoicing that Paul's nightmarish reign had ended.

Paul's reign revealed the potential dangers and weaknesses of autocracy. Absolute power wielded irresponsibly and inconsistently endangered the entire state. Noblemen now realized that autocratic power could destroy privileges as well as grant them. Paul's efforts to outlaw some of the worst abuses of serfdom and to introduce legislative controls over it had only slight impact but dramatized the pressing need to alleviate the crushing weight of peasant obligations. Alexander I had to grapple with autocracy and serfdom, twin pillars of the old Russian system, but he proved no more successful than his predecessors in finding solutions to their inherent contradictions.

Alexander I (1801–25) mounted the Russian throne at the age of 23, confused, grief-stricken, and guilt-ridden. His entire life had been plagued with contradictions: caught between a grandmother who supervised his education and a father who feared him as a rival, Alexander tried to love these strong-willed and antagonistic persons. He was thrust back and forth between the sophisticated St. Petersburg court life of Catherine and Paul's crude and vulgar barracks life at Gatchina. The moral laxity, self-indulgence, and hypocrisy at court appalled him no less than the brutality and pettiness of Gatchina. In trying to please both grandmother and father, Alexander led a chameleon-like existence, constantly shifting moods to please one or the other. It proved even harder to reconcile Russian reality with his liberal education in the humanitarian principles of the Enlightenment under his Swiss tutor, F. C. La Harpe. Harsh military training under Paul's trusted lieutenant, Count A. A. Arakcheev, contrasted wholly with La Harpe's progressive views. To characterize Alexander as weak, docile, vacillating, and contradictory, however, is superficial. On the contrary, once he became emperor, Alexander proved single-minded, imperious, stubborn, and domineering.

A staggering array of problems faced the new ruler. Paul's rule had left the country morally and physically exhausted, the economy in disarray, corruption and inefficiency endemic, and foreign policy confused and contradictory. Inexperienced and with few trusted friends, Alexander was temporarily at the mercy of the conspirators. They were eager to stabilize the new regime, and Alexander cooperated. His first acts aimed to restore confidence in government and promote economic recovery. A general amnesty freed some 12,000 persons sentenced without trial under Paul. To stimulate the economy, all restrictions on imports and exports were lifted. Educational institutions were given support after languishing for years without funds. The Charter of the Nobility was officially reaffirmed. Once again nobles could travel abroad, take service with friendly powers, use private printing presses, elect their officials, and form provincial assemblies. Nobles were guaranteed freedom from corporal punishment, the poll tax, and from having to billet troops. These measures aimed to restore noble confidence and foster security and stability.

Alexander soon recalled several youthful friends sent abroad by his distrustful father. Returning to Russia, Prince Adam Czartoryski, Nicholas Novosiltsev, and Count Victor Kochubei, together with Count Paul Stroganov, constituted the Unofficial Committee, an informal group which met with Alexander over coffee to discuss general policy. These young Anglophile aristocrats (except Novosiltsev) favored abolition of serfdom and advocated enlightened absolutism, but neither they nor Alexander were democrats or desired a constitutional regime in the British sense. They and Alexander aimed to establish the rule of law in place of Paul's arbitrary despotism and orderly, efficient government with separation of functions, not powers. All of them, including Alexander, wished to transform Russia into a more modern country, but gradually and without radical change. Alexandrine "constitutionalism," therefore, operated within narrow confines and did not include any limitations on the emperor's autocratic powers.

Alexander has often been portrayed as a liberal whose reform plans were frustrated by Russia's backwardness and entrenched upper class privileges and vested interests. Allen McConnell, however, recently has argued persuasively that the liberals were the conspirators who lifted Alexander into power. The Zubovs and Pahlen in particular planned to transform the Empire's basic political structure by granting genuine legislative powers to the Senate, powers traditionally exercised by the sovereign alone. Such a program if implemented would have imposed crucial limitations on the ruler and altered the state structure. Alexander, however, never sanctioned such drastic change and opposed vigorously and successfully all efforts to limit his authority. Once he felt secure, was assured of a loyal army, and was surrounded by his youthful friends, he moved against the conspirators who posed a threat to his power. They were removed or exiled by the end of 1801. Once rid of the conspirators, the tone of Alexander's administration changed. Liberal-sounding initial measures were halted abruptly, and plans to reform the Senate, revise the law code, and issue an earlier promised Charter of the Russian People were shelved. Now in full control, Alexander resolved to preserve full traditional monarchical authority. This decision may have been a crucial turning point in Russian political development, a turning away from constitutional or representative government.

Alexander drew closer to his young friends and discussed state affairs with them in secret. They all agreed that serfdom was inequitable and odious, but they failed to suggest serious measures to reform or abolish it. To be sure, members of the professional and merchant classes were given the right to purchase estates with serfs (formerly only nobles could) on the ground that they would be more humane serf-owners, and public advertisement of serfs for sale without land was prohibited. Alexander, however, continued to turn over state lands and peasants to private individuals, though not as rapidly as Paul had done.

Only the Free Agriculturalists' Law of 1803, permitting landowners voluntarily to free their peasants individually or in groups, was intended to benefit private serfs. This decree, however, did not confront the fundamental issues of serfdom and affected very few serfs. Perhaps recalling the fate of his father and grandfather (Peter III), Alexander would not risk measures which would have provoked intense noble hostility.

Alexander's most important and lasting administrative reform was the creation in September 1802 of government ministries. The Petrine administrative colleges, some of which had atrophied, were replaced by eight ministries: Foreign Affairs, War, Navy, Finance, Interior, Justice, Commerce, and Education. In theory the ministers were accountable to the Senate, which was to be a mediator between the sovereign and the administration. In practice the ministries completed the creation of a bureaucratic, centralized system administered by powerful officials directly responsible to the emperor. The new ministers were not to form a cabinet and consulted little among themselves on broad issues of policy. Each minister, heading a centralized department organized on military lines, reported directly to and received orders directly from Alexander. Confirming that Alexander did not conceive of the Committee of Ministers as a cabinet was his appointment of liberals, conservatives, and even reactionaries as ministers, men who could not possibly act collectively with unanimity. Members of the Unofficial Committee were all appointed to positions within the ministries: Czartoryski became deputy minister of foreign affairs, Novosiltsev deputy minister of justice, Stroganov deputy minister of interior, and Kochubei Minister of Interior. Admiral N. S. Mordvinov, the Navy Minister, shared the political views of the Unofficial Committee, whereas G. R. Derzhavin, Minister of Justice, was a confirmed reactionary.

The Committee of Ministers, however, did meet with Alexander to discuss important policy issues. The group with its conflicting political views remained largely a sounding board with the tsar deciding all matters personally. Once Alexander became embroiled in conflict with Napoleon, it was empowered to decide all but the most important questions by majority vote. Absorbed in foreign policy, Alexander late in 1803 even ceased to meet with the Unofficial Committee. As relations between the tsar and his young friends grew strained, they began resigning their government positions to go into the army, education, or private life.

Education was a bright spot in an otherwise uninspired domestic policy. The shortage of adequately trained personnel, Alexander realized, hampered the proper functioning of bureaucratic monarchy because the educational system could not supply enough educated men to run the country. Creation of the Ministry of Education in 1802 showed that Alexander was determined to remedy this deficiency. This ministry supervised all educational institutions including libraries, museums, printing presses, and censorship. Early in 1803 a new school statute divided the Empire into educational districts, each of which was to have a university. A district curator was to be the district's chief educational authority responsible directly to the minister of education. Previously the only functioning university had been in Moscow (founded in 1755). Existing universities in Vilna (largely Polish) and Derpt (German) were revived, and new ones were founded in Kharkov and Kazan. St. Petersburg University was founded in 1819, bringing the total to six. Each university was to train teachers, disseminate knowledge, and supervise preparatory schools in its district. The educational system was open in theory to all classes, to anyone with the academic qualifications. Such egalitarianism offended the nobility, which wished education restricted to the privileged. Clearly, few serfs or non-nobles possessed the necessary interest or qualifications and scarcely threatened the upper classes. Nevertheless, a stated goal of the new system was to uncover and develop talent and skills useful to the state. Educational advances were perhaps modest in absolute terms, but relatively progress was significant. Those officials with even a rudimentary education, however, remained few, and educational deficiencies continued to hamper bureaucratic efficiency.

Involvement in the coalition wars against Napoleon (1805–07) distracted Alexander's interest from even modest domestic changes. Only after the Tilsit Treaty (1807) did he again consider projects for internal reform. His unpopular alliance with France, however, made the atmosphere at home less favorable for reform than in 1801–04

The spearhead for reform came from a remarkable non-noble bureaucrat, Michael Speranskii, son of an Orthodox priest. Born in a small village of Vladimir province in 1772, Speranskii had been educated at the local seminary, then owing to his unusual ability and interest was sent to the Alexander Nevskii seminary in St. Petersburg to continue his education. Within two years his progress at what was then the best ecclesiastical school in Russia was such that he was appointed to the faculty. By 1795 he was already among the best educated men in Russia, thoroughly familiar with advanced concepts of law, philosophy, politics, mathematics, and rhetoric as well as theology. Though assured of a brilliant academic career, he entered government service in 1797. A born bureaucrat, he possessed the ability to make even the most complex materials simple and understandable. His extraordinary stylistic brilliance made his memoranda and reports models of elegance, grace, and precision. Within three months he had risen to the eighth civil rank, which conferred hereditary nobility; by 1798 he occupied the sixth rank, equivalent to the rank of colonel in the army.

Count Kochubei, becoming Interior Minister in 1802, requested Speranskii's transfer to his ministry. As head of its Second Department, he handled police functions and internal welfare and drafted important measures such as the decree on Free Agriculturalists. In 1807 he attracted Alexander's personal attention when he began, in Count Kochubei's absence, to brief the tsar regularly on the Ministry's activities. Impressed with Speranskii's ability to prepare succinct reports and to administer the Ministry's complex affairs, Alexander relied on him increasingly for advice. In 1808 when Alexander met Napoleon at Erfurt, Speranskii was there as a civilian observer. In a famous remark Speranskii told Alexander: "They [the French] have better institutions, we have better men." Soon Speranskii became Deputy Minister of Justice, headed a commission to codify Russian laws, and was commissioned by Alexander to draw up a plan to improve Russia's institutions.

By 1809 Speranskii had prepared a comprehensive plan for an entirely new governmental system which would have transformed Russia from an autocracy based on the sovereign's arbitrary whim into a true monarchy based on the rule of law. The plan featured a proposal for the separation of functions. The executive branch would be headed by ministers, the judicial by the Senate, and the legislative branch would have several levels of elected assemblies, culminating in an indirectly elected State Duma. Above this was to be a Council of State of the tsar's closest advisers. All bills were to be submitted to the State Duma, which would pass acceptable ones on to the emperor for confirmation and invalidate unacceptable bills. Alexander, however, found totally un-acceptable any proposal limiting his authority, and so the only section of Speranskii's plan to be implemented was for the creation of a Council of State (1810). This body functioned as a sounding board for new legislation to the end of the Empire. Speranskii was appointed Secretary of State responsible for the State Council's operation.

Speranskii's power was second only to that of the Emperor himself. Concentration of such power in the hands of a single person, especially a social upstart, naturally produced enmity and jealousy. Speranskii's foes among the nobility multiplied as his responsibilities and Alexander's dependence on him grew. Intent on improving the efficiency of the bureaucracy, Speranskii introduced compulsory examinations as the only entree into state service and for promotion to the higher ranks. Speranskii's efforts to resolve the financial crisis by proposing a progressive tax on noble property infuriated the aristocracy. Speranskii had enemies even within the tsar's own family: a conservative circle formed around Catherine Pavlovna, Alexander's favorite sister. A leading figure associated with this circle was N. M. Karamzin, author of a spirited and patriotic defense of Russia's past traditions, *A Memoir on Ancient and Modern Russia,* which defended unlimited autocracy and stressed the role and status of the nobility. Karamzin's analysis of Russia's past and present, a classic expression of Russian conservative thought, articulated the views of the privileged class.

Speranskii's most vocal enemies, not content with attacking his political views, resorted to slander and innuendo to undermine his position and accused him of being a French agent, negotiating secretly with Napoleon and trying to subvert Russia by introducing French legal and administrative practices. Alexander evidently recognized these accusations to be ridiculous, but faced with rising anti-French feeling, he could ill afford to keep Speranskii in office. In March 1812 Alexander capitulated reluctantly to "public opinion" and dismissed Speranskii, ending the reform era prematurely. There had been little concrete accomplishment as preparations for the confrontation with Napoleon shunted reform into the background, nor would the reforms be revived after the war.

The last decade of Alexander's reign has customarily been viewed as one of unmitigated reaction associated with the sinister figure of Count A. A. Arakcheev. Indeed, the period is often called the Arakcheevshchina, or the time of Arakcheev. Accurate assessment of these years requires proper perspective, taking into account the atmosphere prevailing in Russia and the personalities of Alexander and his associates.

Russia's decisive contribution to Napoleon's defeat gave it unprecedented prestige abroad. Alexander "the Blessed," "the Savior of Europe," personified this new glory and renown. Victory, of course, had been achieved by the sacrifice and courage of the Russian people among whom, in all social ranks, arose a mood anticipating major internal changes. Peasants yearned for reward in the form of emancipation and a lessening of their burdens. Educated society hoped for freer institutions and more cultural freedom. To satisfy such high expectations would have required radical reforms, which Alexander considered impractical and dangerous.

The traumatic events of the Napoleonic wars had altered Alexander's political outlook. He was influenced deeply by the religious mysticism of Baroness von Krüdener, who had revealed that he was God's chosen instrument for the redemption of mankind. Alexander had been introduced by Prince A. N. Golitsyn to Bible study in 1812. Golitsyn then founded the Russian Bible Society with close ties to Protestant and Catholic circles.

Alexander did not renounce his hopes of reform, but he became more fearful of revolution. Insisting upon constitutions for defeated France and the restored Kingdom of Poland, he continued to consider reform for Russia. Speranskii, recalled from exile and appointed Governor General of Siberia, hoped that a reformed bureaucracy and thorough reorganization of the legal code would gradually change the empire into a semiconstitutional monarchy. Alexander remained sympathetic with Speranskii's views, and in 1819 requested Novosiltsev to draw up a constitutional proposal. The Emperor enthusiastically approved his draft constitution but then failed to proclaim it. Disturbing events in Europe contributed to growing malaise in Russia. Student associations, secret societies, assassinations, and minor revolts in Europe worried Alexander and made him unwilling to permit the people any voice in the process of government.

While he toyed with constitutional ideas, Alexander depended heavily on Count Arakcheev, who occupied a position similar to that held by Speranskii earlier. Arrogant, cruel, power hungry, and vindictive, Arakcheev, though doggedly loyal, represented the dark side of the political forces of Alexander's last decade; he is associated with the military colonies which he administered. Their precise origin is unknown, but there were many precedents in Russia, Austria, and Prussia. Arakcheev had organized his own estates along quasi-military lines, and Alexander may have derived the concept of military colonies from them. The tsar aimed to improve the military and reduce costs of a huge standing army. He voiced humanitarian concern for his troops who had to serve 25 years, separated from their families. The military colonies were designed to remedy all these problems. Army recruits with their families were to be settled on state lands, combining military training and exercises with agricultural pursuits.

Begun on an experimental basis before the Napoleonic invasion, colonies became widespread afterward. Initially, they were an experiment in social reform designed to improve living conditions and the socioeconomic status of recruits. Colonists were to be granted inviolability of property and sufficient land to till free of charge. Freed from all state taxes and forced labor service, each was to be given a horse and living quarters, and the infirm were to be cared for. This experiment might have served as a model for future emancipation, except that reality did not conform to theory. A chief aim of military colonies was to reduce the costs of a huge standing army, equal to those of Austria and Prussia combined. The provisions outlined above would have bankrupted an already overburdened treasury. Under Arakcheev's administration, moreover, occurred merciless exploitation, misery, mismanagement, and open resistance. Alexander denounced military colonists for being ungrateful for the opportunities provided by the state. "There will be military colonies whatever the cost, even if one has to line the road from Petersburg to Chudovo with corpses," he thundered when informed of open unrest in the colonies. He expanded these infamous institutions to almost a third of the million-man Russian army.

Military colonies were unpopular with inmates, who suffered draconian discipline and frequent corporal punishment. The colonies combined some of the worst features of serfdom and the army barracks and were bitterly denounced by liberals as barbaric. As violent protests by military colonists increased, even conservative elements expressed fear that uprisings in the colonies might touch off a general insurrection. The notorious military colonies revealed again Alexander's callousness toward a peasantry which had served him so well in war.

Alexander's fear of the lower classes promoted distrust of all social groups, notably the youthful noblemen who had served as junior officers in the Russian advance across Europe. As many of them abandoned military careers and entered universities, Alexander took alarm at the rapid spread of "Jacobinism," of liberal and radical ideas tolerable perhaps when discussed secretly by top government leaders but potentially explosive when debated publicly. There was also a growth of obscurantist, reactionary views tinged with religious mysticism. Alexander selected as Minister of Education Prince A. N. Golitsyn, director of the Bible Society and Procurator of the Holy Synod. Education and religion thus became inextricably connected. As head of the Bible Society, Golitsyn was tolerant toward Protestant and Catholic churches and toward religious sectarians, but as Minister of Education he espoused reactionary and intolerant views and unleashed a host of obscurantist bureaucrats upon the educational system. He aimed to root out all liberal and controversial influences from the schools and universities. Universities were purged of professors who disagreed with Golitsyn's bureaucrats or were dismissed for "teaching in a spirit contrary to Christianity and subversive of the social order." Such men as Michael Magnitskii and Dmitri Runich, curators respectively of Kazan and St. Petersburg school districts, sought to transform educational institutions into docile purveyors of official rhetoric and conservatism. Magnitskii recommended that Kazan University, as a dangerous and unnecessary institution, be closed completely. Alexander would not go that far, but he encouraged increasing vigilance and control. The universities were emasculated and the cause of learning suffered severe blows.

With the peasantry ground down by serfdom and military colonies, what opposition there was developed within the aristocracy. In the tradition of Radishchev and Novikov, educated noble army officers recognized the glaring contradictions and shocking injustices of the Russian system. These young men, upon returning home, were struck by the enormous gulf separating European social and political life from Russia's. These officers, mostly veterans of the Russian army of occupation in France, had absorbed liberal and radical ideas there and experienced the freer atmosphere of Western Europe. These experiences equipped them with a heightened social consciousness and greater interest in public affairs. They were acutely conscious of contradictions in Alexandrine policies: Alexander the Blessed abroad was Alexander the Despot at home. Constitutions and civil liberties for foreign countries, and even for Poland and Finland within the Russian Empire; serfdom and military colonies for Russia. The most powerful country in Europe, Russia was shamefully backward in domestic affairs. European events also stimulated Russian thought as revolts in Spain, Naples, and Piedmont in 1820–21 reflected popular opposition to reactionary postwar governments.

In such circumstances idealistic, liberal-minded young Russian aristocrats naturally sought to act in defense of freedom and justice. In Russia public debate of fundamental issues was impossible, and this situation promoted the formation of the first secret society in 1816, the Union of Salvation. Founded by elite Guards officers, all members of prominent and distinguished noble families, the Union of Salvation, like similar secret societies springing up in Western Europe, resembled a Masonic lodge with a constitution and degrees of initiation. Prominent among its small membership were Nikita Muraviev, Prince Sergei Trubetskoi, and Paul Pestel, young men who hoped to revivify Russia by abolishing serfdom and military colonies and introducing a constitutional regime. They disagreed, however, on how to achieve these broad aims. In 1818 this informal group was reorganized as the Union of Welfare with an elaborate apparatus but a vague political creed ranging from mild reformism to radical revolution. Members were urged to spread enlightenment through philanthropic activity similar to that of Masonic lodges. The Union of Welfare attracted some 200 members, mostly from the Guards regiments and chiefly veterans of the Napoleonic wars. By 1820 the government knew of its existence, and faced with official threats, the Union decided to disband. A few members maintained a smaller supersecret society with headquarters in St. Petersburg. Colonel Pestel, who had been transferred to the south, organized a second secret group.

Three major groups of what were subsequently called Decembrists emerged after 1820: a Northern Society in St. Petersburg, a Southern Society in the south, and the Society of United Slavs on the southwestern frontier, separated by distance and differing political views. The Northern Society, representing the upper gentry, tended to be more moderate, while the more radical Southern Society sought to enlist the support of ordinary soldiers scorned by their northern brethren. The Society of United Slavs was largely composed of poor gentry and was the only Decembrist element to favor a mass revolution; soon it merged with the Southern Society.

Nikita Muraviev, leader of the Northern Society, produced a constitution for Russia which incorporated the moderate views of his wealthy gentry colleagues. Its preamble summarized his political philosophy:

> The experience of all nations and of all times has proved that autocratic government is equally fatal to rulers and society; that it is not in accordance either with the rules of our sacred religion or with the prin-

ciples of common sense; it is not permissible to let the basis of government be the despotism of one person; it is impossible to agree that all rights shall be on one side and all duties on the other.[3]

Muraviev demanded abolition of serfdom and military colonies and prohibition of all social distinctions. Freedom of speech, religion, and assembly were guaranteed, and landowners were assured of the right to own their estates. Following the American Constitution, Muraviev envisaged Russia divided into thirteen states and two provinces. A bicameral National Assembly consisting of a Supreme Duma and a Chamber of Representatives would exercise legislative power, but the franchise and officeholding would be restricted to men of wealth and property. Each state and province was to have both state and local assemblies. Executive power would be entrusted to a hereditary emperor with powers similar to those of the American president. Muraviev envisioned a liberal constitutional monarchy run by the nobility.

Pestel and the Southern Society rejected Muraviev's constitution as "legalized aristocracy." This son of the Governor General of Siberia and the first dedicated Russian revolutionary composed *Russkaia Pravda* (Russian Justice) to guide a provisional government after the revolution had overthrown tsarism. All existing social institutions would be abolished: serfdom, military colonies, and aristocratic privileges and titles. All men were to be considered equal. Pestel advocated a centralized government, a single culture and a single language, which clearly was to be Russian. Except for the Poles, who would become independent, national and religious minorities must abandon their institutions and faiths in a Russia "one and indivisible," in contrast with the federalism implicit in Muraviev's constitution. Pestel would concentrate legislative authority in a unicameral National Assembly with wide powers and elected by universal male suffrage. Executive power was to be held by a five-member State Council elected by the National Assembly (like the French Directory of 1795–99). To implement this political program, Pestel envisioned the need for an authoritarian provisional government for a decade or so. Then it would yield its powers to a centralized republic which would exert absolute control over its citizens' behavior and thoughts through the clergy and police. Like the French Jacobins, Pestel would bar card playing and all dissipation. Private property was to be "sacred and inviolable," but half the land, much of it confiscated from the large serf owners, would be state-owned and distributed to those who wished to work it in accordance with need. Pestel's vision fused in strange combination Great Russian nationalism, Jacobin republicanism, dictatorship, and elements of socialism.

Most members of the Northern Society were horrified at Pestel's political and social program, especially at the violent minority seizure of power which he advocated. Persuasion and peaceful change were the principles upon which Muraviev wished to act. Still, vague discussions

[3] Cited in A. G. Mazour, *The First Russian Revolution, 1825* (Stanford, Calif. 1937), pp. 88–91.

were held between the two groups and there was tacit agreement that some action would be taken in 1826. Early in 1825, Muraviev and Trubetskoi were temporarily replaced as leaders of the Northern Society by Kondraty Ryleev, a radical poet sympathetic with Pestel's views. While in Kiev, Trubetskoi agreed with Pestel to establish closer ties between the two societies, and that fall he began to arrange a closer alliance with the southerners. Soon events interrupted all theoretical planning. On November 19, 1825, Alexander I died unexpectedly in Taganrog on the Sea of Azov.

Alexander and his wife were childless, and normally the throne would have passed to Constantine, his younger brother. Unknown to virtually everyone, Constantine had renounced all rights to the throne in 1820 after divorcing his first wife to marry a Polish countess. Continuing to reside in Poland, he took little interest in Russian court affairs. In 1823 Alexander had formally designated his youngest brother Nicholas as heir apparent. A sealed copy of a manifesto to that effect was kept in Moscow; others were deposited in state institutions with instructions to open them in the event of Alexander's death. Though vaguely aware of all this, Nicholas was uncertain of his status, and so he immediately swore allegiance to Constantine and ordered that this oath be administered throughout the Empire. When Constantine failed to accept or renounce the throne and remained in Warsaw, the resulting confusion and uncertainty afforded the conspirators opportunity to act. They had agreed that Alexander's death by natural causes or assassination would trigger an attempt to overthrow the government. Nicholas learned of a possible conspiracy in St. Petersburg and the south and resolved to have himself proclaimed emperor on December 14, 1825, and then have the oath of allegiance administered to the troops. The Northern Society's leaders agreed to stage a revolt on December 14. Trubetskoi, selected as "dictator," had just three days to prepare an uprising.

The conspirators made no definite plans and few preparations, anticipating that their troops would follow orders at the appointed time. Many clearly recognized the hopelessness of their cause. "We are destined to die!" Ryleev announced melodramatically. December 14th was a comedy of errors. Ryleev was ill, and "Dictator" Trubetskoi failed to appear. Only about 3,000 troops on Senate Square in St. Petersburg refused the oath of allegiance to Nicholas, and even they did not understand why. The conspirators made no attempt to enlist support from a sympathetic crowd of commoners, which had gathered on the edge of the square. After the government had failed to disperse the rebel troops peacefully, Nicholas ordered his men to fire. In the volley of canister shot which followed, many rebels were killed or wounded and even more innocent bystanders. The rebels fled, and the abortive revolt reached an ignominious end. The Southern Society, out of touch with events in the capital, acted somewhat later but with similar lack of success. Pestel had been arrested even before December 14, and the two companies of the Chernigov Regiment which rebelled under the Muraviev-Apostol brothers were soon subdued. Nicholas set up a commission of inquiry to investigate the entire Decembrist affair. It interrogated more than 600 persons of whom 121 were brought to trial before a special tribunal of five judges (one was Speranskii). Five leaders were sentenced to death, 31 were exiled to Siberia for life, and the remaining 85 were exiled for shorter periods.

The Decembrist Revolt is often considered the last of the palace coups common in the 18th century, but the revolt on Senate Square aimed at a fundamental alteration of the system of government, not the mere replacement of one ruler by another. In this sense, the Decembrist Revolt began a genuine revolutionary movement led by the intelligentsia which would culminate in the Revolution of 1917. The Decembrist Revolt was unique as the only time until 1917 that revolutionary ferment would center in the army. For the balance of the century the army would support the autocracy. The Revolt became a powerful myth inspiring generations of Russian radicals, who saw the Decembrists as heroic defenders of the rights of man. Soviet historians have hailed these noble revolutionaries as the first Russians to build a revolutionary organization and prepare armed action against tsarism. The revolt failed for lack of preparation and adequate leadership, but also because it was premature. Only a tiny minority of the population had any comprehension of the ideas which motivated the Decembrists to act. Like their successors, the Decembrists, isolated from the populace, did not represent and could not articulate popular needs except in the vaguest way.

The Alexandrine era closed, as it had opened, on a note of violence. The promise of fundamental reform enunciated in 1801 was blocked by Alexander's stubborn insistence on maintaining his full autocratic powers. Speranskii's approach, which might have prepared the way for a constitutional monarchy based on law, was not given a chance. Serfdom and autocracy remained as the apparently unshakable core of the Russian imperial system.

Suggested Additional Reading

ALMEDINGEN, E. M.   *The Emperor Alexander I* (London, 1964).

JENKINS, M.   *Arakcheev: Grand Vizir of the Russian Empire* (New York, 1969).

LANG, D.   "Radishchev and the Legislative Commission of Alexander I," *ASEER*, vol. 6 (1947), pp. 11–24.

LOEWENSON, L.   "The Death of Paul I. . . ," *SEER*, vol. 29 (1950), pp. 212–32.

McCONNELL, A.   "Alexander I's Hundred Days," *SR*, vol. 28 (1969), pp. 373–93.

———.   *Tsar Alexander I: Paternalistic Reformer* (New York, 1970).

McGREW, R.   "A Political Portrait of Paul I. . . ," *JfGO*, vol. 18 (1970), pp. 503–29.

NARKIEWICZ, O.   "Alexander I and the Senate Reform," *SEER*, vol. 48 (1969), pp. 115–36.

PALMER, A.   *Alexander I: Tsar of War and Peace* (London, 1974).

PIPES, R.   *Karamzin's Memoir on Ancient and Modern Russia . . .* (Cambridge, Mass., 1959).

RAEFF, M.   *Michael Speransky, Statesman of Imperial Russia* . . . (The Hague, 1957).

————.   *Siberia and the Reforms of 1822* (Seattle, 1956).

STRAKHOVSKY, L.   *Alexander I of Russia* (New York, 1947).

"The Reign of Paul I," *Canadian-American Slavic Studies,* vol. 7, no. 1 (1973).

VERNADSKY, G.   "Reforms Under Alexander I . . . ," *RoP,* vol. 9 (1947), pp. 47–64.

21

War and Diplomacy, 1796–1825

RUSSIA PLAYED a vital role in European power politics during the French Revolution and Napoleonic era. Under Paul I it joined European efforts to block French expansion and began a successful Mediterranean policy, while under Alexander I Russia fought Napoleon in central Europe (1805–07), repelled the Napoleonic invasion of 1812, and headed the European resurgence which overthrow him in 1814. Victory over Napoleon brought Russia to its peak of power in the tsarist period and gave it predominance in eastern Europe. Personal shortcomings prevented Alexander from exploiting Russian victories fully, and afterwards, in upholding the Vienna Settlement, he followed in Austria's wake. What were Russian aims in Europe? Why the alternating cooperation and conflict with Napoleon? Which factors defeated the French invasion of Russia? How did Russia's great victory over Napoleon affect its foreign policy afterwards?

PAUL I

Paul hated and feared revolutionary France even more than his mother and sought by every means to bar Jacobin principles from Russia. At first he refused to join an anti-French coalition partly because his advisers feared foreign war would worsen Russia's financial and administrative problems, and he negotiated with the French Directory to restore the relations which Catherine had suspended. Assuming an increasing role in foreign policy, Paul sought to consolidate his empire, remain neutral in the Anglo-French struggle, and avoid binding commitments abroad.

A French challenge to Russian interests in the eastern Mediterranean and central Europe upset his cautious approach. In 1798 Napoleon launched a program of conquest: he seized Malta, the Ionian Islands, and Egypt and invaded Syria. The deeply religious Paul had long been interested in the Maltese Order of the Knights of St. John, and his first foreign agreement (January 1797) was with the Order's grand master after the French had confiscated its assets in France. That November he became protector of Malta, and French seizure of the island in June 1798 triggered Russian intervention in the Mediterranean. Imbued with a mystic aim to revive chivalry in Russia and Europe, Paul wished to lead a crusade against the "infidel" French Revolution. He viewed the Order as the vanguard of counterrevolution and strove to build an international movement to support traditional churches and monarchies. In October 1798 he was chosen Grand Master of the Order, the first and only non-Catholic ever so honored.

The Second Coalition against France, headed by Russia and Britain, also included Austria, the Ottoman Empire, and Naples. The unprecedented Russo-Turkish alliance, provoked by the French threat, was the basis for anti-French action in the eastern Mediterranean. After Napoleon's invasion of Egypt caused the Porte to declare war on France and seek Russian aid, a Russo-Turkish expedition under Vice Admiral F. F. Ushakov liberated the Ionian Islands. While the war lasted, Russia sent its warships freely through the Turkish Straits and used Ionian bases to exert strong influence in the eastern Mediterranean. Simultaneously, Russia established important political ties with the Balkan Christians (Paul decorated and subsidized the Prince of Montenegro). On land Austro-Russian forces fought the French in Italy as General Suvorov scored repeated victories, but growing suspicion soon estranged the allies. In the war's most dramatic (but futile) episode, Suvorov's army struggled heroically through the Swiss Alps, but Austria's withdrawal from Switzerland induced Paul to recall Suvorov, and the Second Coalition dissolved without real result.

In 1800 Paul's policy shifted as Anglo-Russian tension grew over the enhanced Russian role in the Mediterranean. After the British captured Malta from the French, Russia seized British property and sailors and suspended commercial and diplomatic relations. A Russo-Swedish alliance (October 1799) became the cornerstone of a second League of Armed Neutrality to protect neutral seaborne trade against British seizures. Britain and Russia drifted toward war while Paul undertook rapprochement with Napoleon's Consulate, which he believed, was no revolutionary threat. Responding to Napoleon's peace overtures, Paul allied with him against Britain and proposed a Franco-Russian expedition against British India as part of plans for southward expansion. Napoleon, approving the Indian venture, delayed sending troops, but in February 1801 Paul ordered 22,000 Cossacks through the Central Asian deserts toward India. His murder, preventing full implementation of this fantastic scheme, averted war with Britain.

Paul's foreign policy lacked coherence or overall planning. Except in the Mediterranean, where Russian power was increased temporarily, little was accomplished. Paul's hatred of revolution drew him initially into an anti-French coalition similar to the Holy Alliance of his son, Alexander, but in his foreign policy whim, not national interest, predominated.

ALEXANDER I: ORIENTATION AND INITIAL POLICIES (1801–1804)

Alexander and his chief advisers, defending monarchical and aristocratic values, were profoundly oriented to Europe and sought to preserve a balance of power. At times they sought to promote peace abroad in order to concentrate on domestic reform; at others they involved Russia deeply in European power struggles. Alexander himself made the chief policy decisions and often conferred with foreign ambassadors and heads of state. Viewing foreign relations theoretically, he stressed neither pragmatic security nor commercial interests. He considered war a justifiable extension of diplomacy, but entered it reluctantly, mostly for defensive reasons. "If I make use of arms. . . ," he stated in 1801, "it will be only to repulse an unjust aggression. . . ." "What need have I to increase my empire?" he asked Chateaubriand in 1823. "Providence has not put 800,000 soldiers at my orders to satisfy my ambition but to protect religion and justice and to preserve those principles of order on which human society rests."[1]

At first, Alexander, anxious to pursue domestic reform, sought general European peace. To avert war with Britain, he recalled the Cossacks sent to India and freed British property in Russia. Lord Nelson's destruction of the Danish fleet (April 1801) damaged the Russian-led League of Armed Neutrality; but only two months later an Anglo-Russian convention was signed, and normal relations were restored. In October Alexander and Napoleon reached an agreement to respect Ionian independence and Neapolitan neutrality, and the tsar promoted Anglo-French talks culminating in the Peace of Amiens. To achieve rapprochement with England, Alexander then sacrificed the League of Armed Neutrality. Russia also resumed good relations with Austria while continuing to protect the small German states. Acting Foreign Minister Victor Kochubei's "passive system" of nonintervention appeared to be successful.

Alexander, preferring a weak Porte under Russian protection to partition of the Ottoman Empire, continued the Russo-Turkish alliance, which guaranteed Russia's position in the eastern Mediterranean. Rejecting suggestions for a partition, he declared that Russia favored Ottoman integrity. Meanwhile Russia's Black Sea commerce, protected by her fleet, rose from 5.5 percent of her total seaborne trade in 1802 to 12.9 percent in 1805.

Anti-French feeling soon developed at the Russian court, however, fostered by Alexander I's Anglophile "young friends." As Napoleon's ambitions unfolded and relations with Britain improved, Russian ties with France deteriorated. Viewing himself as the champion of liberty, Alexander came to identify Napoleon with despotism, especially after the abduction of the Duke d'Enghien from neutral Baden in March 1804. Napoleon's insulting response to Russian protests over this inci-

---

[1] Cited in Patricia Grimsted, *The Foreign Minister of Alexander I* (Berkeley, 1969), pp. 44–45.

dent led to the severing of diplomatic relations, and Russia moved into the waiting arms of England.

COALITION WARS (1805–1807)

Britain resumed war with Napoleon in 1803 and eagerly sought continental allies. When Russia and Austria responded favorably, a Third Coalition formed against France, organized chiefly by Prince Adam Czartoryski, assistant Russian foreign minister and Alexander's intimate friend. Czartoryski, a Polish aristocrat, aimed at maximum Russian involvement abroad in order to reconstruct Europe and resurrect Poland under Russia's wing. N. Novosiltsev, bearing Czartoryski's instructions, went to England on a secret mission (November 1804) to arrange an alliance against Napoleon. His instructions advocated an Anglo-Russian league to restrict France to its natural frontiers, while assuring the French that their national interests would be secured, and outlined ambitious Russian territorial goals: all of Poland, Moldavia, Malta, Constantinople, and the Turkish Straits. If the Ottoman Empire collapsed, Britain and Russia were to confer on its partition. Prime Minister William Pitt raised objections over Malta and the Straits, then consented to an Anglo-Russian alliance to liberate non-French regions from Napoleonic rule. In return for British subsidies, Russia would supply most of the land forces. Some Russian leaders opposed this alliance, but Alexander finally ratified it. Austria and Russia had agreed earlier that in a war with France, Austria would raise 235,000 men and Russia 115,000. Sweden and Naples also joined the Third Coalition.

The campaign of 1805 brought disaster to the allies. Napoleon, marching eastward, forced an Austrian army at Ulm to surrender. General M. I. Kutuzov's Russian army joined the main Austrian force in Bohemia, but poor Austrian generalship, and Alexander's impatience for military glory wrecked allied prospects. Kutuzov's sound advice to await reinforcements was rejected, and at Austerlitz (December 1805) Napoleon won a decisive victory. Kutuzov extracted the bulk of his army, but Austria made peace and Prussia became pro-French while the Third Coalition expired ingloriously.

Napoleon next expanded in the Balkans, inducing Austria to cede Dalmatia, Istria, and Kotor (Cattaro) to his Kingdom of Italy. Admiral D. N. Seniavin, commanding Russia's Mediterranean fleet, resolved to deny the French use of Kotor, persuaded the Austrians to yield it to him, and allied Russia with Montenegro. Dominating the Adriatic, Seniavin blockaded the French in Dubrovnik and tightened Russian ties with the Balkan Slavs. Napoleon's agents, bribing the Sultan with promises of territorial gain, however, persuaded the Turks to fight Russia. After the Sultan's arbitrary removal of the rulers of the Danubian Principalities provoked Russia to occupy them, the Porte declared war on her (October 1806) and closed the Straits. Alexander then authorized his Balkan commanders to cooperate with Serbian insurgents under Karadjordje and secure Serbia's autonomy from the Turks.

Late in 1806 a Fourth Coalition formed against France as Prussia replaced fallen Austria. King Frederick William III, angered by arbitrary French actions in west Germany and swayed by Alexander, demanded a French withdrawal to the Rhine. Napoleon responded with a lightning stroke, destroying the main Prussian forces at Jena and capturing Berlin before the slow moving Russians arrived. The Poles greeted Napoleon as their liberator and flocked to his banners. That winter the Russians and French fought two bloody, indecisive battles in East Prussia. Finally, at Friedland (June 1807) Napoleon won a hard-earned victory. Alexander, distracted by wars against the Porte and Persia and dissatisfied with British subsidies, decided on peace. He was influenced by court pressures and Russia's financial and military exhaustion.

TILSIT AND THE FRANCO-RUSSIAN ALLIANCE (1807–1812)

In June 1807 Napoleon and Alexander met alone on a raft in the Niemen River, separating French and Russian forces. Reportedly the tsar declared that he hated the English as much as Napoleon. "If so," Napoleon supposedly declared, "then peace is concluded," and at Tilsit they concluded peace and a secret alliance against Britain. Alexander made his own decisions and was not duped by Napoleon as some contemporaries believed. For Alexander survival of his empire was paramount: Russia needed peace and friendship with France, he believed, in order to recover her strength. In the Tilsit bargaining, Alexander proved a more stubborn, calculating negotiator than Napoleon had anticipated.

The Tilsit accords created a rough division of Europe into French and Russian spheres of interest, and Russia became Napoleon's junior partner in his efforts to force Britain to submit. Prussia lost all her territory east of the Elbe, and from its Polish lands Napoleon erected the Duchy of Warsaw, a French satellite state. Russia received the Polish district of Belostok but yielded her Mediterranean foothold to France and recognized Napoleon's brothers as kings of Naples and Westphalia. Admiral Seniavin's fleet, losing its bases and blocked from the Black Sea, surrendered to the British. Alexander pledged secretly to mediate between France and England and to declare war on Britain if he failed; in return, Napoleon would try to mediate a Russo-Turkish settlement, or failing that would "make common cause" with Russia. A secret alliance treaty committed France and Russia to fight side by side in any European conflict with all their resources.

The French alliance proved so unpopular in Russia that some called Alexander "Napoleon's henchman," and there was even talk of a palace coup; but Alexander persisted in his dealings with Napoleon. As foreign minister, he appointed N. P. Rumiantsev, a wealthy serf owner who favored ties with France. While Tilsit allowed France to dominate most of the continent, establish a French base on Russia's borders, and win Polish support, it nonetheless gave Russia an urgently needed breathing spell, preserved shrunken Prussia's independence, and enabled Russia to acquire Finland. For Russia, the worst consequences of Tilsit were conflict with Britain and membership in the French Continental System, which sought to bar British goods from Europe.

A breach with Britain soon followed. After the British destroyed the Danish fleet to prevent its use against them, Russia broke relations and then declared war. Early in 1808 Napoleon proposed to Alexander a joint campaign against British India and possible partition of the Ottoman Empire, promising Russia the Danubian Principalities and northern Bulgaria; France would take Albania and much of Greece. France and Russia, however, clashed over Constantinople and the Straits (Rumiantsev insisted on these), negotiations broke down, and the expedition against India was abandoned.

One consequence of Tilsit was a Russo-Swedish war. Because King Gustav IV of Sweden, allied with Britain, remained stubbornly anti-French, Napoleon encouraged Alexander to seize the Swedish province of Finland, and Rumiantsev persuaded him to move in order to assuage Russian patriotic opinion and protect St. Petersburg. Within six months the Swedes were driven from Finland and ceded it to Russia (1809), though guerrilla warfare revealed Finnish hostility to Russia. To calm this resistance, Alexander pledged to respect Finnish laws, religion, and institutions; Finland became a grand duchy within the Russian Empire.

At their Erfurt meeting (1808) Napoleon tried to tighten his alliance with Alexander by recognizing Russia's claims to Finland and the Danubian Principalities, but Alexander refused to join France in a war against Austria. In fury Napoleon threw down his hat and stamped on it, but to no avail. Talleyrand, the French foreign minister, forseeing Napoleon's ultimate fall, urged the tsar secretly to resist his demands. When Austria rose in 1809, Russian troops on the Galician frontier only moved in to prevent the Poles from uniting Galicia with the Duchy of Warsaw. Napoleon finally defeated Austria, but he deeply resented Russia's inaction and was angered further by the refusal of Alexander's sister to marry him.

The Franco-Russian alliance broke down for many reasons. Like Hitler after him,[2] Napoleon aimed to control all Europe. His bloated ambitions and arrogance conflicted with vital Russian interests in the Balkans, the Straits, and Poland, and his arbitrary annexation of Oldenburg, a north German state ruled by a relative of the tsar, confirmed their divergence. Their economic differences also increased because Russia had joined the Continental System most reluctantly and its participation remained halfhearted. Anglo-Russian trade dwindled, but Alexander did not enforce measures against British contraband. Russian merchants and landowners, hurt by the Continental System, complained vehemently. Alexander's decree of December 1810 imposed heavy customs duties on French imports, and he refused to close Russian ports to neutral vessels. Franco-Russian economic interests proved incompatible, and trade with Britain remained vital to Russia. Talley-

---

[2] See below, pp. 556–57.

rand kept exhorting Alexander to form a coalition against Napoleon: "You must save Europe." In 1811–12, though Rumiantsev espoused loyal cooperation with France, both sides prepared for conflict.

NAPOLEON INVADES RUSSIA (1812)

The War of 1812 (Soviet historians call it the "first fatherland war") decided Franco-Russian competition for European supremacy. Western scholars often attribute Napoleon's defeat in Russia largely to distance, bad roads, and climate; whereas the Soviets emphasize General Kutuzov's brilliant strategy and generalship and the heroism and patriotism of the Russian people. All these, Russia's size and manpower reserves, and Alexander I's courage and persistence, contributed to victory in a campaign described graphically in Leo Tolstoy's immortal novel, *War and Peace*.[3]

Napoleon hoped by conquering Russia to deny all continental markets to Britain and encompass her defeat. "In five years I shall be ruler of the world; there remains only Russia, but I shall crush her," he declared in 1811. Europe's fate rested upon Russia's ability to resist a French invasion. By pressure and force, Napoleon had built a formidable European coalition based on military alliances with weakened Austria and Prussia. (Privately their rulers assured Alexander that their participation would be only nominal.) Most Poles, believing that French victory would restore their independence, supported Napoleon. On the eve of the invasion, Russia managed to erase potential threats in the north and in the south. Welcoming a Russian pledge to help her recover Norway, Sweden allied with Russia secretly; and the Turks, whom Napoleon had hoped would tie up Russian forces and even invade the Ukraine, were defeated repeatedly by General Kutuzov. Russian willingness to return most of the Danubian Principalities and Turkish losses outweighed French pressure. The Treaty of Bucharest (May 1812), giving Russia Bessarabia and part of the Caucasian Black Sea coast, released sizable Russian forces and contributed to victory over the French. Once the war began, Russia allied with Britain and Spain, Napoleon's other enemies.

On June 24, 1812 without declaration of war the Grand Army of some 400,000 men (almost 600,000 with later reinforcements) invaded Russia. It included about 250,000 French, many Poles (who fought willingly), and Germans, Italians, and Spaniards (mostly recruited forcibly). Facing them were some 200,000 Russians in three armies: one under the supreme commander, Barclay de Tolly, a second under Prince Bagration, and reserves under General Tormazov. The Russians, though heavily outnumbered, were roughly equal in armament and superior in morale. Initial numerical inferiority compelled them to adopt the wise strategy of retreating into the interior, avoiding a decisive battle, and destroying foodstuffs and supplies.

Napoleon's precise objectives in Russia remain obscure, though evi-

---

[3] See below, pp. 417–18.

MAP 21–1
Napoleonic Wars and Russia

Russian military activity against French forces
in Italy 1798–1799

Russian military attack on Turkey 1806–1812

Napoleon's march to Moscow 1812

Russian advance from Moscow to Paris 1813–1814

❋   Battle sites

dently he wished to engage and destroy the Russian army near the frontier and restore Russia to obedient partnership. Soviet historians affirm that Napoleon (like Hitler later) aimed to exclude Russia from the Baltic and Black seas, take away its western lands, and thrust it into Asia. Moving through friendly Lithuania and eastern Poland, Napoleon reached Vilna on June 28th. He decided against emancipating the Russian serfs, explaining that rousing such savages against the nobility would make orderly government impossible. The possible effects of such a proclamation are hard to gauge. In mid-August when Napoleon reached Smolensk on the road to Moscow, there was heavy fighting but no decisive battle, and the Russian armies linked up and withdrew eastward. Personal friction among Russian commanders and public outcry at their retreat induced Alexander to remove Barclay and name the aged but popular Fieldmarshal Kutuzov commander in chief.

Plunging eastward, Napoleon met Kutuzov's forces at Borodino, about 75 miles west of Moscow, where on September 7 was fought the greatest battle of the campaign and Napoleon's career.[4] The French captured key positions, but Napoleon withheld his Guard, which might have destroyed the battered Russian army. Withdrawing to Fili near Moscow, Kutuzov consulted his generals at a council of war, then decided to abandon Moscow. This unpopular but wise move brought Alexander I's prestige to its nadir. He turned over the army to Kutuzov and the government to his ministers, but his unwavering determination to resist and his refusal to negotiate while the French remained on Russian soil contributed significantly to ultimate victory.

Napoleon entered Moscow September 14th expecting supplies and Russian peace offers, but as the French occupied the largely deserted city, fires broke out and, fanned by a strong wind, destroyed most of it. Napoleon had to flee the Kremlin in haste. Probably the fires broke out spontaneously as French soldiers looted the city. To Napoleon's dismay, Alexander and Kutuzov refused to parley, while at Tarutino, southwest of Moscow, lay Kutuzov's army guarding armament and supply centers and the unconquered south. Kutuzov was being steadily reinforced while French strength dwindled and numerous partisans and mobile Cossack units raided their communications. Napoleon's position in Moscow became untenable.

On October 19th Napoleon abandoned Moscow intending to retreat southward, but Kutuzov's army barred the way; and after a bitter battle at Maloiaroslavets, the French retreated westward toward Smolensk, harried by the Russians. Poor Russian coordination, hesitancy by their generals, and Napoleon's ability permitted his escape across the frozen Berezina River. Then the cold completed the Grand Army's destruction, and fewer than 30,000 ragged, half-frozen troops recrossed the Niemen. The Russian campaign undermined Napoleon's strength,

---

[4] According to H. Seton-Watson, (*The Russian Empire*, p. 132), the Russians lost nearly 40,000 men and the French more than 30,000. Florinsky's figures in *Russia: A History*, vol. 2, p. 676, are 58,000 Russians lost and 50,000 French. A recent Soviet account lists French losses at 58,500 against 38,500 Russians. *Isstoriia SSSR* (Moscow, 1967), vol 4, p. 131.

but his escape prolonged his rule for two years and required a costly war to liberate Europe.

LIBERATION OF EUROPE AND THE VIENNA SETTLEMENT (1813–1815)

Russian leaders split over whether merely to expel the invader or to free Europe. Kutuzov favored a nationalist policy of concentrating on Russia's affairs because, as far as he was concerned, "that accursed island [England] could sink out of sight." The sentiments of Rumiantsev and Count Arakcheev, were similar but Alexander, encouraged by the British ambassador and vom Stein, the liberal German statesman, resolved to deliver Europe from Napoleonic tyranny. His decision launched Russia on expensive wars abroad as his sense of mission blended with the desire for revenge upon Napoleon and to liberate Paris. Neglecting urgent need of reform at home, he turned his face toward Europe.

Russia's victory over the Grand Army and awakening patriotism in Germany triggered a national rising there against French rule. As Russian troops moved into Prussia, the King and people greeted them enthusiastically. Supported by Russia, Prussia declared war on France and led a German war of liberation. As Prussian and Russian forces sparred with Napoleon, Austria temporized. Emperor Francis did not wish to fight Napoleon, his new son-in-law, and Foreign Minister Metternich opposed a liberal, national German war of liberation. During a summer truce Metternich tried in vain to arrange a compromise peace, then reluctantly brought Austria into the anti-French coalition. This decision turned the scale, and at Leipzig (October 1813) an allied force almost half Russian defeated Napoleon decisively and threw him into France.

Determined to crush Napoleon, Alexander led his forces into France, and the Allies (Britain, Russia, Prussia, and Austria) pledged in the Treaty of Chaumont (March 1814) to fight until final victory. On March 30 Alexander and his Prussian junior partner, Frederick William III, entered Paris. Talleyrand, having already abandoned Napoleon, persuaded Alexander to demand Napoleon's abdication and the Bourbons' return as French constitutional monarchs. Alexander, enjoying paramountcy in Europe, failed to exploit or retain it, and in a state visit to Britain alienated the Court with tactless support of the Whig opposition. Inconsistency, idleness, and deepening mysticism cost him diplomatic leadership, which was seized instead by Metternich and the clever Talleyrand.

Alexander's determination to restore a Polish kingdom under his rule alienated west European governments and public opinion and almost broke up the Vienna Congress, which convened in the Austrian capital to work out a European settlement. At its first session, the Polish-Saxon question was hotly debated. Sympathetic in a sense with Polish national aspirations, Alexander treated kindly the Poles who had fought for the French and with Czartoryski drew up plans for a constitutional Poland, including the former Duchy of Warsaw, Prussian Poland, and Austrian Galicia. Prussia and Austria were to be compensated; the former with Saxony, but Metternich strongly opposed strengthening Russia and Prussia so much. Lord Castlereagh of Britain, fearing Russian domination of Europe, seconded Austrian objections, and Talleyrand exploited this opening to secure full French participation at the Congress by backing Russia's opponents. The Polish-Saxon issue provoked a secret Austro-British-French alliance in January 1815 against the claims of Russia and Prussia, and war threatened until a compromise had been negotiated. Prussia kept some of its Polish lands, Austria retained Galicia, and Cracow became a free city, while Russia obtained the rest of Poland as a constitutional kingdom.

Napoleon's escape from Elba temporarily reunited the powers. The British and Prussians defeated Napoleon at Waterloo in June 1815 without Russian participation, but Russian troops entered Paris and joined in a subsequent Allied occupation of France (1815–18). The Vienna Congress confirmed Russia's claims to Finland and Bessarabia and its status as the greatest European land power.

THE CONCERT OF EUROPE

Russia played a major though quieter role in European affairs during Alexander I's final decade. Anxious to preserve the great power alliance and the balance of power, Alexander sought good relations with the eastern monarchies (Austria and Prussia) and with more liberal France. In his idealistic, mystical quest for European peace and harmony, he composed in 1815 a Holy Alliance based on Christian principles for signature by his fellow monarchs in order to insure peace and mutual aid. Signed eventually by most European rulers, it lacked practical significance but symbolized the unity of the conservative European monarchies.

More substantial was the Concert of Europe (1815) to bring together periodically leaders of the great powers to preserve peace and the Vienna Settlement. Once the unifying menace of French expansion disappeared, however, rifts deepened, especially between Russia and Britain. At the Aix-la-Chapelle Congress (1818), Castlereagh of Britain rejected a Russian proposal for regular, intimate great power cooperation, and France was evacuated and granted equality in European affairs. At subsequent congresses at Troppau, Laibach, and Verona (1820–22), the powers discussed what to do about revolutions against legitimate rulers. Convinced that revolutionary conspiracy threatened all European regimes, Alexander proposed common action against it. At Verona he declared: "My sword is at the service of France," but the French showed no desire to use it. He offered Russian troops to crush revolts in Italy and Spain, but Austria demurred. Britain refused to sanction intervention in domestic affairs of continental states and blocked the eastern monarchies' efforts to restore Latin America to Spanish control. Verona was the final congress, but the eastern powers still collaborated closely to uphold the Vienna Settlement.

Continuing to control foreign policy closely, Alexander between 1815 and 1822 pursued a flexible course of cooperation with France and Austria. In the foreign office, he maintained both I. A. Capodistrias, a liberal Greek aristocrat, and Karl Nesselrode, a conservative Austrophile. Capodistrias, favoring constitutionalism and moderate reform, espoused Greek independence; Nesselrode, self-effacing and obedient, established close ties with Metternich.

The abortive Greek Revolt of 1820–21 severely tested Alexander's balancing act between constitutionalism and status quo conservatism. The Greek question, preoccupying European diplomacy in the 1820s, revealed Russia's acute dilemma over the Eastern Question and threatened to involve her in war with the Porte. Dominating commercial and intellectual life in the Ottoman Empire, the Greeks in 1814 at their colony in the Russian port of Odessa founded *Philike Hetairia* (Society of Friends) to liberate Greece from Turkish rule. Early in 1821 Alexander Ypsilanti, a Greek officer in the Russian army, left Russia illegally and invaded Turkish-held Moldavia, sparking revolts in Greece and appeals for Russian support. Capodistrias, some army officers, and expansionists in St. Petersburg advocated war against the Porte. Alexander I remained passive, torn between sympathy for Orthodox Christians and opposition to revolts against legitimate rulers. Ottoman collapse, he realized, might destroy the Concert of Europe and provoke intolerable great power rivalries. In 1822 Capodistrias' approach was repudiated: the tsar, fearing revolution, turned toward Austria and sent a secret mission to Vienna to reach agreement about Greece with Count Metternich.

Russia's relations with the United States improved after a severe crisis in the early 1820s. Russians had moved south from Alaska and had founded Fort Ross in 1812 near San Francisco Bay; between 1815 and 1817 there were indirect Russian efforts to influence or control Hawaii. Alexander's desire to restore Spanish rule in Latin America provoked Anglo-United States opposition, expressed in the U.S. Monroe Doctrine of December 1823. Alexander, an admirer of the U.S. Constitution who had corresponded with President Jefferson, decided to negotiate rather than provoke complications with the United States. A treaty of April 1824 restricted Russian claims in Alaska to the region north of 54°40′, and Russia pledged to respect freedom of navigation and fishing in North American coastal waters and renounced intervention in Latin America. By abandoning expansion in North America, he facilitated subsequent friendly Russo-United States relations.

During his final years Alexander withdrew largely from governmental affairs and left ordinary diplomacy to Nesselrode. This withdrawal signified a partial surrender to Metternich, although Alexander never wholly abandoned his constitutional aspirations. He continued to oppose Metternich indirectly by sending liberal envoys abroad, such as Pozzo di Borgo, and through direct contacts with French leaders. Metternich, by siding with the Porte, blocked his efforts at a compromise solution of the Greek problem.

The Alexandrine epoch coincided with the peak of Russian power and influence in Europe. Russian prestige was high after the defeat of Napoleon's invasion and the liberation of Europe, partly because of Alexander's able diplomacy and continuing commitment to European affairs.

Suggested Additional Reading

BOOKS

DUFFY, CHRISTOPHER. *Borodino and the War of 1812* (New York, 1973).

BOLKHOVITINOV, N. N. *The Beginnings of Russia-American Relations, 1775–1815,* tr. E. Levine (Cambridge, Mass., 1976).

GRIMSTED, PATRICIA. *The Foreign Ministers of Alexander I* (Berkeley, 1969).

KUKIEL, MARIAN. *Czartoryski and European Unity, 1770–1861* (Princeton, 1960).

PURYEAR, VERNON J. *Napoleon and the Dardanelles* (Berkeley, 1951).

SAUL, NORMAN. *Russia and the Mediterranean, 1797–1807* (Chicago, 1970).

TARLE, EUGENE. *Napoleon's Invasion of Russia, 1812* (N.Y., 1942). (Soviet view).

TOLSTOY, LEO. *War and Peace* (Outstanding historical novel of Russia and the Napoleonic wars).

Ministerstvo Inostrannykh Del SSSR. *Vneshniaia Politika Rossii XIX i nachala XX veka* (Moscow, 1960), *Seriia Pervaia 1801–1815* (A wealth of diplomatic documents, some in French, on the period).

ARTICLES

ANDERSON, M. S. "British Public Opinion and the Russian Campaign of 1812," *SEER,* vol. 34, June 1956, pp. 408–25.

CHANDLER, DAVID. "The Russian Army at War, 1807 and 1812," *Hist. Today,* vol. 20, 1970, pp. 867–74.

McNALLY, R. T. "The Origins of Russophobia in France, 1812–1830," *ASEER,* vol. 17, April 1958, pp. 173–89.

MORLEY, CHARLES. "Czartoryski's Attempts at a New Foreign Policy under Alexander I," *ASEER,* vol. 12, Dec. 1953, pp. 475–85.

GRIMSTED, PATRICIA. "Czartoryski's System for Russian Foreign Policy, 1803: A Memorandum," *Cal.Sl.Stud.,* vol. 5, pp. 19–91.

PERKINS, DEXTER. "Russia and the Spanish Colonies, 1817–1818," *AHR,* vol. 28 (July 1923), pp. 656–72.

QUESTED, R. "Further Light on the Expansion of Russia in East Asia: 1792–1860," *Journal of Asian Studies,* vol. 29 (1969–70), pp. 327–45.

RAGSDALE, H. "A Continental System in 1801. . . ," *JMH,* vol. 42 (1970), pp. 70–89.

22

The "Iron Tsar"

In 1839, the Marquis de Custine wrote in his *Journey for Our Time* (translation, Chicago, 1951).

> The more I see of Russia the more I agree with the Emperor when he forbids Russians to travel and makes access to his own country difficult for foreigners. The political system of Russia would not resist 20 years free communication with western Europe.

Ruling Russia from 1825 to 1855 was Nicholas I, called the "Iron Tsar" for his tightfisted militarism. This final epoch of autocracy combined with serfdom was comparable in its absolutism and personal monarchy to the reign of Peter the Great. Recent Soviet accounts depict Nicholas I as a rigid status quo conservative, but Western and some tsarist Russian historians point out that he carried through, mostly early in his reign, some cautious but constructive reforms. Nicholas' personal autocracy notwithstanding, Russian society displayed a remarkable moral and intellectual ripening. This circumstance helps explain the apparent paradox that an era of rigorous censorship and repression could also be one of great intellectual and literary vitality and achievement. Was Nicholas a reactionary or a reform conservative? Did his regime prepare the way for subsequent reform or render it more difficult? How did his militarism affect Russian government and society? Why, despite his devotion to the army and the resources he lavished upon it, was Russia defeated in the Crimean War, and what did that defeat signify?

THE RULER AND HIS IDEOLOGY

Nicholas I epitomized his autocratic, militaristic regime. He ascended the throne at the age of 29, competently educated though not prepared as specifically as his elder brothers to rule. General M. I. Lamsdorf, his chief tutor, was a narrow, strict disciplinarian, who had developed Nicholas' sense of military duty to an extreme degree. Though intelligent, Nicholas was narrow-minded and unimaginative, and during his visits to Europe as grand duke, he preferred authoritarian, militaristic Prussia. Whereas Alexander I had observed Russia theoretically from above, Nicholas scrutinized it from below like a piece of machinery in need of repair. As a third brother he had never been given much official responsibility. Profiting from free discussions with those waiting to see his brother, he came to power with a few simple, realistic political ideas.

Nicholas looked so impressive that the French ambassador, struck by his bearing, called him an educated Peter the Great. Nicholas kept Peter's bust on his desk and claimed to emulate him as a ruler, but unlike Peter his severe appearance concealed fear and deepening pessimism as he sought to make Russia an impregnable fortress. Orderly, precise, and duty-bound, his chief delights since childhood had been army reviews, formal parades, and the minutiae of military life. Stated the French observer, Custine: "The Emperor of Russia is a military commander and each one of his days is a day of battle." Only God was his superior, Nicholas believed; all others owed him unquestioning loyalty and obedience. Such divine right absolutism was virtually dead in western Europe.

After removing his brother's worst advisers—Arakcheev, Runich, and Magnitskii—Nicholas selected some capable and some incompetent subordinates. The conservative but cultured Count S. S. Uvarov as minister of education and the able reformers, Counts P. D. Kiselev and Speranskii, were counterbalanced by such a boastful failure as Prince A. S. Menshikov.

The official creed was Autocracy, Orthodoxy, and Nationalism, the famous trilogy proclaimed in Uvarov's circular of 1833 and reiterated constantly for the next 20 years. Orthodoxy, believed Nicholas and his followers, represented the true faith of all rightminded citizens. Assisted by state, family, and school, the Church was to inculcate Christian virtues of obedience, humility, and morality, and Russians should learn only what was proper for their station in life. The non-Orthodox were liable to persecution. Of autocracy, the Empire's basic law declared: "The tsar of all the Russias is an autocratic and unlimited monarch. God Himself commands us to obey the tsar's supreme authority, not from fear alone, but as a point of conscience." Anyone blaspheming or insulting the emperor could be decapitated. Russian autocracy combined Western divine right theory with the awesome authority of the Mongol khans. Russia, many asserted, required autocracy and its whole history justified it. "The Russian people," wrote Michael Pogodin in 1826, "is marvelous, but only in potential. In actuality it is low, horrid and beastly"—and must be led firmly. Nationalism, the least defined of the three doctrines, portrayed Russia as a youthful, pure, and separate entity with a unique past and a brilliant future. Russian customs and language, it was suggested, were superior to those of the decadent West. Under Nicholas were anticipated the subsequent concepts of Russification and Panslavism.[1]

---

[1] See below, pp. 359–62, 384.

ADMINISTRATION

Nicholas sought to strengthen, improve, and repair the existing administrative system bureaucratically, without public participation. He examined personally the complaints and proposals of the Decembrists and, rejecting reactionary advice to repeal Alexander I's administrative reforms, he encouraged moderates to suggest some changes. A secret committee of leading officials was set up in 1826 to study papers left from Alexander's reign. After three years work it proposed modest improvements in the administrative and social structure, leaving autocracy and serfdom intact. Legislative, judicial, and executive organs in national and provincial government were to be clearly separated. The State Council would advise the Emperor on legislation; the Senate, yielding administrative tasks, would become a supreme court. The Revolutions of 1830 interrupted the committee's work, and few of its recommendations were implemented, but Nicholas did consider them.

Impatient with regular official channels, Nicholas from 1826 built up a private bureaucracy of several sections—His Majesty's Own Imperial Chancery—which bypassed ordinary administrative organs and enhanced the tsar's personal power. The Second Section, dominated by Count Speranskii, undertook to codify Russian law. All decrees and acts since the *Ulozhenie* were collected, ordered chronologically, and published as *The Complete Collection of Laws of the Russian Empire* (1833). Speranskii also codified military law and the laws of the western borderlands. Codification, perhaps Speranskii's greatest achievement, marked a significant and essential step toward the rule of law, a basis for the improvement of justice, and spurred development of the Russian legal profession.

The Chancery's Third Section, the most notorious to many Russians, symbolized Nicholas' entire regime. Count A. K. Benkendorf had warned Alexander I about secret societies and proposed a special elite political police recruited from moral men of breeding which would be "feared and respected." The Third Section was established under Benkendorf in 1826 to coordinate regular and political police, gather information, and conduct surveillance of heretical religious groups, subversive or suspect persons, and all foreigners. It administered political prisons, handled censorship, and arrested and exiled subversives. Benkendorf was an unusual police chief: kindly, humane, and so forgetful that it was said that he sometimes forgot his own name! The Third Section, with agents scattered over the empire, watched state institutions and submitted reports on the public mood. Nicholas hoped that it would also promote efficiency and reduce red tape. The gendarmes' blue uniforms appeared wherever domestic trouble existed or was suspected. The Third Section was independent and powerful but uncovered very little subversion.

Aiming at efficient government, Nicholas tried to reduce personnel and paperwork. His personal inspections of St. Petersburg offices caused panic among their bureaucrats. Trusted officials were sent to the provinces to conduct rigorous inspections (see Nicholas Gogol's humorous literary version in *The Inspector General*), and one report of a tax official ran to 15,000 pages. Forty carts, hired to bring the report from Moscow to St. Petersburg, disappeared en route without trace! Efforts to create an efficient, European bureaucracy failed despite the tsar's best efforts largely because poorly educated officials could not apply complex laws which they often misunderstood. Poorly paid provincial officials stole or took bribes to support their families. Because lower officials evaded responsibility, trivial matters came to ministers or the emperor for decision. At the top were some able, patriotic men, but in the provinces where bureaucracy proliferated, the wheels of state often turned largely by corruption.

THE ARMY

Nicholas I's military despotism rested on the pillars of bureaucracy, church, police, and army. To Nicholas the last was the most important, and he lavished on it great attention and resources. His system must be judged therefore partly on the army's effectiveness and showing in war. As supreme commander Nicholas sought to improve its efficiency, but he always suspected intelligent, educated officers, fearing a repetition of the Decembrist Revolt. He relied instead largely on the 18th century traditions of General Suvorov: "The bullet is a fool, the bayonet is a hero." Technology, strategy, and tactics were neglected.

Field Marshal F. I. Paskevich, Russia's top military man from 1827 to 1855 and greatly admired by Nicholas, epitomized the shortcomings in the army command. A harsh disciplinarian, he guarded a swollen reputation won in easy victories over Persia, the Porte, and the Poles. Despite sporadic objections by Nicholas, he emphasized formal regulations, parade ground routine and precise marching over realistic combat training:

> Uniformity and organization reached the point where a whole infantry division of four regiments of 12 battalions (9,000 men) formed in columns, performed all the movements, marching in step. . . , and keeping the ideal alignment in rank and depth. The manual of arms by whole regiments struck one by their "purity." . . . [Here], according to the views of the times, lay the guarantee of success in war.[2]

Promotions were based solely on seniority, while the most innovative military minds and daring commanders were unused or forced into premature retirement. The motto of General N. O. Sukhozanet, fussy commander of the General Staff Academy: "Without knowledge victory is possible, without discipline never," epitomized a conservative, anti-intellectual military establishment. Brutal, unreasoning discipline reduced the Academy's low enrollment to a trickle and deprived Russia of the able staff officers it needed so badly during the Crimean War.

The Russian army, the largest in Europe, numbered 859,000 in the peacetime year of 1850, but many troops were tied down in garrison duty and internal security (some 145,000 in 1853). Thus Russia's field

---

[2] Quoted in J. S. Curtiss, *The Russian Army under Nicholas I, 1825–1855* (Durham, N.C. 1965), p. 119.

army was not much larger than the French or the Austrian. The stifling restrictions of serfdom made an effective reserve system impossible, and the huge standing army and an unwieldy, overcentralized military bureaucracy overburdened taxpayers and unbalanced the budget. Even trivial decisions often had to be made by the minister of war. Enlisted men, mostly serfs, served 25 years and were punished brutally by their noble officers. In 1827 Nicholas ordered two Jewish escapees whipped 12 times through a column of 1,000 men. "God be thanked," commented the tsar. "There has been no death penalty with us and I shall not introduce it."[3]

The army command, overconfident and self-satisfied after victories over weaker opponents (Poles and Turks), turned its back on technical innovation. Their successes had been achieved by discipline, numbers, and the stoic courage of the Russian soldier. Infantrymen were supplied with antiquated muskets and given virtually no target practice. Marching on the paradeground could not prepare men for battle. The cavalry, except for the Cossacks, was clumsy and loaded down with heavy, useless equipment. Its horses were pampered, over-fed, and lacking in endurance. Only the artillery and engineers, containing some of the ablest officers, remained innovative and abreast of their western colleagues. While western European armies adopted modern weapons and had trained reserves, Nicholas' army—his pride and joy—reflected Russia's backward economy and the worst features of autocracy and serfdom. Tested severely for the first time in the Crimean War, it was found wanting.

THE INTELLIGENTSIA

Intellectually, Nicholas' reign was a strange combination of stifling censorship and highly creative literature and thought. The full weight of reaction, however, hit literature and the press only from 1848 to 1855, and even then it lacked the thoroughness of Soviet censorship. Particularly from 1838 to 1848 a wide variety of material was published with the aid of liberal censors.

Suppression of the Decembrist Revolt temporarily blighted the bright promise of the Petersburg intelligentsia. Executions or exile of Decembrist leaders frightened other intellectuals, and this first decade was marked largely by intellectual emptiness, fear, and somnolence. Nonetheless, some remarkable writers—Pushkin, Zhukovskii, Gogol, and Lermontov—lived and worked in Petersburg and wrote some of their finest works. In these years Russian intellectuals renounced the French Enlightenment for Germanic theories as Schelling's and especially Hegel's dialectical idealism came into vogue. Schelling's writings stimulated both the doctrine of official nationalism[4] and later idealistic theories of purposeful evolution. In Petersburg, however, the bureaucracy and police were too omnipresent for a free development of ideas,

---

[3] Ibid., p. 49.

[4] See above, p. 294.

and the government sponsored or watched over the leading press organs.

Moscow was freer, its university more distinguished, and a sizable group of leisured, cultured noblemen resided there. In the 1830s Moscow University became the center of Russian intellectual life and inspiration. Groups of professors and students earnestly discussed moral and philosophical problems, and many published their views in the *Moscow Telegraph* (1825–34). Of the three major groups, two were associated directly with the University. One, headed by Alexander Herzen[5] and N. P. Ogarev, espoused the views of early western socialists until denounced to the police in 1834. A second, the so-called Stankevich Circle (from a leader, N. V. Stankevich), included Professor T. N. Granovskii, whose lectures on general history aroused widespread interest for their liberal viewpoint. Its leading Hegelian, until he emigrated in 1840, was Michael Bakunin, later a founder of anarchism, and it also included V. G. Belinskii, the first professional Russian man of letters not from the gentry.[6] A third group, later called the Slavophiles,[7] contained A. S. Khomiakov, and the Kireevskii and Aksakov brothers, all landowners knowledgeable about agriculture and the peasantry.

A few Russians were turning to socialism as derived from the French Utopians and centered on a peasantry whose discontent was rising. Wrote Count Benkendorf, head of the Third Section: "Every year the idea of freedom spreads and grows stronger among the peasants owned by the nobles. In 1834 there have been many examples of peasant insubordination to their masters . . . purely from the idea of obtaining the right to freedom."[8] Responding to peasant yearnings for land and liberty, members of the intelligentsia laid the foundations of Populism. Alexander Herzen, the leading early Russian socialist, combined elements of Slavophilism and Westernism,[9] and suggested agrarian socialism as the solution to Russia's problems. In his memoirs Herzen described how the Decembrists' sacrifice had inspired him: "The stories of the revolt and the trial . . . shook me deeply. A new world opened for me and became the center of my spiritual life. . . . The execution of Pestel and his comrades woke me forever from my youthful dreams."[10] He and his young friend, N. P. Ogarev, vowed to dedicate their lives to the struggle which the Decembrists had begun, and they adopted many of the ideas of Charles Fourier and other European socialists. Sharing the Westernizers' passion for science and the belief that Russia must be Europeanized, Herzen called Hegel's philosophy of development, "the algebra of revolution," but he rejected Western industrialism, urbanism, and materialism. While denouncing the Slavo-

---

[5] See below, p. 382.

[6] See below, pp. 308–9.

[7] See below, pp. 306–8.

[8] Quoted in Franco Venturi, *Roots of Revolution* (New York, 1960), p. 65.

[9] See discussion of these ideologies below, pp. 305–9.

[10] Ibid., p. 2. See *The Memories of Alexander Herzen*, 6 vols. (New York, 1924–28) vol. 1, p. 61.

philes' Orthodoxy and nationalism as "fresh oil for anointing the tsar, new chains laid upon thought," he shared their veneration of Russian institutions and faith in the peasantry. Unlike them he viewed the commune, purged of feudal elements, as the basis for Russia's socialist regeneration.

The Petrashevskii Circle of the late 1840s reflected the narrow, abstract and Utopian nature of nascent Russian socialism. This small group, mostly lesser gentry in government service, discussed socialist ideas and built paper Utopias but made no concrete plans to implement them. M. V. Petrashevskii was an idealistic, eccentric dreamer and minor foreign office official, who adopted Fourier's ideas wholeheartedly. His pamphlets urged emancipation of the serfs and setting up phalansteries combining private property and collective ownership. The Russian commune minus its feudal aspects, he believed, equalled Fourier's phalanstery. Within this circle, N. A. Speshnev's small Communist faction advocated a tightly organized, centralized organization to direct a peasant revolt to be followed by dictatorship and large-scale collective agriculture. Petrashevskii summarized his difference with Speshnev: "Fourierism leads gradually and naturally to what Communism wishes to impose immediately and forcibly."

The Revolutions of 1848 alarmed Nicholas I as the French Revolution of 1789 had frightened Catherine II. To quarantine Russia from revolutionary contagion, his Buturlin Committee policed the press so carefully that little could be published. Even Count Uvarov, the regime's official spokesman, was removed as minister of education for defending the universities against reactionaries who wanted to close them down! In April 1849 the police uncovered the Petrashevskii Circle. Though it was harmless, the authorities sentenced many Petrashevtsy to death, including the young writer, Fyodor Dostoevskii. Moments before execution, their sentences were commuted. In 1850 universities were forbidden to teach philosophy and European constitutional law. As Orthodoxy, Autocracy, and Nationalism were enforced rigidly by a militaristic regime, gloom and despair settled over the Russian intelligentsia.

FOREIGN AFFAIRS

Until the Crimean War, Russia, believed to be the strongest European land power, with its Austrian and Prussian allies, upheld Metternich's system of conservative absolutism. Nicholas stood ready to use his powerful army to repress foreign revolutions, but his foreign policy, though aggressive in tone, aimed to preserve the status quo, not extend Russian boundaries. To avoid general European conflict Nicholas kept lines of communication open with the Western powers. Even strong suspicion of his policy in Britain did not prevent practical cooperation at times. Among his specific goals were to regulate Russia's relationship with Poland and consolidate Russia's favorable position in the Balkans. Like his predecessor, Nicholas maintained personal control over foreign policy. Foreign Minister Count Nesselrode, inherited from his brother, remained an obedient mouthpiece. Later, a breakdown in communications between them helped involve Russia in the Crimean War. In foreign affairs Nicholas was direct, blunt, stubborn, and often rigid.

The Polish Revolt (1830–31) brought Russia closer to the other eastern powers but alienated her from France. Nicholas had upheld reluctantly his obligations as constitutional king of Poland until the French Revolution of 1830 encouraged Polish nationalists and radicals to overthrow the Warsaw government. The Poles received only sympathy from the West, and Nicholas' commander, General Paskevich, captured Warsaw (September 1831); but Polish resistance helped prevent Russian intervention in western Europe, and Nicholas had to accept a neutral Belgium and the July Monarchy in France. As thousands of Poles fled into exile in France, Nicholas' Organic Statute (1832) divided Poland into provinces and incorporated it directly into the Empire.

In the Caucasus, Russian expansion continued as Paskevich defeated Persia (1826–28). The Treaty of Turkmanchai gave Russia most of Persian Armenia with Erivan and moved the frontier to the Araxes River. The Caucasian lowlands had been won fairly easily, but Russia's control of the mountain regions remained insecure. In the late 1820s there developed in Daghestan a strong Moslem resistance movement known in Russia as Muridism. Its leader, Kazi Mullah, proclaimed a holy war on Russia. Religious and national hatred of Russians combined with resentment at their occupation of mountain lands. After Kazi Mullah's death (1834), Shamil led the mountaineers in guerrilla warfare and for two decades inflicted humiliating defeats on Nicholas' troops. Shamil's movement, encouraged by the British, prevented firm Russian control of the Caucasus.

In Central Asia by 1850 small Russian forces, sometimes without official initiative, had established firm control over the broad Kazakh steppe and its nomadic population. Major revolts by Isatai Taimanov (1836–38) against local Kazakh rulers and by Kenesary Kasimov (1837–47) against the Russians were quelled. Russian forces, occupying Fort Perovskii on the Syr River and Fort Vernoe (the future Alma-Ata) further east, brought the ill-defined frontier close to rich oases ruled by the semifeudal khanates of Khiva, Kokand, and Bukhara. In the Far East, N. N. Muravev (Amurskii), governor general of eastern Siberia (1847–61), advanced into the Amur region, claimed but not settled or firmly controlled by decaying Manchu China. Captain G. I. Nevelskoi, authorized to explore the Amur River, raised the Russian flag at the river's mouth. Nicholas I, dismissing Nesselrode's cautious objections, declared: "Where once the Russian flag has flown, it must not be lowered again." Muravev founded Khabarovsk on the Amur (1854) and penetrated Sakhalin Island offshore, and the delighted emperor made him a count. Simultaneously, Admiral E. V. Putiatin entered Nagasaki, Japan, weeks after Commodore Perry of the United States reached Tokyo, opening Japan to external influences. The Russo-Japanese treaty of 1855 provided for extraterritorial rights, trade, diplomatic relations, and joint administration of Sakhalin Island.

The Eastern Question remained the chief focus of Russian foreign policy. Nicholas regarded relations with the Sultan as more important than wooing rebellious Balkan Christians. "The advantages of maintaining the Ottoman Empire in Europe," he affirmed, "exceed the inconveniences which it presents . . ." A weak, pliant Ottoman Empire under Russian protection still seemed preferable to a partition which might provoke a European war. At times Nicholas dealt with the Sultan unilaterally; at other times he supported the Christians, but usually he cooperated in the Balkans with the European powers. He and Nesselrode, however, fearing that the "sick man," the Porte, might die, believed that plans must be made for that eventuality.

In the late 1820s, Russian influence in the Ottoman Empire increased greatly. In 1826 Russia, backed by France and Britain, secured domestic autonomy for the Greeks. Russia and Turkey concluded the Akkerman Convention, which confirmed autonomy for Serbia and the Danubian Principalities under the Sultan and provided free passage through the Straits for Russian merchant ships; but when a Turkish fleet was destroyed at Navarino Bay (1827), the Sultan repudiated Akkerman and declared war on Russia. At first the Russians made little headway in the Balkans, but in the Caucasus Paskevich conquered some of the southern Black Sea coast and captured the powerful Kars fortress. In 1829, Field Marshal I. Dibich's forces took Adrianople and threatened Constantinople while Paskevich conquered Erzerum in Anatolia. In the ensuing Treaty of Adrianople (1829), the Sultan had to reaffirm Akkerman, make the Danubian Principalities a Russian protectorate, and cede to Russia the southern Danube delta and more Black Sea coastline. Merchant ships of all countries at peace with the Porte could now use the Straits. In 1830 the Powers arranged the independence of Greece, and the Porte became virtually a Russian satellite.

Ottoman dependence upon Russia increased still further after Mehemet Ali, pasha of Egypt, revolted in 1832, invaded Syria, and defeated a Turkish army. In desperation the Sultan turned to Russia, which prevented Mehemet from taking Constantinople and helped the powers arrange peace. The Treaty of Unkiar-Skelessi (July 1833) provided that Russia would aid the Porte militarily upon request and that the Turks would close the Dardanelles to foreign warships. By this treaty with the Ottoman Empire, Russia safeguarded its vulnerable Black Sea coast and claimed the right to intervene at will in Turkish affairs. Unkiar-Skelessi marked a high point of Russian power in the Straits question. At Münchengrätz (September 1833), the Austrian emperor and the Prussian crown prince met with Nicholas and accepted Unkiar-Skelessi. Austria and Russia agreed to preserve the Ottoman Empire and prevent Mehemet from taking any of European Turkey.

Russia could not keep the Porte in subjugation for long. The British ambassador, Lord Ponsonby, counterbalancing Russian influence in Constantinople, helped the Sultan regain freedom of maneuver. Whereas Nicholas remained moderate and defensive, Ponsonby and a journalist, David Urquhart, whipped up anti-Russian feeling in Britain. When Mehemet Ali revolted again and another Near Eastern crisis erupted (1839–40), the powers restricted him to Egypt and Unkiar-

Skelessi lapsed. The powers signed a Straits Convention (1841) with the Porte which barred foreign warships from the Straits while the Sultan was at peace. Russia remained secure unless the Porte were a belligerent. This compromise delayed a confrontation between Russia and the western powers.

Early in 1848 the French July Monarchy and Metternich's regime fell as revolution engulfed Paris, Vienna, Berlin, and Budapest. Nicholas feared that it might spread to Russian Poland and wished to restore the July Monarchy by force, but the outbreaks in central Europe prevented him from doing so. Instead, he guarded Russia's position in Turkish affairs and supported the Austrian Habsburgs. When radicals took power in Wallachia, Russian troops occupied neighboring Moldavia and aided the Turks to suppress the rebels. Nicholas grew convinced that the Hungarian Revolution, led by Lajos Kossuth's liberal nationalists, was part of an anti-Russian conspiracy. He wrote Paskevich: "At the head of the rebellion . . . are our eternal enemies, the Poles." In May 1849, responding to a request by the young Austrian emperor, Franz Josef, Paskevich crushed the Hungarian Revolution. Russia restored Austrian leadership in German affairs, blocked Prussian action, and upheld the Vienna Settlement. These successes made Nicholas I grossly over-confident.

THE CRIMEAN WAR (1853–1856)

The Crimean conflict, the diplomatic and military climax to Nicholas' reign, revealed the disastrous failure of Nicholas' policy. Clashing Russian and Franco-British interests in the Ottoman Empire, inept diplomacy, and miscalculations on both sides led to war. A trivial "quarrel of monks" sparked a costly, useless war between Russia and Turkey, backed by several European powers. Roman Catholic and Orthodox priests argued over rights at the Holy Places in Jerusalem, and their respective claims were backed by France and Russia.

In February 1853 Nicholas sent Prince A. S. Menshikov on a diplomatic mission to Constantinople to reassert Russian prestige against France. Menshikov secured the resignation of the Turkish foreign minister and reached agreement on the Holy Places, but the Turks, supported by Stratford de Redcliffe, the British ambassador, rejected his haughty demands for a secret Russo-Turkish alliance and denied Russia's rights to "protect" their Orthodox Christians. Soviet accounts suggest that Redcliffe provoked war deliberately. In May Menshikov left Constantinople angrily, severing Russo-Turkish relations; in July Nicholas ordered Russian troops into the Danubian Principalities.

Menshikov's demands drew Britain and France together behind the Turks. To Nicholas' dismay they and the German powers protested Russia's occupation of the Principalities. The Porte blocked a European attempt at compromise (the Vienna Note), and London also rejected a revised version. A Franco-British fleet sailed through the Dardanelles, and the Porte declared war on Russia (October 1853). Emotional British reactions to Admiral N. S. Nakhimov's destruction of the Turkish fleet at Sinop ended chances to localize the conflict. Though the Turks had been the aggressors, London denounced the Russian action as a "massacre." When Nicholas ignored a Western ultimatum to evacuate the Principalities, France, Britain, and, later, Sardinia joined the Turks in the war.

The causes of the Crimean War remain debatable, but evidently neither the allies nor Russia planned aggression nor desired war. London believed that Russian intervention in the Ottoman Empire would threaten its vital interests; Napoleon III of France needed success abroad to prop up his regime at home. Hostility toward and suspicion of Russia, especially in Britain, contributed to the war. Western leaders believed that they had to stop Russia and restore Europe's balance of power. For his part, Nicholas overrated Russia's strength and sought by bluster to reassert undefined Russian rights to "protect" the Christians. He apparently did not intend to seize Constantinople or partition the Ottoman Empire, but only to consolidate Russian influence there.

During the war Russia's strategic position was unfavorable. Nicholas had planned to invade the Balkans with the aid or friendly neutrality of the German powers. Instead, they allied with one another (April 1854); Austria mobilized against Russia and agreed with the Turks to occupy the Danubian Principalities jointly. Austria's "monstrous ingratitude" (for Russian aid in 1849) rendered Russia's position there exposed, and Nicholas' efforts to rouse the Balkan Christians failed. Field Marshal Paskevich, the commander in chief, considered the Austrian threat awkward and kept many troops in Poland. Other Russian forces fought the Turks in the Caucasus and watched Shamil, and still others protected St. Petersburg against possible invasion. Such a dispersal of troops and cautious Russian commanders prevented proper use of Russia's huge army.

In the campaigns of 1854–55 the Russians won in the Caucasus but lost on the Danube and in the Crimea. After making probing attacks along the Danube and suffering minor setbacks, Russian forces withdrew behind the Pruth, and Austria occupied the Principalities. Then a Franco-British expeditionary force of 60,000 men landed in the western Crimea (September 1854). After Prince Menshikov's smaller Russian force, marching northward to meet it, suffered defeat at the Alma River, only hasty fortification of Sevastopol on the landward side and Allied slowness saved the chief Russian naval base from immediate capture. Menshikov, reinforced from the Danuban front, tried to throw the Allies off Inkerman Heights near Sevastopol into the sea, but he failed to use his numerical superiority. Poor coordination and ignorance of the terrain (a detailed map of the region reached Menshikov *after* the battle!) contributed to a major Russian defeat. In the ensuing siege of Sevastopol, the defenders fought heroically, but superior Allied firepower pulverized their positions while both armies suffered severely from disease and cold. Early in 1855 Nicholas, knowing that his huge military machine could not even protect Russian soil, died of pneumonia and was succeeded by his son, Alexander II. In September the Allies captured key Malakhov Hill and compelled the Russians to

MAP 22–1
Russia and the Crimean War, 1853–1856

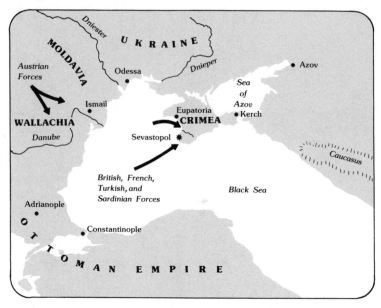

evacuate Sevastopol, but the Russian capture of Kars in the Caucasus somewhat offset the Crimean defeats.

Throughout the war the diplomats tried to arrange a compromise settlement. In August 1854, France, Britain, and Austria agreed upon Four Points as a basis for peace: all powers, not just Russia, should regulate the status of Serbia and the Principalities; all states were to navigate the Danube freely; the Straits Convention of 1841 was to be revised; and Russia was to renounce claims to exclusive protection of Orthodox Christians. In December 1855 Austria threatened to enter the war unless Russia accepted the Four Points and two additions. Realizing that Russia could not fight Austria too, Alexander II agreed to a peace conference in Paris and accepted the Four Points. Russia ceded southern Bessarabia to Moldavia and consented reluctantly to "neutralize" the Black Sea by dismantling her fleet and naval bases there.

The Crimean defeat and the Paris treaty, though galling, did not threaten Russia's great power status, but Russia had lost the predominance on land which she had enjoyed since 1814. Ottoman disintegration was arrested, and Russian prestige in the Balkans was reduced. Russia's defeat and Austria's support of the Western powers destroyed the unity of the three eastern monarchies. Timid and incompetent leadership, inferior weapons, and inadequate communications had caused Russia's defeat. The complete lack of railroads south of Moscow had complicated the supply problems of the Crimean army. The war revealed Russia's technological and economic backwardness compared to the Western powers and the need for drastic internal reform. The new ruler, Alexander II, and his advisers learned these harsh lessons and were determined to restore Russan power and influence.

PROBLEM 6: WHITHER RUSSIA? SLAVOPHILES VERSUS WESTERNIZERS

After publication in Russia (1836) of Peter Chaadaev's first *Philosophical Letter* (Herzen called it: "a pistol shot in the dead of night"), a great debate erupted within the intelligentsia over Russia's past history and future role. Two major schools of thought emerged, known generally as Slavophiles and Westernizers, which criticized the regime of Nicholas and were suspected by it. Sir Isaiah Berlin, an English historian, believes Chaadaev's *Letter* began "a marvelous decade" of effort by a small intelligentsia, in attitude half-Russian and half-foreign, cut off from the populace and standing between an oppressive regime and a sea of wretched but disorganized peasants.[11] Few ideas presented in this debate were original: Russian intellectuals seized eagerly upon European ideas, often considering them the ultimate truth. Russian thinkers of the 1840s compare in outlook and by their raising of major issues to the late 18th century French philosophes. Below are summarized Chaadaev's *Letter* and some views of the Slavophiles and Westernizers from their principal spokesmen.

CHAADAEV: THE FIRST PHILOSOPHICAL LETTERS

Peter Ia. Chaadaev (1793–1856), a veteran of the Napoleonic wars, had lived in western Europe. Embittered by the post-1815 reaction, the Decembrists' failure, and Nicholas' oppressive regime, he kept apart from the discussion circles of the 1830s. In 1829 he wrote the *Philosophical Letters* in French; the first and most spectacular one was published in Russia by Nadezhdin's *Telescope* in 1836. Chaadaev's views were strongly pro-European and pro-Catholic:

> It is one of the most deplorable traits of our peculiar civilization that we are still discovering truths which other peoples, even some much less advanced than we, have taken for granted. The reason is that we have never marched with the other peoples. We do not belong to any of the great families of the human race; we are neither of the West nor of the East, and we have not the traditions of either.

Chaadaev's view of Russia's history was very negative:

> A brutal barbarism to begin with, followed by an age of gross superstition, then by a ferocious and humiliating foreign domination, the spirit of which has passed into the national state—that is the sad history of our youth. . . . We live in a narrow present, without a past and without a future, in the midst of a dead calm.

---

[11] Isaiah Berlin, "A Marvellous Decade, 1838–48," *Encounter,* vol. 4 (June 1955), pp. 27–39.

That was bad enough, but the following passage infuriated the authorities and nationalists who had glorified Russian traditions and institutions:

> We are alone in the world, we have given nothing to the world, we have taught it nothing. We have not added a single idea to the sum total of human ideas; we have not contributed to the progress of the human spirit, and what we have borrowed of this progress we have distorted. . . . Not one useful thought has sprung from the arid soil of our fatherland; not one great truth has emerged from our midst; we have not taken the trouble to invent anything ourselves, and of the inventions of others we have borrowed only empty conceits and useless luxuries.

Neither Peter I nor Alexander I, though exposing Russia to European civilization, had been able to civilize her:

> There is something in our blood that resists all real progress. In a word we have lived, and we live now, merely in order to furnish some great lesson to a remote posterity . . . We are a blank in the intellectual order.

Chaadaev attributed this cultural vacuum to the fact that "we went to wretched Byzantium," whereas Europe had been schooled by Catholicism. He held out only the vague hope that in the future Russia might save European civilization.[12]

The government responded by closing down the *Telescope*, exiling its editor, and, concluding that Chaadaev must be mad, placed him under a physician's care. In his *Apology of a Madman* (1837), Chaadaev expressed some hope about the future of Russia but refused to recant his negative view of its past. Protesting his patriotism, he added that love of truth must precede love of country.

Chaadaev's writings helped spark the development of the Slavophiles and Westernizers, both of which groups objected to the existing social and political system in Russia. Repelled by bureaucratic absolutism, serfdom, the atmosphere of fear, and suppression of thought, they joined at first to demand civil liberties and social and political reform. They believed that Russia could solve issues like the peasant question, but they argued sharply about religion and history. During the early 1850s the publications of both groups were suppressed by Nicholas' regime.

THE SLAVOPHILES

The leading Slavophiles—A. S. Khomiakov and the Kireevskii and Aksakov brothers—were romantic nationalists who idealized Russian Orthodoxy and the institutions of old Muscovy, notably the *zemskii sobor* and the peasant commune, which they believed exemplified the distinct, superior qualities of the Russian people: unity, obedience, and harmony of tsar and people. For them Orthodoxy was the only true

---

[12] From *Russian Intellectual History: an Anthology*, edited by Marc Raeff, copyright © 1966 by Harcourt Brace Jovanovich, Inc. and reprinted with their permission. P. 162 ff.

faith, spiritually superior to western Christianity, and they considered non-Orthodox Slavs, especially the Poles, to be traitors. Rejecting a Westernization which they associated with the Petrine reforms, they denounced the bureaucracy for alienating the tsar from his people. The Slavophiles opposed constitutional government as alien and divisive, but their more liberal members (Iu. Samarin, V. Cherkasskii) later were leaders in emancipating the serfs. Wrote K. S. Aksakov in a memorandum submitted to Alexander II in 1855:

> The Russian people is not a people concerned with government. . . . It has no aspiration now toward self-government, no desire for political rights . . . [or] power. [This had been proven at the dawn of Russian history] when the Russians of their own free will invited foreigners to rule over them—the Varangians. . . . [In 1612 the people] chose a tsar and having wholly entrusted their fate to him, they peaceably laid down their arms and returned to their separate homes. . . . The spirit of the people is the guarantee of tranquility in Russia and security for the government. . . . For Russia to fulfill her destiny, she must follow her own ideas and requirements, and not theories which are alien to her. . . . The Russian people *has no concern for government.* . . , has no desire to limit in any way the power of the authorities. . . , is apolitical and consequently does not contain so much as an embryo of revolution or a trace of desire for a constitutional order. . . .

What then does the Russian people desire?

> To retain their internal communal life, their way of life. . . . The essential qualities of the Russian people are good, its beliefs are holy, its way is righteous. . . . The Russian people, having renounced the political realm and given unlimited powers to the government, reserved for themselves *life*—their moral and communal freedom, the high purpose of which is to achieve a Christian society.

Aksakov, while advocating absolute monarchy and noting the ancient and traditional division in Russia between "tsar's business" and "people's business," also glorified the old Muscovite *zemskii sobor*:

> The power of the state must be absolute . . . it must be a monarchy. . . . In recognizing the absolute power of the monarch, [the Russian] retains complete independence of spirit, conscience and thought. . . . It is one of the state's duties to protect freedom of public opinion. [The *zemskii sobor*] consisted of representatives of all the social classes. . . . Their only purpose was to elicit expression of *opinion*. . . . The people of Russia gathered at these assemblies at the summons of the tsar and not out of a vainglorious desire to orate, as they do in Parliament, or to seek power. . . . Our [Muscovite] tsars gave full rein to public opinion among the peasantry . . . by asking them to elect judges . . . and by giving full latitude to peasant meetings to decide all matters pertaining to their own administration.

On the other hand, Aksakov argued that the West had "abandoned the spiritual path," had been "lured by vanity into striving for power," and was thus on the verge of collapse. Consequently, Russian rulers had been wrong to adopt "false" Western principles, as during the reign of Peter I:

We must now speak of a period when tne government—not the people —violated the principles of Russia's civil order and swerved Russia from her course. . . . The revolution wrought by Peter, despite all its outward brilliance, shows what immense spiritual evil can be done by the greatest genius. as soon as he acts alone, draws away from the people, and regards them as an architect does bricks. Under Peter began that evil which is still the evil of our day. . . . Contempt for Russia and for the Russian people soon became an attribute of every educated Russian intent upon aping Western Europe. That is how the breach between the Tsar and the people occurred. . . .

Turning to the present condition of Russia, Aksakov described what should be done to remedy its shortcomings:

. . . Internal dissension glossed over by unscrupulous lies. . . . The general corruption and the weakening of moral principles in society have reached vast proportions. Bribery and organized robbery by officials are terrifying. . . . The main root of the evil is our repressive system of government—repression of freedom of opinion and of moral freedom. . . . A man is not even expected to think right, he is expected not to think at all. . . . The specific remedy for the ills of modern Russia is . . . to revert to the essential principles which are consonant with her spirit. . . . Let there be reserved for the government unlimited freedom to *rule*, which is its prerogative, and for the people full freedom of social and spiritual life under the government's protection. Let the government *have the right to action* and consequently the power of law; let the *people have the right of opinion* and consequently freedom of speech.[13]

THE WESTERNIZERS

Headed by T. N. Granovskii and V. Belinskii, the Westernizers believed that Russian development should follow that of western Europe, not pursue its own path. Most were atheists or deists who repudiated Orthodoxy and all established churches. Contrary to Slavophile claims, Westernizers were patriotic Russians who wished not to substitute Western for Russian institutions, but to lift Russia to Europe's level by educating Russian society. Less unified in ideology than the Slavophiles, the Westernizers were positivists with deep faith in science and technology. Besides freedom of speech and press, many espoused constitutional government. Some, like Professor Granovskii, were political moderates; others, like Belinskii, became socialists. They admired Peter I as their founder but deplored his cruelty and rejected the autocracy which succeeded him.

Vissarion Belinskii (1811–48) became the Westernizers' most militant spokesman. A radical and an atheist, he is much quoted and admired by Soviet historians. At first an ardent Hegelian and social conservative, Belinskii became the leading Russian advocate of freedom, democracy, and humanitarianism. Expelled from Moscow Uni-

---

[13] Raeff, *Russian Intellectual History*, pp. 231 ff.

versity for attacking serfdom, he developed into the most brilliant, incisive literary critic of his age. In his *Letter to Gogol* (1847) written in Austria, his best known political work, he castigated the famous conservative writer for his *Selected Passages from Correspondence with Friends*, a defense of Nicholas I's regime:

> One cannot remain silent when, under the cloak of religion and the protection of the knout [whip], falsehood and immorality are being preached as truth and virtue. . . . You know Russia well only as an artist and not as a thinking man.

Like Voltaire, to whom he compared himself implicitly, Belinskii denounced the Orthodox Church as a corporate entity:

> Russia sees her salvation not in mysticism, not in asceticism, not in pietism, but in the achievement of civilization, enlightenment, and humanitarianism. What she needs is neither sermons (of which she has heard enough!) nor prayers (she has mumbled enough of those!), but an awakening in her people of the sense of human dignity. . . ; she needs rights and laws conforming not to Church doctrine but to common sense and justice. . . . Instead, she offers the dreadful spectacle of a country in which men trade in men. . . ; a country, finally, which not only affords no guarantees for personal safety, honor, and property but which cannot even maintain internal order and has nothing to show but vast corporations of officeholding thieves and robbers.

Belinskii attacked boldly the official doctrines of Nicholas' regime in this work, which circulated widely inside Russia:

> [The Orthodox Church] has ever been the support of the knout and the toady of despotism. [It had nothing in common with Christ], the first to teach men the ideals of liberty, equality, and fraternity. . . . Our clergy is held in general contempt by Russian society and the Russian people. . . . Take a closer look and you will see that the Russian people are deeply atheistic by nature. They still have many superstitions, but not a trace of religious feeling. [The public] holds the Russian writers to be its only leaders, its only defenders and saviours from the black night of Autocracy, Orthodoxy and Nationalism. . . .

Finally, Belinskii sought to point the way forward toward the achievement of a new and freer Russia:

> The most topical, the most vital national questions in Russia today are the abolition of serfdom, the repeal of corporal punishment, and the introduction as far as possible, of the strictest possible application of at least those laws which are already on the books.[14]

CONCLUSION

The Crimean War revealed the traditional system of autocracy, serfdom, and Orthodoxy to be hollow and incapable of meeting Russia's domestic problems or of maintaining its power abroad. Nicholas' critics, notably Belinskii, pointed the way toward the reform of Russian institu-

---

[14] Raeff, *Russian Intellectual History*, pp. 253–58.

tions, especially the abolition of serfdom. In the midst of the war a new tsar, Alexander II, had mounted the throne. Although conservative and traditional in some ways, he was realistic enough to attempt major reforms in order to save the imperial regime.

Suggested Additional Reading

BOOKS

BADDELEY, J. F.   *The Russian Conquest of the Caucasus* (London, 1908).

BARKER, A. J.   *The War Against Russia, 1854–1856* (New York, 1971).

BELINSKII, V. G.   *Selected Philosophical Works* (Moscow, 1956).

CHRISTOFF, P.   *An Introduction to 19th Century Slavophilism: Khomjakov* (Hague, 1961).

CURTISS, J. S.   *The Russian Army under Nicholas I, 1825–1855* (Durham, N.C., 1965).

EVANS, J. L.   *The Petrashevsky Circle, 1846–1848* (Hague, 1974).

HERZEN, A.   *My Past and Thoughts* (6 vols., London 1924–27).

MALIA, M.   *Alexander Hersen and the Birth of Russian Socialism* (Cambr., Mass. 1961).

MONAS, S.   *The Third Section* (Cambridge, Mass. 1961).

MOSELY, P. E.   *Russian Diplomacy and . . . the Eastern Question in 1838 and 1839* (Cambridge, Mass., 1934).

PURYEAR, V. J.   *England, Russia and the Straits Question, 1844–56* (Berkeley, 1931).

PRESNIAKOV, A. E.   *Emperor Nicholas I of Russia . . .* (Gulf Breeze, Fla., 1974).

RIASANOVSKY, N. V.   *Nicholas I and Official Nationality . . .* (Berkeley, 1959).

SQUIRE, P. S.   *The Third Department . . .* (Cambridge, Eng., 1968).

ARTICLES

BALMUTH, D.   "The Origins of . . . Censorship Terror," *ASEER,* vol. 19, pp. 497–520.

BERLIN, I.   "Russia and 1848," *SEER,* vol. 26, pp. 341–60.

BOLSOVER, G. H.   "Nicholas I and the Partition of Turkey," *SEER,* vol. 27, pp. 115–45.

GOOCH, R.   "A Century of Historiography on the Origins of the Crimean War," *AHR,* vol. 62, pp. 33–58.

HORVATH, E.   "Russia and the Hungarian Revolution, 1848–49," *SEER,* vol. 12, pp. 628–45.

KAPLAN, F.   "Russian Fourierism of the 1840's. . . ," *ASEER,* vol. 17, pp. 161–72.

LENSEN, G.   "Early Russo-Japanese Relations," *FEQ,* vol. 10, pp. 3–37.

LEWAK, A.   "The Polish Rising of 1830," *SEER,* vol. 9, pp. 350–60.

MCNALLY, R.   "The Origins of Russophobia in France, 1812–30," *ASEER,* vol. 17, pp. 173–89.

PIPES, R.   "The Russian Military Colonies, 1810–31," *JMH,* vol. 22, pp. 205–19.

PINTNER, W.   "The Social Characteristics of the Early 19th Century Russian Bureaucracy," *SR,* vol. 29, pp. 429–43.

23

Social, Economic, and Cultural Development, 1796–1855

IMPERIAL RUSSIA reached a lofty plateau in its development in the era after the defeat of Napoleon. Internationally, it was unchallenged by rivals, the dominant military power, epitomizing stability and legitimacy, the unyielding bastion against unorthodox and revolutionary ideas. The Empire enjoyed tremendous prestige and exercised great power and influence in Europe. Though beset with sporadic outbursts of peasant discontent and rumblings from disgruntled officers and intellectuals, the autocracy controlled internal developments firmly and blocked all organized opposition. The Empire's external power, however, concealed grave social and economic problems. Among the perceptive there was a nagging uneasiness, a vague disquietude about the future. With the Empire's rapid growth came new and perplexing problems.

The period from Paul's accession to Nicholas I's death in 1855 brought a very rapid growth of population, from 37.2 million to 59.2 million without Finland, Russian Poland, or the Caucasus (they brought the total to 72.7 million).[1] The peasantry numbered 32.6 million "souls" in 1795, or 90 percent of the population; by 1857 it had increased to 48.4 million, still almost 84 percent. This mass of humanity was divided almost equally between privately owned serfs and state peasants. Whereas in 1719 private serfs had accounted for 71 percent of the total population and state peasants only 19 percent, by 1857 the landowners' serfs comprised only 51 percent of the peasant class and 46 percent of the population, revealing a significant change in the composition of the peasantry. In the mid-19th century Russia remained an overwhelmingly peasant, agrarian country.

The nobility, increasing in absolute numbers, decreased as a percentage of the population. By the fifth revision (census) of 1795, male nobles numbered 363,000 (2.2 percent of the population); the tenth revision of 1858 recorded 464,000 (1.5 percent).[2] Only about 700 families could trace their noble status back before 1600. Noble status,

---

[1] Ia. Vodarskii, *Naselenie Rossii za 400 let*, p. 54.
[2] *Istoriia SSSR*, (Moscow), no. 4, 1971, p. 164.

either inherited or earned through state service, entitled the holder to own populated estates, that is, peasant serfs. Noblemen enjoyed not only high social status but real economic, civic, and judicial privileges. As we have seen,[3] however, there were many impoverished noble families, chiefly because of the traditional and ancient practice of dividing property equally among the male heirs, which produced fragmentation of the estates into smaller and smaller parcels with each generation. Impoverishment and the general economic climate of the early 19th century forced many serf owners to borrow extensively to maintain their living standards and social status and keep themselves afloat financially. Serf owners borrowed by mortgaging their serfs to banks or private individuals. By 1859 fully two thirds of the male serf population was mortgaged. Indebtedness was not confined to small, marginal proprietors. Even great magnates found it increasingly difficult to live within their incomes and were forced to borrow on a grand scale. Count Sheremetiev, Russia's largest landowner, was reputedly six million rubles in debt by 1859. Contributing to this indebtedness were extravagant living patterns, inflation, and low returns from inefficiently run estates.

Despite their economic difficulties, the nobility remained *the* privileged social class with many exclusive rights and privileges. Their income, however inadequate, came chiefly from landed estates rather than government salaries, commercial ventures, or investments. Many commoners aspired to become gentlemen-landowners because a noble title, and hence the right to own serfs, could be earned by talent and hard work. Thus the noble class increased steadily in size despite efforts to prevent this. Between 1795 and 1858 the nobility increased by more than 100,000 males. As long as the government needed more civil servants, there was no reason to abolish the Table of Ranks, which, providing a way to acquire nobility, served as a powerful device to attract the ablest individuals into state service. Nicholas I sympathized with noble demands to restrict access to the nobility and issued a decree in 1845 to tighten up the provisions governing the Table of Ranks. Henceforth, the rank of major in the army (eighth rank) would confer hereditary nobility, while titular councillor (ninth rank) in state service would bestow only personal nobility, a status which could not be transmitted to heirs. Achievement of rank five (actual state councillor) conferred hereditary noble status. These provisions made acquisition of nobility through state service harder but failed to satisfy noble demands for creation of a closed class.

In 1832 the government allayed some of the frustration of those who had acquired wealth or distinction but not nobility by creating the title "honored citizen" to recognize special achievement in business, science, and the arts. The title could be either personal or hereditary and granted to the holder many privileges, including exemption from the poll tax, recruitment, and corporal punishment. Still, the title was con-

---

[3] See above, p. 253.

ferred sparingly and failed to satisfy those intent on the social distinction of noble status.

The Russian urban population grew faster in this period than any
other demographic category. Numbering 1.6 million in 1795, or roughly
four percent of the population, it had risen by 1858 to 5.4 million, or
more than nine percent.[4] Much of the urban population lived in the
two capitals. In 1800 Moscow had about 300,000 inhabitants and St.
Petersburg slightly fewer; by 1864 St. Petersburg had grown to 586,000,
while Moscow had increased to only 378,000. St. Petersburg was clearly
the Empire's economic, cultural, and administrative center. Whereas in
1811 there were few other towns that had more than 25,000 people,
by 1864 rapid urban growth had produced 12 towns with more than
50,000.[5] Clearly, 19th century Russia was urbanizing rapidly, largely
because of a growing internal market and expanding foreign trade and
manufacturing.

Russian towns contained a populace very diverse in wealth and social status. In the capitals lived the wealthiest noblemen who could
maintain splendid town mansions besides their country estates. Many
moderately wealthy noblemen had residences in Moscow, and in a
descending scale in other provincial centers. There was a relatively
small well-to-do merchantry (*kupechestvo*), divided into three guilds
by wealth and social status. Beneath the merchants were artisans and
skilled workers organized into corporations (*tsekhi*) with their own
rules and regulations. A large miscellaneous group of petty bourgeoisie
(*meshchantsvo*) remained a rather vague and imprecise social category. Then there were government bureaucrats and a small group of
intellectuals. Together these non-noble urban residents were the Russian counterpart of the Western middle classes, or bourgeoisie. Yet
there were profound differences between the urban middle class in
Russia and in western Europe. The Russian middle class did not stand
for individualism, free enterprise, and political democracy as did middle classes in the West. The autocracy maintained as tight a control over
townsmen as it did over the rural elements.

The intelligentsia was in the process of formation in this period and
would become the chief advocate in Russia of free institutions and
political liberties. Urban groups—merchants, bureaucrats, artisans, and
intellectuals—did not constitute a Russian equivalent of the western
European bourgeoisie, as has been stated. They were not socially
homogeneous and thus could not wield the influence or pressure which
the European bourgeoisie exercised so successfully.

As urban centers developed, they presented a vivid kaleidoscope of
the extremes of Russian life. The incredible display of ostentatious
wealth by the upper classes with their opulent pleasure palaces and

---

[4] P. G. Ryndziunskii, *Gorodskoe grazhdanstvo doreformennoi Rossii* (Moscow,
1958), p. 334.

[5] Odessa, Kishinev, Saratov, Riga, Vilna, Kiev, Nikolaev, Kazan, Tbilisi, Tula,
Berdichev and Kharkov. W. H. Parker, *An Historical Geography of Russia* (Chicago,
1969), p. 262.

townhouses contrasted with shocking and degrading poverty. The Empire's wealth was poured into building up St. Petersburg, which the rulers resolved to make the most imposing and beautiful city in Europe. Yet alongside stately mansions, impressive official buildings, and resplendent imperial residences stood the distressing slums, hovels, dosshouses, and wretched taverns of the lower classes, portrayed so graphically in Dostoevsky's famous novels, *Crime and Punishment, The Idiot,* and *Poor Folk.*

Russia's industrial development and technological progress stagnated compared to more advanced western Europe. By 1860 Russian industry lagged even further behind the West than in 1800. The government during this era pursued conservative, unimaginative economic policies featuring protective tariffs, fiscal restraint (to prevent excessive debt and inflation), and financial support for noblemen. Officially, the government favored industrial expansion, but in practice did little to promote it, partly because of fears of a host of social problems associated with rapid growth of the factory system, partly from distaste for speculative Western capitalism.

Typifying the conservative state economic policies of this era was Count E. F. Kankrin, Finance Minister (1823–44). A German who had come to Russia as a youth, he served in the quartermaster corps before being appointed Finance Minister through Arakcheev's influence. Kankrin never developed a consistent economic philosophy, but he considered himself a "practical" man able to make adjustments. Primarily, he was a mercantilist and a consistent opponent of free trade. Socially, he favored the status quo and aristocratic predominance. Kankrin's credit policies were clearly anti-industrial: he refused to provide direct state loans to industry, which could readily have been provided through state banks. Instead, he had state banks loan large sums to an indigent nobility who squandered much of the money on luxuries. Kankrin abhorred the idea of an unbalanced budget or private banking; he opposed Admiral N.S. Mordvinov's enlightened projects for private provincial banks. A high tariff policy protected domestic industries, but its main purpose was revenue, not industrial growth. As to railroads, Kankrin saw no benefit in them whatsoever. They separated man from nature, he complained, broke down class barriers (which he wanted to preserve), and increased the restlessness of the younger generation. He seems to have envisioned hordes of disorderly youths tearing around the country in railroad cars! Railroads, concluded Kankrin, were a needless luxury, and anyway they would never carry freight! Kankrin's rigid balance-the-budget conservatism reflected the bureaucrats' approach toward the economy under Nicholas I. The state, as the American historian Walter Pintner points out, was unwilling to foster economic development until forced to do so by painful defeat in the Crimean War.

Despite the sluggish Russian economy of the early 19th century, there were notable achievements in certain areas. According to official statistics, the number of industrial enterprises rose from about 2,400 in 1804 to 15,400 by 1860. These figures are conservative estimates because some types of manufacturing firms were not counted and many small operations may have been concealed by owners to evade taxes. Fewer than ten percent of manufacturing enterprises employed more than 100 workers. Workers in industry, according to official figures, increased from a paltry 95,200 in 1804 to 210,600 in 1825 and 565,000 in 1860. Both hired free laborers and serf workers, mostly state peasants, were employed in industry. A surprising number of serfs became successful industrialists. Serfs of the Sheremetiev family were pioneers of the Russian cotton industry, which developed in the village of Ivanovo, owned by the Sheremetievs.

Soviet historians, recently challenging the official industrial employment figures, argue that they are disproportionately low and substitute higher ones: 225,000 industrial workers in 1804 (only 27% free hired laborers) increasing to 862,000 by 1860 (56% free). Many industrial workers were seasonal laborers working in factories during the off season and returning to the village at the peak agricultural periods, spring and autumn. Whichever figures are accepted, clearly only a tiny minority of the population engaged in regular factory work in 1860.

The leading branches of industry in the early 19th century were woolen, linen, and cotton textiles, leather processing, and the sugar beet industry. Woolen textile manufacturing, largely for the army, with only 29,000 workers in 1804, employed more than 120,000 persons by 1860. The work was carried on largely in primitive estate factories, though enterprising Old Believer merchants in Moscow were beginning to create a basis for a modern woolen industry by mid-century. Cotton textiles with 8,000 employees in 1804 grew even faster to 152,000 workers by 1860. At first Russia depended on imported English cotton cloth, which was printed and sold domestically. During the Napoleonic Wars the flow of English cotton imports was temporarily interrupted, forcing the Russians to develop their own manufacture of cotton cloth. After 1842 the latest spinning machinery was imported from England by thrifty serf craftsmen and Old Believer merchants. A thriving cotton textile industry was established to meet a large internal demand for cotton cloth and to be sold in the Middle East and China. The sugar beet industry, which barely existed in 1804, responding to rising domestic demand, expanded to 65,000 workers by 1860.[6]

The oil and coal industries, so essential to modern industrial societies, remained largely undeveloped in Russia in this period. Iron and steel production lagged, and it was soon evident that Russian iron products could not compete in price or quality with English ones manufactured in mechanized mills. The backwardness of such key industries helps account for the relative stagnation of the Russian economy.

Modest railroad construction, despite Kankrin, was begun in the 1830s. A short line connecting St. Petersburg with the imperial summer residence at Tsarskoe Selo opened in 1837, more as a curiosity for Nicholas I and his family than as an experiment in a new form of

---

[6] P. A. Khromov, *Ekonomicheskoe razvitie Rossii v XIX–XX vekakh* (Moscow, 1967), p. 31.

transportation. Several prominent Russians realized the railway's revolutionary potential and promoted its construction. In 1839 F. Bulgarin, a leading publicist, wrote:

> Are the complaints justified that the industrial spirit of our age has stifled the poetry of life? We do not think so! It seems to us that from the creation of the world there has not been an idea more poetic and majestic than the project for a railroad from Petersburg to Moscow and from there . . . to Odessa."[7]

In 1842 work was begun to link the two capitals by rail, and the project was completed in 1852 with the help of an American engineer, G. W. Whistler, who convinced the Russians to use a wider gauge than that in Europe on the ground that this would prevent enemies from using Russian railroads for invasion. By 1855 about 660 miles of track had been built, only a tiny beginning, and there was no railroad to Odessa.

After victory over Napoleon, Russia took on a modest but significant role in international economic affairs. By 1850 the volume of Russian foreign trade exceeded Austria's, though it was only 18 percent of Britain's. Russia exported largely raw materials and foodstuffs and imported manufactured goods and luxuries. As early as 1822, Russia adopted a high protective tariff, mainly to raise revenue and discourage excessive imports. In spite of a generally backward economy, Russia maintained a favorable balance of trade in most of Nicholas' reign largely by means of grain exports. The outbreak of the Crimean War had a depressing effect on the Russian economy and especially on foreign trade, which dwindled almost to nothing during the war.

The early 19th century Russian economy was characterized by backwardness owing to the persistence of an agrarian economy based on serfdom. Still there were important signs of industrial activity and accumulation of private capital, particularly among Old Believers and Jews and some enterprising serfs. These social outcasts were often persecuted and restricted, forcing them to pool their resources and engage in economic activities scorned by the upper class. Old Believers formed the core of the Russian textile industry, while Jews dominated banking, retail trade, and vodka distribution. Serfs were encouraged to engage in commercial ventures by masters seeking additional revenue. The most enterprising serfs accumulated capital, built factories and shops, some of which became the nuclei of future large enterprises, such as the Ivanovo textile industry. The government, however, remained cautious, failing to recognize the significant social and economic changes that were occurring. The dynamic changes in western Europe became fully evident only with Russia's defeat in the Crimean War, which eventually forced a change in official thinking and policies.

CULTURE

The political conservatism and obscurantism so widespread in Russia early in the 19th century did not preclude a tremendous outburst of

---

[7] Cited in T. Koepnick, *The Journalist Careers of F. V. Bulgarin and N. I. Grech,* unpublished Ph.D. dissertation, Ohio State University.

cultural creativity. Russian literature and music showed unprecedented vigor and originality after a long apprenticeship in the schools of western Europe.

A necessary prerequisite for an original literature was a modern literary language, which owes much to Russia's greatest 18th century scholar and scientist, Michael Lomonosov, often called the "father" of Russian literature for his linguistic reforms. Lomonosov helped shape the Russian language for poetic expression by developing a suitable system of versification and poetic structure. His textbooks of rhetoric and grammar set standards for the modern Russian literary language. His poetry, in a ponderous classical style, demonstrated his theories of versification and became the models for subsequent 18th century Russian poetry. As a nationalist, Lomonosov believed that the Russian language as a vehicle of expression was superior to all others. He distinguished three linguistic levels: high, middle, and low, each characterized by many Old Church Slavonic elements.

The greatest Russian 18th century poet, Gabriel Derzhavin (1743–1816), further elaborated Lomonosov's theories and language. An innovator within the narrow bounds of classicism, Derzhavin's imaginative power set him apart from his predecessors and contemporaries and presaged the romantic movement.

Nicholas Karamzin's literary work[8] helped turn Russian literature away from classical models toward the romantic movement. His *Letters of a Russian Traveler* (1791) introduced a delightfully casual, colloquial style and a genteel, cosmopolitan sensibility to the reading public. His name is associated with the school of sentimentalism and his short novel, *Poor Liza* (1792) won him instant fame as a writer. Karamzin's efforts to use the cultivated conversational Russian of his day, infused with French phrases and influences, was challenged by Admiral A. Shishkov (1753–1841), who passionately defended the purity of the Russian language and attacked Karamzin's cosmopolitan language. Refusing to become involved in polemics, Karamzin abandoned literature in favor of history. From 1803 until his death in 1826 he was official court historiographer and wrote his monumental *History of the Russian State*, which ignored the Russian people but gave dramatic portraits of Russian rulers and eulogized absolute monarchy. The *History* was widely read and inspired generations of Russian artists, notably Alexander Pushkin, who drew heavily on its materials.

The poet, V. A. Zhukovskii (1783–1852) with a few colleagues formed the Arzamas Society, which advanced Karamzin's literary reforms and attacked the conservative Shishkovites with epigrams, puns, and insulting witticisms. Seeking to translate Karamzin's literary reforms into poetics, Zhukovskii in his works helped create a new language of poetry based on that of Karamzin and well suited to the literary romanticism of the period. Zhukovskii portrayed masterfully man's spiritual world and intimate thoughts and feelings. His poetry gained unprecedented popularity and began a Russian cult of poetry which continues to this day.

---

[8] For Karamzin's political views, see above, p. 272.

As a poet Zhukovskii was completely overshadowed by the towering figure of his friend Alexander S. Pushkin (1799–1837). Indeed, one cannot discuss modern Russian literature without dealing with Pushkin, Russia's great national poet. Declared the prominent literary critic, V. G. Belinskii (1811–48): "To write about Pushkin means to write about the whole of Russian literature; for just as previous Russian writers explain Pushkin, so Pushkin explains the writers who followed him." He has always been ranked by Russians with the greatest literary figures of all time, such as Shakespeare and Goethe. Virtually all leading Russian writers of the 19th and 20th centuries have paid homage to Pushkin's artistic genius and have acknowledged their debt to him. Pushkin's genius was manifested in his ability to speak on behalf of all Russians, not just the elite. He embodied the Russian people and articulated the latent creativity of the Russian spirit.

Born in 1799 into an old but undistinguished noble family, Pushkin on his mother's side was descended from Peter the Great's black favorite from Abyssinia, Abraham Hannibal. Pushkin was extremely proud both of his noble origin and his African ancestry. Though he grew up like so many Russian noblemen in an atmosphere of French culture, books and tutors, he developed early and lasting ties with the Russia of the common people from his beloved nursemaid, Irina, who told him traditional Russian folk tales, which he later included in some of his greatest creations.

Even Pushkin's schoolboy verse bore the mark of genius and by the time he had completed his formal schooling in 1817, he was an established poet openly associated with Zhukovskii and the Arzamas Society.

Library of Congress

Alexander S. Pushkin (1799–1837)

His first major work, *Ruslan and Liudmila* (1820), based on a fairy tale heard from his nurse, was brilliant in language and poetic artistry. His reputation rested equally upon radical and irreverent poems known only in manuscript copies because of the censorship: *Ode to Liberty* (1817), *The Village* (1819), and *Hurrah! He's Back in Russia Again* (1818). These attacked evils of Russian society, particularly serfdom and hypocrisy, and induced the authorities to exile the young poet to the south of Russia. He lived in the Caucasus, the Crimea, and settled in Odessa on the Black Sea. These "exotic" places were reflected in such vibrant poems as *The Prisoner of the Caucasus* and *The Fountain of Bakchisarai.*

Pushkin returned to the family estate at Mikhailovskoe in Pskov province in 1824, and in its solitude and isolation produced one masterpiece after another: *The Gypsies;* the great historical drama, *Boris Godunov*, recalling Shakespeare and inspired by Karamzin; and began perhaps his greatest work, *Eugene Onegin*. In that novel in verse Pushkin portrays the classic "superfluous man," an insipid misfit who suffers from boredom and indifference. Eugene inspires the love of the passionate Tatiana, then rejects her love in favor of aimless wandering. Tatiana enters into an arranged marriage with a "fat general." Eugene gradually realizes the value of what he had so casually spurned and returns to declare his love for Tatiana, but she refuses his advances and remains loyal to her husband. Apparently a romantic tale of unrequited love, *Eugene Onegin* in fact indicts shallow and selfish Byronic romanticism. Tatiana, the archetype of the great Russian literary heroine, is passionate yet sensible, honest, loyal, and long suffering.

A shorter, more intense and brilliant work, considered by many as Pushkin's masterpiece is *The Bronze Horseman* (1833), a paean to Peter the Great and his monumental city on the Neva River. It is named from the French sculptor Falconet's majestic equestrian statue of Peter, commissioned by Catherine the Great. Pushkin contrasts the power of nature and the great vision of Peter with the suffering and tragedy of the helpless government clerk, Eugene, pursued by rampaging flood waters which sweep away his fiancée and her family, and by the statue of the bronze horseman which comes to life in his anguished mind. Eugene, too, becomes a literary archetype, a model of the downtrodden, defenseless common man buffeted by forces beyond his control and comprehension, adrift in the murky waters of destiny.

Drawing upon similar sources is *The Queen of Spades*, one of Pushkin's finest short stories. Set in St. Petersburg, it records with mounting psychological tension the adventures of a callous army officer who terrorizes an old lady to death in an effort to obtain her secret of winning at cards. The old woman's spirit appears and reveals to the greedy youth a false version of the secret, causing him to lose instead of win a fortune. His life and reputation destroyed by avarice, he too goes mad. Realistic portrayals of character set against exotic backgrounds and situations won Pushkin enormous and continuing popularity.

At the zenith of his creative powers Pushkin was killed in a senseless duel in 1837. It was as though he foresaw his tragic end when he described in *Eugene Onegin* the duel between Onegin and the poet, Lenskii. After Lenskii has been shot down and killed, Pushkin writes:

> His hand upon his breast lays lightly,
> And drops. His clouded eyes betray
> Not pain, but death. Thus, sparkling whitely
> Where the quick sunbeams on it play,
> A snowball down the hill goes tumbling
> And sinks from sight, soon to be crumbling.
> Onegin frozen with despair,
> Runs to the poor youth lying there,
> And looks and calls him . . . But no power
> Avails to rouse him: he is gone.
> The poet in the very dawn
> Of life has perished like a flower
> That by a sudden storm was drenched;
> Alas! the altar-fire is quenched.[9]

Russian educated society was stunned and outraged by Pushkin's untimely and pointless death. How could such a thing be allowed to happen? None dwelt on that question more intensely than a young army officer, Michael Lermontov (1814–41), who composed a devastating indictment of society for permitting such a senseless waste of genius. Pushkin had been the victim of a system which rewarded mediocrity and ignored talent and artistic brilliance.

> You whose eager flock surrounds the throne,
> You, the slayers of genius and freedom,
> You hide in the shadow of the law;
> But justice and truth, for you, are dead letters![10]

His poem *On the Death of Pushkin* circulated widely in manuscript because censorship prevented critical views from appearing in print. Lermontov's forceful language and heartfelt sentiments touched a chord in educated circles and gave him a recognition his earlier poems hardly deserved.

Descendant of a Scottish soldier of fortune who had entered Russian service early in the 17th century, Lermontov with his restless, romantic spirit and unconventional behavior caused the authorities to exile him repeatedly to remote areas. His greatest poem, *The Demon,* was judged by officialdom to be unfit for publication because of its "blasphemous" theme: love between a demon and a mortal. Unpublished in Lermontov's lifetime, it inspired later generations.

While in Caucasian exile Lermontov completed his greatest prose work, *A Hero of Our Time* (1840), which analyzed vividly and penetratingly contemporary Russian society in an easygoing, natural style. This work contributed much to literary realism and naturalism in Russia. The novel's hero, the proud, passionate, self-reliant Pechorin, inspired both real and fictional imitators. Lermontov, who had condemned

---

[9] Cited in A. Yarmolmsky, (ed.), *The Poems, Prose and Plays of Pushkin* (New York, 1936), p. 240, trans. by Babette Deutsch.

[10] Cited in Henri Troyat, *Pushkin* (New York, 1970), p. 605.

Russian society for Pushkin's death, died precisely the same way at the age of 27, killed in a duel over an absurd point of honor. Lermontov wrote relatively little but is generally considered among the giants of Russian literature.

Nicholas Gogol (1809–52), whose greatest masterpieces epitomized the literary realism which became the hallmark of Russian literature, was born in the Ukraine into a family of lesser gentry. Gogol's education was haphazard, but nonetheless he became briefly professor of history at St. Petersburg University through Pushkin's influence. His literary career began in 1831 with publication of a collection of stories, *Evenings on a Farm Near Dikanka,* based on Ukrainian folktales, legends, and daily life. This first work, winning him immediate acclaim, was a microcosm of his later great works. In later collections of stories, *Mirgorod* (1835) and *Arabesques* (1835), Gogol continued to use folktales and historical tales, producing disturbing and exciting stories such as "Viy," about the devil, and "Taras Bulba," about the Zaporozhian Cossacks and based on their folk legends and songs. Other stories chronicled the lives of lower middle-class St. Petersburg society: "The Portrait," "Nevskii Prospekt," "Memoirs of a Madman." The most famous of these St. Petersburg stories was "The Overcoat" (1842). The poor, lamentable Akaki Akakievich, a petty clerk, makes incredible sacrifices to buy a new overcoat to transform himself from a worm into a human being. Alas, after all his travail, the coat is stolen, and Akaki perishes in a futile effort to recover it. His spirit returns to haunt those who refused to help him find it.

Among Gogol's greatest masterpieces is the comedy, *The Inspector General* (1836), inspired by A. S. Griboedov's famous play, *The Misfortune of Being Clever* (1823), the first great Russian social comedy. *The Inspector General* satirizes provincial Russian life and the self-satisfied inferiority of townspeople (Russians call this *poshlost*) in a humorous fashion. The play centers on a case of mistaken identity as the rascal, Khlestakov, is taken for a powerful government inspector traveling incognito to audit the local administration. The townspeople overwhelm him with hospitality and attention; the ladies flatter him, the gentlemen compliment and try to deceive him. The boorish Khlestakov survives because the townspeople are even stupider than he. He robs them blind, then leaves an insulting letter making fun of their gullibility before disappearing. The play received a mixed response. Nicholas I liked it, but upper class society was outraged, accusing Gogol of undermining the established order. Others saw the play as an accurate portrayal of Russian provincial life. Gogol had held a mirror up to Russian society and some disliked what they saw. The critic Belinskii called Gogol "a great comic painter of real life."

Whereas *The Inspector General* focused on one provincial town, Gogol's epic novel, *Dead Souls* (1842) ranged the length and breadth of Russia. The hero, Chichikov, is a middle-aged scoundrel who travels about buying up the names of dead serfs before they can be removed from official registers in order to use these nonexistent serfs as collateral for a huge bank loan. Gogol again focuses on the greed, stupid-

Nicholas Gogol (1809–1852)

ity, and corruption of much of Russian society. "God, what a sad country our Russia is!" exclaimed Pushkin after reading a draft of *Dead Souls*. Yet it is a comic epic with sidesplitting humor and satire, but black humor and mordant satire. Gogol is generally considered the true founder and leading practitioner of Russian literary realism and occupies a pivotal place in literary history.

Russian achievements in music, painting, and architecture were more limited and little known outside of Russia. Russian music remained imitative in the 18th century. Early 19th century Russian music is chiefly identified with Michael Glinka (1804–57), a composer of genius. He laid the foundations of the national school of Russian music which developed so brilliantly later in the century.

Glinka's operas complemented and drew upon Pushkin's literary works. He was drawn irresistibly to the peculiar musicality of his friend Pushkin's writings, so well suited to musical adaptation. Indeed, most great 19th century Russian composers turned to Pushkin, and many operas were derived from his creations.[11] Without a Russian musical

---

[11] Notably Glinka's *Ruslan and Liudmila*, Dargomyzhskii's *Rusalka* and *The Stone Guest*, Musorgskii's *Boris Godunov*, Tchaikovskii's *Eugene Onegin, Mazeppa*, and *The Queen of Spades*; Rimskii-Korsakov's *Tsar Saltan* and *The Golden Cockerel*, and Rachmaninov's *Aleko* and *The Covetous Knight*.

Michael Glinka (*1804–1857*)

conservatory, Glinka nonetheless received excellent private tutoring in St. Petersburg, and met Zhukovskii, Pushkin, and other leading writers. Because a musical career was then considered unworthy for an aristocrat, Glinka's family tried to dissuade him from it. Eventually, he persuaded them to let him visit Italy, where he continued his musical studies for several years. Returning to Russia in 1834 and impressed with Italian opera, Glinka decided to compose an opera Russian in subject matter and music. Accepting Zhukovskii's suggestion of the story of the peasant hero, Ivan Susanin,[12] Glinka completed his opera, *Ivan Susanin* in 1836. After Nicholas I praised it highly, he renamed it *A Life for the Tsar*. Glinka drew heavily on Russian folk music to depict Ivan's heroic plan to save Michael Romanov from capture by the Poles during the Time of Troubles. Susanin loses his life but saves Russia and the Romanov dynasty. *A Life for the Tsar* was a great popular success and won for Glinka adulation from educated society. Soviet audiences still applaud this opera as a great classic, though the title has reverted to *Ivan Susanin* and the libretto has been partially rewritten to stress Susanin's devotion to country and people, not the tsar.

Glinka's second opera, *Ruslan and Liudmila,* based on Pushkin's fairy tale, was judged a failure by audiences and critics alike. Glinka was bitterly disappointed because he knew that musically it marked a

[12] See above, p. 149.

significant advance over his previous work. Having matured as a composer, Glinka had developed an individual style, and his music had a vitality and richness unprecedented in Russia. *Ruslan and Liudmila* is more truly a Russian opera than *Ivan Susanin*, which is essentially Italian covered with a veneer of Russian folk music. Though misunderstood at the time, *Ruslan and Liudmila* is the great pioneering work of Russian national music and Glinka's masterpiece. A leading Soviet scholar affirms that Glinka was to Russian music what Pushkin was to Russian literature. He set the stage for the musical outpouring later in the century.

Early 19th century Russian painting and architecture produced no towering figures such as Pushkin, Gogol, and Glinka. Nonetheless, significant progress was made toward independence, originality, and national artistic expression, influenced by developments in literature.

The upsurge in national feeling and his desire to foster imperial prestige induced Alexander I to make St. Petersburg a beautiful and splendid city, a capital befitting the most powerful state in the world. Revealing his cosmopolitanism in his preference for European neoclassicism, he selected as architects a Russian, Vasili Stasov (1769–1848); an Italian, Carlo Rossi; and a Frenchman, Auguste Montferrand, all strongly influenced by prevalent Greek classicism. Their style resembled that found in any European capital of the time or in the eastern United States. These architects' works completed the classical configuration of St. Petersburg. In Winter Palace Square, Rossi erected the semicircular and grandiose General Staff building. He also built the Mikhailovskii Palace (now the Russian Museum), Alexandra Theater, and Theatrical Square just off Nevskii Prospect. Stasov, though trained in western Europe, adapted traditional Russian architectural styles to neoclassicism. He renovated the Winter Palace, Peterhof, and the great palace at Tsarskoe Selo and designed its famous Lyceum, where many prominent Russian noblemen, including Pushkin, would study. Several large Orthodox churches testify to Stasov's skill at synthesizing classical and Byzantine styles. In Winter Palace Square, Montferrand added a towering granite monolith erected in 1829 to commemorate Russian victory over Napoleon. His most impressive work is St. Isaac's Cathedral, a very unRussian church but an architectural treasure house in exterior design and interior decoration. These architects completed the carefully planned development of official St. Petersburg.

Early 19th century Russian painting, like architecture, followed European styles rather unimaginatively, adopting an academic style which stressed classical and Old Testament themes and draughtmanship rather than conceptualization. The Russian Academy of Arts, founded in the 18th century, resembled European academies. The academic painter, Karl Briullov (1799–1852), the most famous artist of the age, was called "the Russian Raphael" for his painting "The Last Day of Pompeii," but posterity has not sustained this judgment. Briullov himself realized that his paintings resembled those of many other academic painters.

The fate of Alexander Ivanov (1806–58) resembled Briullov's. The gifted son of a leading Petersburg academic painter, Ivanov received the best art education available in Russia, then settled in Rome to create masterpieces in the style of the Renaissance masters. Stimulated by the "success" of Briullov's gigantic "The Last Day of Pompeii," Ivanov resolved to create a work surpassing all previous religious painting. He labored over his magnum opus, "The Appearance of Christ to the People" for over 25 years, but when it was exhibited in St. Petersburg in 1855, it was a failure, as even he realized.

Early 19th century Russian culture was characterized by a new independence and national consciousness which stimulated a great creative outburst, first in literature, then in music and the fine arts. For all its originality and creativity, this half century was merely a prelude, a portent of the superb accomplishments to come in the arts during the second half of the century.

Suggested Additional Reading

ECONOMY AND SOCIETY

BLACKWELL, W. *The Beginnings of Russian Industrialization, 1800–1860* (Princeton, 1968).

CRISP, O. "The State Peasants Under Nicholas I," *SEER,* vol. 37 (1959), pp. 387–412.

PINTNER, W. *Russian Economic Policy under Nicholas I* (Ithaca, New York, 1967).

PIPES, R., trans. and ed. *Karamzin's Memoir on Ancient and Modern Russia* (Cambridge, Mass., 1959).

CULTURE

ASAFIEV, B. *Russian Music from the Beginning of the Nineteenth Century* (Trans. A. Swan) (Ann Arbor, 1953).

BLACK, J. *Nicholas Karamzin and Russian Society* (Toronto, 1975).

CROSS, A. *N. M. Karamzin: A Study of His Literary Career* (Carbondale, Ill. 1971).

DANIELS, G. (ed.) *A Lermontov Reader* (New York, 1965).

LAVRIN, J. *Lermontov* (New York, 1959).

LEONARD, R. *A History of Russian Music* (New York, 1968).

MAGARSHACK, D. *Pushkin: A Biography* (New York, 1967).

MAGUIRE, R. ed. *Gogol from the Twentieth Century* (Princeton, 1974).

SIMMONS, E. *Pushkin* (Cambridge, Mass., 1937). Still the best biography.

VICKERY, W. *Alexander Pushkin* (New York, 1970).

YARMOLINSKY, A., ed. *The Poems, Prose and Plays of Alexander Pushkin* (New York, 1964).

part III

Modern Russia, 1855 to the Present

SPANNING THE last 120 turbulent years, this section emphasizes the modernization of Russia and the USSR in its political, social, economic, and cultural aspects under the last
three tsars and the Soviet leaders: Lenin, Stalin, Khrushchev
and Brezhnev. The regime of Alexander II implements the
Great Reforms, especially emancipation of the serfs, which
changes considerably the socioeconomic and cultural climate in Russia. Under Alexander III, a conservative autocrat, Count Witte takes the first difficult steps toward rapid
industrialization. After the Revolution of 1905, which nearly
overthrows tsarism, Count Stolypin begins to modernize
agriculture; widespread public education is begun. Alternating periods of reform and reaction under the last tsars is
followed by the calamity of World War I. Russia's defeat contributes to the Revolutions of 1917 in which tsarism yields
to democracy, and democracy to Soviet Communism. Political autocracy, in abeyance during the Revolution and civil
war, is gradually restored in a new guise by Lenin and perfected by the dictator, Joseph Stalin. Stalin transforms agriculture through forcible collectivization and makes the
Soviet Union a powerful industrial state through the Five
Year Plans, but his purges cost millions of lives. After the
terrible travail of the German–Soviet war, the triumphant
USSR emerges as one of the two superpowers with control
of eastern Europe, global interests, great military and industrial strength, and an autocratic and repressive political
system run by the Communist Party.

24

Political Reform and Minorities

THE DEATH OF Nicholas I and the Crimean defeat ended the old regime of undiluted autocracy and serfdom in Russia. Alexander II, the new emperor, pursued from the start more pragmatic enlightened policies than his father. The Great Reforms (1855–74) of his reign released forces of change that gradually transformed patriarchal Russia as it adjusted to rising industrial capitalism. The reforms, which were partial and incomplete, met entrenched conservative interests, which sought, sometimes successfully, to reverse or impede change. This opposition made the half-century after the Crimean War an era of ebb and flow, of conflict between modernizing and traditional elements. The Great Reforms remain controversial. Did the government seek to create a modern, progressive Russia or merely avert revolution and save the nobility by halfhearted concessions? Did the reforms place Russia on the path earlier traversed by western Europe and leading toward parliamentary government and social reform, or were they, as Soviet historians claim, mere palliatives, altered later by a more conservative regime?

ALEXANDER II AND THE EMANCIPATION

The emperor, retaining full autocratic powers, remained the prime mover in the Russian political system. In the midst of the Crimean War Alexander II, well prepared and well intentioned, assumed power at the age of 37. His father and tutors had stimulated his sense of duty and concern for the military; the poet Zhukovskii had reinforced his romantic, humanitarian impulses. Though no scholar, Alexander was well versed in foreign languages, and Count Speranskii had coached him in Russian law and politics. He was the first tsar who had visited Siberia (1837) and had traveled extensively in Russia and Europe. Alexander married a German from Hesse-Darmstadt, christened Maria Alexandrovna in Russia, and Prussia remained his favorite European country. Nicholas I had entrusted him with important state duties and allowed him to run the government during his absences. Alexander's character was a curious mixture of strengths and weaknesses. Tending to shy away from obstacles, he had combated irresolution and weak will since childhood, but he could be very stubborn. He was irritable and emotional but possessed sound common sense, sincere patriotism, and he wanted to do what was right. Generally, Alexander chose able advisers and supported them loyally even against strong opposition.

Emancipation of the serfs, affecting roughly 85 percent of the population, was the most significant and controversial act of his reign. Why did he take this step which his predecessors had shunned? Russian liberal historians stressed the role of an aroused public opinion directed by abolitionist writers. Mounting peasant unrest and fear of revolution, counter Soviet historians, compelled the regime to end serfdom in order to save itself. Between 1859 and 1861, they maintain, a "revolutionary situation" existed which needed only leadership to produce social upheaval. Some Western scholars, notably T. H. von Laue, argue that emancipation aimed to foster economic development and modernization so that Russia could overtake western Europe. The Crimean defeat, wrote Sir Bernard Pares, exposing Russia's military and economic backwardness, induced Russian leaders to undertake this basic reform. Recently, an American, A. J. Rieber, argued that Alexander freed the serfs mainly in order to modernize the army, necessary if Russia were to remain a great power. Probably all these factors were involved in the decision to emancipate.

Designated the "tsar-liberator" by some, Alexander II played a vital, probably decisive part in the Emancipation, one of the 19th century's greatest reforms. He acted more from conservative than liberal motives and sought as Russia's "leading nobleman" to protect legitimate interests of the nobility. Shaking off indecisiveness and weak will, he directed the difficult campaign at every step. War Minister D. A. Miliutin wrote:

> The tsar showed at this time such unshakable firmness in the great state undertaking he had personally conceived that he could ignore the murmurings and grumblings of the clear opponents of innovation. In this sense the soft and humanitarian Emperor Alexander II displayed greater decisiveness and a truer sense of his own power than his father who was noted for his iron will.[1]

Nor was he the frightened man depicted by Soviet accounts. Letters to his trusted friend, Prince A. I. Bariatinskii, emphasized that in an emancipation designed to take Russia along the path of progress, the ruler must seize the initiative: "Autocracy created serfdom and it is up to autocracy to abolish it." In 1856 he warned the Moscow nobility: "It is better to begin to abolish serfdom from above than to wait until it begins to abolish itself from below. I ask you, gentlemen, to think over how all this can be carried out." This speech jolted the nobility out of its apathy but failed to win substantial support for emancipation among noblemen.

Initially the press was permitted to discuss the emancipation issue, but the Emperor, to protect his autocratic powers, had the Emancipation prepared bureaucratically. He appointed a secret committee to ex-

---

[1] Cited in A. J. Rieber, *The Politics of Autocracy* (Paris, 1966), p. 21.

Library of Congress

Alexander II

amine the problem, most of whose members were conservative noblemen, though liberals such as S. S. Lanskoi and N. A. Miliutin, dominated the Ministry of Interior, which prepared the specific statutes. The tsar prodded the reluctant Main Committee and ordered the provincial nobility to create committees to draw up emancipation procedures. Rejecting the landless emancipation favored by conservative gentry, Alexander in 1858 visited key provinces and stressed the need for a landowning peasantry. Soviet accounts attribute his initiatives largely to a rising tide of peasant disorders. Alexander Herzen's emigre newspaper, *The Bell*, rejoiced: "Thou hast triumphed, O Galilean!" When editorial commissions (set up to decide how much land should go to the peasants and on what terms) delayed, Alexander appointed his liberal brother, Grand Duke Constantine, to head them. The emancipation statutes, after a brief discussion in the State Council, were signed by Alexander on February 19, 1861, the sixth anniversary of his accession. To prevent peasant disturbances the authorities announced the Emancipation the Sunday before Lent and it was proclaimed to the peasants in church and in their villages. Their initial joyous reaction at liberation soon yielded to dismay or anger when they realized they would not receive free and clear all lands they had worked previously.

The Emancipation Act of 1861, relating only to private serfs, granted them immediate personal freedom. The statute was so lengthy, complex, and often so vague that it is no wonder that the peasants failed to understand it. The reform was to proceed in three phases: a brief transition era, a phase of "temporary obligation," and a redemption period. For the first two years former serfs were expected to perform traditional services for the landowners while reaching agreements with them on lands, boundaries, and obligations. Such "inventories" were to be drawn up by mutual agreement or with the aid of peace mediators (*mirovye posredniki*), appointed by the Crown from the gentry. If peasants and lords failed to draw up an inventory, the mediator was to do so. Numerous peasant disturbances developed because the peasants were reluctant to accept onerous or unfair terms; some charters had to be completed without peasant approval. Many peasants expected that "real freedom" would follow this two-year interlude, and when such rumors proved false, some refused regular-sized land allotments, instead accepting free of charge dwarf plots ("beggars' allotments"). About one fourth of the maximum norm, these proved insufficient to support a peasant family. Other peasants, once the inventories had been completed, became "temporarily obligated": they paid their usual *obrok* or performed *barshchina* while the lords retained ownership of the land. For the first nine years after 1861 all former serfs, except those taking beggar allotments, had to accept a standard-sized allotment. Household serfs, though personally free, usually received no land and often had to work for the landlord. "Temporary obligation" lasted until both parties agreed on a procedure to redeem the land. Finally, the government set 1883 as the date by which all peasants must begin redeeming their land. After deducting noble debts, the state advanced to the landowners about three fourths of the amount due them in interest-bearing securities. The peasants were to repay the government over a period of 49 years and pay the remaining quarter directly to the lords.

Land allotments varied in size by region—Black Soil, non-Black Soil, and steppe. Maximum and minimum norms were set for each province, but the lord was guaranteed at least one third of his estate. In Great and New Russia the land was transferred generally to the repartitional commune; in the Ukraine where the hereditary commune prevailed, allotments became the hereditary possession of individual households. In the western provinces under the land reform of 1864, because the landlords were largely Polish, the mostly Belorussian, Ukrainian, or Lithuanian peasantry received all land previously worked at below its market price. In the west and infertile north and east, allotments usually equalled or exceeded pre-emancipation standards. In the fertile Black Soil region, however, they were smaller and reductions ("cut-offs") in behalf of the nobility exceeded 25 percent. In the Black Soil zone the land was somewhat overvalued and in the north greatly overvalued to compensate nobles for loss of labor power or peasant side earnings.

Other categories of peasants obtained better terms. In 1863 the imperial peasants (826,000 registered males in 1858) received allotments about equal to the maximum accorded private peasants in their region, and were to begin redemption payments within two years. A law of November 1866 assigned to state peasants—mostly in northern and eastern Russia and Siberia—all lands previously worked in return for higher *obrok* payments; in 1886 redemption payments replaced *obrok*. Since "cut-offs" were rare and state peasants had worked more land than private serfs, these latter groups were considerably better off. For all peasants the household and commune, regarded by the state as guarantors of order and stability, were reinforced: they were given most of the nobility's former judicial and police powers.

The significance of the emancipation settlement is still debated. Most liberal western historians consider it a major step in modernizing Russia, which only an autocratic government could have carried out. For Soviet scholars the Emancipation was a "bourgeois reform" extracted from a reluctant government by peasant pressure. Because former serf-owners executed it, there were many feudal survivals, galling restrictions, and excessive payments imposed on the peasantry. The emancipation settlement, claims a recent Soviet account, created conditions which fueled subsequent revolutionary peasant explosions. Thus some historians emphasize the progress achieved, others the remaining restrictions and problems. The Emancipation did produce a single class of free villagers who were, however, still clearly demarcated socially and administratively from other groups and governed by their own regulations and standards. Emancipation did not and could not solve Russia's longstanding agrarian problem of low productivity.

OTHER REFORMS

The end of serfdom encouraged, and in some cases required, other significant changes. Most were drafted or suggested during the late 1850s; after 1861 their enactment and implementation met increasing opposition from conservative noblemen in and outside the government. During the 1860s contending factions within the bureaucracy and Alexander's indecision caused shifts, delays, and confusion in government policies. Such disputes over reform, affirms a recent Soviet account, were over what concessions had to be made to preserve autocracy against the threat of revolution. On the one hand, magnates with vast estates, such as Count P. A. Shuvalov, favored only minimal concessions to improve existing laws and institutions coupled with repression of radicals and liberals. More liberal officials of the new generation, especially the Miliutin brothers and Count P. A. Valuev, favored basic new institutions and some even suggested a constitutional regime. Alexander's vacillation between these groups helped account for alternating liberalism and repression. Generally, the government adopted a middle course of limited reforms designed to make a constitution unnecessary.

CENSORSHIP AND EDUCATION

Even before the Crimean War ended, the government permitted a revival of Russian intellectual life that had been stifled by the post-1848 repression. Under a liberalized censorship, Russian-language periodicals, some quite radical in approach, increased from 25 to almost 200 between 1855 and 1862. After 1858 the government limited the press in its discussion of controversial policies, especially in foreign affairs, but the press law of 1865, which largely abolished preliminary censorship for books and "thick" journals, generally confirmed the liberal trend. For newspapers a new system of punitive censorship, involving warnings and suspensions, marked an advance over the old system of preliminary censorship. Though the authorities still often seized or suspended radical publications, for most of Alexander II's reign the press enjoyed greater freedom than before or immediately after. Whereas Nicholas I had sought to permit only publications beneficial to the state, Alexander generally permitted whatever did not endanger it.

In higher education there was heartening progress. When the war ended, restrictions on university admissions were lifted, courses in philosophy, European government, and international law were reinstituted, and enrollments increased some 50 percent in four years. Foreign scholarly works were freely imported, and Russian students again traveled and studied abroad. In May 1861, however, strict temporary rules caused serious student disorders at Russian universities, and Admiral E. V. Putiatin, the new Minister of Education, urged that the universities be closed. But in December Alexander dismissed Putiatin and appointed an outstanding liberal, A. V. Golovnin, to his post. The charter of June 1863 gave universities much autonomy and academic freedom. Faculty councils controlled university affairs and elected rectors, and the universities entered a period of growth and creative activity.

For the first time the government sought to educate the Russian masses. In the early 1860s an unofficial public effort established some 500 literacy clinics for adults. In July 1864, the Ministry of Education issued the Public School Statute, the first major proposal in Russia for a national system of primary schools. District school boards were created which included representatives of the Ministry, the Holy Synod and other agencies. The new *zemstva* assemblies[2] also made encouraging progress: by 1880 they supported, at least in part, most of the 23,-000 elementary schools in European Russia. Under their auspices some 1,000 village schools were opened in the latter part of the reign. City councils (*dumy*) did similar work in larger towns.

The Ministry of Education's limited resources were devoted mainly to secondary education based on German and French models. Golovnin's statute of 1864 stated the liberal all-class principle, a vital innovation of this epoch: "The gymnasia and progymnasia are for the education of children of all conditions without social or religious distinction." Classical and modern curricula were considered equally valid, though only graduates of the classical gymnasia had sure access to the universities. Debate continued over the relative merits of classical and practical-scientific studies. Golovnin's liberal approach yielded in 1866 to the rigid discipline of Count Dmitri Tolstoi, minister of education until

---

[2] See below, pp. 335–36.

1880. Tolstoi, a fervent advocate of classicism, by the law of June 1871 imposed the "Greco-Roman bondage" by which the gymnasia stressed Greek and Latin to the detriment of Russian language and history. His purpose was to discipline the students, steer them away from revolution, and make access to universities difficult for nonprivileged elements. Nonetheless, both gymnasia and *realschulen* (practical schools emphasizing science and modern languages) expanded in numbers and improved in quality. A law of 1870 provided for the opening of women's gymnasia, largely locally supported. Women's universities (women were not admitted to the existing ones) were opened in the provincial capitals Kiev and Kazan beginning in 1869.

LOCAL SELF-GOVERNMENT

The highly significant *zemstvo* reform of January 1864, marked a shift from the appointed local officials of Nicholas I to a measure of self-government. The old system of bureaucratic tutelage had led A.M. Unkovskii of Tver province to complain in 1859: without official permission people "dare not repair a miserable bridge or hire a schoolteacher." That same year Alexander instructed a special commission to propose a new system of local government. After the Emancipation ended their direct power over the peasantry, noblemen agitated for a larger role in local affairs. Some liberal gentry urged a national representative assembly like the old *zemskii sobor*. In February 1862 the Tver nobility, renouncing special tax and class privileges, petitioned the tsar to convene an assembly elected by the entire land. Alexander responded angrily by having the Tver leaders imprisoned. Noble assemblies, warned the Ministry of Interior, must submit no petitions going beyond local needs. The central government opposed a national assembly or constitution.

Instead in January 1864 the tsar approved the *zemstva* system, which provided for election by landowners, peasantry, and townspeople of district and provincial assemblies. Introduced in some provinces in 1865, *zemstva* were gradually extended by 1914 to 43 of the 50 provinces of European Russia. Each class group was to elect representatives (*volost* elders selected peasant deputies) to a district assembly primarily on the basis of landownership and property value, a weighted franchise which assured the predominance of landowners. In 1867 at the district level nobles held 42, peasants 38, and townsmen about 20 percent of the seats. District *zemstva* elected delegates to provincial assemblies where the gentry, because of their dominance at the district level, occupied almost three fourths of the seats. At each level the assembly chose an administrative board to execute its decisions. Despite gentry predominance, *zemstva* reflected the all-class principle as for the first time the various class participated together in local government in an elected assembly.

The sphere of *zemstvo* activity was carefully limited by law to local tasks which the central government lacked the personnel or desire to perform. Supervised by police and crown officials, they were to fill the gap between the *mir* (peasant commune) and provincial governors. *Zemstva* were to build roads and bridges, construct and operate village schools, establish public hospitals and clinics, and improve agricultural techniques. Local taxes on landed property and commercial wealth were to finance their activities. Though the taxing power of the *zemstva* was severely restricted, their revenues grew steadily and they employed more and more professional people: agronomists, teachers, and doctors. Despite a jealous bureaucracy, they improved conditions in rural Russia considerably and were far superior to anything which had existed previously. Serving as schools of self-government, the *zemstva* gradually undermined the principle of autocracy and agitated for national representation. Soviet historians, however, quoting Lenin, regard them as a halfhearted gesture by the autocracy: "The *zemstva* were doomed from the very start to play the part of the fifth wheel on the coach of Russian state administration, a wheel tolerated by the bureaucracy only so long as its own powers were not at stake."[3] This statement reflects Lenin's contempt for liberalism but fails to do the *zemstvo* justice.

The municipal law of 1870, based on Russian and European practice, represented progress toward urban self-government. The eight largest cities, accorded the status of provinces, were placed under commandants, while other towns were treated as equivalent to districts and subordinated to provincial governors. Important towns were to elect city councils (*gorodskie dumy*) under a system resembling the Prussian, reserving most influence to the merchant elite, which paid the most taxes. Though provincial governors sharply restricted their competence and tax revenues, city *dumy* accomplished much in elementary education, building hospitals, paving and lighting streets, and creating other city services, especially in the two capitals. The city council elected an executive body consisting of a mayor (*golova*) and several members, which was closely regulated by the Ministry of Interior or provincial governor. Although most city dwellers were excluded from public office and deprived of real influence, the law of 1870 still represented progress toward self-government.

JUDICIAL

Nowhere was reform more urgently needed than in the court system. Under Nicholas I, legal procedure had been antiquated, cumbersome, and corrupt. Frequently judges had been untrained and open to bribery; the accused often languished in jail for years before their cases were tried. Alexander II declared in 1856: "May justice and mercy reign in our courts!" but not until 1862 did he decide to establish a new system of justice. The law of November 1864 introduced enlightened European judicial practices and set up a system of regular courts in each province not subject to administrative control with judges who would serve for life. Justice of the peace courts that were established in the countryside and the towns to try lesser cases became highly popular for their simple,

---

[3] V. Lenin, *Sobranie Sochineniia*, 5th ed. (Moscow, 1960), vol. 5, p. 35.

swift, and impartial procedures. In the regular courts, public jury trials were introduced for more important cases, and a brilliant Russian bar developed. This new judicial system took firm root, but it required decades to extend the new courts from the capitals to more remote parts of European Russia and the borderlands.

Unfortunately many cases fell outside or were removed from the jurisdiction of the new courts. After 1872 crimes against the state were tried, often secretly, by special courts under the Ministry of Interior, and the minister could banish to remote parts of the empire suspicious or politically dangerous persons without trial. Three additional court systems continued to function outside the regular one. *Volost* courts, originally set up for state peasants by Count Kiselev, were extended to former serfs as a part of Emancipation legislation. Using oral customary law and staffed by often illiterate peasant judges, they tried minor civil and criminal cases involving peasants under the Ministry of Interior. Thus peasant contacts with the modern judicial system were minimal (except for the justice of the peace courts) which helped to perpetuate the peasants' separate status. Ecclesiastical courts under the Holy Synod handled all cases involving the clergy, church property, and divorce. Finally, the War Ministry maintained courts for military personnel and areas under martial law. Despite these severe limitations, the judicial reforms of 1864 were strikingly successful and promoted the rise of an able legal profession. The principle of equality before the law helped undermine the old estate system.

MILITARY

Under an able war minister, Dmitri A. Miliutin (1861–81), described by Bismarck as "the most daring and radical spirit among the reformers," the Russian army was transformed and modernized. His long tenure of office, energy, and the tsar's support enabled him to carry through comprehensive changes despite powerful opposition. Earlier, Miliutin had fought against Shamil in the Caucasus and served 15 years as a leading professor at the Military Academy. During travels to western Europe he had pointed out the numerous shortcomings of Nicholas I's army. As chief of staff to Field Marshal Bariatinskii (1856–60), he had reorganized the military command in the Caucasus and contributed greatly to that region's pacification. Appointed War Minister at Bariatinskii's urging, Miliutin acted to create a more efficient, less expensive army and to insure Russia's security. First he reduced the term of service to 15 years and abolished most corporal punishment. In 1864, 15 regional military districts replaced the overcentralized system of Nicholas and strengthened local authority. Miliutin also reorganized the central army command and greatly reduced its personnel and paperwork. A liberal reform of military justice was effected along the lines of the judicial reform of 1864. Military gymnasia, providing a broader education and open to all classes, replaced the exclusive cadet corps for training officers, and primary schools were set up to provide literate recruits.

During the late 1860s growing noble reaction imperiled military and other changes. In April 1866, D. V. Karakozov, a nihilist student, attempted unsuccessfully to assassinate Alexander II, frightening him, and increasing the influence of conservative noblemen and officials. Count P. A. Shuvalov, chief of gendarmes and spokesman for former serfowners, dominated the government for the next seven years. Prussia's decisive victory over France (1870–71), which dramatized the issue of Russia's national security, however, enabled Miliutin to secure approval for universal military training. He had advocated this since the early 1860s, but only in 1874 did he finally overcome vehement opposition from Shuvalov and Bariatinskii, the chief defenders of traditional gentry privileges. The law of January 1874 proclaimed that "the defense of the fatherland forms the sacred duty of *every* Russian citizen." At the age of 20 all able-bodied males, with a few exceptions, were subject to a maximum of six years active service and some years in the reserves. The term of service depended upon one's education (a university graduate had to serve only six months). The tsar, despite his sympathy with the conservatives, supported Miliutin because of the importance of universal training for national security. Universal military service enabled Russia to establish trained reserves, and the Russian army, thanks to Miliutin's dedicated work, became a more effective fighting force with high morale. As subsequent wars would reveal, however, serious shortcomings remained.

SIGNIFICANCE

The Great Reforms, despite their limitations and inconsistencies, changed Russia fundamentally. The all-class principle reduced noble privilege and predominance and increased the rights of other groups. The vast majority of the population, finally released from bondage, was gradually integrated into society. A liberalized censorship and educational progress stimulated the development of public opinion and increased literacy. The concepts of equality before the law, universal liability to military service, and local self-government all weakened autocracy. The reforms created a basis for more rapid social, economic, and even political evolution. Soviet historians, following Lenin, view the reforms as marking Russia's transition from feudalism to capitalism and its adaptation to bourgeois values and a capitalistic economy. They stress correctly that since the regime protected and favored noble interests, there were many survivals of serfdom and feudal inequality. Many of the most liberal changes were later halted or reversed, which revealed the continuing power of conservative interests. Older attitudes and institutions, though shaken, persisted side by side with the new in continual friction and conflict, and the shallowness of political change left the Great Reforms incomplete.

Legally, Alexander remained an unlimited autocrat, and to preserve absolute power he blocked creation of a national parliament or constitution. He controlled the executive branch by keeping in office simultaneously liberal and conservative ministers whom he appointed and dismissed and who were responsible to him alone. He presided over the

Committee of Ministers, a loose, uncoordinated body, whose members rarely consulted one another on their policies and took pride in keeping their colleagues ignorant of their activities. The appointed State Council of 75 to 100 top civil and military officials debated prospective laws, but neither its decisions nor advice was binding, and the Emperor and his ministers initiated all legislation. The effective operation of the central administration depended largely on the Emperor; so chaos threatened if he failed to provide adequate leadership.

MINORITIES TO 1905

Alexander II's attitude toward national and religious minorities remained generally liberal and moderate, but in Poland an armed rebellion caused him to resort to Russification and repression, which heralded official policies after 1881. During the liberal years after 1855 some Polish emigres returned home, and a reform-minded Agricultural Society was created with branches throughout Russian Poland. Though Alexander warned the Poles not to expect political changes, Polish radicals agitated for broad autonomy or independence and opposed the moderate approach of Alexander Wielopolski, appointed head of a Polish commission on religion and education. Wielopolski wished to introduce needed reforms, make Russian rule more tolerable, and cooperate with Russian liberals such as Grand Duke Constantine. Late in 1861 as student and worker demonstrations broke out in Warsaw, Wielopolski's policies were repudiated, and radical defiance of his decree on conscription in January 1863 touched off armed rebellion.

The Polish insurrection against Russia lasted over a year and doomed the hopes of the moderates. Polish lords supported the Warsaw radicals while the enserfed peasantry remained largely passive. The rebels, hopelessly outnumbered and incompetently led, found few sympathizers in Russia and obtained only moral support abroad from France and England. Alexander's government crushed them, then implemented a drastic land reform in 1864, which undermined the nationalistic landowners. Count M. M. Muravev, known subsequently as "the hangman of Vilna," successfully "pacified" Poland. The property of the Polish Catholic Church was mostly confiscated, the clergy put on the state payroll, and the Church subordinated to the Russian Ministry of Interior. In 1875 Russian Poland was divided into ten provinces. Russian regulations on secondary education were extended there in 1872, and at Warsaw University Russian was the required language of instruction. Repression in Poland helped discredit Russian Panslavism,[4] but Alexander had little choice: the romantic Polish nobility had prepared its own ruin.

In Finland, Alexandrine liberalism proved more successful. A reform program stimulated trade, developed communications, and spread education. The Russian governor-general, Count Berg, backed Finnish liberals who favored a railway into the interior to aid the timber industry and agriculture. In 1863 the Finnish Diet, convened for the first time since

---

4 See below, pp. 359–62.

1809, approved plans to modernize the economy and promote public education. Meeting regularly thereafter, the Diet steadily extended Finnish autonomy. Alexander II observed the Finnish constitution scrupulously because the Finns sensibly restricted themselves to measures he would tolerate.

The status of Russian Jews improved considerably under Alexander II. Some categories, notably merchants, doctors and intellectuals, were permitted to reside outside the Pale of Jewish Settlement, urban areas in western Russia where Jews had lived for centuries. Jewish military recruitment was placed on the same basis as for other citizens. As restrictions relaxed, Jews tended to assimilate with the Russian population. Anti-Semitism, however, remained strong in the lower bureaucracy and among the public.

From the mid-1870s, the government adopted more repressive policies, especially toward incipient Ukrainian separatism. The Russian Geographical Society's Kiev branch, whose members studied the Ukrainian language, folklore, and poetry, had been the chief center. Hromada, a mildly socialist and autonomist political group, maintained contacts with Russian radical groups. Mykhaylo Drahomaniv, lecturer in history at Kiev University and an outstanding Ukrainian leader, lost his post in 1875 and went into exile in Vienna. The Geographical Society's Kiev branch was closed, and most Ukrainian publications and theatrical performances were prohibited. Crushed in Russia, Ukrainian national consciousness flourished in freer Austrian Galicia, where Drahomaniv continued to exert influence. Galicia's role as a Ukrainian Piedmont worried and embarrassed Russian authorities in Warsaw. Despite such repression, Alexander II's regime generally pursued more tolerant and constructive policies toward the empire's minorities than did those of Alexander III and Nicholas II.

Following Pobedonostsev's theories,[5] the regime from 1881 to 1905 pursued active discrimination against the empire's national and religious minorities. Favoring Russians and Orthodox everywhere, it sought to turn these elements into Russian Christians. Russification, fostered by a central bureaucracy intolerant of diverse traditions, languages, and faiths, was supported for security reasons by the Orthodox clergy and the military. It represented a conscious attempt in the form of Great Russian domination to achieve Uvarov's vague concept of nationalism,[6] and paralleled policies of some other European countries in the age of neo-imperialism. Among those who suffered most were Baltic Germans, Finns, and Armenians who had shown unswerving loyalty to the imperial regime.

Russification was introduced in Finland and intensified in the western borderlands. Finland, which had enjoyed the broadest autonomy of any region of the empire, began in 1890 to experience gradual Russian encroachment. The independent Finnish postal service was abolished (1890), and the Russian language was later introduced forcibly into

---

[5] See below, p. 384.
[6] See above, p. 294.

certain Finnish institutions. In 1899, in violation of the Finnish constitution, St. Petersburg proclaimed that imperial laws would take precedence over Finnish laws. Under the narrow-minded Governor-General N. I. Bobrikov (1898–1904), the separate Finnish army was abolished and the Finnish Senate had to speak Russian. Such high-handed measures provoked growing Finnish passive resistance and antagonism toward Russia.

In Russian Poland, remnants of autonomy were eliminated. In 1885 the Polish Bank became the Warsaw Office of the Russian State Bank; after 1885 all subjects in Polish schools, except the Polish language, were to be taught in Russian. Repression of Ukrainian nationalism intensified, but nationalist, democratic, and socialist movements, stimulated by literature from freer Ukrainian areas under Austrian rule, continued a slow growth. Mykhaylo Hrushevsky, a Russian-born Ukrainian scholar made professor of Ukrainian history at Lwow University in Austrian Poland in 1894, continued Drahomaniv's tradition. In the Baltic provinces the regime launched a campaign against Lutheranism and separate German schools. The German University of Dorpat was closed, then reopened as the Russian Iurev University. Police and court systems there were Russified, embittering many loyal public servants.

The anti-Semitic Alexander III and Nicholas II enacted stringent laws against Jews. Pobedonostsev, Alexander's one-time tutor and later minister, declared: "One third will die out, one third will become assimilated with the Orthodox population, and one third will emigrate." Pogroms—unofficial mob violence against Jews and their shops—grew more frequent and were often condoned by the authorities. The "Temporary Rules" of 1882, enforced until 1905, forbade Jews to live outside towns or large villages and forced them into business and certain professions. In 1887 the Ministry of Education established Jewish quotas for secondary schools and universities: ten percent in the Pale of Settlement, three percent in the capitals, and five percent elsewhere. Jews were virtually prohibited from becoming lawyers and lost the right to vote in *zemstvo* elections while still having to pay *zemstvo* taxes! Jewish responses were to emigrate, especially to the United States, or enter the revolutionary movement. Bigoted decrees undermined the loyalty of minorities especially in western borderlands and helped stimulate revolutions in 1905 and 1917.

Suggested Additional Reading

AMBLER, EFFIE. *Russian Journalism and Politics 1861–1881: The Career of A. S. Suvorin* (Detroit, 1972).

EMMONS, TERENCE. *The Emancipation of the Russian Serfs* (N.Y., 1970).

———. *The Russian Landed Gentry and the . . . Emancipation* (Cambridge, England, 1968).

GREENBERG, LOUIS S. *The Jews in Russia*, 2 vols. (New Haven, 1951).

HRUSHEVSKY, MICHAEL. *A History of Ukraine* (New Haven, 1941).

MILLER, FORREST. *Dmitrii Miliutin and the Reform Era . . .* (Nashville, 1968).

MOSSE, W. E.   *Alexander II and the Modernization of Russia* (New York, 1958).

PAGE, STANLEY.   *The Formation of the Baltic States* (Cambridge, Mass., 1959).

RIEBER, ALFRED, ed.   *The Politics of Autocracy* . . . (Paris, 1966).

ROTHFELS, H.   "The Baltic Provinces," *JCEA*, vol. 4 (July 1944), pp. 117–46.

THADEN, E. C.   *Conservative Nationalism in 19th Century Russia* (Seattle, 1964).

VAKAR, NICHOLAS.   *Belorussia* . . . (Cambridge, Mass., 1956).

VOLIN, L.   "The Russian Peasant . . . ," in C. Black, *Rewriting* . . . , pp. 292–311.

25

Social and Economic Development

AFTER 1861, political development was slow, but Russia underwent major socioeconomic change as the Emancipation provided a key to modernization. Towns grew and railroads and factories were built at an increasing rate. Profound social alterations accompanied this economic surge. As the nobility and clergy declined, a dynamic professional middle class emerged, a small industrial bourgeoisie, a better-off (*kulak*) peasant element, and an industrial proletariat. The old social system weakened despite state aid to traditional privileged classes designed to enable them to cling to their positions and status. How much capitalism developed in Russia and how deeply it affected the peasantry are questions still debated by Soviet and Western historians. Western scholars emphasize the persistence of traditional communal agriculture, while Soviet historians, following Lenin's *The Development of Capitalism in Russia* (first published in 1898; in final form, 1906), stress peasant differentiation and the triumph of capitalism and the bourgeoisie. What effects did the Emancipation have on the economic and social position of the peasantry and the nobility? What problems did Russia face in industrializing and how did ministers of finance attempt to solve them? How did the Great Reforms affect Russian society and the church?

AGRICULTURE

The Emancipation triggered the development of a money economy and capitalist relationships but failed to solve the problems of the peasantry and nobility. For most peasants the period 1861–1905 was apparently an era of increasing misery and discontent.[1] They were personally free, but whether they had benefited economically from the Emancipation remained unclear. Increasing by almost one million persons per year, the rural population rose from roughly 50 million in 1861 to 79 million in 1897. Especially in the fertile, overpopulated Black Soil provinces there was growing pressure on the land, and land prices rose rapidly. Noble "cut-offs" at the Emancipation had made peasant allot-

[1] G. T. Robinson, *Rural Russia Under the Old Regime* (New York, 1949), p. 111.

343

ments in European Russia in 1877 smaller than those of peasants under serfdom. Between 1877 and 1905, the average allotment per household declined by about one third. Peasant tax burdens with redemption charges and *zemstvo* dues added to their former obligations, rose considerably despite state efforts to reduce them by abolishing the poll tax (1886), lowering redemption debts and granting partial moratoria. Even in the Black Soil region most peasants could not meet their taxes from allotments alone. Their arrears rose until in 1900 they exceeded a peasant's average annual tax assessment for 1896–1900.[2] Peasant woes were compounded by heavy state reliance on indirect taxes, especially on liquor, falling hardest on those least able to pay.

The peasant's problem was less insufficient land than ignorance of and inability to use new techniques to increase productivity. Russian peasant allotments, averaging 35 acres of allotment land per household in 1877, were almost four times as large as the average French farm. To be sure, in the Black Soil region allotments were smaller, ranging down to 16 acres per household in Poltava province. Yields per acre were also far lower than in western Europe or even the United States. Out of ignorance and tradition, Russian peasants failed to fertilize the land thoroughly, plow thoroughly, and diversify and rotate their crops. Under a system of periodic repartition, there was little incentive to improve the land and much reason to exploit it ruthlessly.

Rather than adopting new techniques, Russian peasants found less satisfactory solutions. Communes and individual households bought or rented additional land. By 1900 they rented some 52.7 million acres, mostly in small plots. Aided by the Peasant Bank, created in 1883, peasants between 1897 and 1903 purchased almost 15 million acres.[3] But their land hunger drove up prices so high that fewer could afford to buy subsequently. From rented lands, despite feverish exploitation, they received barely a subsistence wage. This "hunger renting" and an increasing shortage of work animals revealed the peasant's plight. In 1900, workhorses averaged only about one per household.

Many peasants left their villages temporarily or permanently. During the industrial spurt of the 1890s, many, especially in the central provinces, sought seasonal employment. Village authorities usually allowed this practice if they returned in the spring to plow the fields and pay their share of taxes. In the Black Soil provinces, a more common solution was migration, at first to New Russia, the north Caucasus, and the Trans-Volga, later to Turkestan and Siberia. During the 1870s and 1880s many departed illegally; later the state fostered settlement of Russia's vast Asian domains. From 1894 to 1903, emigration to Asia reached a peak of some 115,000 annually, many taking the new Trans-Siberian Railroad. But in rural areas of European Russia, natural population increase was almost 14 times the net loss from emigration. In forest provinces during the off season, peasants relied heavily on traditional handicrafts to eke out their incomes. These crafts were carried on inde-

---

[2] Ibid., p. 96.
[3] Ibid., p. 101.

pendently in peasant huts, by primitive cooperatives, or were organized by outside entrepreneurs. Handicrafts which had to compete with factory industry disappeared or declined, but in 1900 they still employed more people than factory industry.

How far had peasant differentiation and capitalist development proceeded in the Russian village? In *The Development of Capitalism in Russia*, Lenin asserted that about 17 percent of the peasantry had become kulaks ("rural bourgeoisie") and 11 percent "rural proletarians," lacking arable land or livestock. Communal agriculture, he claimed, was disintegrating. Lenin pointed to a marked difference between regions of the north and center following the "Prussian pattern," in which landowners remained dominant and feudal survivals were strong, and the borderlands, where the "American pattern" of an independent farmer class was accelerating capitalist development. Disputing Lenin's findings were Populists who affirmed that the *mir* (peasant commune) remained unshaken and the Russian peasantry was still fundamentally equal in land and wealth. The American scholar, G. T. Robinson, who takes a middle position in this controversy, notes how few Russian farmers, only 150,000 in 1906, had fully consolidated holdings like those in the United States. The collective traditions of the *mir* still predominated: in 1905 about three fourths of peasant allotments in European Russia were still of the repartitional type.

The nobility, despite official favoritism, was declining economically. The Emancipation statutes, though drawn to favor the landowners, brought ruin or decline to most. Technological backwardness, slowness to adjust to new conditions, and lack of initiative were more to blame than shortage of capital. Many lords, unable to compete with more efficient west European producers, sold out. On private non-allotment land in European Russia, half of it noble, the average yield of spring wheat in 1899–1903 was only one third that of lands in Germany. In the south some large plantations operated by hired labor persisted, but noble landownership declined in every province and decade from the Emancipation to 1905 from some 197 million acres in 1877 to 140 million in 1905. At first, townsmen were the chief buyers of noble lands; later, peasant purchases gained much more rapidly.

Russian agriculture, noble and peasant alike, was adversely affected by the late 19th century world agrarian crisis despite some improvements in technology and greater regional crop specialization. Increased European imports of North American grains intensified competition, lowered grain prices, and depressed peasant living standards. Until 1900, Russian grain exports continued to rise but more slowly than before. By 1905 the agrarian problem of Russia was becoming a crisis.

INDUSTRY AND FINANCE TO 1891

The Crimean defeat ushered in a new chapter in Russian economic history marked by the development of a capitalist economy. Soviet historians, regarding the entire period of 1861–1917 as Russia's capitalist phase, assert that the country between 1861 and 1890 was transformed

MAP 25–1

Russian Industry by 1900

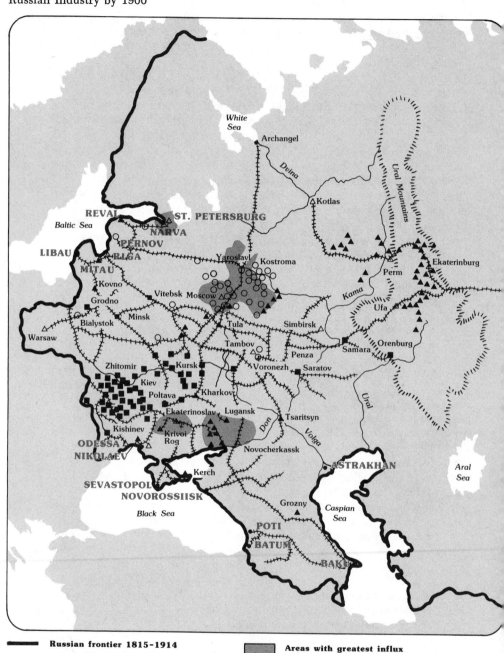

	Russian frontier 1815–1914
┼┼┼┼┼	Railways by 1900
▲	Heavy industry
○	Textiles
■	Manufactured food
△	Important manufacturing centres

Areas with greatest influx of workers from other areas

LIBAU — Ports with flourishing import and export trades by 1900

Adopted with permission of Macmillan Publishing Co., Inc. from *Russian History Atlas* by Martin Gilbert. Cartography by Martin Gilbert. Copyright © 1972 by Martin Gilbert.

swiftly into a capitalist industrial country. On the other hand, Western scholars tend to regard those decades as an era of slow growth preparatory to rapid development after 1890. How did Russia's modernization and industrialization differ from that of western countries? Did Russia pursue a new path and set a pattern for the modernization of backward countries, or was this basically a process of Westernization; that is, of following techniques worked out earlier in western Europe?

Whatever the model, the Russian government played a more prominent role than in the West, especially in railroad construction. Alexander II's government, realizing the disastrous consequences of economic backwardness, quickly eliminated hampering restrictions: tariffs were lowered, and an influx of foreign products and capital was encouraged. The regime promptly recognized the need for railroads, first for strategic and later for economic reasons. The Finance Minister wrote Alexander II: "Without railways and mechanical industries Russia cannot be considered secure in her boundaries. Her influence in Europe will fall to a level inconsistent with her international power and her historic significance."[4] Because the impoverished Treasury could not afford to build railroads, private companies were encouraged to do so. In 1865 the government, deciding that Russia must have an extensive railroad network, provided subsidies and guarantees to numerous small private firms to construct lines which the state considered essential. There ensued an orgy of construction and speculation comparable to the railway boom at the same time in the United States. Many of these private concerns, poorly financed and inefficient, went bankrupt in the depression of 1873–1876, and many others borrowed heavily from the state. In the 1880s, the government reversed its policy, constructed the major lines itself, bought up many private railways, and created an expanding state-owned system. The pace of construction slowed, but by 1890 major economic regions were interconnected and linked with the principal ports. The railway network grew from only 600 miles in 1857 to 11,730 miles in 1876 and more than 22,000 miles in 1895.

Meanwhile the Finance Ministry, seeking to overcome Russia's poverty, faced complex and interrelated problems: stabilizing the currency, balancing the budget, financing railway construction, achieving an active trade balance, and attracting foreign investment in industry. Finance Minister Michael Reutern (1861–1878) took office with a Treasury impoverished by war, a badly unbalanced budget, and a ruble the value of which had been undermined. A new State Bank was established with branches throughout Russia. The creation in 1862 of a unified state budget enabled the Finance Ministry to coordinate the government's economic activities and develop a degree of state planning. Reutern discovered that heavy foreign imports, low tariff rates, and rising state expenditures on railways were producing large budget deficits. To conceal Russia's poverty, he set up an extraordinary budget, financed by foreign loans, for new arms and railroad construction. To

---

[4] T. von Laue, *Sergei Witte and the Industrialization of Russia,* (New York, 1963) p. 9.

attract foreign loans, Reutern tried but failed to make the ruble convertible into a given amount of gold. To increase revenues, he developed indirect taxation and raised the poll tax rates. The balance of trade and payments, however, remained negative, evidence that Russia was living beyond its means. The Russo-Turkish War of 1877–1878 wrecked Reutern's efforts and plunged the country deeply into debt.

Finance Minister N. K. Bunge (1881–1886) tried a different approach. A modest rise in tariff rates restricted imports, produced additional revenue, and helped protect Russian industry. Seeking long-term economic improvement, Bunge abolished most direct taxes on the peasantry, including the poll tax, and set up peasant and noble land banks to assist them with credit. Unable to balance the budget, Bunge resorted to more foreign loans until interest on them consumed more than one third of the budget.

Coming to the Finance Ministry from industry, I. A. Vyshnegradskii (1887–1892) reversed Bunge's policies. He balanced the budget and built up a surplus by reducing expenditures and increasing state revenues. This policy required heavy taxation of the peasantry and forcing grain exports to the limit to pay for imports from abroad. "We must export though we die," declared Vyshnegradskii prophetically. A drastic tariff was enacted in 1891, imposing levies averaging one third the value of imports, which remained the cornerstone of Russian state economic policy until 1917. Providing almost one fourth of state revenues, it improved the balance of payments and increased Russia's bullion reserves. When the harvest of 1891 failed, however, the overburdened peasantry had no reserves. The government admitted: "Our peasant economy has come to a full collapse and ruin . . ." and disastrous famine forced Vyshnegradskii from office. Down to 1892 the Finance Ministry, despite a variety of approaches, had found no formula to overcome Russia's poverty.

Until 1890 industrial development proceeded at a modest pace. At first the emancipation settlement did little to assist it and contributed to the industrial slump of the early 1860s, especially in Ural industries which had employed mostly serf labor. Industrial growth was hampered by low peasant purchasing power, shortage of domestic capital and skilled labor, and an inadequate transportation system. Also the *mir* blocked permanent peasant migration to the cities. Relaxation of restrictions on importation of foreign capital and goods and the judicial and administrative reforms of the 1860s, however, created a more favorable climate for business activity. The government gradually lost its fear of industrialization and in order to strengthen Russia's position in world affairs, accepted it by the 1890s as a central goal.

Before 1890, although small commodity production and handicrafts predominated, strong bases were laid for large-scale industry, especially in textiles and food processing. Among domestic manufactures, only the textile industry had an assured home market. The per capita consumption of cotton goods roughly doubled between 1860 and 1880. Sugar refining expanded markedly, and, stimulated by greater domestic consumption, sugar began to be exported. Metallurgy, however, developed slowly, and Russia's share in world production of cast iron fell during the first post-Emancipation decades. During the 1880s, the Donets Basin became an important iron and steel region. Most of its factories were owned by foreign capitalists, who received favorable prices, especially for iron rails, from the government. The English capitalist, John Hughes, established a large factory at Iuzovka (now Donetsk) in the heart of this region. Southern iron and steel plants were more modern and productive than those of the Urals. Also in the 1870s the oil industry began to grow rapidly at Baku in the Transcaucasus.

Private capitalism now flourished in Russia. Between 1861 and 1873 357 joint-stock companies were formed with a capital of over a billion rubles, a vast increase over pre-Emancipation days. The Russian government strongly encouraged private companies and credit facilities. Native entrepreneurs, however, were too few, their time horizons too restricted, and their methods too antiquated for rapid industrial and commercial development. In the 1880s industrial growth remained sluggish as the impoverished villages checked demand.

FINANCE AND INDUSTRY: THE SPURT OF THE 1890s

The achievements of the preparatory era permitted major financial gains and fostered the industrial boom of the 1890s. Both were attributable largley to Sergei Iu. Witte, Minister of Finance (1892–1903), perhaps the ablest minister of the late tsarist period. Of German background, Witte graduated from the new Odessa University and made a brilliant career in private business before entering state service as a railway expert. Self-confident and dynamic, he moved easily among bureaucrats and business leaders. After being appointed finance minister, he reformed the Ministry into an efficient general staff for economic development. In his first budget report, Witte affirmed that the government was responsible for the whole economy and should develop its resources and "kindle a healthy spirit of enterprise." Firmly backed by Alexander III, he developed the boldest and most ambitious economic program since that of Peter the Great.

The Witte System was based upon considerations of power politics. "International competition does not wait," he warned. Unless Russia developed its industries swiftly, foreign concerns would take root: "Our economic backwardness may lead to political and cultural backwardness as well." Thus Witte's work was filled with a sense of urgency and the belief that Russia's industrialization was a race against time. His plan was to stimulate private enterprise and exploit Russian resources through a vast state-sponsored program of railway construction which would trigger expansion of heavy industry, especially metallurgy and fuels. Developing these industries would spark light industry; eventually agriculture would perk up as growing industrial cities demanded more foodstuffs. General prosperity would raise tax yields and recompense the government for heavy initial capital outlays.

Witte's program, with its concentration on heavy industry and substituting the role of the state for timid and inadequate private capital in many ways presaged Stalin's more ruthless Five Year Plans.[5] An experiment in state capitalism, it suggested a way by which a backward country could overtake the industrial frontrunners. Finance Minister Witte channeled about two thirds of the government's revenues into economic development to fuel Russia's first major industrial boom. His most ambitious project was building the Trans-Siberian Railroad, which was pushed through on schedule on an economy budget. As other parts of his planned development of Siberia, he promoted peasant colonization and new shipping routes and envisioned the Trans-Siberian line as the means to penetrate and dominate Asian markets. Russia's European rail network was doubletracked, and lines were built to major ports. Everywhere construction was carried on at a feverish pace: from 1898 through 1901 more than 1,900 miles of railway line were constructed annually. Such construction stimulated a boom in the iron and steel industry of the Donets Basin, where the plants were large, modern, and used the latest German and American technology. The Witte upsurge seized hold of all industry, but especially heavy industry. The average industrial growth rate in the 1890s was approximately eight percent annually, the highest of any major European country. During that decade pig iron output trebled, oil production rose two and one half times, and coal output doubled.

Witte's financing of the industrial upsurge was masterful. Heavy indirect taxation, falling largely on peasants and lower class townsmen, met most ordinary expenses and a state liquor monopoly with stores throughout Russia increased government revenues considerably. The high tariff of 1891 on imports produced large sums for the Treasury. For extraordinary expenditures, especially railroad construction, Witte relied chiefly upon foreign loans, primarily French. He was favored by an abundance of foreign money seeking investment and by the Franco-Russian Alliance of 1893, which induced the French government to foster private investment in Russia. In order to balance his overall budget, Witte had to continue borrowing abroad, but he maintained a high credit rating there by prompt payment of dividends in gold. To preserve a favorable trade balance, he forced agricultural exports and curtailed imports, and, above all, he sought a stable currency convertible in gold. After stabilizing the paper ruble, he increased the state gold reserves, and in 1897 finally put Russia on the gold standard. This action enhanced Russia's international prestige, created a stable currency, and encouraged foreign investment.

In the late 1890s, however, the Witte system showed signs of strain and came under increasing public attack. Ultranationalist publications blamed it for Russia's supposed agricultural decline and growing foreign economic influence. Witte's vast authority and advocacy of ever wider reforms (notably abolition of the *mir*) in order to promote industry aroused the opposition of conservative and Slavophile officials, especially Pobedonostsev. They and Nicholas II opposed Witte's efforts to streamline the autocracy and adapt it to 20th century needs. Despite

---

[5] See below, pp. 506–12.

his strenuous public relations campaigns and optimistic statistical predictions, his program of industrialization through sacrifice became ever more unpopular. Growing exhaustion of the lower-class taxpayer, agricultural downturn, and the industrial depression which began in 1900 doomed his system. Nonetheless, Witte had proved that rapid economic growth was possible in a backward country if the state mobilized its resources. His system laid a sound basis for subsequent Russian industrial development.

SOCIAL CHANGE

Russia's social structure changed fundamentally after 1861. The old categories of the class (*soslovie*) system[6] persisted in official usage, but traditional privilege was undermined by new elements which did not fit the old patterns: a professional middle class, a capitalist peasant element, and an industrial working class. Industrialization, urbanization, and legislation of the Great Reforms promoted social mobility. The Emancipation deprived hereditary noblemen of their chief privilege, the right to own serfs, and the new courts largely disregarded estate, title, and 'wealth. Universal military service, abolition of the poll tax, and participation in the *zemstva* lessened peasant isolation from society, while increasing sales of noble lands to merchants and peasants reduced the nobility's economic power and social prestige.

After 1880, however, the development of new social groupings was hampered by a conservative government anxious to preserve the traditional order. Separate land banks for peasants and noblemen gave the latter preferential treatment, and some schools were reserved for noble children. The *zemstva* and city *dumy*, in which social groups mingled, were severely restricted in power and function. New groups, such as industrial workers and kulaks, failed to break cleanly with tradition or form economic organizations to promote their interests.

The census of 1897, more informative about social groups than previous ones, nonetheless retained the old categories. Hereditary noblemen, including top civil and military officials and some professional men, with their dependents numbered 1,220,169 persons. Many embodied the attitudes of the novelist Ivan Goncharov's Oblomov, a superfluous, guilt-ridden landowner trained only for leisure who spent most of his day in a bathrobe trying to get up. Most of the 630,119 "personal noblemen" listed were government servants. Ecclesiastics of all faiths numbered 342,927, over two thirds of them Orthodox and about nine percent Catholic. In the Orthodox hierarchy, the small but privileged "black" (monastic) clergy, often of noble origin, held the top positions. The "white" (parish) clergy were not far above the peasantry in social and economic status. Townsmen were divided into three categories according to tax payments. The two top groups, "distinguished citizens" (342,927) and "merchants" (281,179), dominated urban economic and political affairs and included many professional people. Other city

---

[6] See above, p. 155.

dwellers—*meshchane* (13,386,392)—included artisans, petty trades-men, and most urban workers. The bulk of Russia's population still con-sisted of peasants (96,896,648), including industrial workers who still belonged legally to the commune. Cossacks (2,928,842), mostly inde-pendent farmers, were listed separately.

Soviet sources claim that the working class was far larger than offi-cial statistics suggested. The number of industrial workers employed in manufacturing, mining, and transportation in European Russia grew from 706,000 in 1865 to 2,208,000 in the years 1900–03. On the basis of his research, Lenin listed the following breakdown of mass groups under the 1897 census: well-off smallholders, 23.1 million; poor small-holders, 35.8 million; proletarians, 22 million; and semi-proletarians, 63.7 million.[7] In Moscow province about 1900, noted Lenin, 44 percent of peasant families and in Vladimir province 56 percent labored not in agriculture but in industry, trade, or services, but official statistics, to conceal the proletariat's growth, still listed them as peasants.

Western scholars generally adopt a position between these tsarist and Soviet claims. Hugh Seton-Watson, using official figures for 1904, lists 1,663,800 factory workers subject to inspection by the Finance Ministry. More than 80 percent of the workers in large cities by this time were permanent residents who had broken their ties with the village.[8] The Emancipation, notes Gliksman, swelled an industrial labor force of some 800,000 by creating a manpower reservoir of some four million peasants, left landless or with dwarf allotments. They were slower than new workers in the West to learn industrial skills, thus delaying the de-velopment of a modern class of industrial workers. As late as 1900, 90 percent of Russian urban workers were still legally classified as peasants, still belonged to the commune, sent part of their earnings to the village, and returned there periodically. Miserable living conditions and low industrial pay delayed the formation of a hereditary working class. Some 60 percent of workers, noted the 1897 census, lived alone, many in filthy employer-owned barracks. Only skilled and semiskilled workers could afford to maintain a regular family life; the unskilled usually left their families in the village. Slowly conditions improved, and a separate industrial working class took shape; but even in 1917, Gliksman empha-sizes, it represented a small fraction of the population and remained half-proletarian, half-peasant.[9]

Lenin, claims Seton-Watson,[10] exaggerated the extent of differentia-tion among the peasantry before 1905. Kulaks neither comprised a social class nor were they regarded as such by other villagers. Instead peas-ants, mainly conscious of their difference from nobles and townsmen, retained a strong sense of solidarity. Rural class conflict, if it existed, pitted peasant against nobleman, not kulak against poor peasant. On the

[7] V. I. Lenin, *Sobranie sochinenii*, 5th edition vol. 3, p. 505.

[8] H. Seton-Watson, *The Russian Empire* (Oxford, 1967), p. 540.

[9] Jerzy G. Gliksman, "The Russian Urban Worker: From Serf to Proletarian," in Cyril Black, *The Transformation of Russian Society* (Cambridge Mass., 1960), pp. 312–317.

[10] Seton-Watson, *The Russian Empire*, pp. 545–46.

David MacKenzie

Old wooden dwelling in Riazan

eve of the 1905 Revolution, Russia was undergoing profound social change, but new groupings based on economic interest had not yet replaced the old categories. The process was furthest advanced among professional men, least among peasants.

During the post-Emancipation era, the state acted, albeit reluctantly, to protect industrial workers and regulate factory conditions. In 1859 the governor-general of St. Petersburg, supported by progressive manufacturers, favored installing safety devices, improving sanitary conditions in the factories, and forbidding child labor under the age of 12. On the other hand, Moscow industrialists, like the British classical liberals, urged freedom of contract and unrestricted child labor. These attitudes reflected varying local conditions: St. Petersburg recruited labor from distant provinces and had to pay higher wages, whereas in Moscow abundant cheap labor was available from nearby rural districts. Thus St. Petersburg entrepreneurs put more emphasis on skill, labor productivity, and machinery. Finance Minister Bunge's regulatory legislation of 1882 reflected the views of the St. Petersburg group: It forbade child labor under the age of 12 and restricted hours for those under 15. There were too few inspectors to enforce this strictly, but their reports on deplorable factory conditions brought increased governmental intervention. A 14-hour day was the norm, and many workers were paid in kind under a type of industrial serfdom. In 1885, after worker disorders, legislation prohibited night work for women and boys under the age of

17 and required that wages be paid in money. The law of 1897 set a maximum of 11½ hours for all workers and ten hours for night work, but many manufacturers still evaded the regulations and workers opposed them. Before the 1905 Revolution, few Russian workers were unionized, and they lacked the right to strike or bargain collectively.

RELIGION

After 1855 the administration of the Orthodox Church remained stagnant while the need for reform became increasingly evident. The emperor was "the supreme defender and preserver of the dogmas of the ruling faith," but he rarely intervened directly in matters of dogma. The Holy Synod, which included the three metropolitans, the exarch of

Michael Curran

Leningrad—Church of the Savior's Blood—built on the site of Alexander II's assassination in 1881

Georgia, and eight or nine bishops appointed by the tsar, handled matters of dogma and discipline of the clergy, and administered church property and parochial schools. The dominant official in the Church was the Over-Procurator, a layman who since 1824 had enjoyed the status of a minister of state. He acted as intermediary between the tsar and Synod, was the only church official with direct access to the ruler, and really ran its affairs. Pobedonostsev[11] held this key post from 1880 to 1905. In 1914 the Orthodox Church had 64 dioceses and more than 50,000 priests. Lay officials, headed by the secretary of the consistory, a miniature over-procurator, ran diocesan affairs.

---

[11] See below, p. 384.

The Orthodox Church resembled closely the bureaucratic autocracy it served. Even minor matters required decisions by high lay officials so that often it took many months to get the repair of church buildings authorized. Parishioners had no part in selecting their priests nor in disbursing church funds. The priests lived among the villagers, but their seminary education and frequent collection of high fees for their services led to divergence in outlook. Priests were expected by the police to aid the authorities by reporting anything suspicious learned in confession. The moral tone of the monastic clergy was deplorable. A Kazan church publication in 1906 reported that the environs of Russian monasteries were populated largely by the offspring of their monks!

The state church was privileged and wealthy. By law a Russian was automatically considered Orthodox from birth unless he was inscribed officially as a member of another faith. Children of mixed marriages were supposed to be brought up as Orthodox. Salaries of bishops averaged 20 times those of industrial workers, and although sworn to poverty, they received additional revenue from monasteries and diocesan homes. Only the Orthodox could conduct missionary work freely and maintain church-related schools. Despite these manifold advantages, by 1900 the Orthodox Church, corrupt and worldly, was clearly decaying. Its influence with the Russian people was fading. Most intellectuals had left it, although in the early 20th century such conservative intellectuals as P. Struve, N. Berdiaev and S. Bulgakov led a back-to-the-church movement. Factory workers tended to be much less devout than the peasantry they had come from. Serious dissension developed between parish priests and the pampered church hierarchy; yet before 1905 attempts at church reform failed utterly. Russian Orthodoxy, unlike western Protestant and Catholic churches, was bound to a rigid autocracy and failed lamentably to adapt to a new age.

Other religious groups, especially after 1881, suffered discrimination and persecution. Dissenters were forbidden to construct new churches, ring church bells to announce services, and hold open religious processions. But all except extreme Sectarians could practice their faith, engage in trade and industry, and hold minor offices. Some sectarian groups, especially Stundists (similar to Baptists) and Dukhobors, were severely persecuted, and the latter were virtually compelled to emigrate. Official figures issued in 1901 that purposely underestimated the number of Dissenters listed only 1,028,437 Old Believers, 176,199 Sectarians, and 969,102 "others," whereas official data published in 1859 had listed 9,300,000 Old Believers. Curtiss estimates that in 1900 the Old Believers (17,500,000) and Sectarians (1,500,000) constituted more than 15 percent of the population of the Russian Empire, leaving out Poland and Finland.[12] Catholics and Jews were persecuted less for their religion than for national and economic reasons. The regime made no concerted effort to undermine Islam in the Caucasus, Volga valley, and Central Asia where it was widely practiced. Religious discrimination, however,

---

[12] J. S. Curtiss, *Church and State in Russia, 1900–1917* (New York, 1940), pp. 137–39.

doubtless contributed much to rising minority dissatisfaction with the imperial regime.

Suggested Additional Reading

BOOKS

CURTISS, J. S.   Church and State in Russia . . . : 1900–1917 (New York, 1940).
DILLON, E. J.   The Eclipse of Russia (London, 1918).
LENIN, V. I.   The Development of Capitalism in Russia (Moscow, 1956).
LYASHCHENKO, P. I.   History of the National Economy of Russia . . . (New York, 1949).
MAYNARD, JOHN.   The Russian Peasant and Other Studies (London, 1942).
ROBINSON, G. T.   Rural Russia under the Old Regime (New York, 1932, 1949).
ROSTOW, W. W., ed.   The Economics of Take-Off . . . (London, 1963).
TREADGOLD, DONALD.   The Great Siberian Migration (Princeton, 1957).
VON LAUE, T.   Sergei Witte & the Industrialization of Russia (New York, 1963).
WITTE, S. IU.   The Memoirs of Count Witte (New York, 1921).

ARTICLES

HELLIE, R.   "The Foundations of Russian Capitalism," SR, vol. 26, pp. 148–54.
GERSCHENKRON, A.   "Agrarian Policies & Industrialization . . . ," Cambridge Economic History, vol. 6, Pt. 2 (Cambridge, Eng., 1966).
PORTAL, R.   "The Industrialization of Russia," Cambridge Economic History, vol. 6, Pt. 2 (Cambridge, Eng., 1966).
SKERPAN, A.   "The Russian National Economy and Emancipation," in Essays . . . to George Vernadsky (Hamden, Conn., 1964), pp. 161–230.
VON LAUE, T.   "Russian Peasants in the Factory, 1892–1903," JEH, vol. 21, pp. 61–80.
———.   "Tsarist Labor Policy, 1895–1903," JMH, vol. 34, pp. 135–45.

26

Diplomacy and Empire

THE CRIMEAN DEFEAT shook tsarism, damaged its prestige and forced
Alexander II and his advisers to consider new external policies. Revealing the old army's inadequacy, the war exposed Russia to nationalist
agitation in the western borderlands and to British incursions along its
vulnerable southern frontiers. Russia could not maneuver freely until it
restored its Black Sea defenses and cleaned up matters left from Nicholas' reign: unrest in Poland, resistance in the Caucasus, and unstable
boundaries in Central Asia. Absorbed in domestic change, especially
army reform, Russia could not fight a major war and needed to break up
the Crimean coalition. Alexander's closest advisers agreed that the
Crimean defeat must be avenged and prewar frontiers regained but disagreed over means. Generally, the Foreign and Finance ministries advocated caution and traditional diplomacy, while the War Ministry,
Asiatic Department, and army commanders urged expansion along the
southern frontiers to restore Russian prestige by force. Russia's viceroy
in the Caucasus, Prince A. I. Bariatinskii, advocated that region's speedy
pacification and use as a base to conquer Central Asia and threaten
Britain in India. He viewed Russia's mission as bringing European
civilization and Christianity to Asia, but he failed to convert Alexander
II to reckless expansion there. The Emperor believed that the empire's
European and Balkan frontiers were more vital, and the Eastern Question, he noted, "interests us more than all that happens in the rest of Europe." Alexander would not adopt unreservedly Foreign Minister A. M.
Gorchakov's preference for working with the European powers in the
Balkans, yet his hatred of revolutionary movements led him to oppose
a Panslav crusade there. Lacking any overall plan, the Emperor was
pushed this way and that by conflicting advice. Like previous Russian
rulers, he could not separate the Polish and Turkish issues nor overcome Austrian opposition to Russian predominance in the Balkans.

During the half century after 1855 Russia pacified the Caucasus,
conquered Central Asia, and advanced in the Far East. Except between
1894 and 1904, when Russia was preoccupied with its expansion in the
Far East, official Russian diplomacy focused on Europe and the Balkans

and aimed generally to preserve a balance of power and cooperate with other powers to maintain peace. At key junctures (1878 and 1885), Russian leaders, to prevent war with major powers, made concessions which distressed the advocates of a unilateral, forward foreign policy. In 1904, however, the adventurists temporarily dominated the leadership itself with disastrous results, i.e. the Russo-Japanese War. A recent Soviet account claims with exaggeration that "landowner interests" through a court elite still largely determined tsarist policy, though mercantile and industrial influences were growing. How much influence did military and Panslav elements exert on policy decisions? How did the Foreign Ministry's role change during this era? Why did Russia expand in Central Asia[1] and the Far East and become involved in war with Japan in 1904?

RELATIONS WITH EUROPE TO 1875

In the first post-Crimean War years, antagonism toward Austria and Britain drew Russia closer to France. Though Napoleon III refused to cancel the humiliating Black Sea clauses of the Paris Treaty, France and Russia cooperated against Austria to promote Rumanian independence and the nationalist course of Prince Michael Obrenović of Serbia; and Russia's benevolent neutrality and French support of Sardinia against Austria in 1859 contributed to Italian unification. The Polish revolt of 1863[2] ended this Franco-Russian entente and produced Russo-Prussian cooperation against the rebels. This change enabled Gorchakov to defy Western demands for Polish amnesty and autonomy and to emerge as triumphant spokesman of a resurgent Russia. The subsequent Russo-Prussian alliance was cemented by Alexander II's respect for his uncle, King William I of Prussia.

During the 1860s Otto von Bismarck of Prussia exploited Russia's dislike for the Paris Treaty and domestic preoccupation to unify Germany by force. Originally considering Bismarck his pupil, the vain Gorchakov later had to recognize the Prussian statesman as his master. During the Austro-Prussian War of 1866, Russia tied down Austrian troops which might have fought Prussia, thus gaining revenge for similar Austrian action during the Crimean War. Prussia's defeat of France in 1871, aided by Russian benevolent neutrality, enabled Gorchakov, with Bismarck's support, to denounce the Black Sea clauses; the London Conference of 1871 recognized this high-handed action reluctantly. Now Russia could rebuild its Black Sea fleet and Crimean bases. Gorchakov thus achieved the peak of his career, but the price was high: a powerful German Empire, which upset the European balance and stretched ominously along Russia's exposed western frontiers.

Chancellor Bismarck sought to preserve his new Germany by keeping defeated France isolated. The emperors of Germany, Austria-Hungary, and Russia met and in 1873 formed the Dreikaiserbund (Three Em-

---

[1] See Problem 7 below, pp. 370–76.

[2] See above, p. 339.

perors' League), a loose and fragile entente based on similar conservative ideologies and institutions and a determination to keep Poland partitioned.

PANSLAVISM AND THE EASTERN QUESTION TO 1878

The Great Reforms made Russia more attractive to Habsburg and Ottoman Slavs, and Gorchakov's opposition to the Paris Treaty brought official Russian policy closer to nationalist and Panslav desires. In the Balkans in the post-Crimean era, Russia sought to rebuild prestige, regain influence over Orthodox Slavs, and obtain free access to the Turkish Straits. During the 1860s Gorchakov aimed to strengthen the Serbia of Michael Obrenović and encourage Serbian leadership of Balkan Christians against the Turks. Around Serbia formed a Balkan League including Greece and Montenegro, supplied with arms by the Russian War Ministry. Prince Michael, however, tempted by Austrian territorial offers, backed away from conflict, and his murder (May 1868) shattered the League and Russia's hopes of Balkan hegemony.

Bellicose Russian Panslavs exerted increasing influence as official Russia shifted to support the Balkan status quo and embrace the German powers. Panslavism had developed first among western Slavs, notably the Czechs, as a movement to unite Slav peoples culturally and free them from alien rule. Russian Panslavism, the offspring of Slavophilism and resurgent nationalism, renounced a cultural humanitarian emphasis for militant national imperialism. Regarding Russia as the superior "big brother" for "younger" Slav brethren of the west and south, its spokesmen often excluded Poles and other non-Orthodox Slavs from their proposed Slav federations. A small group of Russian noblemen, army officers, and writers, including Fedor Dostoevskii, expounded Panslav doctrines which stimulated sympathy among educated Russians for Slavs under foreign rule. N. Ia. Danilevskii's lengthy *Russia and Europe* (1872), the "Bible" of Panslavism, predicted Slav triumph in an "inevitable conflict" with the German world and formation of an all-Slav federation centering in Constantinople. R. A. Fadeev, a retired major general, proclaimed in 1869: "Russia's chief enemy . . . is the German race"; Russia must "extend her preeminence to the Adriatic or withdraw again beyond the Dnieper." Its historic mission was to lead Orthodox Slavs in war against the Germans until "the Russian reigning house covers the liberated soil of Eastern Europe with its branches under the supremacy of the tsar of Russia. . . ."[3] In western Europe Fadeev's pamphlet, translated into English in 1876, raised the spectre of Russian imperial rule of Slav satellite states all over eastern Europe.

Until 1875 only small, uninfluential groups in Russia advocated Panslav doctrines, but during the Balkan Crisis of 1875–78, using the Slav Committees of Moscow and St. Petersburg, Panslavs achieved temporary dominance. Earlier, the Moscow Committee had merely

---

[3] Fadeev, *Opinion on the Eastern Question* (London, 1876).

MAP 26–1a
Russia and the Balkans, 1876–1885

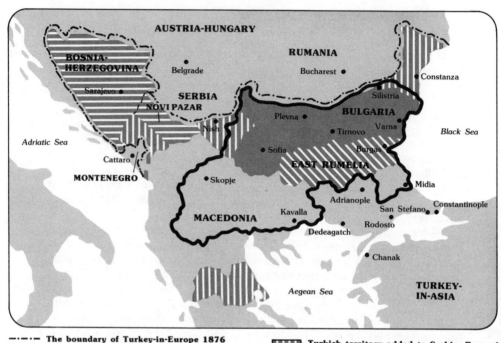

- — · — · — **The boundary of Turkey-in-Europe 1876**

━━━━━ **Russian proposal for an independent "Big Bulgaria", agreed to by the Turks at the Treaty of San Stefano 1878**

Bulgaria, autonomous, not independent, as allowed by Britain and Germany by the Treaty of Berlin 1878

Turkish territory added to Serbia, Rumania and Montenegro (who each gained their independence from Turkey) by the Treaty of Berlin 1878; and to Greece in 1881

Occupied by Austria-Hungary in 1878

Added to Bulgaria in 1885, when Bulgaria became fully independent of Turkey

educated a few foreign Slavs in Russia and aided Orthodox churches abroad. In 1867 it had sponsored a Slav Congress in Moscow, but Russian claims of primacy for Orthodoxy and the Russian language had alienated many western Slav guests. During the Balkan Crisis, the Panslavs exploited official indecisiveness and a divided foreign ministry to achieve unusual influence. Within the Ministry the Diplomatic Chancellery, staffed largely by diplomats of foreign origin with European connections and high social positions, handled relations with the powers and favored cooperation with Europe. The Asiatic Department, responsible for Asia, the Balkans, and the Near East, contained many Russian nationalists and persons of Balkan background. In the Balkans, its work was coordinated by the embassy in Constantinople, run between 1864 and 1877 by Count N. P. Ignatiev, a Panslav and former director of the

MAP 26–1b
Russia and the Balkans, 1912–1914

Countries in which Austrian and German influence
worked against Russia. Greece had a pro-German
King; Turkey a pro-German Minister of War and
virtual dictator; Bulgaria and Rumania had both
accepted alliance with the Central Powers

Russia's only two Balkans allies, both threatened by
Austria. Austria had created the state of Albania in
1912 in order to cut Serbia off from the sea

Adopted with permission of Macmillan Publishing Co., Inc. from *Russian History
Atlas* by Martin Gilbert. Cartography by Martin Gilbert. Copyright © 1972 by Martin
Gilbert.

Asiatic Department, who favored a unilateral Russian solution of the
Eastern Question.

In July 1875, Orthodox Serbs in the Turkish provinces of Herze-
govina and Bosnia revolted and were supported, at first unofficially, by
Serbia, Montenegro, and Russian Slav Committees. Alexander II and
Gorchakov, seeking a compromise European solution, proclaimed Rus-

sia's nonintervention, but Ambassador Ignatiev encouraged Balkan Slavs to aid the insurgents and the Serbian states in their fight against Turkey. Panslav activists in Russia, backed by the Heir and court ladies, organized public medical and financial aid for the embattled Slavs. Coordinating this aid program, the Slav Committees sent the Panslav general, M. G. Cherniaev, to direct Serbia's armies and recruited several thousand Russian volunteers to serve under him. To the Russian public and many Slavs abroad, Cherniaev symbolized unselfish Russian aid to the cause of Slav liberation, though he and his officers actually sought to transform Serbia into a Russian satellite. Finally, the Turks defeated his forces, and to prevent Serbia's destruction, Russia issued an ultimatum to the Turks in October 1876, which halted their advance.

Panslav agitation and Alexander II's sense of honor drew Russia into the costly Russo-Turkish War of 1877–78. Eventually the Russian army, after embarrassing setbacks at the Turkish fortress of Plevna, reached the outskirts of Constantinople. Shelving Gorchakov's program of cooperation with Europe, the tsar allowed Ignatiev to impose on the Turks the Treaty of San Stefano (March 1878), which envisioned a Big Bulgaria under Russian military occupation. This action provoked near panic in England, which feared Russian seizure of Constantinople and the Straits. England and Austria threatened war unless Russia submitted its treaty to the powers for approval. Alexander II, reluctant to fight a European coalition, agreed to the Congress of Berlin, directed by Chancellor Bismarck of Germany, which accorded Russia only its minimum aims: southern Bessarabia and Kars and Batum in the Caucasus. Big Bulgaria was reduced and split up, and Austria-Hungary occupied Bosnia and Herzegovina. Serbia, rebuffed by Russia, turned to Austria-Hungary. The Berlin Treaty recognized the independence of Serbia, Montenegro, and Rumania and Bulgaria's autonomy, but it preserved the Ottoman Empire and let Austria-Hungary dominate the western Balkans. Russian Panslavs and nationalists were furious; they and most government leaders agreed that Russia had been cheated and humiliated at Berlin.

THE CAUCASUS AND CENTRAL ASIA

Under Alexander II, Russia finally pacified the Caucasus. After Field Marshal Bariatinskii and his chief of staff, D. A. Miliutin,[4] had reorganized the Caucasus command, systematic operations by able commanders and assurances to Moslem tribesmen that they could retain their faith and customs brought speedy success. In 1859, Shamil, leader of the mountaineers, was forced to surrender, and by 1864, after many Circassians sought refuge in Turkey, the west Caucasus tribes had also been subdued. The Caucasus now provided Russia with secure natural boundaries in the south and bases for expansion in Asia.

Central Asia, lying east of the Caspian Sea and south of Siberia, became the next arena of Russian imperial expansion. At slight cost a

---

[4] See above, pp. 337–38.

region with vast potential wealth and over twice the size of France was annexed. For reasons resembling those in European overseas imperialism, Russia moved deep into Moslem Asia. No serious geographical or military obstacles hindered Russia from filling the Central Asian power vacuum, a policy favored by the War Ministry, frontier governors and generals, and nationalist diplomats. The Foreign Ministry, fearful of British reactions, opposed major advances, and the Finance Ministry pleaded poverty. Having to make the final decisions, the Emperor backed cautious advances, though at times frontier generals took action independently of the War Ministry, committing the government to unwanted conflicts and territory. The imperial family, tempted by glory and prestige, sanctioned most conquests and rewarded those responsible.

Between 1864 and 1885 small Russian forces seized most of Turkestan in Central Asia from the weak, poorly organized Moslem khanates of Kokand, Khiva, and Bukhara. In 1864, after Colonel Cherniaev and Colonel N. A. Verevkin closed the remaining gap in Russia's steppe defense lines, Cherniaev seized Chimkent fortress on the edge of the oasis region. Foreign Minister Gorchakov pledged publicly that Russia would halt there, but Cherniaev disregarded instructions to capture Tashkent (June 1865), Central Asia's chief commercial center. Though removed for insubordination, Cherniaev had committed Russia to absorb the

MAP 26–2
Central Asia, 1850–1914

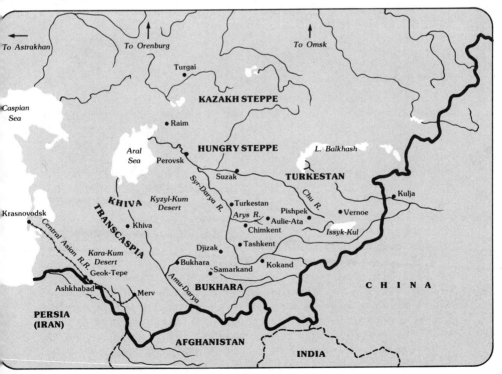

Moslem oases. In 1867 the Emperor appointed General K. P. Kaufman governor general of Turkestan. He built an administration from scratch, won native respect, and began developing Turkestan's resources. In 1873, Khiva became a Russian protectorate, and three years later Kokand khanate became Fergana province, later the empire's chief cotton-growing region. In 1881 General M. D. Skobelev conquered fierce Turkoman tribesmen to the southwest.

Under Alexander III Russia expanded until it reached British controlled areas. The occupation of Merv oasis (1884) caused fears ("Mervousness") in London for India's security. In 1885 Russia's advance to the Afghan border almost provoked war with Britain, but the two countries agreed to a compromise frontier and ended their acute rivalry in Central Asia. An agreement in 1895 gave Russia natural frontiers in the mountainous Pamir region. The Central Asian Railroad (begun in 1881) and the Orenburg-Tashkent line (completed in 1905) linked firmly with central Russia strategic Turkestan, which produced increasing amounts of cotton and silk for Russian industries.

After 1880, Anglo-Russian rivalry grew over weak and corrupt Persia. Military and civilian agents steadily extended Russian influence, and the Cossack Brigade of Persia (founded in 1879), led by Russian officers, served as a spearhead against the British. London considered Persia an outpost in its Indian defense system; Russian leaders saw it as ripe for the plucking. "The entire northern part of Persia," declared Count Witte, "was intended, as if by nature, to turn in the future . . . into a country under our complete protectorate." In Persia the British lost much ground to Russia in competition for trade, influence, and railway construction.

EUROPE AND THE BALKANS, 1881–1905

Under Alexander III, Russia remained at peace. The Emperor rarely interfered directly in foreign affairs and when he did, as in Bulgaria, disaster resulted. Policy was directed by Foreign Minister N. K. Girs, a highly trained, prudent, and experienced Swedish Protestant without fortune. He restrained nationalists and militarists, kept Russia out of war, and induced the Emperor to accept most of his views. Girs favored close relations with Germany, but finally, albeit reluctantly, had to prepare the way for an alliance with France.

A second Dreikaiserbund formed soon after Alexander III's accession. Germany in 1879 had allied with Austria-Hungary. Fearing diplomatic isolation and loathing republican France, Russian leaders swallowed their hurt pride and found Bismarck happy to admit them to "the German club." The three partners pledged neutrality if one were fighting a fourth power. The Dreikaiserbund guaranteed closure of the Straits to foreign warships and enhanced Russia's security, but it cost her freedom of action in the Balkans. Though accepting this policy of Girs, Alexander agreed with the Panslavs that Constantinople must eventually be Russian. Russian nationalists denounced the Dreikaiserbund as treason to Russia's national mission and predicted a Russo-German war.

Bonds linking the three eastern monarchies remained fragile, but the Panslavs could not oust Girs nor undermine his policy.

In the Balkans after 1878, Serbia became an Austrian satellite and Bulgaria a Russian one, but each great power alienated the leaders of its protégé. Commercial and political treaties bound Serbia to Austria, but King Milan's Austrophilism caused rising public sympathy for Russia in Serbia. In Bulgaria, liberated by Russia in 1877, conflicting policies by Russian ministries and tactlessness of Russian officers who dominated the army and administration stimulated national feeling.

In September 1885, a crisis erupted when Bulgarian nationalists seized control in Eastern Rumelia and proclaimed its union with Bulgaria under Prince Alexander of Battenberg. Refusing to recognize an act he had not initiated, Alexander III ordered home all Russian officers. To secure territorial compensation, Serbia attacked Bulgaria but met decisive defeat. Austria intervened to prevent disaster to its Serbian protégé and restored peace without territorial changes. The tsar then had the Bulgarian prince abducted to Russia and forced him to abdicate, while Baron Kaulbars, a Russian general, assumed control of Bulgaria. When the defiant Bulgarians chose Ferdinand of Coburg as their ruler, the tsar recalled his officers and broke relations. Britain and Austria, reversing their position of 1878, protested Russian bullying and supported Bulgarian unification. Russia lost its Bulgarian bastion temporarily, and its Balkan position was weakened. Austro-Russian tension, revealed anew by the Bulgarian crisis, destroyed the Dreikaiserbund. Russian nationalists, led by M. N. Katkov, fanned anti-German feeling, but Bismarck and Girs managed to preserve Russo-German diplomatic cooperation. Though their Reinsurance Treaty of 1887 did not square fully with the Austro-German alliance, it provided Russia and Germany with a measure of security. Russia, however, was already increasing its financial links with France, foreshadowing their subsequent alliance.

Russo-German relations deteriorated rapidly after Bismarck's forced retirement in 1890. When Emperor William II of Germany refused to renew the Reinsurance Treaty, the way lay open for reconciliation between autocratic Russia and republican France on bases of power and national interest. France needed a continental ally against Germany; Alexander III wished to restrict German power. French loans to Russia and fear that Britain might join the Triple Alliance pushed France and Russia together. In 1891, during the French fleet's official visit to Kronstadt, the tsar stood bareheaded while "La Marseillaise," anthem of revolution, was played. Common fear of Germany proved more potent than ideological hostility. France and Russia pledged in 1893 to aid one another with all their forces if either were attacked by Germany. As their defensive military alliance opposed the Triple Alliance of Germany, Austria, and Italy, two formidable power blocs split Europe, although room for diplomatic maneuver remained.

After the Bulgarian crisis a generally pacific Russian policy in the Balkans produced an accommodation with Austria-Hungary. With Russia absorbed in the Far East and Austria-Hungary weakened by domestic problems, they agreed in 1897 that neither power would annex

Balkan territory unless the Turks collapsed in Europe. In that event, Austria could annex Bosnia, Herzegovina, and Novi Pazar, occupied since 1878; other Turkish possessions would be divided so as to prevent predominance by a single Balkan state. The Straits would remain closed to foreign warships. Temporarily the rivals placed the Balkans "on ice," and even bitter rivalry of Serbia, Bulgaria, and Greece over Macedonia and a major uprising there failed to disrupt an accord which the Austrian and Russian rulers reaffirmed at Mürzsteg in 1903.

RUSSIA IN THE FAR EAST TO 1904

In the half-century after the Crimean War, Russia conquered the Maritime Province, penetrated north China, and encroached upon Japanese interests in Korea. In aims and methods, Russia's Far Eastern expansion resembled that of other European powers. At the expense of decaying Manchu China, Russia sought railroad concessions, commercial privileges, warm water ports, and spheres of interest.

Governor-General N. N. Muraviev (Amurskii) of Eastern Siberia (1847–61) exploited China's weakness and absorption in war against Britain and France to seize the Amur and Ussuri regions. Hitherto China had refused to recognize Russian control of the Amur basin, but Muraviev forced the local Chinese commander to confirm in the Treaty of Aigun (May 1858) Russia's claims to the Amur's left bank from the Aigun River to the sea and to place the Ussuri region under joint Sino-Russian administration. In June, Admiral Putiatin exploited the Western powers' defeat of China to conclude the Treaty of Tientsin, which granted Russia trading rights obtained earlier by Britain, France, and the United States. As Western forces prepared to attack Peking, Muraviev advanced southward and near the Korean frontier in July 1860 founded the port of Vladivostok ("Ruler of the East"). In December, Count Ignatiev negotiated the Treaty of Peking with China, which confirmed the previous treaties and gave Russia territory between the Ussuri River and the Pacific. In the 1960's China complained that Russia seized the Maritime Province illegally.

In the 1860s, St. Petersburg liquidated its Alaskan venture. The fur trade there was dwindling and the inefficient Russia-America Company was deeply in debt to the government. During the U.S. Civil War, Russia and the Union government shared hostility to England. Viewing Alaska as an economic burden and as indefensible against British Canada, Russian leaders decided to sell it to the United States. They hoped this action would create a balance of power in North America and increase Anglo-American rivalry. Since 1854 the Russian and American governments had discussed the sale of Alaska informally. In March 1867, Baron E. Stoeckl, the Russian ambassador, and Secretary of State William Seward signed a treaty transferring Alaska to the United States for $7,200,000. Stoeckl used $200,000 to bribe American Senators to ratify the treaty! Considering Alaska's present economic and strategic importance, the United States unwittingly had struck a rare bargain.

MAP 26–3
Russia in the Far East to 1914

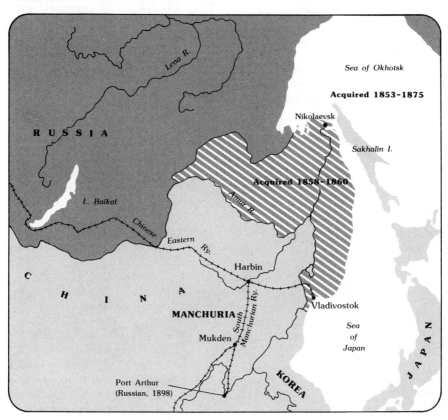

Russia's position in the Far East remained vulnerable. Siberia's settlement lagged, and Russian port facilities, naval bases, and overland communications were inadequate. To be sure, by the Treaty of St. Petersburg (1875) Russia had obtained from Japan the large offshore island of Sakhalin, valuable for oil and fisheries. Japan, however, modernizing rapidly, displayed increasing interest in the Asian mainland.

A group of Russian scholars, journalists, and military men known as Vostochniki (easterners), like the Panslavs for the Balkans, advocated further imperial expansion in Asia. With its essentially non-European culture and values, they argued, Russia was destined to develop or incorporate much of Asia and protect Europe from the "yellow peril." Mongolia and Sinkiang longed to join Russia, affirmed the explorer, M. N. Przhevalskii: "Those poor Asiatics look to the advance of Russian power with the firm conviction that its advent is synonymous with the beginning of a . . . life of greater security for themselves." V. P. Vasiliev, a leading Sinologist, predicted in 1893 that Russia would liberate Oriental peoples "oppressed by the tyranny of internecine strife and impotency." Prince E. E. Ukhtomskii, journalist and student of Oriental philosophy, who influenced Nicholas II deeply, believed that once opened by modern communications, Siberia would become Russia's Eldorado: "For Russia there is no other course than to become . . . a great power uniting the West with the East, or ingloriously and imperceptibly to tread the downward path." Count Witte[5] translated some of these vague imperial dreams into reality. Earlier Muraviev had suggested a transcontinental railroad, but Witte persuaded the government to start building the Trans-Siberian Railroad in 1891. Witte envisioned it as replacing the Suez Canal as the bearer of Russian and European goods to Oriental markets, and his memorandum of 1892 outlined a broad program of Russian economic expansion in the Far East.

The Sino-Japanese War of 1894, revealing China's weakness, stimulated European imperial powers to press forward. In 1895 Witte, to prevent Japan from securing a foothold on the Asian mainland, obtained Franco-German diplomatic support. Posing as guardians of China's "territorial integrity," the three powers insisted that Japan return to China the Liaotung Peninsula containing Port Arthur, a strategic warm-water port. Urging peaceful Russian economic penetration of north China, Witte favored a passive, friendly China as Russia's ally against Japan. By the Li-Lobanov agreement of 1896, negotiated by Witte with China's foreign minister, China authorized a private Russian-controlled corporation to build and operate a Chinese Eastern Railroad across northern Manchuria, shortening the route to Vladivostok by more than 300 miles. In 1898 Nicholas II, over Witte's objections and urged on by War Minister A. N. Kuropatkin, ordered Port Arthur occupied and forced China to grant Russia a 36-year lease of the Liaotung Peninsula, the very region Russia had compelled Japan to renounce in 1895! Constructing the South Manchurian Railroad from Port Arthur northward to Harbin where it joined the Chinese Eastern, the Russians dominated all Manchuria economically. In 1900 the Boxer Rebellion erupted in China against foreign imperialism. After the Boxers attacked Russian railways there, Kuropatkin's troops occupied Manchuria, and he told Witte that it would become a Russian protectorate like Bukhara.[6]

The Russian government was seriously divided over Far Eastern policy. As the Foreign Ministry lost control of the situation, Russia embarked upon an ill-considered, aggressive course. Foreign Minister V. N. Lamsdorf and Finance Minister Witte still favored peaceful economic penetration of China while avoiding conflict with Japan, but an adventurous clique of former Guards officers (A. M. Bezobrazov and V. M. Vonliarliarskii) and titled aristocrats (Grand Duke Alexander Mikhailovich and Count Vorontsov-Dashkov) converted Nicholas II to reckless expansion. Late in 1897 Bezobrazov had obtained a timber concession on the Yalu River on the Manchurian-Korean border, a first move toward Russian annexation of Korea, a region which Japan considered its rightful sphere. Naval leaders seeking Korean bases supported Bezobra-

[5] See above, pp. 349–51.

[6] *The Memoirs of Count Witte* (Garden City, 1921), vol. 1, p. 10.

zov's group. In May 1903 Bezobrazov became Secretary of State for Far Eastern Affairs, and Admiral E. I. Alekseev became Imperial Viceroy over the entire region east of Lake Baikal and responsible for relations with China, Korea, and Japan. Witte had warned the Foreign Ministry in vain that misunderstandings with Japan must be removed since "an armed clash with Japan in the near future would be a great disaster for us."

Japan sought accommodation with Russia. In 1901, the Ito mission visited St. Petersburg but failed to achieve agreement, partly because of Bezobrazov's growing influence with Nicholas II. Japan offered to guarantee Manchuria as a Russian sphere if Russia would respect Japanese predominance in Korea. Russian moderates, such as Witte, favored such a settlement, but Bezobrazov's group was supported by naval and military elements. Interior Minister V. K. Pleve declared that bayonets had made Russia, not diplomats, and that "in order to restrain revolution, we need a little victorious war." Nicholas II, blissfully confident, wrote William II of Germany: "There will be no war because I do not wish it." He and the extremists, grossly underrating Japan, disregarded clear warning of its impending action.

THE RUSSO-JAPANESE WAR (1904–1905)

As in the Russo-Turkish War of 1877, Russia blundered poorly prepared into a war which could benefit her little. Allied defensively with England since 1902 and enjoying American sympathy, Japan held the stronger diplomatic position because the Franco-Russian Alliance did not apply to the Far East. Russia's population, army, and fleet were far larger than Japan's, but the war was fought, more than 6,000 miles from Russia's industrial and population centers, and at the outset Japan was stronger on land and sea. Russian leaders were negligent and overconfident, and Admiral Alekseev, the commander in chief, was incompetent and at odds with the army commander, General Kuropatkin. The incomplete Trans-Siberian Railroad could transport only two divisions of reinforcements per month. From the start, the war was highly unpopular in Russia whose soldiers and officers could not understand why they were fighting on Chinese soil.

War began in January 1904 with sudden Japanese attacks on the scattered Russian fleet. Japanese land forces in Korea defeated weak Russian units on the Yalu River and moved into southern Manchuria. Port Arthur, the main Russian naval base, was besieged. Its Russian garrison fought heroically to repel several Japanese assaults only to have its commander surrender needlessly to the enemy. In Manchuria, the Japanese defeated the indecisive General Kuropatkin repeatedly. After the Battle of Mukden early in 1905, the greatest land battle hitherto in world history, Kuropatkin abandoned the city and retired northward. Japanese resources were nearly exhausted and Russian reinforcements kept arriving, but Russian morale was low from repeated defeats and a rising tide of revolution in European Russia. In February 1905,

Japan requested the president of the United States, Theodore Roosevelt, to mediate.

Then Russia suffered a final devastating blow. In October 1904 the Baltic Fleet was sent around the world to wrest control of the seas from Japan. While crossing the Dogger Bank in North Sea, Russian ships accidentally sank some English fishing boats, almost causing war with Britain. When Admiral Rozhdestvenskii's obsolescent Russian ships engaged Admiral Togo's main Japanese fleet in Tsushima Strait, most of them were destroyed or captured. After this humiliation, the tsar agreed to seek peace.

At the peace conference in Portsmouth, New Hampshire, Count Witte, heading the Russian delegation, rejected Japanese demands for an indemnity and for all of Japanese-occupied Sakhalin Island. Witte won American public sympathy, but the peace terms confirmed Russia's defeat. With the consent of prostrate China, Japan acquired the Liaotung Peninsula with Port Arthur and southern Manchuria. Russia recognized Japanese preeminence in Korea, while Japan permitted Russia to hold northern Manchuria and the Chinese Eastern Railroad.

The Russo-Japanese War, costing each side about $1 billion and 450,000 men killed and wounded, was futile but significant for Russia. Japan had halted Russia's imperial drive in the Far East and weakened her position there, but with northern Manchuria and the Maritime Province, Russia remained an important Pacific power. Her defeat weakened the Franco-Russian alliance and encouraged Germany to pursue an aggressive policy in Europe; but, ending British fears of Russian imperialism, it provided a basis for their subsequent rapprochement. This first major Asian victory over a European power began to undermine European imperialism in the Orient. Defeat by Japan discredited the tsarist regime at home and helped force it to grant important political and economic concessions to the populace.

PROBLEM 7: WHY DID RUSSIA EXPAND IN CENTRAL ASIA?

Between 1850 and 1895 Russians, moving south from the previously conquered Kazakh steppe, occupied the Syr and Amu river valley oases and advanced to the borders of Afghanistan and India. This expansion created Russian Central Asia, a large imperial domain which in 1914 covered 655,427 square miles and contained millions of Turkic Muslims with a culture wholly different from Russia's. Why should already vast tsarist Russia, absorbed by domestic problems and with an impoverished treasury move to the Himalaya and Hindu Kush Mountains? Tsarist accounts, often remarkably frank, stressed considerations of power, trade, and Russia's civilizing mission. Below are statements by conquerors of Turkestan region, a contemporary justification by Foreign Minister Gorchakov, and a retrospective view by an official tsarist source of 1914. Soviet historians, as one would expect, emphasize economic motives: growing appetites of industrial and commercial elements for raw materials and markets, and demands that the government protect their trade caravans and representatives in Central Asia. Soviet authors have stressed the supposedly growing threat of British imperialism to which Russia responded by occupying Turkestan. Recent Soviet accounts also give military, political, and prestige motives. Finally, a recent Western article summarizes and assesses various factors in the Russian expansion.

TSARIST VIEWS: THE CONQUERORS

General M. G. Cherniaev, a leading and reckless frontier general who conquered much of Turkestan (1863–66), played a semi-independent role in Central Asian expansion. Here are a few of his declarations:

> This point [Aulie-Ata] is important to us both commercially and militarily because it lies at the intersection of routes from Kokand and Tashkent. With the capture of Aulie-Ata we have acquired the entire Trans-Chu region . . . (To his parents, June 29, 1864. Cherniaev Archive, Amsterdam.)
>
> In view of the fact that Kokand's concentrations grow daily, that our [native] population is losing confidence in us, . . . I decided, in order to cover Aulie-Ata and the nearby nomads . . . to advance toward Chimkent. . . . (To Diugamel, July 6. *Turkestanskii krai*. Compiled A. G. Serebrennikov (Tashkent, 1908–15), XVII, 213–14).
>
> Chimkent is scarcely known to Europeans even by map and its conquest cannot cause much noise, and having some 5,000 natives with me, we can dress ourselves in the clothing of the defenders of an exploited people. . . . (To Poltoratskii, August 20, *Turk. krai*, XVIII, 113–16).
>
> Everyone feels that it would be calmer for us in Chimkent if [Tashkent] were either independent or belonged to us, but in Petersburg, of course, they know better." (To Poltoratskii, January 22, 1865, *Turk. krai*, XIX, 33).
>
> I could not remain indifferent to the [Bukharan] Emir's machinations and was compelled without awaiting arrival of reinforcements on the line to advance now along the road to Tashkent. . . . (To Kryzhanovskii, May 2, *Turk. krai*, XIX, 146–47).
>
> To withdraw from [Tashkent] would give the Emir [of Bukhara] vast prestige in Central Asia and strengthen him with all the sinews of war concentrated in Tashkent. Consequently, I resolved to seize the city by open force. . . . Please call the attention of the Emperor to this handful of tireless, intrepid warriors, who have established the prestige of the Russian name in Central Asia commensurate with the dignity of the Empire and the power of the Russian people. (To Kryzhanovskii, July 7, *Turk. krai*, XIX, 244–54).

N. A. Kryzhanovskii, governor-general of Orenburg and Cherniaev's immediate superior, sounded the theme of "the white man's burden":

> It seems to me that it is time to stop catering to the languages and customs of our weak neighbors [the khanates]. We can compel them to conform somewhat to our customs and impose our language on them. In Central Asia we alone must be the masters so that with time through us civilization can penetrate there and improve the lives of those un-

fortunate offspring of the human race. (To Stremoukhov, September 3, 1865, *Turk. krai*, XX, 47–48.

General K. P. Kaufman, appointed in July 1867 as the first governor-general of Russian Turkestan and who completed its conquest, spoke of insecurity and disorder there upon his arrival:

> All this indicates *the necessity* to strike at Bukhara and induce it by force of arms to make peace, and then by a single stroke subdue unconditionally the lands occupied by us so far, remove any thought or possibility of subordination to other than the Russian state. (Alexander II commented: "I find this very sensible.") (*Voenno-istoricheskii sbornik*, II (1916), 159–160).

War Minister Miliutin, the superior of the abovementioned conquerors, noted in 1862 Turkestan's significance as a threat to British India:

> In case of a European war we should especially value the occupation of [Kokand khanate] bringing us closer to the northern regions of India. . . . Ruling in Kokand we can constantly threaten England's East Indian possessions. This is especially important since only there can we be dangerous to this enemy of ours. (A. L. Popov, "Iz istorii zavoevanii Srednei Azii," *Istoricheskie zapiski*, IX (1940), p. 211).

OFFICIAL MEMORANDA (1864)

After Russian troops had seized the towns of Chimkent and Turkestan on the fringes of Tashkent oasis, Foreign Minister Gorchakov submitted a memorandum to Alexander II which was soon sent to European powers to reassure them about Russian expansion. It sought to explain and justify Russian conquests:

> The relationship of Russia to Central Asia . . . reveals that, despite our constant wish not to expand our territory with conquests, we, under the influence of the insistent demands of our commerce and some kind of mysterious but irresistible attraction to the Orient, have constantly advanced into the depths of the steppe. . . . The intentions of our government toward this area have undergone continual and fundamental changes. . . . Motivated by a sincere desire not to be drawn into making new acquisitions, we have had to obey willy-nilly the attraction of inexorable necessity. . . . [Russia's] natural and legitimate desire is not to imitate Europe, not to expand her already vast territories, but to retain all her resources for internal development, but a strictly peaceful policy is impossible for a powerful and civilized state bordering upon half-wild tribes. These tribes either must themselves rise because of internal revolt to the same level of civilization or be devoured by a powerful neighbor. (Gorchakov to Alexander II, October 31, 1864, *Turk. krai*, XVIII, 165–67).

Gorchakov stated his opposition to an advance beyond Chimkent because it would create longer Russian frontiers and involve the expense and responsibility of administering millions of Central Asian Muslims.

A memorandum written slightly later by the Foreign and War Ministers suggested that chance had played a major part in Russian expansion:

Until recently all our acquisitions in that region [Central Asia] have been made not on the basis of a definite system, not to achieve a specific goal, but under the influence of temporary circumstances and personal, sometimes one-sided views of local commanders. In view of the vast area of the Kirgiz steppe occupied gradually by us . . . , one involuntarily reaches the conclusion that in Russia's advance to the southeast there is a definite law not yielding to human considerations, and that occupying the middle and lower parts of the Syr-Daria, we inevitably, sooner or later, will also occupy its upper reaches, that is the entire Kokand khanate. Truly, Russian possessions in Central Asia would then achieve natural limits: the Tien Shan Range . . . and the sands of Kyzyl-Kum. . . . At the present time the further extension of our holdings in Central Asia would not accord either with the views of the government or the interests of the country. (Gorchakov and Miliutin to Alexander II, November 20, *Turk. krai*, XVIII, 196–98).

"ASIATIC RUSSIA"

In 1914 this official tsarist source summarized and evaluated Russian expansion in Central Asia a generation after its completion. It emphasized: Muslim hatred and agitation against Russia; attacks on Russian settlers, merchants, and diplomats by savage tribes; and the need for defensible frontiers. Nowhere did it suggest that either the Russian government or frontier commanders had been aggressive or greedy.

. . . The Muslim world with every generation became more hostile to Russia. The khans of Khiva, Bukhara, and Kokand . . . constantly spurred on the Kazakhs to hostile action . . . The khans . . . with Oriental cunning shifted the responsibility for keeping the people quiet on to the Russians and Russia. . . . Only by subduing [the khanates] could the Kazakh country become Russian not only in name but in fact. . . . Pacification of the Steppe was only possible by terrorizing or subduing these khanates who adopted a bold attitude toward Russia. . . . From this followed the conclusion that it was necessary to deliver a decisive blow against the khanates and by the 1850s the Russian government had adopted this course.

. . . It only remained to join the fortified town of Vernoe with a cordon to Fort Perovsk for the Kazakh territory to be cut off from external influences hostile to Russia. . . . By 1864 our troops . . . captured the towns of Turkestan, Chimkent, and others. The line was now closed up. . . . The Steppe had been crossed and the Russians were now established in a very rich and fruitful region. . . .

But our occupation of the new line did not bring peace to the Central Asian steppes. The khanates . . . , in their half-brigandish existence, did not appreciate the significance of the events which had taken place nor did they have a proper understanding of the power of Russia. . . . The Asiatic nomads . . . had no desire to reconcile themsleves to the new situation and to see around them Russian garrison towns. Incited from without, they plundered our merchants, attacked small detachments, and detained not only our traders, but our ambassadors, and incited the native population of the towns captured by us to start a . . . holy war against the infidels. (*Aziatskaia Rossiia* from G. Wheeler, *The Modern History of Soviet Central Asia*, pp. 235–44).

SOVIET VIEWS

For two decades after the Bolshevik Revolution, Soviet historians, led by Pokrovskii, denounced what they called the brutal tsarist imperial conquest of Central Asia, attributing it mainly to typical bourgeois greed for markets, land, and raw materials; they discounted British threats as justifying such moves. After 1937, however, the party line shifted and Central Asia's incorporation into the Russian empire was considered a "lesser evil" than if its peoples had been ruled by the British or had remained under reactionary Muslim khanates. Soviet historians since have stressed the British danger and economic motives for tsarist expansion. Wrote S. S. Dmitriev:

> At this time [1850s] Russia's ancient economic ties with Central Asia increased sharply. Commercial relations between Orenburg, Nizhnii-Novgorod, and Irbit on the one side, and Khiva, Bukhara, and Tashkent on the other, became regular. . . . Russian government policy contributed to this development. . . .
> . . . Central Asia was essential to tsarist Russia not only as a source of raw materials, especially as a cotton base for Russian cotton textile manufactures, but as an important market for the sale of goods produced by Russian industry. The Russian bourgeoisie sought new sources of raw materials, new markets for their industrial products. The narrow domestic market [of Russia] could not satisfy the demands of an industry developing rapidly in the post-reform period. . . . No less than the bourgeoisie, Russian noble landowners were also interested in acquiring Central Asia. The acquisition of new colonies permitted capitalism to develop in breadth relatively easily and thus delayed the inevitable basic destruction of survivals of serfdom in the country's landowning structure. . . .
> . . . Central Asia interested Russian tsarism also as a new region of colonization for the "excess" population of Russia, as a new source of money for the treasury, and as a convenient military base to halt England's expansionist policy directed at the interior of Asia. New conquests in Central Asia also opened to an important and influential group of military and civilian Russian nobles and bourgeoisie easy possibilities for feudal-military plunder of the new colony. . . . The English bourgeoisie [from 1830] sought thirstily to seize more and more new colonies as markets for the goods of its capitalist industry and to obtain valuable raw materials. (S. Dmitriev, "Sredniaia Aziia i Kazakhstan v 1860–1880–kh godakh. Zavoevanie Srednei Azii," in M. V. Nechkina, ed., *Istoriia SSSR* (Moscow 1949), pp. 578–81).

More recently, N. A. Khalfin, a Soviet specialist on Central Asia and British imperialism there, affirmed:

> . . . Rapid industrial development made the question of expanding markets particularly acute. Russian entrepreneurs submitted to the Finance and Foreign Ministries various petitions, requests, and memoranda which solicited the increase of opportunities to sell their products, especially about "creating in Central Asia favorable conditions for the activity of Russian merchants. . . ." The tsarist government responded sympathetically. . . . Through expansion abroad it counted on weakening class contradictions within the country which were becoming ex-

tremely sharp. . . . By an active and successful foreign policy it sought to distract attention of the popular masses from severe internal problems. . . . Advances in Central Asia, where the opponent was weak, gave promise with small expenditures of securing for Russian entrepreneurs profitable markets and sources of raw materials, for military men a chance to distinguish themselves, for the service gentry administrative posts, for landowners reserves of land for resettlement, etc. . . .

In the early 1860s the most important branch of Russian industry—textiles—developed an urgent need for cotton. . . . However, the U.S. Civil War . . . reduced the imports of cotton into Russia, 1861–65. . . . The interruption in the receipt of American cotton compelled the [Russian] government, merchants, and industrialists . . . to view differently the question of turning the Central Asian khanates into sources of raw materials. Though during the cotton famine, prices of Central Asian cotton in Russia jumped upward sharply, its importation increased significantly. . . . The difficulty of obtaining this vital raw material for the Russian textile industry caused sharp concern in commercial-industrial circles and among all those connected with eastern policies. . . . Central Asia, regarded hitherto by Russian merchants and industrialists primarily as a profitable market, now acquired the significance of an important source of industrial raw materials. Russian newspapers and journals were filled with articles and comments about turning Central Asia into the cotton farm of the Russian empire. (N. A. Khalfin, *Prisoedinenie Srednei Azii k Rossii* (Moscow 1965), pp. 137–45).

A WESTERN VIEW

Firuz Kazemzadeh, a leading American scholar, assessed the validity of these tsarist and Soviet explanations for expansion:

Many attempts have been made to uncover the motives behind Russia's expansion in Central Asia and the Middle East . . . Soviet writers have stressed the economic forces which supposedly made it inevitable. . . . Indeed, Russian trade with the khanates of Turkestan had been growing rapidly ever since the middle of the 18th century . . . , however, the volume of this trade was relatively small and there is very little evidence that the Russian bourgeoisie had sufficient influence on the government to induce it to undertake large-scale conquests in the interests of a rather insignificant industry. Moreover, the alleged interests of the bourgeoisie fail to explain the origins of Russia's eastward expansion, a process which had begun long before the post-reform period. . . . In the case of Central Asia Russian expansion cannot be explained exclusively in economic terms. The same objections apply to the assertion that the conquest of Central Asia was in the interests of the serf-owning gentry who hoped that the acquisition of new territories would somehow postpone . . . "the liquidation of the survivals of serfdom. . . ."

. . . Up to 1917 the British habitually referred to a "military party" at St. Petersburg . . . that was supposed to have pushed the tsars, often against their better judgment and will into dangerous Asiatic adventures. Prince A. M. Gorchakov and his successor, N. K. Giers, found it convenient to blame the military for Russia's every embarrassing action, for every unfulfilled obligation, every broken promise. However, in fact, the military were tightly controlled from St. Petersburg, all their moves being decided on at the highest governmental level. . . .

The large-scale advance of 1864 was undertaken on the initiative of [War Minister] Miliutin and his generals and carried out in spite of the objections of Gorchakov and the diplomats. . . . The pressure exercised by the military was perhaps the decisive factor in Russia's conquest of Turkestan and Transcaspia. The generals, frustrated by the Crimean fiasco, were impatient and angry. More than any other group in the Empire they were imbued with a nationalist-imperialist ideology of the Panslavist type . . . and clamored for expansion. It meant everything to them: quick promotion, decorations, fabulous loot, unlimited opportunities for enrichment through dishonest management of army funds, excitement and adventure. ("Russia and the Middle East," in Ivo Lederer, ed. *Russian Foreign Policy* (New Haven, 1962), pp. 493–97).

CONCLUSION

Neither tsarist nor Soviet explanations of Central Asian expansion are wholly convincing, though each contains part of the truth. The advances, though initiated by government decision, greatly exceeded official intentions and plans. Security arguments of tsarist officials and generals seem partly justified and partly spurious, but Russian leaders believed that Russia would be strengthened if India were put under threat. Gorchakov's arguments about the need to protect Russian trade, chance, and a great power's tendency to expand to natural limits likewise appear sincere. Soviet historians, correctly noting Russia's growing economic interests in Central Asia, have exaggerated their importance, the influence of mercantile interests, and ostensible British threats. Tsarist Russia expanded into Central Asia for many reasons, but especially to win prestige and glory for its army and regime.

Suggested Additional Reading

BECKER, SEYMOUR. *Russia's Protectorates in Central Asia* . . . (Cambridge, Mass., 1968).

CURZON, GEORGE. *Russia in Central Asia in 1889* (New York, 1967, Reprint).

FADEEV, R. A. *Opinion on the Eastern Question* (London, 1876).

JELAVICH, CHARLES. *Tsarist Russia and Balkan Nationalism* . . . (Berkeley, 1958).

KALMYKOV, A. D. *Memoirs of a Russian Diplomat* . . . *1893–1917* (New Haven, 1971)

KAZEMZADEH, FIRUZ. *Russia and Britain in Persia, 1864–1914* (New Haven, 1968).

LANGER, WILLIAM. *The Franco-Russian Alliance* (Cambridge, Mass. 1929).

MACKENZIE, DAVID. *The Lion of Tashkent* . . . (Athens, Georgia, 1974).

————. *The Serbs and Russian Pan-Slavism, 1875–1878* (Ithaca, N.Y., 1967).

MALOZEMOFF, A. *Russian Far Eastern Policy, 1881–1904* (Berkeley, 1958).

MEDLICOTT, W. N.   The Congress of Berlin and After . . . (London, 1938).

OKUN, S. B.   The Russian-American Company (Cambridge, Mass., 1951).

PETROVICH, MICHAEL.   The Emergence of Russian Panslavism, 1856–1870 (New York, 1956).

OKAMOTO, SHUMPEI.   The Japanese Oligarchy and the Russo-Japanese War (New York, 1970).

PIERCE, RICHARD.   Russian Central Asia, 1867–1917 . . . (Berkeley, 1960).

ROMANOV, B.   Russia in Manchuria, 1892–1906 (Ann Arbor, 1952).

ROSEN, R. R.   Forty Years of Diplomacy (2 vols., New York, 1922).

SUMNER, B. H.   Russia and the Balkans, 1870–1880 (Oxford, 1937).

———.   Tsardom and Imperialism in the Far East and Middle East, 1880–1914 (London, 1940).

TAYLOR, A. J.   The Struggle for the Mastery of Europe, 1848–1918 (Oxford, 1954).

WITTE, COUNT S. IU.   Memoirs (Garden City, N.Y., 1921).

27

Opposition to Tsarism

A VIBRANT NEW intellectual climate marked the first decade of Alexander II's reign as numerous liberal and radical newspaper and periodicals appeared. "Everyone is talking, everyone is studying, including people who never before read anything in their lives," wrote the historian, K. D. Kavelin. Contacts with Europe, severed by Nicholas I, were renewed; hopes for drastic change soared. In London in 1857 Herzen and Ogarev began publishing a fortnightly newspaper, *Kolokol* (*The Bell*), which called upon the living to bury the dead past, oppose prejudice and oppression, and work for a bright Russian future. *Kolokol* attacked evils of the old system and at first hailed government plans for emancipation. With a remarkable 2,500 subscribers, it was read in Russia by intellectuals, bureaucrats, and the Tsar himself.

In the post-Crimean epoch, a diversified liberal and radical opposition developed against the autocracy. Liberals, aiming to reform and improve the system peacefully, competed with revolutionaries who sought to overthrow it. Liberals found it difficult to pursue their work without a parliament and in the face of governmental repression. Determined radicals, often using despotic methods and organizations, answered police repression with terrorism, secrecy, and ruthlessness. Before 1890 they looked mostly to the peasantry as their army of revolution; afterwards Marxism grew rapidly and its adherents wooed a rising urban working class. Soviet historians devote most attention to Marxist Social Democrats and claim that only a worker's party could have taken Russia to socialism. Recent Western scholars, often rejecting this thesis, have turned more to agrarian socialists and liberals. Why did Russian liberalism remain relatively weak? Why did radical movements develop so many splits? Was a Marxist triumph in Russia inevitable as Soviet accounts suggest? Did the autocracy help determine the opposition's aims and means?

LIBERALISM AND RADICALISM, 1855–1870

The relaxation of censorship, increased contacts with Europe, and government overtures stimulated liberal gentry to advocate reform. The Nazimov Rescript (November 1857), making public the Tsar's intent to free the serfs, urged the Lithuanian gentry to draw up proposals on land reform; similar rescripts went to all Russian provinces. In Tver province, liberal gentry leaders A. M. Unkovskii and A. A. Golovachev composed a memorandum which criticized the bureaucracy and official reform proposals, advocated full and immediate emancipation, and an equal role for gentry committees in working it out. The Tver gentry committee's majority project (1858), incorporating most of this memorandum, urged landowners to favor emancipation with land, abolition of *barshchina* and patrimonial rights, and an all-class, elected local administration. The Kaluga committee's minority proposal also urged reform of army recruitment and the courts, accountability of bureaucrats to the courts, and public primary schooling. Strongly influenced by liberal European thought and Russian university lectures, such liberal views won considerable support among the middle gentry in the provinces.

Liberal gentry ideology evolved further in their provincial assemblies of 1859–60. The Tver assembly protested government violations of noble rights and affirmed a major public role for the gentry. When the authorities exiled Unkovskii for this, he wrote Alexander II:

> I never thought that the problem of peasant emancipation could be decided by the gentry or its representatives, but I have always been convinced that for the success of this transformation the conscious sincere cooperation of the gentry is necessary.[1]

These gentry assemblies, transforming lifeless corporate bodies into vehicles to express independent interests and crystallize public opinion, were unprecedented in Russia. Summoned to discuss national issues in elected bodies for the first time, the provincial gentry discussed economic, political, and legal reform. As official reform plans matured, however, the regime gradually restricted public initiative and in November 1859 forbade gentry assemblies to debate the peasant question. Nonetheless, they continued to voice strong opposition to extension of bureaucratic control and demanded full local self-government in return for the imminent loss of seigneurial rights. The most vocal assemblies, those of Tver, Iaroslavl, Riazan, and Vladimir, advocated immediate obligatory redemption of land by the peasantry, drastic judicial reform, and all-class elective local self-government.

After the Emancipation, gentry assemblies pressed for political and administrative change and criticized the emancipation statutes. The Tver provincial gentry assembly resolved (February 1862):

> . . . Gentry are deeply convinced that the government is not capable of realizing [further reforms]. The free institutions to which these reforms lead can come only from the people. . . . The gentry . . . indicate that the path onto which [the government] must venture for the salvation of itself and of society . . . is the gathering of representatives from the entire people without distinction as to class.

---

[1] Quoted in T. Emmons, *The Russian Landed Gentry* (Cambridge, Eng., 1968), p. 281.

To dramatize gentry demands for local self-government, the Tver Assembly went on to renounce its class privileges:

> The gentry, by virtue of class advantages, have so far escaped fulfillment of the most important public obligations. Sovereign, we consider it a grievous fault to live and enjoy the benefits of the public order at the expense of other classes. . . . We most loyally request Your Majesty to be allowed to take upon ourselves a part of state taxes and obligations. . . .[2]

However, instead of meeting with the Tver leaders or heeding their recommendations, Alexander II ordered their arrest.

During 1861–62 Russian publicists abroad, such as Koshelev and Herzen, fostered a semi-constitutional gentry movement for a consultative assembly, or *zemskii sobor*. Underground leaflets such as *Velikoruss* (June–October 1861), advocating a constitution, responsible ministers, jury trials, and freedom of religion and the press, declared: "The educated classes must take the handling of affairs from the incapable government into their own hands." The regime blocked gentry constitutionalism and punished its leaders while conceding to gentry wishes by facilitating redemption of land and outlining liberal *zemstvo* and judicial reforms.[3] This took the steam out of gentry opposition, and a Moscow petition (1865) for a national consultative assembly was gentry constitutionalism's last gasp.

After 1865 gentry liberalism centered in the new *zemstva*. Leaders such as I. I. Petrunkevich of Chernigov aimed to convert them into "a school of self-government and by this means prepare the way for a constitutional state order." They aimed to expand *zemstvo* activities to the maximum and take from the autocracy most control over rural affairs. In Chernigov, Petrunkevich's program to aid the peasantry included free primary education, improving material conditions, and justice under law.[4] Such liberals sought a society where the individual would be central and self-governing, private property would be guaranteed and law would be supreme. *Zemstvo* liberals strove to persuade the regime to accept their "small deeds" in raising popular cultural and material well-being, hoping that eventually it would grant a national *zemstvo* or even a constitution.

Meanwhile young intellectuals, led by N. G. Chernyshevskii and N. A. Dobroliubov, determined to remake the world through reason, turned enthusiastically to radicalism. Some were priests' sons estranged from existing values and institutions and convinced that partial reforms were useless. Radicals gathered around a journal, *The Contemporary*. Soviet scholars regard Chernyshevskii, a leading contributor, as the chief precursor of Bolshevism and praise his materialism and scorn for liberalism. Chernyshevskii dreamed of changing history's course by building

---

[2] Ibid., pp. 341–43.

[3] See above, pp. 335–37.

[4] Charles Timberlake, "Ivan Il'ich Petrunkevich . . ." *Essays on Russian Liberalism* (Columbia, Missouri, 1972), p. 18 ff.

a perpetual motion machine to abolish poverty. He and Dobroliubov stressed the intellectual's duty to awaken, educate, and lead the toiling masses. Viewing the *mir* (peasant commune) as the basis for decentralized agrarian socialism, Chernyshevskii affirmed that Russia, unlike Europe, could avoid capitalism and move directly to socialism. In *What is to be Done?*, composed in prison (1863), he described a socialist utopia achieved by relentless, practical revolutionaries who would "impose their character on the pattern of events and hurry their course." Now few, they would multiply rapidly, and "in a few years . . . people will call unto them for rescue, and what they say will be performed by all." Chernyshevskii's "toiler's theory" asserted that labor was entitled to all that it produced, but he derived his socialism more from Fourier than from Marx. Twenty years in Siberian exile made him a revolutionary martyr.

Dmitri Pisarev (1840–68) reflected the uncompromising radicalism of intelligentsia "sons" of the 1860s who attacked the values and beliefs of the "fathers" of the 1840s. "Here is the ultimatum of our camp: what can be smashed should be smashed; what will stand the blow is good; . . . at any rate hit out left and right." This thrilled rebellious adolescents fighting the establishment. The writer, Ivan Turgenev, dubbed their ideology Nihilism, and Bazarov, the hero of his novel, *Fathers and Sons*, was Pisarev thinly disguised. A convinced Westernizer, Pisarev believed that an educated elite with modern science and European technology would uplift the masses and destroy autocracy.

During the early 1860s, small groups of intelligentsia discussed ways to spread propaganda and achieve revolution. N. Shelgunov's dramatic leaflet, *To the Younger Generation* (1861), urged the educated youth to reject Western parliamentary models and rely upon the *mir*. "We trust in our own fresh forces. We believe that we are called upon . . . to utter our [own] words and not follow in the wake of Europe." Another leaflet, *Young Russia* (1862), by Peter Zaichnevskii, a Moscow University student, proposed a republic and local assemblies based on the peasant commune: "Russia is entering the revolutionary period of its existence. The interests of the masses are irreconcilable with those of the Imperial party, landowners, officials, and Tsar. Their plundering of the people can only be stopped by a bloody, implacable revolution." The police speedily dissolved such groups.

In the mid-1860s, a small group of Moscow intelligentsia led by Nicholas Ishutin, a follower of Chernyshevskii, plotted direct, violent action. A secret band of terrorists known as Hell was to destroy autocracy. In April 1866 a student, Dmitri Karakozov, Ishutin's cousin, shot at the tsar. He missed (and apologized to Alexander II before being executed!), and the Ishutin circle was broken up.

In the ensuing reaction Russian exiles developed conspiratorial ideas. In 1869 Sergei Nechaev, a Moscow University student in Geneva, Switzerland, and the romantic revolutionary, Michael Bakunin, composed *Catechism of a Revolutionary*, which stressed that revolutionaries must be professional, dedicated, and disciplined:

The revolutionary is a doomed man. He has no interests, no affairs, no feelings, no attachments of his own. . . . Everything in him is wholly absorbed by one sole, exclusive interest . . . revolution. He must train himself to stand torture and be ready to die. . . . The laws, the conventions, the moral code of civilized society have no meaning for him. . . . To him whatever promotes the triumph of the revolution is moral, whatever hinders it is criminal.[5]

Later Lenin, praising the *Catechism* highly, patterned his Bolshevik Party upon it. Nechaev returned briefly to Russia in 1870 and set up a small organization, "The People's Reckoning" (*Narodnaia Rasprava*), which murdered a member for planning to betray it to the authorities.[6]

REVOLUTIONARY POPULISM

In the 1870s, a broader movement of revolutionary intelligentsia heeded Herzen's appeal: "Go to the people." Populism (*Narodnichestvo*) combined idealistic faith in the peasantry with determination to overthrow the old social and political order by force. Lacking central organization or a cohesive ideology, Populism advocated a peasant socialism derived largely from Herzen. The Populists regarded European large-scale factory industry as degrading and dehumanizing, denied that an industrial revolution must precede socioeconomic progress, and believed that only farmers led the good, natural life. Using intelligence and free will, Russians could avoid European errors. Like Rousseau, Populists believed that bad institutions had corrupted men and that the state had fostered inequality, injustice, and oppression. Popular revolution, not parliaments, would produce a decentralized socialist order. Populists idealized the people (*narod*), especially the peasantry, as a mystical, irresistible, and virtuous force whose traditional institutions—the *mir* and the primitive producers' cooperative (*artel*) with their collective landholding and quasi self-government—would become socialist once the old order was destroyed. Convinced that peasants in the *mir* were practicing rudimentary socialism, Populists disregarded clear signs of its disintegration before an advancing money economy. They emphasized ethical and humanitarian values and faith in collective institutions, but they disagreed about revolutionary organization, the intelligentsia's relationship to the people, and how and when to achieve revolution. In the early 1870s the emigrés, Bakunin and Lavrov, had small followings of socialist youth; later Tkachev's views tended to prevail.

Bakunin, a founder of anarchism, advocating an immediate, spontaneous mass uprising (*bunt*) to liberate the people, appealed to feeling, emotion, and mass instincts rather than reason. "The Russian peasantry are socialists by instinct and revolutionaries by nature," and so the intelligentsia should summon them to revolt, destroy the existing state completely, then establish a federation of peasant communes. When

---

[5] A. Yarmolinsky, *Road to Revolution* (London, 1957), p. 156.

[6] Fyodor Dostoevskii based his novel, *The Possessed,* on this incident and the character, Peter Verkhovenskii, on Nechaev.

the anticipated uprisings failed to break out, Bakunin's following in Russia dwindled.

P. L. Lavrov's more moderate, cautious approach grew popular. Lavrov, a mathematics professor, achieved prominence with his legally published *Historical Letters* (1870). For their education, intellectuals owed a debt to the people and should repay it by preparing them for revolution: a "critically thinking" elite should propagandize and agitate among the people. Abroad, in his journal, *Forward!*, Lavrov developed a complete Populist program. He borrowed Marx's tenets of the increasing misery of the masses and the worldwide socialist revolution but was uncertain whether revolution in Russia would precede or follow full capitalist development. He emphasized careful preparation of a peasant revolution by the intelligentsia (Bakuninists derisively dubbed his followers "the preparationists"). Dedicated intellectual revolutionaries were to explain socialism to the masses and recruit members from their ranks. (Lavrov worked it all out mathematically!). Local uprisings, directed by a revolutionary organization, would fuse in a nationwide revolution. Afterwards, a strong central government would be needed temporarily, but Lavrov repudiated dictatorship.

P. N. Tkachev, the heir of Nihilism and Ishutin, led a small Jacobinist faction which rejected Lavrov's patient approach. Tkachev's views in the emigré newspaper, *The Tocsin*, combined Populism, Marxism, and Blanquism. Like Bakunin he urged immediate action but believed that a centralized, elite organization of revolutionaries must lead the masses, a disciplined party able to impose its will. Tkachev's writing was filled with urgency: unless revolution came soon, capitalism would destroy the *mir*. "This is why we cannot wait. This is why we insist that a revolution in Russia is indispensable . . . at the present time." A temporary dictatorship would follow armed overthrow of the old order, but it would wither away once the people had been educated in socialism. Tkachev appealed desperately for immediate revolution until finally he went insane. Later, Lenin described his plan for seizing power as majestic.

Populism's practical achievements were few. Its main early organization, the Chaikovskii Circle (Lavrist) was broken up by arrests. In 1873–74, after a famine in the Volga region, more than 3,000 young urban intellectuals "went to the people" to spread socialist ideas and prepare revolution, but the peasants responded to this unorganized, naive "children's crusade" by turning over many of the ragged agitators to the police; the rest returned home disillusioned, and Lavrism was discredited. In 1876 a broader Populist organization, the second *Land and Liberty* (the first was founded in 1861), demanded all land for the peasants and conducted the first mass revolutionary demonstration in Russia at Kazan Cathedral in Petersburg. The police arrested its leaders and two big trials were held. In 1879 *Land and Liberty* split mainly over the issue of terrorism; moderates founded their own organization and newspaper, *Black Repartition*, which repudiated terrorism and violence, but soon its leaders (Plekhanov, Deutsch, and Zasulich) fled abroad. An extremist, pro-terrorist element created *Narodnaia Volia*, "The People's Will," based on ideas of Nechaev and Tkachev. Its secret "Executive Committee" plotted to assassinate the tsar and other high officials in order to disorganize the regime and trigger popular revolution. In March 1881 The People's Will murdered Alexander II, but within two years the police had destroyed it and broken the revolutionary movement.

REACTION, 1881–1904

The assassination of Alexander II in March 1881 by a terrorist of the People's Will organization, bringing Alexander III (1881–94) to the throne, inaugurated a quarter century of reaction and political stagnation. The new ruler, a powerful, unimaginative, poorly educated man of 36, though honest and straightforward, was strongly conservative, nationalistic, and religious. Alexander relied mainly upon Constantine Pobedonostsev, procurator of the Holy Synod, who until 1905 played a key role in domestic affairs. Tutor to Alexander III and his son, Nicholas II, Pobedonostsev and his ideology largely determined their outlook and policies.

Pobedonostsev elaborated the most complete, consistent theory of autocracy and status quo conservatism Russia had known. As the "grey eminence" of moribund tsarism, he contributed much to the "dogma of autocracy," which helped block essential political change and provoked radical opposition. Basing his views upon Uvarov's trilogy of Orthodoxy, Autocracy and, Nationalism,[7] Pobedonostsev agreed with the earlier English political theorist, Thomas Hobbes, that men were by nature unequal, weak, and vicious. Russians, he believed, required strong leadership and a firm hand. A onetime Slavophile who emphasized the differences between Russian and west European development, he felt that Western ways and institutions were not limbs that could be grafted onto the Russian tree. Favoring concentration of political power in the autocrat and in the central administration, he opposed local self-government and counted instead on traditional romantic bonds between tsar and people. To him constitutional government was anathema: "I hear everywhere the trite, accursed word, 'constitution.' A Russian revolution . . . is preferable to a constitution. The former could be suppressed and order restored . . . ; the latter is poison to the entire organism." Although a distinguished jurist, Pobedonostsev rejected the rule of law and civil liberties as restrictions upon autocracy. Orthodoxy, he declared, was the only true faith, and only one religion could be tolerated in an autocratic state. Rigid censorship by the Holy Synod must shield Russians from Western liberal and radical ideas, while the Orthodox Church imbued them with correct ideas through its press and schools. Unity was indispensable—one tsar, one faith, one language—and therefore national and religious minorities should be converted, assimilated, or expelled by ruthless Russification. Pobedonostsev's program was mainly negative: to preserve paternalistic noble and bureaucratic authority and a rigid status quo. To a remarkable extent, he persuaded Alexander

---

[7] See above, p. 294.

III and Nicholas II to accept and implement principles which intensified revolutionary opposition.

Within a few months of Alexander III's accession, Russia was moving toward political reaction and gentry rule. At Pobedonostsev's demand, M. T. Loris-Melikov's proposals for a consultative assembly, approved by Alexander II, were shelved. Loris-Melikov, D. A. Miliutin, and other liberal ministers resigned. The Slavophile Count Ignatiev was the leading figure for the next year until he was removed for seeking to revive the Muscovite *zemskii sobor*.[8] The ensuing reactionary regime tried to undo the Great Reforms by bureaucratic counter-reforms. The land captain law of 1889 abolished justice of the peace courts except in Moscow and Odessa and transferred their functions to judges appointed by the interior ministry. Land captains (*zemskie nachalniki*), usually hereditary noblemen, were to supervise peasant affairs, exercise administrative and judicial powers, and could rescind decisions of village assemblies and *volost* courts. They were to keep the peasantry under government control and noble tutelage. In 1890, peasant representation in *zemstvo* assemblies (appointed by the governor) was reduced and the Minister of Interior's authority over the *zemstva* was tightened. The law of June 1892 greatly reduced city electorates so that in St. Petersburg only 7,152 persons could vote. Without abolishing local self-government, the central authorities aimed to curtail it and stifle local initiative. Nonetheless, *zemstva* and city *dumy* continued to achieve much. They employed many youthful experts and professional people, who further stimulated their agencies to press for political change. Deep tension persisted between the central bureaucracy and local governmental institutions.

Alexander III's sudden death by stroke in 1894 brought Nicholas II (1868–1918) to the throne amidst widespread expectations of liberal change. Though more intelligent than his father, Nicholas was irresolute and strongly influenced by reactionaries. As heir, he was adequately educated, became an able linguist, and had acquired, during a trip around the world, abiding enthusiasm for Asia and Russia's supposed Asiatic mission. Shortly before his accession he married Alexandra of Hesse, "Alix," a deeply religious woman who dominated him and reinforced his piety and belief in autocracy. Nicholas remained sincerely devoted to his wife and family but became isolated from Russian reality. His chief interests, as reflected in his carefully kept diary, were trivial: hunting, yachting, and military reviews.

The accession of the youthful, personable Nicholas II encouraged liberals to hope for relaxation of restrictions on the press and political activity. In January 1895, however, he dashed these expectations abruptly at a reception for *zemstvo* leaders and warned liberals to abandon "senseless dreams" about an increased role for *zemstva*. ". . . I, devoting all my strength to the welfare of the people, will uphold the principle of autocracy as firmly and unflinchingly as my late unforgettable father." Dominated by Pobedonostsev and the reactionary Prince V. P. Meshcherskii, Nicholas believed that constitutional government

---

[8] See above, pp. 152–55.

Nicholas II and Alexandra

and parliaments were evil. At first he displayed reasonable judgment in
state affairs and retained Witte and other capable men in office, but he
tended increasingly to heed irresponsible adventurers ready to lead the
country to disaster. The first decade of Nicholas II's reign was outwardly quiet and uneventful, but beneath the surface developed Marxist, agrarian socialist, and liberal constitutional movements.

THE DEVELOPMENT OF MARXISM

By 1881 the more naive, idealistic elements of the intelligentsia had
been eliminated or discredited. The Populist movement, after the failure
of the "going to the people" and faced with police persecution following
the Tsar's assassination, was in disarray. Urban-bred revolutionaries,
still idealizing the peasantry, had not bridged the gulf in education, at-

titudes, and life-styles with the rural masses. Economic conditions were changing rapidly, and an industrial working class with more revolutionary potential was emerging. Alexander III's stifling autocracy, allied with rising business, heightened the revolutionaries' despair and isolation. Radical youths of the 1880s, dismayed by Populist defeats and illusions, searched for a new, comprehensive theory to explain disturbing new economic facts. Some found their answer in Marxism, which began to attract intellectuals and link them with the industrial working class.

Karl Marx and Friedrich Engels had derived their cohesive theory of "scientific" socialism from many sources, amalgamating others' ideas ingeniously into a system to explain the "laws of history." Marx owed much to the German philosopher, G. F. Hegel, accepting his method of reasoning (dialectic) and his belief that conflict of opposites and resulting synthesis produces progress. Instead of agreeing with Hegel that ideas create reality, Marx adopted Ludwig Feuerbach's materialism: how man earns his daily bread determines his actions and outlook ("Being determines consciousness"). Antagonistic social classes (e.g., bourgeoisie versus proletariat), affirmed Marx, contend over the means of production (land, factories, and tools). Economic elements (means of production and worker-owner relationships), he argued, were the substructure of society and determined basically its superstructure (government, law, religion, etc.). A person's economic and social status would determine what he or she did, wrote, and thought.

Applying their philosophy to history (historical materialism), Marx and Engels shared Hegel's view of human evolution by inexorable laws through a series of stages toward a goal: freedom. Each successive historical stage—primitive communism, slavery, feudalism, capitalism, and socialism—reflects a more advanced form of production. Passage from one state to the next results from conflict between a class (e.g., slaveholders) controlling the means of production and the one it exploits (slaves). As one mode of production yields to a more advanced one and the exploited class achieves greater freedom, a new stage develops, often by revolution.

Marx stated that capitalism was the historical stage in western Europe when the bourgeoisie (especially factory owners) exploited the proletariat (factory workers). The worker, who creates all value according to Marx, received back in wages only part of the value his labor created, while the capitalist pocketed the rest ("surplus value") as profit. Competitive capitalism would evolve eventually into its opposite, monopoly, as weaker capitalists went bankrupt. The industrial work force would absorb farmers until the proletariat became the vast majority of the population. Overproduction and unemployment would grow, as would worker dissatisfaction and class consciousness. Fully developed capitalism would produce piles of goods which workers could not buy until they seized the means of production in a proletarian revolution.[9]

---

[9] In 1848 Marx believed revolution was the only route from capitalism to socialism; much later he concluded that advanced countries such as Great Britain and the United States might achieve a peaceful transition to socialism.

Revolutions, Marx believed, would occur first in advanced capitalist countries, led by communists: class-conscious workers and bourgeois intellectuals like Marx. Workers the world over would unite, overthrow capitalism, and establish socialism everywhere. Revolutions presumably would be violent because ruling capitalists and feudal lords would not yield wealth and power voluntarily. A transitional era of undefined length—the dictatorship of the proletariat—would follow the overthrow of capitalism. This workers' state would run the government and economy, distribute goods fairly to the people and educate them in socialism. Coercing only former exploiters, it would be more democratic than the former "bourgeois democracy" because it would represent the workers, by then the vast majority. When it had achieved its purposes, the workers' state, at least its coercive aspects, would wither away. Private property, class struggle, and exploitation would disappear, bringing into being a perfect socialist order called "communism," with the principle: "From each according to his ability, to each according to his needs."

Did the Marxian theory, conceived for western Europe, apply to backward Russia? Marx learned Russian, read Chernyshevskii, and corresponded with Russian socialists, but his views on Russia were inconsistent and uncertain. Anxious to see reactionary tsarism overthrown, Marx wrote in 1877 and 1881 that Russia could escape capitalism and move directly from feudalism to socialism *if* capitalist elements within the commune were eliminated and proletarian revolutions occurred soon in western Europe. On Russia, Marx proved a poor Marxist.

In the 1870s Marxist ideas began to circulate in Russia. The abstruse and technical *Das Kapital* (1867, 1885, 1894) was published openly, as were other nonpolitical Marxist works. In 1875 the first significant worker organization in Russia, the South Russian Workers Alliance, opened in Odessa, but soon its leaders were arrested. Three years later the Northern Alliance of Russian Workers with more than 200 active members arose in St. Petersburg, but until the mid-1880s Russia had few Marxists and no Marxist movement.

George Plekhanov (1856–1918), though of noble origin, "reared a whole generation of Russian Marxists," Lenin said. Earlier Plekhanov had sought to create a scientific Populism, but even then he had stressed the industrial workers' revolutionary potential. In 1879 he became editor of *Black Repartition*, but the following year he fled into Swiss exile. Realizing that in Russia the commune was disintegrating and industry developing, Plekhanov converted to Marxism, attracted by its scientific, orderly qualities. In Switzerland he, Paul Akselrod, and Vera Zasulich set up an independent Marxist group, The Liberation of Labor (1883), which for the next two decades acted as an embryo Russian social democratic party. Its members translated Marxist works and sent pamphlets into Russia, but at first Russians remained apathetic. In *Our Differences* (1885), Plekhanov denounced the People's Will for urging terrorism and minority insurrection. Industry was growing in Russia: "We must recognize that in this sphere the present

as much as the [near] future belongs to capitalism in our country."
Plekhanov affirmed that Russia, like western Europe, must pass through
capitalism to reach socialism; only the proletariat, sparked by the intelligentsia, could organize a true socialist revolution. He balanced
between voluntarist and determinist aspects of Marxism: the proletariat
needed knowledge and organization, but the laws of history would
surely bring defeat to the bourgeoisie. "The Social Democrats," he exulted, "are swimming along the current of history."

The Russian intelligentsia viewed Marxism and Populism as separate, competing movements. In 1885 a Bulgarian student, D. Blagoev,
established the first Marxist study group in Russia; soon these became
popular among university students and workers. The famine of 1891,
revealing peasant helplessness, stimulated Marxism's growth as younger
intellectuals such as V. I. Ulianov, later known as Lenin, rejected
Populism and turned to the workers. In St. Petersburg a Central Workers Circle linked worker groups and Marxist intellectuals, and in 1893
Ulianov joined one of them, beginning an illustrious revolutionary
career. Marxist literature then mostly stressed determinism: capitalist
development was undermining the *mir* and proving Populism wrong.
Arkadi Kremer's pamphlet, *On Agitation* (1894), however, warned
that Marxists must not just study and theorize but learn workers'
grievances and exploit them. His associate, Julius Martov, met Ulianov,
and merged his Vilna group with ones in Petersburg. In 1895 major
strikes in the textile industry revealed the workers' revolutionary energy
and dispelled naive faith in Marxist study circles, but many Marxist
leaders including Ulianov and Martov were arrested and exiled to
Siberia.

Some Russian Marxists, influenced by European currents, turned
away from revolution. Eduard Bernstein, a German Social Democrat,
was attacking some of Marx's main premises, claiming that socialism
could be reached by gradual, nonviolent, democratic means. In Russia,
Peter Struve and S. Bulgakov argued that capitalism would evolve
gradually into socialism. The movement of Economism developed,
stressing "spontaneous" development and peaceful agitation to encourage workers to demand economic benefits from employers. Many
Russian workers seemed more interested in shorter hours and higher
pay than in revolution. Meanwhile, an attempt by Russian Marxist
"politicals," who advocated active struggle against the regime, to form
a national social democratic party failed when the leaders of their
secret Minsk congress of 1898 were arrested.

The youthful Lenin (Ulianov) helped reinvigorate Russian Marxism
and turn it back toward revolution. He too was of noble background
(his Soviet biographers gloss this over) because his father as school
inspector in Simbirsk earned hereditary nobility. Vladimir Ilich was
raised in a conservative, disciplined, religious household. In 1887 his
older brother, Alexander, whom Vladimir greatly admired, was executed for trying to kill Alexander III. His brother's death and his
favorite author, Chernyshevskii, influenced Vladimir Ilich greatly.
Chernyshevskii's *What Is To Be Done?* convinced him that "strong per-

sonalities" would impose their pattern on history. Expelled from Kazan University after a student demonstration, Ulianov later passed the bar in St. Petersburg and practiced law briefly in Samara. Though admiring the dedication of the Narodovoltsy (People's Will), he became a Marxist (1892). He attacked the Populists, affirming in *Who Are the Friends of the People?* (1894) that Russia was well along in capitalist development. In his major work written in Siberian exile, *The Development of Capitalism in Russia* (1899), he argued that differentiation of the peasantry into a rural proletariat and bourgeoisie proved that the commune was disintegrating irrevocably.

After his exile, Lenin with Plekhanov became Orthodox Marxism's chief spokesmen against revisionism. Restating Plekhanov, Lenin affirmed that revolution was absolutely essential in Russia and urged Social Democrats to lead an organized, class-conscious working class. Attacking the view of the Economists, a faction of Russian Marxism, that workers could develop cohesion spontaneously while improving their economic status, he argued that by itself the working class could develop only trade unionism. Marxists must provide conscious leadership, not trail behind the masses. In 1900 Lenin and Martov joined older emigrés of The Liberation of Labor (Plekhanov, Akselrod and Zasulich) to found the newspaper, *Iskra* (The Spark) in Stuttgart, Germany to combat revisionism and consolidate Marxist ideology and organization. In its first issue, using his pseudonym for the first time, Lenin stressed the need for active political work:

> The task of Social Democracy is to instill social democratic ideas and political consciousness into the mass of the proletariat and to organize a revolutionary party unbreakably tied to the spontaneous labor movement. . . . We must train people who will dedicate to the revolution not a free evening but the whole of their lives. . . .

In *What Is To Be Done?* (1902), a sizable pamphlet containing his main ideas on party organization, Lenin stressed the need for a small, centralized body of professional revolutionaries from the intelligentsia to serve as the vanguard of the working class in their struggle to achieve socialism. "Give us an organization of revolutionists and we will overturn the whole of Russia."

Iskra's leaders moved to reorganize Russian social democracy. In July 1903, a Second Congress (the abortive Minsk meeting of 1898 was designated the first) convened in Brussels, Belgium. Since *Iskra* controlled 33 of the 43 delegates, its program was mostly approved. After the Belgian authorities compelled the congress to move to London, a struggle developed within the *Iskra* group between Lenin and Martov over party membership and organization. Arguing for an elite party, Lenin insisted that membership be limited to active participants in a party organization. Martov advocated a broad, mass party: "The more widely the title of party member is extended the better." That, Lenin objected, would inundate the party with opportunists. Plekhanov, the party's elder statesman, sided with Lenin, but at first Martov's more democratic formula prevailed 28 to 22. After the congress had rejected the Jewish Bund's demand for autonomy, however, the Bundists

Library of Congress

Vladimir Ilich Lenin (1870–1924)

walked out; they were soon joined by the defeated Economists. These walkouts, engineered by Lenin, who worked frantically to secure victory, gave his "hard" faction a majority of two over Martov's "softs." Lenin promptly dubbed his group Bolsheviks (majority men) and obtained a psychological edge over Martov's faction, which meekly accepted the name Mensheviks (minority men). Lenin sought to exploit his slim majority to impose his views on membership and organization and make the party a centralized organization of professional revolutionaries. Instead, the Second Congress split the Social Democrats irreconcilably. Soon after the congress, the Mensheviks took over *Iskra* and won a majority on the central committee as well. Former *Iskra* colleagues accused Lenin of dictatorial methods and creating a state of siege within the party. Bolshevik-Menshevik differences then were confined to party organization, while young Leon Trotskii (Lev Bronstein), a brilliant polemicist and orator, stood between the factions and sought to mediate their differences.

FROM POPULISM TO THE SOCIALIST REVOLUTIONARIES (SR'S)

Populism recovered slowly from the destruction of the People's Will. Populist ideologists of the '80s and early '90s denounced capitalism and argued desperately that it must never come to Russia. Younger Populists, however, calling themselves Socialist Revolutionaries (SR's), agitated among new factory workers of peasant origin. In the capitals the Marxists outdid them, but in provincial centers the SR's won much support. Some Populist exiles returned, such as Catherine Breshko-Breshkovskaia, who won converts around the country and became known as "the grandmother of the revolution."

In the late 1890s, three centers of SR activity emerged. In 1896 the Union of Socialist Revolutionaries was founded in Saratov and won followers in the Moscow and Volga regions. Declared its Lavrist program, *Our Tasks* (1898): "Propaganda, agitation and organization . . . , such are the tasks of preparatory work at present." It emphasized winning political freedom and deferred revolution to an indefinite future. A southern element from Voronezh and the Ukraine advocated a constitution, agitation among the peasantry, strikes by agricultural workers, and boycotts against landlords. A third group formed in Minsk by Breshko-Breshkovskaia and A. Gershuni, a young Jewish scientist, featured terror as its chief weapon against autocracy. In 1898 the police frustrated an attempt to establish an SR party in Russia, but in 1900 an underground organization and newspaper, *Revolutionary Russia,* were set up in Kharkov. Two years later elements from the various SR groups met in Berlin to establish the Socialist Revolutionary Party.

Its chief ideologist was Victor Chernov (1876–1952), an SR organizer in Tambov province, who accepted some Marxist doctrines and recognized capitalist development in Russia. Urging SR's to agitate in factories and include workers in "the people," Chernov admitted that the proletariat would lead the revolution against capitalism but affirmed that the peasantry would be "the fundamental army." In the new society, socialized enterprise in the towns would complement reorganized socialist communes. Chernov, like the Populists but unlike the Marxists, stressed free will, passion and creativity, but he stood ready to collaborate with Marxists and urban workers to overturn captalism.

The dynamic, rapidly growing SR's formed many local groups and sent a stream of pamphlets to workers and peasants, but they failed to resolve the old dispute between terrorism and preparationism. Within the party operated a Combat Detachment, led by terrorists A. Gershuni and Evno Azev, which between 1902 and 1905 assassinated two interior ministers, the Moscow governor-general, and other officials. The tsarist police considered the SR's more dangerous than the more academic, theoretical Social Democrats.

LIBERALISM ORGANIZES

Nineteenth century Russian liberalism, despite considerable achievements through the *zemstva,* never attained cohesion, but on the eve of the 1905 Revolution, reinforced with former revolutionaries, it broadened into a vigorous, effective national movement seeking a national *zemstva* union, constitutional reform, and civil liberties.

Until 1898, *zemstva* remained the main liberal arena and gradualism their chief approach. *Zemstvo* leaders, anxious to promote public welfare, felt keenly the lack of a national organization, but their activities continued to expand despite official restrictions. By 1900, *zemstva* employed more than 70,000 agronomists, doctors, and teachers. This professional personnel, known as the "Third Element," helped democratize the *zemstva* until both their gentry and professional members supported constitutional reform and civil rights. The Slavophile liberals' chief spokesman, the conscientious D. N. Shipov (1851–1920), chairman of the Moscow provincial *zemstvo* board, favored joint administration of Russia by tsar and people through a national consultative assembly and hoped the tsar would heed his appeals. Petrunkevich, active in the Chernigov and Tver provincial *zemstva* since 1868, led *zemstvo* constitutionalists. Slavophile liberals still awaited governmental concessions, and Shipov, despite official rebuffs, sought to extend *zemstva* to additional provinces and create a national *zemstvo* union. The regime's refusal to permit that, its repressive actions of 1899–1900, and the Slavophile liberals' submissiveness strengthened the constitutionalists.

Defectors from revolutionary socialism reinforced liberalism among the professional intelligentsia. During the 1890s the Legal Populists, led by N. K. Mikhailovskii, stressing ethical principles and the individual, abandoned revolutionary views to cooperate with the liberals. Legal Marxists, headed by N. Berdiaev and P. Struve, likewise rejected revolution. Struve, author of the Marxist manifesto of 1898 at Minsk, broke with the SD's to advocate liberal gradualism. The Economists, S. Prokopovich and his wife, Kuskova, like the English Webbs, advocated "pure trade unionism" to satisfy the workers' economic needs. Kuskova's *Credo* (1899), depicting Orthodox Marxists as narrow sectarians, urged Economists to support the liberals.

At the turn of the century Russian liberals acquired a press and a more cohesive political program. The liberal gentry set up *Beseda*, a private discussion group including Slavophiles and constitutionalists. After 1896 *zemstvo* liberals of all shadings met irregularly to agitate for a national *zemstvo* union, and in May 1902 the first congress of *zemstvo* officials, 52 leaders from 25 provinces, met without official authorization at Shipov's home. This semi-legal action set a pattern for liberals in 1905. The founding in Stuttgart in 1902 of the periodical, *Osvobozhdenie* (*Liberation*), edited by Struve, with money from a Moscow landowner, established a militant liberal press organ. Adopting a radical constitutionalist line, it became almost as influential as Herzen's *Bell*. In 1903 a Union of Liberation, designed to unite the entire non-Marxist intelligentsia, was formed in Switzerland with many outstanding theorists and activists. In January 1904 its leaders met in private apartments in St. Petersburg and pledged to work to abolish autocracy, establish constitutional monarchy, and achieve universal, secret, and direct suffrage in equal constituencies—the "four-tailed" suffrage—for a national parliament. The Union's national council met regularly until the 1905 Revolution.

Before 1905 the opposition movements were developing greater cohesion and clearer programs. The liberals, led by such pro-Western intellectuals as Paul Miliukov, were supported by much of the growing professional middle class and some provincial *zemstvo* gentry. Socialists generally agreed on the need to overthrow the tsarist autocracy and establish a less rigidly centralized popular government. They differed sharply, however, over timing and means, over how their movement or party should be organized, and over which elements should constitute and lead it. The SR's with an urban intellectual leadership and mainly peasant rank and file opposed a Marxist workers' party, the SD's, itself split between Bolsheviks, Mensheviks, and smaller factions.

Suggested Additional Reading

ANDERSON, T.   *Russian Political Thought* (Ithaca, N.Y., 1967).

ASCHER, A.   *Pavel Axelrod and the Development of Menshevism* (Cambridge, Mass., 1972).

BARON, S. H.   *Plekhanov: The Father of Russian Marxism* (Stanford, 1963).

BILLINGTON, JAMES.   *Mikhailovsky and Russian Populism* (New York, 1958).

BYRNES, R. F.   *Pobedonostsev: His Life and Thought* (Bloomington, Ind., 1969)

CARR, E. H.   *Mikhail Bakunin* (New York, 1961).

———.   *Studies in Revolution* (London, 1950).

CHERNYSHEVSKY, N. G.   *What Is to be Done?* (New York, 1961) (Novel).

DAN, FEDOR.   *The Origins of Bolshevism* (New York, 1970). (Translation).

EMMONS, T.   *The Russian Landed Gentry* . . . (Cambridge, Eng., 1968).

FIGNER, VERA.   *Memoirs of a Revolutionist* (New York, 1927).

FISCHER, GEORGE.   *Russian Liberalism* (Cambridge, Mass., 1958).

GETZLER, J.   *Martov* (New York, 1967).

HAIMSON, LEOPOLD.   *The Russian Marxists* . . . (Cambridge, Mass., 1955).

HARE, RICHARD.   *Pioneers of Russian Social Thought* (New York, 1964).

HERZEN, A. I.   *My Past and Thoughts* (6 vols., New York, 1924–28 and reprints).

KEEP, J. L.   *The Rise of Social Democracy in Russia* (Oxford, 1963).

KROPOTKIN, PETER.   *Memoirs of a Revolutionist* (New York, 1927 and reprints).

LAMPERT, E.   *Sons against Fathers* . . . (London, 1965).

———.   *Studies in Rebellion* (London, 1957).

LAVROV, P. L.   *Historical Letters*, ed. J. Scanlan (Berkeley, 1967).

PIPES, RICHARD, ed.   *The Russian Intelligentsia* (New York, 1961).

POMPER, PHILIP.   *The Russian Revolutionary Intelligentsia* (New York, 1970).

RANDALL, F. N.   *N. G. Chernyshevskii* (New York, 1967).

THADEN, E. C.   *Conservative Nationalism in Nineteenth Century Russia* (Seattle, 1964).

TIMBERLAKE, CHARLES, ed.   *Essays on Russian Liberalism* (Columbia, Missouri, 1972).

TREADGOLD, DONALD.   *Lenin and His Rivals, 1898–1906* (New York, 1955).

TURGENEV, IVAN.   *Fathers and Sons* (New York, Modern Library) (Novel).

VENTURI, FRANCO.   *Roots of Revolution* . . . (New York, 1960).

WOLFE, BERTRAM.   *Three Who Made a Revolution* (New York, 1964).

WORTMAN, RICHARD.   *The Crisis of Russian Populism* (London, 1967).

YARMOLINSKY, A.   *Road to Revolution* (London, 1957).

28

Revolution, Reaction, and Reform, 1905–1914

THE DECADE OF 1905–14 witnessed a crucial race in Russia between reform and revolution and alternating periods of radicalism and reaction. The major revolution which erupted in 1905 brought masses of workers and peasants, under intelligentsia leadership, for the first time into a broad, popular movement against the autocracy. Although the revolution failed and was succeeded by iron-handed political reaction, the tsarist system was altered significantly. A semi-constitutional monarchy with a national parliament sought, albeit hesitantly, to grapple with Russia's perplexing problems. Important agrarian reform was undertaken and industrialization resumed. While the armed forces were being reorganized and modernized, a weakened Russia sought simultaneously to recover prestige abroad and avoid conflict. By 1914 a measure of success seemed to have crowned these efforts. Partially industrialized Russia, though plagued by social turmoil, was moving ahead economically and maturing politically. Why did the Revolution of 1905 break out? Why did it fail to overthrow tsarism? How genuine was the constitutional monarchy which succeeded unlimited autocracy? Was Russia in 1914 truly moving toward parliamentary government, prosperity, and social harmony, or toward imminent, massive social revolution?

THE REVOLUTION OF 1905

Historians differ widely over the meaning of the Revolution of 1905. Most Western scholars regard it, like the European revolutions of 1848, as a liberal-democratic movement in which workers and peasants acted largely spontaneously. Early Soviet accounts, such as Pokrovskii's, agreed, but Stalinist historians dramatized and glorified Bolshevik leadership of the proletariat in a "bourgeois-democratic revolution." Most scholars affirm that 1905 was the dress rehearsal for the greater 1917 revolutions because similar parties and mass elements participated, though with less cohesion and militancy in the first case.

Revolution occurred in 1905 because industrial workers, intellectuals, peasants, and ethnic minorities found their repressive, unresponsive

395

The demonstrators are fired upon by Tsarist troups in front of Narva gate

government unbearable. Supporting the government, on the other hand, were a large and cohesive bureaucracy, a vast police network, the nobility, the church, and the army, but until Witte was returned to office (October 1905), the regime used these still powerful elements ineptly. The depression of 1900–03 and bad harvests had brought hard times to Russia, and an increasingly articulate opposition sought political freedom, civil liberties, and social reform. Spurring the revolution were Japanese victories in the Far East, which discredited the government, eroded its prestige, inflated prices, and caused rising disaffection in the armed forces. Each setback in Asia reinforced dissatisfaction and opposition in European Russia.

Pleve's assassination (July 1904) had removed the only energetic government figure. Nicholas II, replacing him with the mild Prince Peter Sviatopolk-Mirskii, made minor concessions to the public. In Paris in October 1904, the Liberation movement and socialists agreed to agitate for the replacement of autocracy with a democratic regime based on universal suffrage, and by December most educated Russians were criticizing the regime. In many cities political banquets were held similar to those before the Paris revolution of 1848.

The revolution began on "Bloody Sunday" (January 9, 1905). With police cooperation, the priest Father George Gapon had organized St. Petersburg factory workers to deflect them from revolutionary ideas. When news came of Port Arthur's fall, a strike of locomotive workers

The demonstrators led by Father Gapon are attacked by the Tsar's cavalry

Taking refuge behind a hastily assembled barricade, the demonstrators fire on the Tsar's troops

BLOODY SUNDAY, JANUARY 9, 1905, ST. PETERSBURG

spread through the giant Putilov plant and several other St. Petersburg factories. Gapon urged the workers to petition the Tsar to end the war, convene a constituent assembly, grant civil rights and establish an eight-hour day, all also goals of the Liberationists. On January 9, a snowy Sunday morning, Gapon led one of several columns of workers from various parts of the city toward the Winter Palace. The marchers —men, women, and children—bore icons, sang hymns, and clearly intended no violence. When they disregarded orders to halt, the Tsar's uncle, Grand Duke Vladimir Aleksandrovich, ordered troops to fire on the crowd and hundreds of the unarmed workers were slaughtered.

Bloody Sunday united the Russian people against the autocracy and undermined its faith in the Tsar. During January half a million workers struck, and noble assemblies and *zemstva* issued sharp protests. As students and professional people joined the workers, St. Petersburg became the center of nationwide agitation. Except for SR terrorists, however, there was no violence. At their congress in March, the Liberationists demanded a constituent assembly, universal suffrage (including women), separation of church and state, autonomy for national minorities, transfer of state and crown lands to the peasants, and an eight-hour day and the right to strike for workers. Revolutionary socialists, mostly in exile, squabbling over tactics, played little part in this movement.

In May and June the opposition organized, the strike movement expanded, and a naval mutiny erupted. Fourteen unions of professional people established the Union of Unions to coordinate their campaign for a constituent assembly. Paul Miliukov, head of the Union of Liberation, was elected its president, giving liberals in 1905 a unity which socialists and conservatives lacked. Although Bolsheviks and many SR's favored armed insurrection, other socialists cooperated with the Union. At the textile center of Ivanovo-Voznesensk, virtually the entire work force struck, some 70,000 workers. Their strike committee, calling itself a soviet (council), took on governmental functions such as price regulation. On June 14, the crew of the new battlecruiser *Potemkin* mutinied under a red flag and forced the government to deactivate the Black Sea Fleet.

Nicholas II's response to all this was to announce the Bulygin Duma (named after the new Minister of Interior, A. G. Bulygin), a consultative assembly to be elected by a limited suffrage favoring rural elements. It would be able to speak but not act, and autocracy would be preserved. This split the opposition temporarily three ways: *zemstvo* moderates favored participating in such elections, the Union of Unions urged a boycott and agitation for a constituent assembly, and revolutionaries advocated an armed uprising.

Spreading mass unrest forced greater governmental concessions. Peasant disorders grew in many regions. Radical demands by the Peasant Union, formed in July, revealed that contrary to official expectations, the peasantry had joined the opposition. The workers forced the government's hand: history's first general strike began spontaneously September 19 with a walkout by Moscow printers, which then was joined by bakers and factory workers. Spreading to St. Petersburg, it halted railroad, telegraph, and telephone service completely. In all Russia only one newspaper, a conservative Kiev daily, was published, and in mid-October mobs controlled the streets of leading cities. The workers' strike committee in St. Petersburg became a soviet and selected a 22-man executive committee under Leon Trotskii and a Menshevik, G. Khrustalev-Nosar.

Powerless to halt the strike, the regime fell into panic and virtual paralysis. Count Witte advised either a military dictatorship or a constitution. Unable to find a dictator and faced with general revolt in town and countryside, the Tsar yielded. His October Manifesto (October 17 old style) promised a constitution, civil liberties, and a national parliament (Duma) elected by a broad suffrage without whose consent no bill was to become law. Two days later Nicholas revived the Council of Ministers, creating a unified executive branch, and named Witte premier. Nicholas was in despair because he had broken his pledge to maintain autocracy unaltered.

The Tsar replaced reactionary ministers, but liberal leaders refused to join the government, and socialists and left liberals spurned the Manifesto. The two months after it was issued were the most disorderly of 1905. In those "days of freedom," the St. Petersburg Soviet, coordinating a growing soviet movement, decreed the end of censorship, newspapers ignored censorship restrictions, and the public began exercising rights which the Manifesto had promised. In October and November, rural violence reached its peak, and national minorities agitated for autonomy or independence. Naval mutinies broke out at Kronstadt, Vladivostok, and Sevastopol, and in November postal and telegraph workers struck, touching off new railroad strikes. Government troops suppressed peasant revolts and arrested the St. Petersburg Soviet's leaders, but the Soviet, supported by the Peasant Union and the socialists, proclaimed economic war against the regime and another general strike. In December the Moscow Soviet led a week-long armed workers' rebellion, but it was suppressed after bitter street fighting reminiscent of the Paris "June Days" of 1848; thousands of Moscow workers were shot or deported. The regime had now recovered its nerve, and after the Moscow Soviet called off its faltering general strike, the Revolution gradually subsided. Opposition newspapers were closed and the "days of freedom" ended.

Tsarism survived 1905 for reasons not present in the fatal crisis of 1917. Quick and honorable conclusion of the war in August localized disaffection in the armed forces, and mutinies were suppressed; most peasant soldiers remained loyal. The timely political and economic concessions of the October Manifesto satisfied most moderates and isolated radical elements. Mass groups were uncoordinated and lacked good leadership, while the bureaucracy and police solidly backed the regime. Finally, at a crucial time Witte secured a large French loan to prop up the government. Nonetheless, the Revolution of 1905 aroused the

Russian people politically and gave them a taste of freedom. The government restored order but not the awe it had formerly inspired in the masses. Tsarism had a last chance but under altered conditions.

CREATION OF THE DUMA MONARCHY, 1905–1906

The most dangerous time for a bad government, noted the 19th century French writer, Alexis de Tocqueville, is when it begins to change for the better. Bloody Sunday had shattered the myth of the Tsar as a benevolent, omniscient father. A new principle of political authority was needed, but as the revolution ebbed, Nicholas II salvaged most of his autocratic powers, fired Witte, and blocked creation of a true parliamentary regime. Further trouble portended between "society" and the government as the Manifesto's promises were hedged about with restrictions, infuriating the left liberals and making them into defiant obstructionists.

Decrees and acts of the next six months laid foundations for a regime satisfying neither side. To the liberals' dismay, an imperial manifesto of February 1906 created a bicameral legislature. The hitherto wholly appointive State Council was reorganized as a conservative upper chamber, half of it appointed by the Emperor, half of it elected by various social bodies (*zemstva,* municipal dumas, the nobility, universities, etc.). Though most males over the age of 25 could vote for deputies to the lower house, the State Duma, the electorate was divided into the traditional classes: landowners, peasants, and townspeople. A weighted, indirect franchise favored landowners and peasants and excluded many workers. It represented the belated realization of Speranskii's scheme of 1809,[1] not the "four-tailed" suffrage of liberal demands. The government expected the Duma to be a conservative assembly.

The Duma's powers were very limited. Russia's constitution, the Fundamental Laws of April 1906, described the emperor now as "autocrat" instead of "unlimited autocrat." He retained power to declare war and appoint and dismiss ministers of state, who were responsible to him alone. Duma members could question ministers, but the latter did not have to give satisfactory replies, and the crown retained all powers not specifically given to the legislature. To become law, a measure had to pass both houses, and the emperor retained absolute veto power. Article 87 of the Fundamental Laws further restricted Duma authority by authorizing ministers to govern by decree during Duma recesses provided the Duma approved such decrees subsequently. The Duma's ability to obstruct the executive was slight because the emperor determined the duration of its sessions and could prorogue it at will if he set a date for new elections. The Duma could not overturn the ministry nor revise the Fundamental Laws, and its control of the purse was severely restricted (It had no control over court expenses and little over

---

[1] See above, p. 271–72.

the army or state debt). Could any legislature operate effectively under such limitations?

Amidst continuing revolutionary disturbances, the electoral campaign for the First Duma began in December 1905. Excitement and expectancy gripped Russia as for the first time political parties, though still not legal, contended in national elections. The SR's, deciding at their first open congress in Finland to boycott the elections and promote violent revolution, demanded socialization of the land and its issuance to peasants on the basis of need and a federal system with full national self-determination for non-Russians. At their Fourth Congress in Stockholm (spring 1906), the SD's restored surface unity, but serious Bolshevik-Menshevik differences persisted. Initially, most SD's favored boycotting the elections, and then the Mensheviks decided to participate. Arguing that Bolsheviks could use the Duma to denounce tsarism, Lenin shocked his colleagues by voting with the Mensheviks. As revolutionary parties scarcely competed in the elections, peasants voted mostly for the Trudovik (Labor) group, largely SR in ideology but peaceful in tactics. Among the non-revolutionary parties, the most radical was the Constitutional Democrats (Kadets, KD), led ably by Miliukov and Struve from the Union of Liberation and Petrunkevich from the *zemstva*. Abandoning temporarily their call for a constituent assembly, the Kadets campaigned for full parliamentary rights for the Duma, alienation of large estates with compensation, and more rights for labor. The Octobrist Party led by A. I. Guchkov, representing moderate *zemstvo* leaders, business, and liberal bureaucrats, accepted the October Manifesto. Aiming to strengthen constitutional monarchy and civil liberties, it opposed real land reform and national self-determination. The extreme Right, especially the ultranationalist Union of the Russian People, denounced the Duma and the Jews, and demanded restoration of unlimited autocracy.

The election revealed Russia's radical mood and dismayed the government. The Kadets (180 seats) with their allies organized and dominated the First Duma, and the peasant Trudoviks had about 100 deputies. There were 18 Menshevik SD's, 17 Octobrists, 15 extreme Rightists, and about 100 deputies from national and religious minorities.

In the Winter Palace's elegant St. George's room, the Tsar opened the First Duma on May 10, 1906. He, his court, and ministers, magnificent and bejeweled, occupied one side of the hall. Opposite sat the staid State Council, and behind them crowded the 500 Duma delegates: bearded peasants, Mensheviks in worker blouses, and minority groups in national costume. The contrast between the élite and popular representatives resembled that at the French Estates-General of 1789. In a brief colorless "Address from the Throne," Nicholas II, like Louis XVI, gave the legislature no directives.

Organizing the Duma, the Kadets elected one of their own, Sergei Muromtsev, as speaker. Their reply to the Tsar's "Address" demanded fully democratic suffrage, abolition of the State Council as an upper house, ministerial responsibility to the Duma, and amnesty for all political prisoners; but Nicholas and his ministers refused such exorbitant demands. Obsessed by European precedents and blind to Russian realities, Miliukov spurned compromise. I. L. Goremykin, the faded and servile bureaucrat who had replaced Witte as premier, responded for the Tsar that the Duma's requests were all "inadmissible." The Duma promptly declared no confidence in the government, which simply ignored it. Because the Kadets failed to use existing Duma powers, vital issues such as land reform, minority rights, and education were neglected. Secret Duma discussions with the Tsar on a Kadet or coalition ministry proved fruitless. The Kadets' doctrinaire approach and Nicholas' suspicion doomed the First Duma and ultimately the constitutional experiment. When the Duma appealed directly to the public on the land question, Nicholas dissolved it without ordering new elections.

The Kadets responded with illegal defiance. When troops closed the Duma, some 180 delegates, mostly Kadets and Trudoviks, went to Vyborg, Finland, where Muromtsev proclaimed it reconvened. Miliukov drew up the Vyborg Manifesto, which urged Russians not to pay taxes or supply army recruits until the Duma met again, but there was little public response and the Manifesto's signers were tried, jailed briefly, and disfranchised. Losing many talented leaders, the Kadets never fully recovered their political leadership.

After the Duma's dissolution, P. A. Stolypin, since July 1906 premier and minister of interior, made frequent use of Article 87, which allowed the executive to rule by decree. This last statesman of imperial Russia dominated the political scene for the next five years. Stolypin, a well-to-do landowner, had been a provincial marshal of nobility who in 1905, as governor of Saratov province, had repressed peasant disorders ruthlessly. He was an impressive orator thoroughly convinced of his rectitude who favored bold measures and strongarmed tactics. Stolypin was a Russian nationalist who viewed repression as the prelude to reform by an enlightened autocracy. Proclaiming a state of emergency, he instituted field courts-martial against SR terrorists who were killing hundreds of police, priests and officials. By the spring of 1907, the trials had broken the revolutionary movement effectively.

To the government's chagrin, the short-lived Second Duma (February–June 1907) was more extreme and less constructive than the first. Both SD's and SR's participated in the elections, but Stolypin declared leftist parties illegal and forbade their campaign literature. Almost half those elected were socialists, but they failed to form a bloc and disdained collaboration with the Kadets, who had lost ground. The Duma debated Stolypin's agrarian reforms[2] heatedly, then refused to approve them. Violent SD attacks on the army infuriated the Tsar who, urged on by the Union of the Russian People, dissolved the Duma. The first constitutional phase ended in complete deadlock between the Duma and the executive.

---

[2] See below, pp. 404–5.

POLITICAL DEVELOPMENT, 1907–1914

Stolypin's decree of June 1907, dubbed a "coup d'etat," altered the original electoral laws arbitrarily to produce a Duma "Russian in spirit." Declared Stolypin: "We don't want professors, but men with roots in the country, local gentry and the like." Blatantly violating the Fundamental Laws, his measure insured that subsequent elections would be far from democratic. The government reduced peasant representation drastically, insuring that noblemen would choose almost half the electors; non-Russians lost most of their seats. Only about one fortieth of the population voted for the Third Duma, in which the Octobrists emerged as the largest party, the Right was greatly strengthened, and the Kadets were further weakened. On the Left, Trudoviks and Social Democrats each had 14 deputies. This "Masters' Duma" proved so satisfactory to the government that it was allowed to serve out its full five year term. Though the State Council blocked many progressive laws, the Duma nonetheless approved Stolypin's agrarian reforms, promoted universal education, extended local self-government and religious freedom, and expanded its control of the budget. Even the Third Duma marked an advance over the Pobedonostsev era: all political points of view were represented, political parties operated openly, and newspapers debated public issues. Whenever possible, the Duma protected and broadened civil liberties by drawing public attention to government abuses.

Outwardly the Fourth Duma (1912–17), more than half noblemen, seemed still more conservative. The strengthening of Right and Left at the expense of the political center revealed dangerous political polarization, but even many conservative deputies defended the Duma and observed parliamentary forms. The Duma's tragedy, notes Thomas Riha, was that "too few were learning too slowly" in a political oasis far from the masses. The government often treated it as a mere department, and the Emperor, until dissuaded by his ministers, considered making the Duma merely advisory.

Until late in 1911 Stolypin ran the executive branch capably if highhandedly. He used Article 87 to bypass the legislature whenever it obstructed his measures. At first he enjoyed Nicholas II's confidence and support; later he offended the imperial family. In September 1911, Stolypin was assassinated in the Kiev opera house by a double agent who received a ticket from the chief of police! Succeeding him as premier was Finance Minister V. N. Kokovtsov, who was able and moderate but lacked his predecessor's independence and dynamism. In late 1913 the Emperor removed him under pressure from the Empress and Gregory Rasputin, whose influence Kokovtsov had opposed consistently. The aged and incompetent Goremykin replaced him.

The revolutionary movement, though plagued by police infiltration, recovered somewhat after 1912 from its eclipse under Stolypin. The SR's were appalled by the exposure of Evno Azev, head of their Combat Detachment, as a police agent. Arrests and double agents also weakened the SD's. According to Trotskii, Bolshevik membership had shrunk in

1910 to 10,000. Early in 1914 Roman Malinovskii, Bolshevik leader in the Duma, was exposed as a police spy. Abroad, Lenin maintained his own organization and blocked efforts to reunite the party. In 1912 he convened a conference in Prague and set up a separate Bolshevik party. Later that year the so-called "August Bloc" under Martov and Trotskii held a separate Menshevik conference, and in 1913 separate Menshevik and Bolshevik fractions were formed in the Duma. The Bolsheviks retained their revolutionary fervor while the Mensheviks tried to create a legal, trade-union-oriented labor movement run by the workers themselves.

How were the Bolsheviks faring in 1914? Some Western accounts, emphasizing their demoralization, cite declining circulation of *Pravda*, their party newspaper, Lenin's isolation in SD ranks, a weak Russian apparatus, and loss of popularity among Russian workers. Only the outbreak of World War I, claims Leonard Schapiro, prevented the Bolsheviks' demise. A Soviet source, however, asserts that by July 1914 the Bolsheviks had the support of four fifths of Russian workers and were leading a militant strike movement in St. Petersburg. Leopold Haimson, an American historian, agrees that Bolsheviks were outdoing Mensheviks in the capitals because their revolutionary program and tactics appealed to many new workers. Bolshevik success, if success it was, reflected worker militancy more than skilful, perceptive leadership.

ECONOMIC AND SOCIAL DEVELOPMENT

Important economic and social change occurred between 1906 and 1914. Industrial growth was lifting Russia out of backwardness, and the Stolypin agrarian reforms was creating a basis for a new class of independent farmers. Social inequality was lessening as workers and peasants obtained higher incomes, greater mobility, and more rights.

Stolypin agreed with the socialists that a communal peasantry was potentially revolutionary. His government's aim therefore was to abolish the *mir* (peasant commune), free the peasant from it, and foster individual farming. Stolypin explained to the Duma in 1908: "The government has put its wager not on the drunken and the weak but on the sober and the strong—on the sturdy individual proprietor." In November 1906, he decreed after the First Duma that in communes without a general repartition since 1882, a householder could claim ownership of all plowland worked in 1906. In case of a repartition, he could demand land held before 1882 plus land received in a repartition provided he paid the commune the original redemption price. This policy encouraged peasants to shift from repartitional to hereditary tenure. The law of June 1910 dissolved all communes with no general repartition since 1861. After one peasant in such a commune applied for an ownership deed, all land in it became private. In repartitional and hereditary communes, the head of the household received ownership of the land, a policy which encouraged or even forced younger males to go to the city. Stolypin's ultimate objective was consolidation of scattered strips into Western-style farms.

How successful were these land reforms? Stolypin stressed the need for 20 years of peace to implement them, but they were halted in 1915. Though the government appointed many surveyors and exerted great pressure, results were inconclusive. By 1915 over half of Russian peasant households had hereditary ownership of their allotments, but less than ten percent were fully consolidated individual farms.[3] Agricultural techniques and output improved considerably on such farms, but village collectivism, though weakened, had not been destroyed by 1917.

Who benefited from the reforms? According to Soviet accounts, only a minority of wealthy peasants. Stolypin sought to end strip farming and carry through an agricultural revolution, reply recent Western accounts. Viewing the process as a race against time, Lenin feared that Stolypin's reforms would transform the dissatisfied peasantry, upon which he counted in the future, into a class of loyal, conservative peasant proprietors.

The government encouraged colonization of Siberia to absorb dispossessed younger peasants and to increase farm output. About half of Siberian wheat was exported abroad or to other parts of Russia. Siberia, however, lacking a local nobility, promoted rugged individualism and a bourgeois ethos which distressed conservatives. After a visit in 1910 Stolypin called Siberia "an enormous, rudely democratic country which will soon throttle European Russia." The government also promoted peasant land purchases through the Peasant Bank. In 1914, European Russian peasantry owned over four times as much land as the nobility (460 to 108 million acres). The vast state and imperial holdings (390 million acres) were mostly unsuited to agriculture. By 1917 most Russian crop land was already in peasant hands.

After 1905, significant industrial progress occurred though the government did not promote it with Witte's singleminded determination. The economy now was more mature, and the official role less marked. The Finance Ministry, despite creation of a separate Ministry of Trade and Industry, still controlled the keys to industrial development but used them more cautiously. Finance Minister Kokovtsov (1906–13), stressing balanced growth, sought to maintain the gold standard and a high tariff, to uphold Russia's foreign credit, and to balance the budget. Thanks to a spurt in new railroad building, the growth rate almost equalled that of the Witte period. Excellent harvests, large exports, and wider prosperity enhanced Russia's overall economic performance, although in 1914 it still had the lowest per capita wealth

---

[3] In 1915 of the some 14,000,000 peasant allotments, some 5,000,000 remained under repartitional tenure. About 1,300,000 were subject to automatic dissolution but had not actually been dissolved, and 1,700,000 had been affected to some degree. About 4,300,000 holdings had fully hereditary title in scattered strips, and more than 1,300,000 had been partially or completely consolidated into farms. Robinson, *Rural Russia* (New York, 1949), pp. 215–16.

of the major powers and its industry trailed those of England, Germany, the United States, and France.[4] Industrial progress now, instead of impoverishing the population, was combined with agricultural growth and modest prosperity. Russia had overcome its backwardness, claimed Kokovtsov, and only the Bolshevik Revolution interrupted its "swift and powerful development."

Geographical distribution of Russian industry changed little, but consolidation and foreign ownership increased. In 1912 the central industrial region produced more than one third of all manufactures, followed by the Ukraine, the northwest, and the Urals. In manufacturing the largest labor force was in metalworking, cottons, and other textiles. Soviet accounts stress that foreign interests initiated most industrial combinations in this "era of imperialism." In 1902 French capitalists fostered creation in southern Russia of Prodameta, a metallurgical cartel, the member firms of which by 1910 produced about three fourths of the empire's iron products and almost half its rails. The Duma, however, prevented it from becoming a full-fledged trust, a circumstance which revealed big industry's limited influence in imperial Russia. Other combinations formed in sugar (1887) and oil (1904). Foreign influence and investment in Russian industry were considerable, but Soviet claims that Russia had become a semi-colonial appendage of Western capitalism seem exaggerated. A tsarist source estimated foreign investment in Russia in 1916 at 2,243 million rubles, over half in mining, metallurgy, and metalworking with the French holding almost one third of this total, followed by the British, Germans, and Belgians.

Railroad construction remained the key to Russian industrial booms. The 6,600 miles of line built between 1902 and 1911 triggered an annual industrial growth rate of almost nine percent between 1909 and 1913 and overall economic growth of about six percent annually between 1906 and 1914. Private railroad lines were more efficient; but the state owned about two thirds of the network, and rising revenues from its lines enabled the government to pay interest on railroad loans and still have a surplus. Nonetheless, in 1914 Russia's external debt (5.4 billion rubles) was one of the world's largest.

Russia's foreign trade increased considerably in volume, but its direction and structure changed little. In 1913 exports were worth more than 1.5 billion rubles and imports 1,374,000,000. Russia still exported mostly agricultural goods (grain 44 percent, and livestock and forest products 22 percent). Industrial exports (ten percent) went mostly to backward Asian lands. Germany bought about 30 percent of Russian exports and supplied 47 percent of its imports; Britain stood second with 17.5 percent and 13 percent respectively.

The empire's population rose by almost one third between 1897 and 1913 to more than 165 million (excluding Finland). Mainly respon-

---

[4] In total volume of industrial production in 1913, France exceeded Russia 2.5 times, England 4.6, Germany 6, and the U.S. 14.3. P. Liashchenko, *History of the Russian National Economy* (New York 1949), p. 674.

sible were a birthrate much higher than in western Europe and a declining deathrate. The east had the highest growth rates, but three fourths of the population resided in European Russia. Despite industrialization and urban growth, cities in 1913 contained only 16 percent of the population.

Russian society in 1914, undergoing transition and with numerous inequities and frictions, remained dominated by a nobility which guarded its privileges jealously against the bourgeoisie. Impoverished lesser gentry were selling their lands rapidly, but large landowners retained much wealth and strengthened their influence at court. After 1906, a pressure group, the Council of the United Nobility, protected their interests. Within the Church the élite black (monastic) clergy remained in control and blocked needed reform. In an expanding bourgeoisie, Moscow entrepreneurs led the commercial and industrial elements; St. Petersburg remained the financial center. Outside the capitals the bourgeoisie was often cautious, stodgy, and engaged mainly in local trade and industry. Within the Russian middle class, liberal professions exceeded industrial and commercial elements in numbers and influence.

Among the peasantry slow differentiation was speeded somewhat by the Stolypin reforms, but the mass of middle peasantry was still growing numerically. There were tensions in the village between an upper crust of kulaks and proletarian and semi-proletarian elements, but the basic rural rivalry pitted peasant against nobleman. Peasant isolation was diminishing, and with freedom of movement gained after 1906, many younger peasants migrated to the cities. Peasant inferiority and poverty was lessening but remained potential dangers to the regime.

Instead of the increased misery Marx had predicted, the Russian industrial worker found his status and economic position much improved. Sharply reduced summertime departures by workers from the city to the village revealed growth of a largely hereditary working class. By 1914 more than three million workers labored in mines and factories, more than half of these in large enterprises. In St. Petersburg more than 70 percent worked in concerns with more than 500 employees. This situation facilitated socialist agitation and enhanced worker consciousness and solidarity. Working conditions were improving: the ten-hour day prevailed after 1912; accident and sickness insurance, paid partially by employers, was instituted; and factory inspection was tightened. Workers' real wages rose considerably, but they still lagged far behind European wages because Russian factory owners could draw on a large agrarian manpower reserve. Only the increasingly unionized skilled and semiskilled workers were paid enough to maintain normal family life; most others lived alone in barracks. Between 1907 and 1911, strikes declined sharply, but a massacre of workers in the British-owned Lena goldfields (April 1912) sparked a strong resurgence of strikes, increasingly political. St. Petersburg metalworkers, the highest paid and most literate, were the most militant Russian workers.

FOREIGN AFFAIRS, 1906–1914

Defeat in the war with Japan, the 1905 Revolution, and indebtedness restricted Russia's freedom of action abroad, and dreams of an expanded Asian empire lay shattered. Settling outstanding disputes in the Far and Near East, Russia concentrated again on Europe and the Balkans in an effort to regain lost prestige. The Foreign Ministry's task was to prevent exploitation of Russia's military weakness by other powers. Until 1914 it averted disaster by repeated diplomatic retreats under German pressure.

In the Far East, relations between Russia and Japan were transformed as Russian leaders learned from their defeat. Both powers were anxious to protect their mainland interests and moved toward partnership. The United States Open Door policy, an apparent screen for economic penetration of Manchuria, fostered a series of Russo-Japanese agreements. In 1910 Russia recognized Japan's special interests in Korea and south Manchuria in return for Japan's pledge to respect Russian domination of northern Manchuria and Outer Mongolia. Russia encouraged Mongolia to escape Chinese control; in 1912 it proclaimed its "independence" and became de facto a Russian protectorate. On the eve of World War I, Russia's position in the Far East was quite secure.

Powerful imperial Germany absorbed much of Russia's attention. In 1904–05, William II, to undermine the Franco-Russian Alliance, had offered the Tsar the defensive Björkö Treaty. Although the naive Tsar signed it, Foreign Minister Lamsdorf and Count Witte persuaded him to ignore it and stick to Russia's alliance with France. When Germany sought to humiliate France in Morocco (1905–06), Russia backed France loyally at the Algeciras Conference in return for a large French loan. The French alliance remained the cornerstone of Russian foreign policy until the end of the empire, and growing German military and naval strength fostered rapprochement between Russia and England. German leaders believed that Anglo-Russian imperial rivalries were insoluble, but Japan's defeat of Russia caused London to abandon fears of Russian expansionism. The friendship of Russia and England with France encouraged the British Liberal cabinet, realizing that it could not defend Persia, to seek agreement with Russia. Foreign Secretary Lord Grey wrote: "An entente between Russia, France, and ourselves would be absolutely secure. If it is necessary to check Germany, it could then be done."

Serious obstacles had to be overcome on the Russian side. Foreign Minister Alexander Izvolskii (1906–10), who reasserted his ministry's role (sometimes rashly), had to neutralize pro-German feeling at court and overcome the old Turkestan military men who coveted all of Persia. The Anglo-Russian Convention of August 1907 left Afghanistan and Tibet in the British sphere, while unfortunate Persia was partitioned into a British sphere in the southeast and a huge Russian zone in the north, separated by a neutral area. Anglo-Russian rivalry in Persia continued but became tolerable and peaceful. By 1914 Russia dominated most of it, but England accepted this as the price of containing Germany.

Izvolskii hoped that Britain would now assist him to revise the Straits Convention to let Russian warships pass through the Bosphorus, but he was disappointed. His interest in the Straits coincided with Austria's more dynamic Balkan policies. Conrad von Hötzendorf, Austrian chief of staff, wished to crush Serbia by preventive war, while Alois von Aehrenthal, the Foreign Minister, aimed to annex Bosnia and Herzegovina, which Austria had occupied since 1878. At Buchlau (September 1908) Aehrenthal and Izvolskii agreed that Russia would support their annexation by Austria in return for Austrian backing to revise the Straits Convention. Austria annexed Bosnia and Herzegovina, but Izvolskii could not win the other powers' consent on the Straits question. Angered by Austria's absorption of two Serbian-speaking provinces, Serbia demanded territorial compensation, but since Germany backed Austria, Russia dared not support Serbia's claims. Russia and Serbia had to back down before the German powers. The Bosnian crisis discredited Izvolskii and gave warning of a general war over the Balkans.

Succeeding Izvolskii as foreign minister was S. D. Sazonov (1910–16), a conscientious diplomat who lacked firm control over his subordinates. As Panslav tendencies revived, Russian consuls N. G. Hartvig in Belgrade and A. Nekliudov in Sofia advocated a forward policy. In 1912 with their warm encouragement, a Balkan League of Serbia, Bulgaria, Montenegro, and Greece was formed. In October, disregarding official Russian and Austrian warnings, the League attacked Turkey and conquered Macedonia. Austria, however, blocked Serbia's aspiration to Adriatic ports, and Russia yielded again to German threats. In a second Balkan war of 1913, Bulgaria, seeking control of Macedonia, attacked the Serbs and Greeks, but they, aided by Rumania and Turkey, defeated Bulgaria and seized Bulgarian Macedonia. This victory smashed the Balkan League, turned embittered Bulgaria toward the Central Powers, and damaged Russian prestige. Serbian nationalism intensified further as the Austrian military awaited an opportunity to crush Serbia completely.

In the Balkans before 1914, Russian and Austrian imperialism clashed and Russo-German tension was sometimes severe, but war between Russia and the Central Powers was far from inevitable. Russo-German friction over the Berlin to Bagdad Railway and over German attempts to dominate the Straits were settled peacefully. The Romanovs remained pro-German, supported by the Duma Right, which sought to buttress autocracy against Western liberal parliamentarism.

Suggested Additional Reading

Bock, Maria. *Reminiscences of My Father, Peter A. Stolypin* (Metuchen, New Jersey, 1970).

Charques, Richard. *The Twilight of Imperial Russia* (London, 1958, 1974).

FLORINSKY, MICHAEL. *The End of the Russian Empire* (New York, 1931, 1961).

GAPON, GEORGE. *The Story of My Life* (London, 1905).

GURKO, V. I. *Features and Figures of the Past* . . . (Stanford, 1939).

HARCAVE, SIDNEY. *The Russian Revolution of 1905* (London, 1970).

HOSKING, GEOFFREY. *The Russian Constitutional Experiment* . . . *1907– 1914* (New York, 1973).

IZVOLSKY, A. P. *Recollections of a Foreign Minister* (New York, 1921).

KOKOVTSOV, V. N. *Out of My Past* (Stanford, 1935).

LEVIN, ALFRED. *The Second Duma* (New Haven, 1940).

———. *The Third Duma: Election and Profile* (Hamden, Conn., 1973).

MCNEAL, ROBERT, ed. *Russia in Transition, 1905–1914* (New York, 1970).

MAKLAKOV, V. A. *The First State Duma* (Bloomington, Indiana, 1964).

———. *Memoirs of V. A. Maklakov* (Bloomington, Indiana, 1964).

MILIUKOV, PAUL. *Political Memoirs, 1905–1917*, ed. Mendel (Ann Arbor, 1967).

———. *Russia and Its Crisis* (Chicago, 1905, 1962).

OBERLANDER, E. *et al. Russia Enters the Twentieth Century* . . . (New York, 1971).

PARES, BERNARD. *Russia between Reform and Revolution* (New York, 1962).

RIHA, THOMAS. *A Russian European: Paul Miliukov* . . . (Notre Dame, Ind., 1968).

SABLINSKY, WALTER. *The Road to Bloody Sunday* (Princeton, N.J., 1976).

STAVROU, T. G., ed. *Russia under the Last Tsar* (Minneapolis, 1969).

THADEN, EDWARD. *Russia and the Balkan Alliance of 1912* (University Park, Pa., 1965).

29

Cultural Developments, 1855–1917

THE LATE 19th century witnessed a spectacular flowering of Russian culture. Nicholas I's death removed an oppressive weight from Russian life and ushered in a relatively liberal era which, combined with a powerful national upsurge, produced remarkable cultural creativity. Individuals in literature, art, music, and architecture began to experiment with new modes of expression. Frank discussion of the plight of the peasantry and emancipation focused attention on this long neglected segment of society. The daily lives of commoners, the drama and pathos of peasant life captured the imagination of Russian artists.

LITERATURE

Russian literature entered a Golden Age associated primarily with Turgenev, Dostoevsky, and Tolstoy, all among the world's greatest novelists. This triumvirate, building upon the legacy of Pushkin, Lermontov, and Gogol, became the most consummate practitioners of literary realism. Under their tutelage, Russian literature achieved great international acclaim.

Turgenev. Ivan Turgenev (1818–83) as a nobleman, received an excellent education first from private tutors, then at Moscow and St. Petersburg universities, and finally at the University of Berlin, where he was exposed to progressive and enlightened ideas and studied philosophy. His sojourn in Berlin made him an ardent Westerner. Always considered the most Western of Russia's major writers, Turgenev, through his works, taught Europeans to appreciate Russian literature and learn about Russian life. Returning to Russia in 1841, Turgenev was briefly in the civil service, then retired in 1845 to devote himself to literature. In 1847 his short stories about peasant life, based on personal observation, appeared in Nekrasov's *The Contemporary;* later they were published in book form as *A Sportsman's Sketches* (1852). This book won him wide recognition as the leading contemporary Russian author. Individually the stories seemed charming, harmless, picturesque ex-

411

Ivan Turgenev (1818–1883)

cursions into the peasant world; collectively they constituted a powerful indictment of serfdom, portraying the serf as full of compassion and dignity, often morally superior to his master. Despite sharp official criticism, the book affected public opinion deeply. Publication that same year of what the authorities considered Turgenev's questionable obituary of Gogol brought arrest, brief imprisonment, and banishment to his provincial estate. A year later he was pardoned and allowed to return to the capital, his reputation enhanced by his brush with the law, and he was regarded as the chief spokesman of literary Russia.

Turgenev embodied the new spirit pervading Russian life. In his first novels, *Rudin* (1856) and *Nest of Gentlefolk* (1859), he described graphically the mentality of the older generation with its misguided idealism, well intentioned but out of touch with reality. In the novel *On the Eve* (1860), he sought to portray the aspirations of the new generation. Each of these works, hailed as a model of literary realism, endeavored to show life as it really was and faced the most burning, controversial issues of the day. In these novels the critics found no sentimentality or fantasy, only beauty and truth, simplicity and sensitivity. Everyone hailed Turgenev, right-wing and left-wing critics admired his descriptive powers, his ability to portray character, and his literary insight.

Following this unprecedented literary success appeared Turgenev's most famous novel, *Fathers and Sons* (1862), which dealt with the eternal problem of conflict between generations. The struggle raged between men of the 1860s—Arkadi and the novel's hero, the nihilist Bazarov—and men of the 1840s represented by Arkadi's father and uncle. The novel was promptly attacked from all quarters. Right-wing critics condemned Turgenev for giving needless publicity to and implied approval of radicalism by depicting Bazarov too positively. The left criticized his portrait of Bazarov as a caricature misrepresenting the younger generation's aspirations. Except for Dmitri Pisarev who praised the novel, most radical critics claimed Turgenev had run out of talent. After an unbroken string of triumphs, the general rejection of *Fathers and Sons* was an unbearable blow to Turgenev's ego. He left Russia for good, except for a few brief visits home, and settled in western Europe. His novel, *Smoke* (1867) expressed his disillusionment with Russia over the reception of *Fathers and Sons*. *Smoke* depicted Russian aristocrats and political emigrés living at European spas, an unflattering portrait stressing their arrogance, narrowmindedness, and deceitfulness.

Turgenev's last novel, *Virgin Soil*, was a literary analysis of the "going to the people" movement of the early 1870s,[1] but neither this book nor *Smoke* had the same ring of authenticity which had given such freshness and charm to his earlier works. Turgenev had lost touch with Russia and Russian life in self-imposed exile, but his reputation grew in Europe as his works were translated there. Turgenev became the first Russian author to gain an international reputation; ultimately, he felt more at ease among Europe's literary elite than among his compatriots whom he treated with haughty disdain. Unreconciled with the Russia he loved so much, Turgenev died in a small French village near Paris.

Dostoevsky.   If Turgenev was the stylistic master of realism, Feodor Dostoevsky (1821–81) strove to be a "realist in a higher sense," plumbing the very depths of man's soul. He sought to penetrate the inner consciousness and lay bare the conflicts within human nature. His stunning metaphysical realism was concerned with the ultimate meaning and purpose of life. Dostoevsky felt ideas as others felt heat, cold, or pain; for him ideas had a tangible, palpable quality. He sought to overcome the divisions in Russian life and in so doing discovered that only by surmounting the more fundamental division between man and God could Russian life be restored to wholeness. Dostoevsky wrote:

> I am a child of the age, a child of unbelief and skepticism; I have been so far, and shall be I know to the grave. . . . If anyone proved to me that Christ was not the truth, and it really was a fact that the truth was not in Christ, I would rather be with Christ than the truth.[2]

He engaged in a lifelong struggle with religious belief, seeking to know and understand Christ. He always believed in Russia and the Russian

---

[1] See above, p. 382–83.

[2] Cited in E. H. Carr, *Dostoevsky* (New York, 1931) pp. 281–82.

Feodor Dostoevsky (1821–1881)

people and he tried in the same way to believe in God. One of his characters in *The Possessed* blurts out: "I believe in Russia, I believe in Orthodoxy . . . I believe that Christ will come again in Russia. And in God? in God? . . . I . . . I shall believe in God." Ultimately, this was Dostoevsky's own conviction and the message he wished to proclaim in his writings.

Dostoevsky was the son of a well-to-do but miserly doctor. In 1839, while he was attending the Military Engineering Academy in St. Petersburg, Dostoevsky learned of his father's murder by vengeful peasants. With the inheritance he received, his financial position improved markedly. In 1843 he was commissioned in the army and appointed to the Engineering Department of the War Ministry. The next year, rather than accept reassignment to a distant post, Dostoevsky resigned to devote himself exclusively to literature. The first period of his literary career began in 1845 with publication of the short novel, *Poor Folk*, and ended with his arrest for alleged subversion in 1849. The second period of his literary activity dates from the appearance of *Notes From the House of the Dead* in 1861 and closes with *The Brothers Karamazov* in 1880, the year before his death.

"We have all sprung from Gogol's 'Overcoat,'" Dostoevsky once remarked. Indeed, the relationship between *Poor Folk* and "The Overcoat" is evident. Dostoevsky uses an exchange of letters between a young girl and an aging government clerk to expose the pathos, self-delusion, and constant struggle of the downtrodden for human dignity. The novel foreshadowed Dostoevsky's intense concern with psychological torment, pity, self-sacrifice, and alienation, which become key themes of his later great novels. At the age of 23, he was hailed as a new Gogol, recognized overnight as one of Russia's most promising authors. His success went to his head. When his second novel, *The Double* (1846) was greeted indifferently, his vanity was deeply wounded. Estranging himself from his literary friends, he joined the radical Petrashevskii Circle.[3] Neither a revolutionary nor a radical, Dostoevsky joined the group partly out of boredom and curiosity. But in the stifling atmosphere of Nicholas I's Russia, any noncomformist behavior was quickly equated with treason. Dostoevsky and his fellow "conspirators" of the Circle were arrested in April 1849. Confined for eight months in Peter and Paul Fortress, he was then convicted of crimes against the state. Dostoevsky's death sentence was commuted at the place of execution to eight years exile in Siberia. Being snatched from the very jaws of death had a profound and lasting effect on him. His already profound interest in human psychology and torments of the mind was further stimulated to extraordinary limits by this shattering experience. For almost a decade Dostoevsky languished in prison and exile, lost to Russian literature.

Dostoevsky recorded his prison sojourn vividly in letters to his younger brother, Michael; then in the famous *Notes From the House of the Dead* (1861), resembling Alexander Solzhenitsyn's account of life in contemporary Soviet prisons.[4] Dostoevsky's work, however, suffers from remoteness, a sense of detachment required by the rigid censorship which is wholly absent in his private letters. He wrote his brother:

> For five years I have lived under the control of warders in a crowd of human beings, and have never been alone for a single hour. To be alone is a necessity of normal existence, like drinking and eating; otherwise, in this forced communal life you become a hater of mankind. The society of people acts like a poison or an infection, and from this insufferable torment I have suffered more than anything these four years.[5]

In spite of harsh conditions, imprisonment was a turning point in Dostoevsky's life and produced an intellectual reorientation which profoundly affected his entire outlook. He discovered two vital sources of inspiration which became bases for his later views: the New Testament and "the people" of Russia.

In 1859 Dostoevsky was allowed to return to Petersburg. In partnership with his brother, he entered the capricious journalistic world. Initial success hardly compensated for the disasters which soon descended upon him: suppression by the authorities, and financial failure. In 1864 the unexpected deaths of his wife and beloved brother plunged him into grief and his debts brought him to the brink of bankruptcy.

That disastrous year Dostoevsky wrote a seminal work in his first venture into philosophy: *Notes From Underground*. He sought to release his own despair and to answer the radical Chernyshevskii's *What*

---

[3] See above, p. 299.

[4] See below, pp. 605, 612–15.

[5] Cited in Helen Muchnic, *An Introduction to Russian Literature* (New York, 1947), pp. 129–30.

Is To Be Done?, a shallow portrait of the utopian future.[6] Chernyshevskii believed that people were inherently good and rational; Dostoevsky argued that man by virtue of his free will was equally capable of choosing good or evil, and presented people as irrational and contradictory, capable of building and destroying, loving and hating, affirming and denying. Man's ability to choose, claimed Dostoevsky, was the very root of his freedom. These ideas were developed more fully in his major novels.

The four great novels *Crime and Punishment* (1866), *The Idiot* (1868–69), *The Possessed* (1871–72), and his final and most profound work, *The Brothers Karamazov* (1879–80) constitute an interrelated cycle. Each deals with issues of contemporary Russian life, reflects a stage in Dostoevsky's elaboration of Christianity, and represents a carefully drawn portrait of the "underground man." *Crime and Punishment* reveals the tragic failure of Raskolnikov, a poor student, to assert his individuality and personal worth "without God" through the senseless murder of a pawnbroker and her sister. Raskolnikov succeeds only in denying his humanity and Christian spirit. In *The Idiot*, Dostoevsky portrays saintly idiocy—a long revered Russian trait—in the Christlike Prince Myshkin, an impotent epileptic, long confined in mental institutions. Returning to society, he becomes enmeshed in the lives of "ordinary" people, who find him amusing, harmless, pure, and wholly gullible. They exploit his kindness and generosity shamelessly and destroy him by making him into a real madman. Myshkin by his actions, attempts to spread Christian compassion and, like Christ, is ridiculed and abused. Unlike Christ, his suffering serves no purpose, but Myshkin remains one of Dostoevsky's most sympathetic characters.

The Possessed deals with what Dostoevsky thought were socialism's destructive qualities. It is based on a sensational incident in which the ruthless nihilist, Nechaev,[7] persuaded his followers to murder in cold blood a fellow-conspirator suspected of wishing to betray the group to the police. The "Nechaev Affair" convinced Dostoevsky of socialism's moral bankruptcy. *The Possessed* dramatized the alienation and estrangement which, he felt, resulted from rejecting Christianity. In *The Possessed* the theater of the struggle between good and evil is all of Russia. Dostoevsky feared that the evil of socialism threatened Russia with destruction just as it destroyed individuals like Raskolnikov or Nechaev. The novel, a powerful indictment of the revolutionary movement, provoked a storm of criticism in the press. Left-wing critics vilified Dostoevsky as a writer devoid of talent, a man who had betrayed his principles. Undaunted, he continued his quest for spiritual peace and salvation for Russia.

In his greatest novel, *The Brothers Karamazov*, Dostoevsky tried to resolve the issues which had so long tormented him. The plot revolves around the murder of old Feodor Karamazov by one of his four sons, which provokes a great theological debate between Ivan Karamazov

---

[6] See above, pp. 380–81.

[7] See above, pp. 381–82.

and his younger brother Alyosha over the existence of God. The debate culminates in the famous "Legend of the Grand Inquisitor," which portrays in parable form the human conflict between material well-being and spiritual struggle for belief in God. In the parable Christ reappears in Spain during the Inquisition, a time of persecution and intolerance. Christ is recognized by the people and by the Grand Inquisitor, who threatens to burn Him at the stake as a public enemy because Christ offers freedom of choice by asking man to grant Him allegiance freely without coercion. Freedom of choice, warns the Grand Inquisitor, threatens man's happiness and well-being. Man, he argues, begs for authoritarianism to be free of the awesome responsibility of freedom. Give man material well-being and he will be happy; give him freedom and he will be tormented and miserable. Socialist revolutionaries, like the Grand Inquisitor, offered man material well-being at the cost of his freedom, contended Dostoevsky. Society was doomed unless it embodied Christ's ideal. The Russian common people, he believed, bore a new spirit of Christlike harmony, which once manifested could redeem mankind. The salvation of Russia and mankind was to be found not in socialism or nihilism, but in man's spiritual rebirth through voluntary acceptance of Christ's spirit. Dostoevsky conveyed this universal message with great power and supreme artistry in *The Brothers Karamazov,* in which, he claimed, "everything will be said."

Tolstoy. Leo Tolstoy (1828–1910), often compared with Dostoevsky, was very different. From a well-to-do noble family with estates south of Moscow, Tolstoy was tutored at home, then attended Kazan University to become a diplomat. He shifted to law but finally decided to abandon his studies and open a school for peasant children on his estate. He joined the army in 1851, served in the Caucasus, and began his literary career there with a semi-autobiographical trilogy, *Childhood, Boyhood,* and *Youth* (1852–57), which won him wide acclaim as a writer. During the Crimean War he participated in the siege of Sevastopol, recording his impressions in his successful *Sevastopol Stories.* After the war Tolstoy resigned from the army, traveled in Europe, and became an advocate of reform. In 1862 he married and settled down on his estate to devote himself to writing and his family.

His great novels, *War and Peace* and *Anna Karenina,* stem from this tranquil period of his life. *War and Peace* (1869) is a vast literary canvas of the momentous events of the Napoleonic period and probes in revealing detail the personal lives of many people from all social groups. Vast panoramas, thousands of men in movement, great battles, agonizing retreats, and the historic encounter between Napoleon and Kutuzov serve as a rich backdrop for Tolstoy's philosophy of history and moral philosophy. The novel's heroine and Tolstoy's ideal woman is Natasha Rostov, an ordinary woman with extraordinary qualities, who becomes the mirror of mighty historical forces. It is ordinary men and women who move history, not supposed great heroes like Napoleon, he believed. In fact, Tolstoy viewed Napoleon not as the arbiter of history, but as a mere puppet, manipulated by forces and circumstances beyond his control. To Tolstoy, history was a process with its own

Count Leo Tolstoy (1828–1910) in his study

inner logic gradually working itself out through people who were its agents, not its creators. Despite its huge cast of characters and the bewildering variety of human experience recorded, *War and Peace* is a remarkably unified masterpiece in which Tolstoy's philosophy is integrated perfectly with his imaginative artistry.

Unlike *War and Peace*, Tolstoy's *Anna Karenina* has different dimensions and smaller confines, but is a truly great social novel. In it Tolstoy expressed his views on such major public issues as judicial reform, emancipation, the Russo-Turkish War, and the nobility's economic decline. The novel's focus is the triangle of Anna, her husband Alexis, and her lover, Count Vronskii, surrounded by numerous other characters. Contrasting with the tempestuous affair between Anna and Vronskii is Kitty's marriage to the idealistic landowner, Levin. Anna and Vronskii struggle against social conventions which refuse to let them pursue happiness together. When her husband refuses divorce, Anna abandons her child to live with Vronskii despite society's scorn. Eventually bitterness and guilt corrupt their relationship until Anna, to achieve peace, throws herself under a passing train. Vronskii's life is utterly ruined.

None of Tolstoy's later works have the same scope, intensity, and depth as the two abovementioned masterworks. In the late 1870s Tolstoy underwent a profound religious conversion, dramatically recounted in *A Confession* (1882). He rejected the dogma, liturgy, and ritual of Orthodoxy for a rationalistic Christianity rooted in belief in nonresistance to evil. He called for a nonviolent moral revolution predicated on rejecting all institutions of coercion: the Church, state, and private property. His critique of contemporary society brought conflict with the Church, which excommunicated him publicly in 1901. Tolstoy's denunciations of the nobles' greed and selfishness and his repudiation of private property caused conflict with them and the state, which viewed his ideas as dangerously revolutionary. His unconventional views on marriage and the family expressed in *The Kreutzer Sonata* (1889) and *The Devil*, published posthumously, provoked bitter dissension within his own family. At the age of 82, signing over his property to his estranged wife, Tolstoy set out on a pilgrimage and died within a few days at a house in Riazan province. Justifiably, he has been called the last "true giant of the reformist aristocratic intelligentsia." His great works were but prologue to his restless, driving ethical search for answers to those "cursed questions"—the meaning of life and history.

Chekhov. The great literary tradition begun by Pushkin ends with Anton Chekhov (1860–1904), the last great figure of 19th century Russian literature. He was born in Taganrog on the Sea of Azov, son of a greengrocer and grandson of a serf. He grew up amidst provincial boredom, middle-class piety, straitened finances, and poor health. When his family had to move to Moscow, Anton remained in Taganrog, supporting himself by tutoring backward children and running errands. Nonetheless, he was a gay, carefree youth with an extraordinary sense of humor, which often appeared in his later stories. His literary career began in 1880 with stories hastily written for pulp magazines under the pseudonym, Antosha Chekhonte. Besides putting him through medical school, his writings gave him by 1884 the reputation of a prolific writer of modest talent. When one of his stories, published in 1885, attracted interest among the literary elite, Chekhov was invited to St. Petersburg and was introduced to Alexis Suvorin, editor of the leading daily, *New Times*. Impressed with Chekhov's obvious abilities, Suvorin urged him to make writing his career. Chekhov, much flattered, continued writing short stories, the quality of which improved as their quantity decreased. In 1888 he received the prestigious Pushkin Prize from the Russian Academy of Sciences. Amidst this growing success came the first signs of tuberculosis, which would end his life prematurely. With premonitions of death, Chekhov wrote many of his finest stories between 1889 and 1897. They reflected growing personal restlessness and the conviction that sweeping changes were required in Russia. Recurrent themes are human vanity, weaknesses, and melancholia. Many of his characters are preoccupied with longing for a richer and more beautiful future.

Anton Chekhov (1860–1904)

Always fascinated by the theatre, Chekhov had written several witty one-act comedies. In 1895 he composed a more serious play, *The Sea Gull,* the performance of which in 1896 was a disaster because the director and actors did not understand it. Chekhov vowed never to write another play, a pledge he fortunately broke. Two years later *The Sea Gull* was performed by a new theatrical company formed by K. S. Stanislavskii and V. I. Nemirovich-Danchenko, the famous Moscow Art Theater. Its directors and actors understood the subtleties of *The Sea Gull,* which became a sensation. In close association with Stanislavskii and the Moscow Art Theater, Chekhov wrote his immortal plays, *Uncle Vania, The Three Sisters,* and *The Cherry Orchard* between 1899 and 1903. Lacking clear plots or dramatic climaxes, they are studies in human character, psychology, and complex human relationships. Understatement, lack of suspense, little action—Chekhov's literary devices —succeed brilliantly on the stage. Despite apparently banal dialogue, Chekhov wrote with tremendous enthusiasm for life and unfaltering optimism about the future. A sense of anticipation and hope pervades almost everything he wrote. Chekhov lived in a Russia moving into the 20th century, an age of momentous change. The words of a character in his last story, "A Marriageable Girl," reflect the anticipation and apprehension he and his generation felt about the future:

> The whole town was so outmoded and antiquated, she felt. Was it awaiting its own end? Or expecting something fresh and original to begin? It was never quite clear which. Oh, if it would only hurry up and begin . . . that brave new world where you can face your own

destiny boldly, where you can be cheerful and free, knowing you're in the right! Now, such a life *will* come about sooner or later.[8]

Chekhov died in the summer of 1904 while optimistically taking a health cure in Germany. He left a rich and varied legacy of plays, stories, letters, and essays which deeply influenced writers in Russia and abroad. He brought the Golden Age to a close, though Russian literature continued to be creative and original. The last tsarist decades witnessed another outburst of creative energy, called the Silver Age. The transitional figure was Maxim Gorkii (1869–1936), whose literary credo evolved from classical realism through neoromanticism to socialist realism.

Gorkii. From a lower middle-class family, Maxim Gorkii (born A. M. Peshkov), saw his modest social status deteriorate rapidly after his father's premature death. On the streets at a tender age, he obtained his education by surviving in the hostile environment of Nizhnii-Novgorod. Gorkii wandered ceaselessly through southern Russia, learning what he could from whomever he met and gaining invaluable insights into life's vicissitudes. He acquired a profound understanding of and sympathy for the downtrodden and wretched. Acquaintances from these early years later appeared in his writings. Gorkii's first published work was *Makar Chudra* (1892), a tale of love, passion, and violence among gypsies. Written in a realistic style, which expressed a deeply felt humanitarianism, his early works reflect his predilection for broad social themes. His stories were well received because they portrayed vividly to the reading public a little known or little understood world. In 1898 his collected stories were issued in two immensely successful volumes, insuring his reputation as a talented and forceful writer. In 1902 he was elected to the Russian Academy of Sciences, only to have the government annul the election on political grounds, an action which endeared him all the more to the public. Long associated with the revolutionary movement and arrested in 1900, he supported the Social Democrats and after 1903 tended toward the Bolshevik position.

Urged on by Chekhov, his friend and benefactor, Gorkii began to write plays. In 1902 Stanislavskii's Moscow Art Theater staged his drama, *The Lower Depths,* with limited success. It is a rather unconventional play set in a dreary, decaying boardinghouse filled with social dregs—drunks, prostitutes, thieves, and other poor people. Quickly translated into several foreign languages, it became a hit in western Europe. In this play Gorkii defended the dignity of people ground down by tsarism. It was a clarion call for freedom, a reaffirmation of human dignity. The authorities banned it in the provinces and branded Gorkii a dangerous radical.

Gorkii's massive and tendentious novels were less successful as artistic creations. One of them, *Mother* (1907) was composed in the Adirondack Mountains of New York on Gorkii's ill-fated visit to the United States after the 1905 Revolution. Participating in the revolution,

---

[8] *The Oxford Chekhov,* R. Hingley trans. and ed. (London, 1975), vol. 9, p. 222.

Maxim Gorkii (1869–1936)

Gorkii had been arrested again, then released provided he left Russia. He was disillusioned with the United States and criticized American society bitterly in a series of stories about New York: *The City of the Yellow Devil* (1907). He finally settled in Italy where his villa on the Isle of Capri became a haven for political exiles and an artists' and writers' colony. His reputation in Russia dwindled in his absence and his novels were poorly received. His great autobiographical work, *Childhood* (1913), followed by *Among Strangers* (1915), restored his faltering renown as a writer of power and depth. He returned to Russia in 1913 during a political amnesty honoring the Romanovs' tercentenary, and plunged again into political activity, writing for the Bolshevik press and editing a Marxist journal, *Annals.* Gorkii rejoiced at tsarism's collapse in March 1917, but was less enthusiastic about the Bolshevik seizure of power in November. He had quarreled with Lenin frequently and their relations grew strained. Eventually, he made his peace with Lenin and continued writing in the Soviet period.

Decadence and Symbolism. Other writers criticized Gorkii not so much for his radical politics as for his continued commitment to a literary realism they considered outmoded. Many rejected literary realism and emphasis on socially significant, didactic art in favor of preoccupation with form and beauty. A general European romantic revival influenced these new trends in Russia. There the revival became known as the Decadent movement and later Symbolism. Decadent or Symbolist writers and poets emphasized esthetics and the principle, "art for art's sake." Mysticism, individualism, sensualism, and demonism were its hallmarks. Language became vague, even obscure in an effort to create symbolic images and sounds, contributing to a resurgence of poetry which had been eclipsed by the prose of recent decades. The older Symbolists included Dmitri Merzhkovskii, Feodor Sologub, Konstantin Balmont, Valeri Briusov, Zinaida Gippius, and Vasili Rozanov. The younger Symbolist generation included the great Alexander Blok, Andrei Belyi, Viacheslav Ivanov, Alexis Remizov, and Nicholas Gumilev. These poets formed a closely knit group which, meeting frequently and contributing to the same journals and reviews, created poetry unsurpassed in technical perfection, pure tonal harmony, and sheer beauty. These writers were mostly unaffected by the outbreak of World War I and growing crises in Russian society. Most welcomed the March Revolution, but the Bolshevik takeover dismayed many writers. Some chose to go into voluntary exile abroad; others remained in Russia hoping to influence revolutionary developments. War and revolution took their toll of Russian culture but pointed it in new and uncharted directions.

In music, painting, and architecture, developments paralleled, though belatedly, those in literature. Painting and music, following literature's lead, responded favorably to the national upsurge following the Crimean War and were influenced by the new realistic esthetics. Architecture was less affected until the turn of the century.

MUSIC

The Russian Music Society, founded in 1859, helped foster musical activity in Russia, promoted conservatory training, and encouraged music appreciation among the public. Anton Rubinstein, a distinguished pianist and composer, was the moving force behind it. With his younger brother, Nicholas, he established branches of the Music Society in Moscow and some 30 provincial centers. Conservatories were founded in St. Petersburg, Moscow, Kiev, Kharkov, Saratov, Tbilisi, and Odessa to provide musical education. The Society organized several symphony orchestras and smaller performing ensembles and sponsored concerts by Russian and foreign artists all over Russia to bring music to wider audiences. Conservative in musical taste and theory, the Society followed the lead of the Rubinsteins, who viewed the German classical and romantic schools of composition as the models to be emulated.

Despite the Society's remarkable popular success and an upsurge of interest in music, its conservative credo did not go unchallenged. A small group of musicians formed to initiate a revolution in Russian music and direct it along new paths; the famous "Five," or the so-called "Mighty Handful." One could scarcely imagine a more unlikely group to revolutionize the field of music. Its leader and organizer was Mily Balakirev (1837–1910), its only trained musician, an excellent pianist and conductor but mediocre as a composer. Cesar Cui (1835–1918) was trained as an engineer and eventually became a general of army engineers. Modest Musorgskii (1839–81) was a Guards officer and later an official in the Transport Ministry. Alexander Borodin (1834–87), trained as a doctor of medicine, eventually became professor of chemistry at the St. Petersburg Medical-Surgical Academy. Nicholas Rimskii-Korsakov (1844–1908) became a naval officer and later a professor of music at the St. Petersburg Conservatory. These men, from diverse backgrounds and differing professional interests, did not always agree on everything, but they shared common musical ideals and attitudes.

The "Five," considering themselves the legitimate successors of Glinka and Dargomyzhskii, aimed to create a Russian national school of music based on native folk and church music. Rejecting strict Western rules of technical form, they preferred a freer, more flexible style associated with folk music. They abhorred imitation of foreign models and scorned the canons of Italian opera as shallow devices to glorify the voice. Italian opera, they believed, was devoid of content and dramatic effect. Not surprisingly, bitter polemics erupted between Rubinstein's conservatives and Balakirev's musical nationalists which failed to resolve their fundamental differences but publicized and popularized music. In 1862, to counter the influence of Rubinstein's Music Society, the "Five" organized the Free School of Music to promote their musical theories in teaching, musical theory, and through performances of their works. The great champion of the "Five," the Free School of Music, and the nationalist musical trend was the distinguished art and music critic, V. V. Stasov (1824–1906), whose caustic polemics and enthusiastic reviews won for the "Five" a large and loyal following.

Balakirev and Borodin were the creators of the Russian symphonic

Modest Musorgskii (1839–1881)

school and both contributed significantly to symphonic theory. Musorgskii, Rimskii-Korsakov, and Borodin were the geniuses of Russian opera, whose works have survived fluctuating tastes and remain in the repertoire throughout the world. Borodin worked 18 years on his great opera, *Prince Igor*, first performed in 1890 with great success. Based on the disputed 12th century epic, *The Tale of the Host of Igor*,[9] it is a heroic national saga. Musorgskii composed his monumental opera, *Boris Godunov*, adapted from Pushkin's play, between 1870 and 1874, one of the greatest works of art ever produced in Russia. Rimskii-Korsakov expended enormous amounts of time and energy to complete Musorgskii's unfinished opera, *Khovanshchina*, another historical drama, which premiered in 1886. Rimskii-Korsakov's own operas, somewhat less well-known outside of Russia, include *The Snow Maiden*, a fantastic Russian fairy tale; *Sadko*, an old folktale of Novgorod; and the well-known, *The Golden Cockerel* (*Le Coq d'Or*), also based on a fairy tale.

Tchaikovsky. Among the first students at the St. Petersburg Conservatory opened in 1862, was Peter Tchaikovsky (1840–1893), destined to become the best known and most beloved Russian composer. His name became synonymous with Russian music, and his works remain favorites throughout the world. Like so many of his contemporaries, Tchaikovsky was trained not for a musical career, but for the civil service and briefly served as a minor official in the Ministry of Justice. Music was his passion, and he studied privately until enrolling in the Conservatory. He soon resigned his civil service post to devote himself to full-time study. He was such a distinguished music student that he was invited to join the faculty of the new Moscow Conservatory in 1866; for the next dozen years he worked and taught there. His association with the Rubinsteins and with Moscow fostered antagonism between him and the "Five" in St. Petersburg, which unfortunately often obscured how much they shared and how close they were in musical tastes and attitudes. Their antagonism often was more personal than professional. Some critics have characterized Tchaikovsky's music as cosmopolitan and Western, while calling that of the "Five" nationalist and Russian. This superficial distinction ignores their common origins and national feelings.

In Moscow Tchaikovsky composed some of his finest and most enduring music. Despite recurring mental crises, he completed four symphonies, many operas, including *Eugene Onegin*, adapted from Pushkin, concertos, and much incidental music, and his greatest ballet, *Swan Lake*. Then followed a period of acute depression and nervous tension, which prevented him from composing with the same intensity and creative power. Another burst of sustained creative energy began in 1889 with his second great ballet, *The Sleeping Beauty*, followed in 1892 by a third, *The Nutcracker*, one of his most popular compositions. Traveling in western Europe in 1892, Tchaikovsky rediscovered his old facility in composition, which had eluded him for years and realized that his Sixth Symphony ("Pathetique") would be his masterpiece.

---

[9] See above, pp. 52, 56.

First performed in St. Petersburg in October 1893, under the composer's direction, it has been acclaimed universally not only as Tchaikovsky's greatest work, but one of the greatest of all Russian musical works.

More than any other 19th century Russian composer, Tchaikovsky acquired even in his lifetime an international reputation. In his last years he traveled extensively, conducting his music all over the world, and was specially honored at ceremonies opening Carnegie Hall in New York City in 1891. Despite or perhaps because of his international reputation, nationalists criticized his music as too Western and imitative of foreign models. This criticism was justified in the sense that Tchaikovsky was influenced by European musical traditions, but it did not mean that his music was not Russian. Igor Stravinsky, his worthy successor, emphasized repeatedly its uniquely Russian quality:

> Tchaikovsky's music, which does not appear specifically Russian to everybody, is often more profoundly Russian than music which has long since been awarded the facile label of Muscovite picturesqueness. This music is quite as Russian as Pushkin's verse or Glinka's song. While not especially cultivating in his art the "soul of the Russian peasant," Tchaikovsky drew unconsciously from the true popular sources of our race.[10]

By the turn of the century, Russian music had achieved unprecedented maturity, international recognition, and respect. A whole group of brilliant teachers took up the cause in Russian conservatories and helped mold a new generation of composers, which carried on the traditions of the "Five" and Tchaikovsky. Among the most talented were Serge Rachmaninov (1873–1943), A. E. Glazunov (1865–1936), A. Liadov (1855–1914), M. M. Ippolitov-Ivanov (1859–1936), and Serge Taneev (1850–1918). None achieved the status or reputation of the "Five" or Tchaikovsky, nor did they possess quite the same creative spark, but they contributed nonetheless many original and creative compositions to Russian music.

Meanwhile a pair of young, innovative Russian composers opened up entirely new vistas, much as the Symbolists had introduced new forms of poetic expression. Alexander Scriabin (1871–1915) came from a musical family and revealed a precocious talent, which was nurtured by excellent teachers. Enrolled at the Moscow Conservatory at the age of 16, he revealed prodigious ability as a pianist and as a composer. He dabbled in mysticism, devoured Decadent poetry, and wrote poetry himself. Scriabin went on a successful concert tour of Russia and Europe, but he suffered from nervous disorders which cut short his career. Influenced by the Symbolists, Scriabin rejected the musical realism of the "Five" and Tchaikovsky's academic conventions and charted a new musical course. Inspired by mysticism, romanticism, the occult, and the Decadents, Scriabin concluded that art must transform life. Pain, ugliness, and evil would be transformed into beauty and joy by art; life would be transformed into the Kingdom of God on earth. He viewed the artist as a new messiah, capable of redeeming mankind

---

[10] Cited in R. A. Leonard, *A History of Russian Music* (London, 1956), p. 197.

and infusing life with new creative energy, lifting man to the level of a god. He composed music, such as *The Poem of Ecstasy,* of eerie, haunting qualities, music which he characterized as mystico-religious, the basis for a new harmonic system. His influence remained limited outside Russia, but his compositions, especially his piano music, affected Stravinsky, Sergei Prokoviev, and Dmitri Shostakovich. Today his music is experiencing a revival in the West.

Stravinsky. Stravinsky (1882–1971) marks a watershed in the history of Russian music because he represents the first tide of musical influence flowing *from* Russia *into* Europe. Unlike most of his contemporaries, Stravinsky was self-taught until tutored by Rimskii-Korsakov. His early career was closely associated with the famous Russian impresario, Serge Diagilev (1872–1929), who heard two of his works at a private concert in 1908 and was deeply impressed. At the time Diagilev was preparing the program for the first season of the revolutionary Ballet Russe de Monte Carlo in Paris, and he asked Stravinsky to orchestrate two Chopin pieces for the ballet. Thus began one of the most revolutionary and productive associations in musical history—Diagilev, the organizer and man of ideas; Stravinsky, the musical innovator whose scores would revolutionize music; Michael Fokine, the choreographer whose ballets would become modern classics against which all other dance was measured; Leon Bakst, the brilliant set and costume designer who with Alexandre Benois revolutionized set design; and finally Vaslav Nijinsky, perhaps the greatest of all ballet dancers.

Library of Congress

Igor Stravinsky (1882–1971)

Together in 1910 they created a stunning and opulent production of *The Firebird,* based on an old Russian folktale, with music by Stravinsky, choreography by Fokine, and sets by Bakst. The result was an international triumph of extraordinary importance. In 1911 the company staged *Petrushka,* a ballet teeming with new ideas and musical forms. Stravinsky introduced a radical orchestral style and boldly innovative music, which shocked many listeners. In 1913 Diagilev staged Stravinsky's even more radical ballet, *The Rite of Spring,* which created a public scandal because of its brutal realism, violence, and extraordinary vitality, which to many was sheer lunacy and cacophony, insulting to a generation still steeped in sentimental romanticism. Stravinsky was the musical descendant of Musorgskii's realism and a musical nationalist in these early works, using the rich tradition of Russian folk music. After these amazing early successes, Stravinsky sought still newer musical forms, which led him away from Russian traditions. Before World War I, he settled in Switzerland, and after the war he lived in France. At the outbreak of World War II he moved to the United States. War and revolution cut him off from Russia which he revisited triumphantly only in his final years. The creativity of Russian music in the last decades of the monarchy, epitomized by Stravinsky, parallels in many ways the flowering of Russian literature during its "Golden Age."

PAINTING

Russian painting developed rapidly during the late 19th century, though less dramatically than music. Painting was finally emancipated from the neoclassical style long imposed by the Academy of Arts. As in literature and music, young artists challenged older artistic conventions and strove to develop realism and nationalism in painting. In 1863, the entire graduating class of the Academy openly challenged the rigid policies of the artistic establishment. Opposition to Academy policies and to its monopoly over art surfaced after "The Festival of the Gods in Valhalla" was decreed as compulsory subject matter for the annual competition to determine those who would be selected to continue their studies in Italy. Refusing to participate in such a competition, the students demanded the right to select their own subjects freely so as best to display their artistic talents. When the authorities demurred, 14 students resigned from the Academy in protest and formed their own artistic cooperative (*artel*), which soon evolved into the Society of Traveling Art Exhibitions. This organization dominated Russian art from 1870 into the 1890s and survived until the 1920s. The Society was organized by young artists who were cultural nationalists and rejected the Academy's cosmopolitan and neoclassical approach. Annual exhibitions were organized in St. Petersburg, which then went on tour throughout Russia. The exhibitions of the "Itinerants" (*Peredvizhniki*), as artist members of the Society were called, were very popular and acquainted wide audiences with recent works by

Russia's best artists. Most talented artists were affiliated formally or informally with the Society. The critic Vladimir Stasov, who had served as public spokesman for the "Five," was a staunch defender of the *Peredvizhniki*.

These "Itinerants," declaring war on the Academy's conventions, promoted artistic realism based on a portrayal and interpretation of Russian life as it existed around them. They emphasized content more than form and composition, but they were by no means indifferent to composition, color, and design. They stressed social comment, often protesting against injustice, inequality, and exploitation, but they recognized that for their art to make serious social statements, it had to display sound form too. They regarded themselves as artists first, not as mere propagandists.

The moving force behind the Society of Traveling Art Exhibitions was Ivan Kramskoi and, to a lesser extent, Vasili Perov. They were organizers and entrepreneurs as well as skillful artists. Kramskoi was a fine portrait painter whose paintings of prominent leaders reveal great psychological insight and understanding. Perov, of humble origin, portrayed most powerfully lower class life and problems. His scathing criticisms of the hypocrisy and moral turpitude of the Orthodox clergy brought him into conflict with the authorities.

The most famous and successful 19th century Russian artist was Ilia Repin (1844–1930), whose canvases still evoke a powerful response. Though of lower class origin, he studied at the Academy of Arts and won a prestigious traveling scholarship to study in Italy. "The Volga Boatmen," painted between 1870 and 1873, and designed as a group portrait of the human beasts of burden who hauled heavy barges up river, against the Volga's current, won him a European reputation. This painting portrayed the brutal exploitation so widespread in Russia. Repin knew each of the characters depicted in the painting and recorded their tragic lives in his memoirs. Equally devastating as a critique of social evils was his "Religious Procession in Kursk Province" (1880–83), which suggested the clergy's arrogance and aloofness, the brutality of the police, the quiet suffering of the peasantry, and the haughty superiority of the nobility. Repin gained a reputation as the most talented Russian painter and an outspoken critic of contemporary society. In the 1880s he turned to history, choosing subjects such as "Tsar Ivan and the Body of His Son" (1881–85), a painting which showed Ivan IV moments after he had clubbed his eldest son to death. It criticized implicitly the corrupting influence of unlimited autocratic power. Repin helped win greater European recognition for Russian art, but after the Bolshevik Revolution he retired to his country house in Finland and refused to return to Soviet Russia.

Such artists as V. V. Vereshchagin (1842–1904) likewise enhanced the growing reputation of Russian painting. A military painter, he sought to promote pacifism and international peace by portraying realistically the horrors of war he had observed firsthand as artist-correspondent in the Russo-Turkish War of 1877–78. Exhibited extensively in Europe and the United States, Vereshchagin enjoyed a

Ilia Repin (1844–1930) self portrait

wider reputation than almost any other Russian artist of the period. Thus Russian artists tried to create a truly national art form, just as the writers sought to guard against foreign influences, yet their work paralleled the genre and historical painting prevalent in many European countries.

Beginning in the 1890s the Russian art world, like literature and music, experienced a revolt against the canons of realism and nationalism by younger artists, notably Michael Nesterov (1862–1942) and Michael Vrubel (1856–1911). Both broke with the realism of the "Itinerants." Nesterov was a deeply religious man whose paintings on religious themes revealed a strength and simplicity, formal structure, and symbolic design reminiscent of iconography. His paintings were studies in mystical idealism, designed to capture the essence of an otherworldly reality revealed in lives of saints, hermits, and monks.

Vrubel's abbreviated and tragic career was perhaps more important in turning Russian art away from realism. He studied philosophy before enrolling in the Academy of the Arts and was interested in esthetic theory and art history, especially classical art and Russian iconography. He became a successful designer and mural painter skilled at church decoration. In an art work every element was important to him: form, line, color, design, and subject matter, not for their total effect but in themselves. Vrubel became an advocate of "art for art's sake," art created for esthetic purposes which the realists considered outrageous. Suffering from serious mental stress, Vrubel was obsessed with demons, particularly after illustrating a commemorative edition of Lermontov's story, *The Demon*. Vrubel produced a powerful, brooding devil, but still unsatisfied, he continued painting devils and finally produced a huge figure with contorted features and an expression of terrifying bitterness and despair, which mirrored his own accelerating breakdown. This figure was placed against a background of dark swirling colors reminiscent of the Art Nouveau movement and Impressionism in Europe. After completing this tour de force, he went insane and was confined in an asylum until his death. In his short career Vrubel did much to shake Russian art loose from crystallized forms of realism and influenced the poets and composers of his age.

The foundations of a new direction in Russian art were firmly established in 1898 with formation of a group known as *Mir Iskusstva* (The World of Art), named after the journal the group published between 1898 and 1904. This group of young, cosmopolitan aristocrats were led by Serge Diagilev, Alexander Benois, Leon Bakst, and Dmitri Filosofov. Diagilev, the moving force and impresario, began his activities with successful exhibitions of advanced Russian and European art. The journal attracted the most talented and avant-garde artists, essayists, and poets who wrote daring, controversial articles on a variety of topics. The journal openly advocated "art for art's sake" and tried to popularize new artistic trends. The success of *Mir Iskusstva* encouraged such similar publications as *Byloe* (Past Years), *The Golden Fleece*, and *Apollon*, which informed their readers of the latest European trends and attempted to reintegrate Russian and European art. The resulting excitement and enthusiasm carried over into every facet of Russian culture. Symbolism, Futurism, Cubo-Futurism, Cubism, and Abstract Impressionism all found supporters and practitioners in Russia. The best known Russian artists of this period included the young Marc Chagall, M. Larionov, N. Goncharova, V. Borisov-Musatov, V. Kandinskii, and K. Malevich, all artists who helped to shape the development of modern art.

ARCHITECTURE

Finally, a few words about Russian architecture. It did not reveal the same originality and striving for national forms as did literature, music, and painting, and it continued to be dominated by foreign architects and styles. Only towards 1900 did some Russian architects seek consciously to create a new national architectural style based upon Russian structures and styles of the medieval period. The Slavic Revival, a rebirth of interest in Russia's past, affected all aspects of Russian culture. Iconography was rediscovered as a developed art form and iconographic principles influenced many artists. The Slavic Revival encouraged architects to turn to traditional Russian wooden structures as a source of inspiration and to translate these traditional styles into stone and brick structures. Slavic Revival architecture, found all over

Library of Congress

A. V. Shchusev (1873–1949)

Russia, was particularly noticeable in Moscow, the traditional center. The Historical Museum there, completed in 1883, is an excellent example of this revival of traditional national forms. A leader in this revival was A. V. Shchusev (1873–1949), who designed a number of Orthodox churches in traditional Novgorod and Pskov style, built Moscow's Kazan Railroad Station, and designed the Russian pavillion at the Venice International exhibition, all in the style of 17th century Muscovy.

The history of Russian culture between the Crimean War and World War I is one of tremendous vitality and originality in most fields of cultural endeavor. This was a period when the world discovered the richness of the Russian accomplishments in the arts. For the first time Russian culture began to influence international culture rather than merely responding to or imitating Western trends. On the eve of World War I, Russian culture was extraordinarily dynamic and diverse, exciting and energetic. War and revolution dampened spirits but did not destroy the creative impulses of the Russian intelligentsia.

Suggested Additional Reading

Benois, A.   *The Russian School of Painting* (London, 1919).
Berlin, I.   *The Hedgehog and the Fox: An Essay on Tolstoy's View of History* (New York, 1953).

EIKHENBAUM, B. M.   *The Young Tolstoy,* trans. G. Kern (Ann Arbor, 1972).

FANGER, D. L.   *Dostoevsky and Romantic Realism* (Cambridge, Mass., 1965).

GRAY, C.   *The Great Experiment: Russian Art 1863–1922* (London, 1962).

GROSSMAN, L.   *Dostoevsky: A Biography.* Trans. M. Mackler (New York, 1975).

HINGLEY, R.   *Chekhov: A New Biography* (New York, 1976).

LEONARD, R.   *A History of Russian Music* (New York, 1968).

SIMMONS, E. J.   *Chekhov: A Biography* (Boston, 1962).

TROYAT, H.   *Tolstoy* (Garden City, New York, 1967).

YARMOLINSKY, A.   *Turgenev. The Man, His Art and His Age* (New York, 1959).

30

War and Revolution, 1914–1917

IN AUGUST 1914 Imperial Russia, though its army was still being reorganized, refused to yield to Austro-German pressure and entered World War I. At first the war produced unity and predictions of quick victory in Russia, but as it dragged on it revealed Russia's persisting backwardness, political weaknesses, and disunity. The economy showed alarming signs of collapse, and military defeats undermined morale in the army and among civilians. In March 1917 in the midst of this conflict, the regime was overthrown by a popular revolution. What caused the sudden collapse of the Romanov regime, which had ruled Russia for 300 years? This chapter and the attached problem[1] will probe the complex relationship between the war and the coming of the revolution in March 1917.

RUSSIA ENTERS WORLD WAR I

On June 28, 1914, a Bosnian student linked with the Serbian national movement assassinated Archduke Francis Ferdinand, heir to the Austrian throne, in Sarajevo, Bosnia, sparking war among the European powers, Japan, and later the United States. The assassination alone did not cause the war. World War I resulted from increasingly rigid alliance systems, which divided Europe between the Triple Alliance (Germany, Austria-Hungary, and Italy) and the Triple Entente (Great Britain, France, and Russia) and involved the prestige of all powers; from a precipitous growth of armaments and militarism; from intense nationalism, especially in Serbia and France, expressed in hatred of their national enemies, Austria and Germany; and from imperial rivalries. In this tense, intolerant atmosphere, diplomats, hampered by the lack of an international organization to preserve peace, could not reach reasonable compromises.

Russian leaders, at first not unduly alarmed by the Sarajevo murder, went on vacation. The Russian public and press, while mostly anti-Austrian and pro-Serbian, were not violently so. In mid-July the Russian government even sent the quartermaster-general on a routine mission

---

[1] See below, pp. 447–51.

to the Caucasus. On July 20, Russian leaders had returned to St. Petersburg to greet President Poincaré of France, who spent three days there on a previously arranged state visit. French and Russian chiefs reaffirmed their solemn obligation under the Franco-Russian Alliance.

No sooner had Poincaré departed than Austria-Hungary issued an ultimatum to Serbia that was so framed as to be unacceptable. Russian Foreign Minister Sazonov exclaimed: "That means European war," but he urged Serbia to make a conciliatory reply, appeal to the powers, and not resist Austria militarily. He requested Austria to give the Serbs more time to answer, but Russia, assured of French support, resolved not to back down.

The mobilization of Russia's army became a vital factor in the last days before war broke out. On July 24 the Council of Ministers empowered the War Minister to mobilize only districts facing Austria. Sazonov saw this as mainly a diplomatic move to back Serbia. War Minister Sukhomlinov and Chief of Staff Ianushkevich agreed to this partial mobilization, though subordinates objected that there were no plans for it and that to improvise them might disrupt full mobilization later. On July 25 the Tsar and his ministers, learning that Serbia's reply had not satisfied Austria, agreed to support Serbia at any cost. Austria mobilized and on July 28 declared war on Serbia, and Sazonov announced that Russia would carry out partial mobilization.

Meanwhile Russian staff officers had convinced their chiefs, and finally Nicholas II and Sazonov, that partial mobilization was impractical. On July 29, with the Austrians bombarding Belgrade, the Russian chief of staff gave General Dobrorolskii the decree of Nicholas II authorizing full mobilization. Nicholas, receiving the Kaiser's telegram warning of the consequences, rescinded this order, but on July 30 Sazonov and the military chiefs persuaded him to authorize general mobilization. Germany demanded that Russia demobilize; when it refused, Germany declared war on Russia, then on France. After Germany violated Belgian neutrality, England joined France and Russia on August 4. The Central Powers (Germany and Austria-Hungary) faced a coalition of Serbia, Russia, France, and England.

Russia's responsibility for World War I remains debatable. German and Western revisionist historians argue that its general mobilization doomed German and British efforts to head off conflict. The tsar and Sazonov, who opposed war, concluded, however, that partial mobilization would disorganize the Russian army. Another retreat in the Balkans, they believed, might destroy Russia's credibility as a great power. Also, Austria was the first to mobilize, declare war, and begin hostilities against Serbia, an ally of Russia. Like all powers in 1914, Russia bore some responsibility, but its leaders went to war reluctantly after failing to find a peaceful solution.

WAR AIMS AND WARTIME DIPLOMACY

Russia entered the war without clear aims except to protect itself and Serbia. At first no specific territorial claims were made against

Germany, and Sazonov merely denounced German militarism and pledged to restore a "free" Poland. In September 1914 he told the French and British ambassadors that Russia advocated reorganziing Austria-Hungary into a triple monarchy, ceding Bosnia, Herzegovina, and Dalmatia to Serbia and restoring Alsace-Lorraine to France. As an afterthought he requested free passage for Russian warships through the Straits. Grand Duke Nicholas, Russia's commander in chief, urged the peoples of Austria-Hungary to overthrow Habsburg rule and achieve independence, but other Russian leaders did not pursue this nationalist tack. Like other members of the Entente, Russian leaders expected victory to provide them with a program of war aims.

Early defeats and Turkish entry into the war ended official Russian reticence. After Germany persuaded the Ottoman Empire to join the Central Powers (November 1, 1914), the Tsar favored expelling it from Europe and solving "the historic task bequeathed to us by our forefathers on the shores of the Black Sea." Nationalists and liberals in the Duma and press took up the refrain. Only securing Constantinople, Professor Trubetskoi of Moscow University declared, would guarantee Russia's independence. Paul Miliukov, leader of the Kadets and the liberal opposition in the Duma, echoing the general nationalist euphoria, demanded that Russia seize the Straits and Constantinople, and to do so became the principal Russian war aim.

The Entente powers pledged in September 1914 not to conclude a separate peace and to consult on peace terms, but they disagreed over war plans and aims. As a basis for a future peace they concluded secret treaties and agreements. In December 1914, Grand Duke Nicholas, lacking forces to capture or garrison the Straits, urged Sazonov to obtain them by diplomacy. London, to keep Russia fighting, responded warmly. "As to Constantinople, it is clear that it must be yours," the English king told the Russian ambassador. In 1915 the British undertook a Dardanelles campaign to force open the Straits and open a supply line to Russia; its failure helped doom Russia instead to eventual defeat. In March 1915 Sazonov insisted that if the Entente won, the Straits and environs go to Russia; England, then France, agreed. The Tsar told the French ambassador, Paléologue: "Take the left bank of the Rhine, take Mainz; go further if you like." Later, secret inter-Allied agreements arranged a partition of the Ottoman Empire. Russia would obtain the Straits, eastern Anatolia, and part of the southern coast of the Black Sea. The former Crimean powers promised this, knowing that without Russia they would lose the war. Thus, the Russian government and liberals were committed to an imperialistic peace, which aroused no popular enthusiasm at home.

THE ARMY AND THE FRONTS

Russia began World War I with unity, optimism, and loyalty to the Crown, a situation unlike the public apathy prevalent at the beginning of the Japanese war. Domestic quarrels and differences seemed forgotten, and the strike movement, so threatening in July, ended abruptly.

Virtually the entire Duma pledged to support the war effort, except for a few socialists who refused to vote war credits. The enthusiasm was largely defensive; Russian opinion believed that the war was being fought to defend Russia and Serbia. In the cities this spontaneous patriotism became anti-German: the name of St. Petersburg was changed to Petrograd and there were anti-German riots. The villages, however, remained ominously silent.

At first the generals and nationalist press proclaimed that the Russian "steamroller" would advance to Berlin and end the war within a few weeks. In the West this myth was widely believed. Actually, the ill-prepared army reflected the backwardness and low standards of Russian life. Faulty strategy and tactics were pursued under incompetent commanders. The impressive six foot six commander in chief, Grand Duke Nicholas, despite semi-dictatorial powers, in General Polivanov's words, "appeared entirely unequipped for the task and . . . spent much time crying because he did not know how to approach his new duties." He was popular with the rank and file, though, which mistook his severity for competence. In August 1915 Nicholas II, who knew even less, replaced him, continuing a disastrous Romanov tradition of placing members of the imperial family in top military posts. Chief of Staff Ianushkevich was undistinguished and War Minister Sukhomlinov incompetent, negligent, and unfit for high office. High army commands were filled by seniority, not proven ability. Abler company grade officers were killed in large numbers during the first months and could not be replaced.

General conscription soon expanded a peacetime army of 1,350,000 men to almost 6,500,000. During the war over 15,000,000 men were called up, some 37 percent of all Allied soldiers, but they were poorly led, equipped, and supplied. Terrible red tape and confusion among the War Ministry and General Headquarters produced growing shortages. The army's rank and file were mostly peasants, two thirds illiterate and ignorant as to why they fought.

Prewar Russian strategy envisioned defensive operations against Germany and an offensive against weaker Austria-Hungary to open the way into the Balkans. Appeals for help from the hard-pressed French and British, however, persuaded the Russian high command to improvise an offensive before mobilization was even complete. Two Russian armies under Generals Rennenkampf and Samsonov plunged into East Prussia and scored initial successes. But inadequate maps, bad intelligence, and poor coordination between the Russian armies and their commanders produced disaster. The Germans rushed reinforcements from France, and General Hindenburg trapped Samsonov's army at Tannenberg. Some 300,000 men were lost, Samsonov shot himself, and Russian morale was damaged irreparably. Tannenberg revealed German superiority and ended Russian dreams of a march to Berlin. But a Russian offensive against Austria, better planned and executed, led to occupation of Galicia, heavy Austrian losses, and smashed the hopes of the Central Powers for quick victory in the east.

Early in 1915, the Germans, reinforcing the eastern front, scored a

MAP 30–1
Russia in World War I, 1914–1918

SWEDEN

Arkhangelsk

Helsingfors Viborg

Petrograd

Reval Vologda

Baltic Sea Pskov Volga

Riga Tver Moscow

Libau

Danzig Dvinsk

Vilna Smolensk Riazan Penza

**Tannenberg
Aug. 1914** Minsk Mogilev

**Sept. 1914
Masurian
Lakes** Bug R U S S I A

GERMANY POLAND Gomel Voronezh Volga

**Front in November
1917**

Kiev Kharkov Don Tsaritsyn

GALICIA **Brusilov Offense
1916** U K R A I N E

AUSTRIA Ekaterinoslav Rostov-on-Don

Budapest **Rumanian and
Russian Forces
1916** Kuban

HUNGARY Odessa Terek

Belgrade RUMANIA **Caucasus**

Sarajevo Bucharest Sevastopol **CRIMEA**

Danube Black Sea Kura

SERBIA BULGARIA Batum

ALBANIA Sofia Bosporus Trebizond Kars

Constantinople

Gallipoli *Farthest Russian Advance
1916* Tabriz

GREECE Dardanelles

Allies, 1915–16 TURKEY

✱ **Major battle sites** ┼┼┼┼ **Major Russian railways** ▬ ▬ ▬ **Farthest Russian advance
1916**

▬▬▬ **Russian border 1914** ᵛᵛᵛ **Farthest Russian advance in
Germany and Austria, 1914**

Adapted from *A History of Russia, Second Edition* by Nicholas V. Riasanovsky. Copyright © 1969 by Oxford
University Press, Inc. Used by permission.

breakthrough and reconquered Galicia. The Russians retreated grudgingly, abandoning Poland and part of the Baltic provinces. An unwise Russian scorched-earth policy produced swarms of refugees and demoralized the population. In a struggle with a superior foe, the Russian army was bled white. Severe shortages of war material and even food plagued the Russian forces, and the Russian artillery had few shells while heavy German cannon fired ceaselessly. In the retreat from Galicia, many Russian soldiers even lacked rifles. Losses and desertion mounted and morale fell as rumors spread: "Britain will fight to the last drop of Russian blood." Only the Russian soldier's subborn courage held the army together. During 1915, while the western front had a long breathing spell, Russia bore the main pressure of the Central Powers.

In the winter of 1915–16 came a surprising recovery. Due largely to unofficial efforts by *zemstva*, Duma deputies, and other public-spirited groups, the army was far better supplied. The new War Minister Polivanov and Chief of Staff Alekseev were abler than their predecessors. The Germans retained superior firepower, but the Russian army's fighting capacity improved. General A. A. Brusilov's sudden attack in Galicia in May 1916 shattered Austrian lines and forced the Germans to send reinforcements. This action revealed Russia's continued ability to fight and induced Rumania to join the Allies. In the Caucasus, Russian forces prevailed against poorly organized Turkish armies, capturing Erzerum and Trebizond in 1916 and penetrating deep into Anatolia.

The Russian army, despite poor command and organization, played a vital part in World War I. It tied down much of the Central Powers' strength and repeatedly saved the western front from disaster, but the cost to Russia was staggering: over 3,000,000 soldiers killed and wounded and 2,700,000 captured and missing. Though coping with Austrians and Turks, Russia was defeated consistently by the Germans. These defeats demoralized the army and contributed greatly to the downfall of the regime.

THE HOME FRONT

Modern war, the supreme test of a nation's soundness, reveals strengths and hidden weaknesses. World War I exposed an underdeveloped Russian industry, inadequate transport, and fumbling government. It showed the tsar's incompetence and isolation and heightened contradictions between a disintegrating regime and a disgruntled public. The terrible weakness of the home front more than military shortcomings produced defeat and revolution.

The Economy. Agriculture suffered less than industry from the ill-considered mobilization of Russian manpower. Because of rural overpopulation and prewar wastage of labor, peasant farms were able to operate almost normally despite the loss of most male laborers. In some unoccupied provinces acreage under cereal crops actually increased as women, children, and old men took up the slack. Large estates, which had produced most of the surplus for home and foreign

Hungry Petrograd in World War I

markets, were harder hit because they could not obtain hired laborers, machinery, or spare parts. Despite increased demand, the total Russian grain and potato harvest and meat production fell by about one third during the war. At first peasant soldiers ate better in the army than they had at home, but by 1917 the front was receiving less than half the grain it required. As commanders searched for food, their soldiers grew hungry and dissatisfied.

Even in 1917 Russia possessed enough food for both civilians and soldiers. The virtual cessation of food exports and diminished use of grain to manufacture vodka roughly balanced production declines. Government policy was largely to blame for shortages because artificially low state prices for grain supplied to the army and later for all grain deprived farmers of production incentives while prices of the manufactured goods they desired rose rapidly. Peasants therefore consumed more grain and brewed their own alcohol, while speculators hoarded grain and awaited higher prices. Because shipping foodstuffs to the cities was complicated by a worsening transport crisis, by 1917 the cities in the northern consuming provinces were hungry while in the Ukraine and Siberia food was relatively abundant.

Transportation, the economy's weakest link, was nearing breakdown by 1917. The railroad system, which had barely met ordinary peacetime needs, had a low carrying capacity and inferior connections with seaports. (Only a narrow gauge line went to Archangel, and not until 1916 was a railroad built to the new port of Murmansk.) Wartime needs virtually monopolized a railway system further overburdened by the retreat in Poland and massive evacuation of civilians. Railroad cars and spare parts, formerly obtained largely in western Europe, became critically short. The government spent 1,500,000,000 rubles to improve the network and build additional lines; it ordered American railway equipment, but this arrived only late in 1917. On the eve of the March Revolution, a crisis in railroad transport worsened the problems of industry and food supply.

Because at first the government had no deferment system, industry was crippled by mobilization of irreplacable skilled labor. Much of the labor force came to be comprised of women, children, and war prisoners. Initially, many factory owners pursued "business as usual," and some curtailed production because of mobilization, disruption of foreign business connections, and expected decreased domestic demand. Unprecedented need for munitions and war supplies (more shells were used in a month than in a year of the Russo-Japanese War) placed an intolerable burden on industry, which could not get essential raw materials and fuel. The loss in 1915 of Russian Poland, the Empire's most industrialized region, reduced production by about one fifth. To be sure, certain branches of industry, spurred by war demand, grew rapidly: metalworking trebled in 1916 and chemicals expanded 250 percent. Rifle production in August 1916 was eleven times that of 1914 but was still insufficient.

Red tape and lack of government planning further complicated industry's problems. The official hands-off policy lasted until appalling munitions shortages spurred public action. During 1915, industrialists, Duma members, *zemstva*, and municipalities formed military-industrial committees which improved the supply picture greatly. But government action was too little and too late. By 1917 industrial production was falling sharply in a growing economic crisis. On the other hand, Soviet accounts exaggerate the wartime growth of monopolies and trusts to support their claims that in Russia finance capitalism was maturing, thus preparing the way for socialism.

The war badly disrupted Russian foreign trade. In the first year, exports fell to about 15 percent of the prewar level and recovered later to only 30 percent. Imports, dropping sharply at first, in 1916 were double the prewar value, mainly war supplies and equipment sent by the Allies through Siberian ports. Instead of the 47,000,000 ruble export surplus of 1913, the wartime Russian trade deficit totalled some 2,500,000,000 rubles.

Incompetent government wartime financing damaged the Russian economy. At the outset Russia seemed in better financial shape than in the Russo-Japanese War, but the Treasury expended as much in a month of World War I as in a year against Japan. A drastic fall in customs and railway receipts cut Treasury revenues and an incredible blunder robbed it of the liquor tax. The Finance Minister ordered state liquor stores closed during mobilization and introduced legislation to raise liquor prices to combat drunkenness. A decree of August 1914 unaccountably kept liquor stores closed throughout the war. Such pioneering in prohibition cost the Treasury about 700,000,000 rubles annually, about 25 percent of its total revenue. Peasants brewed their own liquor, and illicit vodka sales brought huge profits to dealers but nothing to the Treasury. New wartime taxes barely covered this loss, and state revenues fell far short of war expenditures. Income and war profits taxes were low and introduced too late. Huge domestic and foreign loans and massive use of the printing press financed the war. Foreign nations, chiefly Britain, loaned Russia some eight billion rubles, accelerating a sharp decline in the ruble's exchange value, which produced rampant inflation, loss of confidence in the currency, and a rapid rise in living costs. Russia grew ever more dependent financially upon its allies.

The serious economic effects of the war helped make the revolution more profound, though the economic framework, especially of agriculture, remained fundamentally sound. The masses, far from being impoverished, saw their purchasing power rise but found little to buy as Russian resources were wasted and poorly used by incompetent officials.

The Government.   During the war the tsarist regime revealed its inability to govern the country and disintegrated rapidly. Nicholas II, retaining faith in Autocracy, Orthodoxy, and Nationality, failed to supply leadership, believed that constitutional government was evil, and that the public could not be allowed to help run Russia. Though interfering little with the Duma, he largely ignored it and absorbed himself in family affairs and probems. Ever more dominated by Empress Alexandra, he and his family were estranged from the public and the bureaucracy. "The characteristic feature of the imperial family," noted a trusted minister, "is their inaccessibility to the outside world and their atmosphere of mysticism." Empress Alexandra, who hated the Duma and liberal ministers with a passion, was largely responsible for this isolation, and as Rasputin's hold over her grew, she interfered more and more in state affairs. The most influential of several "men of God" to influence the superstitious empress, Rasputin had been introduced at court in November 1905. She found this semiliterate, debauched (his motto was: "Redemption through sin"!) but dynamic Siberian peasant indispensable to preserve her hemophiliac son, Alexis (born 1904), and the dynasty. Rasputin managed through hypnotism to stop the Tsarevich's bleeding, and to the imperial couple he embodied the Russian people.

When Nicholas II took command of the army in September 1915, control over the government passed to the Empress and Rasputin. Believing that she could save Russia from revolution, Alexandra relied completely on Rasputin, who lacked clear political aims and was surrounded with unscrupulous, greedy adventurers. When the more competent, liberal ministers appointed under public pressure early in 1915 protested Nicholas' decision to become army chief, the Empress, to preserve autocracy, removed them from office. A nonentity, Boris Stürmer, was named premier. "A country cannot be lost whose sovereign is guided by a man of God," Alexandra wrote Nicholas. "Won't you come to the assistance of your hubby now that he is absent. . . ?" Nicholas queried. "You ought to be my eyes and ears there in the capital. . . . It rests with you to keep peace and harmony among the ministers."[2] The final disgraceful year of Romanov rule was marked by "ministerial leapfrog" as the Empress and Rasputin shifted ministers with bewildering speed. The last premier, Prince N. D. Golitsyn, begged to be relieved of his tasks, which he did not know how to perform. Late in 1916 Rasputin's disgraceful behavior became intolerable even to loyal monarchists. An ultraconservative Duma delegate, V. M. Purishkevich, and two grand dukes invited Rasputin to a banquet, fed him cake laced with cyanide, shot him, and finally drowned him in a canal. This was a terrible blow to the Empress, but she and A. D. Protopopov continued to rule and hold seances to recall Rasputin from the dead. On the eve of the March Revolution the government was inactive, divided, and in an advanced state of decay.

Meanwhile, the Duma had risen to unprecedented national leadership. After the war began, the Duma set up a provisional committee to aid the wounded and war sufferers and to coordinate its war work. At first the Duma supported the government unconditionally, but early in 1915 it agitated with *zemstvo* and municipal representatives for a responsible ministry. That summer about two thirds of the Duma, excluding the extreme Left and Right, formed a Progressive Bloc led by Kadets and Octobrists, which advocated a government capable of winning public confidence, political amnesty, religious freedom, and freedom for trade unions. Though most of the ministers accepted this program, Premier Goremykin stubbornly rejected it as an illegal attempt to limit the autocrat's power. During 1916 the Duma's relations with the executive branch deteriorated sharply when deputies led by Miliukov accused the government and the Empress of conspiring with the Germans. Censorship deleted the sharpest Duma attacks, but its debates were widely publicized and it was winning a public following. The fatal weakness which prevented the Duma from representing and leading the Russian people in 1917 was the narrow suffrage by which it had been elected.

The Revolutionary Movement. The government's ineffectiveness and inability to win liberal support provided revolutionaries with a rare opportunity. In 1915 after the defeat in Galicia, strikes grew more numerous and continued to mount until the March Revolution, but the socialist parties in Russia remained too disorganized and fragmented to prepare a revolution. Their leaders mostly remained in exile in Siberia

---

[2] *The Letters of the Tsar to the Tsaritsa, 1914–1917* (London, 1929), and *Letters of the Tsaritsa to the Tsar, 1914–1916* (London, 1923).

or Europe, out of touch with Russia. Initially the SD's in the Duma denounced the war as the product of aggressive capitalism and urged the proletariat to oppose it. The Bolshevik deputies, more aggressively anti-war than the Mensheviks, were soon arrested, tried, and exiled to Siberia. Social Democrats abroad were divided by the war. Plekhanov, splitting with Lenin and the majority, urged Russian workers to fight against Prussian imperialism and with the Western democracies to final victory. Lenin in his *Theses on War* (1914), written in Switzerland, denounced World War I as imperialist, and exhorted Russian workers to help defeat tsarism and to turn the conflict into a civil war and prepare revolution. Lenin accused the Second International and its leader, Karl Kautsky, of betraying the proletariat by voting for a fratricidal war. At international socialist conferences at Zimmerwald (1915) and Kienthal (1916), the minority Leninist left urged a civil war of workers against all capitalist governments, but most European socialists supported their governments in World War I.

The Bolsheviks' Russian rivals were likewise divided. The Menshevik organizational committee in Switzerland, including Martov, Akselrod, and Martynov, denounced the war and advocated eventual revolution, but sought to restore unity to international socialism. Rather than favor Russia's defeat, they exhorted workers to exert pressure on all governments to conclude a democratic peace without annexations and indemnities. In Russia an important Menshevik group around the publication, *Our Dawn* (*Nasha Zaria*) advocated noncooperation with the regime without hampering the war effort; later it favored defense of Russia against invasion. The SR's, still dispirited, were split between a right actively supporting the war effort, Chernov's pacifist center, and a sizable left internationalist wing favoring defeat of tsarism. In Russia and abroad, socialists divided into three main groupings: patriots, centrists (defensists and pacifists), and defeatists advocating revolution.

Bolshevik organizations in Russia were tougher and more resilient than their rivals. The British scholar Leonard Schapiro claims that Bolshevik wartime activity was intermittent and ineffective, but Soviet accounts assert that the Bolsheviks led the workers' struggle against the war from the start, steadily expanded their organization and followed Lenin's instructions. Although the police "liquidated" the Petrograd Committee 30 times and arrested more than 600 Bolsheviks, the party nonetheless expanded its membership and activities. By late 1916 the Bolsheviks, numbering perhaps 10,000, were led by A. G. Shliapnikov (Lenin's man), V. M. Molotov, and Zalutskii. Though Soviet historians exaggerate Bolshevik strength and leadership of the workers, the party did represent a considerable force ready, unlike Mensheviks and SR's, to exploit a revolutionary situation.

The March Revolution. In five days—March 8/12, 1917 (February 23/27 Old Style) a mass movement in Petrograd overturned the tsarist government. N. N. Sukhanov's eyewitness account stresses that it was spontaneous and not led by a party or organization. Western historians and early Soviet accounts such as Trotskii's *History of the Russian*

Revolution, accept this view whereas Stalinist historians exaggerate Bolshevik leadership of the masses.

In previous months, the Petrograd strike movement had steadily gathered momentum. A strike by some workers at the Putilov factory, Russia's largest, became general, and on March 7 the management locked out the workers. Though the government and emperor had received numerous warnings of impending revolution (from foreign ambassadors and Duma president, M. V. Rodzianko), they made no concessions. Nicholas II, confident that nothing unusual was afoot, left Tsarskoe Selo on March 7 for military headquarters at Mogilev. The authorities had a detailed plan to suppress an uprising: first the 3,500 police were to be used, then Cossacks with whips, and finally troops from the 150,000 man garrison. The plan, though later implemented, proved ineffective.

Revolution began in Petrograd on March 8, international women's day. In the large factories of Vyborg district, women in bread lines and strikers began spontaneous demonstrations, which spread to the Petersburg side. Women textile workers, the most downtrodden segment of the Petrograd proletariat, supplied the impetus. In the streets appeared placards with slogans: "Down with the war!" "Give us bread!" and "Down with autocracy!" That day, notes Sukhanov, "the movement in the streets became clearly defined going beyond the limits of the usual factory meetings. . . . The city was filled with rumors and a feeling of 'disorders.'" The Bolsheviks who controlled Vyborg Borough Committee, fearing conflict with the authorities while the party was weak, relegated revolution to the indefinite future, not realizing that one was in progress. In March, noted Trotskii, the higher the revolutionary leaders, the further they lagged behind the masses. Next day (March 9), continued Sukhanov, "the movement swept over Petersburg like a great flood. Nevskii Prospect [the main shopping street] and many squares in the center were crowded with workers." Mounted police were sent to disperse the demonstrations; then Cossacks were ordered out. They charged the crowds halfheartedly and often chatted amicably with the workers.

By March 10 "the entire civil population felt itself to be in one camp united against the enemy—the police and the military." Proclamations of the garrison commander, General Khabalov, threatening stern punishment for demonstrators, were torn down, police were disarmed or vanished from their posts, factories and streetcars halted operation. Khabalov sent in troops, but the crowds, avoiding clashes with them, sought to win them over.

Early on Sunday, March 11 workers advanced from outlying districts toward Petrograd's center. Stopped at the bridges, they poured across the solidly frozen Neva River dodging bullets. At the Tsar's orders Khabalov sent thousands of infantry into the streets. On the Nevskii Prospect soldiers fired on crowds, killing many and terrorizing the rest and that afternoon the Vyborg Committee considered calling off the strike. The critical moment of the revolution had come. In the evening, after police fired on a crowd, soldiers of the passing Pavlovskii Regi-

Tsar Nicholas and Family, the Tsar seated second from left

ment mutinied, fired on the police, then returned to barracks, resolved
not to fire again at strikers, and appealed to their comrades to join
them. This was the military's first revolutionary act of 1917.

On the fifth day (March 12) workers streamed into the factories
and in open meetings resolved to continue the struggle. Armed insurrection grew irresistibly from events while the Bolshevik headquarters
staff looked on despondently, leaving the districts and barracks to their
own devices. Soldiers mutinied in growing numbers and joined crowds
of workers.

New centers of authority sprang up before old ones had disappeared.
The government had ordered the Duma prorogued, but on March 12
some members elected a Provisional Committee under the Duma president, Rodzianko, representing all groups except the Right, "to restore
order in the capital and establish contact with public organizations and
institutions." Reflecting views of the Progressive Bloc, the Committee
sought to save the dynasty with a responsible ministry. Simultaneously,
the Petrograd Soviet was reborn while mutinous troops freed worker
and socialist leaders from the city's prisons. Proceeding with the troops
to the Tauride Palace and aided by trade union leaders, they created
the Provisional Executive Committee of the Soviet of Workers' Deputies.
At the Petrograd Soviet's first meeting that evening some 250 delegates
were present, but new ones kept entering the noisy, chaotic session. No

political party proposed a definite plan or took decisive leadership. When soldier deputies asked to join, the organization became the Soviet of Workers' and Soldiers' Deputies. Henceforth, this spontaneous fusion of popular elements led the revolution.

The tsarist government and dynasty came to a swift, unlamented end. By March 14 the entire garrison of Petrograd had defected and the tsarist ministers were arrested. The Duma's Provisional Committee selected a Provisional Government from liberal members of the Progressive Bloc, the "government having public confidence" which the bourgeoisie had long sought. Learning of the deteriorating situation in Petrograd, Nicholas II decided to rejoin his family in Tsarskoe Selo, but railroad workers halted his train and forced him to return to Pskov, headquarters of the northern front. Behind events as usual, he agreed now to a responsible ministry, but his commanders unanimously advised abdication. On March 15 delegates Guchkov and Shulgin, sent to Pskov by the Provisional Committee, secured Nicholas' abdication in favor of his brother, Grand Duke Michael. Rumors of Michael's impending rule caused such indignation among the workers that he wisely renounced his claims and on March 15, 1917 Romanov rule ended in Russia.

PROBLEM 8: DID WORLD WAR I CAUSE THE COLLAPSE OF TSARISM?

What is the relationship between the defeat of a regime in war and its overthrow? What is the connection between war and revolution? Did Germany's defeat of the Russian imperial army cause or trigger the collapse of tsarism in March 1917? Without war was it likely that the regime could have survived in liberalized form, turning perhaps into something resembling the British constitutional monarchy? Or did, conversely, the war delay tsarist collapse by generating a final outburst of Russian patriotism? Was the regime's disintegration so far advanced in 1914 that it would soon have collapsed in any case? Were social and political tensions rising or declining in Russia in 1914? Finally, could either the tsarist regime without war or a liberal successor have confronted 20th century problems successfully?

Soviet historians assert that a "revolutionary situation" existed in Russia in 1914 and that only the outbreak of war prevented the rising strike movement from launching a decisive assault upon autocracy. The revolution, they affirm, was already ripe in 1914. The American scholar, Leopold Haimson, while rejecting their thesis of a revolutionary situation, nonetheless rejects the idea of stabilization and argues that social and political tensions were growing. These accounts reflect the "pessimists' " view of tsarist prospects in 1914.

On the other hand, the "optimists" among Western historians cite the weakness of the revolutionary movement and some argue that a constitutional regime would have succeeded autocracy in Russia had there been no war. Leonard Schapiro emphasizes the impotence of the Bolsheviks in 1914 and claims that without World War I they were doomed to oblivion. The cautious economic historian, Alexander Gerschenkron, stresses Russia's economic growth after 1906 and discerns a lessening of tensions among peasantry and workers which promoted social and political stabilization.

THE SOVIET POSITION

History of the Communist Party of the Soviet Union (Moscow, 1960): This official Soviet account written during the rule of N. S. Khrushchev, emphasizes the approaching collapse of tsarist Russia and the revolutionary upsurge just before World War I as well as the growing strength and cohesion of the Bolsheviks in leading the discontented masses:

> The cost of living was rising and the position of the worker was deteriorating. An official industrial survey revealed that while annual wages averaged 246 rubles, annual profit per worker averaged 252 rubles. . . . Incredible poverty reigned in the countryside. Stolypin's agrarian policy had, as its direct result, the mass impoverishment of the peasants and enrichment of the kulak [better-off peasants] bloodsuckers. . . . The Russian countryside presented a picture of omnipotent feudal landlords, bigger and richer kulak farms, the impoverishment of a vast mass of middle peasants, and a substantially increased mass of landless peasants. . . . The situation left no doubt whatever that the Stolypin policy had collapsed.

> Its collapse brought out more saliently than ever the profound contradictions throughout Russia's social and political system. It demonstrated anew that the tsarist government was incapable of solving the country's basic social and economic problems. . . . Poverty, oppression, lack of human rights, humiliating indignities imposed on the people—all this, Lenin emphasized, was in crying contradiction to the state of the country's productive forces and to the degree of political understanding and demands of the masses. . . . Only a new revolution could save Russia. . . .

> The Bolsheviks' prediction that a new revolutionary upsurge was inevitable proved to be true. Everywhere there was growing discontent and indignation among the people. The workers saw in the Bolshevik revolutionary slogans a clear-cut expression of their own aspirations. . . . Of all the political parties then active in Russia, only the Bolsheviks had a platform that fully accorded with the interests of the working class and the people generally. . . .

> The workers' movement continued to grow in scope and strength. There were over one million strikers in 1912, and 1,272,000 in 1913. Economic struggles were intertwined with political ones and culminated in mass revolutionary strikes. The working class went over to the offensive against the capitalists and the tsarist monarchy. . . . In 1910–1914, according to patently minimized figures, there were over 13,000 peasant outbreaks, in which many manor houses and kulak farmsteads were destroyed. . . . The unrest spread to the tsarist army. . . . Mutiny was brewing in the Baltic and Black Sea fleets. A new revolution was maturing in Russia.

Together with the rise of the working-class movement, the party of the working class, the Bolshevik Party, grew and gained in strength. . . . Amidst the difficulties created by their illegal status, the Bolsheviks *reestablished a mass party*, firmly led and guided by its Central Committee. . . . Everywhere—in mass strikes, street demonstrations, factory gate meetings—the Bolsheviks emphasized that revolution was the only way out, and put forward slogans expressing the people's longings: a democratic republic, an eight-hour working day, confiscation of the landed estates in favor of the peasants.

Meanwhile the waves of the working-class movement rose higher and higher. In the first half of 1914 about 1,500,000 workers were involved in strikes. . . . On July 3 the police opened fire on a workers' meeting at the Putilov Works in St. Petersburg. A wave of indignation swept over the country. The St. Petersburg Bolshevik Committee called for immediate strike action. . . . Demonstrations began in protest against the actions of the tsarist authorities and the war, which everyone felt was about to break out. The strike wave spread to Moscow; barricades were thrown up in St. Petersburg, Baku, and Lodz.

Russia was faced with a revolutionary crisis. The landlords and capitalists were accusing each other of inability to put out the flames of revolution. . . . The tsarist government adopted "emergency" measures, the capital was turned into a veritable military camp. . . . The advance of the revolution was interrupted by the outbreak of the world war. (pp. 163–64, 167, 169–70, 173, 175–76, 182–83)

THE PESSIMISTS' VIEW

Leopold Haimson in "The Problem of Social Stability in Urban Russia, 1905–1917, II," *Slavic Review*, vol. 24 (March 1965), No. 1, presents an interesting analysis of conditions in Russia on the eve of World War I in some ways refuting and in others supporting the above Soviet assertions:

The four-day interval between the last gasps of the Petersburg strike and the outbreak of war may not altogether dispose of the thesis of Soviet historians that only the war prevented the strike movement of July, 1914, from turning into a decisive attack against the autocracy. . . . Yet surely much of the conviction of this argument pales in the light of the two glaring sources of political weakness that the strike revealed from its very inception . . . the failure of the clashes in St. Petersburg to set off anything like the all-national political strike which even the Bolshevik leaders had considered . . . a necessary condition for the armed assault against the autocracy . . . [and] the inability of the Petersburg workers to mobilize, in time, active support among other groups in society. . . . No demonstrations, no public meetings, no collective petitions—no expressions of solidarity even barely comparable to those that Bloody Sunday had evoked were now aroused. . . . Thus, . . . the most important source of the political impotence revealed by the Petersburg strike was precisely the one that made for its "monstrous" revolutionary explosiveness: the sense of isolation, of psychological distance, that separated the Petersburg workers from educated, privileged society.
    . . . The crude representations to be found in recent Soviet writings

of the "revolutionary situation" already at hand in July, 1914, can hardly be sustained. Yet when one views the political and social tensions evident in Russian society in 1914 in a wider framework and in broader perspective, any flat-footed statement of the case for stabilzation appears at least equally shaky. . . .

By July, 1914, along with the polarization between workers and educated, privileged society. . . , a second process of polarization—this one between the vast bulk of privileged society and the tsarist regime—appeared almost equally advanced. Unfolding largely detached from the rising wave of the labor movement, this second process could not affect its character and temper but was calculated to add a probably decisive weight to the pressure against the dikes of existing authority. By 1914 this second polarization had progressed to the point where even the most moderate spokesmen of liberal opinion were stating publicly, in the Duma and in the press, that an impasse had been reached between the state power and public opinion, which some argued could be resolved only by a revolution of the left or of the right. . . .

Indeed, by the beginning of 1914 any hope of avoiding a revolutionary crisis appeared to be evaporating even among the more moderate representatives of liberal opinion. Under the impact of the blind suicidal course pursued by the government and its handful of supporters, the Octobrist Party had split at the seams. . . .

Indeed, many signs of economic and social progress could be found in the Russian province of the year 1914—the introduction of new crops, new techniques and forms of organization in agriculture, and the industrialization of the countryside; growing literacy among the lower strata and invigorated cultural life among the upper strata of provincial society. But no more than in the major cities were these signs of progress and changes in the localities to be viewed as evidence of the achievement or indeed the promise of greater social stability. . . . "Official" and "unofficial" Russia had now turned into two worlds completely sealed off one from the other. . . . (pp. 1, 2, 3, 8, 9, 10)

THE OPTIMISTS' VIEW

Leonard Schapiro, a British historian in *The Communist Party of the Soviet Union* (New York, 1959) stresses the weakness and disorganization of the Bolsheviks on the eve of World War I, providing a sharp contrast to Soviet accounts:

The Bolsheviks, or those of them who supported Lenin, could now [1914] no longer persist in their policy of maintaining the split [with the Mensheviks] at all costs. . . . There was also more unity now on the non-Bolshevik side than ever before. . . . If Lenin were isolated in his intransigence, there was every chance that many of his "conciliator" followers, who had rejoined him in 1912, would break away again. The Bolshevik organization was, moreover, in a poor state in 1914, as compared with 1912. The underground committees were disrupted. There were no funds, and the circulation of *Pravda* had fallen drastically under the impact of the split in the Duma "fraction."

Intensive propaganda for unity now began inside Russia. The Mensheviks and organizations supporting them drew up an appeal to the Russian workers, blaming the Bolsheviks for the split and urging support for the efforts of the International to reunite the whole party. But it was too late. War broke out . . . and before long the Russian social democrats were rent asunder by new and even less reconcilable dissensions. (pp. 139–140)

Alexander Gerschenkron, an American economic historian, argues that Russia was following the path that western Europe had taken earlier and suggests that without war, it would have avoided revolution:

> Russia before the First World War was still a relatively backward country by any quantitative criterion. . . . Nevertheless . . . Russia seemed to duplicate what had happened in Germany in the last decades of the 19th century [in industrial development]. One might surmise that in the absence of the war Russia would have continued on the road of progressive westernization. . . . The liklihood that the transformation in agriculture would have gone on at an accelerated speed is very great. . . .
> . . . As one compares the situation in the years before 1914 with that of the 90s, striking differences are obvious. In the earlier period the very process of industrialization with its powerful confiscatory pressures upon the peasantry kept adding . . . to the feeling of resentment and discontent until the outbreak of large-scale disorders became almost inevitable. The industrial prosperity of the following period [1906–1914] had no comparable effects, however. Modest as the improvements in the situation of peasants were, they were undeniable and widely diffused. Those improvements followed rather than preceded a revolution and accordingly tended to contribute to a relaxation of tension. . . .
>
> Similarly, the economic position of labor was clearly improving. . . . There is little doubt that the Russian labor movement of those years was slowly turning toward revision and trade-unionist lines. As was true in the West, the struggles for general and equal franchise to the Duma and for a cabinet responsible to the Duma, which probably would have occurred sooner or later, may well have further accentuated this development. . . .
> . . . It seems plausible to say that Russia on the eve of the war was well on the way toward a westernization or, perhaps more precisely, a Germanization of its industrial growth. ("Patterns of economic development," in C. Black, *The Transformation of Russian Society* [Cambridge, Mass., 1960], in excerpts, pp. 57–61.)

Suggested Additional Reading

BOOKS

BERNSTEIN, H. *The Willy-Nicky Correspondence, 1914–17* (New York, 1918).

BRUSSILOV, A. A. *A Soldier's Notebook, 1914–18* (Westport, Conn., 1971).

CHERNIAVSKY, M. *Prologue to Revolution . . . 1915* (Englewood Cliffs, 1967).

FLORINSKY, M. *The End of the Russian Empire* (New Haven, 1931).

FRANCIS, S. R. *Russia from the American Embassy* (New York, 1971). Reprint of 1921.

GANKIN, O. and H. FISHER, eds.   *The Bolsheviks and the World War* (Stanford, 1940).

GOLDER, F.   *Documents of Russian History, 1914–17* (New York, 1927).

GOLOVIN, N. N.   *The Russian Army in the World War* (New Haven, 1931).

MASSIE, R.   *Nicholas and Alexandra* (New York, 1967).

PALEOLOGUE, M.   *An Ambassador's Memoirs*, 3 vol. (New York, 1972).

PARES, B., ed.   *The Letters of the Tsar to the Tsaritsa, 1914–17* (London, 1929).

———.   *The Letters of the Tsaritsa to the Tsar* . . . (London, 1923).

PAVLOVSKY, G.   *Agricultural Russia on the Eve of Revolution* (London, 1930).

RODZIANKO, M. V.   *The Reign of Rasputin* (London, 1927).

SENN, A. E.   *The Russian Revolution in Switzerland* (Madison, Wisc., 1971).

SMITH, C. J.   *The Russian Struggle for Power, 1914–17* (New York, 1956).

SOLZHENITSYN, A.   *August 1914* (New York, 1972) (historical novel).

ARTICLES

DURNOVO, P.   "Memoir to Nicholas II," in Riha, *Readings*, vol. 2, pp. 457–70.

HAIMSON, L.   "The Problem of Social Stability . . . 1905–17," *SR*, vol. 33, pp. 619–42; 34, pp. 1–22.

LEVIN, A.   "P. A. Stolypin. . . ," *JMH*, vol. 37, pp. 445–63.

VON LAUE, T.   "The Chances for Liberal Constitutionalism," *SR*, vol. 24, pp. 34–46.

31

From March to November 1917

THE FREEST, most exciting year in Russian history was 1917, and it has generated more controversy than any other. Bolshevik victory in November brought to power an intransigent, anti-liberal element. Ever since 1917 Soviet and Western historians have debated why the Bolsheviks won and what it signified for mankind. The Soviet view, now more flexible and sophisticated, presents Bolshevik victory as the inevitable result of historical development. The Bolsheviks, it notes, assumed power for the proletariat under Lenin, their revered leader. A few Western historians, such as E. H. Carr, agree that the Bolsheviks were bound to triumph because of their clear purpose and determination. Some Western accounts, especially Robert Daniels' *Red October,* stress spontaneity and the role of chance in 1917. Others cite conspiracy as the decisive factor, but most Western histories reject an explanation of the outcome on the basis of a single factor.

How do the Revolutions of 1917 compare with other revolutions in modern history, especially the French and Chinese? Were the events and outcome in 1917 predetermined? Did the Provisional Government's liberal democratic experiment founder because of Russia's weak constitutional tradition, because it failed to keep its promises, or because it kept Russia in World War I? What produced Bolshevik victory: Lenin's and Trotskii's leadership, superior organization, an attractive program, mass action, or a combination of these elements? Did the Bolsheviks win because of their strengths or their opponents' weaknesses and blunders?

THE "DUAL POWER"

In March 1917 a "Dual Power," to use Trotskii's phrase, succeeded tsarism. Dual power, he notes, does not necessarily imply equal division of authority or a formal equilibrium, and it arises from class conflict in a revolutionary period when hostile classes rely upon incompatible ruling institutions—one outlived, the other developing. The Provisional Government, argued Trotskii, represented a Russian bourgeoisie too weak to govern long; the Petrograd Soviet was a proletarian organ which surrendered power initially to the bourgeoisie. Both convened at first in the Tauride Palace, where they competed for loyalty and popular support.

The Provisional Government represented landed and industrial wealth, privilege, and educated society. Its Premier and Interior Minister, Prince G. E. Lvov, a distinguished aristocrat and wealthy landowner, had been a prominent *zemstvo* leader and member of the right wing of the Kadet party. "I believe in the great heart of the Russian people filled with love for their fellow men. I believe in this fountain of truth, verity, and freedom," declared this idealistic Slavophile liberal. "An illustrious but notoriously empty spot," commented Trotskii. Lvov's government, despite good intentions, was poorly equipped to maintain order or to govern Russia. Its dominant figure and real brains was Foreign Minister Paul Miliukov, the erudite but unrealistic history professor who had led the Kadet Party since 1905. War Minister Guchkov, a big Moscow industrialist, strove to preserve army discipline and create reliable military support for the regime. Finance Minister M. I. Tereshchenko owned property worth some 80 million rubles, spoke excellent French, and was a ballet connoisseur. Only A. F. Kerenskii, Minister of Justice, who joined the SR party, represented even vaguely those who had unseated the Tsar. A young lawyer of rare oratorical power and febrile energy, he believed fully in the revolution and his own destiny, but Kerenskii, noted Trotskii, "merely hung around the revolution." The Petrograd Soviet had barred its members from the Government, but Kerenskii, a vice-chairman of the Soviet, after a dramatic speech, secured permission to enter the cabinet.

This liberal Provisional Government, lacking in power, was to exercise authority only until a democratically elected constituent assembly could establish a permanent regime. "Its orders," Alexander Guchkov, the War Minister, noted, "are executed only insofar as this is permitted by the Soviet . . . which holds in its hand the most important elements of actual power such as troops, railroads, the postal and telegraph service." The Provisional Government pledged to prepare national elections with all possible speed, and the constituent assembly became an article of faith—the holy grail of Russian democracy—for moderates and revolutionaries, including Bolsheviks. Meanwhile the Government took what steps it could toward democracy by granting full freedom of speech, press, assembly, and religion, and equality to all citizens. An amnesty released political prisoners and allowed exiles to return. Provincial governors were abolished, and local governmental officials were to be elected. Unprecedented freedom and euphoria prevailed in Russia.

The Petrograd Soviet, hastily formed and ill-defined in membership, powers, and procedure, promptly took charge in the capital and coordinated other soviets which sprang up throughout Russia. On March 15 it had 1,300 members; a week later soldier delegates swelled the number to more than 3,000. Even when reduced to its former size, it was too large and noisy to do much real business. A small Executive Com-

Library of Congress

A. F. Kerenskii (1881–1970)

mittee, chaired by the Menshevik N. S. Chkheidze, was chosen to reach
and implement important decisions. Moderate socialists dominated it
and the Soviet, with Bolsheviks in opposition. At first party affiliations
were unimportant in the Soviet.

The Soviet approved the Government's initial program and measures,
but their relations soon grew strained over control of the army and
foreign policy. On March 14 the Soviet's army section issued Order No.
1, which authorized all army units to elect soldier committees and send
representatives to the Soviet. Enlisted men were to obey their officers
and the Government only if their orders did not conflict with the Soviet.
This Order, confirmed most reluctantly by War Minister Guchkov, prevented the Government from controlling the army and further undermined army discipline. Meanwhile, Foreign Minister Miliukov insisted
that the March Revolution had not changed Russian foreign policy:
Russia would fulfill its commitments to the Allies and fight for "lasting
peace through victory." Allied governments and the United States,
which had entered the war in April, quickly recognized the Provisional
Government and supplied it generously with war credits. Russia, in-

sisted Miliukov, must obtain Constantinople and the Straits and "merge the Ukrainian provinces of Austria-Hungary with Russia." This expansionist program based on secret inter-Allied treaties provoked a Soviet appeal on March 27 to European peoples to overthrow their imperialist governments and achieve a just and democratic peace "without annexations and indemnities." Meanwhile, until peace came, the Russian revolution must defend itself. Within the Government, Miliukov and Guchkov contended with ministers who repudiated an annexationist peace, though for the time being an atmosphere of democratic unity muted these differences.

THE BOLSHEVIKS GAIN LEADERS AND A PROGRAM

Moderates controlled the Government and Soviet, but the Bolsheviks grew into a formidable opposition. Late in March L. B. Kamenev and Joseph Stalin (I. V. Djugashvili) returned to Petrograd from Siberian exile. Briefly turning the Bolsheviks to the right, they pledged to support the Provisional Government in a defensive struggle against Germany. (Later Stalin blamed Kamenev for this rightist orientation, claiming that he had always opposed the Provisional Government and the war.) Though described by N. N. Sukhanov in 1917 as "a grey blur," Stalin was an able organizer and contributed from behind the scenes to Bolshevik victory, but neither he nor Kamenev supplied dynamic leadership.

Lenin's return to Russia in mid-April proved vital to Bolshevik success. In Switzerland, directing a small group of socialist émigrés, he had feared that he would not live to see the revolution. Though taken unawares by the March Revolution, he grasped its significance immediately and telegraphed his party comrades: "Our tactic: absolute lack of confidence, no support to the new Government. . . ." His "Letters from Afar" to *Pravda*, the Bolshevik newspaper, envisioned an armed seizure of power by the proletariat fused with an armed populace. To arrange his return home, Lenin negotiated through Swiss socialists with the German government, which readily consented to send home socialists dedicated to overthrowing a pro-Allied government and ending Russia's participation in the war. Temporary identity of interests and even Lenin's receipt of "German gold," though, does not prove his opponents' assertion that he was a German agent. Lenin was prepared to accept help from whatever source (only the Germans provided it) without compromising his principles or altering his goals. He and other Russian socialist exiles passed through Germany on a sealed train.

At Petrograd's Finland Station on April 16, the Bolsheviks gave Lenin a triumphal welcome, although he had been in neither the Soviet nor the Duma. The Soviet's chairman, Chkheidze, greeted him: "We think that the principal task of the revolutionary democracy is now the defense of the revolution from any encroachment, either from within or without . . . , the closing of democratic ranks. We hope that you will pursue these goals together with us." Lenin, disregarding Chkheidze, turned to the entire Soviet delegation:

> Dear Comrades, Soldiers, Sailors and Workers! I am happy to greet in your persons the victorious Russian revolution, and greet you as the vanguard of the worldwide proletarian army. . . . The piratical imperialist war is the beginning of civil war throughout Europe. . . . The worldwide socialist revolution has already dawned. . . . Germany is seething. . . . Any day now the whole of European capitalism may crash. The Russian revolution accomplished by you has prepared the way and opened a new epoch. Long live the worldwide socialist revolution.[1]

Lenin's exhortation caused dismay and incredulity among Bolshevik leaders.

The following day (April 17) Lenin presented his "April Theses" to the Petrograd Bolshevik Committee, but they were rejected 13 to two. Denouncing Soviet leaders for cooperating with the Provisional Government, Lenin urged Russians to turn the "imperialist war" into a civil war against capitalism. The Bolsheviks should lead the proletariat and poor peasants and seize power from the bourgeoisie while the soviets, after rejecting "liquidator" (Menshevik-SR) leadership, should replace the Provisional Government. All power would pass to the soviets, the peasants would take the land and the workers the factories. *Pravda* dubbed these theses "unacceptable," and Plekhanov, father of Russian Marxism, declared: "A man who talks such nonsense is not dangerous." Lenin argued, cajoled, and persuaded until three weeks later an all-Russian Bolshevik congress approved his program by a wide margin. The Bolsheviks took over the initial soviet program: bread, land, and peace.

In May, Leon Trotskii returned from exile in New York and in July joined the Bolsheviks with his followers. Lenin had adopted (or stolen) Trotskii's idea of permanent revolution: instead of awaiting full development of capitalism, Russia could move on directly to socialism by revolution. Becoming the most popular and effective orator of the Revolution, Trotskii by joining Lenin, its ablest strategist and organizer, gave the Bolsheviks a great advantage in leadership.

THE REVOLUTION MOVES LEFT (MAY-JULY)

As Lenin won control of the Bolsheviks, a severe crisis shook the Provisional Government. Foreign Minister Miliukov's May 1st note to Allied governments, rejecting any separate peace and pledging that Russia would fight to secure "sanctions and guarantees", touched it off. The Soviet viewed this as a thin disguise for an annexationist peace. Massive, spontaneous demonstrations of workers and soldiers erupted in Petrograd and Moscow with slogans, "Down with Miliukov!", "Down with the Provisional Government!" The demonstrators could have over-

---

[1] N. Sukhanov, *The Russian Revolution* (New York, 1962), vol. 1, pp. 272–73.

turned the Government, but the Soviet forbade this. After the Government had disavowed Miliukov's note, the Soviet prohibited street demonstrations for three days. Nonetheless, Miliukov's position had become untenable, and the Government's weakness was evident.

After Miliukov and Guchkov resigned, the cabinet was reorganized to include moderate socialists (Mensheviks and SR's) since the Soviet's Executive Committee now permitted its member parties to join the Government. On May 18 a coalition government was formed with nine non-socialist (mainly Kadet) and six socialist ministers. The new cabinet's dominant figure was Alexander Kerenskii as war and navy minister, while Victor Chernov, the SR's chief ideologist, became minister of agriculture. Apparently the bourgeoisie (Kadets) had joined with the masses (socialists). By far the largest Russian party was the SR's, supported by peasants, many soldiers, and some officers, but their leadership remained moderate and ineffective. The coalition government advocated "peace without annexations and indemnities," but it was vague on how to achieve it. By entering the Government the moderate socialists became vulnerable to Bolshevik criticism of mistakes and of the continuing war. The extremist Bolsheviks, like the French Jacobins earlier, profited from the moderates' incompetence as rulers and war leaders.

The coalition ministry's policies differed little from its predecessor's. Caught between Allied insistence upon a total military effort and Soviet pressure for a democratic peace, the Government issued vague statements to mask internal divisions. War Minister Kerenskii, Foreign Minister Tereshchenko, and Premier Lvov advocated an active war role. Responding to French pleas to tie down German troops in the east, Kerenskii prepared a great offensive in Galicia, hoping thereby to revive army morale, provide the regime with reliable troops, and secure Allied financial and political support. A patriot and a democrat, he believed that a free Russia was linked indissolubly with the Allied cause. Conservatives of the Kadet Party expected an offensive to restore order in Russia and perhaps bring military victory. Kerenskii toured the front to whip up patriotic enthusiasm. Special volunteer "shock battalions" were recruited to lead the way. Kerenskii's oratory was applauded warmly, but it had little lasting effects on the war-weary Russian troops.

In June 1917, moderate socialists seemed securely in control of the Government and the Soviet. When the first all-Russian Congress of Soviets opened on June 16, the Bolsheviks and their allies had only 137 out of 1,000 delegates. The Menshevik Tseretelli told the delegates that the Government was safe; no party in Russia would say: "Give us power!" To his surprise Lenin shouted: "Yes, there is one!" and attacked the bourgeoisie, demanding that the war be ended and capitalist aid repudiated. The moderate majority disregarded Lenin, but in the factories Bolshevik strength and worker radicalism were rising. On June 23 the Bolsheviks, pressed by workers and soldiers, agreed to lead a demonstration against the Government, but next day the Congress of Soviets called it off. A week later, however, a demonstration organized by the Congress to display revolutionary unity was dominated by such

Bolshevik slogans as "End the war!" The Bolsheviks, not the Soviet, now clearly led the Petrograd workers.

On July 1 Kerenskii's much heralded offensive began in Galicia with a great artillery barrage. After initial gains against the Austrians, it was halted after 12 days, and on July 19 German and Austrian forces counterattacked and easily broke through Russian lines. Demoralized Russian troops threw down their weapons and fled. Their panicky retreat ended only after all Galicia had been lost and enemy attacks ceased. On July 25 the Government restored the death penalty for desertion, but this action failed to revive the army's will to fight.

As the Russian offensive faltered, disorders broke out in Petrograd (July 16–18). Troops of the garrison, sailors from the Kronstadt naval base, and factory workers clashed with Government supporters. The Bolshevik-dominated First Machine Gun Regiment, after refusing to leave for the front, began the demonstrations. Soon some 500,000 soldiers and workers marched on the Tauride Palace to force the Soviet to assume power. Radical Bolsheviks from the Military Organization and Petersburg Committee supported this movement, but more cautious Central Committee leaders considered it premature. The Bolshevik Party finally decided reluctantly to lead the demonstration. The Soviet's Executive Committee, though frightened, refused to take power or implement Bolshevik demands. Without clear purpose, the demonstrators, after roughing up some ministers, gradually dispersed and the July Days petered out. Later Stalin explained the curious Bolshevik tactics: "We could have seized power [in Petrograd] . . . , but against us would have risen the fronts, the provinces, the soviets. Without support in the provinces, our government would have been without hands and feet." Lenin, too, believed that national support for the Bolsheviks was still inadequate. Their unwillingness to lead damaged the Bolsheviks temporarily among militant soldiers and workers.

KORNILOV AND THE RIGHTWARD SHIFT (JULY-SEPTEMBER)

As the July Days ended, the Provisional Government and Petrograd Soviet regained control. Guards regiments in Petrograd, told that Lenin was a German agent, rallied to the Government, and a reaction set in against the Bolsheviks as newspapers published documents accusing their leaders of treason. The Government disarmed the First Machine Gun Regiment and occupied Bolshevik headquarters. The next day troops searched *Pravda*'s editorial office, wrecked its press, and closed down Bolshevik newspapers. The Bolshevik Military Organization wished to resist, but the workers were cowed. Realizing that the party had suffered a severe setback, Lenin convinced the Central Committee of the need to retreat. He considered standing trial to refute the Government charges, but fearing that he might be murdered in prison, Lenin took refuge in Finland. Trotskii and some other Bolshevik leaders were arrested.

Kerenskii, reshuffling the coalition cabinet on July 25, replaced Prince Lvov as premier. Mensheviks and SR's held most ministerial posts, but the moderate Government failed to implement the measures which the impatient masses demanded. Kerenskii, the democrat, began his rule with halfhearted repression. Insurgent troops and civilians mostly retained their arms, and though the central Bolshevik apparatus was shaken, Bolshevik support in Petrograd's factories continued to grow. By mid-August the Bolshevik Party numbered about 200,000 members compared with 80,000 in April and had outstripped the Mensheviks, whose support declined partly because of the inactivity of the Provisional Government.

Early in August Kerenskii again reshuffled his cabinet and moved into the Winter Palace, seat of the tsars. To build support for his shaky regime before the elections to the Constituent Assembly, he convened the Moscow State Conference drawn from Russia's elite: members of the four Dumas, the soviets, the professions, and army leaders. The Bolsheviks boycotted the Conference (August 26–28) and sought to embarrass it with a general strike in Moscow. Instead of strengthening Kerenskii's government, the Conference exposed the chasm between conservatives and moderate socialists.

As the Moscow State Conference met, General Lavr Kornilov emerged as leader of the conservatives. The son of a Siberian Cossack with a reputation for bravery and rigid discipline, he had been appointed commander in chief of the army by Kerenskii on July 31. Though Kornilov lacked political acumen (General Alekseev described him as "a man with the heart of a lion and the brains of a sheep"), he headed a movement of bourgeoisie, landowners, and the military organized by Rodzianko and Miliukov. About August 20 he ordered his Cossacks and Caucasian Wild Division to take up positions within striking distance of Moscow and Petrograd. After talking with Kerenskii, Kornilov told his chief of staff: "It is time to hang the German supporters and spies with Lenin at their head and to disperse the Soviet . . . once and for all." When Kornilov entered the chamber of the Moscow State Conference, the Right cheered wildly; the Left applauded Kerenskii with equal warmth. The Conference convinced Kornilov that Kerenskii was too weak to restore order in Russia. Supported by conservative Duma leaders, financiers, and the Allied powers, Kornilov pushed plans to march on Petrograd and crush the revolution. Learning of the conspiracy, Kerenskii secured authorization from socialist members of his cabinet to take emergency measures, but the Kadet ministers resigned. Kerenskii's dismissal of Kornilov as commander in chief on September 9 forced the general's hand.

The threat of a military coup united Petrograd socialists, who mobilized workers and soldiers to defend the revolution. While Kerenskii postured equivocally hoping that Kornilov would crush the Bolsheviks and leave him in command, the Soviet's Executive Committee set up a "Committee for Struggle against Counterrevolution" to coordinate resistance. Bolshevik leaders were released and directed the Committee's work, and arms were gathered everywhere to equip the Red Guard, a workers' militia. Kronstadt sailors, pouring in to defend Petrograd, swiftly rounded up Kornilovites. The Executive Committee instructed army committees and railroad and telegraph workers to obstruct

Kornilov's advance; his small forces were enveloped and never reached Petrograd. His troop trains were delayed or derailed while Bolshevik agitators turned his soldiers against their officers. The Wild Division, won over by a Moslem delegation, elected a committee which apologized to the Petrograd Soviet for participating in a counterrevolutionary plot. Kornilov and his supporters were arrested, and the only serious rightist attempt in 1917 to seize power fizzled out ingloriously.

THE RISING TIDE (SEPTEMBER-NOVEMBER)

After Kornilov's defeat, the Bolsheviks rode a wave of mass discontent which finally overwhelmed the weak Provisional Government. In the Kornilov affair the party had displayed leadership and control of the workers who were becoming increasingly radical. On September 13, the Petrograd Soviet approved a Bolshevik resolution for the first time; five days later this action was repeated in Moscow. On September 22, when the Petrograd Soviet again voted Bolshevik, the moderate Executive Committee, interpreting this as a vote of no confidence, resigned and soon thereafter Trotskii was elected chairman. Control of the principal soviets gave the Bolshevik Party a strategic base as important as the Paris Commune was for the French Jacobins in 1792.

Kerenskii's moderate regime might still have survived had it acted swiftly to begin land reform, end the war, and convene the Constituent Assembly, but it did none of these. Alexander Verkhovskii, the new War Minister, urged Russia and the Allies to conclude a just peace and carry out immediate social reforms; but the Provisional Government, ignoring his suggestions, soon removed him. Instead, Kerenskii made more cabinet changes and proclaimed Russia a republic. On September 27, he convened a 1,200-man Democratic Conference in Petrograd, drawn from soviets, trade unions, *zemstva,* and cooperatives. Representing mostly the Russian educated classes whose influence and popular support were dwindling, this Conference voted to establish the Council of the Republic, or Preparliament, dominated by moderate socialists but including non-socialists and some Bolsheviks. At the Council's first meeting on October 20, Trotskii denounced it, the Bolsheviks walked out, and the other deputies took no action.

Extreme elements were growing at the expense of the moderates. Between July and October while the Bolshevik vote in Moscow city elections rose from 11 to 51 percent, and the Kadets (now the conservatives) from 17 to 26 percent, the moderate SR's dropped from 58 to 14 percent. Chernov, the only SR leader of real stature, was a theoretician, not a practical politician. Its other leaders (Kerenskii and Savinkov) grew more conservative, whereas the militant rank and file drew closer to the Bolsheviks. As the SR's neared an open split, the Mensheviks were losing worker support to the Bolsheviks. The radical masses were rejecting moderate leaders and parties and moving the revolution to the left.

The breakdown of the army, which had been developing since March, contributed much to extremism. Kornilov's fiasco hastened the collapse of discipline among the war-weary troops; the men regarded officers as enemies of the revolution. For months thousands of peasant soldiers had been deserting their units and filtering back to their villages, ragged, hungry, and disgruntled. Soldier soviets in most army units swung toward the Bolsheviks, who accelerated the trend with leaflets and agitation. National groups demanding independence also helped dissolve the army until by November few reliable units remained.

The peasantry moved spontaneously during 1917 to seize and divide up landowners' estates, though at first they had waited and listened to Government promises. In May, the first National Peasant Congress in Petrograd, wholly SR-dominated, outlined a program: all property in land was to be abolished, even for smallholders, and land was to belong to the entire people. Anyone might use land if he tilled it himself; hired labor was to be prohibited. Final solution of the land question was to be left to the Constituent Assembly. By midsummer, angered by official grain requisitioning, shortages of manufactured goods, and postponement of land reform, the peasants began to act. Violent land seizures and murders of landowners grew in number week by week, reaching a peak in October and November. The Bolsheviks did not lead the peasants but exploited their discontent. The Government, helpless to protect landlord property, reluctantly recognized local peasant committees and soviets, which controlled much of the countryside. By November most peasants backed leftist SR's who were cooperating with the Bolsheviks.

The workers grew more discontented as they were squeezed by galloping inflation, dwindling food supplies, and shrinking real wages. Food riots and long lines of hungry workers became common in the cities. Disorder mounted in factories as strikes intensified and industrial sabotage and murders of hated foremen by workers increased. The owners, lacking essential raw materials and fuel, shut down many factories, but the workers believed that this kind of action was to prevent strikes for higher wages. The Government could neither mediate between workers and employers nor coerce the workers. By November the rapidly growing trade union movement had more than two million members. Moderate socialists retained influence in central trade union conferences, but by June more radical local factory committees were endorsing Bolshevik proposals for worker control of the factories; by November factory committees and district soviets in Petrograd were firmly Bolshevik. The largely spontaneous and militant worker movement converged with the Bolshevik drive for political power and supplied the mass base for the Bolshevik Revolution. By November peasants were seizing the land, workers the factories, soldiers were deserting and making peace, and soviets were taking power. All this coincided with the Bolshevik short-term program.

Kornilov's defeat signalled a sharp upturn in Bolshevik popularity. To Lenin, still hiding in Finland, the achievement of Bolshevik majorities in leading soviets proved that it was time to strike. The soviets could become the foundation for a revolutionary regime. "They represent a new *type* of state apparatus which is incomparably higher, incomparably more democratic," he wrote. Crucial for Lenin were majorities in the chief soviets, not victories in parliamentary elections. The

Bolsheviks now were strong in the capitals, Volga cities, the Urals, Donets Basin, and Ukrainian industrial centers while their allies, the Left SR's, had widespread peasant and soldier support. No longer could an isolated Red Petrograd be crushed by the rest of Russia.

Lenin and Trotskii, certain that it was time to seize power, had to convince the Central Committee in Petrograd. Lenin's slogan was "Insurrection now!" With majorities in the Petrograd and Moscow soviets, he wrote the Central Committee in late September, "the Bolsheviks can and must take power into their own hands." To await the Constituent Assembly, warned Lenin, would merely enable Kerenskii to surrender Petrograd to the Germans. "The main thing is to place on the order of the day *the armed uprising in Petrograd and Moscow* . . . We will win *absolutely* and *unquestionably*." Insurrectionary detachments should be formed and placed in position immediately. Shocked by Lenin's urgent messages, the Central Committee burned one of his letters and disregarded the other.

Early in October, Lenin moved to Vyborg, closer to the capital. Bolshevik leaders in Petrograd were calling for the Second Congress of Soviets, set for early November, to assume power peacefully. In a pamphlet, *Will the Bolsheviks Retain State Power?* Lenin insisted that the masses would support a purely Bolshevik government. Nothing except indecision could prevent the Bolsheviks from seizing and keeping power until the world socialist revolution triumphed. As the Central Committee stalled, Lenin wrote in *The Crisis Has Matured* (October 12): "We are on the threshold of a world proletarian revolution" which the Bolsheviks must lead. If the Central Committee showed misguided faith in the Congress of Soviets or Constituent Assembly, its members would be "miserable traitors to the proletarian cause." When this too was disregarded, Lenin threatened to resign and campaign in the lower ranks of the party.

On October 20, Lenin came to Petrograd in disguise to convert the Central Committee to armed insurrection. He and 11 Committee members argued through the night of October 23–24 in the apartment of the unsuspecting Sukhanov. They approved a Political Bureau (subsequently Politburo) of seven: Lenin, Zinoviev, Kamenev, Trotskii, Stalin, Sokolnikov, and Bubnov. After long debate, the idea of armed uprising was approved in principle, though Zinoviev and Kamenev, arguing that insurrection would be unMarxian, remained opposed and kept the party leadership in turmoil until the November Revolution. Trotskii urged that the insurrection be coordinated with the imminent Second Congress of Soviets, thus giving it a measure of legitimacy, and he stuck to this position despite Lenin's demand for immediate action. Without Lenin's and Trotskii's leadership, it seems unlikely that the Bolsheviks would have taken power.

THE NOVEMBER REVOLUTION

Unlike the spontaneous overthrow of tsarism, the November Revolution was an armed seizure of power by one party under cover of the

Second Congress of Soviets. Had the Bolsheviks not acted in November, Trotskii concludes, their opportunity would have passed.

Preparations for an armed showdown were haphazard on both sides. Trotskii, chairman of the Petrograd Soviet and its Military Revolutionary Committee (MRC), directed the insurrection and was the most active Bolshevik leader at large in Petrograd. The MRC and the Bolshevik Military Organization won over or neutralized the 150,000 man Petrograd garrison. Composed mostly of overage, sick, or green troops, the garrison leaned politically toward the SR's but was loyal to the Soviet and to whomever kept it away from the front. The MRC sent revolutionary commissars to all its regiments, ousted government commissars, and won control. When the garrison recognized MRC and Soviet authority on November 5, the Government was virtually powerless, but the uprising was "postponed" until the meeting of the Second Congress of Soviets on November 7.

The Government remained outwardly confident. Colonel G. P. Polkovnikov, commander of the Petrograd Military District, announced he was ready for trouble. Premier Kerenskii hoped the Bolsheviks would act so that the Government could crush them. The Government had a thorough defense plan which anticipated most Bolshevik moves and concentrated on holding the city center and Neva bridges. Kerenskii had some 1,000 military cadets, officers, and Cossacks—sufficient, he believed, to paralyze Bolshevik centers if used boldly.

As both sides waited, Government strength ebbed. On November 5 Trotskii and Lashevich harangued the garrison at Peter and Paul Fortress, persuaded it to surrender, and procured weapons there for 20,000 Red Guards. Next morning the Government sent military cadets to close down Bolshevik newspapers and moved the Women's Battalion of Death, which Kerenskii had recruited to shame Russian males into fighting. Accusing Lenin of treason and ordering MRC leaders arrested, Kerenskii sought plenary powers from the Preparliament to crush the Bolsheviks.

Government moves and Lenin's exhortations prodded the MRC into counteraction. "The situation is impossibly critical . . . A delay in the uprising is equivalent to death," Lenin told the Central Committee. Early on November 7, Red Guards and sailors occupied railroad stations, the State Bank, and the central telephone exchange without resistance. Kerenskii lacked troops which would defend his regime and left Petrograd to locate loyal units outside. The capture of the Winter Palace that evening was prosaic, anticlimactic, and virtually bloodless. About 10 P.M. when the Women's Battalion tried a sortie, the besiegers rounded it up, raped a few, and dispersed the rest. The ministers surrendered meekly to invading Red Guards and were placed under house arrest. In this "assault," unduly glorified in Soviet accounts, only six attackers and no defenders were killed. The Provisional Government had fallen almost without resistance.

Bolshevik Petrograd withstood Kerenskii's counterattack combined with an internal revolt. At Pskov, Kerenskii had persuaded General N. N. Krasnov to move on Petrograd with about 700 Cossacks, and on

United Press International

Leon Trotskii (1879–1940)

November 12 they occupied Tsarskoe Selo, just to the south. The previous day, however, an uprising in Petrograd by military cadets organized by moderate socialists had been crushed. Red Guards and sailors repelled Krasnov's feeble attack on Petrograd, and his force, neutralized by Red propaganda, melted away. Kerenskii escaped in disguise and eventually reached England.

In most of Russia the Bolsheviks established control in a few weeks. In Moscow there were several days of severe fighting before the Red Guards[2] overcame military cadets and stormed the Kremlin November 15, but there was no active defense of the Provisional Government elsewhere. Georgian Mensheviks set up a nationalist regime, and in Kiev the Ukrainian Rada took over, but these actions did not then threaten Bolshevik rule.

Screened by the Second Congress of Soviets, the Bolsheviks created a new regime even before the Government yielded. Lenin emerged from hiding the afternoon of November 7 to tell the Petrograd Soviet: "The oppressed masses themselves will form a government. The old state

---

[2] The Red Guards numbered about 20,000 in Petrograd and between 70,000 and 100,000 in all Russia. D. N. Collins, "A Note on the Numerical Strength of the Russian Red Guard in October 1917," *Soviet Studies*, vol. 24, No. 2 (October, 1972), pp. 270–80.

apparatus will be destroyed root and branch. Now begins a new era in the history of Russia." That evening the Second Congress of Soviets convened with Bolsheviks predominating (390 out of 650 delegates). After verbal fireworks, the moderate socialists denounced the Bolshevik coup as illegal, walked out, and went into opposition. The remainder (Bolsheviks and Left SR's) set up an all-Bolshevik regime: Lenin became president of the Council of People's Commissars, Trotskii foreign commissar, and Stalin commissar of nationalities. Lenin read his decree on Peace, which urged immediate peace without annexations and indemnities, the end of secret diplomacy, and publication of all secret treaties. To win peasant support, he issued the Decree on Land, which confiscated state and church lands without compensation. Lenin was acting swiftly to implement his promises.

The Russian Revolution, unlike the French or the American, occurred in wartime amidst military defeat and governmental disintegration. The Provisional Government set up in March lacked leadership, could not build reliable military or political support, and delayed too long the elections it had promised to a constituent assembly. Its decision to remain in World War I and the weakness of Russian democratic traditions contributed to its downfall. The Bolsheviks' triumph in November resulted from their strengths and their opponents' weaknesses and mistakes. Alone of the major parties, the Bolsheviks had not joined the weak Provisional Government and were free to criticize its shortcomings and blunders. Lenin and Trotskii provided abler leadership, got their ideas across better than their rivals, and possessed a short-term program that was clear, readily comprehensible, and attractive to the war-weary Russian masses.

Suggested Additional Reading

ADAMS, A., ed.   *The Russian Revolution and Bolshevik Victory* (Boston, 1972).

BROWDER, R. and A. KERENSKY, eds.   *The Russian Provisional Government, 1917*, 3 vol., (Stanford, 1961).

CARR, E. H.   *The October Revolution: Before and After* (New York, 1971).

CHAMBERLIN, W. H.   *The Russian Revolution, 1917–1921*, 2 vol. (New York, 1935).

CHERNOV, VICTOR.   *The Great Russian Revolution* (New Haven, 1936).

CURTISS, J. S.   *The Russian Revolution of 1917* (Princeton, 1957).

DANIELS, ROBERT.   *Red October: the Bolshevik Revolution of 1917* (New York, 1967).

———.   *The Russian Revolution* (Englewood Cliffs, 1972).

HEALD, EDWARD.   *Witness to Revolution: Letters from Russia, 1916–1919* (Kent, Ohio, 1972), ed. Gidney.

KERENSKY, A. F.   *Russia and History's Turning Point* (London, 1965).

MELGUNOV, S. P.   *The Bolshevik Seizure of Power* (ABC-Clio, 1972).

PALEOLOGUE, M.   *An Ambassador's Memoirs*, 3 vols. (New York, 1972).

PIPES, RICHARD, ed.   *Revolutionary Russia: A Symposium* (New York, 1969).

RABINOWITCH, A.   *Prelude to Revolution: . . . the July Uprising* (Bloomington, 1969).

RADKEY, O. H.   *The Agrarian Foes of Bolshevism: . . . Russian Socialist Revolutionaries . . .* (New York, 1958).

REED, JOHN.   *Ten Days That Shook the World* (New York, 1919, and reprints).

SERGE, VICTOR.   *Year One of the Russian Revolution* (New York, 1972).

SUKHANOV, N. N.   *The Russian Revolution of 1917*, ed. J. Carmichael, 2 vol. (New York, 1962).

TROTSKY, LEON.   *The History of the Russian Revolution*, 3 vol. (New York, 1932).

WADE, REX.   *The Russian Search for Peace: February–October 1917* (Stanford, 1969).

32

The First Soviet Decade

AFTER THE November Revolution it took the Bolsheviks, governing a divided, wartorn country, a decade to achieve full military and political control and begin to build a new autocracy. After making peace with the Central Powers, they defeated their domestic opponents (Whites) in a bitter civil war (1918–21) complicated by foreign intervention. They moved simultaneously to destroy the old state, political parties, society, and economic order and erect new socialist ones. In 1927 they had succeeded in their destructive mission but had taken only initial and tentative steps in socialist construction. One can divide this first decade of Bolshevism in power into the hectic initial months, a period of extremism and revolutionary fervor (1918–21), and one of recovery, compromise, and power struggle (1921–27). In 1918–19 it seemed dubious that the Soviet regime could retain power in semi-backward Russia without revolutions abroad. Provided they succeeded, could the Bolsheviks build socialism in isolated Soviet Russia? Why and how did they win the Civil War? Why did the Allies intervene and how did this affect the outcome? Was "War Communism" an unplanned response to the war crisis or a conscious effort to build socialism? Did the New Economic Policy of 1921 represent a retreat toward capitalism or the initial stage of socialist construction? How did Stalin defeat his rivals and achieve absolute power?

FIRST STEPS, 1917–1918

After the Bolshevik coup in Petrograd many people believed that their rule would be but a brief interlude and that Lenin could not implement his program of bread, land, and peace. Predicting that 240,000 Bolsheviks, running Russia for the poor, could "draw the working people . . . into the daily work of state administration," Lenin counted on imminent European revolutions to preserve his infant regime; otherwise its prospects appeared dim. Bolshevik leaders recalled the Paris Commune of 1871, crushed by conservative France, and their initial measures seemed designed to make a good case for posterity in case world capitalism overwhelmed them.

Michael Curran

Bolshevik Headquarters, Smolny Institute in Leningrad, where the Revolution was first declared won.

Bolshevik power spread swiftly from Petrograd over central Russia, but it met strong opposition in borderlands and villages,[1] from other socialist parties and even from some Bolsheviks. Lenin, however, acted decisively to crush other socialist parties, dissident Bolsheviks, and workers' groups in Russia proper. Mensheviks and Right SR's were demanding a regime of all socialist parties without Lenin and Trotskii, who had led the "un-Marxian" November coup. Right Bolsheviks under Gregory Zinoviev and Lev Kamenev temporarily left the Central Committee proclaiming: "Long live the government of Soviet parties!" Retorting that the Congress of Soviets had approved his all-Bolshevik regime, Lenin called the rightists deserters and until they submitted, threatened to expel them from the party. Bringing a few Left SR's into his government, Lenin hailed it as the dictatorship of the proletariat (Bolsheviks) and poor peasantry (Left SR's). This action completed the split of the SR's.

The Constituent Assembly represented a severe political challenge because during 1917 the Bolsheviks had pledged to convene it. Even after November *Pravda* proclaimed: "Comrades, by shedding your blood, you have assured the convocation of the Constituent Assembly." Lenin

---

[1] See below, pp. 473–75.

knew his party could not win a majority, but he found it too risky to cancel the scheduled national elections, the only free ones ever held in Russia. Despite some intimidation and restrictions imposed on the Kadets and the Right, the elections were remarkably fair and orderly. The SR's obtained about 58 percent of the vote, the Bolsheviks 25, other socialists four, and the Kadets and the Right 13 percent. Soviet accounts stress that major cities returned Bolshevik majorities and that many SR votes were cast for pro-Bolshevik Left SR's. Nonetheless, non-Bolshevik parties had won the elections.

Lenin swiftly neutralized, then dissolved the Assembly. In December the Kadets were banned as counterrevolutionary, and their leaders and many right-wing socialists were arrested. The Constituent Assembly, warned Lenin, must accept the Soviet regime and its measures or be dissolved. When the Assembly convened in Petrograd January 18, 1918, it was surrounded with sharpshooters, and armed Red soldiers and sailors packed its galleries. After Bolshevik resolutions were defeated and Chernov, a moderate SR, was elected president, the Bolsheviks walked out. Early next day on Bolshevik orders, a sailor told Chernov to suspend the session because "the guards are tired." Red troops then closed down the Assembly and dispersed street demonstrations in its behalf. Moderate socialists during the Civil War tried to use the Assembly as a rallying point only to find that most peasants knew nothing about it. The Constituent Assembly's dissolution marked the demise of parliamentary democracy in Russia.

Old political agencies, principles, and parties were crushed ruthlessly. Decrees abolished the Senate, *zemstva*, and other organs of local self-government. Even before counterrevolutionary threats materialized, the Cheka (Extraordinary Commission) began Red terror under the dedicated Polish revolutionary Felix Dzerzhinsky. The imperial family, transported to Ekaterinburg (Sverdlovsk) in the Urals, was murdered at Lenin's orders in a cellar in July 1918.[2] The Left SR's, who left the cabinet after Brest-Litovsk and sought to overthrow the regime, were expelled from the soviets and proscribed. At the December 1920 Congress of Soviets, individual Mensheviks and SR's appeared legally for the last time.

At first Lenin sought to achieve his short-term economic program without antagonizing mass elements. The peasantry were allowed to seize and divide up the land into small holdings. Worker committees were authorized to take over factories. "Workers' control" undermined private capitalism, dislocated production, and fed economic chaos. All banks, railroads, foreign trade, and a few factories were nationalized, but a mixed economy functioned for the time being. The Supreme Council of National Economy (*Vesenkha*) was created to coordinate economic affairs and supervise regional economic councils (*sovnarkhozy*), which ran local activities. These initial economic policies proved rather ineffective and impractical.

---

[2] Reports abound that the Tsar's daughter, Anastasia—or even the entire family —escaped execution and went abroad, but these remain unsubstantiated.

The Bolsheviks acted promptly to destroy the traditional family, army, and church and clear the way for a new socialist society. Marriage and divorce were removed from church control, and only civil marriage was recognized. One spouse could cancel a marriage before a civil board without citing reasons, and then notify the absent partner of the "divorce" by postcard. Incest, bigamy, and adultery were no longer considered crimes. In the army, ranks and saluting were abolished, and officers were to be elected. A major campaign against the Orthodox Church began because Lenin, like Marx, considered religion as superstructure which must reflect economic conditions. Declared Lenin: "God is before all a complex of ideas produced by the stupefying oppression of man;" he predicted a struggle between religion and the socialist state until the former disappeared. Orthodoxy's link with tsarism, the Bolsheviks believed, made it counterrevolutionary and an obstacle to building socialism. Lenin warned, however, that attacking religious "superstitions" directly might alienate the masses from the Soviet state. Instead a multi-faceted campaign began to pen the church in a corner until it withered and died. A decree of February 1918 separated church and state and deprived churches of property and rights of ownership. The church hierarchy was destroyed and its lands, buildings, utensils, and vestments nationalized. Believers had to apply to a local soviet to secure a place of worship and religious articles, and parish churches could operate only with irregular donations of believers. Twenty years of Soviet persecution of all religions had begun.

Lenin had promised peace, and the Russian army had disintegrated to the point where it could no longer fight. When the Allies failed to respond to his Decree on Peace,[3] Lenin urged a separate peace, but only German advances on Petrograd in February 1918 overcame Central Committee opposition to such a peace. Lenin considered the Treaty of Brest-Litovsk, despite its severity, essential for his regime's survival.[4] As he predicted, it provided a breathing space, allowed demobilization of the army and perhaps saved the Soviet regime.

CIVIL WAR AND "WAR COMMUNISM," 1918–1921

The Russian Civil War between the Bolsheviks (Reds) and their political opponents (Whites), affirms a recent American work,[5] did as much to create the USSR as the Revolutions of 1917. Bolshevik objectives in November 1917 were unclear, but in the merciless civil strife between Reds and Whites were laid the foundations of the autocratic Soviet system. The Bolshevik Party was hardened and militarized, systematic terror began, extreme economic policies were adopted, and implacable hostility developed toward the West. The Civil War, though not wholly responsible for these, made Bolshevik policies much more draconian.

---

[3] See below, p. 548.

[4] See below, ibid.

[5] Peter Kenez, Civil War in South Russia, 1918, (Berkeley, 1971).

MAP 32–1

The Civil War, 1919

■ **Fronts of Civil War, October, 1918**

▬ **Line of Red Army, March 1920**

Source: Treagold, Donald W., *Twentieth Century Russia*, Fourth Edition, © 1976, 1972, 1959, by Rand McNally College Publishing Company, Chicago. Map, page 114.

After moving to Moscow early in 1918, Lenin's regime came under intense military and political pressure. As White forces approached, Lenin set up a ruthless emergency government, which sought to mobilize central Russia's total resources. "The republic is an armed camp," Nicholas Bukharin declared. "One must rule with iron when one cannot rule with law." Relatively democratic norms of party life in 1917 yielded to dictatorship, and local popular bodies were suppressed. Lenin made major political and economic decisions and reconciled jealous subordinates. Wisely he let Trotskii handle military affairs, confirmed his decisions, and defended the able war commissar against intrigues by Stalin and others. Jakob Sverdlov ran the party organization until his death in 1919 when Stalin assumed that role. The Eighth Party Congress in 1919 created the first operating Politburo with five full members (Lenin, Trotskii, Stalin, Kamenev, and N. M. Krestinskii) and three candidates (Bukharin, Zinoviev and M. Kalinin) constituting Bolshevism's general staff.

In January 1918 Lenin, proclaiming the Third Congress of Soviets the supreme power in Russia, had it draft a constitution. At the Congress some delegates advocated genuine separation of powers and autonomy for local soviets, but the successful Stalin-Sverdlov draft outlined instead a highly centralized political system which concentrated all power in top government and party bodies. The Constitution of 1918, disfranchising former "exploiters" (capitalists, priests, and nobles) and depriving them of civil rights, supposedly guaranteed all democratic freedoms to the working class. Urban workers received weighted votes to counteract the peasantry's huge numerical superiority. Between congresses of Soviets, a 200-member Central Executive Committee was to exercise supreme power and appoint the executive, the Council of People's Commissars. A hierarchy of national, regional, provincial, district, and local soviets was to govern Soviet Russia. The Constitution, however, omitted mention of the Bolshevik Party, possessor of all real political power!

As the Soviet regime consolidated political control over central Russia, long repressed national aspirations for independence disintegrated the former tsarist empire until Russia was reduced virtually to the boundaries of 1600. The Civil War, like the Time of Troubles,[6] brought political conflict, social turmoil, foreign intervention, and ultimate national Russian resurgence and reunification. Soviet accounts stress heroic Russian resistance in both instances to foreign aggression. The southern frontier—the "Wild Field"—again became a refuge for rebels against a shaky regime in Moscow, and western borderlands broke away to secure independence. Anti-Communist Finns defeated Bolshevik-supported Red Finns to create an independent Finland, and the Baltic states of Latvia, Lithuania, and Estonia, assisted by German occupiers, declared independence and retained it until 1940. In the Ukraine a moderate General Secretariat signed a treaty with the Germans who occupied that region and set up a puppet regime under "Hetman" Skoropadski, opposed by Bolsheviks and many Ukrainian nationalists. In Belorussia an anti-Communist Hromada declared independence, but the national movement there was less developed and lacked a broad popular following. In the Caucasus a Transcaucasian Federative Republic existed briefly in 1918 before yielding to separate regimes in Georgia, Armenia, and Azerbaijan under foreign protection. In Central Asia Tashkent was an isolated Bolshevik fortress in a sea of disunited Moslems. The SR's created regimes in western Siberia and at Samara on the Volga, while Cossack areas of the Urals and the North Caucasus formed a Southeastern Union. Russia had almost dissolved.

The Bolsheviks had used national self-determination to weaken

---

[6] See above, pp. 138–50.

V. I. Lenin and sister in Moscow, 1920

tsarism and the Provisional Government but opposed a permanent fragmentation of the empire because without the western borderlands
Soviet Russia might not be a major power. Lenin strove to reconcile
support of national self-determination with Soviet Russia's unity.
Wherever possible the Bolsheviks overthrew new national regimes:
dissolving the Belorussian Rada, invading the Ukraine, and closing the
Constituent Assembly grossly violated self-determination and the expressed will of the Russian people. Stalin then formulated a Bolshevik
doctrine of "proletarian self-determination" limited to "toilers" and
denied to the bourgeoisie. National independence would be recognized
only "upon the demand of the working population . . ." (meaning in
fact the Bolshevik Party).

Opposition to Lenin's government began in November 1917 but at
first was disorganized and ineffective. Many Russians believed that the
Soviet regime would soon collapse, and an ideological gulf divided
conservative military elements from moderates and socialists. In the
Don region General M. V. Alekseev, former imperial chief of staff, began
organizing anti-Bolshevik elements soon after November into the Volunteer Army, which became the finest White fighting force. Before the
Bolsheviks seized Russian military headquarters at Mogilev, some leading tsarist generals (Kornilov, A. I. Denikin, and others) escaped and
joined Alekseev. The anti-Bolshevik White movement included socially
and ideologically disparate elements lacking in unity and coordination.

Former tsarist officers exercised military and often political leadership and played a disproportionate role. Though some were of humble origin, their education and status separated them from a largely illiterate peasantry. White soldiers were mostly Cossacks, set apart from ordinary peasants by independent landholdings and proud traditions. Officers and Cossacks had little in common ideologically with Kadet and SR intellectuals except antipathy for Bolshevism.

Facing this motley opposition was a Red Army, created in January 1918. At first an undisciplined volunteer force, after Trotskii became War Commissar in April, it became a regular army with conscription and severe discipline imposed by former imperial officers. Trotskii defended this risky and controversial policy as "building socialism with the bricks of capitalism." To get Red soldiers to obey their officers, he appointed political commissars whose families were often held hostage to insure the officers' loyalty. Trotskii raised uncertain Red Army morale by appearing in his famous armored train at critical points. In August 1918 at Sviiazhsk near Kazan he rallied dispirited Red troops and helped turn the tide against the SR's. Soviet historians still give him no credit for this brilliant feat of inspiration and organization, which saved the regime.

Full-scale civil war and Allied intervention followed an uprising in May 1918 of the Czechoslovak Brigade in Russia. The Czechs had joined the imperial Russian army during World War I and, surviving its collapse, remained perhaps the best organized military force in Russia. Wishing to go to the French front to fight for an independent Czechoslovakia, the Czechs quarreled with Soviet authorities. Then they seized the Trans-Siberian Railroad, cleared the Reds from most of Siberia, and aided their White opponents. The Allies, claim Soviet accounts, employed the Czechs to activate all enemies of Red power and with the United States intervened militarily to overthrow the Soviet regime. Western accounts affirm that Allied intervention was to restore a Russian front against Germany. President Wilson allowed United States participation in the Allied expeditions to north Russian ports in the summer of 1918 only after the Allied command insisted it was the only way to win World War I.[7] Such individual Allied leaders as Winston Churchill and Marshal Foch, however, did aim to destroy Bolshevism through intervention. The Soviet-Western controversy over its nature and purpose still rages.

The Civil War, fought initially with small Russian forces of uncertain morale, grew in scope and bitterness. Villages and entire regions changed hands repeatedly in a fratricidal conflict in which both sides committed terrible atrocities. At first the main threat to the Soviet regime came from the east. In August 1918 SR troops, encouraged by the Czechs' revolt, captured Kazan and the tsarist gold reserve and formed SR regimes in Samara and in Omsk in western Siberia. After the Red Army regained Kazan, the SR's in Omsk were ousted by Admiral A. Kolchak, who won Czech and later Allied support, for his con-

---

[7] George Kennan, *Russia and the West under Lenin and Stalin* (Boston, 1960), p. 64.

servative Siberian regime. Early in 1919, pledging to reconvene the Constituent Assembly, Kolchak moved westward toward Archangel and Murmansk, controlled by the Allies and the White Russian army of General E. Miller. By late summer, however, the Red Army had forced him back across the Urals. White and Allied armies hemmed in the Bolsheviks on every side. In the west General Iudenich, commanding a British-equipped White army in Estonia, advanced close to Petrograd in October 1919, but Trotskii rallied its defenders and Iudenich's army dissolved. The chief military threat came from the south. Early in the fall of 1919, General Denikin, commanding Don Cossacks and the elite Volunteer Army equipped with British tanks, reached Orel, 250 miles south of Moscow. Then numerically superior Red forces counterattacked and drove him back, and in March 1920 the British evacuated the remnants of his army from Novorossiisk.

By then the Allies, except for the Japanese in Vladivostok, had departed and White resistance had weakened, but a Soviet-Polish war prolonged Russia's agony. To reconstitute a Greater Poland, the forces of Marshal Joseph Pilsudski invaded the Ukraine and captured Kiev in May 1920. A Soviet counteroffensive carried General M. N. Tukhachevskii's Red Army to Warsaw's outskirts, and Lenin sought to communize Poland. The Poles, however, rallied, drove out the Red Army, and forced Soviet Russia to accept an armistice and later the unfavorable Treaty of Riga (March 1921). Soviet preoccupation with Poland enabled Baron Peter Wrangel, Denikin's successor and the ablest White general, to consolidate control of the Crimea. Wrangel employed capable Kadet leaders to carry through land reform, won peasant support, and occupied considerable areas to the north. After the Soviet-Polish armistice in October 1920, the Red Army smashed Wrangel's resistance and forced the evacuation of some 150,000 Whites to Constantinople.

The Whites had lacked coordination and were plagued by personal rivalries among their leaders. They denounced Bolshevism but affirmed nothing. Denikin and Kolchak were moderates who lacked effective political or economic programs. Their slogan: "A united and indivisible Russia" alienated national minorities and played into Bolshevik hands. White generals made military blunders, but their political mistakes and disunity proved decisive. Allied intervention was of dubious value: foreign arms and supplies aided the Whites but were insufficient to insure victory and let the Reds pose as defenders of Mother Russia. Bolshevik propaganda portrayed White generals (wrongly) as reactionary tools of Western imperialism, and (more correctly) as aiming to restore the landlords. Conversely, the Reds possessed able leadership, a disciplined party, clever propaganda, and a flexible policy of national self-determination. The Red Army had central positions, better discipline, and numerical superiority. Retaining worker support in the central industrial region, the Bolsheviks won the Civil War as they had won power in 1917 with superior leadership, unity, and purpose.

During the Civil War the government adopted War Communism, an emergency program of nationalization, grain requisitioning, and labor mobilization. With the Whites holding the richest food producing regions, in Lenin's words: ". . . Hunger and unemployment are knocking at the doors of an ever greater number of workers . . . , there is no bread." In May 1918 he launched a "crusade for bread," and in June all large-scale industry was nationalized and labor conscripted. This development marked the true beginning of War Communism. State administration of industry by the Supreme Council of National Economy (*Vesenkha*) and its numerous boards proved to be inefficient. Almost one fourth of Petrograd's adult population became officials, perhaps outnumbering actual factory workers. According to Maurice Dobb, representatives of some 50 boards surrounded a dead mare in the streets of Petrograd and disputed responsibility for disposing of its carcass! Later Lenin admitted:

> Carried away by a wave of enthusiasm . . . , we thought that by direct orders of the proletarian state, we could organize state production and distribution of products communistically in a land of petty peasants. Life showed us our mistake.

By 1920 industrial production had fallen to one fifth of the 1913 level.

In the countryside, as the Bolsheviks denounced "rich" peasants (kulaks), Sverdlov warned that the Soviet regime would survive "only if we can split the village into two irreconcilably hostile camps, if we succeed in rousing the village poor against the village bourgeoisie." Red Army detachments aided "committees of the poor" (*kombedy*) to seize "surplus" grain—everything above a bare minimum for subsistence—from kulaks and middle peasants. Compulsory grain deliveries, though later regularized, amounted to virtual confiscation because peasants were paid in almost worthless paper currency. When farmers hid their grain, sold it on the black market, or brewed vodka, the government responded with forcible seizures. Lacking incentives, the peasantry reduced sowings, and agricultural output under War Communism fell to about one half of what it had been. Government attempts to organize collective farms and cooperatives failed because few peasants would enter them voluntarily, and only fear that the Whites would restore landlordism kept some peasants loyal to the Bolshevik regime.

With most state expenditures financed by the printing press, the ruble was undermined and paper currency became almost worthless. Worker rations were free, and wages were paid mostly in kind. As doctrinaire Bolsheviks rejoiced at an increasingly moneyless economy, production plummeted. With the government unable to obtain enough food for the cities, illegal bagmen brought foodstuffs to city dwellers in return for consumer goods.

Once the Civil War ended, the population found War Communism unbearable. In the winter of 1920–21 in the Don and Volga regions, Ukraine and north Caucasus peasant uprisings broke out. Soviet sources blame SR-led kulaks, but most middle peasants joined the revolts as the worker-peasant alliance, the cornerstone of Soviet power, tottered. Grain requisition detachments were attacked everywhere, and the Cheka in February 1921 reported 118 separate peasant uprisings. In Tambov province, Antonov, a former SR, led almost 50,000 insurgent peasants demanding "Down with Communists and Jews!" and "Down with requisitioning!" From all over Russia peasant petitions demanded a fixed tax on agricultural produce instead of grain seizures. In the towns the situation was equally dismal: industry and transport lay idle, workers starved, and city life was falling apart. Despite the Reds' military victory, Soviet Russia seemed about to collapse.

The Kronstadt Revolt confirmed Lenin's decision to yield to peasant demands. Responding to worker strikes in Petrograd, Kronstadt, the chief base of the Baltic Fleet, revolted in March 1921. Kronstadt sailors, avid revolutionaries in 1905 and 1917, tore up party cards and demanded a government of all socialist parties. Their Petropavlovsk Resolution condemned War Communism, demanded elections to soviets by secret ballot, and abolition of grain requisitioning. Despite Bolshevik efforts to depict Kronstadt as a White-émigré plot, it was clearly native and spontaneous. Advocating anarcho-populism, the insurgents demanded land, liberty, and a federation of autonomous communes. Trotskii's Red Army suppressed the uprising only after bitter fighting. Kronstadt, noted Lenin, "lit up reality better than anything else." Revealing the need for new economic policies and the repressive nature of the Soviet regime, it marked the end of the Russian revolutionary movement.

NEW ECONOMIC POLICY AND POWER STRUGGLE, 1921–1927

Lenin had written that tactical retreats would sometimes be necessary. To save the regime, the peasantry had to be wooed and the worker-peasant alliance restored. To achieve this Lenin, overcoming objections to "compromise with capitalism," persuaded the Tenth Party Congress to end grain requisitioning and approve a fixed tax in kind per acre. Initially the New Economic Policy (NEP) was a limited move to stimulate peasant production for the urban market, but by late 1921 private buying and selling had swept the country. Private ownership was restored in consumer sectors while the state retained control over the "commanding heights"—large industry, transport, and foreign trade. Lenin viewed NEP as a tactical retreat toward capitalism to prepare a later strategic advance toward socialism.

Postponing socialist agriculture indefinitely, NEP stimulated small private farming. Class war in the village was abandoned and richer peasants were allowed to prosper. Once they had paid their tax in kind, farmers were free to dispose of their surplus and were guaranteed secure tenure. Within limits they could lease additional land and hire labor. With these stimuli, agriculture recovered rapidly until threatened by the "scissors crisis" of 1922–23. Marketing their grain in order to buy consumer goods, farmers found that industrial prices, kept up by inefficient state trusts, were three times higher relative to agricultural prices than before World War I. Farmers again curtailed marketings and purchases of manufactures. When this threatened economic recovery by reducing urban food supplies and piling up consumer goods,

Red Army passing in review before Trotskii (third from left) in Red Square, c. 1918

the government forced state industry to lower prices and to prune excess staff. The worst effects of the scissors were overcome.

Scrapping War Communism also fostered industrial recovery. Denationalization began in May 1921, and soon about 4,000 small firms controlled three fourths of retail and 20 percent of wholesale trade. Inefficient state enterprises were forced to close, and free contracts among remaining state firms gradually replaced centralized allocation of raw materials and equipment. State-owned big industry employed more than 80 percent of all workers, but handicrafts and small firms with up to 20 employees were private. Real wages recovered roughly to prewar levels, but unemployment became an increasing problem. By 1923 the USSR possessed the first modern mixed economy with state and private sectors. A degree of economic planning was achieved by Gosplan (State Planning Commission).

In 1924–25 the mixed NEP economy, overcoming currency difficulties and the price scissors, reached its peak. As state-controlled big industry coexisted with individual and family enterprises, production in industry and agriculture neared prewar levels. In 1927 about 25 million individual farms comprised 98.3 percent of all agricultural units, while state and collective farms included only a tiny minority of peasants and land. Some 350,000 peasant communes with their village assemblies, not local soviets, dominated rural life. More than 90 percent of the peasantry belonged to *mirs* and had reverted to traditional strip farming and periodic land redistribution. Millions of households still used wooden plows, and half the 1928 grain harvest was reaped by scythe or sickle! Whereas Soviet sources divide the peasantry neatly into kulaks, middle peasants, and poor peasants, actually each group shaded into the next. Middle peasants, poor by European standards, often lacked horses. Redefined to suit political convenience, kulaks were estimated at five to seven percent of the total, yet only one percent of households employed more than one laborer. Nonetheless, the kulak increase suggested peasant differentiation and capitalist revival. Individual farmers sought to consolidate their land and increase production for the market, but success meant being labeled "kulak exploiters." In 1925 the sown area was about that of 1913, but the grain harvest was some ten percent smaller. Whereas Stalin claimed that only half as much grain was marketed in 1927 as in 1913, recent studies affirm that marketings in 1927 almost equalled the 1909–13 average. Urban demand for grain was rising while peasants, discouraged by low prices, ate better and sold less. Grain exports, which reached 12,000,000 tons in 1913, were only 300,000 tons in 1927–28.

Party moderates led by Bukharin advocated continuing NEP indefinitely in order to reach socialism. Peasant prosperity, they argued, would stimulate rural demand for industrial goods and increase marketable agricultural surpluses. In 1925 Bukharin declared: "Peasants, enrich yourselves!" but soon had to repudiate that slogan. The party's goal, he stated, was "pulling the lower strata up to a high level," because "poor peasant socialism is wretched socialism." Lower industrial prices would spur peasant demand and achieve socialism without coercion "at a snail's pace."

Serious economic problems still faced Russia in 1927. A primitive peasant agriculture barely surpassed prewar levels of productivity. An overpopulated countryside inundated towns with unskilled workers, threatening Bolshevik industrial goals and urban-rural market relationships. As industrial growth leveled off, the economy, unable to live indefinitely off capital accumulated under tsarism, faced hard decisions on how to generate more investment and savings. Grain marketings were insufficient to support industrial progress, yet short of coercion, the only ways to increase them were to provide more cheap consumer goods or to raise farm prices significantly.

Under NEP, though a degree of freedom persisted, political controls were tightened. Remaining Menshevik and SR leaders were exiled, and late in 1921 a party purge excluded about one fourth the Bolshevik membership. Within the party, factions were banned and political dissent became more dangerous. Punitive powers of the expanding central party apparatus over the members increased, and decision-making by top leaders grew more arbitrary. Party decrees, however, failed to end debate or factions during NEP, even though the defeated might be expelled or lose their posts.

The Constitution of 1918 had proclaimed federalism, but relations among Soviet republics remained undefined until in December 1922 a unified, centralized Union of Soviet Socialist Republics replaced the several independent republics. Within the huge Russian Republic (RSFSR) were 17 autonomous republics and regions for national minorities, all ruled from Moscow. Other republics, such as Ukraine and Belorussia, had to accept the RSFSR's constitution verbatim. Because the soviets were subordinate to party direction and other Communist parties were Russian-led, the Russian Party's Central Committee exercised full de facto power everywhere. The RSFSR government became the highest state authority in all areas occupied by the Red Army. Recent Soviet histories, minimizing national resistance to integration in Soviet Russia, attribute the USSR's formation partly to "imperialist" pressure and foreign plots to overthrow Soviet power. Actually, it resulted mainly from the Red Army's subjugation of tsarist borderlands. Georgia's conquest in 1921 after severe resistance brought Transcaucasia under full Soviet rule. When Red troops entered Vladivostok in 1922 following Japanese withdrawal, the Far Eastern Republic dissolved instantly and merged with the RSFSR. The nominally independent republics of Khiva and Bukhara in Central Asia were abolished in 1924 and their territory distributed arbitrarily among five new Soviet republics: Uzbek, Turkmen, Tajik, Kazakh, and Kirghiz.

The new USSR was an apparent compromise between Bolshevik desires for centralization and autonomist aims of nationalists and federalists in the borderlands. The Bolsheviks viewed the USSR as a stage in the advance toward an ultimate worldwide Soviet state. Within it national minorities often enjoyed less autonomy than under tsarism. Gone were their political parties and separate religious and cultural institutions, though they received linguistic autonomy, distinct national territories, and political representation—a fake federalism concealing complete Russian and Bolshevik predominance.

Once Lenin achieved power his doctrines changed considerably. Before the November coup he had declared in *State and Revolution:*

> To destroy officialdom immediately, everywhere, completely—this cannot be thought of. . . . But to *break up* at once the old bureacratic machine and to start immediately the construction of a new one which will enable us gradually to reduce all officialdom to naught, this is *no* Utopia, it is the experience of the [Paris] Commune, the . . . direct and urgent task of the revolutionary proletariat.[8]

Capitalism had so simplified governmental functions, Lenin believed, that ordinary workers could perform such "registration, filing and checking." He had conceived of a "state apparatus of about ten if not 20 million" class-conscious workers as part-time civil servants (How poorly he understood the problems of running an industrial society!). Once in power, the flexible Lenin discarded former views which proved inapplicable. The transition to socialism, he admitted in 1918, would require bourgeois experts, and in 1920 he conceded sadly: "We have to administer [the proletarian state] with the help of people belonging

---

[8] Lenin, *Polnoe Sobranie Sochineniia*, 5th ed. (Moscow, 1962), vol. 33, pp. 48–49.

to the class we have overthrown" and pay them well. In his final years Lenin grew evolutionary and reformist. Criticizing War Communism's "furious assaults," he described "exaggerated revolutionism" as dangerous in domestic policy and advocated "conquering peacefully" by cautious economic construction. The contrast between his militant views in 1917–20 and the reformism of 1921–23 makes one wonder which was the "real" Lenin.

Nonetheless, Lenin bequeathed an elitist doctrine and party as foundations of a new autocracy. His central doctrine—the dictatorship of the proletariat—he defined as "power won and maintained by the proletariat against the bourgeoisie, power unrestricted by any laws." Having designed a centralized party able to strike quickly and ruthlessly and outlawing factions within it, he hoped that "democratic centralism" would permit free intra-party debate, then unanimous action. Discussion was to be free until a decision was reached, then all party members were to execute it loyally. Lenin had prevailed by persuasion and charisma, not force. Bukharin recalled: "Lenin was a dictator in the best sense of the word." He was "leader, organizer, captain, and a stern iron authority. . . . But he was for us all Ilich, a close, beloved person, a wonderful comrade and friend . . ."[9] Nevertheless, Lenin gave Stalin the tools to build his brutal dictatorship: a centralized party, predominant central organs, subservient soviets, and police terror. Stalin merely applied these more ruthlessly and vindictively than his mentor.

In May 1922 Lenin suffered his first stroke. By theoretical grasp, pragmatic leadership, and ability to handle people, he had dominated Bolshevism since its inception, and his semi-retirement sparked a struggle for succession within the party. Lenin named no successor, and his "Testament" found fault with all the leading contenders. Increasingly dismayed by Stalin's Great Russian chauvinism and brutal domination of the party apparatus, Lenin wrote: "Comrade Stalin, having become *gensek* [General Secretary] has concentrated boundless power in his hands, and I am not sure that he will always manage to use this power with sufficient caution." In January 1923 he added: "Stalin is too rude. . . . I propose to the comrades that they devise a way of shifting Stalin from this position. . . ." Apparently, only a third stroke in March 1923 prevented Lenin from removing Stalin. Concern for the party and their own positions induced other contenders at first to form a collective leadership and present a united front. Behind the scenes the succession struggle went through several phases until Stalin triumphed. Issues debated fiercely included: Where was the Revolution heading? Would NEP lead to capitalism or socialism? How should Russia be industrialized? Factions, though illegal, were too ingrained in party traditions to be easily eradicated, though politics grew ever more dangerous and secretive. At Lenin's death in 1924, four major groups had formed: a Stalin faction, the Trotskii Left, Bukharin's moderates, and a Zinoviev-Kamenev group based in Leningrad.

Joseph Stalin, the eventual winner, was born in 1879 as Iosif Vis-

<hr>

[9] S. Cohen, *Bukharin* (New York, 1974), p. 224.

sarionovich Djugashvili of semiliterate Georgian parents descended from serfs. As a boy, Soso was devoted to his mother and rebelled against a drunken father and all authority. An excellent student who expected to excel in everything, he idealized Koba, a fearless 19th century Caucasian mountain chieftain, and adopted his view of vindictive triumph as a worthy goal in life. He resented the strict discipline at the Tiflis Orthodox seminary and was expelled as a socialist in 1899. Between 1902 and 1917 he was arrested and exiled repeatedly for underground revolutionary activity. Becoming a Bolshevik soon after the faction's formation, as Lenin's admiring disciple, he modeled himself after his hero and adopted the name, Stalin, partly because it resembled Lenin. Stalin became a Great Russian in outlook and dedicated his life to revolution. His *Marxism and the National Question* (1913) established him as a major leader and a mature Marxist. In 1917 as party organizer and close colleague of Lenin, he belonged to the Bolshevik general staff. The SR memoirist, N. Sukhanov, however, recalled Stalin then as "a grey blur, looming up now and then dimly and not leaving any trace." During the Civil War he gained military experience and political influence but was intensely jealous of Trotskii, who overshadowed him. The traditional Western view of Stalin as a non-intellectual "organization man," building the party state, however, fitted Sverdlov better. Stalin handled crises well, but he was too impatient, hot tempered, and uncooperative to be a gifted organizer or administrator. In 1923 he confided to Kamenev: "The greatest delight is to mark one's enemy, prepare everything, avenge oneself thoroughly, and then go to sleep."

Aiming to control the Bolshevik movement, Stalin achieved his commanding position by the politics of power and influence and by culti-

Michael Curran

Stalin's birth place, surrounded by the Stalin museum, in Gori, Georgia

vating a political following built up over the years. In exile, studying the strategy and tactics of politics, his primer was Machiavelli's *The Prince.* He had an intuitive eye for men's strengths and weaknesses and how to exploit them. After Sverdlov's death in 1919, Stalin acquired key posts in the Orgburo (concerned with organizational matters), Politburo, and Secretariat, and election as General Secretary consolidated his organizational position. Stalin dominated the party apparatus which Sverdlov had built, forged his personal machine, and obtained a controlling voice on party bodies which selected and placed personnel.

Stalin exploited cleverly the cult of Lenin, which developed during the leader's final illness. Lenin had prohibited public adulation of himself and detested ceremony, but after his death his teachings—Leninism—became sacred doctrine. Official decrees ordered monuments to Lenin erected all over the USSR, renamed Petrograd as Leningrad, and authorized a huge edition of his writings. Stalin urged that Lenin's body be embalmed and placed on public display in a tomb on Red Square over indignant protests by his widow, Trotskii, and Bukharin that this was un-Marxian. As Lenin's devoted disciple, Stalin gathered the reins of power and won public acclaim.

Before achieving full power Stalin survived some tense moments. In May 1924, a Central Committee plenum heard Lenin's "Testament," which urged Stalin's removal as General Secretary. Zinoviev and Kamenev, who had formed a triumvirate with Stalin in 1922, however, supported him from fear of Trotskii. Stalin used the triumvirate to undermine Trotskii, whose inept tactics and arrogance antagonized many party members and who spurned overtures from Kamenev and Zinoviev when Stalin's rise might still have been prevented. Only after his rivals had voted him into all his positions of power did Stalin begin an open struggle with them. His repetitious, catechistic style won support from younger, semi-educated Bolsheviks who sought a single authoritative chief to lead their party forward.

In 1925 the triumvirate broke up: Zinoviev and Kamenev drifted belatedly toward Trotskii, while Stalin joined Bukharin's moderates. At the Fourteenth Congress, Kamenev, too late, challenged Stalin's credentials as the new party chief, but Stalin's machine defeated him and broke up Zinoviev's Leningrad organization. Because Stalin still lacked enough prestige to seize sole power, his alliance with Bukharin proved most advantageous. As chief theorist and spokesman for NEP, Bukharin shielded Stalin from accusations that he was usurping Lenin's place and compensated for his lack of ideological clout. Through 1927 Stalin supported Bukharin's gradualist economics and his ideological warfare against Trotskii.

During the growing debate over socialist construction,[10] Stalin developed his major theory: socialism in one country. He had declared at a Bolshevik conference in April 1917: "The possibility is not excluded that Russia will . . . blaze the trail to socialism." In 1925 Bukharin affirmed that the USSR could build its own socialism gradually but added: "Final practical victory of socialism in our country is

---

[10] See below, pp. 500–502.

not possible without the help of other countries and of world revolution." Stalin, posing as a moderate and Lenin's true interpreter, in *Foundations of Leninism* (1924) restated the Leninist view:

> To overthrow the bourgeoisie the efforts of one country are sufficient; for the final victory of socialism, for the organization of socialist production the efforts of one country, particularly of a peasant country like Russia, are insufficient; for that the efforts of the proletariats of several advanced countries are required.[11]

To prove that Trotskii and his theory of world revolution were anti-Leninist, however, Stalin later that year suddenly asserted that Russia alone could organize a completely socialist economy with advanced industry and high living standards. He developed the nationalistic view that Russia alone might blaze the trail of socialist construction. Soviet Russia, the pioneer of proletarian revolution, could construct a fully socialist society by its own exertions with or without revolutions abroad. To insure that the old order would not be restored, however, the proletariat must win power in "at least several other countries." Carefully selecting his quotations, Stalin insisted that this was Lenin's theory too. Stalin's program of Russian self-sufficiency in building socialism proved highly effective, especially among new, young party members. The doctrine of socialism in one country made Stalin an authoritative ideological leader who could shrug off his opponents' belated criticisms.

In 1926–27 Stalin defeated and silenced the Left with support from the Bukharinists. Trotskii and Zinoviev were removed from the Politburo, and the latter was ousted as Comintern chief. Trotskii's denunciations of the Stalin-dominated Politburo as "Thermidorean," his critique of its blunders in foreign policy, and his street demonstration of November 1927 hastened his expulsion from the party and exile. As Zinoviev and Kamenev recanted their views to save their party membership, only the Bukharinists stood between Stalin and complete power.

Soviet Russia under NEP was a one-party dictatorship modified by social pluralism, an economic compromise between socialism and capitalism. Though the state sector predominated in industry and was growing, the private sector remained vital and dominant in agriculture. Most Soviet citizens, especially peasants, worked and lived far from party or state control, which did not extend far outside the urban centers. NEP was an era of rival theories, contention, and exciting experiments. Tolerance of political, economic, and social diversity marked it as a period of liberal Communism, recovery, and civil peace. As Stalin built his party autocracy, however, these compromises could not long endure.

Suggested Additional Reading

CARR, E. H. *The History of Soviet Russia: the Interregnum, 1923–24* (London, 1954).
———. *Socialism in One Country, 1924–26*, 3 vol. (Baltimore, 1970–72).

---

[11] Quoted in R. Tucker, *Stalin as Revolutionary* (New York, 1973), p. 371.

COHEN, STEPHEN.   *Bukharin: A Political Biography* (New York, 1974).

DANIELS, ROBERT.   *The Conscience of the Revolution* (Cambridge, Mass., 1960).

DEUTSCHER, ISAAC.   *The Prophet Unarmed: Trotsky, 1921–29* (Oxford, 1951).

FISCHER, LOUIS.   *The Life of Lenin* (New York, 1964).

KENNAN, GEORGE.   *Soviet-American Relations, 1917–1920,* 2 vol. (New York, 1967).

KRUPSKAIA, NADEZHDA.   *Memories of Lenin* (London, 1942).

LEHOVICH, DMITRY.   *White against Red: The Life of General Denikin* (New York, 1974).

LEWIN, MOSHE.   *Lenin's Last Struggle* (New York, 1968).

MEYER, ALFRED.   *Leninism* (Cambridge, Mass., 1957).

PAGE, STANLEY.   *Lenin and World Revolution* (New York, 1959).

PIPES, RICHARD.   *The Formation of the Soviet Union* (Cambridge, Mass., 1954).

SCHAPIRO, LEONARD.   *The Origin of the Communist Autocracy, 1917–1922* (Cambridge, Mass., 1955).

SHOLOKHOV, MIKHAIL.   *And Quiet Flows the Don* (New York, 1966) (historical novel of Civil War).

TROTSKY, LEON.   *The Revolution Betrayed* (Garden City, 1937).

TUCKER, ROBERT.   *Stalin as Revolutionary 1879–1929* (New York, 1973).

ULAM, A.   *The Bolsheviks* (New York, 1965).

ULLMAN, R. H.   *Intervention and the War: Anglo-Soviet Relations 1917–1921,* 2 vol. (Princeton, 1961, 1968).

ZALESKI, EUGENE.   *Planning for Economic Growth in the Soviet Union, 1918–1932* (Chapel Hill, 1971).

33

The Politics of Stalinism,
1928–1941

STALIN, having ousted Trotskii and the "Left Opposition" by 1928, had taken major steps toward personal rule in a totalitarian system and away from the collective leadership and freer intra-party debate of Lenin's earlier years. After 1928 Stalin moved to secure total power over party and state by crushing the "Right Opposition" and purging other colleagues of Lenin who retained positions of influence. He manipulated the Lenin cult and created the monstrous myth of his own omniscience. To win autocratic power, the Stalin regime crushed passive opposition by the petty bourgeois peasantry and secured control over the countryside by forcibly collectivizing agriculture. With the rapid industrialization of the Five Year Plans it won support from an increasing working class.[1] The state swallowed society as most Soviet citizens became state employees subject to increasing party supervision and controls. After all significant opposition had seemingly been overcome, Stalin launched the Great Purge of 1936–38, which eliminated the Old Bolsheviks and left his elite triumphant over a purged party, army, and state, and over a supine and frightened populace. In the Stalinist political system, theory and practice were often totally at odds. The federal system and Constitution of 1936 gave national minorities and the Soviet people the appearance of self-government and civil rights while all power resided in fact in a self-perpetuating party leadership in Moscow. Did Stalin's aims and methods resemble those of Ivan the Terrible? Was he a loyal Marxist and heir of Lenin, or an Oriental despot paying only lip service to Marxism-Leninism? How did the Soviet political system function under Stalin? Why was the Great Purge undertaken and what were its effects?

INTRA-PARTY STRUGGLES AND CRISES, 1929–1934

A growing personality cult aided Stalin's drive to dominate the party and rule the USSR. Launched cautiously at the Fourteenth Congress in 1925, it developed notably after Stalin's 50th birthday (December 21,

---

[1] For collectivization and industrialization see below, pp. 500 ff.

Joseph Stalin (1879–1953)

1929), celebrated as a great historic event. In contrast with Lenin's modest, unassuming pose, the Stalin cult by the mid-1930s took on grandiose, even ludicrous forms. At a rally during the Purges in 1937, N. S. Khrushchev, Stalin's eventual successor, declared:

> These miserable nonentities wanted to destroy the unity of the party and the Soviet state. They raised their treacherous hands against Comrade Stalin . . . , our hope; Stalin, our desire; Stalin, the light of advanced and progressive humanity; Stalin, our will; Stalin, our victory.[1]

Within the party the area of dissent narrowed, then disappeared. As he crushed the "Left" in 1926–27, it became clear that Stalin would exclude factions or individuals who opposed his personal authority. But though Trotskii and the rest were stripped of influential positions, they still underestimated Stalin. Trotskii's expulsion from the USSR in 1929 brought predictions that power would pass to a triumvirate of Bukharin, Alexis Rykov, and M. P. Tomskii, which appeared (mistakenly) to dominate the Politburo selected after the 15th Congress.

Once the "Left" had been broken, Stalin adopted a moderate stance and split with the "Right" led by Bukharin. The Stalin-Bukharin struggle developed behind the scenes during a growing economic crisis: better-off peasants (kulaks), taxed heavily by the regime, withheld their grain from the market. Whereas Bukharin favored further concessions to the peasantry, including raising state grain prices, Stalin began urging strong action against the kulaks and officials who sympathized with them. Denouncing the still unnamed opposition for blocking industrial-

---

[1] Quoted in E. Crankshaw, *Khrushchev's Russia* (Harmondsworth, Eng., 1959), p. 53.

ization, Stalin used his control of the Secretariat and Orgburo to remove Bukharin's supporters from key party and government posts. Belatedly contacting Kamenev from the broken "Left," Bukharin warned: *"He* [Stalin] will strangle us." He added:

> Stalin . . . is an unprincipled intriguer who subordinates everything to the preservation of his power. He changes his theories according to whom he needs to get rid of at any given moment. . . . He maneuvers in such a way as to make us stand as the schismatics.[2]

By early 1929 Stalin attacked the "Right" openly and told a Politburo meeting: "Comrades, sad though it may be, we must face facts: a factional group has been established within our party composed of Bukharin, Tomskii, and Rykov" which was blocking industrialization and collectivization. Though the "Right" controlled the Moscow party organization, Stalin won majority support in the Politburo, bypassed the Moscow leaders, and broke their resistance. In April 1929 the Central Committee condemned the "Right" and removed its leaders from their posts; in November they surrendered, recanted their views, and bought themselves a few years of grace.

Open political opposition in the party ended, but during 1932–33 Stalin faced a grave economic and political crisis. Forced collectivization had brought on famine and hunger in the cities, and provoked widespread nationalist opposition especially among Ukrainian peasants. As Stalin's popularity fell to its nadir, Trotskii's *Bulletin of the Opposition* declared abroad: "In view of the incapacity of the present leadership to get out of the economic and political deadlock, the conviction about the need to change the leadership of the party is growing." Trotskii reminded his readers of Lenin's "Testament," which had urged Stalin's removal as General Secretary. In November 1932 after Nadezhda Allilueva, Stalin's second wife, spoke out about famine and discontent, the overwrought Stalin silenced her roughly, and she apparently committed suicide. Victor Serge notes that Stalin submitted his resignation, but none of the Politburo's obedient Stalinist members dared accept it. Finally, Molotov said: "Stop it, stop it. You have got the party's confidence," and the matter was dropped.

Stalin surmounted this personal danger and the economic and political crisis in the country. Opposition remained unfocused, confused, and leaderless. In 1932 Stalin had Kamenev and Zinoviev expelled from the party and exiled to Siberia, but after more abject recantations, they were allowed to return. After similar admissions of guilt, other Old Bolsheviks received responsible posts. They might have tried to kill Stalin, but there seemed to be no viable alternative to his rule. Even Trotskii declared: "We are concerned not with the expulsion of individuals but the change of the system." Stalin adopted temporarily a moderate, conciliatory course: his speech of January 1934 called for consolidating earlier gains and inaugurated a brief period of relative liberalism. Within the Politburo the youthful and popular Leningrad

---

[2] Quoted in I. Deutscher, *Stalin* (London, 1949), p. 314.

party chief S. M. Kirov, backed by Voroshilov and Kalinin, supported concessions to the peasantry and an end to terror; hard liners such as Molotov and Kaganovich opposed this. During 1934 Stalin apparently wavered between these groups.

THE GREAT PURGE

This interlude ended with Kirov's murder in December 1934. The supposed assassin, Nikolaev, and his accomplices were promptly apprehended, tried secretly, and shot. They were described officially as Trotskyites working for the clandestine, foreign-directed "United Center," which had allegedly plotted to kill Stalin and other top leaders. Zinoviev and Kamenev, supposedly implicated in the plot, were sentenced to penal servitude.

Ominous changes proceeded in the political police. Early in 1934 the secret police (GPU), which had gained a sinister reputation, was dissolved. Its tasks were assumed by the People's Commissariat of Internal Affairs (NKVD), which combined control over political, regular, and criminal police. Henrikh Iagoda, its first chief, perhaps fearing that Kirov's liberal line threatened his power, may have engineered the assassination at Stalin's order. NKVD employees were highly paid and obtained the best apartments and other privileges. This "state within a state" maintained a huge network of informers, kept dossiers on millions of persons, and spied on all party agencies. Special sections watched the NKVD's own regular personnel, whose members were expected to show primary loyalty to the NKVD and only secondarily to the party. Special NKVD courts, exempt from control by government or judicial agencies, were set up to conduct secret trials.

While surface calm prevailed, Andrei Zhdanov, Kirov's successor as Leningrad party chief, conducted a ruthless purge there, deporting tens of thousands of persons to Siberia, and the NKVD prepared the greatest mass purge in history. In May 1935 a Special Security Commission was created to investigate all party members, "liquidate enemies of the people," and encourage citizens to denounce suspected counterrevolutionaries and slackers. Its members included Stalin, N. I. Ezhov (later head of the NKVD), Zhdanov, and Andrei Vyshinskii, subsequently chief prosecutor at the public trials. That spring 40 members of Stalin's personal bodyguard were tried secretly for conspiracy, and "terrorists" were hunted in every party and Komsomol agency. As the rapidly growing NKVD justified its existence by uncovering conspiracies everywhere, Stalin ordered careful surveillance even of Politburo members.

A reign of terror was unleashed dwarfing that of the French Revolution. Perhaps that precedent had previously deterred Stalin who once remarked: "You chop off one head today, another one tomorrow. . . . What in the end will be left of the party?" Unlike the French case, terror in Russia reached its murderous peak two decades after the Revolution. The French terror claimed a few thousand victims; Stalin's from 1935 to 1938 killed hundreds of thousands and sent millions into exile. Stalin, not the NKVD, initiated the Great Purge and approved executions of prominent figures. A Stalinist account explained:

> The Trotsky-Bukharin fiends, in obedience to the wishes of their masters—the espionage services of foreign states—had set out to destroy the party and the Soviet state, to undermine the defensive power of the country, to assist foreign military intervention . . . [and] to bring about the dismemberment of the USSR . . . , to destroy the gains of the workers and collective farmers, and to restore capitalist slavery in the USSR.[3]

The party must become an impregnable fortress to safeguard the country and the gains of socialism from foreign and domestic enemies. Stalin added: ". . . As long as capitalist encirclement exists, there will be wreckers, spies, diversionists, and murders in our country, sent behind our lines by the agents of foreign states." The Soviet public found this distorted view credible.

Three great public trials of party leaders accused of treason were held in Moscow. At the "Trial of the Sixteen" (August 1936), Prosecutor Vyshinskii accused Kamenev, Zinoviev, and others of conspiring to overthrow the regime and to remove Stalin and other Politburo leaders. After confessing and incriminating the "Right" Opposition, the defendants were convicted and shot. When this severe treatment of Lenin's old colleagues provoked opposition in the Central Committee, Stalin removed Iagoda and appointed as NKVD chief, Ezhov, under whom the purge reached its bloody climax. Each group of defendants incriminated the next in a chain reaction of denunciations. At the "Trial of the Seventeen" (January 1937), featuring Piatakov, Muralov and Radek, the accused confessed to treasonable dealings with Germany and Japan. The greatest public spectacle of them all, the "Trial of the Twenty-One" (March 1938) included Bukharin, Rykov, and Iagoda. Foreign espionage agencies, claimed the prosecutor, had set up a "bloc of Rightists and Trotskyists" on Soviet soil to bring a bourgeois-capitalist regime to power and detach non-Russian regions from the USSR. Allegedly Bukharin had been a traitor ever since 1918. Vyshinskii concluded his prosecution with the invariable appeal: "Shoot the mad dogs!", and the leading defendants would be executed.

Why did the accused, many of them prominent, courageous revolutionaries, publicly admit crimes they could not have committed when their confessions constituted the only legal basis for conviction? Most had recanted several times already, each time admitting greater guilt, and hoped to save their lives, positions, and families. Some believed that the party, to which they had dedicated their lives, must be right. The defendants, mostly middle-aged, were broken down by lengthy NKVD interrogations, sleeplessness, or hypnotized by the terror. Doubtless they hoped to save something from blasted careers by bowing to Stalin's tyranny.

Those who were tried or died by other means included all surviving members of Lenin's Politburo except Stalin and Trotskii, the defendant in chief tried in absentia. A former premier, two former chiefs of the

---

[3] *Short History of the Communist Party* (New York, 1939), p. 347.

Comintern, the trade union head, and two chiefs of the political police were executed. Survivors must have wondered how the great Lenin could have surrounded himself with so many traitors and scoundrels. In 1914, to be sure, Roman Malinovskii, Lenin's close colleague, had been exposed as a police agent. The legacy of police infiltration of revolutionary organizations under tsarism provided some basis for believing the revelations of the 1930s.

The Great Purge decimated the leadership corps of the Soviet armed forces. The military chiefs, especially Marshal Tukhachevskii, who had made the Red Army an effective fighting force, apparently had been highly critical of the early trials. In May 1937 he and other prominent generals were arrested, accused of treasonable collaboration with Germany and Japan, and shot. None of them resisted or attempted a military coup. Purged later were most members of the Supreme War Council, three of five marshals, 14 of 16 army generals, and all full admirals. About half the entire officer corps was shot or imprisoned, a terrible insult to Red Army patriotism and a grave weakening of the armed forces. (After Stalin's death all leading military figures who were purged were rehabilitated, many posthumously, and declared innocent of all charges brought against them.)[4]

Not only Old Bolsheviks but many Stalinist party leaders were eliminated. Purged were 70 percent of the Central Committee members and candidates chosen in 1934. At the Eighteenth Party Congress in 1939, only 35 of 1,827 rank and file delegates from the previous congress were present! From the party and army the purge reached downward into the general populace as friends and relatives of purgees were arrested, and orders were issued to arrest a specific percentage of the population. Stalin's bloodthirstiness grew as people of all social groups were rounded up.

Why this terrible bloodbath? wondered the survivors. Some victims were scapegoats for economic failures of the early 1930s. Stalin's chief motive, suggests Deutscher, was to destroy those who might lead an alternate regime or criticize his policies. This policy required killing or exiling party and military men trained by purged leaders, then rebuilding the chief levers of Soviet power: the party, the army, and the security forces. The general public may have been involved deliberately to create the climate of fear essential to Stalin's total control. The need for millions of forced laborers in the Arctic and Siberia supplied a reason for mass deportation of workers and peasants. Perhaps Stalin became utterly mad, making pointless the search for rational explanations. Certainly casualties were too great to be justified by ordinary political or social aims. Robert Conquest's estimate of about 8,000,000 purge victims in camps by 1938, plus another million in prisons seems reasonable. During the 1930s a huge NKVD empire of forced labor camps and prisons, begun in the White Sea area under Lenin and described graphically in Alexander Solzhenitsyn's work *The Gulag Archipelago*, mushroomed in European Russia and Siberia. Major projects

---

[4] See problem 10 below, pp. 589–96.

included constructing the White Sea and Moscow-Volga canals, double-tracking the Trans-Siberian Railway, and gold mining in the Kolyma wastefields. Usually fed below the subsistence level and working under extremely arduous conditions, the inmates died off rapidly only to be replaced by new millions.

In December 1938 with the arrest of master purger Ezhov, blamed for excesses ordered by Stalin, the purge's intensive phase ended. Large-scale terror, however, remained endemic to the Soviet system until Stalin's death. The epilogue to the Great Purge was the axe murder of Trotskii in Mexico (August 1940) by an NKVD agent, the son of a Spanish Communist. Besides terrorizing the USSR, the purge opened up numerous vacancies in civil and military posts, filled by obedient but often inexperienced men who insured Stalin's omnipotence. The Politburo lost most of its power and became Stalin's rubber stamp, while his private Secretariat became a modern Oprichnina. Otherwise the purge altered the Soviet political system remarkably little.

The Great Purge necessitated the rewriting of Communist Party history. Directed by Zhdanov and Stalin's secretaries, historians prepared the *Short History of the Communist Party of the Soviet Union* (1938). Apparently, Stalin corrected the manuscript and wrote the section on philosophy. Portraying Stalin as Lenin's only true disciple, the *History* claimed that other Old Bolsheviks had conspired against Lenin and the party since 1917. Thus the all-powerful dictator had altered history to serve his present purposes. After 1938 Stalin worked intensively to foster patriotism, restore unity, and rebuild the army leadership and the armed forces.

GOVERNMENT AND PARTY

The Stalin regime combined systematic terror and massive use of force with a democratically phrased constitution, apparent federalism, and representative institutions. Operating ostensibly through a hierarchy of soviets, the political system was run actually by the party leadership and NKVD. Often theory and practice were wholly at odds, and in many ways Stalinism marked a return to tsarist autocracy. Stalin himself, no longer the patient, humble, and accessible party functionary of the early 1920s, retreated into the Kremlin's recesses or to his country villa at nearby Kuntsevo. Rarely appearing in public, he clothed himself in mystery, and many in the younger generation regarded him and his oracular pronouncements with awe and reverence. Once his rivals had been eliminated, he grew more dictatorial and after 1938 becams an all-powerful father figure. His Politburo contained bureaucrats and party officials, not active revolutionaries or creative ideologists as in Lenin's time. Men such as Molotov, Kaganovich, and Kuibyshev, though able administrators, were narrow and ignorant of foreign lands. In the Politburo Stalin listened impatiently to their arguments, then often decided an issue with a sarcasm or vulgar joke. All important matters were decided there under the dictator's jealous eye.

The legal basis of this Soviet political system was the Constitution of 1936. Constitutions under Marxism were supposed to reflect existing socioeconomic conditions and had to be altered as this situation changed. Earlier Soviet constitutions (1918 and 1924), with a franchise heavily weighted to favor urban elements and excluding "exploiters," represented the proletarian dictatorship's first phase. In November 1936 Stalin explained to the Eighth Congress of Soviets that because rapid industrialization and collectivization had eliminated landlords, capitalists, and kulaks, "There are no longer any antagonistic classes in [Soviet] society . . . [which] consists of two friendly classes, workers and peasants." Restrictions and inequalities in voting could be abolished and a democratic suffrage instituted. The Stalin Constitution, he claimed, would be "the only thoroughly democratic constitution in the world."

The promises of the Stalin Constitution (still in force with amendments) often meant little in practice. "The USSR," it proclaimed, "is a federal state formed on the basis of a voluntary union of equal Soviet socialist republics." Most republics, however, had been conquered or incorporated forcibly, and the predominance of the Russian Republic with about half the population and three fourths the area of the Union negated equality. Theoretically, a republic, as formerly, could secede, but to advocate secession was a crime and a "bourgeois nationalist deviation." Only the working class through its vanguard, the Soviet Communist Party, could approve secession or create and abolish republics. In 1936 Transcaucasia was split into Azerbaijan, Armenia, and Georgia, which were admitted as separate republics; then the Kazakh and Kirghiz republics in Central Asia were added. A Karelo-Finnish Republic was created partly out of territory taken from Finland in 1940, but it was abolished equally arbitrarily in 1956. Also in 1940 the Moldavian Republic was established, mostly from territory acquired by treaty with Hitler, and the formerly independent Baltic countries of Estonia, Latvia, and Lithuania were occupied and became Soviet republics. An amendment of 1944 permitted republics to establish relations with foreign countries (none has ever done so), and the Ukraine and Belorussia obtained separate United Nations representation in 1945. Smaller national groups (more than 100 in the Russian Republic alone) obtained autonomous republics and national areas plus legislative representation.

Soviet federalism provided an illusion of autonomy and self-government, but the central government, retaining full power, repressed any group or individuals who advocated genuine autonomy or independence, especially in the Ukraine, the most populous non-Russian unit. Each nationality received its own territory, language, press, and schools, but the Russian-dominated all-Union Communist Party supervised and controlled them. This federal system, in Stalin's words: "national in form, socialist in content," though preferable to tsarism's open Russification and assimilation, perpetuated Russian rule over most areas of the old empire. National feeling persisted nonetheless among many minority peoples of the USSR.

Under the Stalin Constitution a bicameral Supreme Soviet became the national legislature and supposedly the highest organ of state authority. The Council of the Union was directly elected from equal election districts, one deputy per 300,000 population. The Council of Nationalities represented the various administrative units: 25 deputies from each union republic, 11 from autonomous republics, and so on. Delegates elected for four-year terms by universal suffrage received good pay during brief sessions, but unlike United States Congressmen retained their regular jobs and had no offices nor staffs. A Presidium, elected by both houses, could issue decrees when the Soviet was not meeting, and its chairman was titular president of the USSR. Bills became law when passed by both houses, but the Supreme Soviet has never recorded a negative vote. It was a decorative, rubber-stamp body without real discussion or power of decision. Below it lay a network of soviets on republic, regional, provincial, district, and village or city levels—over 60,000 soviets in all—with some 1,500,000 deputies elected for two year terms. Sovereign in theory, soviets were controlled in fact at every level by their party members and parallel party organizations.

The Constitution entrusted executive and administrative authority to the Council of People's Commissars (called the Council of Ministers since 1946). Some ministries operated only on the all-union level, others there and in the republics, and still others in the republics only. Theoretically, but not in practice, these ministries were responsible to the soviets. Coordinating the administrative and economic system, the Council of People's Commissars possessed more power than the Constitution suggests. The Supreme Court of the USSR headed a judicial system including supreme courts in the republic, regional, and people's courts. Lower courts were elected and higher ones chosen by the corresponding soviet. Judges, supposedly independent, were subject to party policies, and many important cases were tried in secret by the NKVD.

Article 125 of the Constitution promised Soviet citizens freedoms of speech, conscience, press, assembly, and demonstrations "in conformity with the interests of the working people and in order to strengthen the socialist system." Citizens were guaranteed the right to work, education, rest, and maintenance in sickness and old age. Article 127 pledged freedom from arrest except by court decision. In fact, the Soviet people have never enjoyed most of these rights. As the new constitution was printed, the NKVD was conducting mass arrests and deportations without trial. The state assigned workers to jobs arbitrarily and prohibited strikes and independent trade unions. Constitutional rights could (and can) be used only to support the regime, not to criticize it.

The Stalin Constitution, unlike its predecessors, at least suggested in Article 126, the true role of the Communist Party:

> . . . The most active and politically conscious citizens in the ranks of the working class, working peasants, and working intelligentsia voluntarily unite in the Communist Party of the Soviet Union, which is the vanguard of the working people in their struggle to build com-

munist society and is *the leading core of all organizations of the working people, both public and state.* (Italics added for emphasis)[5]

Still organized on Leninist principles, the party remained the élite force of about four percent of the population in which intellectuals and bureaucrats outnumbered ordinary workers. Operating supposedly by democratic centralism, it exercised decisive authority over domestic and foreign affairs. Under Stalin all power passed to higher party organs coopted by the leaders, not elected democratically as the party rules stipulated. The rank and file could merely criticize minor shortcomings and lost all influence over the self-perpetuating leadership. The party became Stalin's monolithic, disciplined, and increasingly bureaucratic instrument. Intra-party debate, avoiding major issues, was limited to *how* to implement decisions, not to discuss alternative policies or leaders.

The all-union congress, periodic gatherings of leaders from the entire USSR, theoretically exercised supreme authority within the party. Once factions were banned (1921) and the "Right" was defeated (1929), however, congresses lost power to initiate policies. Important decisions were made in advance by the Politburo and approved unanimously by the congress, which merely ratified policies of the leadership pro forma. In Lenin's time, the Central Committee, supposedly elected by the congress to direct party work between congresses, was an important decision-making body; under Stalin it grew in size (to 125 full members and 125 candidates in 1952) but declined in power. It comprised mostly regional party secretaries and ministers from the all-union and republic governments.

The Central Committee, stated the party rules, elected three subcommittees: the Politburo, Orgburo, and Secretariat; in fact they determined the Committee's membership and policies. With about a dozen full members and a few candidates, the Politburo ostensibly "directs the work of the Central Committee between plenary sessions." It has always included the most powerful party and state officials, decided the chief domestic and foreign policy issues, and has been since 1920 the main power center in the USSR. Its meetings have been secret, and its debates presumably free. Stalin purged the Politburo, refilled it with his own men, and made it an instrument of his personal power. During the 1930s it experienced great insecurity and high turnover; since then its members have enjoyed much stability of tenure. The Orgburo, Stalin's original power base, directed the party's organizational work until its merger with the Politburo in 1952. The Secretariat directed the party's permanent apparatus. Stalin as General Secretary with four assistants managed its professional staff and controlled all party personnel and appointments.

With four or five levels the party, like the soviets, was directed centrally by its all-Union organs. Thus the Ukrainian Party, run generally by Great Russians, was controlled from Moscow, which decided its policies and personnel. Lower party officials were often sacrificed as

---

[5] *Constitution (Fundamental Law) of the Union of Soviet Socialist Republics* (Moscow, 1957), p. 103.

scapegoats for unpopular or mistaken national policies. Some regional party secretaries became miniature Stalins, who dictated to frightened subordinates. At the bottom of the party hierarchy stood some 350,000 primary organizations, or cells, composed of at least three members, in villages, collective farms, factories, offices, and military units. Acting like nerves of the human body, they permeated and controlled all organizations and agencies.

Party membership was open in theory to all persons over 21 years of age (over 18 for Komsomol [Young Communist League] members). Applicants filled out a detailed questionnaire, submitted recommendations from three members in good standing to a primary party organization, and served at least a year's candidacy. Applications had to be approved by the primary organizations and ratified by the district party unit. Rank and file members performed party work besides their regular jobs. They had to pay dues, work actively in agitation and propaganda among their fellows, explain Marxian theory and the party line, and set examples of leadership and clean living. Their main reward was power and influence because the party was the only road to political success. Disobedient or undisciplined members were reprimanded, censured, or in graver cases expelled. Periodic purges were designed to cleanse the party of opportunists, slackers, and the disloyal. Under Stalin, Communists occupied the key positions in most walks of life; factory managers, collective farm chairmen, school superintendents, and army officers were generally Party members. Within the Party urban elements predominated over rural ones and Great Russians over national minorities.

The highly centralized Stalinist political system was based on interlocking presidia of the party and the state. The main decisions, made by Stalin personally and approved by the Politburo, were transmitted by lower party organs, soviets, trade unions, and media of mass communication to the people. The party manipulated the soviets skillfully to maintain links with the population and provide a semblance of legitimate rule. The main weaknesses were lack of local initiative and the absence of any legal means to transmit power from one leader or group of leaders to another. This intensified intrigue, suspicion, and power struggles behind the scenes at the top.

STALINISM

Stalin had risen in the party as an organizer and administrator, not an ideologist. Marx had been a theorist, not an active revolutionary; in Lenin the two aspects were in rare balance. At first Stalin marched carefully in Lenin's footsteps (his chief work was *Problems of Leninism*), but once in power he altered and gravely distorted the doctrines of Marx and Lenin. Stalin's major doctrinal innovation—socialism in one country[6]—had developed accidentally and pragmatically during his struggle with Trotskii. Trotskii's apparently contrasting theory of "permanent revolution" stressed using the Comintern (Communist Inter-

---

[6] See above, p. 485.

national, organization of Communist parties) to foment revolutions abroad; Stalin emphasized building socialism in Russia first. They differed somewhat over means and tactics but shared the goal of an eventual global triumph of Communism. But could socialism be *completely* built in a single country? Stalin claimed in 1936 that it had already been *essentially* constructed in Russia, although final victory must await worldwide revolution. Stalin's national emphasis won him continuing support from industrial workers, the intelligentsia, and military men as well as from a party anxious to believe that Russians could build socialism themselves. Socialism in one country provided the ideological basis and social support for forced collectivization and the five year plans.

Because Stalin affirmed that socialism had triumphed in the USSR and that class enemies had been broken, why was proletarian dictatorship not withering away as Marx had predicted? Stalin had already answered this question in rather cynical fashion at the 16th Party Congress in 1930:

> We are in favor of the state dying out, and at the same time we stand for the strengthening of the dictatorship of the proletariat, which represents the most powerful and mighty authority of all forms of state which have existed up to the present day. The highest possible development of the power of the state with the object of preparing the conditions of the dying out of the state? Is this contradictory? Yes, it is contradictory. But this contradiction is a living thing and completely reflects Marxist dialectics.[7]

Apparently Stalin derived this view from Lenin's statement that state machinery must be perfected in the lower phase of socialism before withering. To justify strengthening the proletarian state Stalin argued that hostile capitalist powers, surrounding the USSR, threatened armed intervention. Until "capitalist encirclement" was replaced by socialist encirclement of capitalism, the proletarian state must remain strong and alert, eliminate "bourgeois survivals," and hasten the transition to the final goal—Communism.

Stalin was reacting instinctively against a Marxian internationalism which had already been undermined by the apparent failure of world revolution. For Stalin the interests of the Soviet fatherhood clearly preceded those of the international proletariat and foreign Communist parties. Thus in the years before World War II, Soviet nationalism and patriotism were developed partly as an affirmation of what the working class had built in the USSR, partly to counter separatism in the borderlands. Pride in Soviet industrial and technological achievements was fostered by the regime with considerable success among workers and the younger generation. The shift away from internationalism was reflected in the repudiation by the Stalin regime of the works of the Marxist historian M. N. Pokrovskii, who had condemned Russian tsars and imperialism unreservedly. From the mid-1930s occurred a selective rehabilitation and even praise of such rulers as Peter the Great and

---

[7] *Problems of Leninism* (Moscow, 1933), vol. 2, p. 402.

Ivan the Terrible for unifying and strengthening Russia. Tsarist generals such as Suvorov and Kutuzov and certain admirals in the Crimean War were glorified for defending their country heroically. New Soviet patriotism contained elements of traditional Great Russian nationalism, which Stalin had adopted. Through Soviet nationalism—one positive aspect of socialism in one country—Stalin sought to overcome and replace narrower national loyalties within the USSR.

The Stalinist political system established patterns of authority many of which—but not its cult of personality—have persisted to the present. With maximum use of force and terror, Stalin crushed all political opposition, as Ivan the Terrible had sought but failed to do. Stalin created perhaps the most powerful, centralized state in history with a developed industry and a vast bureaucracy. In so doing he, though a believing Marxist, perverted Marxist ideology almost beyond recognition by accumulating personal power analogous to that of Oriental despotism. The Communist Party, though supreme over obedient soviets, was itself transformed into a bureaucracy of frightened automotons by the Great Purge. Mass terror and the cult of individual dictatorship would be repudiated by Stalin's successors but not centralized autocracy.

Suggested Additional Reading

ADAMS, ARTHUR. *Stalin and His Times* (New York, 1972).

ARMSTRONG, JOHN. *The Politics of Totalitarianism: The Communist Party of the Soviet Union from 1934 to the Present* (New York, 1962).

AVTORKHANOV, A. *Stalin and the Soviet Communist Party* (New York, 1959).

BAUER, R., INKELES and KLUCKHOHN. *How the Soviet System Works* (Cambridge, Mass., 1956).

CONQUEST, ROBERT. *The Great Terror* (New York, 1968).

DALLIN, DAVID and B. NICOLAEVSKY. *Forced Labor in Soviet Russia* (New Haven, 1947).

DANIELS, ROBERT, ed. *The Stalin Revolution* (Lexington, Mass., 1972).

DEUTSCHER, ISAAC. *Stalin: A Political Biography*, 2d ed. (New York, 1967).

ERICKSON, JOHN. *The Soviet High Command . . . 1918–1941* (New York, 1962).

FAINSOD, MERLE. *Smolensk under Soviet Rule* (Cambridge, Mass., 1958).

KOESTLER, ARTHUR. *Darkness at Noon* (novel relating to Great Purge).

KOLARZ, WALTER. *Russia and her Colonies* (London, 1952).

LEVYTSKY, BORYS, comp. *The Stalinist Terror in the Thirties: Documentation from the Soviet Press* (Stanford, 1974).

ORWELL, GEORGE. *1984* (novel on totalitarianism).

SCHWARTZ, SOLOMON. *The Jews in Soviet Union* (Syracuse, New York, 1951).

SOLZHENITSYN, ALEXANDER. *The Gulag Archipelago, 1918–1956* (on Soviet concentration camps), 2 vols. (New York, 1974–75).

———. *One Day in the Life of Ivan Denisovich* (New York, 1963), (novel).

ULAM, ADAM. *Stalin: The Man and His Era* (New York, 1973).

VON LAUE, THEODORE. *Why Lenin, Why Stalin? . . . 1900–1930* (Philadelphia, 1964).

34

The Great Transformation

ONCE THE ECONOMY recovered to prewar levels and Stalin had consolidated his power, he launched the "Second Socialist Offensive" of rapid industrialization and forced collectivization of agriculture. This policy followed a bitter debate within the party over how to modernize the Soviet economy. In the decade after 1928 the USSR became a major industrial country, collectivized its agriculture, and acquired the basic economic and social forms which characterize it today. The price paid for these advances by the Soviet people, however, was very high. Did Stalin's "revolution from above" reflect Marxist-Leninist principles or betray the ideals of 1917? Were rapid industrialization and forced collectivization necessary and worth their terrible cost, or was Bukharin's alternative of gradual evolution toward socialism preferable? Should Stalin be called "the great" for overcoming Russia's backwardness and weakness? If so, then 1929 marks a greater turning point in Russian history than 1917. After smashing or remodeling traditional social pillars, the family, school, and church, why did Stalin retreat toward tsarist patterns in the later 1930s and make concessions to the church?

THE GREAT INDUSTRIALIZATION DEBATE, 1924–1928

During the mid-1920s, leading Soviet politicians and economists debated Russia's economic future. They agreed on goals of socialism and industrialization but disagreed on how they could best be achieved. The success of New Economic Policy (NEP) meant that survival was not at issue, but in a largely hostile world, the USSR, unlike tsarist Russia, had to rely on its own resources to industrialize.

The party "Left," led by Trotskii but with Evgeni Preobrazhenskii as chief economic spokesman, advocated rapid industrial growth at home while promoting revolutions abroad. The key to industrialization and socialism, Preobrazhenskii argued, was "primitive socialist accumulation": lacking colonies to exploit, the USSR must obtain necessary investment capital by keeping farm prices low and taxing private farmers heavily. NEP, he believed, could restore the economy, but it could not produce the vast capital required for industrialization and the development of transportation and housing. Central state-planning would permit immediate major investment in heavy industry. The "Left" accused the Stalin-Bukharin leadership of favoring kulaks, "surrendering" to NEP-men, and isolating the USSR. It stressed the intimate connection between developing Soviet socialism and ending "our socialist isolation." Opposing forcible expropriation of kulaks, Trotskii believed that revolutions in advanced countries would promote Soviet industrialization.

Bukharin, chief official spokesman and later leader of the "Right," urged the continuation of NEP until the USSR gradually "grew into" socialism. Leftist "superindustrializers and adventurers" would alienate better-off peasants, undermine the worker-peasant alliance, and threaten the regime. Taxing peasants heavily would price industrial goods beyond their reach and induce them to market less grain. Instead, industrial prices should be cut and peasants encouraged to produce and save freely. Agricultural surplus would provide investment capital, expand the internal market, and stimulate industrial production. Citing Lenin's last writings, Bukharin advocated gradual "agrarian cooperative socialism." He overestimated peasant economic power and considered the peasant-worker alliance inviolable. Unless Soviet industrialization were more humane than under capitalism, he warned, it might not produce socialism. "We do not want to drive the middle peasant into communism with an iron broom." Bukharin spoke of "moving ahead slowly . . . dragging behind us the cumbersome peasant cart," and of creeping "at a snail's pace. . . ."

All leading Bolsheviks viewed industrialization as a vital goal and realized that it must rely mainly on internal resources. Agreeing that investment capital must be shifted from agriculture into industry, they differed over how much to take and how to take it. Bukharin emphasized the development of the internal market, imposition of progressive income taxes, and voluntary savings. Such methods, retorted the "Left," would produce too little capital because peasants would consume most of the surplus. Bolsheviks agreed that central planning was needed, but what did this involve? The "Left" advocated a single state-imposed plan stressing rapid growth of heavy industry. Bukharin called that "a remnant of War Communist illusions," which disregarded market forces of supply and demand; instead he would stress consumer industry.

The factions also argued about capitalist elements in the countryside. Official figures of 1925 stated that poor peasants comprised 45, middle peasants 51, and kulaks four percent of the peasantry. Asserting that more than seven percent were kulaks, who were exploiting and dominating the village, the "Left" argued that continuing NEP would restore capitalism. Peasant differentiation had increased, replied Bukharin, but kulaks were still less than four percent, and state control of big industry prevented any serious capitalist danger. Class conflict in the countryside, he predicted, would subside as the economy approached socialism.

As the debate continued, these differences lessened. Bukharin began to admit the need for rapid growth; Preobrazhenskii warned of its considerable risks. The chief beneficiary of this apparent synthesis was Stalin. Supporting Bukharin during the debate, he expelled the "Left" and stole its plank of rapid industrialization. To break peasant resistance, he combined it later with forced collectivization and demanded industrial goals far higher than those of the "Left."

Bukharin's gradualist solution was doomed as the private sector lost its ability to compete with the state sector. Taxing heavily the profits of private producers, imposing surcharges for transportation and exorbitant levies on kulaks, the state squeezed private producers severely. By cutting industrial prices despite severe shortages of industrial goods, the state undermined the basis of NEP, which was based upon a free market and incentives. To the party the stagnation of the restored Russian economy by 1926 was intolerable because without rapid growth the party's élan and morale would deteriorate.

Recent Soviet accounts claim that the demise of NEP was natural and inevitable. Unlike capitalist countries, the USSR could not exploit colonies, conduct aggressive wars, or obtain foreign credits. To achieve socialism the state had to industrialize quickly by concentrating resources in its hands and tapping all sources of internal capital, especially agriculture. Accepting most of Preobrazhenskii's theory of primitive socialist accumulation, Soviet historians conclude that the populace, especially the peasantry, had to make major sacrifices in order to achieve industrialization. Recent Western studies, however, conclude that NEP agriculture could have satisfied immediate urban needs; they question the necessity and value of collectivization, either to solve the grain problem or to increase capital formation.[1]

COLLECTIVIZATION

Stalin's adoption in 1929 of a policy of forced collectivization of agriculture provoked a grim struggle between the regime and the peasantry. One factor in his decision was an apparent grain crisis in 1927–28. Farm output had reached prewar levels, but grain marketings remained somewhat lower (though higher than Stalin claimed), largely because of government price policies. Better-off peasants, awaiting higher prices, withheld their grain, and the state could not obtain enough to feed the cities or finance new industrial projects. Peasants, roughly 80 percent of the Soviet population, operated about 25 million small private farms; collective and state farms were few and unimportant.[2] Most peasants still carried on traditional strip farming and remained suspicious of the Soviet regime. Kulaks tended to be literate, enterprising, and hard working, envied by other peasants for their relative prosperity but respected for their industry. Employing a hired worker or two and perhaps renting out small machines to poorer neighbors,

---

[1] J. Karcz, "From Stalin to Brezhnev . . . ," in J. Millar, *The Soviet Rural Community*, p. 36 ff.

[2] In 1928 individual farmers tilled 97.3 percent of the sown area, collectives 1.2 (of which 0.7 percent were of the loose *toz type*), and state farms 1.5 percent.

kulaks performed most of their own labor and scarcely qualified as capitalists or semi-capitalists, as Soviet historians describe them.

Marx and Lenin—and even Stalin before 1928—had never suggested *forced* collectivization. Marx intimated that large industrial farms would evolve gradually. Lenin considered collective, mechanized agriculture essential to socialism but warned that amalgamating millions of small farmers "in any rapid way" would be "absolutely absurd." Collective farming must develop "with extreme caution and only very gradually by the force of example without any coercion of the middle peasant."[3] Following this advice closely, Stalin told the 15th Party Congress in 1927:

> What is the way out? The way out is to turn the small and scattered peasant farms into large united farms based on cultivation of the land in common, go over to collective cultivation of the land on the basis of a new higher technique. The way out is to unite the small and dwarf peasant farms *gradually but surely, not by pressure but by example and persuasion,* into large farms based on common, cooperative collective cultivation of the land. . . . There is no other way out.[4] [italics added for emphasis]

Perhaps from ignorance or misinformation, Stalin disregarded Lenin's warnings and his own statements. Touring the Urals and Siberia in January 1928, he arbitrarily closed free markets, denounced hesitant officials, and had grain seized forcibly from the peasants. His "Urals-Siberian method" marked a return to War Communism's forced requisitioning. Faced with strong "Rightist" protests, Stalin retreated temporarily, but during 1928–29 this brutal method was used repeatedly in scattered areas. Bukharin objected to it as "military-feudal exploitation" of the peasantry and referred to Stalin as Chingis-khan. Until he had destroyed the "Right," Stalin refrained from a general assault on private agriculture, and the First Five Year Plan approved in 1929 proposed that state and collective farms provide only 15 percent of agricultural output. The predominance of private farming seemed assured indefinitely.

Late in 1929, after crushing the "Right," Stalin moved abruptly to break peasant resistance and secure resources required for industrialization. Voluntary collectivization had clearly failed, and most Soviet economists doubted that the First Plan could be implemented. Recalled N. Valentinov, a Menshevik: "The financial base of the First Five Year Plan *until Stalin found it in levying tribute on the peasants in primitive accumulation by the methods of Tamerlane,*[5] was extremely precarious." Stalin may have viewed collectivization also as a means to win support from younger party leaders opposed to kulaks, NEP-men, and the free market. Privately, he advocated "industrializing the country with the help of *internal* accumulation," à la Preobrazhenskii. Once the peasantry had been split and rural opposition smashed, Stalin believed that rural

---

[3] Lenin, *Collected Works,* vol. 30, p. 196.

[4] Stalin, *Works,* vol. 10, p. 312.

[5] Ruthless Central Asian conqueror of the early 15th century.

proletarians would spearhead collectivization under state direction. The grain shortage induced the Politburo to support Stalin's sudden decision for immediate, massive collectivization.

A great turn was underway, Stalin asserted in November. The Central Committee affirmed obediently that poor and middle peasants were moving "spontaneously" into collectives. In secret Stalin and his colleagues had ordered local officials to try out massive collectivization in selected areas. When results seemed positive (the number of collective farmers had allegedly doubled between June and October), Stalin ordered general collectivization, led by some 25,000 urban party activists. Entire villages had to deliver their grain to the state at low prices. Kulaks were deliberately overassessed for grain deliveries, then expropriated for failure to obey. The party had not discussed how to implement collectivization, and so initial measures were sudden, confused, and ill-prepared. Many officials interpreted them to mean incorporating all peasants in *kolkhozy* (collective farms). Stalin and Molotov pressed for speed, overruled all objections, and rejected proposals for private peasant plots and ownership of small tools and livestock. Local officials took Stalin at his word.

The initial collectivization drive provoked massive peasant resistance and terrible suffering. Isaac Deutscher notes that rebellious villages, surrounded by Red Army detachments, were bombarded and forced to surrender. So much for voluntary, spontaneous collectivization! Within seven weeks about half the peasantry had been herded into collectives, but bringing in as little as possible, they slaughtered over half the horses, about 45 percent of the large cattle, and almost two-thirds of the sheep and goats in Russia. In December 1929 Stalin authorized liquidation of the kulaks:

> Now we are able to carry on a determined offensive against the kulaks, eliminate them as a class. . . . Now dekulakization is being carried out by the masses of poor and middle peasants themselves. . . . Should kulaks be permitted to join collective farms? Of course not, for they are sworn enemies of the collective farm movement.[6]

Poor neighbors often stole kulaks' clothing and drank up their vodka, but Stalin prohibited their dividing kulak land because they would be reluctant to enter collectives. By a decree of February 1930, "actively hostile" kulaks were to be sent to forced labor camps, "economically potent" ones relocated, and their property confiscated. The "least noxious" kulaks, receiving poor land and some farm equipment, were heavily taxed. A recent party history claims that only 240,757 kulak families were deported, but eventually deportation overtook nearly all so-called kulaks, up to five million persons counting family members. Few ever returned, thousands of families were broken up, and millions of peasants were embittered. Soviet sources claim that such excesses reflected peasant hatred of kulaks, but there is little evidence of this. In March 1930, with the spring sowing threatened, Stalin in an article, "Dizzy with Success," called a temporary halt and blamed overly zealous

---

[6] Cited in *Istoriia KPSS* (Moscow 1959), p. 441.

local officials for excesses he had authorized. Interpreting this as repudiation of compulsory collectivization, the majority of peasants hastily left the *kolkhozy*.

After a brief pause, peasants were lured into collectives by persuasion and discriminatory taxation. By 1937 nearly all land and peasants were in *kolkhozy*, and remaining individual peasants worked inferior land and paid exorbitant taxes. But *kolkhoz* peasants were demoralized: crops lay unharvested, tractors were few, and farm animals died of neglect. Large grain exports in 1930–31 exhausted reserves and city requirements increased. In 1932, amidst widespread stealing and concealment of grain, collectivization hung by a thread and was maintained by force. In the Ukraine and north Caucasus, the state seized all the grain. In the terrible famine of 1933, the nadir of Soviet agriculture, millions of peasants died, but the Soviet press failed to report it. Table 1 reveals the impact of collectivization.[7]

TABLE 1

Agricultural Output during Collectivization

Category	1928	1929	1930	1931	1933	1935
Grain (million tons)	73.7	71.7	83.5	69.5	68.4	75.0
Cattle (millions)	70.5	67.1	52.5	47.9	38.4	49.3
Pigs (millions)	26.0	20.4	13.6	14.4	12.1	22.6
Sheep and goats (millions)	146.7	147.0	108.0	77.7	50.2	61.1

At first collective farm organization and management were confused. The city activists sent to supervise collectivization and manage the farms misunderstood the peasantry and made many blunders. Peasant rights in *kolkhozy* were few and vague, and pay was low. The regime initially favored state farms (*sovkhozy*) as being fully socialist, but their inefficiency and costliness provoked second thoughts, and after 1935 they received less emphasis.

The "Model Statute" of 1935 described the *kolkhoz* as supposedly a voluntary cooperative whose members pooled their means of production, ran their own affairs, and elected their officials in a general meeting. Actually, local party organizations nominated farm chairmen and issued orders to farms, while state procurement agencies and Machine Tractor Stations (MTS) assured party control. The state-controlled MTS received all available machines and tractors and rented them to *kolkhozy*. Only after fixed requirements were met (taxes, insurance, capital fund, administration and production costs) were *kolkhoz* members paid from what remained according to labor units (*trudodni*) earned. Wages varied sharply according to skill and the farm's success, but as late as 1937, 15,000 *kolkhozy* paid their members nothing at all. The Statute recognized the peasant's right to a private plot of up to one acre per household and some livestock. This grant created the chief private sector in the economy. After 1937 *kolkhozy* produced mainly grain and

---

[7] Adapted from Nove, *The Soviet Economy*, 2d ed. (New York, 1967), p. 186.

industrial crops (cotton, sugar beets, flax); private plots provided most meat, milk, eggs, potatoes, fruits, and many vegetables. Low state prices, however, discouraged agricultural output. Industrial prices in 1937 were far higher than in 1928–29, a recurrence of the price "scissors" against the peasant. On *kolkhozy* there was much coercion and unhappiness, but as the output of private plots increased, living conditions gradually improved.

During the last prewar years, arbitrary state decisions, ignoring local conditions, caused agriculture to stagnate or decline. In 1939 the party reduced the allowable size of private plots and transferred millions of acres to collective control. Stricter discipline and compulsory minimums of labor days were instituted for collective farmers, and fodder shortages brought a decline in already low *kolkhoz* livestock production. Crop yields and private livestock ownership declined substantially. Providing few incentives, collectivization remained very unpopular with Soviet peasants. To achieve rapid industrialization and socialism, Stalin had sacrificed Russia's best, most enterprising farmers. No other east European country chose forced collectivization, which suggested that less compulsory methods might have proved more effective and less costly.

INDUSTRY: THE FIVE YEAR PLANS

One rationale for collectivization was to insure food supplies adequate to support the rapid industrialization of the Five Year Plan, which aimed immediately to provide a powerful heavy industry and only later an abundant life. The Plans' psychological purpose was to induce workers and young people to make sacrifices by holding before them a vision of the promised land of socialism in their own lifetimes. The state would benefit because the economy would become fully socialist, production and labor would be wholly state-controlled, and security against capitalist powers would be strengthened. Stalin stated in February 1931: "We are 50 to 100 years behind the advanced countries. We must cover this distance in ten years. Either we do this or they will crush us." Ten years and four months later Hitler invaded the USSR!

The First Five Year Plan did not inaugurate Soviet economic planning. Under NEP, Gosplan, (State Planning Commission) had operated and there had been annual control figures.[8] As private market forces declined, central economic control increased. The goods famine of 1926–27 promoted state distribution of key commodities, especially metals, and regulation of production. Soviet economists had long discussed a five year plan, but serious work on one began only in 1927.

Realistic early drafts of the First Plan yielded to optimistic (and fantastic) variants. In 1927 Gosplan's mostly non-party professional staff outlined a plan for relatively balanced growth, with industry to expand 80 percent in five years, and which recognized probable obstacles. Party pressure, however, soon forced estimates upward, and resulting variants represented overoptimistic predictions made largely for

---

[8] See above, p. 479.

psychological purposes. S. G. Strumilin's version allowed for possible crop failures, little foreign trade or credits, and potentially heavier defense spending, but it set goals far exceeding those of the "Left," which Stalin had denounced as superindustrialist. Stalin boasted in 1929:

> We are going full steam ahead toward socialism through industrialization, leaving behind our century-old "racial" background. We are becoming a land of metals . . . , automobiles . . . , tractors, and when we set the USSR on an automobile and the muzhik on a tractor, let the noble capitalists . . . attempt to catch up. We shall see then which countries can be labeled backward and which advanced.[9]

Because 1928 was a successful year, goals were boosted higher. In April 1929, the Sixteenth Congress approved an optimal draft of the Plan which assumed that no misfortunes would occur. Gross industrial output was to increase 235.9 percent, labor productivity 110 percent, production costs were to fall 35 and prices 24 percent. To fulfil such goals would require a miracle (in which Stalin presumably did not believe!). In December 1929, a congress of "shock brigades" urged the Plan's fulfillment in four years; soon this became official policy. Constantly sounding notes of urgency, Stalin forced the tempo and brought former party oppositionists into line. Riding a wave of overoptimism, party leaders chanted: "There is no fortress that the Bolsheviks cannot storm." Perhaps Stalin knowingly adopted impossible targets largely for political reasons. Those urging caution were denounced as "bourgeois" wreckers working for foreign powers.

During the First Plan some wholly unanticipated obstacles appeared. The Great Depression made Soviet growth look more impressive, but it dislocated world trade and made imported foreign machinery more expensive relative to Soviet grain exports. Defense expenditures, instead of declining, were increased by Japanese expansion in east Asia. Ignorance and inexperience of workers and managers caused destruction or poor use of expensive foreign equipment, blamed on deliberate wrecking and sabotage. Resources were used inefficiently: industrial plants often lacked equipment or skilled workers. The inexorable drive for quantity brought a deplorable decline in quality as strains and shortages multiplied.

The First Plan had mixed results. Vast projects were undertaken, but many remained unfinished. Some, such as the Volga-White Sea Canal, were built by forced labor; others reflected genuine enthusiasm and self-sacrifice. At Magnitogorsk in the Urals, previously only a village, a great metallurgical center arose as workers and technicians labored under primitive conditions to build a bright socialist future. As industrial output rose sharply, the regime announced late in 1932 that the Plan had been basically fulfilled in four years and three months, but goals were surpassed only in machinery and metalworking and then

---

[9] Quoted in Maurice Dobb, *Soviet Economic Development Since 1917* (New York, 1948), p. 245.

partly by statistical manipulation.[10] Nonetheless, the new powerful engineering industry reduced Soviet dependence on foreign machinery. Fuel output rose considerably, but iron and steel fell far short because necessary plants took longer to complete than anticipated. Supposed increases in consumer production concealed sharp declines in handicrafts. To the party, the First Plan was a success (though goals for steel were fulfilled only in 1940, for electric power in 1951, and for oil in 1955) because industrial expansion and defense output could now be sustained from domestic resources. Lifting itself by its own bootstraps, the USSR was vindicating Stalin's idea of socialism in one country. Consumer production, agriculture, and temporarily military strength, however, were sacrificed to a rapid growth of heavy industry.

Labor was mobilized and lost much freedom. Once the state controlled all industry, Stalin declared trade union opposition anti-Marxist: how could the proletariat strike against its own dictatorship? Early in 1929 Tomskii and other trade union leaders were removed and replaced by Stalinists. Henceforth trade unions were to help build socialist industry by raising labor productivity and discipline. Unions exhorted workers to raise production and organize "shock brigades." Factory directors took control of wages, food supplies, housing, and other worker necessities. Russian workers, losing the right to strike or protest against their employer, reverted to their status of 75 years earlier, and Stalin's attitude toward labor resembled that of early Russian capitalists. By 1932 unemployment disappeared in towns and a seven-hour day was introduced, but real wages fell sharply. As millions of untrained peasants, escaping collectivization, sought industrial jobs, labor discipline deteriorated. Machinery was ruined and workers hunted for better conditions (In 1930 the average worker in the coal industry shifted jobs three times!). Cities grew rapidly, housing construction lagged, and urban services were grievously overtaxed.

Huge investments in heavy industry, raising incomes without a comparable rise in consumer goods or services, and burgeoning industrial employment spurred inflation. Seeking to achieve impossible goals, managers hired more and more labor, sending wage bills skyrocketing. Rationed goods remained cheap, leaving people much money but little to buy. By 1929 a wide gap opened between official and private prices. To absorb excess purchasing power, the government in 1930 instituted the turnover tax in place of many excise levies. Generally imposed at the wholesale level, it amounted to the difference between the cost of production and the retail selling price. In 1934, for instance, the retail price of rye was 84 rubles per centner (100 kilograms) of which 66 rubles was turnover tax. Its burden fell mainly on the peasantry because the state paid them so little for their grain; so agriculture indirectly financed the Plan.

A recent Soviet account, claiming that the situation at home and abroad required rapid industrialization, barely mentions Stalin's crucial

---

[10] Overfulfillment in machinery resulted chiefly from assigning high prices in 1926–27 rubles to many new machines. See Nove, *The Soviet Economy* (New York, 1967), p. 192.

MAP 34–1

Industry and Agriculture to 1939

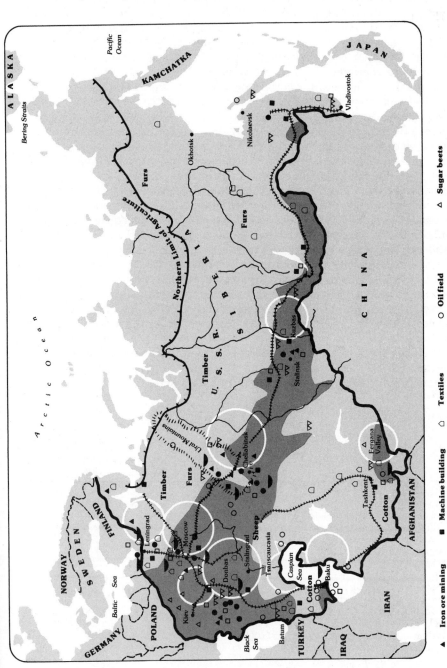

Adapted from *A History of Russia, Second Edition* by Nicholas V. Riasanovsky. Copyright © 1969 by Oxford University Press, Inc. Used by permission.

role in launching it. The First Plan, it continues, erecting the foundations of a socialist economy, turned the USSR into an industrial-agrarian state as enthusiastic shock workers completed the Plan ahead of schedule. The workers themselves, resolving to complete the Plan in four years, were supported by the party and the Plan's success represented a great victory for socialism. While admitting serious shortcomings, Soviet historians assert that the party quickly remedied the difficulties.[11]

By 1932 the Soviet economy was badly overstrained; 1933 brought shortages and privation. The Second Five Year Plan, redrafted during its first year, was adopted in February 1934 by the Seventeenth Congress. More realistic than the First Plan, its execution was aided by more experienced planners and managers. Unlike its predecessor, final goals were lower than preliminary ones. Heavy industrial targets were mostly met, and machinery and electric power output rose dramatically. Labor productivity surpassed expectations and technical sophistication improved as the First Plan's investments bore fruit. The Second Plan stressed consolidation, mastering techniques, and improving living standards. Initially, a greater increase was planned for consumer goods than for heavy industry, but then came a shift toward heavy industry and defense. Consumer goals were underfulfilled and per capita consumption fell below the 1928 level. Completed metallurgical works in Magnitogorsk, Kuznetsk, and Zaporozhe further reduced Soviet dependence on foreign capital goods, relieved the strain on the balance of payments, and permitted repayment of earlier debts. By 1937 the basic tools of industry and defense were being made in the USSR. Growth followed an uneven pattern: after a bad year, 1933, came three very good ones in industry and construction, and then relative stagnation began in 1937 (between 1937 and 1939 steel production actually declined). Table 2 shows some results of the two plans:[12]

TABLE 2

First and Second Plan Results

Category	1927–8	1932 (target)	1932–33 (actual)	1937 (target)	1937 (actual)
National income in 1926–27 rubles (billions)	24.5	49.7	45.5	100.2	96.3
Gross industrial output (billions of rubles)	18.3	43.2	43.3	92.7	95.5
Producers' goods	6.0	18.1	23.1	45.5	55.2
Consumers goods	12.3	25.1	20.2	47.1	40.3
Gross agricultural production (billions of 1926–27 r.)	13.1	25.8	16.6	—	—
Electricity (100 million Kwhs.)	5.05	22.0	13.4	38.0	36.2
Hard coal (million tons)	35.4	75.0	64.3	152.5	128.0
Oil (million tons)	11.7	22.0	21.4	46.8	28.5
Steel (million tons)	5.9	19.0	12.1	17.0	17.7
Machinery (million of 1926–27 r.)	1,822.0	4,688.0	7,362.0	—	—

[11] *Istoriia SSSR*, vol. 8, pp. 475–83.
[12] Adapted from Nove, pp. 191, 225.

During the Second Plan, labor productivity rose substantially and industrial employment fell below estimates as training programs gradually created a more skilled labor force. Pay differentials widened, rationing was gradually abolished, and more consumer goods was made available. After 1934 high prices of necessities stimulated harder work under the prevailing piece work system. Labor productivity was improved by Stakhanovism, a byproduct of "socialist competition." In September 1935 Alexis Stakhanov, a Donets coal miner, by hard work and intelligent use of unskilled helpers, produced 14 times his norm. Fostered by the Party, Stakhanovism spread to other industries and low labor norms were raised. Harsh penalties for absenteeism and labor turnover reduced these and improved labor discipline. The Great Purge, however, Soviet historians now admit, swept away managers, technicians, statisticians, and even foremen. The shaken survivors were often hysterical and rejected responsibility. This reaction and the growing shift of resources into arms production created an industrial slowdown after 1937.

The diversion of resources into defense plagued the Third Five Year Plan (1938–41), which was interrupted by the Nazi invasion. Industrial output increased an average of less than two percent annually compared with ten percent under the first two plans. Progress remained uneven, with much growth in production of machinery but little in steel and oil. New western frontier territories considerably increased productive capacity. Labor was severely restricted in mobility and choice of occupation, the work week rose to 48 hours, and workers required permission from their enterprise to change jobs. A million high school students were conscripted for combined vocational training and industrial work.

In summary, rapid industrialization (1928–41) brought increases in heavy industrial production unprecedented in history for a period of that length as shown in Table 3.[13]

The USSR became a leading industrial power, but living standards, real wages, and housing conditions declined. Dire predictions made during the industrialization debate came true: Bukharin foresaw the human sacrifices and inflation; Preobrazhenskii's contempt of primitive socialist accumulation was implemented by methods which appalled him (he was executed for protesting the excesses of collectivization).

SOCIAL POLICIES

A continued assault on social institutions associated with the old regime accompanied the Second Socialist Offensive. After 1933 or 1934, policy shifted to consolidation of Soviet institutions which often resembled their tsarist models and emphasis on discipline and social stability was renewed to overcome unfavorable effects of the preceding offensive. Social policies of 1934–41 represented "a great retreat,"[14] or

[13] Stanley H. Cohn, *Economic Development in the Soviet Union* (Lexington, Mass., 1970), p. 39.

[14] See Nicholas Timasheff (New York, 1946), *The Great Retreat*.

TABLE 3
Selected Statistical Indicators, 1928–40 (1928 = 100)

Category	1940 output (in percent of 1928)
Industrial production	263
Industrial materials	343
Ferrous metals	433
Electric power	964
Chemicals	819
Machinery	486
Consumer goods	181
Agricultural production	105
Crops	123
Animal products	88
Individual consumption (per capita)	93
Real wages	54
Capital stock	286
Urban housing space (per capita)	78

Soviet Thermidor, except that they coincided with the bloody terror of the purges.

Efforts to undermine the traditional family continued during the First Five Year Plan. Husbands and wives were often assigned to different cities, yet any available job had to be accepted. When a teacher complained of being separated from her husband, the Labor Board advised her to find a husband at her new job. In Stalingrad "socialist suburbs" featuring single rooms were built, but only bachelors would live in them. Such policies did weaken family ties, but the byproducts were grim. Free divorce and abortion caused a serious decline in birth rates, which threatened the supply of labor and army recruits. In Moscow medical institutions in 1934 there were only 57,000 live births and 154,000 abortions. Early in 1935 divorces numbered more than 38 per 100 marriages. Deteriorating parent-child relationships confronted communities with spiraling juvenile delinquency and hooliganism. Neglected children were beating up their schoolteachers!

In 1934–35 the regime shifted course abruptly. "The family," it was now stated officially, "is an especially important phase of social relations in socialist society" and must be strengthened. Marriage is "the most serious affair in life" and should be regarded as a lifelong union; men who changed their wives like shirts were threatened with prosecution for rape. In 1939 the journal of the Commissariat of Justice proclaimed:

> The State cannot exist without the family. Marriage is a positive value for the Socialist Soviet State only if the partners see in it a lifelong union. So-called free love is a bourgeois invention and has nothing in common with the principles of conduct of a Soviet citizen.[15]

Marriage was now dignified with well staged ceremonies in comfortable registration centers. Soon wedding rings were being sold again, and

---

[15] Quoted in ibid., p. 198.

non-Communists frequently reinforced the civil ceremony with a church wedding. Strict regulations, replacing the quickie divorce of earlier days, greatly curtailed divorces and raised fees sharply. Divorce became more difficult to obtain in the USSR than in many of the United States, and unregistered marriage, instituted in 1926, was abolished. After June 1936 abortion was permitted only if the mother's life were endangered or to prevent transmission of serious illness. Parental authority was reinforced, and young people were urged to respect and obey parents and elders. Motherhood was glorified (Stalin made a pilgrimage to Tiflis to show how much he loved his old mother), and mothers of large families were compensated. After destroying the old patriarchal family, the authorities reinforced the new Soviet nuclear family.

Experimentalism in education yielded during the First Plan to a structured, disciplined school program. Not Leninist theory but industry's insistent demands for trained specialists triggered the shift. Applicants to higher educational institutions were found to be woefully deficient in reading skills and parroted vague generalizations. In 1929 A. Lunacharskii, chief exponent of experimentalism, was removed, and a shift to serious study began under the slogan, "Mastery of knowledge." In 1931–32 came partial curricular reforms: teaching of Marxism was reduced, history revived, and "progressive education" was largely abandoned. Book learning, academic degrees, systematic textbooks, and traditional grading practices were reemphasized. Examinations were reinstituted after a 15-year lapse. Noisy, undisciplined classrooms disrupted by hooligans yielded to quiet, disciplined ones as the authority of teachers and professors was restored. Decrees from above specified every detail of instruction and school administration as a new Soviet school emerged, patterned after the conservative tsarist school of the 1880s. Curricula resembled tsarist and European ones, and pupils were dressed in uniforms like those of the 1880s. For pragmatic reasons, a retreat to traditional models began earlier in education than in other fields. The authoritarian school reflected the Stalinist autocracy.

Soviet religious policies fluctuated. During the First Plan there was a widespread campaign to close churches. In 1930 the Soviet press reported the burning of icons and religious books by the carload, and restrictions, disfranchisement, and discriminatory taxation plagued the clergy. The atheist League of Militant Godless, growing to almost six million members, induced many collective farms to declare themselves "godless." Then between 1933 and 1936, partly to allay peasant discontent, came some relaxation of persecution. The Stalin Constitution of 1936 restored the franchise to clergymen and gave them full civil rights. The Purge of 1937–38 brought another wave of persecution, but few priests were executed. After 1938 developed a more tolerant religious policy to win popular support and counter the rising threat of Nazi Germany. Christianity was now declared to have played a progressive, patriotic role in Russian history. Violence against churches and believers was forbidden, and the closing of churches and political trials of clergymen were halted. The regime adopted a subtler approach of emphasizing that scientific advances had made religion outmoded. Soviet leaders, recognizing the persistence of religious belief, sought to use it to consolidate their power. The Soviet census of 1937 had revealed that more than half the adult population still classified themselves as believers (the census takers were sent to Siberia!). Meanwhile the Orthodox Church recognized the regime and wished to cooperate with it to achieve greater social discipline, a strong family, and restriction of sexual activity. Twenty years of official persecution greatly weakened the church as an organization and reduced markedly the numbers of the faithful but strengthened their faith. Marxism-Leninism proved no substitute for religion.

During the 1930s the Stalin regime, abandoning romantic attitudes, experimentalism, and radical policies, retreated toward tradition and national and authoritarian tsarist patterns. There emerged an increasingly disciplined, status-conscious society headed by a new élite of party bureaucrats, economic managers, engineers, and army officers which differed sharply in attitudes and habits from the revolutionary generation.

PROBLEM 9: COLLECTIVIZATION: WHY AND HOW?

The transformation of Russian agriculture under Stalin from 25 million individual farms into several hundred thousand collective and state farms was one of the 20th century's most dramatic and important events. It involved a massive conflict between the Soviet regime and the peasantry, the destruction of many of the best Soviet farmers and much of the livestock, and produced a terrible famine in 1933. Soviet collectivized agriculture, plagued by low productivity, lack of farmer incentives and incompetent organization, has sought ever since without conspicuous success to satisfy domestic needs. Was forced collectivization necessary or wise? Why was it undertaken? Was it properly implemented? Who was responsible for the accompanying mass suffering? Here these issues are explored in Stalin's contemporary speeches, in a recent Soviet account and in the work of a Soviet historian published in the West.

STALIN'S VIEW

Stalin and his Politburo colleagues claimed at the time that it was necessary to collectivize agriculture to achieve economic progress and socialism. They affirmed that the decision to collectivize was imposed upon them by kulak treachery and the insistent demands of an expanding industry. Poor and middle peasants, Stalin claimed, were entering collective farms voluntarily and en masse. Declared Stalin as forced collectivization began:

> The characteristic feature of the present collective farm movement is that not only are the collective farms being joined by individual groups of poor peasants . . . but . . . by the mass of middle peasants as well. This means that the collective farm movement has been trans-

formed from a movement of individual groups and sections of the laboring peasants into a movement of millions and millions of the main mass of the peasantry. . . . The collective farm movement . . . has assumed the character of a mighty and growing *anti-kulak* avalanche . . . paving the way for extensive socialist construction in the country-side (speech of December 27, 1929).

At the beginning of forced collectivization, Stalin, summarizing the party's problems and achievements in agriculture, stressed the rapid development of a new socialist agriculture against desperate resistance from "retrograde" elements:

The party's third achievement during the past year . . . [is] the *radical change* in the development of our agriculture from small, backward *individual* farming to large-scale advanced *collective* agriculture, to joint cultivation of the land . . . , based on modern technique and finally to giant state farms, equipped with hundreds of tractors and harvester combines.

. . . In a whole number of areas we have succeeded in *turning* the main mass of the peasantry away from the old, *capitalist* path . . . to the new *socialist* path of development, which ousts the rich and the capitalists and reequips the middle and poor peasants . . . with modern implements . . . so as to enable them to climb out of poverty and enslavement to the kulaks onto the high road of cooperative, collective cultivation of the land. . . . We have succeeded in bringing about this *radical change* deep down in the peasantry itself, and in securing the following of the broad masses of the poor and middle peasants in spite of incredible difficulties, in spite of the desperate resistance of retrograde forces of every kind, from kulaks and priests to philistines and Right Opportunists.

. . . In the coming year, 1930, the marketable grain output of the state farms and collective farms will amount to over 400 million puds, or more than 50 percent of the marketable grain output of the *whole* of agriculture. . . . Such an impetuous speed of development is *unequalled* even by our socialized large-scale industry. . . . All the objections raised by "science" against the possibility and expediency of organizing large grain factories of 40,000 to 50,000 hectares each have collapsed. . . .

What is the new feature of the present collective-farm movement? . . . The peasants are joining the collective farms not in separate groups, as formerly, but as whole villages, *volosts*, districts and even *okrugs*. And what does that mean? It means that *the middle peasant is joining the collective farm.* (November 1929).

Stalin's speech a month later, however, hinted that forcible means were having to be employed after all:

It is necessary . . . *to implant* in the village large socialist farms, collective and state farms, as bases of socialism which, with the socialist city in the vanguard, can drag along the masses of peasants. . . .

In March 1930, at his colleagues' insistence, Stalin temporarily halted forced collectivization. His article, "Dizzy with Success," blamed local Party workers and extremists for errors and perversions of official policy:

. . . People not infrequently become intoxicated by such successes, . . . overrate their own strength. The successes of our collective-farm policy are due . . . to the fact that it rests on the *voluntary character* of the collective-farm movement and *on taking into account the diversity of conditions* in various regions of the USSR. Collective farms must not be established by force. That would be foolish and reactionary. The collective-farm movement must rest on the active support of the main mass of the peasantry. . . . In a number of the northern regions of the consuming zone . . . , attempts are not infrequently made. to *replace* preparatory work for the organization of collective farms by bureaucratic decreeing . . . , the organization of collective farms on paper. . . . Who benefits from these distortions, . . . these unworthy threats against the peasants? Nobody, except our enemies! In a number of areas of the USSR . . . attempts are being made . . . to leap straight away into the agricultural commune. . . . They are already "socializing" dwelling houses, small livestock, and poultry. . . .
How could there have arisen in our midst such blockhead excesses in "socialization," such ludicrous attempts to overleap oneself? . . . They could have arisen only in the atmosphere of our "easy" and "unexpected" successes on the front of collective farm development . . . as a result of the blockheaded belief of a section of our Party: "We can achieve anything!" (March 2, 1930).

In his report to the Seventeenth Congress in January 1934 Stalin hailed the results of rapid collectivization in the USSR:

. . . From a country of small individual agriculture it has become a country of collective, large-scale mechanized agriculture. . . . Progress in the main branches of agriculture proceeded many times more slowly than in industry, but nevertheless more rapidly than in the period when individual farming predominated. . . . Our Soviet peasantry has completely and irrevocably taken its stand under the Red banner of socialism. . . . Our Soviet peasantry has quit the shores of capitalism for good and is going forward in alliance with the working class to socialism. . . . We have 204,000 tractors . . . working for the collective farms and state farms. This . . . is a force capable of pulling up all the roots of capitalism in the countryside. . . .[16]

THE OFFICIAL POSITION

The *History of the USSR* (Moscow 1967), while defending the necessity and correctness of collectivization and stressing the voluntary entry of many peasants into *kolkhozy*, admits the widespread use of force and "administrative methods" (secret police). It credits the party (not Stalin) with successfully implementing collectivization but criticizes the extremism of some party leaders. Stalin is reprimanded mildly and his role in deciding upon and implementing collectivization is deemphasized.

Under conditions of worsening international relations, increasing economic difficulties, and the growth of class struggle within the USSR,

---

[16] J. Stalin, *Works*, (Moscow, 1955), vol. 12, pp. 131–38, 147, 155, 198–206; vol. 13, pp. 243–61.

the Communist Party had to achieve simultaneously industrialization and the socialist reconstruction of agriculture. Life demanded a colossal application of energy by party and Soviet people and sacrifices. . . .

In the course of fulfilling the First Five Year Plan, the Communist party came out decisively for speeding the tempo of constructing socialism. Collectivization was part of that construction. The decision that it was necessary to reduce the period of implementing it ripened gradually. . . . In the spring of 1929 were heard the words "full collectivization" for the first time as a practical task. . . . *Kolkhoztsentr* RSFSR declared Volovskii raion of Tula province . . . as the first region in the country of complete collectivization. . . . In the second half of 1929 the village seethed as in the days of the revolution [of 1917]. At meetings of the poor peasants, at general village assemblies only one question was raised: organizing *kolkhozy*. From July through September 1929 were attracted into kolkhozy as many peasants as during the whole 12 years of Soviet power. And during the last three months of 1929 the numerical growth of *kolkhozy* was twice as fast again. This was, as the Party emphasized, "an unprecedented tempo of collectivization, *exceeding the most optimistic projections."* . . .

The choice of the moment for a transition to massive collectivization was determined by various reasons. Among them the most important was the spurt in the country's economy. Socialist construction was advancing at an accelerating pace. The industrial population was growing considerably faster than had been assumed. The demand for commercial grain and raw materials rose sharply. The inability of small peasant production to supply a growing industry with food . . . became unbearable. It became clear that the economy of the country could not be based on two different social foundations: big socialist industry and small individual peasant farming. . . .

One of the new methods of struggle of the kulaks against the policy of the Soviet state in 1928–29 was so-called kulak self-liquidation. The kulaks themselves reduced their sowings, sold their stock and tools. "Kulak self-liquidation" thus began before the state shifted to a policy of consistent liquidation of the kulaks as a class. . . . "Self-liquidation" of farms began to take on a massive character . . . leading to the reduction of the productive forces of agriculture. . . . Before the state which hitherto had merely limited the private capitalist structure. . . arose the need to save the productive forces of agriculture from destruction. . . . It would have been easiest to have retreated before the petty bourgeois element and the kulak and remove economic and other restrictions from private capitalist production. . . . The party followed a different path. . . . It considered it necessary to hasten collectivization of production in agriculture and on that basis force the liquidation of the kulaks as a class. . . .

Along with the achievements in socialist reconstruction of the village, inadequacies were revealed. . . . Such a leap was to a significant degree caused by serious extremes, by the broad use of administrative measures. Some leaders believed that it would suffice to draw half the peasants into the *kolkhozy* and the rest would enter voluntarily. . . . In a majority of cases local leaders themselves forced by every means the process of collectivization. . . . Leaders of one region issued at the beginning of 1930 the following slogans: "Collectivize the entire population at any cost! Dekulakize no less than seven percent of all peasant farms! Achieve all this by February 15 [1930] without delaying a moment!" . . . Administrative methods, violation of the voluntary principle in *kolkhoz* construction, contradicting the Leninist cooperative plan caused sharp dissatisfaction among the peasantry . . . All that represented a serious danger for the country, for the alliance of the working class with the peasantry. In the struggle against these extremes rose all the healthy forces of the party. The Central Committee was inundated by letters of local Communists, workers, and peasants. . . . Numerous signals of the dissatisfaction of the peasantry with administrative methods of *kolkhoz* construction caused serious concern in the Central Committee. Thus the party and government in February and March 1930 took a series of emergency measures to correct the situation in the countryside. . . . On March 2, 1930 was published the article of I. V. Stalin, "Dizzy with Success" . . . against leftist extremes. . . . Many people noted, to be sure, that it had come too late when extremes had taken on a massive character. . . . One must note that in describing the causes of the extremes, I. V. Stalin was one-sided and not self-critical. He placed the entire blame for mistakes and extremes on local cadres, accused them of dizziness and demanded harsh measures against them. This caused a certain confusion among party workers, which hampered the task of eliminating excesses.[17]

A DISSIDENT SOVIET HISTORIAN

Roy Medvedev, a Soviet historian, in *Let History Judge* (New York, 1973), still unpublished in the USSR, castigates forced collectivization and Stalin's role in it. Unlike the previous selection which ascribed "mistakes" mainly to a few "leftists," Medvedev points directly at Stalin and the Politburo and suggests that forced collectivization was unwise and unnecessary. He ascribed Stalin's decision for forced collectivization and elimination of the kulaks mainly to economic conditions for which he and his colleagues were responsible:

> The economic miscalculations of Stalin, Bukharin, and Rykov and the kulaks' sabotage of grain procurement brought the USSR at the end of 1927 to the verge of a grain crisis. . . . Mistakes . . . in the previous years did not leave much room for political and economic maneuvering, [but] there were still some possibilities for the use of economic rather than administrative measures, that is for the methods of NEP rather than War Communism.

Medvedev attributed the traumatic implementation of collectivization to Stalin's incompetent and disastrous leadership:

> . . . His inclination toward administrative fiat, toward coercion, instead of convincing, his oversimplified and mechanistic approach to complex political problems, his crude pragmatism and inability to forsee the consequences of alternative actions, his vicious nature and unparalleled ambition—all these qualities of Stalin seriously complicated the solution of problems that were overwhelming to begin with.
> . . . Stalin could not appraise correctly the situation taking shape in the countryside. At the first signs of progress [of collectivization] he em-

---

[17] *Istoriia SSSR* (Moscow, 1967), vol. 8, pp. 443, 541–43, 553–57.

barked on a characteristically adventurous course. Apparently, he wanted to compensate for years of failures and miscalculations in agricultural policy and to astonish the world with a picture of great success in the socialist transformation of agriculture. So at the end of 1929, he sharply turned the bulky ship of agriculture without checking for reefs and shoals. Stalin, Molotov, Kaganovich, and several other leaders pushed for excessively high rates of collectivization, driving the local organizations in every possible way, ignoring . . . difficulties. . . .

Although at the beginning of the 30s, grain production decreased, bread was in short supply, and millions of peasants were starving, Stalin insisted on exporting great quantities of grain. . . . Moreover, Soviet grain was sold for next to nothing. . . . The most galling aspect of the sacrifices that the people suffered—the peasants most of all—is that they were unnecessary. . . . The scale of capital investment in industry, with Stalin forced in the early 1930s, was too much for the economy to bear . . .

Stalin was likewise responsible, claims Medvedev, for the extreme tempo and excessive socialization of the initial collectivization drive. The Central Committee's draft decree had suggested a slower pace:

At his [Stalin's] insistence the draft was stripped of rules indicating what portion of livestock and farm implements should be collectivized. In the final version the period of collectivization was reduced in the North Caucasus and Mid-Volga to one to two years and rules were omitted concerning socialization of the instruments of production. . . . The peasants' right to keep small livestock, implements, and poultry was omitted. Also deleted were guidelines for liquidating the kulaks. . . . Material and financial resources needed to organize hundreds of collective farms had not been set aside. . . . Most of the local party, soviet, and economic organs . . . were not prepared for total collectivization in such a short time. In order to carry out the orders that came from above . . . , almost all party and Soviet organs were forced to put administrative pressure on the peasants and also on the lower officials. . . . Such methods absolutely contradicted the basic principles of Marxism-Leninism.[18]

CONCLUSION

During recent years Soviet historians have greatly revised the idyllic picture of collectivization presented under Stalin's regime, but sharp critiques, such as Medvedev's, have not been published in the USSR. The outstanding recent Western study of collectivization by Moshe Lewin,[19] generally endorses Medvedev's findings. Lewin notes that Stalin, in affirming that the middle peasant was entering the *kolkhoz* voluntarily, was arguing from false premises:

There were no grounds for suggesting that there had been a change of attitude among the mass of the peasantry with regard to the *kolkhozes*.

18 Roy Medvedev, *Let History Judge* (New York, 1973), p. 69 ff.

19 *Russian Peasants and Soviet Power: A Study of Collectivization* (New York, 1975).

The supposed change was a product of Stalin's peculiar form of reasoning which consisted of taking the wish for the deed. It followed that the peasants were being won over because this spring *there would be* 60,000 tractors in the fields, and in a year's time there would be over a hundred thousand.

As to the results of forced collectivization, Lewin concludes:

The rash undertaking of the winter 1929–30 cost the country very dearly. . . . Indeed, it is true to say that to this day Soviet agriculture has still not fully recovered from the damaging effects of that winter.

The cost of collectivization was enormous: "seldom was any government to wreak such havoc in its own country."[20] It is revealing that forced collectivization à la Stalin was not tried elsewhere in eastern Europe. Instead, wealthier farmers were squeezed out, as Lenin had suggested, by economic measures and their managerial talents used in the collective farms.

Suggested Additional Reading

BELOV, FEDOR. *A History of a Soviet Collective Farm* (New York, 1955).

BLACKWELL, WILLIAM. *The Industrialization of Russia . . .* (New York, 1970).

BROWN, EMILY. *The Soviet Trade Unions and Labor Relations* (Cambridge, Mass., 1966).

CARR, E. H. *Foundations of a Planned Economy, 1926–1929* (New York, 1972).

CHAMBERLIN, W. H. *Russia's Iron Age* (London, 1935).

CURTISS, JOHN S. *The Russian Church and the Soviet State* (Boston, 1953).

DANIELS, R. V., ed. *The Stalin Revolution* (Lexington, Mass., 1972).

DEUTSCHER, ISAAC. *The Prophet Outcast: Trotsky, 1929–1940* (Oxford, 1963).

ERLICH, A. *The Soviet Industrialization Debate . . .* (Cambridge, Mass., 1960).

GERSCHENKRON, A. *Economic Backwardness in Historical Perspective* (Cambridge, Mass., 1962).

INKELES, ALEX and R. A. BAUER. *The Soviet Citizen . . .* (Cambridge, Mass., 1959).

JASNY, NAUM. *Soviet Industrialization, 1928–1952* (Chicago, 1961).

KRAVCHENKO, VICTOR. *I Chose Freedom* (New York, 1946).

LEWIN, MOSHE. *Russian Peasants and Soviet Power . . .* (London, 1968).

MALE, D. J. *Russian Peasant Organization before Collectivization . . .* (Cambridge, Eng., 1971).

NOVE, ALEC. *Was Stalin Really Necessary?* (London, 1964).

SCOTT, JOHN. *Behind the Urals* (Boston, 1943).

SHOLOKHOV, MIKHAIL. *Virgin Soil Upturned* (New York, 1959) (novel).

STALIN, JOSEPH. *Problems of Leninism* (Moscow, 1940).

SWIANIEWICZ, S. *Forced Labor and Economic Development . . .* (London, 1965).

TIMASHEFF, NICHOLAS. *The Great Retreat* (New York, 1946).

[20] Ibid., pp. 457, 515.

35

Culture in the Soviet Era, 1917-1953

FROM THE very outset of the new Soviet state, culture has been the handmaiden of politics, and therefore its history cannot be viewed or understood in isolation from politics. Soviet culture has passed through a number of clearly defined stages of development since 1917. During the first years of the Soviet regime (1917–21), there was no real official policy on cultural affairs. From 1921 to 1928, what are often referred to as the New Economic Policy (NEP) years, there was an effort to develop a policy which recognized and accepted experimentation and debate as essential ingredients of cultural life. The consolidation of the Stalinist dictatorship and the industrialization and collectivization campaigns spelled the end of toleration and diversity in the arts. Stalinist policy in the arts became harshly rigid, unyielding, and deadening. Culture was reduced to a dull, catechistic recitation of Soviet virtues and successes designed to inspire and sustain the "new Soviet man." Beginning in 1934 "socialist realism" became the central core of Soviet policy in the arts (and remains so today). Although subject to differing interpretations as political demands shifted, socialist realism has traditionally insisted on two contradictory qualities: a constant and unequivocal revolutionary enthusiasm combined with an objective portrayal of reality. Stalin's own tastes reflected a hidebound traditionalism consisting of a vulgarized version of the "realism" of the 1860s. Many a Soviet artist would stumble badly (or worse) trying to juggle the mutually exclusive principles of "socialist realism." World War II brought, paradoxically, a brief respite from the rigors of Stalinist culture. In an effort to harness the arts to the demands of total war and the struggle for survival, the rigid bonds of control were temporarily relaxed, and a freer atmosphere emerged in a war-torn Soviet Union. The controls, however, were immediately reintroduced with a vengeance in the postwar period, the era of the ascendancy of Andrei Zhdanov, Stalin's cultural watchdog. Associated with Zhdanovism was anti-cosmopolitanism, the Soviet euphemism for the intellectual cold war with the West. The period 1946 to 1953 was one of the dreariest and most dismal in all of Soviet culture.

521

THE FIRST STAGE 1917–1929

The November Revolution that catapulted the Bolsheviks into power did not precipitate an immediate and abrupt break with established cultural patterns and traditions. Indeed, during the first years of the Soviet regime and particularly after the Civil War and the period of liberalization represented by the New Economic Policy introduced in 1921, the Russian cultural scene appeared little changed from what it had been before the Revolution. This static condition was due in part to the fact that the Bolsheviks, once they had seized power, were intent on retaining it and were thus preoccupied with critical questions of political consolidation, economic reconstruction, and military preparedness, all of which left little time or energy to devote to the arts. Even if inclined to introduce wide-ranging control of all aspects of social and cultural activity, the Bolsheviks realized that they could not do so with the limited cadres of trained and experienced personnel at their disposal. On the other hand, the disruptions of war, revolution, and civil war meant that for a time little of enduring cultural value was produced. Relatively little was published as scarce reserves of paper were quickly consumed to print militant propaganda leaflets and revolutionary tracts designed to persuade the populace of the advantages of Bolshevism. Painters and sculptors who managed to continue work found little demand for or even interest in their output. Basic materials—paints, clay, canvas, paper—were all in short supply and what was available was usually of poor quality. Composers and musicians were faced with similar problems. Concert halls, instead of ringing with symphonic melodies and rousing choruses, were more often filled with raucous political debates and revolutionary agitation. Moreover, the intelligentsia, had been reduced by deaths from hunger, disease, war, and execution. Emigration was one avenue of escape from what must have appeared to many as the beginnings of the apocalypse. Many prominent artists chose to live abroad as transients or permanent exiles rather than face the uncertainties of life in the Soviet Union. The list of émigrés was impressive, including such prominent names as Maxim Gorkii, Ivan Bunin, Ilia Ehrenburg, Alexis Tolstoy, Dmitri Merezhkovskii, Zinaida Gippius, Igor Stravinskii, Serge Prokofiev, Serge Rachmaninov, Serge Diagilev, Marc Chagall, and Vasili Kandinskii. Some returned to the Soviet Union later, while others became permanent residents abroad.

The chaos and the uncertainty of the early years of Soviet rule constituted only part of the larger obstacle to elaborating a coherent cultural policy. From an ideological or theoretical vantage point there was equal confusion and uncertainty. In the Marxist scheme culture and the arts constitute part of the superstructure rather than the material base. Only changes in the substructure—in the mode or method of production—would bring about corresponding changes in culture and the arts. A new socialist culture would emerge only gradually after a new economic order had been established and a genuinely proletarian society achieved. Nevertheless, it would be an error to think that Russian culture was unaffected by the Revolution or that the Bolsheviks were uninterested in culture and formulation of policy for the arts.

Lenin outlined his none too radical view of the arts as follows:

> Art belongs to the people. It must have its deepest roots in the broad masses of the workers. It must be understood and loved by them. It must be rooted in, and grow with their feelings, thoughts, and desires. It must arouse and develop the artist in them. Are we to give cake and sugar to a minority while the mass of workers and peasants still eat black bread? So that art may come to the people, and people to art, we must first of all raise the general level of education and culture.[1]

There was really nothing very new nor even particularly Marxist about this view. In many ways it echoed what had been espoused by Vladimir Stasov in his defense of the art of the "Itinerants" and the music of "The Five" during the 19th century. Art had to be rooted in the life of the people, it had to be clear and understandable, and it had to serve a useful purpose: to educate the people. Such was to become the essence of the Soviet concept of art.

The man responsible for translating Lenin's views on culture and art into reality was Anatol Lunacharskii (1875–1933), son of a successful tsarist civil servant, who spared no sacrifice or expense to provide him with the best education available in Russia and western Europe. Lunacharskii studied philosophy and literature and became refined, sophisticated, and urbane, his tastes cosmopolitan and progressive. He joined the Bolshevik Party in 1904 and often described himself as "an intellectual among Bolsheviks, and a Bolshevik among the intelligentsia." As the Bolshevik Party's leading cultural authority, Lunacharskii was the natural choice to be the first People's Commissar of Education. From 1917 to 1929 Lunacharskii guided the Soviet regime's efforts to improve education and develop a socialist culture in conformity with Lenin's views. Lunacharskii proved to be a skillful and imaginative administrator, who exercised his considerable authority with flexibility and tolerance. The tasks facing him were formidable: first to initiate and oversee a program of basic education designed to teach the illiterate masses, variously estimated at 60 to 70 percent of the population, to read and write. He had also to begin winning the allegiance of the artistic intelligentsia and persuade intellectual workers of their social responsibilities, obligations to the state, and need for a common purpose. Finally, he had to convince the hardpressed party leadership of the paramount importance of the arts in order to secure financial backing to carry on an effective cultural program. He recognized the need to maintain a delicate balance between traditional values of more conservative elements of society and fanatical enthusiasm for entirely new directions and demands for a complete break with the past by more radical supporters of the regime. He had to work frantically at times to prevent wanton destruction of cultural monuments by those

---

[1] Cited in Sheila Fitzpatrick *The Commissariat of Enlightenment* (New York, 1971), p. 24.

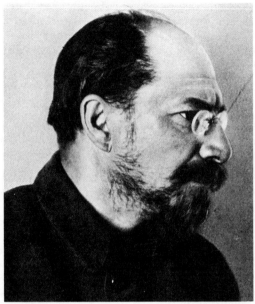

Anatol Lunacharskii (1875–1933)

who wished to obliterate old "bourgeois culture." Although determined to preserve the best of the old heritage, Lunacharskii refused to be limited by it.

His immediate efforts among the intelligentsia were not confined to attempts to restrain enthusiasm by proletarian supporters of the regime. At the same time he had to persuade opponents of the Bolsheviks to forsake open hostility in favor of neutrality or support. Persuasion and patience, he believed, were superior to pressure and coercion. His was a voice of calm and reasonableness in an era of impatience and often frenzied intolerance. Lunacharskii's actions were generally sensible and humane in an inhumane and often irrational age. While he was Commissar of Education, he encouraged a give-and-take which would contrast sharply with later rigid Stalinist authoritarianism. The 1920s were in many ways the "golden era" of Soviet culture. It was an age of experimentation and innovation in many spheres, and Lunacharskii was able to chart a reasonable course through turbulent waters.

Social life and schools were soon affected by the "ideological reorientation" implied by the revolution. Some radical social reformers predicted the "withering away" of the traditional family and encouraged a breach with bourgeois patterns of social behavior. In education the curriculum was drastically revised to give learning practical value by promoting economic specialization and material production, and to develop socially responsible individuals. Schools were to be socially nondiscriminatory, free, secular, and compulsory to the age of 17. Schooling and work experience were to be integrated, and ideological loyalty and Soviet patriotism became integral parts of the curriculum. Schools were designed to be political and economic instruments to overcome Russia's backwardness. Lunacharskii's Commissariat made significant progress in education in a very short time despite shortages of buildings, teachers, and books. By 1926 an estimated 51 percent of those over age nine were literate.

In order to implement a wide-ranging program in education and culture, Lunacharskii saw the need to recruit "bourgeois specialists" of the pre-revolutionary era. A comprehensive educational system could not be organized without experienced personnel. "Bourgeois specialists" were needed to train "socialist specialists" of the future. Wishing to alienate no one, Lunacharskii authorized and helped finance numerous literary, artistic, and educational groups which retained much freedom and autonomy. Cultural groups proliferated. Among the leading groups sponsored by Lunacharskii's Commissariat was the Association of Proletarian Cultural and Educational Organizations (Proletkult). Proletkult had been founded in 1917, before the November Revolution by A. A. Bogdanov to provide an outlet for working-class cultural activity and leadership and to give direction to a broad educational program. Proletkult promoted establishment of workers' clubs (to foster literature, art, drama, and music) and workers' universities and palaces of culture to introduce proletarians to culture and education. In August 1918 Proletkult sponsored a conference of proletarian writers which called for setting up an All-Russian Union of Writers of "working class origin and viewpoint," the first effort to organize proletarian cultural workers into a unified group. This resolution was not acted upon then, but the idea was not forgotten. The aggressive stance of Proletkult caused friction with Lunacharskii's Commissariat, and the two institutions often worked at cross purposes. Their overlap and competition finally persuaded Lenin to intervene in 1920. He ordered Proletkult merged with the Commissariat, ending the former's autonomy. Proletkult was always far more radical and ideological than the Commissariat. Lenin would not allow Proletkult to undermine Lunacharskii's more traditional program.

In contrast to Proletkult's aim of drastic reorientation of culture, a group of writers, dubbed the "fellow travelers" by Trotskii, emerged. These were the "bourgeois specialists" in literature, mostly established pre-revolutionary writers who remained in Soviet Russia. They sought in their works to analyze the acutely felt problems of adjustment in a new and alien world. They wrote of the Revolution, the Civil War, and their effects on individual human beings. They were less interested in cosmic historical forces than the more ideologically oriented proletarian writers were. The "fellow travelers" wrote about romantic love, violence, and passion. In 1921 a group of "fellow travelers" formed a fraternity known as the Serapion Brotherhood (borrowing the name from a hermit-like character created by the early 19th century German Romantic writer, E. T. A. Hoffmann). This rather loosely organized group had no clearly articulated esthetic doctrine to which they all subscribed, but it sought to preserve artistic freedom. "Most of all," wrote one of the founders, "we were afraid of losing our independence, of suddenly finding ourselves a 'Society attached to the People's Commissariat of Public Enlightenment' or to some other institution." They wished to write according to their own principles and convictions. Interest in literature and the belief that it could be produced only in a totally free atmosphere bound the members together. The Serapion Brotherhood's unity though began to crumble as early as 1924.

Another literary group of this period was *Pereval* (The Mountain Pass), more closely aligned with the party than the Serapion Brotherhood. Founded in 1924 with the active cooperation of the Old Bolshevik, Alexander Voronskii, editor of *Red Virgin Soil*, the first important Soviet "thick" journal with essays on politics and economics as well as literature and the arts. The circumstances of the *Pereval* group's emergence reveal the confusion and uncertainty of the early 1920s. The group consisted largely of young writers dedicated to the Revolution and over half were party members. They looked upon emerging Soviet society as transitional between old and new. Their writing probed Soviet society, criticizing as well as praising. Favoring artistic freedom, they advocated literary "sincerity" and artistic "realism" and stressed each writer's unique personality and psychological insight as critical in developing literary talent. Theirs was a humanistic outlook uncomplicated by doctrinaire ideology. The *Pereval* writers' individualism and humanism brought them into conflict with the militant proletarian writers, who accused them of "defeatism," and lack of revolutionary enthusiasm. Lunacharskii had to monitor such disputes and prevent them from becoming disruptive.

Opposed to the Serapion Brotherhood and *Pereval* were larger, more influential organizations of proletarian writers which grew from the Proletkult movement. The Moscow Association of Proletarian Writers (MAPP) was founded in 1923, the Russian Association of Proletarian Writers (RAPP) in 1925, and the All-Union Combined Association of Proletarian Writers (VOAPP) in 1928. These groups claimed to be the only true spokesmen for the working class in literature. From the beginning they were aggressive, attacking the "fellow travelers" and *Pereval* writers in their journal, *On Literary Guard*. Early in 1925, the proletarian groups organized the first all-Union Conference of Proletarian Writers as a forum to attack non-proletarian writers. "Fellow travelers" were accused of writing works against the revolution and of espousing bourgeois values of nationalism, mysticism, and individualism. Many of their accusations against the "fellow travelers" were groundless. Still there was open debate, not intimidation: the "fellow travelers" responded with a ringing defense of their literary freedom and intellectual integrity.

These debates became so intense that the party intervened and issued "The Policy of the Party in the Field of Artistic Literature," the first formal party statement on cultural affairs. It revealed that many Bolsheviks in positions of authority were sophisticated culturally and understood that development in the arts could not be dictated. The party acknowledged that a variety of literary trends existed, reflecting the diversity of the NEP period, and it refused to endorse a single literary trend as "correct." The party announced it would remain aloof from partisan debate and advocated free competition between the groups. This guaranteed that cultural ferment would persist and that the "fellow travelers" would not be devoured by the proletarian writers.

Painting and music revealed similar patterns. The 1920s witnessed a struggle between "left" and "right" factions in art and music. The Soviet musical world was split by the intense, often vitriolic debates between two warring factions: the modern-oriented Association for Contemporary Music (ACM) and the Russian Association of Proletarian Musicians (RAPM). The members of the former were dubbed proponents of the *asmovskii* position, signifying decadent-modernist formalism. Members of RAPM were known as adherents of the *rapmovskii* position, that signified simplistic musical primitivism. These adjectives concealed deep practical and ideological differences. ACM maintained close ties with the musical life of western Europe and thus assured Soviet composers contact with the most advanced and progressive Western ideas. At the same time, ACM sought to acquaint the West with the best music of Soviet composers. These Western contacts were especially stimulating to young composers such as Dmitri Shostakovich (1906–1975). Furthermore, the members of ACM completely rejected the idea that music was a political tool. One member declared, "Of course I am not a 'proletarian' composer in the sense that I do not write commonplace music 'for the masses.'" He went on to argue that, "Music is music, not ideology."

The opponents of the ACM were the proletarian musicians, many of whom had participated in the ill-fated Proletkult movement, which had collapsed in 1920. The Russian Association of Proletarian Musicians was founded in 1923 to organize proletarian ideology in music. The members of RAPM rejected most past composers and displayed a thoroughly negative attitude toward the classical heritage. They declared war on the more traditional composers of ACM and announced a life and death struggle between their "revolutionary realism" and "decadent formalism" of the "bourgeois" composers. Lunacharskii tried to mediate and cautioned the proletarian musicians not to press too hard in efforts to "revolutionize" Russian music. Uneasy coexistence prevailed in music until the end of the 1920s.

LITERATURE (1917–1929)

A mood of uncertainty and ambiguity pervaded Russian literature during the early Soviet period. This ambiguity was clearly expressed in the last works of the brilliant Symbolist, Alexander Blok (1880–1921), considered by many the greatest Russian poet of the 20th century. Well-established and respected in 1917, Blok welcomed the Revolution as the painful birth of a new world order. Yet the violence that accompanied it sickened and frightened him. He stood precariously over a widening gulf between old and new, uncertain where to leap.

He wrote two famous poems in 1918, amidst revolution and civil war, which reflected his—and the intelligentsia's—ambiguous reaction to the Revolution. Blok's *The Scythians* celebrated the Revolution as an elemental expression of the Russian national spirit. "Yea, we are Scythians,/ Yea, Asians, a slant-eyed, greedy brood." Russia, he proclaimed, had long shielded a haughty and ungrateful Europe from the ravages of the Mongol hordes. Now she would collect on that debt and beckoned to Europe to join and promote peace and cooperation, and the welfare of humanity. "Come unto us from the black ways of war,/ Come to our peaceful arms and rest./ Comrades, before it is too late,/ Sheathe the old sword; may brotherhood be blest." Should Europe refuse to heed this call to peace, he warned, a Scythian and Asiatic horde would descend upon it to destroy corrupt and dying western civilization. Warned *The Scythians:* join us in the pursuit of social justice, peace, and harmony or face annihilation.

Even more sombre and controversial was Blok's brilliant poem *The Twelve*, which elicited enormous interest and impassioned debate. *The Twelve* is ambiguous—we are not certain whether Blok intended it to affirm the Revolution or predict destruction of a refined and ancient culture. Was it a hymn of praise or a deceitful blasphemy? The "twelve" are Red Army soldiers tramping through Petrograd in a blizzard, intent on murder and pillage against the hated bourgeois enemy. The poem begins forebodingly: "Black night,/ White snow./ The wind, the wind!/ It all but lays you low./ The wind, the wind,/ Across God's world it

Alexander Blok (1880–1921)

blows!" The Revolution, like the wind, sweeps all before it. Having recorded the soldiers' bloody acts, the poem ends cryptically: "Forward as a haughty host they tread./ A starved mongrel shambles in the rear./ Bearing high the banner, bloody red,/ That He holds in hands no bullets sear—/ Hidden as the flying snow veils veer,/ Lightly walking on the wind, as though/ He Himself were diamonded snow,/ With mist-white roses garlanded!/ Jesus Christ is marching at their head."[2] Thus 12 terrorists are transformed into the 12 apostles, vanguard of a new era, following Christ and leading mankind forward to a new millenium, justifying a destructive revolution. Is this what Blok had in mind?

These were Blok's last two poems. He died in 1921, a victim of chaotic times. His final diary entries confirm his despair and personal incompatibility with the Soviet era. "At this moment, I have neither soul nor body; I am ill as I have never been before. Vile, rotten Mother Russia has devoured me, . . . as a sow gobbles one of its suckling pigs."[3] Having tried to leap to the new, he had slid into the abyss.

Another major poet destined to be devoured by Mother Russia and the Revolution was Vladimir Mayakovskii (1893–1930). No other writer was so closely identified with the Revolution, none was the object of such adulation. A prominent and respected Futurist poet before 1917, Mayakovskii hailed the November Revolution, joined the Bolshevik Party, and confidently set out to create a new "proletarian art" appropriate and appealing to the masses. He was one of the "cultural radicals" who rejected all bourgeois art as obsolete. He insisted: "The White Guard is turned over to a firing squad: "Why not Pushkin?" A new age required a new art, an art to celebrate the Revolution, the proletariat, the machine, the city, all modern life. The Futurists viewed themselves as the vanguard of proletarian culture, and Mayakovskii was in the forefront. To accomplish these grandiose aims, Mayakovskii and his friends organized LEF (Left Front in Art). Its members shared no uniform theoretical doctrine, but LEF proclaimed a functional, utilitarian art, useful to the state. "I don't want to be a wayside flower," Mayakovskii intoned, "plucked after morning in an idle hour." "Art for the sake of art" repelled him: to engage in idle dilletantism during historic change was to betray art. Instead, he commented on current issues, practiced poetic journalism, and even put his poetry to work selling goods and products. His poetry was enlisted in the service of the people and the Revolution.

Typical of his approach was the poem *150,000,000*, published in 1920. "150,000,000 [the 1919 population of the USSR] is the name of the creator of this poem./ Its rhythms—bullets,/ its rhymes—fires from building to building./ 150,000,000 speak with my lips. . . ./ Who can tell the name/ of the earth's creator—surely a genius?/ And so/ of this/ my/ poem/ no one is the author."[4] The poem portrays the struggle

[2] A. Yarmolinsky, ed., *An Anthology of Russian Verse, 1812–1960* (New York, 1962), pp. 109, 120. Translated by Babette Deutsch.

[3] Cited in Marc Slonim, *Modern Russian Literature* (New York, 1953), p. 206.

[4] Cited in Edward J. Brown, *Russian Lietrature Since the Revolution* (New York, 1969), p. 54.

between good and evil, socialism and capitalism, Ivan and Woodrow Wilson, Moscow and Chicago, between 150,000,000 Russians and the rest of the world. These blatantly propagandist works were failures. Lenin chastised Lunacharskii for issuing *150,000,000* in 5,000 copies —1,500 for "libraries and cranks" would have been enough, Lenin thought.

Among Mayakovskii's most popular works are two plays, *The Bedbug* and *The Bath* performed in 1929 and 1930 respectively. Both reveal Mayakovskii's growing disillusionment with the Soviet regime, which seemed to him increasingly remote from the heroic dreams of the Revolution. In *The Bedbug* a worker, Prisypkin, becomes a self-important bureaucrat who indulges his bourgeois tastes and values. A fire set by his drunken guests disrupts his wedding day. Everyone except Prisypkin and a lone bedbug are incinerated. Fifty years later, Prisypkin and the bedbug are found perfectly preserved in a block of ice. Prisypkin makes a full recovery after being thawed out, but his miraculous resurrection is a mixed blessing for the purified and refined communist society of the future into which he is now introduced. His bourgeois attitudes and habits—drinking, smoking, swearing, etc.— and especially the "ancient disease" of love, are all dangerously contagious and potentially disruptive. As a result of these fears, the authorities incarcerate him and the bedbug in a cage and they are displayed as curiosities. Prisypkin symbolized everything Mayakovskii hated in himself and in the Soviet citizen of the late 1920s. Already the revolutionary fervor and willingness to make sacrifices was beginning to fade, to be replaced by what he considered to be bourgeois values—self-satisfaction and complacency and the pursuit of material happiness. Soviet society, he feared, was fostering a whole generation of Prisypkins. *The Bath* was an even more direct indictment of Soviet life and particularly the emerging Stalinist bureaucracy, which already was radiating the pettiness and vulgarity characteristic of the Stalinist dictatorship at its worst, with all its anti-intellectualism, crudeness, and sterility. The inspiring dreams given substance by the Revolution were beginning to dissipate, in Mayakovskii's view, like so many bubbles in the air. The enthusiasm and spontaneity of the NEP period was rapidly giving way to a soulless bureaucratic state supported by a vast police apparatus reminiscent of tsarist times. Mayakovskii's sincere efforts to publicize and expose to public ridicule what he felt to be the dangers and shortcomings of Soviet society were viciously attacked, as could be expected, by the petty and narrow-minded bureaucrats who had themselves felt the sting of his sharp criticism. Their attacks on him only served to convince him of the accuracy of his assessment.

Harassed by enemies and opponents, adrift in a society that no longer met his high standards and expectations, beset with personal problems, and suffering from boredom and isolation, Mayakovskii shot himself in April 1930. His suicide note was entirely rational and devoid of despair and self-pity. "Don't blame anyone for my death, and please don't gossip about it. The deceased hated gossip." His tragic death sent shock waves through the entire intelligentsia. He had always been *the* poet of the Revolution, the poetic spokesman of the working class, the leading proponent of socially useful literature, and yet his suicide seemed to many to be a slap in the face to the Revolution. Whether it was or not we shall never know, for even in death Mayakovskii served the Revolution. His legacy as a poet and a symbol has been enormous and despite all the vicissitudes of Soviet cultural policy since 1930, his image remains untarnished and his poetic genius unchallenged.

The prose counterpart of Mayakovskii was Eugene Zamiatin (1884–1937), author of the brilliant and influential anti-utopian novel *We*. As a young man Zamiatin joined the Bolshevik Party but quickly found the atmosphere sectarian, petty, and doctrinaire, and so he left the party before the 1917 Revolution. He was never an enthusiastic supporter of the Bolsheviks or the November Revolution. He was trained as a naval engineer and ship-builder, although his first love and real interest was literature. He began publishing stories in 1911 and was a well-known author at the outbreak of World War I. During the war he spent a great deal of time in England, supervising the construction of ships for the Russian navy. After the Revolution he found it difficult to fit into the new Soviet society and only with the help of his friend and fellow writer, Maxim Gorkii, was Zamiatin finally able to secure employment as a lecturer on literature at the Petrograd House of the Arts. Zamiatin continued to publish and eventually became the spiritual godfather of the Serapion Brotherhood, although not a formal member of the group. *We*, completed in 1920, and circulated but never published in the USSR, was published in English translation in 1924, the first of a series of Soviet writings which have enjoyed great success in the West.

Zamiatin revealed in *We* a frightening vision of the society he saw emerging in the Soviet Union. He foresaw a degeneration of Communism and feared the destruction of human freedom and individuality by the monolithic state. *We* is a satirical portrait of a future utopian city in which science and technology have provided every convenience (including an Astrodome-like glass cover to protect the city from the elements), but the inhabitants have been reduced to ciphers rather than individuals (men are known by consonants and numbers, women by vowels and numbers). Every facet of human activity—work, thought, leisure activity, sexual love—is carefully controlled by the "wise authorities." Transparent living quarters and constantly monitored activity make privacy or any concept of privacy a thing of the past. Every thought, action, and utterance is recorded; every deviation from the norm is ruthlessly suppressed. The main character of the novel is D-503, who has rebelled against the sterile conformity and has dared to engage in free thought, to entertain feelings of genuine love, and to develop a passionate interest in nature and the world about him—he is a more sophisticated Prisypkin. D-503 is eventually destroyed, or, more accurately, reprogrammed, and his "irrationality" is destroyed by the "wise authorities."

Zamiatin's novel may be interpreted as a warning, an alarm about the potential dangers of the future, stemming from the regime's unethical manipulation of science and technology to deprive man of his freedom and individuality. Such a document was, of course, unacceptable for publication in the Soviet Union. (*We* was the forerunner of Aldous Huxley's *Brave New World* and George Orwell's *1984*.) Many of Zamiatin's other writings annoyed the Soviet authorities, and a vicious campaign of vilification and denunciation (practices later all too familiar) was mounted against him in 1929. *We* was singled out as the worst example of Zamiatin's malicious attacks on Soviet society. He was prevented from publishing, forced to resign his teaching position, and ostracized by friend and foe alike. His old friend Gorkii finally came to his assistance in 1931 and delivered Zamiatin's letter of appeal to Stalin himself. Zamiatin began with dignity:

> The writer of this letter, a man condemned to the supreme penalty, appeals to you . . . to commute that penalty. You probably know my name. For me as a writer to be deprived of the opportunity to write is a sentence of death. Matters have reached a point where I am unable to exercise my profession because creative writing is unthinkable if one is obliged to work in an atmosphere of systematic persecution that grows worse every year.[5]

(Boris Pasternak or Alexander Solzhenitsyn could have written similar lines later). Owing to Gorkii's personal intercession with Stalin, Zamiatin and his wife were finally allowed to leave the Soviet Union in 1932. He died in Paris in 1937, conscious that his impact on Russian literature had been slight and that his major contribution had been training a generation of young writers. He proudly claimed that he taught them to write with "90-proof ink."

Zamiatin's contemporary, Boris Pilniak (the pen name of Boris Vogau, 1894–1938?), was one of the most popular and influential of the "fellow-travelers." His influence on Soviet literature in the 1920s was probably greater than that of any other writer. A productive author, his works were widely read and discussed and became extremely popular with the reading public. His first and in many ways his greatest achievement was his novel, *The Naked Year* (1922), woven out of a series of vignettes of the revolutionary era. These sketches, rather loosely tied together, recount the intense cruelty and impassioned hatreds unleashed by the Revolution, and portray the terrible suffering, unbelievable heroism, and optimism of the age with compelling pathos and energy. Pilniak's sympathies were not with the Bolsheviks (though he wrote about them positively), but with those seeking to free man from all compulsion and restraints, whether they were anarchists, Social Revolutionaries, or disillusioned Bolsheviks. He shared Zamiatin's concern about the dangers to human freedom and individuality engendered by efforts to organize all life according to some preconceived plan. Pilniak's clearest statement of his concerns was "The Tale of the Unextinguished Moon" (1926), which closely resembles the actual death of the Red Army's commander in chief, Michael Frunze. A Red

---

[5] Cited by Michael Glenny in "The Introduction" to E. Zamiatin's *We* (New York, 1972), p. 12.

Army hero of the Civil War falls ill and is ordered by the party to undergo surgery even though he knows instinctively such surgery will kill him. The party leader, known as Number One, insists that the hero, as a useful worker, ought to be repaired to continue being useful just like a piece of machinery. Pilniak castigates this callous, dehumanizing attitude, and in the story the Red Army commander dies on the operating table as if he had been cut down on the field of battle. This provoked a storm of criticism, the journal in which the story appeared was recalled, and Pilniak and the journal's editors were forced to denounce the story publicly as "a gross error."

Pilniak was thus already suspect when his short novel, *Mahogany*, appeared in Germany in 1929. Pilniak had, like many Soviet writers, sent his manuscript to Germany to be published simultaneously with the Soviet edition in order to gain international copyright protection (the Soviet Union did not subscribe to the International Copyright Convention). Unacceptable as written in the Soviet Union, the novel was only published in 1930 after complete rewriting, under the title *The Volga Falls to the Caspian Sea*. It deals with the construction of a dam and a hydroelectric plant that will destroy an ancient, historic town. The theme is the struggle between the "old" and the "new," between "history" and "technological progress." Pilniak's sympathies were clearly with "history," and his heroes were not the construction workers, but the mahogany collectors who cherish true craftsmanship and traditions and preserve what they can of the "old" in face of the advance of the "new."

THE SOVIET CINEMA (1917–1929)

Lenin was among the first to recognize the value of the cinema: "The cinema is for us the most important of all the arts." As a means of communication in an era of mass culture, the cinema is unsurpassed. Highly sophisticated messages can be recorded on film, duplicated in countless copies, distributed throughout a country, and projected on screens for millions of people with a minimum of technical equipment and trained personnel. Thus, the atmosphere was right for the development of Soviet cinema. There had been a well established Russian cinema industry before the Revolution, but almost all film directors and actors and technical personnel gathered up their equipment and left Russia after the Revolution. The Soviet cinema had no "bourgeois specialists" to depend upon or worry about as was the case in literature, music, and painting. The Soviet cinema was free to develop without opposition or tradition. Young enthusiasts were the first Soviet directors, and their spontaneity, ingenuity, and artistic sense left a deep impression on the Soviet cinema.

Two of the earliest Soviet directors of importance were Lev Kuleshov, who directed his first film at the age of 17, and Dziga Vertov, placed in charge of film coverage of the Civil War when he was 20. Vertov's documentary accounts of the Civil War helped to shape future Soviet films. Vertov developed the concept of the "camera-eye" (*kinoglaz*), which records what has occurred. Beyond that, it is the director's task to give meaning to the raw experience recorded by the camera through the process of cutting and arrangement of the film. In this manner the film becomes a powerful instrument of interpretation and education. Vertov carried his techniques further after the Civil War, recording scenes from Soviet life all over the country, editing them, and arranging them into the equivalent of filmed newspapers. He called these documentaries "film truth" (*kino-pravda*) after the newspaper of the same name.

The director Lev Kuleshov sought to apply Vertov's techniques to the feature film. He attempted to use Vertov's documentary realism to stimulate imagination and anticipation in the viewer, to make film an intellectual as well as a visual experience. The technical sophistication of his equipment may not have been very high, but he used it very creatively and intelligently. He combined documentary footage with pure fiction to create an artistic montage, which paved the way for the greatest of all Soviet film directors, Serge Eisenstein.

Eisenstein was trained as an architect, worked as a poster artist during the Civil War, and joined the Proletkult theater as a set designer where he came under the influence of the director V. E. Meierhold. Eventually he staged his own theatrical productions and moved to cinema only in 1924. He combined Meierhold's theatrical techniques, including a stress on the purely visual, caricature, contrast and contradiction, and combined them with Kuleshov's imaginative documentary montage to develop an original and imaginative style of his own. Eisenstein's first film, *Strike* (1924), began as a documentary but evolved into a powerful and imaginative portrait of the inequities of capitalist Russia. Eisenstein's use of visual symbolism enhanced the psychological impact of the film. He wanted to jolt his audiences with powerful scenes, shock them with startling visual effects, to create a "film-fist" (*kino-kulak*) to pummel the viewer with imaginative and thought-provoking images. *The Battleship Potemkin* (1926) was Eisenstein's greatest cinematic triumph. The film portrayed the brief revolt of the crew of the battleship *Potemkin* in Odessa during the Revolution of 1905. The hero of the film is the battleship itself, which gives birth to and sustains the revolutionary enthusiasm of the crew. The film was a powerful indictment of the callousness and inhumanity of the tsarist regime represented by such powerful images as the mechanical march down the famous steps of Odessa harbor by a coldly mechanical phalanx of tsarist troops and the unforgettably repulsive image of maggot-infested meat being given to the battleship crew by inhumane officers. *Potemkin* demonstrated just how powerful a political instrument the cinema could be. Still, Eisenstein's films, including *Potemkin*, were not great popular successes during the 1920s. Audiences seemed to prefer the lighter touch of foreign imports, and party censors and critics were always suspicious of Eisenstein's unorthodox methods. By the late 1920s he was beginning to have difficulties with the authorities.

Another great Soviet director of the 1920s was Vsevolod Pudovkin, whose works were less original than Eisenstein's but more accessible to audiences and thus more popular. He attempted to transfer the theater to film. He relied on professional actors and a clear story line, assets which gave his works a smoothness and continuity lacking in Eisenstein's more experimental films. Pudovkin drew his subject matter from works of fiction and attempted in his films to involve the viewer in the pyschological development of individual characters rather than in great historic events. His films were often sentimental and unsophisticated but were extremely influential in the development of Soviet cinema.

By the late 1920s party authorities began to take a greater interest in the cinema and attempted to control it as they did other aspects of culture. The party supported Vertov and his followers, advocates of the "filmeye" documentary techniques, now to be harnessed to the industrialization drive of the 1930s. Eisenstein and other more imaginative directors, along with a number of prominent film actors, emigrated in protest.

STALINIST CULTURE (1929–1953)

The political ambiguity of many works of the "fellow travelers" in literature and the lack of conformity in other cultural fields could no longer be tolerated in Stalinist Russia. By 1929 Stalin's personal dictatorship began to impinge directly on the lives of Soviet citizens as industrialization and collectivization began in earnest. Stalinist controls were now extended over culture. One sign of the shift away from the tolerance of NEP days was Lunacharskii's removal as Commissar of Education early in 1929. Shortly after came the first signs of tightening Party control over literature.

Literature.   The technique by which party control was extended to literature became the classic Stalinist pattern, repeatedly used and continually refined: to settle on scapegoats who could be used to intimidate and terrorize an entire group into acquiescence. The scapegoats on this occasion were Pilniak, Chairman of the All-Russian Union of Writers, and Zamiatin, Chief of the Leningrad Union of Writers. The attack on them and, by implication, on all "fellow travelers," signaled a sharp change in literary policy. The charges against Pilniak and Zamiatin, that they had arranged for publication of their works abroad to avoid Soviet censorship, were totally bungled by the prosecution (a mistake not so readily made in the future). Both writers presented solid evidence that works of theirs published abroad were totally unauthorized by them. The embarrassed accusers shifted their attack to the alleged anti-Soviet nature of these works. Attention was drawn to the supposedly anti-Soviet nature of "fellow travelers'" works. "Anti-Soviet" was defined as any hostile or neutral position. One was either for socialist construction in the USSR or was considered an "enemy of the people." The message was clear: the "fellow travelers" must cease to write unless they changed their ways and wrote "correct," politically acceptable literature.

Zamiatin and Pilniak, along with their supporters, were removed from leadership of the Union of Writers, over half its membership was purged, and its name was changed to All-Russian Union of Soviet Writers with the emphasis on "Soviet." The freedom and tolerance of NEP ended abruptly, the era of "party-oriented" literature began. The "fellow travelers" were henceforth expected to participate fully in the mighty industrialization effort, to prove their "solidarity" with the proletariat; their literary efforts were to serve the party and help in the construction of socialism. The Russian Association of Proletarian Writers (RAPP) won virtual control over the literary scene. Pilniak recanted, but Zamiatin stood his ground and eventually wrote his courageous and successful appeal to Stalin. RAPP, led by Leopold Averbakh, Alexander Fadeev, and Iuri Libedinskii, exerted heavy pressure on the "fellow travelers" and attacked "neo-bourgeois elements" in literature.

RAPP proved a disappointing weapon of literary control because its members did not accept the party view that literature could be produced on demand or by directive, nor the simplistic approach of a 1930 *Pravda* editorial. "Literature, the cinema, and the arts are levers in the hands of the proletariat which must be used to show the masses positive models of initiative and heroic labor." The emphasis was on the "positive," too simple and one-sided a view even for sincere proletarian writers like Averbakh and Fadeev. To them literature had to present honest, full-scale portraits of life—the bad and the good, the corrupt and the virtuous, the negative and the positive. Despite their enthusiastic support of the regime and willingness to serve as literary watchdogs, Averbakh and the proletarian writers of RAPP were out of step with party authorities who wanted literature and art to portray the heroic struggles to industrialize and collectivize the country only in the positive and optimistic fashion. Culture was conceived as a weapon in the hands of party leaders to propagandize, inspire, and mobilize the masses. Despite their proletarian biases and sympathies, RAPP writers were still too wedded to "objective art" and individualism. The next step in bringing literature to heel was to dissolve RAPP in 1932. Diverse literary groupings were abolished; henceforth all writers were to be members of a single national Union of Soviet Writers completely dominated by the party. To some "fellow travelers" these developments came as a welcome respite from arrogant goading by RAPP. Others, more perceptive and attuned to what was happening, saw this situation as the beginning of direct interference by Stalin and the party in the creative process.

More than two years passed before the full impact of the 1932 decisions was felt. Clearly, a great deal of opposition to party control of literature had to be overcome before the authorities could venture to convene an open congress of writers to formalize the situation. The First All-Union Congress of Soviet Writers met in August 1934. Of the 590 Soviet delegates attending, more than 60 percent were party members. There were many prestigious foreign guests. At this First Writers' Congress Andrei Zhdanov (1893–1948) first emerged as the Party's new authority on cultural affairs. He presented the main address, which clearly outlined the current status of the literary scene and outlined the future form and content of Soviet literature:

Our Soviet literature is not afraid of being called tendentious, because it *is* tendentious. In the age of the class struggle a non-class, non-tendentious, apolitical literature does not and cannot exist. In our country the outstanding heroes of literary works are the active builders of a new life. . . . Our literature is permeated with enthusiasm and heroism. It is optimistic, but not from any biological instinct. It is optimistic because it is the literature of the class which is rising, the proletariat, the most advanced and most prospering class.[6]

This was the genesis of "socialist realism," the aesthetic which still dominates every facet of Soviet culture. Zhdanov defined "socialist realism" as the portrayal of "real" life in all its revolutionary development, the aim of which was to promote the ideological reeducation of the masses in the spirit of socialism. The new doctrine was given respectability by the endorsement of Gorkii who presided over the Congress and lent his enormous prestige to the new policy. Delegate after delegate rose almost mechanically to reiterate Zhdanov's remarks and endorse the new party-oriented literary principle. So carefully orchestrated was the Congress that even the most prominent and respected writers dared not protest openly against a conception of literature so closely and completely identified with the party's political and economic goals. It was not known just how far Stalin was prepared to go to assure conformity to his "literary" and "cultural" views. In 1934, it was evident that if one expected to be a practicing writer, one had to be a member of the Writers' Union; to be a member one had to accept its statutes, which embodied Zhdanov's concept of literature as a weapon in the party's hands. How sharply this contrasted with the tolerant attitude of the 1925 party resolution on literature!

The enormous significance of the First Congress of Soviet Writers was not immediately recognized, nor was the full impact of socialist realism immediately felt. For one thing, literary contacts with Western writers increased and a flurry of flattering literary criticism and many translations of progressive Western authors appeared in the Soviet Union. (More than a hundred works by American authors alone were translated into Russian, including works by Hemingway, Dreiser and Dos Passos.) Moreover, despite the imposition of the narrowly defined socialist realism and the paralyzing atmosphere of the Great Purges in the mid 1930s, some tolerably good literature was produced during this period, a testimony to the indomitable spirit and vitality of literary traditions and to the skill of some authors in skirting around socialist realism as defined by Zhdanov. One example is Iuri Krymov's *Tanker Derbent* (1938), which superficially applied socialist realism in recounting the personal problems and uncertainties of men engaged in intense competition in the oil shipping business on the Caspian Sea. Many themes and concerns of the pre-socialist realism period continued to find a place in the literature of the 1930s. One genre in which socialist realism tended to be less obtrusive was historical fiction, which enjoyed a real renaissance in the 1930s.

---

[6] A. Zhdanov et al., *Problems of Soviet Literature* (New York, n.d.), p. 21.

Russian nationalism was stimulated powerfully by the rise of Nazism in Germany and gathering war clouds in the 1930s. In the year of the ideological reorientation of literature a new orientation in the writing of history was also decreed. M. N. Pokrovskii (1868–1932), friend and collaborator of Lunacharskii, had almost singlehandedly created a Marxist orientation among professional historians in the Soviet Union and had been responsible for virtually eliminating national history from school curricula. History was thus reduced to vague sociological categories involving the class struggle. National heroes ceased to play any meaningful role in history texts, and a whole generation of Soviet school children grew up with little knowledge of their past. Beginning in 1934, Pokrovskii and his historical school were denounced as anti-Marxists who failed to appreciate the progressive character of Russian historical development. The upshot was a reintroduction of national history and a cult of national heroes, which was reflected in the arts. Patriotic themes were developed by many authors who chose historical settings for their plays and novels. Many of these works dealt with the great military struggles of the Russian people against foreigners. Sergei Borodin wrote about the struggles against the Tatars in his novel *Dmitri Donskoi* (1937); Sergei Sergeyev-Tsenskii's portrayal of the Crimean War, *The Ordeal of Sevastopol* (1937–38), was well received, and Alexis Novikov-Priboi used the site of the famous naval battle of the Russo-Japanese War as the setting for his novel *Tsushima* (1932–35). Perhaps the most successful historical novel of the period was Alexis Tolstoy's unfinished three volume *Peter I* (1929–44), which became one of the great popular successes of Soviet literature, often considered a worthy companion of another great historical novel by a distant relative, Leo Tolstoy's *War and Peace*. Based on extensive historical research, *Peter I* presented a very positive portrait of the "Great Transformer of Russia," one which Stalin greatly admired.

Other themes emphasized were World War I, the Revolution, and the Civil War. Comparable to Tolstoy's novel, *Peter I*, was the simultaneous appearance of Michael Sholokhov's *Quiet Don* (1928–1940), which portrayed masterfully the lives of peasants and Cossacks during war, revolution, and civil war. He was less concerned with the nation's heroic struggle than with the moral and psychological problems of individuals struggling to grasp the significance of events which were engulfing them. Soviet critics have always claimed that *The Quiet Don* is the classic example of socialist realism, but in fact it bears little resemblence to the socialist realism of Zhdanov and the hack writers of the 1930s. Conceived on a scale comparable to *War and Peace*, *The Quiet Don* begins in 1912 and traces life in a quiet Cossack village before World War I. The outbreak of war disrupts the village and Sholokhov tries to measure the war's impact on individuals and families. The second volume deals with the difficulties of war, growing discontent, and the Revolution and its impact on the village and individual lives. The last two volumes record the bitter fighting of the Civil War. The novel touched a responsive chord in the Soviet reading public which discovered in Sholokhov's writing more substance, originality, and power than in all the five-year-plan novels of the proletarian writers put together. Indeed, so powerful and moving was the impression left, especially in the first parts of the novel, by an unknown writer that skepticism about the work's authorship was widespread. Wondering at the enormous ability of the author, some claimed that Sholokhov had obtained a manuscript written by a White army officer killed during the Civil War and had passed it off as his own work. Such charges have been investigated and officially denied, but still rumors persist (hinted at most recently by Solzhenitsyn) that Sholokhov is not the author of *The Quiet Don*. In the absence of concrete evidence to the contrary it must be assumed that Sholokhov wrote the novel and that he is a major writer whose study of human resiliency and fortitude represents one of the few bright spots of Soviet literature in the Stalin era.

The period of the Great Purges (1935–38) was one of the most frightening, debased, and sterile periods in Soviet history when virtually no one felt safe. The purge eventually cut deeply into the ranks of the Soviet intelligentsia (Solzhenitsyn claimed in the 1970s that more than 600 writers disappeared during the purges). Many established writers were publicly branded Trotskyite "enemies of the people" and disappeared without trace until hastily rehabilitated in the post-Stalin period. Many others simply disappeared. The literary intelligentsia was encouraged, indeed ordered, to devour itself as the Soviet cultural world was terrorized. The history of those terrible years was a picture of awesome contrasts—enormous heroism, abject cowardice and hypocrisy, and shrewd maneuvering. Some stumbled over themselves in their haste to denounce friend and foe alike as traitors, spies, saboteurs, and Trotskyites. Others tried to remain unnoticed and uncontaminated. Still others merely waited with patient resignation. The result was disastrous for Soviet literature and culture in general as the untalented and unscrupulous came to the fore as spokesmen for Soviet culture. The list of great talents lost during the Purges reads like a Who's Who of Soviet literature.

Prominent among these distinguished literary victims of Stalinism was Osip Mandelshtam (1892–1938), a highly educated poet of Jewish birth and one of the most talented writers of the 20th century. His elaborate poetry was replete with magnificent archaisms which revealed strong Greek Orthodox influence. In 1933–34 his work was criticized for not reflecting Soviet life and "distorting reality." Unusual outspokenness doomed Mandelshtam. Recalled the writer, V. Kataev: "He was a real opponent of Stalin . . . [In 1936 or 1937] he was shouting against Stalin; what a terrible man Stalin was." For an acid poem about the dictator, he was arrested during the Great Purge and died in a labor camp in 1938.

The Nazi invasion of June 1941 offered some respite from the terror of the purges and the concerns of socialist realism. The struggle for national survival against the Nazi onslaught required unity, cooperation, and common purpose only possible in a more tolerant and flexible atmosphere. Literature and the arts were enlisted in the war effort.

party controls, including censorship, were relaxed, and writers and artists found themselves freer to develop their talents. Many writers became war correspondents, went to the front, and sincerely appealed to the national spirit of the people, reporting countless stories of personal heroism, great battles, and partisan activities. Some of this was sheer propaganda to bolster morale, while some was first-rate eyewitness reporting. On occasion pieces would appear which qualified as literature. Ilia Ehrenburg (1891–1967) wrote a memorable two-volume collection of pieces entitled simply *War* (1941–42), an extraordinarily moving portrait of a nation struggling to survive the Nazi *Blitzkrieg*. There was no lack of motivation for writers as the Soviet people rallied to defend Mother Russia. The sieges of Leningrad and Stalingrad (especially K. Simonov's *Days and Nights* on the siege of Stalingrad), the transfer of industry, countless cases of personal sacrifice and unbelievable heroism provided raw materials for hundreds of war novels, narrative poems, plays, and short stories which inspired and informed the masses. This literary outpouring reflected the party's greater tolerance and flexibility early in the war, reminiscent for some of the diversity of the 1920s. As long as the writers and artists contributed to the war effort, they were allowed greater latitude than they had enjoyed since the 1920s.

As the war drew to a victorious end, the war-weary Soviet people anticipated a more relaxed and humane era in which to pursue their interests without interference. Terrible sacrifices had brought victory and unprecedented prestige to the Soviet Union. Most people believed it was time to reap the benefits, a loosening of the heavy-handed Communist dictatorship and a better way of life for all. There were hints of change to be found everywhere during the war. Strident party ideology was toned down during wartime cooperation with the Western democracies. The Soviet people anticipated a continuation of these trends, only to be disillusioned by a rapid return to prewar harshness. The siege mentality of the war years was to be continued into the postwar era.

Shrewd observers were aware how transitory was wartime liberalism as early as 1943, when the immediate threat to the survival of the Soviet Union had been removed and the Red Army went on a sustained offensive. As the tide of battle turned, the party began to express concern over erosion of ideological orthodoxy which might undercut the political reliability of the Soviet intelligentsia. The first indication of renewed party vigilance on the ideological front was an attack, at the end of 1943, on the popular satirist and short-story writer Michael Zoshchenko (1895–1958) whose short, humorous autobiographical sketches, *Before Sunrise,* were being successfully serialized in a Soviet journal. Abruptly, they were attacked in party publications as insipid, unpatriotic, and examples of "vulgar philistinism" (a favorite term of opprobrium in the postwar period). Publication of further installments was immediately halted. Several other prominent writers also came under fire for not following party guidelines with sufficient enthusiasm. This was a chilling reminder that there were limits to the party's tolerance. Even though it was preoccupied with the war, there was still time to watch the writers. The policies of cultural control remained. Still, many hoped that liberal changes in party policies toward culture could be encouraged in the postwar period. Some delegates to the first postwar conference of Soviet writers (May 1945) even went on record against any resumption of party interference in literature and culture in general. The party, it was argued, should not try to create a "miracle" in literature, a polite way of saying that great works of art could not be produced on command.

Such harmful attitudes had to be quickly corrected before they got out of hand. The party lost no time in making it clear that any temporary lapses of discipline during the war would no longer be tolerated. On August 14, 1946 the party's Central Committee issued a resolution condemning two prominent Leningrad journals, *The Star* and *Leningrad* for publishing ideologically harmful, apolitical works, adopting a servile attitude toward contemporary bourgeois culture, and disparaging Soviet life and the Soviet people. This party resolution contained the essential ingredients of the so-called *Zhdanovshchina*, the era of Andrei Zhdanov's ideological dominance. After the Central Committee attack, *Leningrad* was closed down, and *The Star* was saddled with a party bureaucrat as editor who was admonished to clean house and banish from the pages of the journal the "debased" works of authors like Zoshchenko, the poetess Anna Akhmatova (1888–1966), and others who shared their "anti-party" views. Once again, the party singled out "scapegoats" to initiate a new policy of strict control. The choice of scapegoats was not arbitrary. The focus was on Leningrad, its journals and authors, revealing the fear of party authorities, more accurately of Stalin, of the traditional Western orientation of Leningrad and its peculiar sense of independence, stemming from heroic survival of a three-year siege during the war. The choice of Zoshchenko and Akhmatova was no accident either. Both were influenced by pre-revolutionary models, both had won recognition in pre-revolutionary times, neither had been enthusiastic about the Soviet regime. Furthermore, Zoshchenko had come under fire earlier as a literary maverick.

The Central Committee resolution was elaborated on by Zhdanov at a meeting of Leningrad writers. His language was more virulent and vulgar than that of the original resolution. He bitterly denounced Zoshchenko's story "The Adventures of a Monkey," which had appeared in *The Star* in 1945. The story was a harmless satire about a monkey who escapes from a zoo. Zhdanov saw something sinister in the story.

> If you will read that story carefully and think it over, you will see that Zoshchenko casts the monkey in the role of supreme judge of our social order, and has him read a kind of moral lesson to the Soviet people. The monkey is presented as a kind of rational principle having the right to evaluate the conduct of human beings. The picture of Soviet life is deliberately and vilely distorted and caricatured so that Zoshchenko can put into the mouth of his monkey the vile, poisonous anti-Soviet sentiment to the effect that life is better in the zoo than at liberty, and that one breathes more easily in a cage than among Soviet

Anna Akhmatova (1888–1966)

people. Is it possible to sink to a lower political and moral level? And how could the Leningraders endure to publish in their journals such filth and nonsense.[7]

Zhdanov concluded that Zoshchenko's work was "a vile obscenity." Unless he changed his ways there would be no place for him in Soviet literature.

Zhdanov turned, with even greater vituperation to Akhmatova, a most distinguished Russian poetess. The main themes of her poetry were love and religion, which required her to remain silent during most of the 1930s. She began publishing again during and after the war in Leningrad journals. Zhdanov said about her poetry:

> [Her] subject matter is throughout individualist. The range of her poetry is pathetically limited. It is the poetry of a half-crazy gentlelady who tosses back and forth between the bedroom and the chapel. . . .

---

[7] Cited in Edward J. Brown, *Russian Literature Since the Revolution*, pp. 226–27.

Half-nun and half-harlot, or rather both nun and harlot, her harlotry is mingled with prayer.[8]

This was no idle criticism, but a lethal vendetta.

These official denunciations were quickly translated into action. Both writers were expelled from the Writers' Union. Zoshchenko was a broken man who lived in poverty and loneliness until he died in 1958. Akhmatova, too, was forced to remain silent, living in isolation and poverty, sustained only by her great moral courage until she could publish again in the post-Stalin period.

Anticosmopolitanism and the Arts.   The campaign against nonconformity was not limited to the literary sphere; it engulfed also cinema and the arts. Numerous films and other artistic works were pilloried as insufficiently ideological or too Western-oriented. To make sure there was no doubt about the party's new ideological policies, the Central Committee began publishing a weekly newspaper *Culture and Life,* which announced in its very first issue that "all the forms and means of ideological and cultural activity of the party and the state—whether the press, propaganda and agitation, science, literature and art, the cinema, radio, museums, or any cultural and educational establishment—must be placed in the service of the communist education of the masses." *Culture and Life* spearheaded the attack on the "degenerate bourgeois culture of the West," which, party authorities felt, had too strong a following in the Soviet Union. One of the most serious accusations against nonconformists was "cosmopolitanism," defined as servility before Western bourgeois culture. As part of the campaign against "cosmopolitanism" came demands to glorify everything Soviet and stress Stalin's genius." The creation of *Culture and Life,* Zhdanov's speeches, and the growing "cult of personality" were all part of a program designed to spell out within narrow limits what cultural workers must do. The results were disastrous. Soviet culture was reduced to a parody of itself. Everything in Soviet life was idealized, and the Soviet people were touted as the world's most advanced and progressive people, enjoying the most creative and original culture. The harsh facts of life in the postwar Soviet Union were ignored. Any attempt to provide a realistic picture of Soviet life was branded a "slander."

The "anti-cosmopolitan campaign" did not get underway fully until after the mysterious premature death of Zhdanov in 1948. Anti-cosmopolitanism had its roots in the immediate postwar period and received its first elaboration in Zhdanov's 1946 speeches. "Cosmopolitan" became synonymous with "unpatriotic," with "anti-Soviet." Everything in the West was decried, and imitation of Western models was considered "toadyism" or servility before Western bourgeois culture. Any deviation from approved party policies could be labeled "cosmopolitanism," the equivalent of treason. Writers ceased to write or wrote for "the desk drawer" (not for publication), or produced party approved drivel, then tried to make peace with themselves.

---

[8] Ibid., p. 227.

Music. The only branch of cultural activity to survive the deadening party directives was music, perhaps because the Soviet Union possessed some of the most talented and famous composers in the world: Prokoviev, Shostakovich, Khachaturian, and Miaskovskii—and a host of remarkable musicians—the violinist Oistrakh, the pianist Richter, the cellist Rostropovich, to mention only a few. Until the beginning of 1948, the Soviet musical world enjoyed a degree of artistic freedom and creative independence well out of reach of the literary and artistic intelligentsia. The Big Four—Prokofiev, Shostakovich, Khachaturian, and Miaskovskii—were idolized by the party and the Soviet public as the finest examples of Soviet creativity, justly deserving their international reputations. They were awarded every honor and prize the Soviet Union could bestow year after year. Suddenly, in January 1948, Zhdanov announced that this adulation had been a terrible mistake, that these "great" composers were anti-Soviet hacks, unworthy to use the title "Soviet composer." How did this abrupt about-face occur?

A curious silence descended over the Soviet musical world beginning in December 1947 when some long-awaited premiere performances went practically unnoticed in the press and a number of secondary musical figures simply disappeared without mention. Then in January 1948 Zhdanov presided over a turbulent meeting of composers and musicians. On February 10th the party Central Committee issued a resolution on music comparable to that on literature of 1946. This resolution on music viciously attacked long-honored and respected artists. The resolution announced:

> The state of affairs is particularly bad in the case of symphonic and operatic music. The Central Committee has here in mind those composers who persistently adhere to the formalist and anti-people school —a school which has found its fullest expression in the works of composers like Comrades Shostakovich, Prokofiev, Khachaturian, Shebalin, Popov, Miaskovskii, and others. Their works are marked by formalist perversions, anti-democratic tendencies which are alien to the Soviet people and their artistic tastes.[9]

The composers were further accused of creating music incomprehensible to the masses. "Disregarding the great social role of music, [these composers] are content to cater to the degenerate tastes of a handful of esthetizing individualists." The intent of the resolution was to drag serious music down to the level of "pop music."

> The divorce between some Soviet composers and the people is so serious that these composers have been indulging in the rotten 'theory' that the people are not sufficiently 'grown up' to appreciate their music. They think it is no use worrying if people won't listen to their complicated orchestral works, for in a few hundred years they will. This is a thoroughly individualist and anti-people theory, and it has encouraged some of our composers to retire into their own shells.[10]

---

[9] Cited in A. Werth, *Russia: The Postwar Years* (New York, 1971), p. 356.
[10] Ibid., p. 358.

Thus, music was not serving as a vehicle to reeducate the masses in the spirit of socialism! Give the people what they want, Zhdanov told the composers—simple ditties they could sing and hum while they merrily filled or overfilled their production quotas!

The impact of the decree on Soviet music was as disastrous as that of the 1946 decree had been on literature. Khachaturian and Prokofiev adapted themselves as best they could to the new party demands. Shostakovich, publicly repented for past "errors," then went right on composing as he always had, making an occasional obeisance to the party authorities. Miaskovskii, already an elderly man whose career stretched back into pre-revolutionary times, was destroyed by the resolution and died embittered and defeated in 1951. Prokofiev's work deteriorated in his last years, a change for which the resolution on music of 1948 was at least in part responsible. Furthermore, these decrees on music and literature must be viewed as part of a general anti-intellectual policy designed to drag culture down to the level of the masses rather than lift the masses up to the level of a sophisticated, creative culture. The *Zhdanovshchina* represented the triumph of the Stalinist bureaucratic mentality, which enjoyed kicking around those with genuine talent and ability. Zhdanov died in August 1948, but unfortunately his policies did not die with him. One of the supreme ironies of the postwar era was the renaming of the famous University of Leningrad to honor this man who had done so much to poison the intellectual climate of the Soviet Union. It took the death of Stalin to unleash winds of change and usher in a more tolerant and creative atmosphere.

Suggested Additional Reading

BOWRA, C. M. *Poetry and Politics, 1900–1960* (Cambridge, Eng., 1966).

BROWN, E. J. *The Proletarian Episode in Russian Literature, 1928–1932* (New York, 1953, 1971).

HAYWARD, M. and L. LABEDZ, eds. *Literature and Revolution in Soviet Russia, 1917–1962* (New York, 1963).

MAGUIRE, R. *Red Virgin Soil: Soviet Literature in the 1920's* (Princeton, 1968).

POGGOLI, R. *The Poets of Russia, 1890–1930* (Cambridge, Mass., 1960).

RÜHLE, J. *Literature and Revolution . . .* (New York, 1969).

SLONIM, M. *Soviet Russian Literature . . . , 1917–1967* (New York, 1967).

STRUVE, GLEB. *Russian Literature Under Lenin and Stalin, 1917–1953* (Norman, Okla., 1971).

KREBS, S. D. *Soviet Composers and the Development of Soviet Music* (New York, 1970).

SCHWARZ, BORIS. *Music and Musical Life in Soviet Russia, 1917–1970* (New York, 1972).

STEWART, B. H. *Mikhail Sholokhov: A Critical Introduction* (Ann Arbor, 1967).

YARMOLINSKY, A., ed. *A Treasury of Russian Verse* (New York, 1949).

36

Soviet Foreign Relations to 1941

SINCE THE Bolshevik Revolution, Soviet foreign policy has been an intricate combination of national and ideological elements. Some Western historians, stressing the elements of continuity, argue that geography and historical experience determine a country's basic interests regardless of regime. Emphasizing such persistent aims as the desire for security, urge to the sea, manifest destiny in Asia, and leadership of the Slav peoples, they contend that Soviet policy has been pragmatic and power-oriented. Other foreign scholars (notably former Communists) consider Marxism-Leninism paramount and a blueprint for world domination. Soviet leaders, they contend, have sought by every means to create a world Communist system run from Moscow and regard relations with the capitalist world as a protracted conflict lasting until one side triumphs. Believing that all Soviet moves aim to promote world revolution, this group concludes that it is fruitless, even harmful, for the West to make agreements with the USSR. A middle course views Soviet foreign policy as combining traditional and ideological features: revolutionary beliefs and ideology were uppermost at first; then pragmatic nationalism increased as Soviet leaders reverted to more conservative policies based on power, geography, and history.

What were the major aims of Soviet foreign policy down to 1941? At first Lenin and Trotskii strove to foment revolution abroad because they believed that otherwise world capitalism would crush Soviet Russia. War-weary Europe, especially Germany, seemed ripe for revolution, and Comintern leaders long remained confident that one would occur. A second, apparently conflicting aim soon emerged and became paramount: to preserve the Soviet regime and power base, if need be at the expense of foreign Communists. Moscow therefore sought to divide capitalist powers, prevent anti-Soviet coalitions, and woo colonial peoples. As long as their military weakness persisted, Soviet leaders aimed to avoid war with major capitalist powers.

To achieve these goals Soviet leaders forged a variety of instruments. The Comintern and Soviet party coordinated the Communist parties which developed in most foreign countries. Because until 1945 the

USSR was the only Communist power, most foreign Communists looked to Moscow for inspiration and direction. Especially under Stalin, Communist parties abroad became subservient to Soviet policy. Each had a legal organization which propagated Soviet views in democratic countries, was represented in legislatures, led labor unions, and criticized anti-Soviet cabinets. Illegal underground bodies, operating if the open ones were suppressed, conducted subversion and sabotage. Soviet commercial missions and skillful radio and newspaper propaganda supplemented the work of these parties.

The Soviet regime instituted a new diplomacy. As commissar of foreign affairs, Trotskii believed initially that diplomacy would soon disappear because world revolution was supposedly imminent. He declared confidently: "We'll issue a few decrees, then shut up shop." At Brest-Litovsk he had repudiated the norms and dress of old secret European diplomacy, but once the revolutionary wave subsided, Soviet diplomacy became important and its diplomats donned traditional formal dress. Moscow, however, scorned permanent accommodation with other nations, and Soviet diplomacy prepared the way for future expansion by lulling capitalist countries into false security, winning temporary concessions, and splitting the capitalist camp. Whereas under Lenin diplomacy remained innovative and flexible, Stalin bound his diplomats with rigid, detailed instructions.

The Soviets before 1941 made little use of force—the ultimate sanction in foreign policy—because of military weakness. During the Polish-Soviet War of 1919–20 they attempted unsuccessfully to spread revolution on Red Army bayonets, but only in 1939–40 was force used effectively against weaker Finland and the Baltic states.

In matters of foreign policy, Lenin's voice proved decisive. In the first months of the regime, policies were debated freely in the Central Committee and Politburo, and sometimes he was outvoted. Then the Politburo, under Lenin's direction, became the chief policymaking body in foreign affairs, and its decisions were transmitted to *Narkomindel* (People's Commissariat of Foreign Affairs) for implementation. Lenin formulated foreign policy, built up the Soviet diplomatic service, and the foreign commissar had no more independence than a tsarist foreign minister. Noted Foreign Commissar George Chicherin:

> In the first years of the existence of our republic, I spoke with him by telephone several times a day, often at length, and had frequent, personal interviews with him. Often I discussed with him all the details of current diplomatic affairs of any importance. Instantly grasping the substance of each issue . . . , Vladimir Ilich [Lenin] always provided in his conversations the most brilliant analysis of our diplomatic situation and his counsels . . . were models of diplomatic art and flexibility (*Izvestiia*, January 30, 1924).

The autocratic tsarist tradition in foreign affairs was restored fully by Stalin. Let us now examine Soviet policies chronologically. Each of the five periods between 1917 and 1941 reflected a different approach toward the antagonist, the capitalist world.

FIRST REVOLUTIONARY ERA, 1917–1921

Lenin inaugurated a new foreign policy immediately: his Decree on Peace proclaimed an end to secret diplomacy and, echoing President Wilson's Fourteen Points, pledged to "carry on all negotiations absolutely openly before all people." His government began publishing secret treaties of previous Russian regimes. Lenin hoped that the Decree would ignite revolution in Europe or induce the Allies to join the peace negotiations so that his weak regime need not face the Central Powers alone. After firing diplomats of the Provisional Government, Trotskii ran the new *Narkomindel* haphazardly with inexperienced personnel until George Chicherin, a former Menshevik, replaced him in March 1918 and restored order and efficiency.

Although the Allies ignored Lenin's appeal and his regime, peace was concluded quickly. At the Brest-Litovsk conference the Soviets proposed peace without annexations and indemnities. General Max Hoffman of Germany, however, aiming to erect satellite states in western Russia, insisted that German-occupied areas be separated from Russia. To obtain Ukrainian resources, the Germans reached agreement with the Rada and detached the Ukraine from Russia. Stiff German territorial demands caused Trotskii to suspend negotiations. Within the Central Committee, Left Bolsheviks and Left SR's urged revolutionary war to promote world revolution. Lenin advocated accepting German terms to save the Soviet regime, but the Committee approved Trotskii's compromise formula of "no war, no peace": Russia would not fight nor sign a treaty with imperial Germany. The Germans, however, advanced swiftly toward Petrograd until Lenin convinced the Central Committee's majority to accept new, harsher German terms. The Treaty of Brest-Litovsk (March 1918), a severe, imperialist peace, deprived Russia temporarily of its western borderlands and restored boundaries of the early 17th century. Though Russia lost about one third of its population and much industry and mineral resources, the Bolsheviks did not control the lost regions, and Lenin viewed the Treaty as only a temporary expedient. Brest-Litovsk gave the Soviet regime a desperately needed breathing spell, and the Paris Conference annulled it in 1919.

In the summer of 1918 the Allies intervened militarily in Russia's civil war.[1] According to Soviet historians, they sought to overthrow Bolshevism, set up spheres of interest, and exploit Russia's resources. Claimed *Pravda* in September 1957:

> The organizer and inspirer of armed struggle against the Soviet Republic was international imperialism. . . . [which] saw in the victory of the socialist revolution a threat to its own parasitical existence, to its profits and capital. To throttle the young Soviet republic, the imperialists, led by the leading circles of England, the USA, and France, organized military campaigns against our country.

George Kennan, a leading American diplomat, however, affirmed that the Allies aimed to restore an eastern front, win the war, and keep

---

[1] See above, pp. 475–77.

their supplies out of German hands. British and French military leaders pushed for intervention, but President Wilson sent token forces most reluctantly. Their troops did little fighting in Russia, but the Allies equipped and supplied Russian White forces long after World War I ended. Proponents (Churchill) argued that Allied intervention prolonged White resistance and stalled world revolution; recent opponents (Kennan) claim that it helped alienate Soviet Russia from the West. Allied intervention produced international stalemate because neither Soviet Russia nor the West could destroy the other; this situation suggested that outside powers cannot decide a civil war in a major country.

Allied hostility fed the extreme Soviet policies of those years. As German revolutionary socialists (Spartacists) fought for power in Berlin, Lenin in January 1919 invited leftist European socialists to the First Comintern Congress. Of 35 delegates who attended, only five came from abroad, and even they did not truly represent their parties. Russian-dominated from the start, the Comintern, or Third International, gave Lenin a nucleus for a world Communist movement, though it was too feeble then to organize revolutions abroad. During the Second Comintern Congress of August 1920, as the Red Army advanced in Poland, delegates from 41 countries waxed optimistic over prospects for world revolution until Soviet defeat before Warsaw dashed their hopes. Twenty-one conditions for admission which sought to impose the Russian party's tight discipline, were approved, but for some years the Comintern remained a loose collection of parties with factions and heated debates. By 1924, when it became a disciplined tool of Soviet policy, revolutionary opportunities abroad had dwindled.

The Allies excluded wartorn Soviet Russia from the Paris Peace Conference of 1919. Their ideological and military antagonism were at their peak, and in the West people were searching for Communists under every bed. Before the Conference, Prime Minister Lloyd-George of Britain wrote:

> Personally, I would have dealt with the Soviets as the de facto government of Russia. So would President Wilson. But we both agreed that we could not carry to that extent our colleagues at the Congress nor the public opinion of our countries which was frightened by Bolshevik violence and feared its spread. . . .[2]

Preoccupied with Germany, the Allies neglected Soviet Russia and its relationship with Europe. This rebuff fed Bolshevik hostility to the peace settlement and the League of Nations, which the Soviets regarded as a potential capitalist coalition against them, and drew the two outcasts—Weimar Germany and Soviet Russia—together.

In 1919 halfhearted private Allied overtures to Soviet Russia failed, but during 1920 relations began to improve. Once the Allies withdrew from Russia and the White armies were defeated, the Bolsheviks sought Western aid to restore Russia's wrecked economy. Lloyd-George, favoring recognition of Soviet Russia and restoration of normal economic

---

[2] Quoted in George Kennan, *Russia and the West Under Lenin and Stalin* (Boston, 1960), p. 124.

ties, helped end the Allied blockade. "We have failed to restore Russia to sanity by force. I believe we can save her by trade," he told Parliament. The Polish-Soviet War delayed normal relations, but by early 1921 Red Army defeats in Poland and Western desires to win Russian markets laid a basis for accommodation.

ACCOMMODATION, 1921–1927

Lenin warned Moscow leftists late in 1920 that an era of coexistence with capitalism was dawning. European capitalist economies were reviving, and even the intransigent Trotskii admitted: "History has given the bourgeoisie a fairly long breathing spell. . . . The revolution is not so obedient, so tame that it can be led on a leash as we imagined." The Polish conflict, ended by the Treaty of Riga (March 1921), left Soviet Russia weakened. The Ukraine proper became a Soviet republic, but Poland acquired parts of Belorussia and the western Ukraine. After seven years of strife, Russia's economy faced collapse. Lenin, confronting peasant uprisings and the Kronstadt revolt, launched the New Economic Policy at home and a conciliatory policy toward the West.

To strengthen itself for subsequent conflict, Soviet Russia now sought diplomatic recognition, trade, and credits from the West. Recognition would provide some security against attack and aid Soviet efforts to divide capitalist countries and win trade concessions. The West reacted favorably because European industries lacked sufficient markets and their governments, never truly committed to overthrow the Soviet regime, longed for normal relations. Obstacles to settlement included Comintern propaganda in the West and its colonies and especially Russian debts. Western claims, totalling about 14 billion rubles (roughly 7 billion dollars), included pre-World War I tsarist debts, wartime borrowing, and compensation for nationalized European property; the Soviets made huge counterclaims for damage done by Allied intervention. The West agreed that wartime debts and Allied damage to Russia about cancelled out, but the French especially sought repayment of the prewar debt, most of which they held, and reimbursement for confiscated property. When Russia demurred, debt negotiations broke down; but the Soviets, making token concessions on propaganda, obtained some short-term credits, trade agreements, and diplomatic recognition from all major powers except the United States. Even this refusal of recognition did not prevent extensive U.S. technological assistance and some Soviet-American trade during the 1920s.

The shift to accommodation enhanced the role of Soviet diplomacy, though Chicherin, the able foreign commissar (1918–30), faced severe problems. He had to compete with the Comintern, Profintern (international trade union organization), secret police, and foreign trade and tourist agencies, and the *Narkomindel* lacked even the authority of the tsarist foreign office. Nonetheless, these multiple agencies made Soviet policy flexible, helping compensate for economic and military weakness. Chicherin's Menshevik background and low party rank further complicated his position. The Politburo frequently bypassed the *Narkomindel*, the rival Comintern did not keep it informed, and the government, affirming that the Comintern was an independent agency, disclaimed responsibility for its moves. Nonetheless, Chicherin achieved real successes by able, persistent diplomacy.

The Genoa Conference (April 1922) marked his, and Soviet Russia's, diplomatic debut. Chicherin advocated general disarmament and tempted Europeans with prospects of trade and investment in Soviet Russia. Exploiting Allied-German antagonism, Chicherin agreed with the Germans at Rapallo to cancel economic claims, begin trade, and recognize each other diplomatically. Initiating independent postwar German foreign policy and splitting capitalist Europe, Rapallo reduced danger of economic or military action against Soviet Russia and ended its isolation. During the severe German crisis of 1923, the *Narkomindel* supported the Weimar regime (which survived), while the Comintern backed German Communists who sought in vain to overthrow it. In early 1924 the British Labor government recognized Soviet Russia as did most European countries.

Chicherin also suffered some setbacks. The "Zinoviev Letter" of October 1924, containing supposed instructions from the Comintern president to British Communists to subvert the armed forces, ruined budding relations with Britain. In 1925 the Locarno agreements between Germany and the former Allies, excluding the USSR, produced a shortlived European unity, but the Soviet-German Treaty of Berlin (April 1926) reaffirmed Rapallo and stipulated neutrality if either were attacked by a third power. In the 1920s Chicherin's *Narkomindel*, starting from weakness, scored important successes while the Comintern suffered reverses which tended to discredit the USSR. Their rivalry reflected differing tactics, not a conflict of basic aims.

Asia had remained secondary in Soviet policy. Lenin recognized the revolutionary potential of colonial peoples in undermining Western imperialism, but Soviet Russia was too weak to exploit it. Soviet Russia promptly repudiated tsarist imperial privileges and spheres of interest, most of which it could not retain anyway. To weaken Franco-British influence in the Near East and enhance Soviet security, Lenin supported such nationalists as Kemal Pasha of Turkey. The Soviets appealed to colonial peoples, notably at the Comintern-sponsored Baku Congress of September 1920. Zinoviev told delegates from 37 nationalities: "The Communist International turns today to the peoples of the East and says to them: 'Brothers, we summon you to a Holy War first of all against British Imperialism.' " This was purely a propaganda campaign, but later many Asian revolutionaries were trained in the USSR with profound consequences for the West.

Justifiably Soviet leaders regarded China as the key to Asia. They promptly condemned European imperialism there and renounced most special Russian privileges, though in 1921 the Red Army entered Outer Mongolia, ostensibly pursuing White generals, and established a Communist puppet government. Mongolia has served ever since as a buffer and Russian base on China's frontier. During the early 1920s Moscow maintained formal relations with the weak Peking government while

Soviet agents, led by Michael Borodin, penetrated the Canton regime. Its leader, Sun Yat-sen, who had led the Chinese Revolution of 1912, aimed to expel foreign imperialism and to achieve national unity and social reform. With Borodin's aid, he built the Kuomintang (Nationalist Party) on the model of the Soviet Communist Party. Sun's death in 1925 left a vacuum in Canton soon filled by Chiang Kai-shek, a young Moscow-trained nationalist officer. The Stalin-Trotskii struggle affected Soviet policy: convinced that China was entering her bourgeois-democratic revolution, Stalin favored proletarian participation in a national bloc including peasants and bourgeoisie and urged the Communists to enter the Kuomintang. Trotskii, however, advocated an armed Communist uprising and a direct transition to socialism in China. Stalin's policy prevailed, but during his northward expedition in 1926, Chiang slaughtered Communists in Shanghai, expelled Soviet advisers, and soon ruled much of China. Soviet policies there, based on inadequate knowledge of the situation, had plainly failed.

NEO-ISOLATIONISM, 1928–1933

Stalin's predominance brought a return to autocracy at home and abroad. Eliminating potential rivals, Stalin stressed the danger of imminent capitalist attacks on the USSR. He distrusted and envied cosmopolitan, intellectual Old Bolsheviks and moved to sever their ties with European socialism.

At the Fifteenth Party Congress, announcing that capitalist stabilization had ended, Stalin affirmed that capitalist powers were rearming rapidly and preparing to attack the USSR as Europe began a new revolutionary upsurge. The Sixth Comintern Congress of September 1928, an obedient Stalinist body, proclaimed the USSR the bastion of world revolution, and stressed that all Communist parties owed exclusive allegiance to Moscow and that their local interests must be subordinated to preserving the USSR. Communist parties must shun Social Democrats ("social Fascists"), the mortal enemies of Communism. This policy was a deliberate attempt to split the working class movement, cut European connections, and subject foreign Communist parties to rigid Soviet control. Despite Stalin's intransigent, alarmist tone, Soviet policy remained cautious and pacific, avoiding confrontations with capitalist powers. He apparently counted on world peace during the First Five Year Plan, and it is unlikely that he believed France would attack the USSR. Indeed, the Great Depression, beginning in 1929, convinced him that world capitalism faced imminent doom.

Stalin's doctrine of "social Fascism" helped undermine Weimar Germany, the only Western country with a large Communist party. Stalin detested the German Social Democrats' democratic, pro-Western policies, but distrusting German Communists, he doubted he could control them if they took power. Hoping to increase German dependence on the USSR, he played Communists against Social Democrats as German Communists collaborated with the Nazis to destroy the Weimar Republic. Believing that a Communist revolution would follow a Nazi victory, Stalin concluded that the road to a Soviet Germany lay through Hitler, and he thus bears some responsibility for Hitler's rise, which proved so costly to the USSR. Even after Hitler took power, Stalin underestimated him and regarded France as the USSR's main foe, apparently out of ignorance about German conditions and excessive faith in Leninism.

In the Far East Stalin pursued a cautious, defensive course. In 1928 he severed relations with Chiang's nationalist regime, and the next year, after local authorities seized the Chinese Eastern Railway, the Red Army restored it to Soviet control. Once Japan seized Manchuria in 1931 and turned it into the puppet state of Manchukuo, Stalin became gravely concerned about Japanese militarism. Reinforcing the Red Army in the Far East, he sought agreement with Japan, even offering to sell it the Chinese Eastern Railway. He restored relations with Chiang, tried to prevent Sino-Japanese cooperation against the USSR, and sought rapprochement with the United States.

Meanwhile the USSR was advocating peace and disarmament for Europe. Maxim Litvinov, Chicherin's longtime assistant who succeeded him as foreign commissar in 1930, proposed total disarmament at the Geneva Disarmament Conference of 1932 but found little response. In January 1933, Hitler assumed power in Germany and confronted Stalin with another shift in his foreign policy. Deep in the Depression, the West no longer threatened the USSR, but the chief beneficiaries were not Communism but aggressive German Nazism and Japanese militarism.

COLLECTIVE SECURITY, 1934–1937

Worried by the rising Nazi threat, Stalin gradually abandoned isolationism and opposition to the Versailles system to seek reconciliation with the West. During 1932 the Soviets had normalized relations with such neighbors as Finland, Estonia, and Poland, and with France. In 1934 Soviet diplomacy tried to erect an eastern Locarno to protect its western borders, but Poland demurred. Meanwhile normal relations were established with the United States. Soviet leaders, admiring American enterprise and efficiency, had long desired United States recognition, but conservative Republican presidents, Communist propaganda, and debts had blocked it. Invited to Washington by President Franklin Roosevelt, Litvinov provided assurances on propaganda and legal protection for Americans in the USSR. In November 1933, the United States recognized the USSR, and William Bullitt, who had led an unofficial mission to Russia in 1919, became the first American ambassador there. Receiving him warmly and ignoring strong American isolationism, Stalin mistakenly expected the United States to block Japanese penetration of China.

By 1934 Stalin realized that Nazism represented a real danger to the USSR. Though holding out an olive branch to Hitler, he noted that "revanchist and imperialist sentiments in Germany" were growing.

Hitler's nonaggression pact with Poland roused Soviet fears that he might encourage the Poles to seize the Ukraine. Growing concern over Germany accelerated a Soviet shift toward the Western democracies.

In September 1934, the USSR finally joined the League of Nations and abandoned its hostility to the Paris peace settlement. Maxim Litvinov, a Jew, a sincere anti-Nazi and a pro-Westerner, became a convincing spokesman for Soviet cooperation with the West. He used the League of Nations to proclaim a Soviet policy of peace, disarmament, and collective security against aggression. Contrary to assumptions in the West, Litvinov never made policy but merely executed Stalin's orders. His sincere belief in the new line won the confidence of Western liberals and socialists, but the League's failure to halt Italy in Ethiopia in 1935 revealed its weakness as a peacekeeping instrument.

Stalin also sought security through mutual defense pacts. In May 1935, France and the USSR, driven together again by fear of Germany, concluded a mutual assistance pact, but it lacked the military teeth of the old Franco-Russian Alliance; politically divided France took almost a year to ratify even a watered down version. The USSR pledged to aid Czechoslovakia militarily against a German attack if the French did so first as Stalin insured cautiously against being drawn into war with Germany while the West watched.

The Comintern obediently adopted a new Popular Front policy. Its Seventh (and last) Congress of July–August 1935 announced that all "progressive forces" (workers, peasants, petty bourgeoisie, and intelligentsia) should cooperate against Fascism, the most dangerous form of capitalist imperialism. Communists were instructed to work with socialists and liberals while retaining their identity within the Popular Front.

Failures of collective security in 1936 caused growing Soviet disillusionment. In March Nazi troops marched into the Rhineland in clear violation of the Versailles and Locarno treaties, using French ratification of the pact with the USSR as justification. Disregarding feeble French and British protests, the Germans refortified the Rhineland. This action shattered the collective security approach, undermined the Franco-Soviet Pact, and shifted the balance of power to Germany. Stalin realized that he could not count upon the West to resist Nazi aggression, which was now likely to turn eastwards. Soon Stalin began the Great Purge, eliminating rivals in case he later had to deal with Hitler. The West's apathy toward the Spanish Civil War, beginning in July, reinforced Stalin's suspicions. While Germany and Italy supported General Franco's Fascist revolt against the Spanish Republic, the West proclaimed nonintervention. The USSR, explaining that it was aiding the Popular Front against Fascism, provided important military aid to the Republic, saved Madrid from early capture, and greatly prolonged the conflict. Stalin may have hoped to draw the West into the war or that lengthy Fascist involvement in Spain would delay a move against the USSR, but during 1937 he withdrew most military aid from Spain and purged Russian Communists associated with it as Trotskyites.

Soviet efforts to cooperate with the West against Hitler before World War II virtually ended.

THE NAZI-SOVIET PACT

The formation of the Axis (Germany and Italy) in October 1936 and its conclusion of the Anti-Comintern Pact with Japan in November apparently deepened antagonism between Communism and Fascism, but Stalin was already abandoning collective security. For him 1937 was a year of watchful waiting abroad and relentless purge at home. Litvinov covered his retreat by continuing to advocate collective resistance to Fascism.

Nazi gains during 1938 destroyed the remnants of collective security and alienated the USSR from the appeasement-minded West. Hitler's annexation of Austria drew only ineffectual Western protests, and Stalin doubtless concluded that the West would not fight Hitler to save eastern Europe. Litvinov warned repeatedly that time was running out if the West wanted Soviet cooperation against Fascism. Collective security's last gasp was the May Crisis between Germany and Czechoslovakia: the Czechs mobilized, the West and the USSR pledged aid if Czechoslovakia were attacked, and Hitler backed down. At the Munich Conference in October, with the USSR excluded, however, France and Britain surrendered the Czech Sudetenland to Hitler and made Czechoslovakia indefensible. Western appeasement and Stalin's purge of the Red Army had destroyed collective security.

Tension with Japan stimulated Stalin's desire to settle with Hitler. He had tried to appease Japan by selling her the Chinese Eastern Railway in 1935. The outbreak of the Sino-Japanese War in 1937 temporarily relaxed pressure on the USSR, and Stalin signed a friendship treaty with China and supplied Chiang with arms and credits. When the Japanese army probed the Soviet border in major attacks at Changkufeng (July 1938) and Nomonhan (May 1939), it was repulsed with heavy losses, apparently convincing Tokyo that expansion into Siberia would be too costly.

By 1938 Stalin had eliminated all opposition and could dictate to the Politburo. "Stalin thought that now he could decide all things alone and that all he needed were statisticians," recalled N. S. Khrushchev. "He treated all others in such a way that they could only listen to and praise him." In May 1939, V. M. Molotov, Stalin's loyal secretary, replaced Litvinov as foreign commissar, suggesting that Stalin was preparing a major move in foreign policy. Molotov imposed rigid conformity upon the hitherto flexible and cosmopolitan *Narkomindel*.

During early 1939 the West and the Nazis vied for Soviet support. In March, Hitler's occupation of the rest of Czechoslovakia finally ended Western appeasement. France and Britain belatedly guaranteed the integrity of Poland and Rumania but failed to convince Stalin that they would really fight Hitler. In a speech to the Eighteenth Party Congress in March, Stalin, accusing the West of trying to provoke a Soviet-

German conflict, warned that the USSR would not be drawn into a war "to pull somebody else's chestnuts out of the fire." In August the West finally sent military missions to Russia, but it had moved too slowly and indecisively. Hitler, having decided to attack Poland, had already begun intensive negotiations with the USSR. On August 23, 1939 the Nazi-Soviet Pact, concluded in Moscow between the former ideological archenemies, shocked the world.

This fateful agreement contained both open and secret provisions. A public nonaggression pact pledged absolute neutrality "should one of the high contracting parties become the object of belligerent action by a third power." By securing Hitler's eastern flank, it encouraged him to invade Poland. A secret territorial protocol delimited Soviet and German spheres: Poland would be partitioned, with the USSR getting roughly the eastern third. Latvia, Estonia, Finland, and Bessarabia were assigned to the Soviet sphere; Lithuania was added later in exchange for some Polish territory originally occupied by Soviet forces. The two dictators' cynical bargain, in the worst tradition of the old diplomacy, resembled closely the Tilsit Agreement between Napoleon and Alexander I.[3] Once again Russia, bribed with temporary peace and territory in eastern Europe, gave a western tyrant a free hand to deal with Europe and England. Stalin may have interpreted the Pact then as a diplomatic masterstroke securing the USSR from invasion, giving it a buffer zone, splitting the capitalist world, and encouraging its parts to fight it out while Russia became arbiter of Europe.

If so, Stalin's hopes were soon shattered. He was appalled at the awesome Nazi *Blitzkrieg* which rolled over Poland and France and watched helplessly as the Soviet Union became economically dependent on Germany. At Hitler's insistence the Comintern repudiated the Popular Front. Seeking compensation, Stalin incorporated the Baltic states and demanded Finnish territory near Leningrad in exchange for part of Soviet Karelia. When the Finns refused, the Red Army attacked but met heroic resistance, suffered huge casualties, and displayed embarrassing weakness in the aftermath of the military purge. This unprovoked Soviet aggression, which the Soviets justify as an essential defensive measure, brought sharp Western condemnation, expulsion from the League of Nations, and almost provoked war with the West. Once Finnish defenses had been broken, Stalin hastily concluded peace, taking much of the Karelian Isthmus and Finnish bases. Later in 1940 he seized Bessarabia and northern Bukovina from Rumania to protect the vulnerable Ukraine.

Despite their large and mutually profitable trade, friction increased between Germany and the USSR. As early as July 1940 Hitler apparently decided to invade Russia, and Soviet stubbornness during the Molotov-Ribbentrop talks in November merely confirmed his decision. The German foreign minister tried in vain to turn Soviet aspirations southward to the Persian Gulf against Britain. Molotov insisted in pragmatic, un-Marxian fashion on Soviet domination of the Turkish

---

[3] See above, pp. 284–85.

Straits and German withdrawal from Finland. This tension resembled the growing differences between Napoleon and Alexander before the French invasion of 1812. Stalin's response to deteriorating relations with Germany was to appease Hitler. In April 1941, with war imminent, Stalin concluded a nonaggression pact with Japan which provided the Soviet Union with relative security in the east but facilitated the Japanese attack on Pearl Harbor eight months later.

Suggested Additional Reading

ADAMS, ARTHUR. *Readings in Soviet Foreign Policy* . . . (Boston, 1961).

BELOFF, MAX. *The Foreign Policy of Soviet Russia, 1929–1941*, 2 vol. (London, 1947–49).

BRANDT, C. *Stalin's Failure in China, 1924–1927* (Cambridge, Mass., 1958).

CARR, E. H. *The Soviet Impact on the Western World* (London, 1946).

DEGRAS, JANE, ed. *Soviet Documents on Foreign Policy, 1917–1941*, 3 vol. (New York, 1951–53).

———, ed. *The Communist International, 1919–1943* (New York, 1956).

EUDIN, X. and H. FISHER, eds. *Soviet Russia and the West, 1920–1927* (Stanford, 1957).

——— and R. NORTH, eds. *Soviet Russia and the East, 1920–27* (Stanford, 1957).

——— and R. SLUSSER, eds. *Soviet Foreign Policy, 1928–1934*, 2 vol. (University Park, Pa., 1966–67).

FISCHER, LOUIS. *Russia's Road from War to Peace* . . . (New York, 1969).

———. *The Soviets in World Affairs* . . . *1917–1929*, 2d. ed. (New York, 1960).

KENNAN, G. F. *Russia and the West under Lenin and Stalin* (Boston, 1960).

MOSELY, P. E. *The Kremlin and World Politics* (New York, 1961).

PONOMARYOV, BORIS. *History of Soviet Foreign Policy, 1917–45* (Ontario, 1970).

RUBINSTEIN, A. Z., ed. *The Foreign Policy of the Soviet Union* (New York, 1972).

SONTAG, R. J. and J. BEDDIE, eds. *Nazi–Soviet Relations* (Washington, D.C., 1948).

ULAM, ADAM. *Expansion and Coexistence* . . . *1917–1973*, 2d ed. (New York, 1974).

WEINBERG, G. *Germany and the Soviet Union, 1939–41* (New York, 1972).

37

War and Reconstruction, 1941-1953

BETWEEN 1941 and 1945 the USSR fought the greatest war in Russian history. Despite poor military preparation and massive popular hostility to the Stalin regime, Soviet Russia eventually defeated the Nazi invasion, and the Red Army advanced triumphantly into central Europe. The USSR was joined by Britain and the United States, but Soviet relations with the West were complicated by suspicion and differences over strategy and war aims. The Soviet role in World War II and Stalin as wartime leader remain controversial:[1] Was Soviet Russia caught by surprise in 1941, and if so, why? Why did the Red Army suffer terrible early defeats, then recover and defeat Germany? How important was Allied aid in the Soviet victory, and how great were the respective Soviet and Western roles in defeating Germany and Japan?

When the war ended, Stalin reimposed tight controls over a Soviet people yearning for liberalization and relaxation. Reindoctrinating or imprisoning millions exposed to Western influences during the war, he again isolated the USSR and blamed the West for domestic hardships. Heavy industry was stressed again at the consumer's expense, but reconstruction was rapid, and the USSR soon produced atomic and hydrogen weapons. Soviet Russia achieved dominance over eastern Europe, except for Yugoslavia, which escaped Stalin's grasp in 1948. Soviet expansion and Western resistance produced the Cold War between the two superpowers, and in Asia Red China emerged as a huge Soviet ally. How did postwar Stalinism compare with the prewar regime? How and why did the Soviet Union win control of eastern Europe? Was Stalin mainly responsible for the Cold War?

INVASION

At dawn on June 22, 1941 more than three million German and satellite troops crossed the Soviet frontier on a 2,000-mile front. Their

---

[1] See below, pp. 590–96.

MAP 37–1
USSR in World War II

Axis and occupied areas
June 22, 1941

Front lines in Russia

Russian and allied
drives 1941–1945

1938 boundaries

—·—— 1941 ——··— 1942

Russian boundary, 1941

—···— 1943 ——····— 1944

unprovoked attack inaugurated what the Soviets call "the great father-land war," the greatest land conflict in world history, and tested the Soviet regime and people to the limit. Despite warnings of impending attack from Soviet spies and foreign intelligence, the Nazis achieved complete tactical surprise. At first, uncertain whether it was invasion or a provocation, Moscow ordered Soviet troops to remain passive. Apparently Stalin believed that Hitler would not attack if the USSR fulfilled its commitments under the Nazi-Soviet Pact. When Ambassador Schulenburg delivered the German declaration of war, Foreign Minister Molotov queried: "Do you believe that we deserved this?"

Hitler's aim in Operation Barbarossa was to crush the USSR by crippling the Red Army in encirclements near the frontier, then to advance to the Archangel-Astrakhan line. Moscow, Leningrad, and most of European Russia would be occupied and Russian remnants expelled into Asia. Nazi Germany would obtain sufficient resources and manpower to dominate Europe and defeat England. Hitler and his commanders were confident that this could be achieved before winter.

At first, Nazi victories exceeded even Hitler's expectations. Soviet frontier forces were overwhelmed, many planes destroyed on the ground as Soviet soldiers and civilians were stunned by the suddenness and power of the German onslaught. In four weeks General Heinz Guderian's tank forces pierced to Smolensk, only 225 miles from Moscow, while the northern armies sliced through the Baltic states toward Leningrad. Hundreds of thousands of demoralized Soviet troops surrendered; border populations in eastern Poland, the Baltic states and the Ukraine welcomed the Germans with bread and salt as liberators from Stalinist tyranny.

Overconfidence and fanaticism caused Hitler and his associates to overlook or fumble golden military and political opportunities. On July 19, Hitler rejected Guderian's plea for an immediate strike against Moscow, ordering him instead against Kiev. That operation netted more than 600,000 Soviet prisoners but produced fatal delay in assaulting Moscow, the key to Soviet power, as Hitler insisted on a slower advance along the entire front. By October the Germans had occupied most of the Ukraine and surrounded Leningrad, but Red Army resistance was stiffening. Guderian was now unleashed, and by early December reached Moscow's outskirts, but an early winter, lack of warm clothing and tracked vehicles, and Siberian reinforcements stalled his advance. The year 1941 ended with a Soviet counteroffensive which drove the Nazis back from Moscow, opened a relief route into Leningrad, and recaptured Rostov in the south. Hitler's attempt to achieve quick victory in Russia had failed.

The Germans wasted unique chances to overturn Stalin's regime. Nazi agencies in Russia pursued conflicting policies. Many German army leaders and foreign office officials sought Russian popular support, but Nazi party and SS elements treated the people as subhumans, exterminating or exploiting even those ready to cooperate with Germany. Alfred Rosenberg's Ministry for the East favored autonomous German-controlled satellite states in non-Russian borderlands, but Goering's economic agencies grabbed their resources for Germany. No single course was implemented consistently, but German eastern policy (*Ostpolitik*) was brutal and inefficient. The Nazis aimed to colonize choice areas with Germans and exploit Soviet resources, but they achieved remarkably little. Occupying some 400,000 square miles of Soviet territory with 65 million people and rich grain areas, the Germans obtained only a fraction of what they secured from France or from Nazi-Soviet trade agreements. Incompetent and corrupt German officials, who flooded the USSR like carpetbaggers, contributed to this economic failure as they disregarded popular aspirations for religious freedom, self-government, and decollectivization. Himmler's extermination detachments liquidated not just Bolsheviks but thousands of innocent men, women, and children.

Why the initial Soviet collapse followed by recovery? Stalinists blamed setbacks on the Nazi surprise attack and credited recovery to a loyal populace which rallied to the motherland. Later, Khrushchev blamed early defeats mainly on Stalin's deafness to warnings of attack and inefficiency in using the breathing spell of the Nazi-Soviet Pact. In the West many attributed Soviet collapse to a revolt of the borderlands, and Soviet recovery mainly to Nazi brutality. George Fischer suggested that Stalin's initial paralysis of will had left an army and population used to dictation without instructions; once he reasserted leadership, the Soviet people again obeyed the regime.

By the end of 1941, the Soviet leadership had regained widespread public support. After two weeks of silence and seclusion (some reports claim he suffered a near nervous breakdown), Stalin appealed to the Soviet people by radio for national resistance to an invader seeking to turn them into "the slaves of German princes and barons" and restore the tsar and the landlords. A scorched earth policy must deny the Germans factories, food, and material. Stalin's call for guerrilla warfare behind German lines was reinforced by skillful nationalistic propaganda. Soon forests in the German rear were infested with partisans who tied down many German troops and disrupted communications. A State Committee for Defense, headed by Stalin and including Molotov, Voroshilov, Beria and Malenkov, became a war cabinet. Stalin as de facto commander in chief, concentrated military and political leadership in his own hands. He was arbitrary and made tactical blunders but generally proved an able wartime leader. Late in 1941 his decision to remain in threatened Moscow stopped panic, which had begun at the news that diplomats and government offices were moving to Kuibyshev on the Volga.

The Grand Alliance, formed against the Nazis and their allies in 1941, sent significant aid to the USSR. The day after the invasion Prime Minister Churchill of England offered the USSR friendship and military aid while refusing to recant his earlier attacks on Bolshevism. After Harry Hopkins' mission to Moscow in July, the United States began Lend-Lease assistance to Russia, which totalled some 15 million tons of supplies worth over $11 billion. Anglo-United States aid was important in repelling German attacks in 1942 and indispensable in subsequent Soviet counteroffensives. Japan's attack on Pearl Harbor in December 1941 brought the United States into the European war as well.

THE 1942 CAMPAIGN—THE TURNING POINT

In 1941 German losses had been so heavy that in 1942 Hitler's offensive had to be more limited. The Nazis still retained the potential to reach the Archangel-Astrakhan line and knock out the USSR, but Hitler removed most of his high command and interfered frequently in military decisions with disastrous results. Instead of trying to envelop and capture Moscow, he sought economic and psychological objectives which could not produce victory: seizing the Caucasus oilfields and Stalingrad on the Volga.

In June the Germans broke through the Don front, but Soviet resistance at Voronezh prevented an advance to the mid-Volga. Nazi armies rolled east, then southward into the Caucasus, but were halted short of the main oil fields. Stalingrad became the focus of the entire Soviet-German war. In bitter street fighting, General von Paulus' Sixth Army captured most of the city, but his army was bled white in frontal assaults instead of crossing the Volga and encircling the city. Heroic Soviet defense, reinforcements, and United States equipment turned the tide. In November a massive Soviet counteroffensive broke through Rumanian and Italian lines on the exposed northern German flank and cut off the entire Sixth Army. After relief efforts failed, von Paulus and the hungry remnants of his army surrendered. Here was the psychological and perhaps military turning point of the Soviet-German war. After Stalingrad, the Nazis were mostly on the defensive and ultimate Allied victory in World War II became a matter of time and blood.

In 1942 the Nazis again neglected a major political weapon. In July, Lieutenant General Andrei Vlasov, an able Soviet commander, surrendered with his men and agreed to help Germany achieve a free, non-Bolshevik Russia. He denounced the Soviet regime, collective farms, and Stalin's mass murders. Some on the German General Staff wished to use him and several million Soviet war prisoners against Stalin. Named head of a Russian National Committee, Vlasov sought to form an army of liberation (ROA), but Hitler blocked its use until German defeat was inevitable. The Germans employed more than a million Soviet volunteers as cooks, drivers, and orderlies but not in combat.

To counter an appalling desertion rate, Stalin appealed to Russian traditions and achieved reconciliation with the Orthodox Church. Soviet soldiers were told to serve the fatherland without socialist obligations. The army restored ranks, saluting, insignia, and officer privileges reminiscent of tsarist times and the regime's tone became strongly nationalist. At the 25th anniversary of the Bolshevik Revolution (November 1942), Soviet leaders, instead of calling for world revolution, stressed Slav soildarity. To convince the West that the USSR had abandoned world revolution, Stalin abolished the Comintern in 1943 and rewarded the loyal Orthodox hierarchy by restoring the patriarchate under state supervision. A church synod unanimously elected Metropolitan Sergei patriarch in September 1943; Sergei then proclaimed Stalin "the divinely annointed." These moves promoted unity and countered German efforts to foment disloyalty but did not signify changes in Stalin's domestic or foreign aims.

Inter-Allied relations remained good in 1942 primarily because the USSR badly needed Lend-Lease supplies. Even then, friction developed over a second front and over Poland. Throughout 1942 Stalin pressed for a cross Channel invasion; he was only partially mollified by the Allied invasion of North Africa in November. Stalin sought Western recognition of the USSR's June 1941 frontiers, but England and the United States, though making concessions, refused to sanction Soviet annexation of eastern Poland and the Baltic states.

SOVIET OFFENSIVES AND ALLIED VICTORY, 1943–1945

After Stalingrad, with brief exceptions, Soviet armies were on the offensive everywhere and bore the heaviest military burden until victory was achieved. After the failure of a German offensive at Kursk in July 1943, the Red Army attacked, jabbing ceaselessly at various points. U.S. tanks, trucks, and planes insured the success of the Soviet drive westward by making the Red Army highly mobile. The Red Army's numerical superiority grew steadily: by the summer of 1944, the Germans were outnumbered about three to one, and the Soviets commanded the skies and used their artillery effectively. The Germans could merely delay the Soviet advance and hope to exploit Allied divergences.

Once the Allies were advancing everywhere, their relations cooled. Both the Soviets and West feared that the other might make a separate peace, though there is little evidence that either planned to do so. As Soviet armies advanced, Stalin's attitude hardened as he sought to dominate eastern Europe and Germany. The Western allies, still sensitive in 1943 over the absence of a true second front, proved vulnerable to Stalin's diplomacy. Hitherto Soviet war aims had been defensive: to preserve Soviet frontiers, the Communist system, and Stalin's total control. Now Stalin sought also the Carpatho-Ukraine from Czechoslovakia to forestall Ukrainian disaffection. The USSR joined in the formation of the United Nations and approved its high-sounding declarations, but Stalin never accepted Western democratic aims. He refused to alter his views or make major concessions to his partners. Stalin realized that the surest way to achieve his aims was to advance westward as far as possible, then secure what he wanted from the West. Stalin and Molotov, notes Kennan, played their cards skillfully and carefully while the Western allies, holding a stronger hand, remained confused, divided, and unrealistic and let the Soviets score large gains.

Poland was the stickiest issue in inter-Allied relations. Early in 1943 the Germans discovered the corpses of thousands of Polish officers in the Katyn Forest near Smolensk. The Soviets accused the Nazis of the murders, but evidence is strong that Soviet security forces had killed the Poles in 1940. Assertions of this by the London Poles induced Stalin to sever relations with them. At Teheran in November 1943 Churchill proposed the Curzon Line of 1920 as Poland's eastern frontier with Poland to be compensated in the west at German expense. Stalin promptly agreed and suggested the Oder-Neisse Line as the western boundary. Poland's drastic shift westward would make it dependent on Soviet favor. Churchill finally persuaded the London Poles to accept this bargain; but when their new leader, Stanislas Mikolajczyk, went to Moscow in July, the USSR had already recognized the Communist-dominated Lublin Committee and turned over to it liberated Polish territory. Because the Western allies took no firm stand, Mikolajczyk was powerless. In August 1944, with the Red Army in Praga, across the Vistula River from Warsaw, Poles aligned with the London exiles rose against the Nazis: General Bor's men fought heroically, but the Soviet army did not aid them. Once the Germans had destroyed this core of potential opposition to a Soviet-dominated Poland, the Red Army drove the Nazis from Warsaw.

The second front issue caused serious inter-Allied friction until the Normandy invasion of June 1944. At the Moscow foreign ministers' conference (October 1943), the Soviets sought a definite Western pledge to invade France by the next spring. At the Teheran Conference in November, Churchill's idea of invading the Balkans, partly to prevent Soviet control there, was blocked by Stalin, whose support of Overlord, the American plan to invade France, insured its adoption. The Normandy invasion relieved Soviet fears of a Nazi-Western separate peace and speeded the end of the war. Later, Soviet historians claimed that Normandy was invaded to prevent a Soviet sweep to the Atlantic but had contributed little to Germany's defeat.

As Soviet forces advanced through Poland and the Balkans, Churchill sought to delimit postwar spheres of influence which Roosevelt repudiated. In June 1944 Churchill proposed a numerical formula for influence in eastern Europe: 90 percent Soviet influence in Rumania and Bulgaria and similar British control in Greece; Yugoslavia and Hungary would be split 50–50. Such formulas, however, meant little: the USSR could gain total control in its sphere by military occupation.

In February 1945, with Allied armies at the border of or inside Germany, the Big Three met at Yalta in the Crimea to outline a postwar settlement. Because the Red Army controlled most of Poland, only united and determined Western action might have salvaged some Polish independence. The West (especially Roosevelt), however, wished to continue cooperation with the USSR after the war. In regard to Polish frontiers Stalin insisted on the Curzon Line, overcoming halfhearted Western efforts to obtain Lwow and the Galician oilfields for Poland. In the west, Poland was to administer the region to the Oder-Neisse Line until the peace conference, and more than seven million German residents were expelled. Stalin insisted that the West repudiate the London Poles and recognize the Lublin Committee as the core of a new Polish government; the West proposed a wholly new regime formed from all political parties. Finally, the Allies agreed to broaden the

Churchill, Roosevelt, and Stalin at Yalta

Soviet-dominated Polish provisional government and hold "free and un-fettered elections" as soon as possible, but Stalin secured his basic aim: a Soviet-dominated Poland. Germany was to be de-Nazified, demilitarized, and occupied, and France was to receive an occupation zone from the Western share. The USSR would obtain half of a suggested total of $20 billion in German reparations. The Allies also agreed on voting in the United Nations and, by secret protocols, to Soviet entry into the Far Eastern war. Soviet gains at Yalta resulted from a strong military position, shrewd bargaining, and Western uncertainty.

After Yalta, Allied armies advanced swiftly. The Red Army overran Hungary, much of Austria, and crossed the Oder River. The Americans surged across the Rhine, and as Nazi resistance collapsed, the British urged them to occupy Berlin. General Eisenhower, however, halted at the Elbe River, then turned south to destroy the reputed German fortress in Bavaria. On April 17, Marshal Zhukov began his final offensive against Berlin, and on the 25th Soviet and American forces joined on the Elbe. While the Red Army was storming Berlin, Hitler committed suicide, and on May 8, 1945 his successors surrendered unconditionally.

THE USSR AND THE FAR EASTERN WAR

The United States had long sought Soviet participation in the war against Japan, but until victory in Europe was in sight, Stalin avoided the issue. Japanese neutrality in the German-Soviet war had permitted him to bring in Siberian troops to stop the Germans at Moscow and Stalingrad. Late in 1943, Stalin hinted to the United States that the USSR would enter the Pacific conflict soon after Germany's defeat. At Teheran Roosevelt assured Stalin that Russia could recover territories lost in the Russo-Japanese War. U.S. military chiefs estimated before Yalta that without Soviet participation, it would take the United States 18 months and cost up to a million casualties to subdue Japan after Germany's surrender. Consequently, at Yalta Roosevelt accepted Stalin's demands for territory in China and agreed to secure Chiang Kai-shek's consent to them.

On August 8, 1945, two days after the American atomic attack on Hiroshima, the USSR declared war on Japan. Justifying his action, Stalin cited somewhat lamely the "treacherous Japanese attack" in 1904 and the "blemish on the tradition of our country" left by Russia's defeat. "For 40 years we, the men of the older generation, have waited for this day." Stalin omitted to mention that in 1904 Russian Social Democrats had encouraged the Japanese to beat Russia quickly and later had celebrated Russia's defeat! Large Soviet forces overwhelmed the Japanese in Manchuria, continuing operations even after Japan's surrender on August 14. Soviet accounts claim that the Red Army's invasion of Manchuria, not the atomic bomb, caused Japan's surrender and brought subsequent victory to the Chinese Communists. For one week's participation in the fighting, the USSR was rewarded generously: it recovered southern Sakhalin, Port Arthur, Dairen, and the Manchurian railways and secured all the Kurile Islands. General MacArthur, however, rejected Soviet demands for an occupation zone in Japan.

Soviet gains in World War II, though large, were obtained at enormous human and material cost. About 193,000 square miles of territory with some 60 million people were added to the USSR of 1939: the Baltic states, eastern Poland, Bessarabia, northern Bukovina, eastern Karelia, the Carpatho-Ukraine, northern East Prussia, and Far Eastern territories. Almost 20 million Soviet citizens were killed; some 25 million more were homeless, and western European Russia lay devastated. The USSR emerged from the war a superpower whose economy and manpower were severely depleted.

POSTWAR STALINISM

Domestic affairs. As World War II ended, the exhausted Soviet people hoped for liberal change, freedom, and well-being. Instead, Stalin restored total control, resumed rapid industrialization, and isolated the USSR from the West. After the brief euphoria of victory celebrations, Stalin reimposed terror and party dominance, concealing rather successfully from the West signs of mass discontent revealed early in the war.

At war's end some five million Soviet citizens were outside Soviet borders. At Yalta the Allies agreed to help one another repatriate their nationals abroad. About three million Soviet war prisoners, forced laborers, and defectors resided in areas under Western control, mostly Germany, and about two million in Soviet-occupied regions, who were nearly all recovered. Until 1947 Western authorities cooperated by urging or forcing (as with General Vlasov) Soviet citizens to return home. In displaced persons camps, U.S. troops forced many to leave with Soviet officials. Western leaders believed naively that with the war over, all but traitors and criminals would happily return home. About half a million "non-returnables" stayed in the West by claiming they were Baltic or Polish nationals or by melting into the populace of disorganized Germany. The formerly pro-Soviet American journalist, Louis Fischer, noted that when Soviet Russians had a choice, they "voted against the Bolshevik dictatorship with their feet." Others committed suicide or redefected on the way to the USSR. Between 1945 and 1948, some 20,000 Soviet soldiers and officers defected from occupation forces, though until 1947 they were usually turned over to the Soviets for execution by their units. By 1948 Western cooperation ceased, but so did most opportunities to defect.

Returning Soviet soldiers and civilians, having seen Europe at first hand, confronted Stalin with a massive "debriefing" problem comparable with that of the tsarist regime after the Napoleonic Wars. Both governments solved it by repression and cutting ties with Europe, not with needed reforms. Isolation was essential for Stalin because Soviet living standards had fallen sharply while Russia's productive capacity had grown. His regime could not admit failure to produce abundance. Refusing economic dependence upon the West, Stalin found an alternative in quarantining his people.

Even before the war ended, a campaign began against the supposedly decaying "bourgeois" West. Closed party meetings learned: "The war on Fascism ends, the war on capitalism begins" anew. Stalin's victory toast to the Russian people began the glorification of everything Russian while minimizing or ignoring debts to the West. In a February 1946 speech, Stalin reaffirmed that while capitalism survived, war was inevitable; he revived the bogey of capitalist encirclement to justify internal repression and economic sacrifice. In 1946 the *Zdhanovshchina* began,[2] an ideological campaign associated with Andrei Zhdanov, who emerged during the war as heir apparent to Stalin. Zhdanov, who had proclaimed socialist realism *the* acceptable art form in 1934, urged a struggle against foreign influences in Soviet life which amounted to ideological war with the West in order to demonstrate socialism's cultural superiority. "Our role . . . is to attack bourgeois culture, which is in a state of miasma and corruption." Soviet intellectuals were denounced for subservience to Western influence or using Western themes or sources. The economist, Eugene Varga, was castigated for doubting there would be a postwar depression in the United States. Zhdanov's campaign, demanding absolute conformity to party dictates, stifled Soviet intellectual development.

Stalin's assertions of Russian achievement reached absurd extremes. Russian or Soviet scientists were credited with almost every major scientific discovery of modern times. The desire to prove Russian self-reliance reflected a persistent Russian inferiority complex toward the

---

[2] See above, pp. 541–45.

West. In 1950, Stalin, attacking the late N. Marr's linguistic theories, suggested that in the socialist future a single superior language, presumably Russian, would prevail. T. D. Lysenko, an obscure plant breeder, was encouraged to denounce Western genetic theories and Soviet scientists who accepted them. Stalin combined xenophobic Russian nationalism and anti-Semitism: Jews were "homeless bourgeois cosmopolitans." Connected with Israel's emergence as a state and the desire of Soviet Jews to emigrate there, this campaign featured ugly anti-Semitic cartoons and severe persecution, though certain prominent Jews such as Lazar Kaganovich and the writer Ilia Ehrenburg were spared to "prove" that the regime was not anti-Semitic.

Soviet economic problems in 1945 were staggering. About one quarter of the nation's capital resources had been destroyed, including some two thirds in Nazi-occupied regions. Industrial and agricultural outputs were far below prewar levels; railroads were damaged or disrupted. United Nations relief and British and Swedish credits aided reconstruction, as did reparations from Germany and former Axis satellites such as Finland. Newly sovietized eastern Europe had to supply minerals, foodstuffs, and machinery, and German war prisoners helped rebuild devastated cities. Without major U.S. credits which Stalin had hoped for, however, the reconstruction burden fell largely on the Soviet people. The Fourth Five Year Plan, stressing heavy industry and mineral production, aimed to complete rebuilding and exceed prewar levels in industry and agriculture. Prewar "storming" and rigid labor discipline were revived; NKVD (the secret police) slave labor was used extensively. Heavy investment in construction sought to overcome a catastrophic urban housing shortage. In heavy industry the Plan was largely fulfilled, although spectacular industrial growth rates partly reflected restoration of existing capacity in western Russia. Over half the 2,500 industrial plants shifted eastward during the war remained there, heightening the importance of new Siberian industrial areas. Consumer production and agriculture, however, lagged seriously, and during Stalin's lifetime Soviet living standards remained among the lowest in Europe.

With drought and severe shortages of livestock plaguing agricultural recovery, grain rationing continued until December 1947. Wartime peasant encroachments on collective farms were ended, and Khrushchev vigorously recollectivized the western borderlands. By 1950 the 250,000 prewar collectives had been amalgamated into about 125,000, but Khrushchev's ambitious scheme to build agricultural cities (*agrogoroda*) with peasants living in massive housing projects foundered on peasant opposition and lack of funds. In 1948 in the eastern Ukraine, Stalin inaugurated a giant afforestation program, called modestly his "plan to transform nature," to stop drought and sandstorms, but it achieved little. Stalin continued to neglect agriculture as, ensconced in the Kremlin, he apparently believed stories of agricultural prosperity related by fearful subordinates. Meanwhile collective farmers remained miserably poor and lacked incentives to produce.

Nonetheless, Stalin's draconian policies brought major heavy industrial growth and some agricultural recovery. By 1953 the USSR, the world's second greatest industrial power, was moving toward Stalin's seemingly fantastic 1960 goals of 60 million tons of steel, 500 million metric tons of coal, and 60 million metric tons of oil.

Foreign affairs. In the first postwar years, the USSR greatly expanded its influence in Europe and Asia. Stalin, despite a United States atomic monopoly until 1949, built a bloc of satellite states in eastern Europe and promoted Communist victories in China, North Korea, and North Vietnam. His blustering tone and actions, however, then caused the West to rearm and ended opportunities for advances. Soviet expansion clashed with United States containment to produce the Cold War.

Between 1945 and 1948 the Soviet Union established complete control over eastern Europe. According to Soviet accounts, Communist states there emerged from native revolutions against exploitative landlords and capitalists. To construct a security shield against a German resurgence or possible Western action, Stalin insured control in eastern European countries by "progressive elements," i.e. pro-Soviet regimes. Stalin wished to use these countries' resources to rebuild the Soviet economy and their territory to influence events in central Europe.

Soviet methods of achieving control varied, but the general pattern was similar, except in Yugoslavia where Marshal Tito won power independently. Red Army occupation was the first step, except in Czechoslovakia and Yugoslavia. National Communist parties, decimated during the war, were rebuilt and staffed mainly with Soviet-trained leaders subservient to Moscow. Usually the Soviets secured key levers of power for Communists—the army, police, and information media. Then coalition governments were formed from all "democratic, anti-Fascist" parties. With NKVD aid, political opposition was intimidated, disorganized, and fragmented. Conservative parties, accused (often falsely) of collaborating with the Nazis, were banned while socialist parties were split, then merged forcibly with the Communists. Resulting socialist unity parties allowed Communists to control the working class movement. Elections were often delayed until the Communists and their allies were assured of victory.

Poland, whose control was vital for Soviet domination of eastern Europe and influence in Germany, reflects these techniques clearly. Despite Yalta guarantees, Poland succumbed to Soviet domination after mild Western protests. During the war, the Nazis and Soviets had decimated its intelligentsia and officer class. Then the Red Army occupied Poland and the Communist-dominated Lublin Committee formed the nucleus of a coalition government. Mikolajczyk and three other London Poles were included, but they were powerless against Communists, who controlled the chief ministries and forced the socialists into a coalition. Mikolajczyk, very popular with peasants, democrats and conservatives, probably would have won a free election, but the police intimidated members of his Peasant Party, and in the manipulated elections of 1947, the leftist bloc won, and Mikolajczyk escaped into exile.

In Czechoslovakia the script was different but the results similar. It was the only eastern European country with an advanced industry and strong democratic traditions. A genuine democrat, Eduard Beneš, returned as president. At first the Communists (and the USSR) were popular, won 38 percent of the vote in the 1946 elections, and took over several key ministries. Under Beneš, Czechoslovakia was friendly toward the USSR and sought to be a bridge between East and West, but Stalin could not tolerate a democracy on his borders. In February 1948, when democratic elements tried to force the Communist interior minister to resign, the Communists, supported by armed workers and a Red Army demonstration on the frontier, seized power and forced Beneš to resign. Klement Gottwald established a Communist regime subservient to Moscow.

Soviet expansion in eastern Europe and tension over Germany helped produce the Cold War. In March 1945, Stalin and Roosevelt had exchanged heated notes over Poland; the Potsdam Conference in July revealed widening Soviet-Western differences. President Truman (who succeeded to the presidency after Roosevelt's death) and Foreign Minister Ernest Bevin of Britain (who replaced Churchill during the Conference) criticized Soviet policies in eastern Europe which violated the Yalta accords. Rapid deterioration of Soviet-Western relations stemmed partly from suspicion left after Western intervention in Russia in 1918–19 and partly from deepened differences between Soviet and Western ideologies and political systems after Stalin renewed autocracy in Russia. With the common enemy defeated, there was little to hold the USSR and the Western powers together. Stalin's xenophobia and paranoia were contributory: he considered the cessation of Lend-Lease in May 1945 and refusal of postwar American credits unfriendly acts. In his speech in February 1946, Stalin blamed the West for World War II and was pessimistic about prospects of future Soviet-Western friendship. Churchill's "Iron Curtain" speech at Fulton, Missouri, cited by Western revisionist historians as having launched the Cold War, came a month later. Churchill described the Soviet domination of eastern Europe:

> From Stettin on the Baltic to Trieste on the Adriatic an iron curtain has descended across the Continent. All these famous cities and the populations around them lie in the Soviet sphere and are subject, in one form or another, not only to Soviet influence, but to a very high and increasing degree of control from Moscow.

The Iranian crisis was the first skirmish in the Cold War. During World War II Allied troops had occupied Iran to guard supply routes to the USSR, but they were supposed to withdraw afterwards. Soviet troops, however, remained in Iran ostensibly to protect the Baku oilfields while in the north the Soviets, barring Iranian troops, fostered a Communist-led movement for autonomy. Accusing the USSR of interfering in its domestic affairs, Iran appealed to the United Nations, where it received strong support from the United States and Britain. In April 1946, the Soviets, after signing an agreement with Iran for joint exploitation of its oil resources, reluctantly pledged to withdraw.

Once the Red Army had left, Iran suppressed the northern separatists, and its parliament rejected the Soviet-Iranian treaty.

In the eastern Mediterranean, Soviet pressure and British weakness produced another crisis. Demanding "the return" of Kars and Ardahan (Russian from 1878 to 1918) and bases in the Turkish Straits, Stalin massed Soviet troops on Turkey's borders and conducted a war of nerves, but Turkey refused concessions. In neighboring Greece, the Soviets, Yugoslavia, and Bulgaria supported a Communist-led guerrilla movement against the conservative British-backed government. Because Roosevelt had hinted at Yalta that U.S. forces would withdraw from Europe within two years, Stalin hoped to dominate the region once Britain pulled out of Greece. To his surprise President Truman in March 1947 pledged economic and military support to Greece and Turkey, describing the issue as a struggle between democracy and Communism. Reversing traditional U.S. isolationism, the Truman Doctrine began a permanent United States commitment to Europe. The USSR denounced it as subversive of the United Nations and a "smokescreen for expansion."

In June 1947, the U.S.-sponsored Marshall Plan for European recovery confronted Stalin with a difficult decision because all European states were invited to participate. Molotov attended preliminary meetings, and Poland and Czechoslovakia showed deep interest until Stalin abruptly recalled Molotov, forbade east European participation, and denounced the Marshall Plan as concealed American imperialism. Doing so was a serious blunder: Soviet acceptance probably would have doomed the Plan in the U.S. Congress, thus enhancing Soviet prospects of dominating western Europe.

George Kennan, a leading U.S. expert on the USSR, advocated in July long-term containment of the Soviet Union by strengthening neighboring countries until Soviet leaders abandoned designs of world domination. "For no mystical Messianic movement—and particularly not that of the Kremlin—can face frustration indefinitely without eventually adjusting itself in one way or another to the logic of that state of affairs."[3] Kennan urged the West to adopt a patient policy of strength and await changes in Soviet conduct.

Creation of the Soviet-dominated Cominform (Communist Information Bureau) in Belgrade in September 1947, ostensibly to coordinate Communist parties of France, Italy, and eastern Europe, deepened ideological rifts with the West. At its founding congress Zhdanov, confirming the end of Soviet-Western cooperation, described the division of international political forces into two major camps: imperialist (Western) and democratic (Soviet). Zhdanov, stating that coexistence between them was possible, warned that the United States had aggressive designs and was building military bases around the Soviet Union.

Soon the breach widened further. The Czech coup of February 1948 ended any Western illusions about Soviet policy in eastern Europe. Early that year the British and U.S. zones in Germany merged and a

---

[3] "The Sources of Soviet Conduct," *Foreign Affairs* (July 1947), pp. 575–82.

currency reform was implemented. Stalin responded in June by cutting off rail and road traffic to Berlin in order to expel the West from that city. Some U.S. generals, such as Lucius Clay, favored forcing the blockade, but instead the United States flew in necessary supplies until Stalin lifted the siege in May 1949. Separate German regimes were soon formed: the Federal Republic in the west and the German Democratic Republic, a Soviet satellite, in the east. Alarmed and united by the Berlin crisis, the countries of western Europe and North America formed the North Atlantic Treaty Organization, a collective security system to counter huge Soviet conventional forces with European and American armies and atomic weapons.

In June 1948 Stalin's expulsion of the Yugoslav Communist Party from the Cominform opened a breach in east European Communism. Previously, Tito had been a loyal Stalinist, but for Stalin his independent policies and tight control over his party and state proved intolerable. The Soviets accused the Yugoslavs of slandering the Red Army and the USSR and deviating from Marxism-Leninism. Behind the verbiage lay more fundamental conflicts: Tito, already dominant in Albania, aspired to lead a Balkan federation which would break Soviet domination. Stalin overrated Soviet power ("I will shake my little finger and there will be no more Tito. He will fall."), tried to remove Tito, and ordered his satellites to blockade Yugoslavia. But the Yugoslavs rallied behind Tito, who turned to the West for support, and danger of general war probably restrained Stalin from invading Yugoslavia. Tito developed a national Communism which diverged markedly from that of the USSR in ideology, economy, and politics.

Stalin promptly purged other potential eastern European Titos. In Poland Wladyslaw Gomulka was removed in 1949 as the party's general secretary; in other satellites there were show trials and forced confessions resembling the Soviet purges of 1937. Soviet control was insured by an elaborate network that included Soviet troops, diplomats, secret police agents, and "joint companies" under Soviet control. Bilateral treaties enabled the USSR to exploit the satellites economically while Stalin's towering figure dominated a monolithic eastern European bloc.

In October 1949 the Chinese Communist victory over the Nationalists created a huge Eurasian Communist bloc of more than one billion people. Moscow, while aiding the Communists secretly, maintained formal ties with Chiang Kai-shek to the end. Mao Tse-tung, like Tito, had controlled a party and territory before achieving power, and China was too vast to become a satellite. In February 1950, after two months of tough bargaining in Moscow, Stalin and Mao concluded a mutual defense treaty against Japan and the United States. The USSR retained its privileges, treaty ports, and control of Outer Mongolia in return for modest amounts of economic aid, but a united Communist China would clearly be harder to control than a weak Nationalist China.

In his last years Stalin continued a forward policy while carefully avoiding war. Soviet support for national liberation movements tied down large British and French forces in Malaya and Indochina. In

June 1950, after Secretary of State Acheson hinted that the United States would not defend South Korea, Stalin encouraged the Soviet-equipped North Koreans to invade it, but a prompt military response by the United States and other United Nations members prevented a Communist victory. Subsequent Chinese intervention in Korea, probably arranged by Stalin, produced a stalemate but enhanced China's independence of Moscow. The United States in 1951 concluded a separate peace with Japan, which emerged as their partner in the Pacific. Stalin's miscalculations in Asia revealed limitations of Soviet power and the fact that opportunities for expansion had vanished.

The Nineteenth Party Congress and Stalin's Death. Stalin in October 1952 convened the Nineteenth Congress, the first party congress in 13 years. It approved the Fifth Five Year Plan, which featured the development of power resources, irrigation, and atomic weapons. The party now numbered more than six million members, but its top organs had become self-perpetuating and it had lost its proletarian character. Stalin instructed Khrushchev, former party boss of the Ukraine, to revise party statutes and carry through reform. Top party bodies were recast: a larger Presidium replaced the Politburo and the Orgburo and Secretariat were merged. George Malenkov had been Stalin's heir apparent since Zhdanov's sudden death in 1948. His 50th birthday in January 1952 had been celebrated with much fanfare, and he delivered the chief report at the Congress. But his position was under challenge, and before Stalin's death there was much jockeying for position within the party hierarchy.

Stalin had drawn the party line for the Congress in *Economic Problems of Socialism in the USSR.* Often considered his political testament, it discussed the transition from socialism to communism in the USSR without setting a timetable and emphasized the deepening crisis of capitalism. Stalin predicted that wars among capitalist states had become more likely than an anti-Soviet coalition. Stressing this theme at the Congress, Malenkov hinted that Soviet expansion would end temporarily while the USSR overtook the United States in military technology.

In January 1953 *Pravda* claimed that nine Kremlin doctors, six of them Jews, had hastened the deaths of high Soviet officials including Zhdanov. This "Doctors' Plot," part of Stalin's crude anti-Semitic campaign, may have been engineered partly by Alexander Poskrebyshev, sinister head of Stalin's personal secretariat. Seemingly, it was one event in a power struggle between the nationalist former adherents of Zhdanov and the more internationally oriented Malenkov-Beria faction. The atmosphere of suspicion and fear in Moscow suggested strongly that Stalin was planning a new purge. On March 4, however, Stalin, who long had suffered from heart trouble and high blood pressure, had a massive stroke and died the next day. The Malenkov-Beria group, facing demotion or destruction at his hands, may have speeded his demise, ending a quarter century of personal dictatorship and bloody brutality unmatched in world history. Unlike Hitler who left only ruins, however, Stalin bequeathed to his successors a powerful industrial state which owed much to his determination and satanic energy. Because Stalin failed to designate a successor, and the Soviet system provided no legal means to select one, a ruthless power struggle was inevitable.

Suggested Additional Reading

ARMSTRONG, J. A.   *Soviet Partisans in World War II* (Madison, 1964).

BIALER, S.   *Stalin and His Generals* . . . (New York, 1969).

CARRELL, P.   *Scorched Earth: The Russian-German War, 1943–44* (Boston, 1970).

CRAIG, W.   *Enemy at the Gates:* . . . *Stalingrad* (New York, 1973).

DALLIN, A.   *German Rule in Russia, 1941–45* (New York, 1957).

ERICKSON, J.   *The Soviet High Command* . . . *1918–41* (New York, 1962).

FEIS, H.   *Churchill-Roosevelt-Stalin* (Princeton, 1957).

FENNO, R. F. ed.   *The Yalta Conference* (Boston, 1955).

FISCHER, G.   *Soviet Opposition to Stalin* (Cambridge, Mass., 1952).

GALLAGHER, M. P.   *The Soviet History of World War II* . . . (New York, 1963).

HERRING, G.   *Aid to Russia, 1941–46* . . . (New York, 1973).

JORAVSKY, D.   *The Lysenko Affair* (Cambridge, Mass., 1970).

MAISKY, IVAN.   *Memoirs of a Soviet Ambassador:* . . . *1939–43* (New York, 1968).

NETTL, J. P.   *The Eastern Zone and Soviet Policy in Germany* . . . (New York, 1951).

PETROV, V. compiler.   *June 22, 1941* (Columbia, S.C., 1968).

SALISBURY, H.   *The 900 Days: The Siege of Leningrad* (New York, 1969).

SEATON, A.   *The Russo-German War, 1941–45* (New York, 1971).

SHERWOOD, R.   *Roosevelt and Hopkins* (New York, 1948).

SIMONOV, K.   *Days and Nights* (novel on Stalingrad).

SNELL, J., ed.   *The Meaning of Yalta* (Baton Rouge, La., 1956).

STEENBERG, S.   *Vlasov* (New York, 1970).

WERTH, A.   *Russia at War, 1941–45* (New York, 1964).

WHAELY, B.   *Codeword BARBAROSSA* (Cambridge, Mass., 1973).

ZHUKOV, G. E.   *Marshal Zhukov's Greatest Battles* (New York, 1969).

38

The Khrushchev Era

STALIN'S DEATH in March 1953 touched off a power struggle involving the major power levers in the Soviet system: the party, the state, the army, and the police. As Stalin's successors tried new methods of rule and sought public support, controls over the USSR and eastern Europe were relaxed considerably. Nikita S. Khrushchev, the eventual winner, lacked Stalin's absolute authority and wooed the public by denouncing Stalin's crimes, improving living standards, and barnstorming around the country. Khrushchev retained the chief features of the Soviet system, but he instituted important changes. Abroad, revolts in Poland and Hungary loosened Soviet control over the satellites. Between the USSR and Red China ideological and political conflict erupted which produced a Communist world with several power centers and varying approaches. How and why did Khrushchev win the power struggle in the USSR? How great was his authority afterwards? Why did he institute de-Stalinization and what were its effects? How fundamental were differences between Khrushchev's Russia and Stalin's? How did the Soviet position in world affairs change under Khrushchev?

POLITICAL

After Stalin's death the principle of collective leadership revived, and individual dictatorship was repudiated. As Stalin was placed in the Lenin-Stalin Mausoleum, his chief pallbearers—George Malenkov, Lavrenti Beria, and Molotov—appealed to the populace for unity and to avoid "confusion and panic." Briefly Malenkov held the two chief power positions of premier and first party secretary, but within two weeks he resigned as first secretary, and in September Khrushchev assumed that post. Marshal Zhukov, the World War II hero, became deputy defense minister as genuine collective rule and surface harmony prevailed.

In April 1953 *Pravda* announced that the "Doctors' Plot" had been a hoax. There was a shake-up in the secret police, and its chief, Beria, suddenly posed as a defender of "socialist legality" and urged liberal revisions of the criminal code. In June his security forces apparently tried a coup, but party, state, and army leaders combined against him. Beria was arrested and may have been shot in the Kremlin by Marshal Zhukov. In December his "execution" was announced and he became an "unperson." Subscribers to the *Great Soviet Encyclopedia* were instructed to remove his biography and paste in an enclosed article on the Bering Sea! The secret police came under closer party control.

For the rest of 1953 the Soviet press featured a jovial-looking Malenkov as the principal leader, who stressed consumer goods production and pledged that Soviet living standards would soon rise markedly. *Izvestiia*, the government newspaper, pushed this pro-consumer line until December 1954, but *Pravda*, the party organ controlled by Khrushchev, denounced it as "a belching of the Right deviation . . . , views which Rykov, Bukharin, and their ilk once preached." (And they had been executed!). In February 1955 Malenkov resigned as premier, citing "inexperience" and accepting blame for agricultural failures. Marshal N. A. Bulganin, a political general and Khrushchev appointee, replaced him as premier.

Khrushchev, like Stalin, consolidated his power behind the scenes. A genuine man of the people, he epitomized the revolutionary principle: careers open to talent. Born in Kalinovka, a village in Kursk province near the Ukrainian border, his ancestors were serfs, his father a peasant, then a coal miner, and his own childhood full of hardships. Attending the parish school, Khrushchev was the first member of his family to become literate. He joined the Bolshevik party in 1918, worked by day and attended school at night, fought in the Civil War, and revealed leadership and strong ambition. In 1929, still rough and uncouth, he was sent to the Moscow Industrial Academy to complete his education. By sheer ability and drive he came to lead its party organization. Three years later he became a member of the Central Committee and in 1935 headed the key Moscow party organization and guided it through the Great Purge. Invaluable to Stalin, he kept making speeches while others fell silent. In 1938 he was assigned to the Ukraine, completed ruthless purges there, and the next year entered the Politburo as a full member. During and after World War II he served as boss of the Ukraine. Throughout his career Khrushchev displayed toughness, resourcefulness, practicality, and a frank independence uncharacteristic of Stalin's henchmen. In 1950, surviving the failure of his untimely agricultural cities scheme, he stormed again into the inner circle of power.

After Malenkov's fall, Khrushchev as the most powerful member of the collective, shared power with Premier Bulganin and Defense Minister Zhukov. During 1955–56 he and Bulganin traveled to eastern Europe and Asia and undermined the power position of Foreign Minister Molotov. Meanwhile Khrushchev was replacing his rivals' supporters in the Secretariat with his own men.

Khrushchev dominated the Twentieth Party Congress of February 1956. In a dramatic secret speech, he denounced the crimes of the Stalin era and began building up his own image as Lenin's loyal follower as steps toward full power.[1] He overcame strong conservative opposition to the proposed speech by threatening to denounce Stalin publicly. In the speech he accused Stalin of fostering a personality cult, claiming infallibility, and out of paranoidal suspicion liquidating thousands of honest Communists and military leaders. Stalin, he claimed, had gravely weakened the Red Army by executing its top leaders, and his inaction in June 1941 had brought the USSR to the brink of defeat. Khrushchev's speech established him as a reform leader campaigning for basic political changes and won him wide support from younger, provincial party leaders. He sought to break the hold which Stalin retained over the party even from the grave, absolve himself of responsibility for Stalin's crimes, and dissociate himself from the dictator's closest lieutenants, Molotov and Malenkov. Khrushchev depicted Stalinism as an aberration and urged a return to Leninism and collective leadership. Molotov's resignation as foreign minister in June 1956 confirmed the power of Khrushchev's forces.

Opposition to Khrushchev was weakened, not broken. The upheavals in Poland and Hungary in late 1956[2] temporarily lowered his prestige. Khrushchev, by creating regional economic councils (*sovnarkhozy*), aimed to break the technocrats' hold over the central economic ministries, but this action stimulated his opponents to desperate countermeasures. In June 1957, while Khrushchev and Bulganin visited Finland, his rivals united, secured a Presidium majority and voted him out of office. Returning hastily, Khrushchev proved his mastery over the party apparatus. He weaned waverers (Voroshilov, Bulganin, Saburov, and Pervukhin) from his chief opponents (Malenkov, Molotov, Kaganovich, and Shepilov) and insisted that the Central Committee vote on his removal. With Marshal Zhukov's support, Khrushchev's provincial supporters were flown to Moscow. The Central Committee then reversed the Presidium's action and expelled his chief rivals, henceforth dubbed the "anti-Party group." Through maneuver and compromise, Khrushchev had won a decisive though limited victory.

During the next months Khrushchev consolidated his power. Marshal Zhukov, accused of building a personality cult in the Red Army, was removed from the Presidium and as defense minister and replaced by Marshal Rodion Malinovskii. In March 1958 Bulganin resigned and Khrushchev became premier. This rise confirmed his ascendancy, but during his six years of personal rule Khrushchev never possessed Stalin's authority. He could not dictate to the Presidium and he needed almost four years to remove his opponents from their posts. The "anti-party" leaders were exiled but not imprisoned, and even then Khrushchev's reform program was opposed strongly by a conservative group led by Michael Suslov.

Once in power Khrushchev reduced the apparatus of terror and rebuilt the party as his chosen instrument of power. Malenkov had released some political prisoners, but Khrushchev virtually closed down

---

[1] See problem 10 below.
[2] See below, p. 585.

Nikita Khrushchev

the labor camps, releasing millions, especially in 1956. Victims of Stalin's terror were rehabilitated, often posthumously, notably Marshal Tukhachevskii and other Red Army leaders purged by Stalin. Police influence declined, and a more relaxed and hopeful political climate developed. Khrushchev sought popularity by mixing with the people, traveling around the country, and delivering homely speeches to workers and peasants. Unlike Stalin, the Kremlin recluse, Khrushchev remained informal, jovial and talkative, bringing new and able people from industry to revive the party, which Stalin had demoralized by terror. Promoting his youthful provincial supporters, he increased party authority over the technocrats. Like Lenin, Khrushchev stressed persuasion, not coercion, and party congresses, rare under Stalin, now met regularly.

In January 1959 Khrushchev convened the extraordinary Twenty-First Congress to approve a Seven Year Plan[3] to begin building communism. Khrushchev launched a miniature personality cult, which described him as "Lenin's comrade-in-arms" and architect of the transition to communism. Urging preparation of a new party program, he stressed that the state's coercive aspects were "withering away" and

---

[3] See below, p. 581.

that some administrative and police functions could be transferred to "public" organizations such as the *Komsomol*. Opponents, however, objected to any premature dissolution of the state, and after the Congress Khrushchev's erratic behavior and policy shifts revealed his continuing problems with the opposition.

The Twenty-Second Congress of October 1961 convened mainly to adopt a new Party program, which proclaimed: "The present generation of Soviet people shall live under communism." But at the Congress Khrushchev renewed his anti-Stalin campaign and depicted Stalin's atrocities publicly in greater depth and detail. He accused Stalin of authorizing Kirov's assassination in 1934, which led to the Great Purge, and linked Molotov and Voroshilov with him in that affair. "Anti-party" elements, he claimed, had executed Stalin's repressive policies whereas his own regime had broken cleanly with the past. In response to demands of some delegates, Stalin's body was removed from the mausoleum and reburied in the Kremlin wall. Moderates in the Presidium (Alexis Kosygin, Suslov and Mikoian), however, blocked Khrushchev's efforts to expel "anti-party" leaders from the party. Then the Cuban missile crisis shattered his prestige, and only at the Central Committee's June 1963 plenum, which named Leonid Brezhnev and Nicholas Podgorny, his allies in the Presidium as party secretaries, did Khrushchev seem to recover his authority. The "anti-party" leaders were expelled from the party but not tried. Khrushchev's 70th birthday in April 1964 was appropriately celebrated by the Soviet press, but he was not portrayed as absolute or indispensable. His struggle with the opposition remained inconclusive and his victory incomplete.

After 1953 the relaxation of some totalitarian controls enhanced the Soviet regime's legitimacy for most of the population. With the overpowering authoritarian image of Stalin gone and with brutal police repression ended, a political reform movement developed among younger intellectuals and those released from Stalin's camps, which aimed at democratization, civil liberties, and preventing a reversion to Stalinism. Marxist-Leninist ideology became less effective and credible. The critical reaction of youthful dissidents ("sons") to the values of Stalinist "fathers" was reflected by reactions of Vladimir Osipov, later editor of the underground journal, *Veche*, to Khrushchev's secret speech:

> Overthrown was the man who had personified the existing system and ideology to such an extent that the very words "the Soviet power" and "Stalin" seemed to have been synonymous. We all, the future rebels, at the dawn of our youth, had been fanatical Stalinists [and] had believed with a truly religious fervor. . . . Khrushchev's speech and the 20th Congress destroyed our faith, having extracted from it its very core . . . , Joseph Stalin.[4]

The ensuing Hungarian Revolution profoundly affected Soviet university students. In Leningrad alone some 2,000 were disciplined or ex-

---

[4] Quoted in H. Morton and R. Tökes, *Soviet Politics and Society in the 1970's,* (New York, 1974), p. 10.

pelled for condemning Soviet armed intervention in Hungary. They formed a number of political and literary groups which produced *samizdat* journals.[5]

ECONOMY

After 1953, despite some major policy changes, the Soviet economy retained the chief strengths and weaknesses of the Stalin period and was run by men trained under Stalin. It remained a centrally planned economy in which heavy industry and defense were emphasized, though the consumer sector now received more resources. Under Malenkov, the collective leadership, to win public support, pledged that for the first time since 1928 consumer industry would grow faster than heavy industry. In April 1953 food prices were considerably reduced, but since key items such as meat were in short supply, the result was long lines and shortages. Compulsory bond purchases were reduced, and the worker's takehome pay increased but not the supply of available goods.

Khrushchev emphasized agriculture and began with a frank statement on its sad condition. Soviet collective farming in 1953 was unproductive and unworthy of a great power: half the population barely fed the other half. Soviet livestock herds, noted Khrushchev, were smaller than in 1928 or even 1916. Heavy taxes on private peasant plots discouraged production of desperately needed meat, milk, and vegetables. These shortcomings must be overcome in two to three years, warned Khrushchev, always in a hurry. During the next five years many steps were taken to foster agricultural growth. State prices for farmers' compulsory deliveries and over-quota shipments were raised sharply, especially for grains. In 1954 the average price paid for all agricultural products was more than double the 1952 level; in 1956 it was two and one half times higher. The state assumed most collective farm transportation costs, wrote off their old debts, and reduced taxes on private plots and limitations on private livestock holdings. Tractor and fertilizer production were expanded. Greater incentives to farmers and increased state investment in agriculture stimulated a 50 percent rise in output between 1953 and 1958.

Khrushchev's most controversial gamble was plowing up millions of acres of semi-arid soil in the virgin lands of northern Kazakhstan. Reviving a plan of 1940 which had never been implemented, he sought to solve the grain shortage by greatly increasing the cultivated area of the USSR. By the end of 1956, 88.6 million acres had been placed under cultivation, an area equal to the total cultivated land of Canada. Hundreds of new state farms were created, some 300,000 persons permanently relocated in Kazakhstan, and additional hundreds of thousands helped bring in the harvest. Leonid I. Brezhnev, then second party secretary of Kazakhstan, directed this campaign. In 1955 drought brought a poor crop, but an excellent 1956 harvest apparently vindicated Khrushchev's risky experiment.

---

[5] See below, p. 609.

The Sixth Five Year Plan, approved in 1956 by the 20th Congress, set ambitious goals for agriculture, including a grain output of 180 million tons. In 1957 began a hectic campaign to overtake the United States in per capita production of meat, milk, and butter as Khrushchev toured the country, made many speeches, and dismissed numerous officials. He pushed the development of state farms at the expense of collectives (*kolkhozy*) and amalgamated the latter into larger units. (*Kolkhozy* decreased from 125,000 in 1950 to 69,100 in 1958.) In 1958, Machine Tractor Stations[6] were abolished and *kolkhozy* were forced to purchase their machines.

Industrial growth in the 1950s continued to be rapid despite management problems. The Fifth Plan's goals were mostly fulfilled, and the Sixth Plan prescribed creation of a third major metallurgical base in Kazakhstan and western Siberia. Industrial management, however, became entangled with Khrushchev's drive for political supremacy. In February 1957 Khrushchev's scheme to scrap central industrial ministries in Moscow and replace them with regional economic councils (*sovnarkhozy*), eventually 107 in number, under Gosplan was approved. Causing a massive exodus of ministry personnel to the provinces, it made regional party secretaries virtual economic dictators. Khrushchev achieved his political aim of weakening the ministerial hierarchy but not the economic goal of greater industrial efficiency. The *sovnarkhozy* were supposed to overcome supply problems, avoid duplication, and improve regional planning, but they catered to selfish local interests, and individual enterprises often received no clear directives or got conflicting orders from various agencies. In the partial recentralization of 1963, *sovnarkhozy* were reduced in number and 17 larger economic planning regions were created. Khrushchev's insistence in 1962 on splitting party organizations into industrial and agricultural hierarchies caused much confusion and uncertainty especially because *sovnarkhozy* rarely corresponded with the new party units. By 1963 industrial and agricultural management were chaotic.

Meanwhile in 1959 the Sixth Five Year Plan had been scrapped in mid-course in favor of Khrushchev's grandiose Seven Year Plan "to construct the bases of communism."[7] It featured heavy investment in the chemical industry, nonsolid fuels, and development of Asiatic Russia. In 1961 Khrushchev raised some of the Plan's goals, such as steel output. During its first years, industrial progress remained impressive, but thereafter declining growth rates in industry and agriculture made a mockery of Khrushchev's 1961 party program, which foresaw the attainment by 1980 of industrial output and living standards far exceeding those of capitalist countries. In 1963 the Seven Year Plan was abandoned as impossible of achievement, a tacit admission that the party program likewise was unrealizable.

---

[6] See above, p. 505.

[7] Khrushchev's Plan called for an increase of 62 to 65 percent in national income (58 percent was achieved); 80 percent in gross industrial output (84 percent achieved); grain, 164 to 180 million tons (121 million achieved); and meat, 6.13 million tons (5.25 million achieved).

Agricultural stagnation after 1958 and lagging labor productivity slowed overall Soviet economic growth. Agricultural output, supposed to rise 70 percent during the Seven Year Plan, increased only 14 percent (crops only seven percent). Bad weather was a factor, especially in 1963, but other reasons were more important. Abolishing the MTS and selling their machinery had overburdened collective farms financially, and the machinery, dispersed among the farms, could not be properly maintained or repaired. Since meat and milk prices were set too low by the state to compensate *kolkhozy* adequately, these products were often sold at a loss. Renewed official pressure on private plots induced farmers to sell their livestock to the *kolkhozy*, reducing output of meat, milk and vegetables. Khrushchev's personal campaigns, interference, and hasty reorganizations did considerable harm. He did not create agricultural problems, but his policies often made them worse. In March 1962 he told the Central Committee:

> Communism cannot be conceived of as a table with empty places at which sit highly conscious and fully equal people . . . It is necessary to double and triple the output of major farm products in a short period . . . The development of agriculture is an integral part of the creation of the material and technical bases of communism.

Instead, Soviet grain production in 1963 fell 27 million tons below the high point reached in 1958, and millions of tons had to be imported from the United States and Canada. Poor economic performance after 1958 made Khrushchev increasingly vulnerable politically.

Beginning in 1958, the Soviet wage system was reformed with a trend away from the piece rates that had been prevalent under Stalin. New minimum wages in town and country gave the lowest paid workers substantial increases. To cut pay differentials, some higher salaries (e.g., professors) were reduced. The work week was gradually shortened, maternity leaves were lengthened, and industrial pensions and disability benefits were much improved. The currency reform of 1961 exchanged one new ruble for ten old ones; the rate of four rubles to the dollar was altered arbitrarily to 0.90 rubles per dollar. As direct taxes were further reduced, the turnover tax remained the chief source of state revenue.

In foreign trade important changes occurred under Khrushchev. The USSR abandoned Stalin's policy of exploiting the European satellites economically, scrapped the joint companies which had done so, and paid fairer prices for eastern European goods. In 1954 the multilateral Council for Mutual Economic Assistance (COMECON) had been revived, though most Soviet trade with eastern Europe remained bilateral. The USSR had moved into the foreign aid field, and in 1953 China received a long-term Soviet credit of 520 million rubles (The Soviets had removed equipment worth more than three times that much from Manchuria in 1945!). After Khrushchev visited India in 1955, a major program of foreign economic aid to it began, partly to compete with the United States in the Third World. The Soviets supplied goods on credit, especially to India and Egypt, for later repayment in goods. Soviet imports and exports both increased sharply. Using 1955 as the base year (100), imports in 1950 had been 54.6 and exports 56.7. By 1958 they were 148.4 and 130 respectively.[8]

Living standards of most Soviet citizens improved considerably under Khrushchev, but this rise whetted their appetites for more. Beginning in 1956, housing construction spurted and private home building received more state support. Even millions of new apartments, mostly in massive, ugly blocks, however, could not satisfy demand. Between 1953 and 1964 the Soviet population rose from 188 to 228 million, mostly in cities. Just before his fall, Khrushchev declared that the chief task of the near future was "a further rise in the living standard of the people. . . . Now when we have a mighty [heavy] industry, the party is setting the task of the more rapid development of the branches that produce consumer goods. . . ." Performance did not match these promises.

FOREIGN AFFAIRS

Soviet foreign policy quickly discarded its rigid Stalinist mold to adopt flexible, varied tactics. Malenkov began the shift, and Khrushchev, stressing peaceful coexistence with the West from February 1956, continued and extended this new approach. It had to overcome a conservative hard-line opposition, led first by Molotov and later apparently by Suslov, which favored a more aggressive, anti-Western course. Stalin's successors found it increasingly difficult to maintain leadership of the Communist bloc and world Communist movement in the face of Chinese and Yugoslav challenges.

After Stalin's death the collective leadership promoted détente with the West and China as Premier Malenkov warned that nuclear war might destroy all mankind, not just capitalism. In July 1953 an armistice ended the Korean War, and at the Geneva Conference of 1954 the USSR supported settlement of the Indochina conflict. The tone and manners of Soviet diplomacy began to mellow. Unable to coerce Red China, Soviet leaders courted it, promising technical aid, loans, experts to assist Chinese industrialization and agreed to end special privileges, abolish joint companies, and return Port Arthur to China.

Soviet leaders wished to prevent West Germany from rearming and entering NATO, but they refused to sacrifice their East German satellite. Early in 1954, a four-power conference called to reach a general German settlement ended in stalemate. After West Germany joined NATO, the Soviets set up the Warsaw Pact in May 1955, a defensive alliance of the satellites and the USSR with the latter commanding all the military forces and legalizing the presence of Soviet troops in eastern Europe.

Foreign trips by top Soviet leaders, beginning in 1955, fostered a new image of Soviet foreign policy. Khrushchev made a pilgrimage to Belgrade, blamed the Soviet-Yugoslav breach of 1948 on Beria, and

---

[8] A. Nove, *An Economic History of the USSR* (London, 1969) p. 352.

MAP 38–1
USSR and Eastern Europe since 1945

FINLAND
• Viborg
• Leningrad

SWEDEN

Baltic Sea
• Reval

ESTONIA
• Pskov

• Riga
LATVIA

North Sea

Annexed by Poland from Germany
Memel **LITHUANIA**
• Kovno

Königsberg • **EAST**
• Vilna
• Bremen   Stettin •   **PRUSSIA**
• Minsk

GERMANY   • Poznan   Warsaw   • Bialystok
Berlin •

• Bonn   Erfurt •   Dresden •   **POLAND**   • Pinsk
• Breslau

SILESIA

• Prague   • Przemysl   • Lvou   **SOVIET UNION**
Nuremburg •   **CZECHOSLOVAKIA**   Crakow   *Galicia*

FRANCE   • Munich   **AUSTRIA**   • Uzhgorod   Chernovtsy
Vienna •

SWITZ.   • Budapest   Jassy •   • Kishinev
Bessarabia

Trieste •   **HUNGARY**

RUMANIA
Semi-independent since 1963

Belgrade •   • Bucharest
ITALY   *Black Sea*
YUGOSLAVIA
Independent since 1948

Adriatic Sea   **BULGARIA**
Sofia •   *Strongly pro-Soviet*

Tirana •
ALBANIA
Aligned with China since 1961   **GREECE**   *Aegean Sea*   **TURKEY**

Russian occupied zones in Austria (evacuated in 1955) and Germany	Former German and Czechoslovak territory annexed by Russia in 1945
British, French, and American occupied zones	Principal areas of anti-Soviet protest and revolt 1953–1968 crushed by Soviet military intervention (East Germany, Hungary, Czechoslovak and by strong political pressure (Poland)
The "Iron Curtain" in 1948	

Adapted with permission of Macmillan Publishing Co., Inc. from *Russian History Atlas* by Martin Gilbert. Cartography by Martin Gilbert. Copyright © by Martin Gilbert.

over Molotov's strong objections, achieved reconciliation with Marshal Tito. The expanding Soviet foreign aid program and the wooing of such neutral countries as India signified the replacement of Zhdanov's two-camp thesis (socialism vs. capitalism) with a more flexible three-camp concept. In May 1955 the USSR signed an Austrian peace treaty which ended four-power occupation and made Austria a neutral country. Apparently Moscow hoped that West Germany would leave NATO in order to achieve German reunification on a similar basis. This policy culminated in the Geneva Summit Conference (July 1955) between President Eisenhower and a smiling Khrushchev and Bulganin. The amiable "Geneva spirit" produced no substantive agreements but reduced Cold War tensions and enhanced Khrushchev's prestige.

A crisis confronted the USSR in eastern Europe in 1956. Without Stalin's awesome image, the unpopular satellite regimes proved vulnerable to public agitation for change. As Soviet controls relaxed and a degree of diversity appeared, a workers' uprising in East Germany (June 1953) had to be crushed by Soviet tanks. Khrushchev's secret speech further undermined the satellite regimes. In June 1956, riots in the Polish industrial city of Poznan swelled into a national movement of liberalization and brought the hasty restoration of Wladyslaw Gomulka, purged by Stalin, as first secretary of the Polish Communist Party. When top Soviet leaders stormed into Warsaw on October 19th, the new Polish leadership presented a united front. In a compromise solution Poland won domestic autonomy while remaining in the Warsaw Pact and pledging loyalty to the USSR in foreign affairs. Such "domesticism" became a model for other eastern European countries. Preserving Soviet domination of the region, it freed the USSR from detailed supervision of domestic affairs in the satellites.

Meanwhile in Hungary a broad popular movement led by students and intellectuals demanded drastic political reforms. Premier Imre Nagy failed to halt Stalinist Hungary's rapid disintegration. After a revolt in Budapest (October 23), Nagy announced that Hungary would leave the Warsaw Pact, become a neutral country and restore a multiparty system. Much of the Hungarian army joined the insurgents who appealed to the West for aid. Janos Kadar, hastily named as the new first secretary of the Hungarian Party, "invited" in Soviet troops, which soon crushed the Hungarian rebels as thousands of Hungarians fled into exile. The Soviet Union showed in Hungary that it would act militarily in its sphere of interest whenever Communist rule was threatened, a move that demonstrated anew the existence of Communist control in eastern Europe based not on consent but on Soviet bayonets and the unreliability of satellite armies.

Toward the West, Khrushchev combined "peaceful coexistence" with bluster and threats. To him coexistence meant avoiding war and preventing nuclear rearmament of West Germany. The USSR sponsored the Rapacki Plan (October 1957), named after the Polish foreign minister, for a nuclear free zone in central Europe. Khrushchev's caution during crises over Taiwan and Lebanon involving the United States in 1958 distressed hard-liners in Moscow and Peking. The growing Chinese challenge helped provoke Khrushchev to deliver an ultimatum to the West over Berlin in November 1958, hoping to force it out of that city. When his ultimatum instead stimulated Western unity and determination, Khrushchev backed down. His erratic policies toward the West reflected his weakness at home and vulnerability to conservative critics.

At a meeting in November 1957 to celebrate the 40th anniversary of the Bolshevik Revolution, the 12 ruling Communist parties issued the Moscow Declaration, which stressed the unity of the socialist camp headed by the USSR. The Yugoslavs, affirming that every country should determine its own road to socialism, refused to sign and accused the USSR of bureaucracy and departures from true Marxism-Leninism; Moscow retorted that Tito was a revisionist kowtowing to U.S. imperialism. Although the second Soviet-Yugoslav dispute (1958–61) avoided an open breach, Yugoslav independence and the potential threat of national Communism to Soviet leadership were reaffirmed.

After 1957 Soviet foreign policy was influenced strongly by the triangular Soviet-U.S.-Chinese relationship. Khrushchev was caught between his desire for détente with the West and the maintenance of Soviet leadership of the Bloc against more militant China. Seeking to score points against "American imperialism" in the Middle East, he backed Arab states against pro-Western Israel and Turkey and rattled his rockets. The growing Soviet commitment to the Arabs proved expensive, especially the construction for Egypt of the Aswan Dam, which the United States had refused to finance.

Renewed Soviet overtures to the United States ended in failure. After his Berlin ultimatum had failed to budge the West, Khrushchev at the 21st Congress (January 1959) made warm references to the United States, and in September he became the first Russian ruler to visit the United States. This trip was a personal triumph for Khrushchev but produced no concrete agreements except a plan to hold a summit conference with President Eisenhower. When a U.S. U-2 reconnaissance plane spying over Soviet territory was shot down and its pilot captured, and Eisenhower took responsibility for the flight, however, an angry Khrushchev sabotaged the summit and withdrew his invitation to Eisenhower to visit the USSR.

More serious was the growing rift between the USSR and China, which now became public and disrupted Bloc unity. Between 1957 and 1960, though their relations seemed harmonious, mounting Soviet criticism of China's industrial "Great Leap Forward" suggested that China might reach Communism before the USSR. Khrushchev's party program of 1961 was in direct response to this Chinese challenge. The Chinese also condemned Soviet détente with the West. In 1960 began thinly concealed mutual vilification: the Chinese attacked Yugoslav "revisionism," the Soviets denounced Albanian "dogmatism," but clearly they were striking at each other. Sino-Soviet tension was only partly ideological. Mao was now the senior leader of world Communism and in intrabloc disputes the Chinese adopted an orthodox, Stalinist line, which was supported by some of the Soviet "anti-party group." Militance in promoting revolution and national liberation won the Chinese widespread support in Asia and Africa. A unified Red China challenged the Soviet position in Asia and posed a potential threat to underpopulated Siberia. Noting niggardly Soviet economic aid to them, the Chinese complained that Khrushchev was more generous to nonaligned India and Egypt. Asserting that tsarist Russia in the 1850s had acquired the Maritime Province unfairly, Chinese maps showed portions of the Soviet Far East as Chinese territory. Khrushchev withdrew some Soviet technicians from China and sought to dissuade the Chinese from developing nuclear weapons, but in 1959 Peking decided to manufacture its own. In April 1960, *Red Flag* of Peking, denouncing Khrushchev's policy of coexistence with capitalism, affirmed that nuclear war would destroy imperialism but not the socialist camp. At the Rumanian Party Congress in June, Khrushchev, quarreling violently with the Chinese delegates, castigated their leaders as nationalists, adventurists, and "madmen" seeking to unleash nuclear war.

Attempts to resolve the Sino-Soviet dispute failed. In the summer of 1960, a world Communist Congress in Moscow, representing 81 parties, sought to restore unity. Khrushchev, however, clashed with the Chinese over power-political issues. Soon afterward Albania, smallest and most backward of European Communist states, defied Khrushchev openly, praised Stalin, relied upon Chinese support, and boycotted the Soviet 22nd Congress. Chou En-lai, after defending Albania at the Congress, left suddenly and was greeted demonstratively in Peking. Rumania also began to assert independence of the USSR, especially in economic matters, and established good relations with China. In 1963 Rumania proclaimed virtual neutrality in the Sino-Soviet dispute and even voted occasionally against the Soviet Union in the United Nations. The Sino-Soviet quarrel promoted polycentrism in the Communist world and disintegration of the Bloc.

After President Kennedy's inauguration in 1961, Khrushchev sought concessions from the United States to compensate for his troubles in the Bloc. The key issues were Cuba and Berlin. In April 1961 the defeat of U.S. supported Cuban exiles in the inept Bay of Pigs invasion revived Khrushchev's self-assurance. Meeting Kennedy in Vienna that June, Khrushchev threatened to sign a separate peace with East Germany unless an overall German settlement were reached soon. The ensuing Berlin crisis revealed Kennedy's coolness and determination, though East Germany built the Berlin Wall to halt the westward flow of refugees. Khrushchev removed his time limit and advocated nuclear free zones in Europe and the Far East.

In the fall of 1962 the Cuban missile crisis threatened to provoke nuclear war between the USSR and the United States. Khrushchev had been seeking to conclude a German peace treaty and prevent China and West Germany from acquiring nuclear weapons. His decision to install medium range missiles in Cuba was apparently a gamble to solve mounting domestic and foreign problems with one bold stroke: Once

Khrushchev meeting Kennedy in June 1961

his missiles were installed, he might bargain with the West over Berlin and nuclear free zones. U.S. aircraft detected the Soviet installations, however, and President Kennedy ordered a sea blockade of Cuba (October 22). Khrushchev had the choice of withdrawing the missiles or fighting a United States far superior in long-range missiles and local naval power. Khrushchev prudently chose withdrawal only to be taunted by the Chinese for "adventurism" in placing the missiles in Cuba and cowardice in removing them!

Peaceful resolution of the missile crisis improved Soviet-American relations. In 1963 they and Britain agreed to ban the testing of nuclear weapons in the atmosphere. A "hot line" was set up between Washington and Moscow to reduce the danger of accidental nuclear war. Khrushchev's freedom of maneuver was sharply restricted by the Sino-Soviet quarrel. During 1963–64 he tried but failed to round up support for a world Communist conference to expel the Chinese and reassert Soviet hegemony over world communism.

KHRUSHCHEV'S FALL

In October 1964 Khrushchev was suddenly removed from power. The official statement of October 16 in *Pravda* declared:

> The plenum of the Central Committee satisfied the request of N. S. Khrushchev to relieve him of the duties of first secretary of the Central

Committee, member of the Presidium of the Central Committee and chairman of the Council of Ministers of the USSR in connection with advanced age and poor health.

Actually his health was good and many statesmen older than he were directing their countries' destinies. Subsequently his successors accused Khrushchev of "harebrained schemes," recklessness at home and abroad, fostering a new personality cult, undignified behavior, and dangerous experimentation. His prestige had suffered severely from the Cuban crisis, and between 1960 and 1963 he had almost been toppled on several occasions, but in 1964 his power still had far exceeded that of other Presidium members. Apparently Leonid Brezhnev had organized a powerful coalition of interest groups against him. While Khrushchev was on vacation in the Crimea, the Presidium voted him out of office after he had refused to depart gracefully and refused his demand to submit the issue to the Central Committee. Having antagonized the military leaders by reducing the size of the ground forces, Khrushchev this time lacked the army support to reverse this verdict. Overnight Khrushchev became emeritus, an unperson rarely mentioned and relegated to obscurity but granted a fine apartment and limousine. The transfer of power, smooth and orderly, marked a peaceful evolution of the Soviet political system away from Stalinist terror. The Presidium had become a society of relative equals whose collective weight exceeded that of an individual leader.

A combination of foreign and domestic failures caused Khrushchev's unexpected downfall. His Presidium colleagues blamed him for the Cuban fiasco and setbacks in Berlin. The intensifying conflict with China had split the world Communist movement and encouraged Albania and Rumania to assert full or partial independence. The Soviet position in eastern Europe and with it Soviet security were imperilled. At home the Soviet economy was stumbling. Industrial growth rates were falling, agriculture had stagnated, and Khrushchev's boasts of soon overtaking the United States sounded hollow. His decision in 1962 to split the party into industrial and agricultural segments had created confusion and antagonized party traditionalists and technocrats. Reduction of Soviet ground forces and efforts to promote détente with the West had alienated influential military men. Khrushchev's hasty reforms and mistakes welded together a potent conservative coalition. His basic policies, however: de-Stalinization, reducing terror, aiding agriculture and the consumer and increased contacts with the West, apparently were sound. Khrushchev had led the Soviet Union through the difficult post-Stalin transition, insured the party's predominance, and maintained the Soviet Empire without resort to mass terror.

PROBLEM 10: DE-STALINIZATION—STALIN'S ROLE IN THE PURGES AND IN WORLD WAR II

Was Joseph Stalin a "great revolutionary despot" (Deutscher) or a monster worse than Caligula, as his successor, Khrushchev, suggested in 1956? Did Stalin exemplify Soviet Communism or represent an aberration from it because of his "cult of personality" after 1934? Why was the Great Purge launched, and what were its results? Was Stalin or his generals to blame for Soviet defeats early in World War II and for eventual victory? Should Stalin be praised for his wartime leadership or should he have been shot for failing to prepare or lead the country adequately? These and similar issues were debated inside and outside the Soviet Union after Khrushchev's "secret speech" in February 1956 at the 20th Party Congress lifted part of the veil which had shrouded Stalin's actions.

STALINIST DEFENSE

The following sources glorify Stalin's leadership and contend that he was a genius and that what he did was necessary and correct. The first is an excerpt from the *History of the All-Union Communist Party (Bolshevik), Short Course*, published originally in 1938. Approved by Stalin and sometimes attributed at least partly to him personally, this official party history seeks to explain and justify the Great Purge, then underway:

> The successes of socialism in our country gladdened . . . all honorable citizens of the USSR . . . , but infuriated more and more the . . . yesmen of the defeated classes—the miserable remnants of the Bukharinites and Trotskyites. These gentlemen . . . sought revenge upon the party and people for their failures. . . . On December 1, 1934 in Leningrad at Smolny, S. M. Kirov was most foully murdered with a shot from a revolver. The murderer, arrested at the scene of the crime, turned out to be a member of an underground counterrevolutionary group which was organized from members of the anti-Soviet Zinovievite group in Leningrad. . . . This group set itself the aim of murdering the leaders of the [Soviet] Communist Party. . . . From the depositions of the participants . . . it became evident that they were connected with representatives of foreign capitalist states and received money from them. The participants in this organization who were uncovered were sentenced by the Military Tribunal of the Supreme Court of the USSR to the extreme punishment—shooting.
>
> Soon thereafter the existence of an underground counterrevolutionary "Moscow center" was established. Investigation and trial clarified the vile role of Zinoviev, Kamenev, Evdokimov, and other leaders of this organization in arousing among their followers terrorist inclinations and to prepare the murder of members of the Central Committee and the Soviet government. . . . Already then in 1935 it became clear that the Zinovievite group was a hidden White Guardist organization which fully deserved to be dealt with like the White Guardists. . . .
> The chief inspirer and organizer of this whole band of murderers and spies was the Judas, Trotskii. Aiding Trotskii and executing his counterrevolutionary instructions were Zinoviev, Kamenev, and their Trotskyist yesmen. They prepared the defeat of the USSR in case of an attack on it by the imperialists, they became defeatists toward the worker-peasant state, they became the despicable servants and agents of the German and Japanese fascists.[1]

---

[1] *Istoriia VKP(b). Kratkii kurs* (Moscow 1946), pp. 309–12.

The following excerpts from Khrushchev's speech in 1939 show him as the loyal follower of Stalin, praising the dictator and his work slavishly and included in a volume of similar speeches dedicated to Stalin:

> Today, on the 60th anniversary of Comrade Stalin's birth, all eyes will be turned on our great leader of nations, on our dear friend and father. Working people all over the world will write and speak words of love and gratitude about him. Their enemies will foam at the mouth with rage when . . . speaking on this theme. The working men of the world see in Comrade Stalin their leader, their liberator from the yoke of capitalism. . . . The imperialists of all countries know full well that every word uttered by Comrade Stalin is backed by a people of 183,000,000 strong, that every idea advanced by Comrade Stalin is endorsed by the great and mighty multinational Soviet people. . . .
>
> The biography of Comrade Stalin is the glorious epic of our Bolshevik party. . . . Lenin together with Stalin created the great Bolshevik party. . . . In Comrade Stalin the working class and all toilers possess the greatest man of the present era, a theoretician, leader, and organizer of the struggle and victory of the working class. . . . All nations of the Soviet Union see in Stalin their friend, their father, their leader. . . . Stalin is the father of his people by virtue of the love he bears them. Stalin is the leader of nations for the wisdom with which he guides their struggle. . . . The army and the navy are the creation of our great Stalin, who increases their might with every day. . . .[2]

KHRUSHCHEV'S CRITIQUE

In his "secret speech" of February 1956 Khrushchev detailed Stalin's crimes and blunders, concealing the fact that he himself had been Stalin's loyal follower and had participated in them. Even Khrushchev did not condemn Stalin unconditionally—to have done so would have meant repudiating such achievements of the Soviet regime as industrialization, collectivization, and social benefits. Therefore he affirmed Stalin's positive contributions in the Revolution, Civil War, and in building socialism until 1934. Khrushchev focused on what he claimed was an aberration: the cult of the individual leader and its destructive results. He was under strong pressure from World War II generals led by Marshal Zhukov to rehabilitate purged military men and the Red Army's reputation, partly by discrediting Stalin's wartime leadership. Engaged in a bitter power struggle, Khrushchev may have believed that he could undermine such conservative opponents as Molotov by destroying Stalin's monstrous image. He glorified Lenin as embodying socialist modesty, comradely behavior, and socialist legality and posed as his true follower. In his speech Khrushchev discussed the origins and nature of the personality cult, Stalin's character and despotism after 1934, Stalin's responsibility for the Great Purge and its impact, Stalin's failure to prepare the USSR adequately for World War II, and his incompetence as Soviet wartime leader.

[2] Cited in Marin Pundeff, ed., *History in the U.S.S.R.* (San Francisco 1967), pp. 135–39.

Marx and Lenin, Khrushchev reminded the delegates of the 20th Congress, had denounced any cult of an individual leader; Lenin had invariably displayed great modesty and had emphasized the role of the people and the party in making history. Instead of dictating to his colleagues, Lenin had explained and persuaded patiently. He had realized Stalin's grave defects of character, but his premature death had prevented his removing Stalin from office. Lenin's fears soon proved justified. Stalin's negative qualities turned into grave abuses of power "which caused untold harm to our party." Instead of collegiality, Stalin employed capricious and brutal violence against all who opposed or differed with him. Those who refused complete submission to his dictates were removed from their posts and physically annihilated, especially after the 17th Party Congress of 1934 when many dedicated Communists "fell victim to Stalin's despotism."

During the Great Purge, Khrushchev continued, Stalin had grossly violated socialist legality and the principles of Leninism. He used mass repression first against "the enemies of Leninism"—Trotskyites, Bukharinites, etc., then against numerous ordinary loyal party members (Khrushchev failed to mention the millions of non-party people who were liquidated!). Coining the epithet, "enemy of the people," Stalin had unleashed cruel repression which fostered general insecurity and fear. Generally, the only proof of guilt was a "confession" extorted by force and torture. Such incongruous methods, noted Khrushchev, were employed when the Revolution had already triumphed, the exploiters had been wiped out, and socialism had been firmly established ". . . In the situation of socialist victory there was no basis for mass terror in the country." This terror had been blamed on N. I. Ezhov, chief of the security police, but clearly Stalin had made the decisions and issued the arrest orders.

Khrushchev sought to discredit utterly Stalin's role as the chief Soviet leader in World War II. He accused Stalin of failing to prepare the USSR for war, of disregarding numerous clear warnings of impending German attack, and of gross incompetence and negligence in directing military operations. Moreover, after victory Stalin had denied the crucial role of his generals and people in achieving victory, taking all the credit for himself. Khrushchev noted the improbable role which many Soviet war novels and films had attributed to Stalin. Supposedly harkening to Stalin's "genius," the Red Army had retreated deliberately, then counterattacked and smashed the Nazi invaders. Such works ascribed the glorious victory achieved by the heroic Soviet people solely to Stalin's brilliant strategy. Stalin had blamed early severe Soviet defeats on the German surprise attack though Hitler had announced his intent to destroy Communism back in 1933. In the months before the attack came numerous warnings from the West and from Soviet diplomats and military men that a Nazi invasion was imminent, but Stalin had paid them no heed. "Despite these particularly grave warnings, the necessary steps were not taken to prepare the country properly for defense and to prevent it from being caught unawares." The USSR had had enough time and capacity to prepare for war, affirmed Khrushchev, but Stalin did not properly mobilize Soviet industry or equip the Red Army.

Khrushchev was equally critical of Stalin's performance as wartime commander in chief. When the Nazis invaded, Soviet troops had orders not to return fire because Stalin just could not believe that war had really begun. In border areas much of the Soviet air force and artillery were lost needlessly and the Germans broke through. Believing that the end was near, Stalin declared in panic: "All that Lenin created we have lost forever." For a long time Stalin neither directed operations nor exercised real leadership. He was ignorant of the true situation at the front, which he never visited except for one brief look at a stabilized sector, yet his constant interference with military operations caused huge manpower losses. Exclaimed Khrushchev derisively: ". . . Stalin planned operations on a globe . . . and traced the front line on it!" As a result, early in 1942 the Germans surrounded large Red Army units in the Kharkov area and hundreds of thousands were lost. Yet Stalin believed that he was always right and never made mistakes. "This is Stalin's military genius; this is what it cost us," declared Khrushchev.

Right after Soviet victory Stalin began unfairly to denigrate the contributions to victory of many top Red Army commanders. "Stalin excluded every possibility that services rendered at the front should be credited to anyone but himself." All Soviet victories, Stalin claimed, had been due solely to his courage and genius. In the postwar Soviet film, *The Fall of Berlin* (1949), only Stalin issued orders; there was no mention of the military commanders, the Politburo, or the government. "Stalin acts for everybody . . . in order to surround Stalin with glory, contrary to the facts and to historical truth."[3]

POST-KHRUSHCHEV DEBATE ON STALIN

On February 16, 1966, a discussion was held at the Institute of Marxism-Leninism in Moscow of the book by A. M. Nekrich, *June 22, 1941*, which had used the "secret speech" to blame Stalin for Soviet unpreparedness. The debate was wide-open by Soviet standards, though most participants and the audience believed that Nekrich had not gone far enough in criticizing Stalin. Note Professor G. A. Deborin's critical attitude toward the fallen Khrushchev and his partial defense of Stalin.

> *Deborin:* Nekrich adopts an erroneous position; he explains everything by the obstinate stupidity of Stalin himself. That is a superficial analysis. . . . Stalin was not the only person involved. . . . It is unnecessary to refer to Khrushchev's declarations which are not objective. . . . Insofar as [Stalin] received false information, Stalin reached false conclusions. He placed too much hope in the German-Soviet pact, . . . but Stalin's estimate of German intentions was endorsed by all those around him. So Stalin cannot be considered solely responsible for his mistakes.
>
> *Anfilov* (General Staff): And now let us come to the beginning of the war. If all our forces had been completely ready for action, which

---

[3] N. S. Khrushchev, "The Crimes of the Stalin Era," *The New Leader*, 1956.

was entirely Stalin's responsibility, we should not have begun the war with such disasters! And in general the war would not have been so long, so bloody, and so exhausting. . . . Stalin remains the chief culprit.

Dashichev (General Staff): [Nekrich] should have gone deeper. . . . It was [Stalin] who made the situation in which the country then found itself [in 1941]. Stalin's greatest crime was to have eliminated the best cadres of our army and our party. All our leaders understood the international situation, but not one of them was courageous enough to fight to get the necessary measures taken for the defense of the country. That is their terrible guilt before the party and the people. There are people who still say that one ought not to speak badly of Stalin, that he was not the only one. That is not true. The driver of the bus is responsible for every accident that happens through his fault. Stalin assumed the responsibility of sole driver. His guilt is immense. . . .

Vasilenko (Institute of Marxism-Leninism): Objectively, we possessed everything necessary for resisting the German attack. But Stalin ruined everything. And afterwards to explain away his disgraceful defeat, he advanced the ridiculous theory that the aggressor is always better prepared for war.

Slezkin (Institute of History of the Academy of Sciences): I was at the front and took part, at the age of 19, in the June 1941 fighting. There can be no hesitation in saying that Stalin's behavior was criminal. There was a vicious circle of personality cult, provocation and repression. Everyone tried to please his superior by supplying only the information that might gratify him. . . . All this was the cause of immeasurable damage to the country and everyone is guilty in his own way. . . . And the responsibility is heavier in proportion to one's place in the hierarchy. . . . Stalin is the chief culprit. . . . It was a crime to base any hopes on this [Nazi-Soviet] pact and, above all, to stop the fight against fascism. And that is what Stalin ordered.

Peter Yakir (Institute of History of the Academy of Sciences): Some of the speakers . . . have referred to "Comrade Stalin.". . . Stalin was nobody's comrade and above all, not ours. Stalin impeded the development of our armaments by eliminating many eminent technicians, and among them the creators of our artillery. . . . In the concentration camps there were millions of able-bodied men, specialists in every department of the country's economic and military life. And the task of guarding them absorbed considerable forces.

Snegov: Nekrich's book is honest and useful. If a unit is disorganized on the eve of combat, . . . then that unit suffers a defeat. The head of such a unit is generally shot by order of the high command. . . . Stalin was both the supreme commander, and the head of the unit and that unit, in a state of disorganization, was our whole country. Stalin ought to have been shot. Instead of which, people are now trying to whitewash him. Why is Nekrich's book, which accuses Stalin, so hurriedly criticized and even condemned, while the book by the notorious falsifier of history, V. Petrov, [no relation to the editor of this collection] which credits Stalin with merits he never possessed, has still, after years, not come up for criticism? Why has Deborin tried to justify Stalin? . . . How can one be a Communist and speak smoothly about Stalin who betrayed and sold Communists, who eliminated nearly all the delegates of the Eighteenth Congress . . . , and who betrayed the Spanish Republic, Poland, and all Communists in all countries?

Deborin: It has not been my task to defend or justify Stalin. What is needed is to examine the personality cult more deeply in all its aspects. . . . It is strange that Snegov should hold the same view [as West German Professor Jacobson]. Comrade Snegov, you ought to tell us which camp you belong to!

Snegov: The Kolyma [concentration] camp.

Nekrich: . . . It is Stalin who bears the chief responsibility for the heavy defeat and all the tragedy of the first part of the war. All the same, nobody ought to provide his superiors with inexact information because it will give them pleasure. Stalinism began because of us, the small people. Stalin wanted to trick Hitler; but instead of that he got himself into a maze which led to disaster. He knew better than anyone about elimination of the leading cadres and the weaknesses of the army.[4]

A WESTERN EVALUATION

The U.S. scholar, Severyn Bialer, in his introduction to Soviet wartime memoirs, seeks to strike a balance between exaggerated praise of Stalin and Khrushchev's one-sided and partisan denunciation. Up to 1953, he points out, Soviet war history had glorified Stalin as an infallible and omnipotent genius. Soon after Stalin's death "war history came to serve the cult of the party" whose infallibility replaced Stalin's. Khrushchev's attack in 1956 had aimed to use Stalin's crimes as a lever to achieve power:

> The singlemindedness with which Khrushchev concentrated on his goal . . . led him to seek not comprehension, not rectification, but destruction of Stalin's role as war leader. . . . Soviet war memoirs testify to Stalin's complete control over the political, industrial, and military aspects of the Soviet war effort. . . . The Soviet dictator personally made every wartime decision of any importance. He alone seems to have possessed the power to impose his will on both civilian and military associates alike. . . .
> . . . It appeared to [Western observers] that Stalin had an extraordinary grasp of war goals and major long-range plans for conducting the war and a talent for adjusting the conduct of military operations to political realities. . . . On the second level, that of tactical and technical expertise, Western observers were struck by Stalin's mastery of detail. . . . Their descriptions are corroborated in the memoirs of Soviet commanders and industrial managers. . . .
> The task of military leadership is located to an overwhelming extent, however . . . in the area of operational leadership which involves

---

[4] Selected excerpts reprinted from *June 22, 1941, Soviet Historians and the German Invasion* by Vladimir Petrov, pp. 250–61, by permission of The University of South Carolina Press. Copyright © 1968 by The University of South Carolina Press in cooperation with the Institute for Sino-Soviet Studies, The George Washington University, Washington, D.C.

planning and control of large-scale military operations—battles and campaigns. In this middle area . . . , Stalin made no real contribution. . . . Stalin's crucial contribution to victory . . . [derived] from his ability to organize and administer the mobilization of manpower and material resources. . . . Stalin . . . regarded his role as that of arbiter and ultimate judge of his generals' strategic plans and operational designs. His major asset as a military leader was the ability to select talented commanders and to permit them to plan operations, while reserving for himself the ultimate power of decision. . . .

Khrushchev recognized Stalin's vulnerability in the crucial operational area and attempted to discredit [his] . . . entire war leadership by demonstrating the weakness of one of its parts. . . . While Soviet generals aired their alleged wartime misgivings about Stalin's judgment and behavior in military matters . . . , the memoirs clearly show that many of them regarded their leader with genuine respect, admiration or awe. . . . Clearly the Soviet generals feared Stalin more than they feared the Germans. . . .

Thus what was crucial to Soviet survival and eventual victory was Stalin's ability to mobilize Soviet manpower and economic resources over a sustained period, his ability to assure the political stability of his armed forces and the population at large despite disastrous initial defeats, and his ability to recognize and reward superior military talent at all levels under his command. . . . It was in just the area of Russia's greatest need that Stalin showed his greatest strength. . . . He was above all an administrator better suited to directing the gigantic military and civilian bureaucracy than to initiating and formulating military plans.[5]

Suggested Additional Reading

BRANT, STEFAN.   *The East German Rising* (New York, 1957).
Columbia University.   *The Anti-Stalin Campaign and International Communism* (New York, 1956).
———.   *National Communism and Popular Revolt* (New York, 1956).
BRZEZINSKI, Z.   *The Soviet Bloc: Unity and Conflict* (New York, 1960).
BRUMBERG, A., ed.   *Russia under Khrushchev* (New York, 1962).
CRANKSHAW, E.   *Khrushchev: A Career* (New York, 1966).
DALLIN, D. J.   *Soviet Foreign Policy After Stalin* (Philadelphia, 1961).
FRANKLAND, M.   *Khrushchev* (New York, 1967).
GITTINGS, J.   *Survey of the Sino-Soviet Dispute, 1963–1967* (New York, 1968).
GRIFFITH, W. E.   *Albania and the Sino-Soviet Rift* (Cambridge, Mass., 1963).
HILDEBRANDT, R.   *The Explosion* (New York, 1955) (Berlin uprising).
HYLAND, W. and R. SHRYOCK.   *The Fall of Khrushchev* (New York, 1969).
KHRUSHCHEV, N. S.   *Khrushchev Remembers* (Boston, 1971).
———.   *Khrushchev Remembers: The Last Testament* (Boston, 1974).
LEONHARD, W.   *The Kremlin Since Stalin* (New York, 1962).
LINDEN, C. A.   *Khrushchev and the Soviet Leadership, 1957–1964* (London, 1967).
PETHYBRIDGE, R. W.   *A History of Postwar Russia* (New York, 1970).

---

[5] *Stalin and his Generals: Soviet Military Memoirs of World War II*, ed. Severyn Bialer, (New York: 1969), pp. 34–44.

PISTRAK, L.   *The Grand Tactician: Khrushchev's Rise to Power* (New York, 1961).

ROTHBERG, A.   *The Heirs of Stalin. Dissidence and the Soviet Regime, 1953–1970* (Ithaca, New York, 1972).

SCHOLMER, J.   *Vorkuta* (New York, 1955) (uprising in the labor camp).

SMOLANSKY, O.   *The Soviet Union and the Arab East under Khrushchev* (Lewisburg, Penn., 1974).

SOBEL, L. A.   *Russia's Rulers: the Khrushchev Period* (New York, 1971).

SYROP, K.   *Spring in October: the Polish Revolution of 1956* (New York, 1958).

TATU, M.   *Power in the Kremlin: From Khrushchev to Kosygin* (New York, 1969).

WOLFE, B.   *Khrushchev and Stalin's Ghost* (New York, 1957) (on the secret speech).

ZAGORIA, D.   *The Sino-Soviet Conflict, 1955–1961* (Princeton, 1962).

ZINNER, P.   *Revolution in Hungary* (Cambridge, Mass., 1961).

39

Culture in the Soviet Era, 1953-1976

THE DEATH of Stalin ushered in the first of a series of "thaws" in Soviet culture. An almost spontaneous outburst of activity in the arts, coupled with efforts by the party authorities to rid the Soviet Union of the worst aspects of Stalinism, produced a remarkable cultural revival. Soviet cultural policies under Khrushchev and Brezhnev fluctuated between "thaws" and "freezes," but no wholesale return to the Stalin-Zhdanov approach occurred. Socialist realism persists as the guiding principle in literature and the arts, however, and the regime has made it clear that it will intervene decisively when deemed necessary to prevent undue expression of dissident points of view. The careers of Alexander Solzhenitsyn, Amalrik and Andrei and Zhores Medvedev demonstrate this thesis.

One of the first cautious reactions against Zhdanovism was an article in May 1953 deploring a lack of human emotion in Soviet films. The depersonalized "human machines," which were standard in Soviet films, were decried as not "true to life." The heroine agreeing to marry the hero only if he overfulfilled his production norm was a travesty on human feelings, the article claimed. Socialist construction and production quotas were admittedly important for socialist realism, but individual lives consisted of more than that. Such a view could not have been expressed openly, nor even discussed privately, in Stalin's final years for fear of swift reprisal. The air was freer now and bold ideas began cautiously to find their way into print. The precarious post-Stalin Soviet leadership must have recognized the utter sterility of Soviet culture under Zhdanovism and decided to permit more open discussion of alternative approaches in the realm of culture.

A more important example of intelligentsia disaffection was an article in November 1953 by the composer, Aram Khachaturian. "On Creative Boldness and Imagination" squarely confronted the problem of bureaucratic interference in the creative process, which had all but destroyed Soviet musical culture. "We must, once and for all, reject the worthless interference in musical composition as it is practiced by musical establishments. Problems of composition cannot be solved by official bureaucratic methods." Khachaturian's intent was not to reject socialist realism but to insist on the integrity of the artist and his own conception of his art. "Let the individual artist be trusted more fully and not be constantly supervised and suspected."

Others quickly joined in the burgeoning criticism. Alexander Tvardovskii, editor of the prestigious Soviet journal, *New World*, and himself a widely respected poet, denounced Soviet literature as arid, "contrived and unreal," devoid of life and reality. These were sharp and telling words. Ilia Ehrenburg, a well-known author and a leading apologist for Stalin and the party line for many years, boldly compared contemporary Soviet literature to the Russian classics and sadly concluded that the classics were more popular with the reading public because they dealt with living human emotions and feelings, the inner life of real people. He added, "Such books [as the classics] cannot be ordered or planned." Could anyone, he asked, "imagine ordering Tolstoy to write *Anna Karenina?*"

Not everyone shared these liberal views. The Stalinist hard-liners, with much to lose, had their spokesmen too, and there must have been some sharp infighting behind the scenes. That the party leadership was prepared to allow the artistic intelligentsia free rein, at least up to a point, cannot be doubted. Representative of the mood of the times was Ehrenburg's short novel published in 1954, *The Thaw*, which gave a name to the post-Stalin period. It was an apt name, for Stalinist Russia had been frozen solid, rigid, immobile, and somber. What was occurring in the post-Stalin era was an intellectual spring, heralded by the melting of the rock-hard ice, which had so long prevented growth and development. After a dormant period Soviet culture was on the threshold of a new season, rich with the promise of growth. Ehrenburg's short novel set the tone for the post-Stalin era and marked out the paths Soviet culture could follow in the future. Ehrenburg and other writers of "the thaw" insisted on a greater recognition of the gulf between the real and the ideal, a greater emphasis on truth in all its complexity, a rejection of tyranny, arbitrariness, and the politics of fear, recognition of individual human dignity, concern for the private lives of individuals, and an honest acknowledgement of the shortcomings of Soviet society and life. These fundamental artistic aims, shared by many, could best be achieved, Ehrenburg believed, within the framework of socialist realism. The tremendous enthusiasm with which these issues were discussed gave rise to an outburst of literary activity between 1954 and 1956. A number of poetry annuals and literary almanacs appeared without the prior approval of the Writers' Union. New poetic talents began to emerge in these years: Yevtushenko, Voznesenskii, Okudjava, Akhmadulina, and a host of others. New prose writers abounded: Tendriakov, Nagibin, Kazakov, Aksionov, and many others.

There was high optimism among Soviet writers and artists during these years, especially among the young, but conservatives and Stalinists among the literary intelligentsia did not slink away in disgrace and embarassment. They fought hard to maintain the principles of Zhdanovism and their own ascendency within the institutions of control. At the Second Congress of Soviet Writers (the first held since the notorious Congress of 1934) in December 1954, the hard-line Stalinist and Secretary of the Writers' Union, A. Surkov, delivered a ringing denunciation of the new mood and trends and demanded a return to the cold, rigid ideological purity of the Zhdanov era. Others, however, refused to toe the line and insisted, at the Congress, on even greater freedom, the rehabilitation of disgraced writers, the recognition of émigré writers, and publication of works previously deemed unacceptable for one reason or another. These debates at the Congress represented two major factions within the Writers' Union: the liberals, who looked to Ehrenburg and the young writers; and the conservatives, who depended on the old-line Stalinists who controlled the Union. The party authorities were reluctant to intervene; so the two factions manuevered as best they could in what became a stalemate.

At the 20th Party Congress in February 1956, the pendulum seemed to swing in the direction of the liberals. When Surkov gave another hard-line speech similar to that of two years earlier, he was answered by Michael Sholokhov, who viciously attacked literary bureaucrats and hack writers who claimed to speak for all Soviet literature. He concluded, "there isn't anything that a writer can learn from Surkov. Why do we need such leaders?" This was not a backroom squabble in the Writers' Union building, but the 20th Party Congress! During the following months, the liberals seemed to enjoy the upper hand. Khrushchev's secret speech denouncing Stalin's crimes had, by implication at least, compromised many Stalinist hard-liners in the literary establishment. This situation undoubtedly weakened, at least temporarily, their ability to exercise influence and control in the Writers' Union. The result was publication of some works which sharply criticized aspects of contemporary Soviet life. In 1956 the journal *New World* published Vladimir Dudintsev's novel *Not By Bread Alone,* which served as a clear example of the liberal trends in culture. The novel dealt with a nefarious aspect of Soviet life, the exploitation and victimization of talent by stupid and arrogant Soviet bureaucrats, a theme which could not help but offend and outrage literary bureaucrats like Surkov.

In this optimistic atmosphere of 1956, Boris Pasternak (1890–1960) submitted his now famous novel *Dr. Zhivago* to the editors of *New World.* Pasternak like Akhmatova, had made his reputation as a poet even before the Revolution and in the 1920s, but he had remained silent for much of the Stalinist period, publishing occasional poems and essays or translating from English into Russian. His translations of Shakespeare are extraordinary and still the standard for all translations in the Soviet Union. For more than two decades he had remained largely aloof from the events and issues swirling about him. Being a loner and an internal exile, he had time to work on his novel, which he completed in 1955. He fully expected *New World* to publish his novel, which showed his political naiveté and like Zamiatin and Pilniak, 30 years before, he gave a copy of the manuscript to a left-wing Italian publisher, Feltrinelli, with instructions to prepare an Italian translation for publication after the work appeared in the Soviet Union. Much to Pasternak's dismay, the editors of *New World* politely refused to publish the novel. Meanwhile, Feltrinelli was preparing to publish the work, and even the personal intervention of Surkov (Secretary of the Writers' Union, who flew to Italy) could not dissuade Feltrinelli from bringing out the Italian translation in November 1957. *Dr. Zhivago* was quickly translated into English and even the original Russian version was published in the West. *Dr. Zhivago* was hailed everywhere as a masterpiece, comparable to the Russian classics, and Pasternak was awarded the Nobel Prize for literature in October 1958. He modestly accepted the award, the first Soviet author to be so honored, but he was pressured by party authorities to reject it. He was viciously denounced in the Soviet press, expelled from the Writers' Union, and constantly hounded by the authorities. Physically and morally crushed by this harrowing experience, within two years he was dead, another victim of the Soviet literary inquisition.

Dr. Zhivago is an intensely personal statement which traces the story of Dr. Zhivago from pre-revolutionary times through the Soviet period. Zhivago's life is a failure—his personal life is a shambles, and he never makes use of his medical training. His life work is a slender volume of poetry, included at the end of the novel, Zhivago's legacy, his behest to all men. Pasternak was proclaiming that although he had produced nothing of practical value, his poetry, like Zhivago's, could enrich people's lives by stimulating them to think and act in creative and original ways. Zhivago's poems, among the most interesting and profound Pasternak ever wrote, contain the distilled essence of the novel. They affirm life and its constant renewal, as suggested by Zhivago's very name, meaning "living" or "lively" (*zhivoi*). Pasternak served as a living bridge, connecting the values of the pre-revolutionary Russian literary tradition, which emphasized the spiritual qualities of man, with contemporary Soviet life. In *Dr. Zhivago* Pasternak revealed an essentially religious conception of the future, based on an optimistic and unwavering faith in resurrection, renewal, and ultimately salvation—not only for Zhivago, but for Russia as a whole.

Party authorities believed that the Soviet reading public was not prepared for such a message; so Pasternak's novel has never been published in the Soviet Union (the music from the film version of *Dr. Zhivago*, "Lara's Theme," became a popular hit in Moscow though the film has never been shown in the Soviet Union). Even before the Pasternak "affair" had become a *cause célèbre*, it was evident that the pendulum was swinging back and the screws were being tightened again on Soviet culture. Things had moved too far, too quickly. Khrushchev's secret speech, though never published, was widely known and elicited much debate and soul searching, soon translated into demands for complete repudiation of the past and exposure of corruption, arbitrariness, and injustice. Calls were made for the abolition of all the dreary and oppressive formulas which had so long stifled free inquiry and the open exchange of ideas. The spark of revolt ignited violent rebellion first in Poland, then in Hungary in the autumn of 1956. Soviet

The Lenin State Library, Moscow on May Day

armed intervention in Hungary had a sobering impact on the burgeoning de-Stalinization program in Russia. The Soviet regime blocked any possible spread of the contagion of revolt. The more relaxed atmosphere of the thaw ended as Khrushchev moved decisively to halt a headlong race toward liberalization rather than a cautious, methodical, careful advance. Addressing the students of Moscow University, Khrushchev warned them not to go too far or they would face the full force of the regime. Two hundred students were expelled and the remainder were thoroughly intimidated by Khrushchev's threats. Stalinism was still fresh in people's minds.

The brief interlude of the thaw was over. Khrushchev's position was difficult: his de-Stalinization campaign had been a gamble, which had loosened the Soviet grip on the international Communist movement. Hard-pressed by party conservatives, he moved away from a liberal to a more conventional militancy in the cultural sphere. Changes in official policy are often abrupt in the Soviet Union, catching many off guard. Thus, late in 1956, Yevtushenko published a provocative poem with the following telling lines: "Certainly there have been changes; but behind the speeches/ Some murky game is being played./ We talk and talk about things we didn't mention yesterday;/ We say nothing about the things we did ourselves." This devastating criticism of the party leadership and particularly Khrushchev also pointed up a major obstacle to continuation of de-Stalinization: the more that Stalin's activities were revealed and discredited, the more the present leadership was implicated in those crimes. Such embarrassing comments could not go unchallenged. Yevtushenko was summarily dismissed from the *Komsomol* (Young Communist League), and forced to give up many privileges he had enjoyed as a prominent poet.

In spite of Khrushchev's "get tough" policy to demonstrate his control of affairs and determination to police the intellectuals, they were slow to respond to insistence on greater ideological conformity. In May 1957, Khrushchev, in his own ebullient style, took matters into his own hands and personally demanded compliance with his directives. He invited the Moscow writers to a garden party at his summer house outside Moscow and told the writers plainly that they were expendable, and that if they failed to cooperate, he would use force against them. He flatly stated that Hungary's difficulties in the 1956 revolt could have been avoided if its authorities had shot some of the intellectuals who had stirred up rebellion. The message was clear: Stalinist methods could still be applied when necessary. Khrushchev assured the stunned writers, "My hand will not tremble" if it were to apply force. The first phase of the post-Stalin thaw was over, sacrificed to Khrushchev's political requirements and ambitions.

Khrushchev had taken a calculated risk with de-Stalinization and had survived—barely, perhaps, but he had survived. In June 1957, he survived an attempt to oust him as First Secretary of the party and let him rid himself of the "anti-party" group. In March 1958, he consolidated his victory by assuming the premiership. With his political fences mended, he could revive, cautiously, the de-Stalinization campaign and build some bridges to the West. Some foreign travel was permitted, and cultural exchanges were negotiated with a number of Western countries, including the United States. The struggle against "the cult of personality" (Stalinism) continued in an undramatic, low key. The brutal treatment of Pasternak in 1958 revealed its limits, but the thaw, which had refrozen in 1956 and 1957, began to resume. A host of young writers published poems, stories, and novels that revealed great promise and genuine talent. They tended to focus on the problems and concerns of individuals in a complex industrial society. They were less concerned with "building socialism" than with its effects on individuals. They picked up the threads of the earlier thaw and began to weave them into a new, more sophisticated literature. In the party apparatus, however, many conservatives were fearful of liberal developments and were particularly suspicious of cultural rapprochement with the West, the source of dangerously unorthodox cultural influences. While things were kept within strict limits, the liberals maintained their ascendancy. Debate and disagreement, innovation and experimentation were tolerated within limits. At the Third Congress of Soviet Writers in 1959, Khrushchev declared that he was again satisfied with the cultural state of affairs. He was prepared to be liberal, in Soviet terms, so long as the writers and artists supported the party ideologically.

Many stories and novels appearing during the next few years testified to the imaginative power of such young, unknown Soviet writers as Aksionov, Nagibin, Kazakov, Tendryakov, and Voinovich. Discarding the literary didacticism and moralizing tone of so much socialist realist literature, their stories and novels revealed a renewed concern for style, literary imagination, psychological impact, and above all a deep desire to probe human emotions. Their works attracted much popular attention and were avidly read and discussed, not always favorably by literary conservatives. Subjects long held taboo were now openly discussed and debated. In 1961, for example, Yevtushenko published his famous "Babi Yar," a technically flawed but extraordinarily powerful poem about the 33,000 Soviet Jews slaughtered by the Nazis in 1941 in Babi Yar ravine near Kiev. The poem not only memorialized the innocent Jews but castigated anti-Semitism, whether in Fascist or Communist guise. He proclaimed that Russian anti-Semitism still "rises in the fumes of alcohol and in drunken conversations." The poem elicited a flood of controversy and was violently attacked by conservatives as a slander on the gallant and heroic Russian people who had sacrificed so much to destroy Hitlerite Germany and Nazi anti-Semitism. Others lauded Yevtushenko's courage and honesty in confronting squarely a problem with deep roots in the Russian psyche.

The liberal tendency gained ground elsewhere as well. Early in 1962, a highly respected art critic, Michael Alpatov, published an article defending modern, abstract art. Others quickly followed, suggesting that "the 20th century is becoming an age of triumphant abstractions," and implying that it was ridiculous for the Soviet Union to be so backward in appreciating modern art. The venerable Tretiakov Gallery in Moscow cautiously began to open up its vaults and exhibit some works of early 20th-century Russian art innovators such as Kandinskii. The poet, Bella Akhmadulina, wife of Iuri Nagibin, proclaimed optimistically in 1961: "I think that the time has become happy for us, that it now runs in our favor. Not only can my comrades work, but they are given every encouragement in their endeavor." Very important was "official" encouragement to the young artists, writers, and composers.

The liberals pushed their advantage during the summer and autumn of 1962. In October, Yevtushenko's poem "Stalin's Heirs" appeared in *Pravda.* It is worth quoting from this remarkable commentary on the times:

> He [Stalin] was scheming.
> Had merely dozed off.
> And I, appealing to our government, petition them to double
> and treble,
> the sentries guarding this slab,
> and stop Stalin from ever rising again
> and, with Stalin
> the past.

Yevtushenko bluntly confronted the possibility of the revival of Stalinism:

> No, Stalin has not given up.
> He thinks he can
> outsmart death.
> We carried him from the mausoleum.
> But how carry Stalin's heirs
> away from Stalin.
> Some of his retired heirs tend roses,
> thinking in secret
> their enforced leisure will not last.
> Others,
> from platforms, even heap abuse on Stalin
> but,
> at night,
> yearn for the good old days.
> No wonder Stalin's heirs seem to suffer
> these days from heart trouble.
> They, the former henchmen,
> hate this era
> of emptied prison camps
> and auditoriums full of people listening
> to poets.[1]

Khrushchev acknowledged that he had personally authorized the publication of Yevtushenko's poem. Khrushchev seemed about to announce a new round of de-Stalinization, and publication of "Stalin's Heirs" was the clarion call.

Further confirmation of this change was Khrushchev's authorization of the publication, without deletions, of Alexander Solzhenitsyn's *One Day in the Life of Ivan Denisovich* in the November issue of *New World*. Solzhenitsyn's first published work was a powerful and shocking portrayal of everyday life in a Stalinist prison camp. Solzhenitsyn's account, based on his personal experiences in the camps, was understated, dispassionate, and nonpolemical in tone. It brought to life in vivid and searing detail one day—and not a particularly hard or difficult day—in the life of Ivan Denisovich. It is the record of the agony of one day's survival of an inmate reduced to the level of an animal but whose dignity and humanity remain intact. Ivan Denisovich was more than an individual, he was a symbol of the indomitable courage of the Russian people in their continuing struggle for freedom and human dignity. *One Day* became an instant sensation, touching profoundly sensitive chords in millions of Soviet citizens who had experienced in one form or another endless days just like Ivan Denisovich's. Public sentiment about the brutality, terror, and inhumanity of the Stalin terror was once again stirred as though in preparation for a new stage in the process of de-Stalinization.

Just as this new campaign of cutting away the distortions of the

---

[1] Cited in Priscilla Johnson, *Khrushchev and the Arts* (Cambridge, Mass., 1965), pp. 93–95. Translated by G. Reavey.

past got under way, Khrushchev was again plunged into extremely stormy political waters. The Cuban Missile Crisis, in which Khrushchev was forced to back down, occurred in October 1962. The Sino-Soviet dispute was about to break into the open. These foreign policy failures combined with growing economic problems at home to create a very dangerous political atmosphere, which again threatened Khrushchev's control of party and government. Sharp price increases for consumer goods in the summer and autumn of 1962 caused outbreaks of violence among workers in various parts of the country. These political difficulties must have persuaded Khrushchev of the need to renounce any more de-Stalinization. The unstable political atmosphere would not tolerate the strain of new revelations about the Stalin era, which might compromise Khrushchev's political allies and infuriate his growing number of enemies.

In the cultural sphere, "Stalin's heirs" were poised for a counterattack by late November 1962. The occasion was a retrospective art exhibition, "Thirty Years of Soviet Art," including 2,000 art works, at the huge Manezh Gallery near the Kremlin. After the exhibition had opened, a group of about 75 modernistic canvases and sculptures assembled for a private showing were added. In retrospect, it appears that these modernistic works were added to the exhibition as part of an elaborate "provocation" by cultural conservatives. On December 1, Khrushchev, with several Presidium members paid a surprise visit to the Manezh Gallery. Most of his time was spent in three small rooms housing modernistic works by contemporary Soviet artists. His reaction was the one conservatives had anticipated—violent, vulgar, and vicious. Khrushchev's sudden verbal attack startled liberals, who were enjoying a heyday. That Khrushchev's support of the liberals had been politically motivated became clear to everyone as the tables were now turned.

Khrushchev's remarks at the art exhibition were unprecedentedly crude. Pausing in front of an abstractionist painting, Khrushchev remarked:

> I would say this is just a mess. . . . Polyanskii [Presidium member] told me a couple of days ago that when his daughter got married she was given a picture of what was supposed to be a lemon. It consisted of some messy yellow lines which looked, if you will excuse me, as though some child had done his business on the canvas when his mother was away and then spread it around with his hands.

Further on, he lashed out against jazz music.

> I don't like jazz. When I hear jazz, it's as if I had gas on the stomach. I used to think it was static when I heard it on the radio.

His comments became even more vulgar as he proceeded through the exhibition.

> As long as I am chairman of the Council of Ministers, we are going to support a genuine art. We aren't going to give a kopeck for pictures painted by jackasses.

Speaking to one artist but obviously referring to all modernist painters, Khrushchev fulminated:

> You've either got to get out [of the Soviet Union] or paint differently. As you are, there's no future for you on our soil. . . . Gentlemen, we are declaring war on you.[2]

Within hours of Khrushchev's visit to the Manezh exhibition, the war for "ideological purity" began. Editorials appeared in the press demanding that all unions of writers, artists, composers, and cinema workers be amalgamated into a single union in order to prevent nonconformity. The word was out: centralize and control. A number of Stalinist bureaucrats ceased "tending roses" and returned to positions of prominence. Within weeks, a meeting was held between Party authorities and writers, artists, and other intellectuals to discuss the current cultural situation. Leonid Ilyichev, Chairman of the Ideological Commission of the Central Committee, gave the main speech, although Khrushchev himself was present. Ilyichev deplored recent trends which had been carried too far, ending in demands for an end to all censorship. He attacked the continuing and inexorable advance of Western influences, "bourgeois" influences on Soviet culture. This hard-line speech was followed by remarkably candid informal exchanges between party officials and writers and artists. Ehrenburg boldly defended the new freedoms and insisted that modern trends in art were not covers for political reaction. Yevtushenko, too, defended the abstract painters, arguing that they were only beginning and needed time to straighten out problems and difficulties in their art. Khrushchev reportedly broke in and shouted: "The grave straightens out the hunchback." Yevtushenko, perhaps shocked by the threatening tone of Khrushchev's remark, was not to be intimidated. He responded: "Nikita Sergeevich [Khrushchev], we have come a long way since the time when only the grave straightened out hunchbacks. Really, there are other ways." The assembled writers and artists broke into applause and reportedly even Khrushchev joined in. Writers and artists, poets and composers demonstrated a sense of unity and common purpose at this meeting, which provided the conservatives with useful ammunition in the battle against modernist trends in culture.

The tenseness of the situation was further revealed by the affair of Shostakovich's *13th Symphony*, which had been sanctioned by Khrushchev himself. The first movement consisted of Yevtushenko's poem "Babi Yar" set to music. The new symphony was scheduled for a premiere performance on the evening following the great gathering of party officials and intellectuals. Ilyichev is said to have demanded the withdrawal of the symphony, but Shostakovich refused. The premiere went forward as scheduled, although many musicians and the entire choir hesitated, fearing reprisals. An impassioned plea from Yevtushenko gave them sufficient courage, and the performance was given

---

[2] Ibid., pp. 101–5.

as scheduled. After a second performance two nights later, all further performances were cancelled. Not only the icy cold of Moscow winter chilled the intellectual community, but also that of a new ideological freeze.

Its culmination came in March 1963 at a gathering of more than 600 writers, artists, and other intellectual workers. Again it was Ilyichev who led the attack on the writers in general and Ilia Ehrenburg in particular. Somewhat earlier Ehrenburg had argued in his published memoirs, *People, Years, Life* (1960–61), that he and many others had known full well what was going on in the Soviet Union during the 1930s, but were compelled to remain silent, living with "clenched teeth." Ilyichev accused Ehrenburg of enjoying special privileges and protection during the Stalin era, of having openly and frequently praised Stalin as one of his chief apologists. One could assume that almost any survivor of the Purges had done the same things. But Ilyichev drew a dubious distinction between himself and his colleagues and the venerable Ehrenburg, arguing that he and his colleagues had flattered Stalin out of sincere conviction. They had not been hypocrites, prostituting their art. Ehrenburg, on the other hand, had written flattery of Stalin without believing in his infallibility. Doing so made Ehrenburg a hypocrite, devoid of principles and intellectual courage. Ehrenburg believed that Ilyichev's remarks rang so patently false that a reply was unnecessary.

Khrushchev then mounted the rostrum and delivered a devastating speech which partially rehabilitated Stalin's tastes in art and literature (simple, straightforward, and uncomplicated) and to a degree rehabilitated Stalin himself. Khrushchev further sought to exonerate Stalin's entourage (especially himself) of complicity in his repressions and crimes. Khrushchev, more than most, certainly more than Ilyichev, realized the dangers of further de-Stalinization which would raise such questions as "Where were you? What were you doing during Stalin's criminal rampages?" The choice of answers was not particularly appealing. One could argue, as did Ilyichev, that he did not know what was happening—an admission of political naiveté or downright stupidity. Or one could argue, as did Ehrenburg, that he knew of Stalin's crimes but remained silent—an admission of complicity or abject cowardice. It was better to leave Stalin's ghost alone. De-Stalinization came to an end, the conservative heirs of Stalin had used the issue of abstract art to induce the party to prevent further liberalization. Khrushchev was in a political position where he had to yield to mounting pressure within the party. Perhaps, Khrushchev's personal cultural tastes were closer to the conservatives' than to the liberal's anyway. In any case, the lid was slammed down again.

Throughout 1963, at a series of meetings organized by party authorities, the leading cultural figures acknowledged their "errors" and promised to abide by the party's wise and benevolent guidance in all matters. Shostakovich, Yevtushenko, Voznesenkii, and many others knuckled under. The open ferment came to an end or gradually drifted beneath the surface. A light frost, if not a hard freeze, ushered in late autumn with occasional rays of sunshine. Even Khrushchev's fall in October 1964 did not herald a new thaw. The new regime of Brezhnev and Kosygin found it expedient to maintain the status quo, maintaining the comprehensive cultural controls and inflexible conformity which had emerged out of the 1962–63 period. Writing for the "desk drawer" or painting for "the closet" continued as before, becoming, if anything, more widespread after a few fleeting moments of freedom. Literary works in increasing numbers passed from hand to hand in manuscript copies, and artists gave private showings of their latest abstract works. An organized Soviet counter-culture began to emerge. In these circumstances occurred two new developments in liberal literary circles: *samizdat* and *tamizdat.*

Samizdat, a play on *Gosizdat,* the acronym for the all-powerful State Publishing House, means literally "self publication" by authors rather than the state. Because individuals do not have access to printing presses, most *samizdat* material is produced on typewriters or occasionally mimeograph machines. Smudged carbon copies circulate from hand to hand and new copies are made when needed. *Tamizdat* refers to materials published abroad—*tam* means "over there" or more specifically the West—and then smuggled into the Soviet Union. A considerable body of clandestine literature has accumulated in the Soviet Union, literature not subject to official control or censorship.

Writing for the "desk drawer" was for many a frustrating and unrewarding task, and so other avenues of uncensored expression were sought. Publishing works abroad had always been dangerous, as the fate of Zamiatin, Pilniak, and Pasternak had shown. Their works had been published abroad because of confusion and misunderstanding, not as the result of conscious intent to avoid Soviet censorship. Even that excuse did not save these authors from villification and abuse, but none of them was put on trial. The distinguished literary critic Andrei Siniavskii, and the young writer and translator Iuli Daniel consciously sought to evade party literary controls by smuggling manuscripts out of the Soviet Union for publication abroad under the pseudonyms Abram Tertz (Siniavskii) and Nikolai Arzhak (Daniel), beginning in 1956 when the first thaw was ending. For nine years they escaped detection and published a series of stories, short novels, and essays, all highly critical of Soviet life. These became the first examples of *samizdat* and *tamizdat.*

Siniavskii's writings published abroad included a long essay "On Socialist Realism" (1959), a general indictment of the doctrine as old-fashioned and wholly inappropriate for the 20th-century Soviet Union. Soviet literature, he believed, was "a monstrous salad" in which content was distorted by form and party officials interfered continually in literary affairs. He urged abandoning socialist realism in favor of a return to the literary experimentation of Mayakovskii and the 1920s. Also published abroad was *The Trial Begins* (1960), a fictional exposé of the Soviet system of justice, portrayed as fraudulent, cynical, repressive, and arbitrary. Other works either poked fun at Soviet foibles or satirized Soviet life. None, however, could be construed as anti-

Soviet in any strict sense of the word, although all criticized Soviet institutions.

Daniel's works were basically harmless literary exercises, less sophisticated and profound than Siniavskii's. Of Daniel's four stories published abroad, "This is Moscow Speaking" and "Hands" are the most interesting. "This is Moscow Speaking" is a macabre tale about a Public Murder Day decreed by the Politburo. On August 10, 1961, all citizens over the age of 16 are authorized to kill anyone they wish (with some exceptions) between the hours of 6:00 A.M. and midnight. When the population fails to respond to the license to kill, the party condemns this as sabotage. [This implied that mass terror could be reintroduced in the Soviet Union with the same kind of terrifyingly passive response from the population.] The story "Hands" deals indirectly with the psychological impact of terror. A former Cheka officer suffers from chronically shaking hands because as a young secret police officer he had been ordered to shoot down a group of priests accused of counterrevolutionary activities. His friends had played a joke on him by loading his pistol with blank cartridges. When the priests implored the young officer not to shoot and advanced on him with outstretched hands, the officer had shot repeatedly but the priests "miraculously" had continued to advance. This experience had so unnerved the officer that his hands never ceased to move convulsively.

The KGB (security police) mounted an intense campaign to identify Tertz and Arzhak (computers were used to analyze and compare their writing styles). Finally, Siniavskii and Daniel were arrested in September 1965 and charged under the infamous Article 70 of the Soviet Criminal Code of disseminating "slanderous" and "defamatory" inventions about the Soviet system. The trial opened in February 1966 after the accused had been convicted in the press. Both defendants were quickly convicted. Siniavskii was sentenced to seven years hard labor, (the maximum sentence), and Daniel to five years.

The trial of Siniavskii and Daniel was unique in the annals of Soviet justice. Never before had writers been tried for what they had written. Many writers had been publicly denounced and accused of a variety of "crimes"—Zamiatin, Pilniak, Zoshchenko, Akhmatova, and Pasternak—and many writers had simply disappeared during the Purges, but none had been tried in open court. The brilliant young Leningrad poet Joseph Brodskii had been tried in 1964, not for what he had written, but as a "parasite," someone without gainful employment (he claimed to be a poet but was not a member of the Writers' Union). He was convicted and sentenced to five years exile. Furthermore, unlike many other public trials in Soviet history, Siniavskii and Daniel, instead of pleading guilty, defended themselves valiantly.

The harsh sentences shocked the Soviet intellectual community. In a remarkable show of unity, liberal-minded intellectuals from various branches of the arts and sciences, addressed letters to party authorities, protesting the treatment of Siniavskii and Daniel. The only major Soviet writer to give unqualified support to the regime in this matter was Michael Sholokhov, who had been awarded the Nobel Prize for literature the year before. He stated publicly that the sentences meted out to Siniavskii and Daniel were not nearly harsh enough and intimated that the death penalty would not have been too severe. The party authorities were undaunted by the storm of protest that accompanied announcement of the sentences. The trial had been designed to halt dissent and intimidate the dissenters. Siniavskii and Daniel were scapegoats used to announce a new "get tough" policy. The trial was to warn all intellectuals that no work produced by a Soviet citizen was exempt from censorship. To have succumbed to public pressure would have undermined this purpose.

The trial of Siniavskii and Daniel backfired. It became a milestone in the long struggle between party leaders and the intellectual elite. From its very beginning in the 1920s, the literary intelligentsia was in the forefront, preoccupied with a search for truth predicated on the conviction that truth could be found only in an atmosphere of artistic or intellectual freedom. The literary intelligentsia had sought to liberate the creative process from the arbitrary interference of party bureaucrats or watchdogs. The writers tried to advance the artistic and moral values of traditional Russian literature, a deep concern for the individual, psychological truth, intellectual honesty and sincerity, and a multifaceted realism. Siniavskii's and Daniel's struggles for these traditional values brought them into sharp conflict with the Soviet authorities. After the trial, the Soviet intelligentsia had to recognize that the intellectual and artistic freedom Siniavskii and Daniel sought could not be achieved without basic political freedoms.

This new consciousness, brought to the surface by the Siniavskii and Daniel affair, created a genuine dissent that went well beyond anything before that time in the Soviet Union. Questions were asked that had always been taboo even during the most liberal periods of Soviet history. The lack of basic rights, such as freedom from fear, intimidation and terror, freedom of speech, press, and assembly, all guaranteed by the Soviet Constitution, began to be discussed by numerous groups of intellectuals. A consciousness developed that the fundamental rights of Soviet citizens were daily being violated. The Soviet Constitution does not authorize any kind of censorship. By what right, then, had the Soviet government presumed to tell writers what they could and could not write? By what right did the Soviet government proscribe freedom of assembly and freedom of peaceful protest? These were deeply disturbing questions to many intellectuals.

Four young Soviet citizens, Alexander Ginzburg, Iuri Galanskov, Alexis Dobrovolskii, and Vera Lashkova, as part of a campaign to protest the verdict and harsh sentences in the Siniavskii-Daniel trial, put together an astonishingly comprehensive collection of materials on the trial, including a verbatim transcript of the trial itself. The collection was aimed at persuading the authorities to reopen the case and review the procedures used against the defendants and the sentences. In January 1967, copies of *The Collection of Materials on the Siniavskii and Daniel Trial* were sent to the KGB and to deputies of the Supreme Soviet. The authorities responded by arresting the four young compilers, but not before a copy had reached the West, where it was published. The four were tried in January 1968 and quickly convicted under Article 70. The sentences of Galanskov and Ginzburg were even harsher than those of Siniavskii and Daniel. The Galanskov-Ginzburg trial evoked an unprecedented public protest and led directly to the Human Rights (or Democratic) Movement.

The Human Rights Movement was formally organized in early 1970 by the prominent Soviet nuclear physicist and so-called "father of the Soviet H-bomb," A. D. Sakharov. Its purpose was to protest current Soviet policies which violated fundamental individual freedoms specifically protected in the Soviet Constitution and provided for in the United Nations Declaration of Human Rights, a document subscribed to by the Soviet government. Prominent figures from Soviet science, literature, art, cinema, music, and scholarship joined in the clamor of protest. The official response was to proceed with further arrests and repression without public fanfare. The official effort to project an image of legality and respect for individual rights by public trials was abandoned. The movement of dissent tried to keep the public informed of illegal actions of the government by publishing a remarkable *samizdat* account of arrests, beatings, harassments, and exiles, *The Chronicle of Current Events*. It became increasingly difficult for the Soviet government to hide behind a veil of secrecy.

The Human Rights Movement was not organized as an anti-Soviet movement bent on overthrowing the regime, nor to alter the basic Soviet legal structure, but rather to have existing laws enforced on a fair and uniform basis. These patriotic Soviet citizens wished to see the provisions of the Soviet Constitution (proudly proclaimed the most liberal in the world) observed in practice.

The person most closely identified with the movement of dissent in the late 1960s and early 1970s was the author Alexander Solzhenitsyn. His renown had steadily increased since publication of his extraordinary novel *One Day in the Life of Ivan Denisovich* in 1962, although only a few additional stories of his had appeared in print. Born in 1918, he studied mathematics and physics, became a teacher, and served with distinction as an artillery officer in World War II. Towards the end of the war he was arrested and sentenced to the labor camps after referring to Stalin in a personal letter intercepted by the security police as "the man with the moustache." Solzhenitsyn spent eight years in the labor camps and three additional years of exile in Central Asia. In 1956 he was fully rehabilitated during de-Stalinization, all charges against him were declared groundless, and his full civil rights were restored. The publication of his novel and several short stories in 1962–63 won him immediate fame in the Soviet Union and abroad. He was recognized as a writer of great power and moral authority. His few published works, however, represented everything party authorities feared about de-Stalinization and in the subsequent crackdown it was decided that no more of his works should be published. Nevertheless, Alexander Tvardovskii, editor of *New World*, who had persuaded

United Press International

Alexander Solzhenitsyn

Khrushchev to allow publication of *One Day,* accepted for publication a major Solzhenitsyn novel, *The Cancer Ward,* which was to begin appearing in *New World* in January 1968. The type was set and the first run was about to begin when party authorities hastily informed Tvardovskii of their decision to halt publication. The uneasy atmosphere of the Galanskov-Ginzburg trial and the accompanying protest was viewed as an inappropriate time for the publication of a novel dealing with secret police, repression, abuse of power, and moral decay. In the meantime a copy of the manuscript reached the West, and was immediately published over the sincere objections of the author, who refused to accept responsibility for what was published without his consent. Nevertheless, a well orchestrated and vicious attack on Solzhenitsyn appeared in the Soviet press.

The Cancer Ward deals with the terrifying experiences of a highly placed Soviet official, Rusanov, who is suffering from cancer. The powerful Rusanov has no time after discovering his condition to exploit his connections to enter an elite clinic. Instead he is confined to an ordinary cancer ward, overcrowded with inconsequential and unsympathetic people whom he resents and despises. The antithesis of

Rusanov is another cancer patient, Kostoglotov, who has spent many years in the labor camps and exile in Central Asia. He has suffered and survived, but he no longer values life nor does he fear death. He has literally nothing to lose, and this is his strength in his fight against cancer. Rusanov, by contrast, has everything to lose—position, wealth, and family,—and his fear of death makes him desperate. He cannot accept his condition or fight against it rationally.

Another Solzhenitsyn novel, *The First Circle*, an extension on a different level of *One Day*, was published in the West in 1968, but has never appeared in the Soviet Union. *The First Circle* deals with a prison that houses scholars, scientists, and engineers, all convicted of state crimes. Required to work on various scientific projects for the state, they do not feel the physical anguish of Ivan Denisovich, they are well-fed, well-housed, and enjoy many physical comforts, but their mental anguish is worse, more degrading and ultimately more destructive because it can destroy the human spirit. Here too, Solzhenitsyn is concerned with a central theme which reappears constantly in his works, the indomitable human spirit triumphant over adversity.

Solzhenitsyn's third great novel is the broad historical panorama *August 1914*, published in the West in 1971, the first of a projected series of historical works dealing with Russia's travails during World War I and the revolutions that followed. The heroic struggle of the Russian people is contrasted sharply with the criminal incompetency of the tsarist government. The historical parallel between Russia in World War I and the Soviet Union in World War II is impossible to ignore.

None of these great works has appeared in the Soviet Union, but are well-known in manuscript copies in the literary underground. The publication of these works in the West led to a mounting campaign of harassment, persecution, and public vilification of Solzhenitsyn. His international reputation and the Brezhnev regime's sensitivity to international opinion provided the great author with a security not enjoyed by other dissenters, with the possible exception of Sakharov. Like the character Kostoglotov in *The Cancer Ward*, Solzhenitsyn had suffered all the Stalinist regime could subject him to and life held no terrors for him. He could not be frightened, intimidated, or shut up short of physical annihilation. He courageously spoke out against censorship, repression, and injustice. "No one can bar the road to truth," he proclaimed in a famous letter circulated at the Fourth Congress of Soviet Writers in 1967, "and to advance its cause I am prepared to accept even death." He called for an end to all censorship and insisted on absolute freedom for all writers and artists. He concluded his letter with a warning:

> Literature cannot develop in between the categories of "permitted" and "not permitted," "about this you may write" and "about this you may not." Literature that is not the breath of contemporary society, that does not transmit the pains and fears of that society, that does not warn in

time against threatening moral and social dangers—such literature does not deserve the name of literature; it is only a facade. Such literature loses the confidence of its own people, and its published works are used as wastepaper instead of being read.[3]

In 1970, Solzhenitsyn was awarded the Nobel Prize for literature. The anti-Pasternak scenario of 1958–59 was reenacted as party hacks venomously attacked Solzhenitsyn as a "leper" and engineered his expulsion from the Writers' Union. The withering public assault did not intimidate Solzhenitsyn as it had Pasternak. Solzhenitsyn proudly accepted the Nobel award, although he declined to travel to Stockholm to receive it for fear of being denied reentry to the Soviet Union, his homeland for better or worse. His eloquent Nobel lecture, written for delivery at the acceptance ceremonies, was smuggled out of the Soviet Union and published in the West in 1972. It was a restrained and dignified plea for freedom throughout the world and a ringing statement of the moral responsibility of the writer and artist who can help "to conquer falsehood." The campaign of harassment of Solzhenitsyn was stepped up in 1973, and he began to fear for his life. He managed to transmit a number of important manuscripts to friends in the West as a means of preventing his enemies from silencing him even by death. He instructed his friends to publish the manuscripts if anything were to happen to him.

In September 1973 the KGB managed to intimidate one of Solzhenitsyn's typists into revealing the secret hiding place of a copy of a major underground manuscript which she had typed. Haunted by a sense of weakness and betrayal, the distraught woman committed suicide. With a copy of the manuscript in the hands of the KGB, Solzhenitsyn signaled his Western friends to proceed with publication of the book, which had previously been smuggled abroad. Thus, the first volume of the monumental *The Gulag Archipelago, 1918–1956* was published in Paris in December 1973, and in numerous translations, including English, in the spring of 1974. A second volume was published in 1975. Subtitled "An Experiment in Literary Investigation," *The Gulag Archipelago* is not a work of fiction, but a powerfully moving history of the Soviet prison camp system. Solzhenitsyn dedicated the book "To all those who did not survive." He traces the origin of the prison camp system back to Lenin, although it was developed into the monstrous structure it became only under Stalin. This remarkable account of man's inhumanity to man is based on Solzhenitsyn's own personal experiences in the camps, and on the personal experiences of hundreds of former prisoners, (*zeks*), who wrote or told their stories to Solzhenitsyn after the publication of his *One Day in the Life of Ivan Denisovich*. Publication of *The Gulag Archipelago* in the West resulted in an unprecedented campaign of slander and abuse of Solzhenitsyn in the Soviet Union and an equally unprecedented international outpouring of support for him. The Soviet government

[3] Quoted in *Problems of Communism* (Washington, 1968), no. 5, p. 38.

hesitated momentarily in the face of world opinion, but then in February 1974, the police arrested Solzhenitsyn and charged him, not with violations under article 70 of the Criminal Code, but with treason, a crime carrying the death penalty. On the following day, however, Solzhenitsyn was escorted to the Moscow airport, where he was put on a plane for West Germany and involuntary exile. Shortly after, he was joined by his family and settled down in exile where he continues to write and speak out against tyranny and injustice.

Recently he has identified himself more closely with Christianity and the Russian Orthodox Church and has become equally critical of injustice, prejudice and corruption in the West. He has become a sharp critic of the policy of détente, which he argues aids the Soviet regime to perpetuate its cruel dictatorship. He has broken with many of his fellow dissenters and become increasingly strident in his tone of criticism of the Soviet Union. Like another famous Russian exile of the previous century, Alexander Herzen, Solzhenitsyn continues from afar his struggle against the tyranny and abuse of power in his native land.

The Soviet government of Brezhnev and Kosygin has found it more expedient to exile the most prominent dissenters to the West rather than incarcerate them in prison camps at home. Some have been forced to leave their homeland; others have left voluntarily with the encouragement of the authorities. Siniavskii, when released from the camps in 1973, was allowed to leave the Soviet Union to teach at the Sorbonne in Paris. Likewise, Valeri Chalidze, a prominent Soviet physicist and an active participant in the Committee on Human Rights, was allowed to make a lecture tour of the United States and then deprived of his Soviet citizenship, making it impossible for him to return home.

The Soviet regime has found the movement of dissent a nuisance and an embarassment, but it does not feel particularly threatened by it. It is small and without much influence internally in the Soviet Union cannot move public opinion in any significant way. The movement of dissent, however, remains a spark of hope for many who believe in cultural freedom, the values of traditional Russian culture, and the dignity of the individual. The written word remains a powerful force, which even the extraordinarily tight Soviet censorship cannot control completely. Literature has always been a powerful weapon in Russia and remains so today. The existence of the movement of dissent has had a positive impact in the sense that it has helped to stretch the limits of the permissible and loosen up the cultural atmosphere. The struggle between liberals and conservatives continues on the Soviet cultural scene, but even the meaning of these terms is changing. Today's conservative can hardly be compared to those of the mid-1950s. Crude Stalinist conformity and rigidity, it may be cautiously hoped, has passed, and the liberals of today will be able to continue to maintain sufficient momentum to open Soviet culture even more to fresh winds of change in order to encourage the creative energies of the Russian people to develop with renewed power.

Suggested Additional Reading

Almost every work of literature and literary dissent mentioned in this chapter has been translated into English. Consult the author and title catalog of your library or the reference librarian for the most recent editions, collections, and anthologies.

BLAKE, PATRICIA and MAX HAYWARD, eds. *Dissonant Voices in Soviet Literature*, (New York, 1962).

BRUMBERG, ABRAHAM, ed. *In Quest of Justice: Protest and Dissent in the Soviet Union Today*, (New York, 1970).

BJÖRKEGREN, HANS. *Aleksandr Solzhenitsyn: A Biography*, (New York, 1972).

DUNLOP, J. B., R. HOUGH, A. KLIMOFF, eds. *Aleksandr Solzhenitsyn: Critical Essays and Documentary Materials*, (Belmont, Mass., 1973).

FIELD, ANDREW, ed. *Pages From Tarusa, New Voices in Russian Writing*, (London, 1964).

GERSTENMAIER, CORNELIA. *The Voices of the Silent*, (New York, 1972).

GIBIAN, GEORGE. *Interval of Freedom: Soviet Literature During the Thaw, 1954–1957*, (Minneapolis, 1960).

HAYWARD, MAX, ed. *On Trial: The Soviet State Versus "Abram Tertz" and "Nikolai Arzhak"*, (New York, 1966).

JOHNSON, PRISCILLA. *Khrushchev and the Arts: The Politics of Soviet Culture, 1962–1964*, (Cambridge, Mass., 1965).

KIRK, IRINA. *Profiles in Russian Resistance*, (New York, 1975).

LITVINOV, PAVEL. *The Trial of the Four: A Collection of Materials on the Case of Galanskov, Ginzburg, Dobrovolsky & Lashkova, 1967–68*, (New York, 1972).

MEDVEDEV, ZHORES A. *The Medvedev Papers: The Plight of Soviet Science Today*, (New York, 1971).

MEDVEDEV, ZHORES A. *Ten Years After Ivan Denisovich*, (New York, 1973).

REAVEY, GEORGE, ed. and trans. *The New Russian Poets, 1953–1966: An Anthology*, (New York, 1966).

REDDAWAY, PETER, ed. and trans. *Uncensored Russia: Protest and Dissent in the Soviet Union: The Unofficial Moscow Journal "A Chronicle of Current Events"*, (New York, 1972).

ROTHBERG, ABRAHAM. *Aleksandr Solzhenitsyn—The Major Novels*, (Ithaca, N.Y., 1971).

ROTHBERG, ABRAHAM. *The Heirs of Stalin: Dissidence and the Soviet Regime, 1953–1970*, (Ithaca, N.Y., 1972).

SJEKLOCHA, PAUL, and IGOR MEAD. *Unofficial Art in the Soviet Union*, (Berkeley, 1967).

SOLZHENITSYN, ALEKSANDR, et al. *From Under the Rubble: Essays*, (New York, 1975).

TÖKES, RUDOLF L., ed. *Dissent in the USSR: Politics, Ideology, and People*, (Baltimore, 1975).

See also the British journals *Encounter* and *Survey*, both of which contain frequent translations of current Soviet stories, poems, and essays from the underground movement of dissent, and articles about the current cultural scene in the Soviet Union.

40

The Brezhnev Era

A COLLECTIVE LEADERSHIP ruled the USSR after Khrushchev's removal in October 1964. Leonid I. Brezhnev soon assumed the most prominent position but did not become a dictator. The new leaders, avoiding Khrushchev's bold experiments, acted soberly, cautiously, and unimaginatively, stressing efficiency, order, and stability. At home, controls over intellectuals were tightened in a partial return to Stalinism, and the regime sought to combine industrial and agricultural growth with impressive military power. Abroad, the USSR consolidated control of eastern Europe and continued détente with the West and ideological and political rivalry with China. Has the Soviet system achieved stability or stagnation? Has dissent been crushed, or does a resurgent nationalism among minority peoples threaten the USSR's very existence? Why has economic growth slowed, and what does this portend?

POLITICS AND DISSENT

After Khrushchev's ouster, an oligarchy in the Presidium headed by Brezhnev, A. N. Kosygin, and N. V. Podgorny assumed power. *Pravda* castigated Khrushchev's methods:

> The Leninist Party is an enemy of subjectivism and drift in Communist construction. Wild schemes; half-baked conclusions and hasty decisions and actions divorced from reality; bragging and bluster; attraction to rule by fiat; unwillingness to take into account what science and practical experience have already worked out—these are alien to the Party. The construction of Communism is a living, creative undertaking. It does not tolerate armchair methods, one-man decisions, or disregard for the practical experience of the masses.[1]

Subsequently Khrushchev was not criticized by name but was relegated to oblivion. The new leaders, at first uncertain about their political line, were absorbed in a power struggle raging beneath a placid

[1] *Pravda*, October 17, 1964, quoted in Dornberg, *Brezhnev*, p. 184.

618

surface. A veil of anonymity, sobriety, and secrecy enveloped them as they jockeyed for position. Group and individual photographs were avoided so as not to reveal their order of prominence. In the Presidium, which soon reasserted primacy over the Secretariat, former Khrushchev supporters retained their posts. Some Western observers did not expect the collective leadership to last, but it proved surprisingly durable and effective. Powerful interest groups: competed behind the scenes: the party apparatus, high State administrators, "steeleaters" (heavy industry), and less influential army and police elements. None of these lobbies could dictate to or ignore the interests of the others; clashes among them ended in compromise. Whereas the successors of Lenin and Stalin soon had achieved complete or modified one-man rule, this time the top posts of secretary-general (Brezhnev) and premier (Kosygin) remained in different hands.

Within 18 months of the October coup, Brezhnev emerged clearly above his rivals. A Western diplomat admitted: "We just didn't give him enough credit. . . . Everybody wrote him off as a party hack, as a colorless *apparatchik*, as a compromise candidate." Beginning with the mere title of first party secretary and some supporters, Brezhnev outmaneuvered and neutralized Podgorny and quickly restored his followers to posts from which they had earlier been removed. In December 1965, Podgorny was "promoted" to titular president of the USSR. An initial confrontation between Brezhnev and Kosygin (May 1965), heading the two most powerful lobbies, produced a standoff, but soon Brezhnev invaded Kosygin's sphere to become a leading spokesman in foreign affairs. The 23rd Party Congress (March–April 1966) gave Brezhnev the title of Secretary-General and confirmed his superior power. No second secretary was named, and Brezhnev had Podgorny and Shelepin removed from the Secretariat, but he proved unable then to purge the Politburo.

Leonid Brezhnev had risen from lowly origins by hard, persistent work, mainly in the party apparatus. Born in 1906 in Kamenskoe (later renamed Dneprozherzhinsk), the Ukraine, of Russian worker parents, he was graduated from a classical gymnasium and later obtained a degree as a metallurgical engineer. From 1938 on, his career was linked closely with Khrushchev's. Serving as a political commissar in World War II, Brezhnev achieved the rank of major general, and once in power his military career was glorified and inflated beyond measure. Leaving the military service in 1946, Brezhnev, as a chosen member of Khrushchev's entourage, became party chief in Zaporozhe where his success in rebuilding a hydroelectric station and a steel plant brought him membership in the Ukrainian Politburo. In the early 1950s he served as party chief in Moldavia, then in Kazakhstan. Under Khrushchev he became a secretary of the Central Committee and a member of the Politburo. Kicked upstairs in 1960 as titular president of the USSR, he alone of Soviet politicians returned from that political graveyard to true power. After Kozlov's stroke in April 1963 (a stroke of fortune for him and Khrushchev!), he was restored to the Secretariat and became Khrushchev's heir apparent. In the brutal world of

Soviet politics Brezhnev succeeded through patronage, intrigue, manipulation, and maneuver. He built a strong political machine called by some in the West the "Dnieper Mafia," consisting of former engineers, factory directors, and officials from his home region. Brezhnev won the reputation of being efficient, quiet, sensible, with a low profile—a man of experience in agriculture, industry, and the military.

Brezhnev's sporadic attempts after 1965 to achieve full power apparently were blocked by other Politburo members representing powerful lobbies. On his 60th birthday he launched a new mini cult of personality (December 1966), and in 1967 he ousted his main rivals from the Secretariat and dominated celebrations of the 50th anniversary of Bolshevik power. In 1970 he reportedly sought to remove Kosygin and become premier but failed. The 24th Congress (March–April 1971) confirmed Brezhnev's personal ascendancy over the party and succeeded in enlarging the Politburo to include his cronies, V. V. Shcherbitskii and D. Kunaev; F. Kulakov, an associate; and V. Grishin, the independent Moscow chief. Brezhnev's summit diplomacy with Premier Brandt of West Germany and President Nixon of the United States reaffirmed his authority. Finally, in 1973 the Politburo's composition was changed: Voronov and Shelest were removed and replaced by Marshal Andrei Grechko (Defense Minister), Iuri Andropov (security police chief), and Andrei Gromyko (Foreign Minister); in May 1975, Alexander Shelepin was removed. These moves appeared to consolidate Brezhnev's position, though army and police representation on the Politburo suggested the growing influence of lobbies in Soviet politics.

At the 24th Congress Brezhnev announced that henceforth party congresses would convene every five years to coincide with five year plans. The Central Committee, no longer a key policy-making body, was expanded to 241 full members and 155 nonvoting candidates. By 1971 the party had grown to almost 15 million members, close to six percent of the population. About 40 percent were workers, 15 percent peasants, and 45 percent "employees," according to official figures; the party apparatus of full-time paid workers numbered about 250,000. Alarmed by events in Czechoslovakia in 1968[2] with the largest Communist Party per capita, Soviet leaders limited the influx of new members and during an exchange of party cards completed in 1974 removed undesirables from the rolls. This action slowed the steady growth in the party's size. Under Brezhnev the party's elite status, especially the apparatus, has been further enhanced. Middle-level party officials are now more difficult to remove than ever.

Western scholars have debated whether the present Soviet regime represents a stable oligarchy or modified one-man rule, whether it is reverting to Stalinist autocracy or is permitting greater latitude of opinion. The present leaders, concealing their rivalries from the public and the outside world, have projected an image of harmony and unity. Some Western scholars (such as Z. Brzezinski), call the Brezhnev regime a "government of clerks" which, seeking to preserve its power and

---

[2] See below, pp. 629–30.

privileges, has lost any desire for social change. Retaining a decaying, dogmatic ideology, the leaders preside, he feels, over a petrifying political order. Other experts, represented by Robert Daniels, note the evolution of "participatory bureaucracy" and institutional pluralism as the chief agencies—party, state, army, and police—all share power. No recent major policies have been adopted which would reduce the influence of any of these key institutions. The "permanent purge" of top officials under Stalin and Khrushchev has yielded to a remarkably stable leadership. With wider ranging debate in the Soviet press, important decisions have been reached only after extensive debate and compromise. The party has become a "political broker," reconciling and compromising differences among various bureaucracies; autocracy is temporarily at least in abeyance.

Indeed, Khrushchev's peaceful removal by the Politburo serves as a precedent and deterrent to a potential dictator. Totalitarian discipline, argues Michel Tatu, can be reimposed only by mass purges, yet the party is anxious to avoid any such police intervention, and Brezhnev has fewer prerogatives than some democratic chief executives. He lacks sole decision-making power and may have policies imposed on him by a Politburo majority which can dismiss him any time. He cannot alter the Politburo's composition without his colleagues' consent. In a sense the Politburo is a democratic island in a totalitarian sea. In 1976 the top five leaders were all elderly: Brezhnev (69), Kosygin (72), Suslov (73), Podgorny (73), and Kirilenko (69), and the first three apparently suffer from chronic ill health. The only dynamic younger man in the top leadership, Shelepin, had been removed from the Politburo, and Brezhnev has been careful not to groom any successor.

After a brief relatively liberal interlude, the Brezhnev regime without reimposing terror adopted a tough stance toward political dissent. De-Stalinization ended, and in the spring of 1965 memoirs by leading World War II generals began praising Stalin's wartime leadership, which Khrushchev had castigated. Stalin and the party, went the new official line, had been fully aware of the Nazi danger in 1941 and had taken essential precautions. A neo-Stalinist supporter of Brezhnev, S. Trapeznikov, described the Stalin era in *Pravda* in October 1965 as "one of the most brilliant in the history of the party and the Soviet state." Supposed nationalism in the Ukraine was severely repressed. In April 1966, two Ukrainian literary critics, Ivan Svetlichny and Ivan Dyuba, were accused of smuggling "nationalist" verses to the West. V. Chornovil, a courageous journalist, who reported Ukrainian trials to the world and denounced KGB tactics, Russification, and discrimination against the Ukrainian language and culture, was sentenced to forced labor. That fall Articles 190/1 and 190/3, used extensively against dissidents, were added to the Soviet criminal code making it a crime to spread "slanderous inventions about the Soviet state and social system" or to "disturb public order."

Frequently the regime resorted to forced incarceration of dissidents in psychiatric hospitals. In 1966 the writer Valeri Tarsis, exiled to England, published *Ward Seven,* which described compulsory treatment in a Moscow psychiatric hospital. "I believe in God and I cannot live in a country where one cannot be an honest man," wrote Tarsis. "This [the USSR] is not a democratic country; this is Fascism." The Politburo declared him insane, a traitor, and deprived him of Soviet citizenship! In 1967 former major general Peter Grigorenko, campaigning for the right of Crimean Tatars to return home from exile, was arrested, committed to a hospital for the criminally insane, and beaten by the KGB. Explained another dissident, Vladimir Bukovskii:

> The inmates are prisoners, people who committed actions considered crimes from the point of view of the authorities . . . but not . . . of the law. And in order to isolate them and punish them somehow, these people are declared insane and kept in the ward of the psychiatric hospital.[3]

Andrei Amalrik, a young historian, has compared dissident trials under Brezhnev with medieval heresy trials. "Recognizing their ideological hopelessness, they [the leaders] cling in fear to criminal codes, to prison camps and psychiatric hospitals." Deprived of his job, Amalrik was convicted of "parasitism" and despite a heart condition served 16 months in Siberia at hard labor. In his *Involuntary Journey to Siberia,* he revealed the ignorance, drunkenness, hatred, and submissive apathy of the Soviet peasantry. In 1969 Amalrik's essay, *Will the Soviet Union Survive until 1984?* was published abroad. It predicted a Sino-Soviet war which would destroy a USSR ruled by unimaginative and incapable bureaucrats and torn by national rivalries. Amalrik's whole life has been a struggle for personal integrity and truth. In July 1976 he was compelled to leave the USSR.

Leaders of the dissident Democratic Movement have sought to inform the Soviet public and the world of what was happening in the USSR in order to block a return to Stalinist terror. More and more scientists and intellectuals joined its ranks. One of its leading statements was the Sakharov Memorandum, issued in 1968 in *samizdat* and published abroad by the father of the Soviet hydrogen bomb, Andrei Sakharov. His protest reflected growing support by Soviet scientists for civil liberties and democratization. Citing the deadly danger to mankind for nuclear war, overpopulation, bureaucracy, and environmental pollution, Sakharov urged Soviet-American cooperation to save civilization. The Soviet and American systems, borrowing from one another, were converging and would end up with democratic socialism. Sakharov strongly attacked Stalinism and its vestiges, advocated democratic freedoms for the USSR, and denounced collectivization as an "almost serflike enslavement of the peasantry." He demanded rehabilitation for all of Stalin's victims: "Only the most meticulous analysis of the [Stalinist] past and its consequences will now enable us to wash off the blood and dirt that befouled our banner." In May 1970 he warned Brezhnev that unless secrecy were removed from science, culture, and technology, the USSR would become a second-rate provincial country.

Heedless of such advice, the Brezhnev regime crushed organized

---

[3] Quoted in A. Rothberg, *The Heirs of Stalin* (Ithaca, N.Y., 1972), p. 301.

Brezhnev and Nixon at Moscow Summit in 1972

dissent. After 1971, with most of its leaders imprisoned or exiled, the Democratic Movement disintegrated. Worldwide fame enabled Sakharov and Solzhenitsyn to continue their protests, but they were increasingly isolated. Brezhnev, while rejecting extremist Stalinist demands for mass purges and terror, achieved political stability based on police repression.

ECONOMY AND SOCIETY

A declining economic growth rate and increasing demands on Soviet resources faced the new leadership. Changing weather patterns caused annual growth rates to fluctuate widely, but the general trend was down.[4] Reformers urged drastic changes: eliminating much central planning of prices and introducing competitive bidding between the State Planning Commission and individual plants. The party apparatus and the technocrats, however, refused to dismantle the central

---

[4] A bad harvest in 1972 reduced the growth rate to 1.7 percent, but a good crop in 1973 raised it to a healthy 7.5 percent. The average rate of growth 1956–60 was 6.5 percent; 1961–65, 5 percent; 1966–70, 5.5 percent; and 1971–74, 4.4 percent. The goal for the 1971–75 period was 5.8 percent.

planning empire, relax controls, or move toward market socialism. Conservative ideologists opposed making concessions to capitalism.

Premier Kosygin, supporting reform, backed many of the ideas of a follower of Oskar Lange of Poland, Evsei Liberman of Kharkov University, who advocated the concept of profitability. Liberman rejected Stalinist economics based on commands from above and absolute obedience from below and its emphasis on physical volume of output regardless of cost or quality. He wished to free the individual enterprise from outside controls except for overall production goals and time of delivery. Wage increases and bonuses for managers and workers would depend on profitability, i.e., on the sale of products, not on fulfilling production norms. Supply and demand would be used, and suppliers and manufacturers would deal directly with one another rather than going through central economic ministries.

In July 1964, Khrushchev authorized an experiment with aspects of Libermanism in two clothing combines. Profits and sales increased sufficiently to encourage the new leaders to try Liberman's theories on a modified basis in some 400 consumer enterprises. Greater flexibility to adjust to consumer demand and more emphasis on quality resulted.

This experiment was underway when Kosygin's proposals for general economic reform, "a new system of planning and incentives," were approved in September 1965. Back in April Kosygin had challenged the party's role in planning:

> We have to free ourselves completely . . . from everything that used to tie down the planning officials and obliged them to draft plans otherwise than in accordance with the interests of the economy. . . . We often find ourselves prisoners of laws we ourselves have made.[5]

The September reforms included Liberman's managerial economics and profit ideas, but Kosygin coupled this with a restoration of the central economic ministries, often under their Stalinist bosses. Khrushchev's *sovnarkhozy*, by now merely another link in the chain of command, were scrapped. They had been defended strongly by local party officials anxious to retain control of regional industry. The Moscow technocrats regained all of their pre-1957 powers: the new head of Gosplan, N. K. Baibakov, had been removed from that post by Khrushchev in 1957!

Opposition from conservative party elements and Stalinist managers watered down the Kosygin reforms and slowed their implementation. Conservatives realized that to free managers from central tutelage would reduce the power of the party, bureaucracy, and the military over industry. To orthodox party men, Libermanism was "goulash communism," and to allow market forces to prevail over central planning would be "unscientific." Many managers, fearful of responsibility, preferred reliable supervisors and acted in the old Stalinist manner. Thus the 1965 reforms, rather than implementing Libermanism, merely took up some slack in the old system. A Soviet economist lamented:

---

[5] Cited in M. Tatu, *Power in the Kremlin* (New York, 1968), p. 447.

I thought they [the leaders] understood from their experience that repressive measures would never achieve results and that they were therefore ready to employ purely economic tools. Now I see there was nothing to it.[6]

As Soviet growth rates continued to fall, the leadership sought other solutions. In the postwar era a sharply expanding labor force and heavy investment in capital goods had fostered rapid economic growth, but by the 1960s labor shortages and rising consumer demand had undermined this old strategy. Because the regime insisted on maintaining a huge military establishment, the only recourse was to raise labor productivity through imported technology. Eventually this might promote inflation, but in the short term rising world prices for Soviet raw material exports, especially oil, manganese, and iron ore, would prevent this.

The Ninth Five Year Plan (1971–75) approved at the 24th Party Congress reflected a dramatic shift toward consumer industry, perhaps partly in response to worker riots in Poland, which forced Wladyslaw Gomulka to resign. For the first time since 1928, consumer industry was supposed to rise somewhat faster than heavy industry. Heavy investments were slated for agriculture, passenger cars, and other consumer durables. The chief future task, noted the Plan, was "to insure a significant increase in the material and cultural standard of living." Stressing this theme at the Congress, Brezhnev emphasized the importance of private garden plots, quality in consumer goods, larger pensions, and higher minimum wages.

Agriculture, though improved, remained the weak link in the Soviet economy. (Solzhenitsyn in his *Letter to the Soviet Leaders* [1973] even urged abolition of the inefficient collective farm system.) Since 1953 per capita agricultural production in the USSR has risen only about one percent annually. Crop failures in 1963 and 1972 affected the entire economy adversely, and there were severe shortages of bread and flour. In 1972 the USSR purchased $750 million worth of U.S. grain, the largest transaction of its kind in the two countries' history. Small private plots, labor intensive and providing strong incentives, still produce at least one third of gross Soviet agricultural output, and their crop yields and livestock output per animal exceed substantially those on collective and state farms. Inadequate investment and mechanization have hampered Soviet agricultural growth. Soviet farmers till lands about 70 percent greater than in the United States with more than seven times the manpower but with only about one third the tractors and trucks and 60 percent of the grain combines. Despite an excellent harvest in 1973 of 222.5 million tons of grain, the USSR has not yet achieved self-sufficiency in grains, and later harvests have been much poorer.

Soviet foreign trade in the 1970s has risen sharply, spurred by im-

---

[6] Cited in Robert Conquest, "A New Russia? A New World?", *Foreign Affairs*, April 1975, p. 487.

ports of Western technology. Between 1971 and 1974 trade grew by 73 percent, at least twice the increase of industrial production. Soviet trade with the capitalist world now exceeds that with the socialist bloc. To finance Western imports, Soviet oil exports rose from 96 million tons in 1970 to an estimated 125 million in 1975, mostly to Europe and Cuba. Détente with the West enhances Soviet growth, which would be much more expensive if the USSR had to rely solely upon its own technology.

The Soviet economy today is impressive but still far smaller than that of the United States. During 1974, according to Soviet figures, over 684 million tons of coal were produced, 459 million tons of oil and gas condensate, 136 million tons of steel (all in excess of U.S. production), 225 million tons of iron ore, and 975 billion kilowat hours of electricity. The Soviet Union possesses huge reserves of raw materials, far greater than those of any other country, though mostly in remote eastern and northern regions. The USSR claims 57 percent of the world's coal reserves, more than 25 percent of natural gas, and 50 percent of oil shale reserves in an energy-short world. The USSR increased its comparative percentage of the United States Gross National Product from 34 percent in 1950 to 45–47 percent in 1969, but since then this percentage has stagnated. Furthermore, in 1962 Soviet industry lagged an estimated 25 years technologically behind the United States. Thus in 1971 the USSR had about 6,000 computers compared to 24,000 in Western Europe and 63,000 more sophisticated ones in the United States. These comparisons suggest some of the reasons why the Brezhnev regime has promoted détente with the United States.

By 1975 the Soviet population exceeded 250 million. According to the 1970 census about 56 percent was urban and 44 percent rural. The Soviet birthrate was 17.5 per thousand in 1968, varying from only 14.2 in the Russian Republic to more than 30 in the five Central Asian republics. Non-Russian elements are generally increasing in numbers much faster than Russians. From 1959 to 1974 the Soviet urban population rose about 50 percent. Moscow (7,528,000) and Leningrad (4,243,000) have grown more slowly than most other large cities. According to official Soviet figures from the end of 1974, Minsk's population, for example, rose from 509,000 in 1959 to 1,095,000 in 1974. In 1975 there were 13 Soviet cities with more than one million population and six more with more than 920,000. This rapid urban expansion has complicated the chronic postwar housing crisis. In 1970 among the 15 largest Soviet cities only Moscow and Donetsk had achieved the minimum housing standard of nine square meters per person. The housing situation has improved markedly in recent years, but rising consumer expectations make waiting lists for desirable apartments longer than ever.

The Soviet standard of living, though it has risen considerably under Brezhnev, remains the lowest of major industrial countries. In 1964 the income per capita in 1964 dollars was $1,289 in the USSR compared with $3,273 in the United States. The average Soviet citizen still has an inadequate diet with too little meat, lives in shabby, overcrowded housing, and leads a dull and drab existence. Compared with earnings, consumer goods remain extremely high-priced. It takes a Soviet worker about 49 hours to earn a pair of shoes compared to 4.5 hours for his American counterpart. There has been growing consumer resistance against low quality goods; yet goals in light industry have rarely been fulfilled.

There has been growing official concern over crime. A new gun control law of February 1974 prescribes up to five years imprisonment for unauthorized possession of firearms. Crimes of violence have been increasing, notably in the southern areas. Severe penalties are now imposed for drug abuse, especially involving marijuana and hashish. Alcoholism remains the number one social problem despite repeated government campaigns and remains the leading cause of low labor productivity. Government spokesmen no longer attribute it to tsarism or the bourgeoisie!

In 1970 women represented 53.9 percent of the Soviet population and 51 percent of the work force. Women, however, comprised only 22.6 percent of party members, only 14 were full or candidate members of the Central Committee, and only one, Ekaterina Furtseva, has ever sat in the Politburo. The USSR has more women doctors, lawyers, and machine operators per capita than any Western country, but women have only token representation in top economic, cultural, and political bodies. This situation appears to reflect passivity of women rather than lack of official encouragement. Demand for their labor has brought women mainly into low-skilled, physical labor job categories. Lingering traditional concepts of women's role in the home and at work promote their dual exploitation. The regime promotes legal equality of women while permitting economic, cultural, and political inequality to persist. This situaton will doubtless continue until women enter the higher reaches of the party in large numbers.

Within Soviet society the "new class" of bureaucrats, officers, and intellectuals continues to enjoy most of its benefits and generally are screened off from much contact with the masses. Industrial workers continue to enjoy high status but low wages. Collective farmers remain at the bottom of the social ladder, though recent welfare increases have raised their living standards somewhat. They now receive guaranteed minimum monthly wages and old age pensions, but they still earn less than state farm workers or blue-collar industrial workers. In most cases collective farmers lack internal passports, preventing them from traveling without permission of the authorities.

FOREIGN AFFAIRS AND ARMED FORCES

Abroad, the prudent Brezhnev regime, carrying a big military stick, has avoided Khrushchev's dramatic initiatives, threats, and violent reversals. Until 1968 Soviet policy seemed adrift and lacking in self-confidence. Successful intervention in Czechoslovakia, halting the erosion of Soviet control over eastern Europe, reversed this picture. Brezhnev thereafter became more decisive and self-assured. Détente

David MacKenzie

Military parade on May Day in Red Square, Moscow

with the West produced important agreements with West Germany and
the United States, while the dispute with China continued to rage.

The new leaders' initial approach abroad was: we are not angry with
anyone. They sought at first to mend their fences with China, but from
1965 on Sino-Soviet competition increased over influence in Asia and
between the bellicose Chinese and moderate Soviet stance in the Vietnam War. Exploiting this quarrel to enhance its autonomy, Rumania
established warm relations with China and increased its trade with the
West. In 1966 as the "Cultural Revolution" began in China, the Chinese
boycotted the Soviet 23rd Party Congress, and Russians in China were
beaten up. Chinese students left the USSR, and Sino-Soviet trade shrank
almost to zero. In January 1969, *Pravda* called Maoism "a great power
adventurist policy based on a petty bourgeois nationalistic ideology
alien to Marxism-Leninism." As friction mounted along the 4,000 mile
Sino-Soviet frontier, the Soviet writer, Evgeni Yevtushenko, compared
the Chinese with the Mongols. War between the Communist giants became a real possibility despite the assertions of Marxist-Leninist doctrine.

Faced with this rising menace in the East, Soviet leaders avoided
major trouble in the West and built up the USSR's military strength.
The Soviets stepped up trade with western Europe and during Charles
de Gaulle's presidency sought to exploit Franco-American coolness to
split NATO. The similar roles of Rumania and France suggested the
weakening hold by the two blocs over their members as contacts increased between eastern and western European countries. The Cuban
crisis had altered Soviet-American relations considerably. Both sides,

noted Hans Morgenthau, renouncing active use of nuclear weapons, retained them as deterrents, aimed at a balance of power and appeared to realize that neither could achieve true predominance. Their rivalry in the Third World cooled as they discovered that neutral countries would not commit themselves totally to either bloc. In their relations, the United States and the Soviet Union de-emphasized ideology and stressed pragmatic power considerations. Between 1965 and 1968 heavy American involvement in Vietnam poisoned their relations; its subsequent decline promoted détente.

In the late 1960s Soviet policy in the Third World produced both setbacks and successes. During 1965 several pro-Soviet regimes collapsed, notably Nkrumah in Ghana and Sukarno in Indonesia; anti-Communist military governments replaced them. The Brezhnev regime shifted to practical economic assistance and military aid. Seeking to build up India as a bulwark against China, Moscow viewed with dismay the Indo-Pakistan war of 1965. Premier Kosygin met with their heads of state in Tashkent early in 1966, and the resulting settlement enhanced the Soviet image as an Asian peacemaker. India's dependence upon Soviet industrial, military, and diplomatic support increased, their trade expanded, and Soviet naval vessels in the Indian Ocean challenged the former Western monopoly. In the Middle East in order to undermine the West's position and keep the region in turmoil and win political influence, the USSR supplied major economic and military aid to Egypt and Syria. Their defeat by Israel in the June 1967 war was a costly setback to Soviet policy, but it increased Arab distrust of the West and dependence on Moscow. After the war the Soviets rebuilt their clients' armies and thousands of Soviet advisers trained Egyptians to use more sophisticated military equipment. Iraq, the Sudan, and Algeria also relied heavily on Soviet arms. Soviet influence in the Middle East reached unprecedented heights, then declined somewhat in the early 1970s.

The Soviet invasion of Czechoslovakia in August 1968 marked a crucial turning point in Brezhnev's foreign policy. Early that year Czechoslovakia under Premier Alexander Dubček had moved rapidly toward democratic socialism, virtually ended domestic censorship, and increased ties with the West. Communist East Germany and Poland became alarmed, and there were reverberations in the Soviet Ukraine. The Soviet decision to intervene followed apparent agreement with the Czech leaders at Cierna. Without political preparation, credible pretext, or support from any Czech group came a massive Soviet invasion with token forces from other east European states. Yugoslav and Rumanian moral support to the Czechs and Western denunciations of the Soviet move were ignored. The military operation was smooth and unopposed and revealed Soviet military efficiency, but the Czech passive resistance and hostility surprised many Russians. The invasion revealed that collective leaderships are not always indecisive. Without hindrance from the United States, the USSR placed six Soviet divisions in Czechoslovakia and altered the strategic balance in central Europe. The Soviet press rather surprisingly quoted Bismarck: "Whoever rules

Bohemia holds the key to Europe." The subsequent Brezhnev Doctrine warned that the USSR would not tolerate internal or external challenges to its hegemony in eastern Europe. The Yugoslavs and Rumanians feared that Brezhnev might apply his doctrine against them, but their clear determination to resist militarily may have dissuaded Moscow. Nonetheless, the Soviet empire in east Europe was consolidated and the Yugoslav and Rumanian challenges muted. Perhaps this situation encouraged the Soviets to confront the Chinese on the Ussuri River frontier early in 1969, a move that induced China to end its military provocations but drove it toward the United States.

Early in 1969 the USSR adopted a more moderate, flexible foreign policy and sought improved relations with the West. To accelerate the sluggish Soviet economy, Brezhnev sought increased trade with the West and U.S. computer technology. The replacement of Konrad Adenauer's hard-line rule in West Germany with the Social Democrat, Willy Brandt, who favored reconciliation with Poland and the USSR, helped Brezhnev heighten his influence in Europe, weaken NATO, and halt movement toward European economic and political unity. During 1970 treaties concluded among the USSR, Poland, and West Germany confirmed their post-World War II boundaries and undercut U.S. bridge-building with individual eastern European countries. Next the Soviets pushed for a general European security conference, again to weaken NATO and relax tensions on their western frontiers. Their hold over eastern Europe, though, remained insecure because of persistent nationalism and the waning force of Marxist ideology. Riots in Poland, which in 1971 forced the conservative Gomulka to resign and brought the more flexible Gierek regime to power, pointed up this continuing problem.

Major increases in Soviet military strength under Brezhnev have enhanced the USSR's power and prestige and have established a new world balance of forces. In 1972 Soviet armed forces of 3.4 million men outnumbered China's (2.9 million) and those of the United States (2.3 million). A Red Army of about two million men (1973) had more than 160 divisions, about 30 percent of which were concentrated on the Sino-Soviet border. Possessing vast numbers of tanks and supporting aircraft, it proved its efficiency and power in invading Czechoslovakia. Whereas in the Cuban Missile Crisis of 1962 the United States held at least a 3 to 1 edge in strategic weapons, by 1969 the USSR had equalled the United States in intercontinental missiles, and later moved well ahead. In deliverable nuclear warheads, the two powers presently are about equal, but the United States still leads in strategic technology. Achievement of approximate nuclear parity has encouraged the two superpowers to reach significant agreements to limit nuclear armaments (SALT). When these talks were first proposed by the United States in 1966, the Soviet military reacted coolly, at first opposing a freeze which would condemn the USSR to strategic inferiority. By 1968 the Soviets had decided to participate in SALT to avoid an excessively expensive competition in nuclear arms. The Soviet commitment to SALT remained tentative until April 1971 when Brezhnev championed

Michael Curran

Leningrad–Palace Square decorated in commemoration of Lenin's 100th Birthday anniversary

détente and apparently accepted the concept of strategic parity. At the Moscow summit of 1972, Nixon and Brezhnev agreed to limit construction of antiballistic missile defense systems and reached an interim accord on offensive missiles. Additional modest steps toward limitation were made at meetings in Moscow and Vladivostok in June and November 1974, which set a ceiling on the number of offensive missiles for both sides. Both powers appear to have recognized their nuclear parity, but the arms race had been merely slowed not halted. Soviet-American cooperation increased also in such nonpolitical areas as space and environmental research, and their trade grew considerably.

Improvement of Soviet-American relations has not halted an ominous Soviet military buildup. After the mid-1960s the Soviet Navy was greatly strengthened and became second only to the American. The Soviets have established a naval presence in all oceans, especially the Mediterranean Sea to support their Middle East policy. *Red Star* declared in 1970: "The age-old dreams of our people have become reality. The pennants of Soviet ships now flutter in the most remote corners of the seas and oceans." Russia's voice must be heard the world over, declared Foreign Minister Gromyko. Russia's merchant fleet has recently become one of the world's largest; some of it is used for intelligence-gathering purposes. A new, more technically trained generation of Soviet army and navy officers has taken command of these growing forces from retiring World War II commanders. The armed forces' role in Soviet politics, however, has remained stable. Military representation in the Politburo and Central Committee remains small, and it seems unlikely that the military will seek to disrupt an existing order which has provided for it so generously.

Whether détente with the West represents a temporary tactic or a permanent policy change remains uncertain. Some observers suggest that having renounced nuclear war as suicidal, Soviet leaders remain committed to achieving world predominance by other means, including subversion conducted by the KGB. The end of American involvement in Vietnam and a continuing Soviet need for American technology have contributed to recently improved relations. During the Arab-Israeli war of 1973, the two powers restricted their competition and avoided a Middle East confrontation. Toward China also, Soviet policy has been more moderate. Since 1969 the danger of war between them has waned as a Soviet preemptive nuclear strike, favored earlier by some Soviet military men, has less and less prospect of success. Nonetheless, China poses a long-term threat to Soviet security and influence in Asia. Under Brezhnev the Soviet Union at terrific cost has taken considerable strides toward becoming the greatest world military power, but the continued rise of China, Japan, and western Europe make prospects of outright Soviet predominance in world affairs uncertain.

Suggested Additional Reading

AMALRIK, A.   *Involuntary Journey to Siberia* (New York, 1970).
————.   *Will the Soviet Union Survive Until 1984?* (New York, 1970).
BRUMBERG, A., ed.   *In Quest of Justice* (New York, 1970).
CHORNOVIL, V.   *The Chornovil Papers* (New York, 1968).
DORNBERG, JOHN.   *Brezhnev: The Masks of Power* (New York, 1974).
GORBANEVSKAIA, N.   *Red Square at Noon* (New York, 1974).
HAMMER, D.   *USSR: The Politics of Oligarchy* (Hinsdale, Ill., 1974).
HODNETT, G. & OGAREFF.   *Leaders of the Soviet Republics, 1965–72* (Canberra, 1973).
KANET, R.   *The Soviet Union and the Developing Nations* (Baltimore, 1974).
KATZ, Z.   *Soviet Dissent and the Social Structure in the USSR* (Cambridge, Mass., 1970).
KOREY, W.   *The Soviet Cage: Anti-Semitism in Russia* (New York, 1973).
LANDIS, L.   *Politics and Oil: Moscow in the Middle East* (New York, 1973).
LITVINOV, P., ed.   *The Demonstration on Pushkin Square* (Boston, 1969).
MARCHENKO, A.   *My Testimony* (New York, 1969).
MEDVEDEV, ROY.   *A Question of Madness* (New York, 1971).
MORTON, H. and TÖKES, R.   *Soviet Politics and Society in the 1970's* (New York, 1974).
ROTHBERG, A.   *The Heirs of Stalin* . . . (Ithaca, 1972).
SAKHAROV, ANDREI.   *Sakharov Speaks* (New York, 1974).
SMITH, H.   *The Russians* (New York, 1975).
SULZBERGER, C.   *The Coldest War: Russia's Game in China* (New York, 1974).
WINDSOR, P. and ROBERTS.   *Czechoslovakia 1968* . . . (London, 1969).

Bibliography

Bibliography

THIS BIBLIOGRAPHY includes only works in English on Russian history. To attempt to include works in foreign languages would have extended it to an unmanageable length. For the same reason, articles have been included only for the section on Early Russia, though some important ones for later periods have been listed in the "Suggested Additional Reading" at the end of each chapter. Older works in English which now seem outdated have likewise been omitted. Consequently, this bibliography does not pretend to be comprehensive; its purpose is to provide the student with a list of the most important and useful works on Russian history.

ABBREVIATIONS OF JOURNALS

AHR = The American Historical Review
ASEER = American Slavic and East European Review
CH = Church History
CQR = Church Quarterly Review
Cal. SS = California Slavic Studies
CSP = Canadian Slavonic Papers
CSS = Canadian Slavic Studies (also Canadian-American Slavic Studies)
DOP = Dumbarton Oaks Papers
EHR = English Historical Review
HSS = Harvard Slavic Studies
HT = History Today
Ind. SS = Indiana Slavic Studies
JAOS = Journal of the American Oriental Society
JCEA = Journal of Central European Affairs
JEBH = Journal of Economics and Business History

JEH = Journal of Economic History
JfGO = Jahrbücher für Geschichte Osteuropas
JHI = Journal of the History of Ideas
JMH = Journal of Modern History
OSP = Oxford Slavonic Papers
PHR = Pacific Historical Review
PP = Past and Present
RoP = Review of Politics
Rus. Rev. = Russian Review
SBB = Studies in Bibliography and Booklore
SEER = Slavonic and East European Review
SEESt. = Slavic and East European Studies
SR = Slavic Review
TRHS = Transactions of the Royal Historical Society
UQ = Ukrainian Quarterly

BIBLIOGRAPHIES

ALLWORTH, E., ed. *Soviet Asia: Bibliographies: The Iranian, Mongolian and Turkic Nationalities.* New York, 1973.

American Bibliography of Russian and East European Studies. Bloomington, Indiana, annually since 1957.

FISHER, H. H., ed.   *American Research on Russia.* Bloomington, Indiana, 1959.

CROWTHER, P.   *A Bibliography of Works in English on Early Russian History to 1800.* New York, 1969.

HAMMOND, T., ed.   *Soviet Foreign Relations and World Communism. A Selected Annotated Bibliography of 7,000 Books in 30 Languages.* Princeton, 1965.

HORAK, S. M.   *Junior Slavica: A Selected Annotated Bibliography of Books in English on Russia and Eastern Europe.* Rochester, N.Y., 1968.

HORECKY, P., ed.   *Basic Russian Publications. A Selected and Annotated Bibliography on Russia and the Soviet Union.* Chicago, 1962.

——.   *Russia and the Soviet Union. A Bibliographic Guide to Western Language Publications.* Chicago, 1965.

HUNT, R. N., ed.   *Books on Communism.* London and New York, 1959.

MAICHEL, K.   *Guide to Russian Reference Books.* Stanford, 1962.

——.   *Guide to Russian Reference Books II: History, Auxiliary Sciences, Ethnography and Geography.* Stanford, 1964.

MARTIANOV, N. N.   *Books Available in English by Russians and on Russia.* New York, 1960.

MAZOUR, A. G.   *Modern Russian Historiography.* Princeton, 1958.

MORLEY, C.   *Guide to Research in Russian History.* Syracuse, N.Y., 1951.

PIERCE, R.   *Soviet Central Asia. A Bibliography.* 3 vols., Berkeley, California, 1966.

SCHULTHEISS, T., ed.   *Russian Studies, 1941–1958: A Cumulation of the Annual Bibliographies from the Russian Review.* Ann Arbor, Mich., 1972.

SHAPIRO, D.   *A Selected Bibliography of Works in English on Russian History, 1801–1917.* New York and London, 1962.

SZEFTEL, M.   "Russia before 1917," in *Bibliographical Introduction to Legal History and Ethnology.* Ed. J. Glissen. Brussels, 1966.

To Russia and Return. Compiler H. Nerhood. *An Annotated Bibliography of Travelers' English Language Account of Russia from the Ninth Century to the Present.* Columbus, Ohio, 1968.

OTHER REFERENCE WORKS

BEZER, C., ed.   *Russian and Soviet Studies: A Handbook.* Columbus, Ohio, 1973.

FLORINSKY, M. T., ed.   *McGraw Hill Encyclopedia of Russia and the Soviet Union.* New York, 1961.

Great Soviet Encyclopedia. A Translation of the Third Edition. 10 vols., New York, 1973.

KEEFE, E.   *Area Handbook for the Soviet Union.* Washington, D.C., 1971.

KERNIG, C., ed.   *Marxism, Communism and Western Society: A Comparative Encyclopedia.* 8 vols., New York, 1972.

KUBIJOVYC, V. et al, eds.   *Ukraine: A Concise Encyclopedia.* 2 vols., Toronto, 1963, Ottawa, 1971.

SCHÖPFLIN, G., ed.   *The Soviet Union and Eastern Europe: A Handbook,* New York, 1970.

UTECHIN, S. V.   *Everyman's Concise Encyclopedia of Russia.* New York, 1961.

WHITING, K.   *The Soviet Union Today.* Revised Edition. New York, 1966.

GENERAL HISTORIES AND ANTHOLOGIES

CHARQUES, R.   *A Short History of Russia*. London, 1956.

CHERNIAVSKY, M., ed.   *The Structure of Russian History: Interpretive Essays* New York, 1970.

CLARKSON, J.   *A History of Russia*. 2nd edition, New York, 1969.

DUKES, PAUL.   *A History of Russia: Medieval, Modern and Contemporary*. New York, 1947.

DVORNIK, F.   *The Slavs in European History and Civilization*. New Brunswick, N.J., 1975.

FLORINSKY, M. T.   *Russia: A History and an Interpretation*. 2 vols. New York, 1953.

————.   *Russia: A Short History*. 2d ed., New York, 1969.

HARCAVE, S.   *Readings in Russian History*. 2 vols., New York, 1962.

HINGLEY, R.   *A Concise History of Russia*. New York, 1972.

————.   *The Tsars, 1533–1917*. New York, 1968.

KLYUCHEVSKY (Kliuchevskii), V. O.   *Course of Russian History*. 5 vols., New York, 1960, translated from the Russian by C. Hogarth.

MILIUKOV, P., et al.   *History of Russia*. Translated C. Markmann. 3 vols. New York, 1968.

PARES, B.   *A History of Russia*. New York, 1953 (1965).

PIPES, R.   *Russia under the Old Regime*. New York, 1974.

PLATONOV, S. F.   *History of Russia*. Translated E. Aronsberg. New York, 1925.

POKROVSKII, M. N.   *Brief History of Russia*. 2 vols., London, 1933.

————.   *History of Russia from the earliest times to the rise of commercial capitalism*. Translated J. Clarkson and M. Griffiths. Second edition. Bloomington, Indiana, 1966.

RAEFF, M., ed.   *Russian Intellectual History: An Anthology*. New York, 1966.

RIHA, T.   *Readings in Russian Civilization*. 2nd ed., 3 vols., Chicago, 1969.

RUBINSTEIN, A. Z., ed.   *The Foreign Policy of the Soviet Union*. 2nd ed., New York, 1960.

SPECTOR, I.   *An Introduction to Russian History and Culture*. 5th ed., Princeton, 1969.

————.   *Readings in Russian History and Culture*. Palo Alto, Calif., 1968.

SUMNER, B. H.   *A Short History of Russia*. New York, 1949.

VERNADSKY, G.   *A History of Russia*. 5th ed., New Haven, 1961.

VERNADSKY, G. and KARPOVICH, M.   *A History of Russia*. New Haven, 1943–69. I. *Ancient Russia* (1943); II. *Kievan Russia* (1948). III. *The Mongols and Russia* (1953); IV. *Russia at the Dawn of the Modern Age* (1959); V. *The Tsardom of Moscow, 1547–1682* (1969).

WALSH, W.   *Readings in Russian History*. Syracuse, N.Y., 1959.

WESSON, R. G.   *The Russian Dilemma: A Political and Geopolitical View*. New Brunswick, N.J., 1974.

WREN, M. C.   *The Course of Russian History*. 3d ed., New York, 1968.

SPECIALIZED HISTORIES

BILLINGTON, J.   *The Icon and the Axe: An Interpretative History of Russian Culture*. New York, 1966.

BLUM, J.   *Lord and Peasant in Russia from the Ninth to the Nineteenth Century*. Princeton, 1961.

CARMICHAEL, J.   *A Cultural History of Russia*. New York, 1968.

CHERNIAVSKY, M.   *Tsar and People: Studies in Russian Myths*. New Haven, 1961.

JELAVICH, B.   *St. Petersburg and Moscow: Tsarist and Soviet Foreign Policy, 1814–1974*. Bloomington, Indiana, 1975.

KERNER, R. J.   *The Urge to the Sea: The Course of Russian History*. Berkeley, Calif., 1946 (1971).

LIASHCHENKO, P. I.   *A History of the National Economy of Russia to the 1917 Revolution*. Translated, New York, 1949.

LOSSKY, N. O.   *History of Russian Philosophy*. New York, 1951.

MASARYK, T. G.   *The Spirit of Russia*. 3 vols., New York, 1955–67.

MILIUKOV, P. N.   *Outlines of Russian Culture*. Ed. M. Karpovich. Translated and abridged. 3 vols., Philadelphia, 1942.

MIRSKY, D. S.   *A History of Russian Literature*. New York, 1927.

———.   *Russia: A Social History*. London, 1931.

PLATONOV, S. I.   *Moscow and the West*. Translated J. Wieczynski. Hattiesburg, Miss., 1972.

PUSHKAREV, S.   *The Emergence of Modern Russia, 1801–1917*. Translated R. McNeal. New York, 1963.

RAUCH, G. VON.   *A History of Soviet Russia*. 6th ed., New York, 1972.

RICE, T. T.   *Russian Art*. London, 1949.

SCHMEMANN, A.   *The Historical Road of Eastern Orthodoxy*. New York, 1963.

SOLOVIEV, A. V.   *Holy Russia: The History of a Religious-Social Idea*. New York, 1959.

STEPHENSON, G.   *Russia from 1812 to 1945: A History*. New York, 1970.

THADEN, E.   *Russia since 1801: The Making of a New Society*. New York, 1971.

WREN, M. C.   *The Western Impact upon Tsarist Russia*. Chicago, 1971.

COLLECTIONS OF ESSAYS

BLACK, C. E., ed.   *The Transformation of Russian Society*. Cambridge, Mass., 1960.

BLACK, E. E., ed.   *Rewriting Russian History: Soviet Interpretations of Russia's Past*. New York, 1956.

BOCIURKIW, B. and J. STRONG, eds.   *Religion and Atheism in the USSR and Eastern Europe*. Toronto, 1975.

CURTISS, J. S., ed.   *Essays in Russian and Soviet History in Honor of G. T. Robinson*. Leiden, 1963.

DRACHKOVITCH, M., ed.   *Fifty Years of Communism in Russia*. University Park, Pa., 1968.

EISSENSTAT, B., ed.   *The Soviet Union: The Seventies and Beyond*. Lexington, Mass., 1975.

FERGUSON, A. and A. LEVIN, eds.   *Essays in Russian History: A Collection Dedicated to George Vernadsky*. Hamden, Conn., 1964.

GERSCHENKRON, A.   *Continuity in History and other Essays*. Cambridge, 1968.

GOLDHAGEN, E., ed.   *Ethnic Minorities in the Soviet Union*. New York, 1968.

HAIMSON, L., ed.   *The Mensheviks from the Revolution of 1917 to the Second World War*. Chicago, 1974.

HENDEL, S. and R. BRAHAM.   *The U.S.S.R. After 50 Years: Promise and Reality*. New York, 1967.

HUNCZAK, T., ed.   *Russian Imperialism from Ivan the Great to the Revolution*. Brunswick, N.J., 1974.

KASSOF, A., ed. *Prospects for Soviet Society.* New York, 1968.

LERNER, W., ed. *The Development of Soviet Foreign Policy: Studies in Honor of W. W. Kulski.* Durham, N.C., 1973.

MCLEAN, H. et al., eds. *Russian Thought and Politics.* Harvard Slavic Studies IV, Cambridge, Mass., 1957.

KANET, R. and I. VOLGYES, eds. *On the Road to Communism: Essays on Soviet Domestic and Foreign Politics.* Lawrence, Kansas, 1972.

LEDERER, I., ed. *Russian Foreign Policy.* New Haven, Conn., 1962.

LEGTERS, L., ed. *Russia: Essays in History and Literature.* Leiden, 1972.

MILLAR, J., ed. *The Soviet Rural Community: A Symposium.* Urbana, Ill., 1971.

MORTON, H. and R. TÖKES, eds. *Soviet Politics and Society in the 1970's.* Riverside, N.J., 1974.

OBERLÄNDER, E. et al., eds. *Russia Enters the Twentieth Century.* New York, 1971.

OLIVA, L. J., ed. *Russia and the West from Peter to Khrushchev.* Boston, 1965.

PIPES, R., ed. *Revolutionary Russia.* Cambridge, Mass., 1968.

————., ed. *The Russian Intelligentsia.* New York, 1961.

RABINOWITCH, A. et al., eds. *Revolution and Politics in Russia: Essays in Memory of B. I. Nicolaevsky.* Bloomington, Ind., 1972.

SIMMONS, E. J., ed. *Continuity and Change in Russian and Soviet Thought.* Cambridge, Mass., 1955.

STAVROU, T., ed. *Russia under the Last Tsar.* Minneapolis, Minn., 1968.

STRONG, J. W. ed. *The Soviet Union under Brezhnev and Kosygin: The Transition Years.* New York, 1971.

TIMBERLAKE, C., ed. *Essays on Russian Liberalism.* Columbia, Miss., 1974.

TÖKES, R., ed. *Dissent in the USSR: Politics, Ideology and People.* Baltimore, 1975.

TREADGOLD, D. W., ed. *The Development of the USSR: An Exchange of Views.* Seattle, 1964.

VUCINICH, W. S., ed. *The Peasant in Nineteenth Century Russia.* Stanford, 1968.

————., ed. *Russia and Asia: Essays on the Influence of Russia on the Asian Peoples.* Stanford, 1972.

EARLY RUSSIA TO 1682

AFANESEV, A. N. *Russian Fairy Tales.* New York, 1945 (1975).

ALEF, G. "The Adoption of the Muscovite Two-Headed Eagle," *Speculum,* 41 (1966).

————. "Muscovy and the Council of Florence," *SR,* 20 (1961).

ALMEDINGEN, E. M. *The Land of Muscovy: The History of Early Russia.* New York, 1972.

ANDERSON, M. S. *Britain's Discovery of Russia, 1553–1815.* London, 1958.

ANDREYEV, N. "Filofey and His Epistle to Ivan Vasilyevich," *SEER, 38* (1959).

————. "Kurbsky's Letters to Vasyan Muromtsev," *SEER, 33,* (1955).

ARBMAN, H. *The Vikings.* London, 1962.

AVVAKUM. *The Life of Archpriest Avvakum by Himself.* New York, 1960.

BACKUS, O. *Motives of West Russian Nobles in Deserting Lithuania for Moscow, 1377–1514.* Lawrence, Kansas, 1957.

————, and H. STAMMLER. "Kievan Christianity and the 'Church Universal,'" *ASEER, 30* (1971).

BARBOUR, P.   *Dmitry Called the Pretender, 1605–06.* Boston, 1966.

BARON, S. H., ed. and trans.   *The Travels of Olearius in Seventeenth Century Russia.* Stanford, 1967.

———.   "The Town in Feudal Russia," *SR, 28* (1969).

BEAZLEY, R.   "The Russian Expansion towards Asia and the Arctic to 1500," *AHR, 13.*

BERRY, L. and R. CRUMMEY, eds.   *Rude and Barbarous Kingdom: Russia in the Accounts of Sixteenth-Century English Voyagers.* Madison, Wisc., 1968.

BIRKETT, G.   "Slavonic Cities, 4: Moscow 1147–1947," *SEER, 25* (1946–47).

BLUM, J.   "The Smerd in Kievan Russia," *ASEER, 12* (1953).

BOLSHAKOFF, S.   *Russian Nonconformity: The Story of Unofficial Religion in Russia.* Philadelphia, 1950.

BRUTZKUS, J.   "The Khazar Origin of Ancient Kiev," *SEER, 22* (1944).

CHERNIAVSKY, M.   "Ivan the Terrible as Renaissance Prince," *SR, 27* (1968).

———.   "Old Believers and the New Religion," *SR, 25* (1966).

———.   *Tsar and People: Studies in Russian Myths.* New Haven, 1961.

CHUBATY, N.   "The Beginnings of Russian History," *UQ, 3* (1946–47).

CHYZHEVSKYI, D.   *Russian Literature from the Eleventh Century to the End of the Baroque.* New York, 1960.

CONYBEARE, F. C.   *Russian Dissenters.* Cambridge, Mass., 1921.

CROSS, S. H.   *Medieval Russian Churches.* Cambridge, Mass., 1949.

———.   "Medieval Russian Contacts with the West," *Speculum, 10* (1935).

CROSS, S. H., trans. and ed.   *The Russian Primary Chronicle.* Cambridge, Mass., 1953.

CRUMMEY, R. O.   *The Old Believers and the World of Anti-Christ.* Madison, Wisc., 1970.

DEWEY, H.   "The 1497 Sudebnik: Muscovite Russia's First National Law Code," *ASEER, 29* (1951).

———.   "Tales of Moscow's Founding," *CSS, 6,* (1972).

———.   "The White Lake Charter: A Medieval Administrative Statute," *Speculum, 32* (1957).

DMYTRYSHYN, B., ed.   *Medieval Russia: A Source Book, 900–1700.* 2nd ed., Hinsdale, Ill., 1973.

DONNELLY, A.   *The Russian Conquest of Bashkiria, 1552–1740.* New Haven, 1968.

DUNLOP, D.   *The History of the Jewish Khazars.* Princeton, 1954.

DVORNIK, F.   "Byzantine Political Ideas in Kievan Russia," *DOP,* Nos. 9 and 10 (1956), Cambridge, Mass.

———.   "The Kiev State and its Relations with Western Europe," *TRHS, 29* (1947).

———.   *The Slavs. Their Early History and Civilization.* Boston, 1956.

ECKARDT, H.   *Ivan the Terrible.* New York, 1949.

ESPER, T., ed. and trans.   *Heinrich von Staden: The Land and Government of Muscovy: A Sixteenth-Century Account.* Stanford, 1967.

———.   "Russia and the Baltic, 1499–1558," *SR, 14* (1966).

FAENSEN, H. et al., trans. by M. Whittall.   *Early Russian Architecture.* London, 1975.

FEDOTOV, G. P.   "Religious Background of Russian Culture," *CH, 12,* (1943).

———.   *The Russian Religious Mind.* vol. I: *Kievan Christianity: The Tenth to the Thirteenth Centuries.* Cambridge, Mass., 1946; II: *The Middle Ages: The Thirteenth to the Fifteenth Centuries.* Ed. J. Meyendorff. Cambridge, Mass., 1966.

FEDOTOV, G. P.   *A Treasury of Russian Spirituality.* New York, 1948.

FENNELL, J., ed. and trans. *The Correspondence between Prince A. M. Kurbsky and Tsar Ivan IV of Russia, 1564–1579* (with Russian text). New York, 1955.

――――. *The Emergence of Moscow, 1304–1359.* Berkeley, 1968.

――――. *Ivan the Great of Moscow.* London, 1961.

――――, ed. *Prince A. M. Kurbsky's History of Ivan IV.* Cambridge, Eng., 1965.

―――― and A. STOKES. *Early Russian Literature.* Berkeley, 1974.

FIELD, C. *The Great Cossack: the Rebellion of Stenka Razin . . .* London, 1947.

FISHER, R. H. *The Russian Fur Trade, 1550–1700.* Berkeley, 1943.

FLETCHER, G. *Of the Russe Commonwealth, 1591.* Cambridge, Mass., 1966.

FLOROVSKY, G. "The Problem of Old Russian Culture," *SR,* 21 (1962).

GREKOV, B. *The Culture of Kiev Rus.* Moscow, 1947.

――――. *Kiev Rus.* Moscow, 1959.

GREY, IAN. *Ivan III and the Unification of Russia.* New York, 1964.

GUDZY, N. K. *History of Early Russian Literature.* New York, 1949.

HALECKI, O. *From Florence to Brest, 1439–1596.* New York, 1959.

HAMILTON, G. H. *The Art and Architecture of Russia.* Baltimore, 1954.

HAMMER, D. "Russia and the Roman Law," *ASEER,* 16 (1957).

HANEY, J. *From Italy to Muscovy: The Life and Works of Maxim the Greek.* Munich, 1971.

HELLIE, R. *Enserfment and Military Change in Muscovy.* Chicago, 1971.

HERBERSTEIN, S. VON *Description of Moscow and Muscovy.* Chicago, 1971 (Reprint).

HONIGMANN, E. "Studies in Slavic Church History," *Byzantion,* 17 (1945).

HOWES, R. C., ed. and trans. *The Testaments of the Grand Princes of Moscow.* Ithaca, N.Y., 1967.

HOWORTH, H. *History of the Mongols from the Ninth to the Nineteenth Century.* 4 vols., London, 1876–1927.

JOHNSON, J. "The Scythian: His Rise and Fall," *JHI,* 20 (1959).

KALMYKOV, A. D. "Iranians and Slavs in South Russia," *JAOS,* 45 (1925).

KAPLAN, F. "The Decline of the Khazars and the Rise of the Varangians," *ASEER,* 13 (1954).

KEENAN, E. *The Kurbskii-Groznyi Apocrypha.* Cambridge, Mass., 1971.

――――. "Muscovy and Kazan: Some Introductory Remarks on the Patterns of Steppe Diplomacy," *SR,* 26 (Dec. 1967).

KEEP, J. "The Decline of the Zemsky Sobor," *SEER,* 36 (1957).

――――. "The Regime of Filaret (1619–1633)," *SEER,* 38 (1960).

KIRCHNER, W. *The Rise of the Baltic Question.* Newark, Dela., 1954.

KLIUCHEVSKY, V. O. "St. Sergius: The Importance of His Life and Work," *Rus. Rev.* (London), 2 (1913).

――――. *A Course in Russian History. The Seventeenth Century.* Trans. of Vol. 3 of Soviet edition of Kliuchevsky's *Collected Works* by N. Duddington. Chicago, 1968.

KONDAKOV, N. P. *The Russian Icon.* Trans. from Russian. Oxford, 1927.

LANGER, L. "V. L. Ianin and the History of Novgorod," *SR,* 33 (Mar. 1974).

LANTZEFF, G. *Siberia in the Seventeenth Century: A Study of Colonial Administration.* Berkeley, 1943.

――――. "Russian Eastward Expansion before the Mongol Invasion," *ASEER,* 6 (1947).

LAZAREV, V. N. *Russian Icons, From the Twelfth to the Fifteenth Century.* New York, 1962.

LOEWENSON, L. "The Moscow Rising of 1648," *SEER,* 27 (1948–49).

LUBIMENKO, I.   "The Correspondence of Queen Elizabeth with the Russian Tsars," *AHR*, *19* (1914).

MALONEY, G.   *Russian Hesychasm: The Spirituality of Nil Sorsky*. Hague, 1973.

MANCALL, M.   *Russia and China: Their Diplomatic Relations to 1728*. Cambridge, Mass., 1971.

MEDLIN, W.   *Moscow and East Rome: A Political Study of the Relations of Church and State in Muscovite Russia*. Geneva, Switz., 1952.

————.   *Renaissance Influences and Religious Reforms in Russia*. Geneva, 1971.

MICHELL, R. and N. FORBES, trans.   *The Chronicle of Novgorod, 1016–1471* in Royal Historical Society Publications, Camden Third Series, *25*, London, 1914.

MILLER, M.   *Archeology in the USSR*. London, 1956.

MINNS, E. H.   *Scythians and Greeks*. Cambridge, Eng., 1913.

MONGAIT, A.   *Archeology in the USSR*. London, 1961.

NABOKOV, V., trans. and ed.   *The Song of Igor's Campaign*. New York, 1960.

NORRETRANDERS, B.   *The Shaping of Tsardom under Ivan Grozny*. Copenhagen, 1964.

OBOLENSKY, D.   "Byzantium, Kiev and Moscow: A Study in Ecclesiastical Relations," *DOP*, *11* (1957).

————.   "Russia's Byzantine Heritage," *OSP*, *1* (1950).

O'BRIEN, C. B.   *Muscovy and the Ukraine: From the Pereiaslavl Agreement to the Truce of Andrusoro*. Berkeley, 1963.

PALMER, W.   *The Patriarch and the Tsar*. 6 vols., London, 1871–76.

PASKIEWICZ, H.   *The Making of the Russian Nation*. London, 1963.

————.   *The Origin of Russia*. London, 1954.

PHILIP, W.   "Russia's Position in Medieval Europe," in L. Legters, ed. *Russia: Essays in History and Literature*. Leiden, Holl., 1972.

PLATONOV, S.   *The Time of Troubles*. Trans. J. Alexander. Lawrence, Kansas, 1970.

POKROVSKY, M. N.   *History of Russia from the Earliest Times to the Rise of Commercial Capitalism*. Trans. and ed. by J. Clarkson and M. Griffiths. New York, 1931.

POLANSKA-WASYLENKO, N.   *Russia and Western Europe in the Tenth-Thirteenth Centuries*. London, 1954.

PRAWDIN, M.   *The Mongol Empire: Its Rise and Legacy*. Trans. E. and C. Paul. 2d ed., New York, 1967.

PRESNIAKOV, A. E.   *The Formation of the Great Russian State*. Trans. by A. Moorhouse. Chicago, 1970.

RABA, J.   "The Fate of the Novgorod Republic," *SEER*, July 1967.

————.   "Novgorod in the Fifteenth Century," *CSS*, Fall 1967.

RAEFF, M.   "An Early Theorist of Absolutism: Joseph of Volokolamsk," *ASEER*, *8* (1949).

RIASANOVSKY, A. V.   "Runaway Slaves and 'Swift Danes' " . . . *Speculum*, *39* (1964).

RIASANOVSKY, N. V.   "The Norman Theory of the Origin of the Russian State," *Rus. Rev.*, Autumn 1947.

ROSTOVTZEFF, M.   *The Animal Style in South Russia and China*. Princeton, 1929.

————.   *Iranians and Greeks in South Russia*. Oxford, 1922.

RUNCIMAN, S.   "Byzantium, Russia and Caesaropapism," *CSP*, *2* (1957).

RYBAKOV, B.   *Early Centuries of Russian History*. Moscow, 1965.

SAWYER, P.   *The Age of the Vikings*. London, 1962.

SEVCENKO, I.   "Byzantine Cultural Influences," in C. Black, ed. *Rewriting Russian History*. Princeton, 1962.

———.   "Intellectual Repercussions of the Council of Florence," *CH*, 24 (1955).

SHULGIN, B.   "Kiev: Mother of Russian Towns," *SEER*, 19 (1939–40).

SMITH, R. E.   "Some Recent Discoveries in Novgorod," *PP*, no. 5, 1954.

SOKOLOV, Y. M.   *Russian Folklore*. New York, 1950.

SOLOVIEV, A. V.   *Holy Russia. The History of a Religious-Social Idea*. New York, 1959.

SPINKA, M.   "Patriarch Nikon and the Subjection of the Russian Church to the State," *CH*, 10 (1941).

SPULER, B.   *The Mongols in History*. New York, 1971.

STENDER-PETERSEN, A.   *Russian Studies*. Copenhagen, 1956.

———.   *Varangica*. Aarhus, 1953.

STOKES, A.   "The Balkan Campaigns of Svyatoslav Igorevich," *SEER*, 41 (1962).

———.   "The Status of the Russian Church, 988–1037," *SEER*, 37 (1959).

STREMOOUKHOFF, D.   "Moscow, the Third Rome: Sources of the Doctrine," *Speculum*, 28 (1953).

SZEFTEL, M.   "Aspects of Feudalism in Russian History," in R. Coulborn, ed. *Feudalism in History*. Princeton, 1956.

———.   "Joseph Volotsky's Political Ideas in a New Historical Perspective," *JfGO*, 13 (1965).

THOMPSON, W. W., ed.   *Novgorod the Great. Excavations of the Medieval City* . . . New York, 1967.

THOMSEN, V.   *Relations between Ancient Russia and Scandinavia and the Origins of the Russian State*. Oxford, 1877.

TIKHOMIROV, M. N.   "The Origins of Christianity in Russia," *History*, 44, (1959).

———.   *The Towns of Ancient Rus* (Translated from Russian) Moscow, 1959.

TOLSTOY, G.   *First Forty Years of Intercourse between England and Russia*. London, 1875.

VASILIEV, A. A.   *The Russian Attack on Constantinople in 860*, Cambridge, Mass., 1946.

———.   "The Second Russian Attack on Constantinople," *DOP*, No. 6 (1951).

———.   "Economic Relations between Byzantium and Old Russia," *JEBH*, 4 (1932).

———.   *The Goths in the Crimea*. Cambridge, Mass., 1936.

———.   "Was Old Russia a Vassal State of Byzantium?", *Speculum*, 7, no. 3 (1932).

VERNADSKY, G.   *Ancient Russia*. New Haven, Conn., 1943.

———.   *Bohdan, Hetman of Ukraine*. New Haven, 1941.

———.   "Feudalism in Russia," *Speculum, 14*.

———.   *Kievan Russia*. New Haven, 1948.

———.   *Medieval Russian Laws*. New York, 1947 and 1969.

———.   *The Mongols and Russia*. New Haven, 1953.

———.   *The Origins of Russia*. Oxford, 1959.

———.   *Russia at the Dawn of the Modern Age*. New Haven, 1959.

———.   *The Tsardom of Moscow, 1547–1682*. New Haven, 1969.

VOYCE, A.   *The Art and Architecture of Medieval Russia*. Norman, Okla., 1967.

———.   *Moscow and the Roots of Russian Culture*. Norman, 1964.

————. *The Moscow Kremlin*. Berkeley, 1954.

VUCINICH, A.   "The Soviet Theory of Social Development in the Early Middle Ages," *Speculum*, 26 (1951).

WEINRYB, B., comp.   "The Khazars: An Annotated Bibliography," *SBB*, 6 (1963).

WEINRYB, B.   "Solving the Khazar Problem: A Study in Soviet Historiography," *Judaism*, 13 (1963).

WILLAN, T.   *Early History of the Russia Company, 1553–1603*, Manchester, England, 1956.

WIPPER, R.   *Ivan Grozny*. Moscow, 1947.

WOLFF, R. L.   "The Three Romes: the Migration of an Ideology and the Making of an Autocrat," *Daedalus*, Spring 1959.

WOODCOCK, G. and I. AVAKUMOVIC.   *The Doukhobors*. New York, 1968.

WREN, M.   *Ancient Russia*. London, 1965.

YANINE, V. L.   "The Dig at Novgorod," *Midway* (Chicago), No. 5 (1961).

ZDAN, M. B.   "The Dependence of Halych-Volyn' Rus on the Golden Horde," *SEER*, 35.

ZENKOVSKY, S. A.   *Medieval Russian Epics, Chronicles and Tales*. New York, 1963.

————.   "The Old Believer Avvakum: His Role in Literature," *Ind.SS, 1* (1956).

————.   "The Russian Church Schism: Its Background and Repercussions," *Rus.Rev., 16*, no. 4 (1957).

————.   "The Spirit of Russian Orthodoxy," *Rus. Rev.*, 22 (1963).

ZERNOV, N.   *The Russians and Their Church*. London, 1945 and 1964.

————.   *St. Sergius, Builder of Russia*. London, 1938.

————.   "Vladimir and the Origin of the Russian Church," *SEER*, 28 (1949–50).

ZGUTA, R.   "Kievan Coinage," *SEER*, 53 (1975).

ZOLKIEWSKI, S.   *Expedition to Moscow: A Memoir*. London, 1959 (Reprint).

IMPERIAL RUSSIA, 1682–1917

ADAMS, A., ed.   *Imperial Russia After 1861: Peaceful Modernization or Revolution?* Boston, 1965.

ALEXANDER, J. T.   *Autocratic Politics in a National Crisis: The Imperial Government and Pugachov's Revolt, 1773–75*. Bloomington, Indiana, 1959.

————.   *Emperor of the Cossacks: Pugachov and the Frontier Jacquerie of 1773–1775*. Lawrence, Kansas, 1973.

ALMEDINGEN, E. M.   *The Emperor Alexander I*. London, 1964.

ALSTON, P.   *Education and the State in Tsarist Russia*. Stanford, 1969.

AMBLER, E.   *Russian Journalism and Politics, 1861–1881: The Career of A. S. Suvorin*. Detroit, 1972.

ANNENKOV, P.   *The Extraordinary Decade: Literary Memoirs by P. V. Annenkov*. Ed. A. Mendel. Ann Arbor, Mich., 1968.

AVRICH, P.   *The Russian Anarchists*. Princeton, 1967.

BADDELEY, J. F.   *The Russian Conquest of the Caucasus*. London, 1908.

BARKER, A. J.   *The War Against Russia, 1854–1856*. New York, 1971.

BARON, S. H.   *Plekhanov: The Father of Russian Marxism*. Stanford, 1963.

BARRAT, G., comp.   *Voices in Exile: The Decembrist Memoirs*. Montreal, 1974.

BECKER, S. *Russia's Protectorates in Central Asia: Bukhara and Khiva, 1865–1924.* Cambridge, Mass., 1968.

BERDIAEV, N. *The Origins of Russian Bolshevism.* London, 1948.

———. *The Russian Idea.* Trans. R. French. London, 1947.

BERLIN, I. *The Hedgehog and the Fox: An Essay on Tolstoy's View of History.* New York, 1953.

BILLINGTON, J. *Mikhailovsky and Russian Populism.* New York, 1958.

BLACK, C. E., ed. *The Transformation of Russian Society: Aspects of Social Change Since 1861.* Cambridge, Mass., 1960.

———, et al. *The Modernization of Japan and Russia: A Comparative Study.* New York, 1975.

BLACK, J. *Nicholas Karamzin and Russian Society.* Toronto, 1975.

BLACKWELL, W. L. *The Beginnings of Russian Industrialization, 1800–1860.* Princeton, 1968.

BOWMAN, H. *Vissarion Belinsky: A Study in the Origins of Social Criticism in Russia.* Cambridge, Mass., 1954.

BROWER, D. R. *Training the Nihilist: Education and Radicalism in Tsarist Russia.* Ithaca, N.Y., 1975.

BROWN, E. J. *Stankevich and His Moscow Circle, 1830–1840.* Stanford, 1966.

BRUSSILOV, A. A. *A Soldier's Notebook, 1914–18.* Westport, Conn., 1971.

BUCHANAN, G. *My Mission to Russia.* 2 vols., Boston, 1923.

BYRNES, R. F. *Pobedonostsev: His Life and Thought.* Bloomington, Ind., 1968.

CARR, E. H. *Mikhail Bakunin.* New York, 1961.

———. *The Romantic Exiles: A Nineteenth Century Portrait Gallery.* London, 1933.

CATHERINE THE GREAT. *The Memoirs of Catherine the Great.* Ed. D. Maroger. Trans. M. Budberg. New York, 1961.

CHARQUES, R. *The Twilight of Imperial Russia.* London, 1958 and 1974.

CHERNIAVSKY, M., ed. *Prologue to Revolution: Notes of A. N. Iakhontov on the Secret Meetings of the Council of Ministers, 1915.* Englewood Cliffs, N.J., 1967.

CHERNYSHEVSKY, N. G. *What is to be Done?* New York, 1961.

CHMIELEWSKI, E. *Tribune of the Slavophiles: Konstantin Aksakov.* Gainesville, Fla., 1961.

CHRISTOFF, P. K. *An Introduction to Nineteenth Century Russian Slavophilism: A Study in Ideas.* Vol. 1: *A. S. Xomjakov.* The Hague, 1961.

CRACRAFT, J. *The Church Reform of Peter the Great.* Stanford, 1971.

CURTISS, J. S. *Church and State in Russia, 1900–1917.* New York, 1940.

———. *The Russian Army under Nicholas I, 1825–1855.* Durham, N.C., 1965.

DALLIN, D. J. *The Rise of Russia in Asia.* New Haven, 1949.

DANIELS, R. V. *V. N. Tatishchev: Guardian of the Petrine Revolution.* Philadelphia, 1973.

DASHKOVA, E. *The Memoirs of Princess Dashkov.* London, 1958.

DILLON, E. J. *The Eclipse of Russia.* London, 1918.

DMYTRYSHYN, B., ed. *Modernization of Russia under Peter I and Catherine II.* New York, 1974.

DOSTOEVSKY, F. *The Diary of a Writer.* Trans. R. Brasol. New York, 1954.

DUFFY, C. *Borodino and the War of 1812.* New York, 1973.

DUKES, P. *Catherine the Great and the Russian Nobility: A Study Based on the Materials of the Legislative Commission of 1767.* Cambridge, Eng., 1968.

EMMONS, T.   *The Emancipation of the Russian Serfs.* New York, 1970.

———.   *The Russian Landed Gentry and the Peasant Emancipation of 1861.* Cambridge, Eng., 1967.

EVANS, J. L.   *The Petrashevsky Circle, 1846–1848.* The Hague, 1974.

FADNER, F.   *Seventy Years of Pan-Slavism: Karamzin to Danilevsky, 1800–1870.* Washington, D.C., 1962.

FISCHER, G.   *Russian Liberalism, from Gentry to Intelligentsia.* Cambridge, Mass., 1958.

FISHER, A.   *The Russian Annexation of the Crimea, 1772–1783.* Cambridge, Eng., 1970.

FLORINSKY, M. T.   *The End of the Russian Empire.* New Haven, 1931; New York, 1961.

FOUST, C.   *Muscovite and Mandarin: Russia's Trade with China, 1727–1805.* Chapel Hill, N.C., 1969.

GARRARD, J. G., ed.   *The Eighteenth Century in Russia.* Oxford, 1973.

GERSCHENKRON, A.   *Economic Backwardness in Historical Perspective.* Cambridge, Mass., 1962.

GETZLER, I.   *Martov: A Political Biography of a Russian Social Democrat.* New York, 1967.

GIERS, N. K.   *The Education of a Russian Statesman: The Memoirs of N. K. Giers.* Ed. C. and B. Jelavich. Berkeley, 1962.

GOLDER, F. A., ed.   *Documents of Russian History, 1914–1917.* New York and London, 1927.

GOLOVIN, N. N.   *The Russian Army in the World War.* New Haven, 1931.

GREENBERG, L. S.   *The Jews in Russia.* 2 vols. New Haven, 1951.

GRIMSTED, P.   *The Foreign Ministers of Alexander I.* Berkeley, 1969.

GRONSKY, P. and N. ASTROV.   *The War and the Russian Government.* New Haven, 1929.

GURKO, V. I.   *Features and Figures of the Past. Government and Opinion in the Reign of Nicholas II.* Stanford and London, 1939.

HAIMSON, L.   *The Russian Marxists and the Origins of Bolshevism.* Cambridge, Mass., 1955.

HARCAVE, S.   *The Russian Revolution of 1905.* London, 1970.

———.   *Years of the Golden Cockerel: The Last Romanov Tsars, 1814–1917.* New York, 1968.

HARE, R.   *Pioneers of Russian Social Thought: Studies of Non-Marxian Formation in Nineteenth Century Russia and of its Partial Revival in the Soviet Union.* New York, 1951.

———.   *Portraits of Russian Personalities between Reform and Revolution.* New York, 1959.

HARRISON, J. A.   *The Founding of the Russian Empire in Asia and America.* Coral Gables, Fla., 1971.

HAXTHAUSEN, A. VON.   *Studies on the Interior of Russia.* Ed. S. Starr, Trans. E. Schmidt. Chicago, 1972.

HERZEN, A. I.   *My Past and Thoughts.* 6 vols. Trans. C. Garnett. New York, 1924–28.

HOSKING, G.   *The Russian Constitutional Experiment: Government and Duma, 1907–1914.* New York, 1973.

HOUGH, R. A.   *The Fleet that Had to Die.* New York, 1961.

IZVOLSKY, A. P.   *Recollections of a Foreign Minister.* Garden City, N.Y., 1921.

JACKSON, W. G.   *Seven Roads to Moscow.* London, 1957.

JELAVICH, B.   *Russia and Greece During the Regency of King Otton, 1832–1835.* Thessalonika, 1962.

———.   *Russia and the Greek Revolution of 1843.* Munich, 1966.

———. *Russia and the Rumanian National Cause, 1858–1859.* Bloomington, Ind., 1959.

JELAVICH, B. and C. *Russia in the East, 1876–1880.* Leiden, 1959.

JELAVICH, C. *Tsarist Russia and Balkan Nationalism: Russian Influence in the Internal Affairs of Bulgaria and Serbia, 1879–1886.* Berkeley, 1958.

JENKINS, M. *Arakcheev: Grand Vizir of the Russian Empire.* New York, 1969.

KAPLAN, H. *The First Partition of Poland.* New York, 1962.

KARAMZIN, N. M. *Letters of a Russian Traveler, 1789—1790 . . . ,* Trans. F. Jonas, ed. E. Simmons. New York, 1957.

———. *Memoir on Ancient and Modern Russia.* Trans. and ed. by R. Pipes. Cambridge, Mass., 1959.

KARPOVICH, M. *Imperial Russia, 1801–1917.* New York, 1832.

KATZ, M. *Mikhail N. Katkov: A Political Biography, 1818–1887.* The Hague, 1966.

KAZEMZADEH, F. *Russia and Britain in Persia, 1864–1914.* New Haven, 1968.

KEEP, J. L. *The Rise of Social Democracy in Russia.* Oxford, 1963.

KENNAN, G. *Siberia and the Exile System.* 2 vols., New York, 1891.

KINDERSLEY, R. *The First Russian Revisionists: A Study of Legal Marxism in Russia.* Oxford, 1962.

KIRCHNER, W. *Commercial Relations Between Russia and Europe, 1400–1800.* Bloomington, Ind., 1966.

KLYUCHEVSKY, V. O. *Peter the Great.* Trans. L. Archibald. New York, 1959.

KOHN, H., ed. *The Mind of Modern Russia: Historical and Political Thought of Russia's Great Age.* New Brunswick, N.J., 1955.

———. *Pan-Slavism: Its History and Ideology.* New York, 1960.

KOKOVTSOV, V. N. *Out of My Past.* Ed. H. Fisher. Stanford, 1935.

KORNILOV, A. A. *Modern Russian History,* 2 vols. in 1. Trans. and continued by A. Kaun. New York, 1924.

KRAVCHINSKY, S. M. (Stepniak). *Underground Russia: Revolutionary Profiles and Sketches from Life.* New York, 1883.

KUCHEROV, S. *Courts, Lawyers and Trials under the Last Three Tsars.* New York, 1953.

LAMPERT, E. *Sons Against Fathers: Studies in Russian Radicalism and Revolution.* London, 1965.

———. *Studies in Rebellion.* London, 1957.

LANE, D. *The Roots of Russian Communism: A Social and Historical Study of Russian Social Democracy, 1898–1907.* University Park, Penn., 1968.

LANG, D. M. *The First Russian Radical: Alexander Radishchev, 1749–1802.* New York, 1960.

LANGER, W. L. *The Franco-Russian Alliance, 1890–94.* Cambridge, Mass., 1929.

LAVROV, P. L. *Historical Letters.* Ed. and trans. J. Scanlan. Berkeley, 1967.

LEDNICKI, W. *Russia, Poland and the West: Essays in Literary and Cultural History.* London and New York, 1954.

LENIN, V. I. *The Development of Capitalism in Russia.* Moscow, 1956.

———. *What is To Be Done?* Peking, 1975.

LENSEN, G. A. *The Russian Push Toward Japan: Russo-Japanese Relations, 1697–1875.* Princeton, 1959.

LESLIE, R. F. *Reform and Insurrection in Russian Poland.* London, 1963.

LEVIN, A. *The Second Duma: A Study of the Social Democratic Party and the Russian Constitutional Experiment.* New Haven, 1940.

———. *The Third Duma: Election and Profile.* Hamden, Conn., 1973.

LONGWORTH, P.　*The Art of Victory: The Life and Achievements of General-issimo Suvorov, 1729–1800.* London, 1965.

LORD, R. H.　*The Second Partition of Poland.* Cambridge, Mass., 1915.

LUKASHEVICH, S.　*Ivan Aksakov, 1823–1886: A Study in Russian Thought and Politics.* Cambridge, Mass., 1965.

———.　*Konstantin Leontiev, 1831–1891: A Study in Russian "Heroic Vitalism."* New York, 1967.

MACKENZIE, D.　*The Lion of Tashkent: The Career of General M. G. Cherniaev.* Athens, Ga., 1974.

———.　*The Serbs and Russian Pan-Slavism, 1875–1878.* Ithaca, N.Y., 1967.

MACMASTER, R. E.　*Danilevsky: A Russian Totalitarian Philosopher.* Cambridge, Mass., 1961.

MADARIAGA, I. DE.　*Britain, Russia and the Armed Neutrality of 1780.* London, 1962.

MAKLAKOV, V. A.　*Memoirs of V. A. Maklakov: The First State Duma: Contemporary Reminiscences.* Ed. M. Belkin. Bloomington, Ind., 1964.

MALIA, M.　*Alexander Herzen and the Birth of Russian Socialism, 1812–1855.* Cambridge, Mass., 1961.

MALOZEMOFF, A.　*Russian Far Eastern Policy, 1881–1904.* Berkeley, 1958.

MANSTEIN, C. VON.　*Contemporary Memoirs of Russia . . . 1727–1744.* New York, 1968.

MASSIE, R. K.　*Nicholas and Alexandra.* New York, 1967.

MAYNARD, J.　*Russia in Flux.* New York, 1948.

———.　*The Russian Peasant and Other Studies.* London, 1942.

MAZOUR, A.　*The First Russian Revolution, 1825: The Decembrist Movement.* Stanford, 1961.

McCONNELL, A.　*A Russian Philosophe: Alexander Radishchev.* The Hague, 1964.

———.　*Tsar Alexander I: Paternalistic Reformer.* New York, 1970.

McGREW, R.　*Russia and the Cholera, 1823–1832.* Madison, Wisc., 1965.

McNEAL, R., ed.　*Russia in Transition, 1905–1914.* New York, 1970.

MEHLINGER, H. and THOMPSON, J. M.　*Count Witte and the Tsarist Government in the 1905 Revolution.* Bloomington, Ind., 1972.

MENDEL, A. P.　*Dilemmas of Progress in Tsarist Russia: Legal Marxism and Legal Populism.* Cambridge, Mass., 1961.

MILIUKOV, P.　*Political Memoirs, 1905–1917.* Ed. A. P. Mendel. Ann Arbor, Mich., 1967.

———.　*Russia and Its Crisis.* Chicago, 1905; New York, 1962.

MILLER, F. A.　*Dmitrii Miliutin and the Reform Era.* Nashville, Tenn., 1968.

MILLER, M. S.　*The Economic Development of Russia, 1905–1914.* London, 1926.

MOCHULSKY, K.　*Dostoevsky: His Life and Work.* Trans. M. Minihan. Princeton, 1967.

MOHRENSCHILDT, D. VON.　*Russia in the Intellectual Life of Eighteenth Century France.* New York, 1936.

MONAS, S.　*The Third Section: Police and Society under Nicholas I.* Cambridge, Mass., 1961.

MOSELY, P. E.　*Russian Diplomacy and the Opening of the Eastern Question in 1838 and 1839.* Cambridge, Mass., 1934.

MOSSE, W. E.　*Alexander II and the Modernization of Russia.* New York, 1958.

———.　*The European Powers and the German Question, 1848–1871.* Cambridge, Eng., 1958.

OBERLANDER, E. et al. *Russia Enters the Twentieth Century, 1894–1917.* New York, 1971.

O'BRIEN, C. B. *Russia under Two Tsars, 1682–1689.* Berkeley, 1952.

OKUN, S. B. *The Russian-American Company.* Trans. from Russian, Cambridge, Mass., 1951.

OLDENBOURG, Z. *Catherine the Great.* New York, 1965.

OLDENBURG, S. S. *Nicholas II: His Reign and His Russia.* 4 vols., vol. 1, Ed. and trans. L. Michalap and P. Rollins. Gulf Breeze, Fla., 1975.

OLIVA, L. J. *Russia in the Era of Peter the Great.* Englewood Cliffs, N.J., 1969.

PALÉOLOGUE, G. *An Ambassador's Memoirs.* 3 vols., London 1925; New York, 1972.

PALMER, A. *Alexander I: Tsar of War and Peace.* London, 1974.

PAPMEHL, K. A. *Freedom of Expression in Eighteenth Century Russia.* The Hague, 1971.

PARES, B. *The Fall of the Russian Monarchy: A Study of the Evidence.* New York, 1939.

———., ed. *Letters of the Tsaritsa to the Tsar, 1914–1916.* London, 1923.

———. *Russia Between Reform and Revolution.* Ed. F. Randall. New York, 1962.

PAVLOVSKY, G. *Agricultural Russia on the Eve of the Revolution.* London, 1930.

PETROVICH, M. B. *The Emergence of Russian Pan-Slavism, 1856–1870.* New York, 1956.

PIERCE, R. A. *Russian Central Asia, 1867–1917: A Study in Colonial Rule.* Berkeley, 1960.

———. *Russia's Hawaiian Adventure, 1815–1817.* Berkeley, 1965.

PINTNER, W. M. *Economic Policy under Nicholas I.* Ithaca, N.Y., 1967.

PIPES, R. ed. *Revolutionary Russia.* Cambridge, Mass., 1968.

———. *Russia Under the Old Regime.* New York, 1975.

———., ed. *The Russian Intelligentsia.* New York, 1961.

———. *Social Democracy and the St. Petersburg Labor Movement, 1885–1897.* Cambridge, Mass., 1963.

PLAMENATZ, J. *German Marxism and Russian Communism.* London, 1954.

POBEDONOSTSEV, K. P. *Reflections of a Russian Statesman.* London, 1898.

POMPER, P. *The Russian Revolutionary Intelligentsia.* New York, 1970.

PRESNIAKOV, A. E. *Emperor Nicholas I of Russia.* Trans. from Russian. Gulf Breeze, Fla., 1974.

PROFFER, C. and E., eds. *The Silver Age of Russian Culture.* Ann Arbor, Mich., 1975.

PURYEAR, V. J. *England, Russia and the Straits Question, 1844–1856.* Berkeley, 1931.

PUSHKAREV, S. *The Emergence of Modern Russia.* Trans. from Russian. New York, 1963.

PUTNAM, P. B. *Peter, the Revolutionary Tsar.* New York, 1973.

PYZIUR, E. *The Doctrine of Anarchism of Michael A. Bakunin.* Milwaukee, Wisc., 1955.

RADISHCHEV, A. N. *A Journey from St. Petersburg to Moscow.* Ed. R. Thaler. Cambridge, Mass., 1958.

RAEFF, M., ed. *The Decembrist Movement.* Englewood Cliffs, N.J., 1966.

———. *Imperial Russia, 1682–1825: The Coming of Age of Modern Russia.* New York, 1971.

———. *Michael Speransky: Statesman of Imperial Russia.* The Hague, 1957.

————. Origins of the Russian Intelligentsia: The Eighteenth Century Nobility. New York, 1966.

————., ed. Peter the Great: Reformer or Revolutionary? Boston, 1963.

————. Plans for Political Reform in Russia, 1730–1905. Englewood Cliffs, N.J., 1966.

————., ed. Russian Intellectual History: An Anthology. New York, 1966.

————. Siberia and the Reforms of 1822. Seattle, 1956.

RANDALL, F.   N. G. Chernyshevskii. New York, 1967.

RANSEL, D.   The Politics of Catherinian Russia. New Haven, 1975.

READING, D. K.   The Anglo-Russian Commercial Treaty of 1734. New Haven, 1938.

REDDAWAY, W. F., ed.   Documents of Catherine the Great. Cambridge, Eng., 1931.

RIASANOVSKY, N. V.   Nicholas I and Official Nationality in Russia, 1825–1855. Berkeley, 1959.

————. Russia and the West in the Teachings of the Slavophiles. Cambridge, Mass., 1952.

RIEBER, A. J. (Ed.)   The Politics of Autocracy: Letters of Alexander II to Prince A. I. Bariatinskii, 1857–1864. Paris, 1966.

RIHA, T.   A Russian European: Paul Miliukov in Russian Politics. Notre Dame, Ind., 1968.

ROBBINS, R. G.   Famine in Russia, 1891–1892: The Imperial Government Responds to a Crisis. New York, 1975.

ROBINSON, G. T.   Rural Russia Under the Old Regime. New York, 1932, 1949.

RODZIANKO, M. V.   Reign of Rasputin. New York, 1927.

ROGGER, H.   National Consciousness in Eighteenth Century Russia. Cambridge, Mass., 1960.

ROMANOV, B.   Russia in Manchuria, 1892–1906. Trans. S. Jones. Ann Arbor, Mich., 1952.

ROSEN, R. R.   Forty Years of Diplomacy. 2 vols., New York, 1922.

SABLINSKY, WALTER.   The Road to Bloody Sunday. Princeton, N.J., 1976.

SAUL, N.   Russia and the Mediterranean, 1797–1807. Chicago, 1970.

SAZONOV, S. D.   Fateful Years, 1909–1916. New York, 1928.

SCHAPIRO, L.   Rationalism and Nationalism in Russian Nineteenth Century Political Thought. New Haven, 1967.

SCHWARTZ, S. M.   The Russian Revolution of 1905: The Workers' Movement and the Formation of Bolshevism and Menshevism. Trans. G. Vakar. Chicago and London, 1967.

SEGEL, H.   The Literature of Eighteenth Century Russia: An Anthology. 2 vols. New York, 1967.

SENN, A. E.   The Russian Revolution in Switzerland. Madison, Wisc., 1971.

SERGE, V.   Memoirs of a Revolutionary, 1901–1941. Trans. P. Sedgwick. London, 1963.

SETON-WATSON, H.   The Russian Empire, 1801–1917. Oxford, 1967.

SHCHERBATOV, M. M.   On the Corruption of Morals in Russia. Ed. and trans. A. Lentin. New York, 1969.

SINEL, A.   The Classroom and the Chancellery: State Educational Reform under Count Dmitry Tolstoi. Cambridge, Mass., 1973.

SMITH, C. J.   The Russian Struggle for Power, 1914–1917. New York, 1956.

SQUIRE, P. S.   The Third Department: The Establishment and Practices of the Political Police in the Russia of Nicholas I. Cambridge, Eng., 1968.

SUMNER, B. H.   Peter the Great and the Emergence of Russia. New York, 1962.

————. *Peter the Great and the Ottoman Empire.* Oxford, 1949.

————. *Russia and the Balkans, 1870–1880.* Oxford, 1937.

————. *Tsardom and Imperialism in the Far East and Middle East, 1880–1914.* London, 1940.

TAI SUNG AN. *The Sino-Soviet Territorial Dispute.* Philadelphia, 1973.

TARLE, E. V. *Napoleon's Invasion of Russia, 1812.* Trans. from Russian. New York, 1942.

THADEN, E. C. *Conservative Nationalism in Nineteenth Century Russia.* Seattle, 1964.

————. *Russia and the Balkan Alliance of 1912.* University Park, Penn., 1965.

THOMSON, G. S. *Catherine the Great and the Expansion of Russia.* London, 1947.

TIMBERLAKE, C. (Ed.). *Essays on Russian Liberalism.* Columbia, Missouri, 1972.

TOMPKINS, S. R. *The Russian Mind: From Peter the Great through the Enlightenment.* Norman, Okla., 1957.

TREADGOLD, D. W. *The Great Siberian Migration.* Princeton, 1957.

————. *Lenin and His Rivals: The Struggle for Russia's Future, 1898–1906.* New York, 1955.

ULAM, A. *The Bolsheviks.* New York, 1965.

VENTURI, F. *Roots of Revolution: A History of the Populist and Socialist Movements in Nineteenth Century Russia.* Trans. F. Haskell. New York, 1960.

VON LAUE, T. H. *Sergei Witte and the Industrialization of Russia.* New York, 1963.

VUCINICH, A. S. *Science in Russian Culture: A History to 1860.* Stanford, 1963.

VUCINICH, W. S. (Ed.). *The Peasant in Nineteenth Century Russia.* Stanford, 1968.

WALISZEWSKI, K. *Paul the First of Russia.* London, 1913.

WALKIN, J. *The Rise of Democracy in Pre-Revolutionary Russia: Political and Social Institutions under the Last Three Tsars.* New York, 1962.

WALLACE, D. M. *Russia on the Eve of War and Revolution.* Ed. by C. Black. New York, 1961. (1880).

WEEKS, A. L. *The First Bolshevik: A Political Biography of Peter Tkachev.* New York, 1968.

WHITE, J. A. *The Diplomacy of the Russo-Japanese War.* Princeton, 1964.

WILDMAN, A. *The Making of a Workers' Revolution: Russian Social Democracy, 1891–1903.* Chicago and London, 1967.

WILSON, E. *To the Finland Station.* New York, 1940.

WITTE, S. IU. *The Memoirs of Count Witte.* Ed. A. Yarmolinsky. Garden City, N.Y., 1921.

WOLFE, B. *Three Who Made a Revolution: A Biographical History.* New York, 1948 (4th ed., 1964).

WORTMAN, R. *The Crisis of Russian Populism.* London, 1967.

YARMOLINSKY, A. *Road to Revolution: A Century of Russian Radicalism.* London, 1957.

ZENKOVSKY, V. V. *Russian Thinkers and Europe.* Transl. from Russian. Ann Arbor, Mich., 1953.

ZETLIN, M. *The Decembrists.* Trans. from Russian by G. Panin. New York, 1958.

SOVIET RUSSIA

ABRAMOVITCH, R.   *The Soviet Revolution, 1917–1939.* New York, 1962.

ADAMS, A. E., ed.   *The Russian Revolution and Bolshevik Victory: Why and How?* Boston, 1972.

——.   *The Bolsheviks in the Ukraine: The Second Campaign.* New Haven, 1963.

ALLILUEVA, S.   *Twenty Letters to a Friend.* New York, 1967.

AMALRIK, A.   *Involuntary Journey to Siberia.* New York, 1970.

——.   *Will the Soviet Union Survive until 1984?* New York, 1970.

ANDREWS, W. G.   *Soviet Institutions and Policies: Inside Views.* Princeton, 1966.

ARMSTRONG, J. A.   *Ideology, Politics and Government in the USSR: An Introduction.* New York, 1962.

——.   *The Politics of Totalitarianism: The Communist Party of the Soviet Union.* New York, 1962.

——.   *The Soviet Bureaucratic Elite: A Case Study of the Ukrainian Apparatus.* New York, 1961.

——.   *Soviet Partisans in World War II.* Madison, Wisc., 1964.

——.   *Ukrainian Nationalism, 1939–1945.* New York, 1955.

AVTORKHANOV, A.   *Stalin and the Soviet Communist Party.* Munich, 1959.

AZRAEL, J. R.   *Managerial Power and Soviet Politics.* Cambridge, Mass., 1966.

BARGHOORN, F. C.   *The Soviet Cultural Offensive.* Princeton, 1960.

——.   *Soviet Russian Nationalism.* New York, 1956.

BAYKOV, A.   *The Development of the Soviet Economic System.* Cambridge, Eng., 1947.

BECK, F. and W. GODIN.   *Russian Purge and the Extraction of Confession.* New York, 1951.

BELOFF, M.   *The Foreign Policy of Soviet Russia, 1929–1941.* 2 vols. New York, 1947–49.

BEREDAY, G. and J. PENNAR, eds.   *The Politics of Soviet Education.* New York, 1960.

BERGSON, A.   *The Economics of Soviet Planning.* New Haven, 1964.

——.   *Planning and Productivity under Soviet Socialism.* New York, 1968.

——.   *Soviet Economic Growth.* Evanston, Ill., 1953.

BERMAN, H. J.   *Justice in Russia.* Cambridge, Mass., 1950, 1963.

—— and M. KERNER.   *Soviet Military Law and Administration.* Cambridge, Mass., 1955.

BIALER, S. (Ed.)   *Stalin and His Generals.* New York, 1969.

BIENSTOCK, G., SCHWARTZ, S., and YUGOV, A.   *Management in Russian Industry and Agriculture.* Ithaca, N.Y., 1944.

BLACKWELL, W.   *The Industrialization of Russia: An Historical Perspective.* New York, 1970.

BORKENAU, F.   *World Communism: A History of the Communist International.* New York, 1939.

BRANDT, C.   *Stalin's Failure in China, 1924–1927.* Cambridge, Mass., 1958.

BROWDER, R. and F. KERENSKY, eds.   *The Russian Provisional Government, 1917.* 3 vols., Stanford, 1961.

BROWN, E. J.   *The Proletarian Episode in Soviet Literature, 1929–1932.* New York, 1953.

——.   *Russian Literature Since the Revolution.* New York, 1963.

BROWN, EMILY.   *The Soviet Trade Unions and Labor Relations.* Cambridge, Mass., 1966.

BRUMBERG, A., ed. *Russia under Khrushchev.* New York, 1962.
————. *In Quest of Justice.* New York, 1970.
BRZEZINSKI, Z. K. *Ideology and Power in Soviet Politics.* New York, 1962.
————. *The Permanent Purge.* Cambridge, Mass., 1956.
————. *The Soviet Bloc: Unity and Conflict.* Cambridge, Mass., 1960, 1967.
BUNYAN, J. and H. FISHER, eds. *The Bolshevik Revolution, 1917–1918: Documents.* Baltimore, 1936.
BUNYAN, J., ed. *Intervention, Civil War and Communism in Russia, April–December 1918: Documents.* Stanford, 1934.
CAMPBELL, R. *Soviet Economic Power: Its Organization, Growth and Challenge.* Boston, 1960.
CANTRIL, H. *Soviet Leaders and Mastery over Man.* New Brunswick, N.J., 1960.
CARRELL, P. *Scorched Earth: The Russian-German War, 1943–44.* Boston, 1970.
CAREW-HUNT, R. N. *The Theory and Practice of Communism.* New York, 1958.
————. *Marxism: Past and Present.* New York, 1954.
CAROE, O. *Soviet Empire: The Turks of Central Asia and Stalinism.* London, 1967.
CARR, E. H. *A History of Soviet Russia.* Vols. 1–3: *The Bolshevik Revolution, 1917–1923.* New York, 1951–53; vol. 4: *The Interregnum, 1923–1924.* New York, 1954; vols. 5–7: *Socialism in One Country, 1924–1926.* New York, 1958; *Foundations of a Planned Economy, 1926–1929.* New York, 1972.
————. *The October Revolution: Before and After.* New York, 1971.
CATTELL, D. T. *Communism and the Spanish Civil War.* Berkeley, 1955.
CHAMBERLIN, W. H. *The Russian Revolution, 1917–1921.* 2 vols. New York, 1935.
CHERNOV, V. *The Great Russian Revolution.* New Haven, 1936.
COHEN, S. *Bukharin: A Political Biography.* New York, 1974.
CONQUEST, R. *The Great Terror.* New York, 1968.
CRAIG, W. *Enemy at the Gates: The Battle of Stalingrad.* New York, 1973.
CRANKSHAW, E. *Khrushchev: A Career.* New York, 1966.
CURTISS, J. S. *The Russian Church and the Soviet State, 1917–1950.* Boston, 1953.
————. *The Russian Revolutions of 1917.* Princeton, 1957.
DALLIN, A. *Soviet Politics Since Khrushchev.* Englewood Cliffs., N.J., 1968.
————. *The Soviet Union at the United Nations.* New York, 1962.
DALLIN, D. and B. NICOLAEVSKY. *Forced Labor in Soviet Russia.* New Haven, 1947.
DALLIN, D. J. *Soviet Foreign Policy After Stalin.* Philadelphia, 1961.
DALLIN, R. (Ed.). *The Stalin Revolution: Fulfillment or Betrayal of Communism?* Boston, 1965.
DAN, TH. *The Origins of Bolshevism.* London, 1964.
DANIELS, R. *The Conscience of the Revolution: Communist Opposition in Soviet Russia.* Cambridge, Mass., 1960.
————. *Red October: The Bolshevik Revolution of 1917.* New York, 1967.
————. *The Russian Revolution.* Englewood Cliffs, N.J., 1972.
————. *The Stalin Revolution.* Lexington, Mass., 1972.
DEGRAS, J., ed. *The Communist International, 1919–1943.* New York, 1956.
————. *Soviet Documents on Foreign Policy, 1917–1941.* 3 vols. New York, 1951–53.
DENIKIN, A. I. *The Career of a Tsarist Officer: Memoirs, 1872–1916.* Trans. M. Patoski. Minneapolis, Minn., 1975.

————. *The Russian Turmoil*. London, 1922.

DEUTSCHER, I., ed.   *The Age of Permanent Revolution: A Trotsky Anthology.* New York, 1964.

DEUTSCHER, I.   *The Prophet Armed: Trotsky 1879–1921*. New York, 1954.

————. *The Prophet Unarmed: Trotsky 1921–1929*. New York, 1959.

————. *The Prophet Outcast: Trotsky 1929–1940*. New York, 1963.

————. *Stalin: A Political Biography*. New York, 1949, 1966.

DE WITT, N.   *Education and Professional Employment in the USSR.* Washington, D.C., 1961.

DINERSTEIN, H. and L. GOURÉ.   *War and the Soviet Union*. New York, 1962.

DMYTRYSHYN, B.   *Moscow and the Ukraine, 1918–1952*. New York, 1956.

DOBB, M.   *Soviet Economic Development since the 1917 Revolution.* London, 1948.

DORNBERG, J.   *Brezhnev: The Masks of Power*. New York, 1974.

DRACHKOVITCH, M., ed.   *Fifty Years of Communism in Russia.* University Park, Penn., 1968.

DUNN, S.   *Cultural Processes in the Baltic Area under Soviet Rule.* Berkeley, 1967.

————. *The Peasants of Central Russia*. New York, 1967.

EHRENBURG, I.   *Memoirs: 1921–1941*. Trans. T. Shebunina. New York, 1963.

ERICKSON, J.   *The Soviet High Command: A Military Political History, 1918–1941*. New York, 1962.

ERLICH, A.   *The Soviet Industrialization Debate, 1924–1928.* Cambridge, Mass., 1960.

EUDIN, X. and H. FISHER, eds.   *Soviet Russia and the West, 1920–1927.* Stanford, 1957.

EUDIN, X. and R. NORTH, eds.   *Soviet Russia and the East, 1920–1927.* Stanford, 1957.

EVTUSHENKO, E.   *A Precocious Autobiography*. New York, 1963.

FAINSOD, M.   *How Russia is Ruled*. Cambridge, Mass., 1953.

————. *Smolensk under Soviet Rule*. Cambridge, Mass., 1958.

FARNSWORTH, B.   *William C. Bullitt and the Soviet Union.* Bloomington, Ind., 1967.

FEIS, H.   *Churchill-Roosevelt-Stalin*. Princeton, 1957.

FISCHER, G.   *Soviet Opposition to Stalin*. Cambridge, Mass., 1952.

FISCHER, L.   *The Life of Lenin*. New York, 1964.

————. *Russia's Road from War to Peace*. New York, 1969.

————. *The Road to Yalta: Soviet Foreign Relations 1941–1945.* New York, 1972.

————. *The Soviets in World Affairs, 1917–1929*. 2 vols., Princeton, 1951.

FISCHER, R.   *Stalin and German Communism*. Cambridge, Mass., 1948.

FLETCHER, W.   *A Study in Survival: The Church in Russia, 1927–1943*. New York, 1965.

FOOTMAN, D.   *Civil War in Russia*. New York, 1961.

FRANKLAND, M.   *Khrushchev*. New York, 1967.

FRIERRICH, C. J. and Z. BRZEZINSKI, eds.   *Totalitarian Dictatorship and Autocracy*. Cambridge, Mass., 1956.

GALLAGHER, M.   *The Soviet History of World War II*. New York, 1963.

GANKIN, O. and H. FISHER, eds.   *The Bolsheviks and the World War: Documents*. Stanford, 1940.

GARTHOFF, R. L.   *Soviet Strategy in the Nuclear Age*. New York, 1962.

GEIGER, H. K.   *The Family in Soviet Russia*. Cambridge, Mass., 1968.

GITTINGS, J.   *Survey of the Sino-Soviet Dispute, 1963–1967*. New York, 1968.

GOLDHAGEN, E., ed. *The State of Ethnic Minorities in the Soviet Union.* New York, 1967.

GRAHAM, L. *The Soviet Academy of Sciences and the Communist Party, 1927–1932.* Princeton, 1967.

GRIFFITH, W. E. *Communism in Europe: Continuity, Change and the Sino-Soviet Dispute.*

GRUBER, H. *International Communism in the Era of Lenin: A Documentary History.* Greenwich, Conn., 1967.

GSOVSKY, V. *Soviet Civil Law.* 2 vols., Ann Arbor, Mich., 1948–49.

GSOVSKY, V. and K. GRYBOWSKI. *Government, Law and Courts in the Soviet Union and Eastern Europe.* New York, 1959.

GURIAN, W. *Bolshevism: An Introduction to Soviet Communism.* Notre Dame, Ind., 1953.

HAIMSON, L., ed. *The Mensheviks: From the Revolution of 1917 to the Second World War.* Chicago, 1974.

HAMMER, D. *The USSR: The Politics of Oligarchy.* Hinsdale, Ill., 1974.

HAYWORD, M., ed. *On Trial: The Soviet State vs. "Abram Tertz" and "Nikolai Arzhak."* New York, 1966.

HAZARD, J. *The Soviet System of Government.* Chicago, 1957.

HENDEL, S., ed. *The Soviet Crucible: Soviet Government in Theory and Practice.* Princeton, 1960.

HENDEL, S. and R. BRAHAM, eds. *The USSR After 50 Years: Promise and Reality.* New York, 1967.

HODNETT, G. and OGAREFF. *Leaders of the Soviet Republics, 1965–72.* Canberra, Australia, 1973.

HOLZMAN, F. *Soviet Taxation.* Cambridge, Mass., 1955.

HYLAND, W. and R. SHRYOCH. *The Fall of Khrushchev.* New York, 1969.

Impact of the Russian Revolution, The: The Influence of Bolshevism on the World Outside Russia. London, 1967.

INKELES, A. *Public Opinion in the Soviet Union.* Cambridge, Mass., 1959.

—— and R. BAUER. *The Soviet Citizen.* Cambridge, Mass., 1959.

—— R. BAUER and C. KLUCKHOHN. *How the Soviet System Works.* Cambridge, Mass., 1956.

JAMGOTCH, N. *Soviet-East European Dialogue: International Relations of a New Type.* Stanford, 1968.

JASNY, N. *Soviet Industrialization, 1928–1952.* Chicago, 1961.

JORAVSKY, D. *The Lysenko Affair.* Cambridge, Mass., 1970.

KANET, R. *The Soviet Union and the Developing Nations.* Baltimore, 1974.

KARCZ, J., ed. *Soviet and East European Agriculture.* Berkeley, 1967.

KASSOF, A., ed. *Prospects for Soviet Society.* New York, 1968.

KATKOV, G. *Russia, 1917: The February Revolution.* New York, 1967.

KATZ, Z. *Soviet Dissent and the Social Structure in the USSR.* Cambridge, Mass., 1970.

KEEP, J., ed. *Contemporary History in the Soviet Mirror.* New York, 1964.

KENNAN, G. F. *Russia and the West Under Lenin and Stalin.* Boston, 1961.

——. *Soviet-American Relations, 1917–1920.* Vol. 1: *Russia Leaves the War;* Vol. 2: *The Decision to Intervene.* Princeton, 1956–58.

——. *Soviet Foreign Policy, 1917–1941.* Princeton, 1960.

KERENSKY, A. *Russia and History's Turning Point.* London, 1965.

KHRUSHCHEV, N. S. *Khrushchev Remembers.* Boston, 1971.

——. *Khrushchev Remembers: The Last Testament.* New York, 1974.

KOLARZ, W. *Russia and Her Colonies.* New York, 1953.

KOLASKY, J. *Education in the Soviet Ukraine.* Toronto, 1968.

KOREY, W.   The Soviet Cage: Anti-Semitism in Russia. New York, 1973.

KRUPSKAIA, N.   Memories of Lenin. London, 1942.

LAIRD, R., ed.   Soviet Agriculture and Peasant Affairs. Lawrence, Kansas, 1963.

LANDES, L.   Politics and Oil: Moscow in the Middle East. New York, 1973.

LAQUEUR, W.   The Fate of the Revolution: Interpretations of Soviet History. New York, 1967.

————.   Russia and Germany: A Century of Conflict. Boston, 1965.

————.   The Soviet Union and the Middle East. New York, 1959.

LEHOVICH, D.   White Against Red: The Life of General A. I. Denikin. New York, 1974.

LENIN, V. I.   Imperialism: The Highest Stage of Capitalism. New York, 1927.

————.   The State and Revolution. New York, 1927.

————.   Collected Works. New York, 1927–42.

LEONHARD, W.   The Kremlin Since Stalin. New York, 1962.

LEVYTSKY, B. (Compiler).   The Stalinist Terror in the Thirties: Documentation from the Soviet Press. Stanford, 1974.

LEWIN, M.   Lenin's Last Struggle. New York, 1968.

————.   Russian Peasants and Soviet Power: A Study of Collectivization. Trans. from French. New York, 1975.

LINDEN, C.   Khrushchev and the Soviet Leadership, 1957–1964. London, 1967.

LITVINOV, P., ed.   The Demonstration on Pushkin Square. Boston, 1969.

LUCKYJ, G.   Literary Politics in the Soviet Ukraine, 1917–1934. New York, 1955.

MacINTOSH, J.   Strategy and Tactics of Soviet Foreign Policy. New York, 1962.

MAISKY, I.   Memoirs of a Soviet Ambassador: The War, 1939–1943. New York, 1968.

MALE, D. J.   Russian Peasant Organization before Collectivization. Cambridge, Eng., 1971.

MARCHENKO, A.   My Testimony. New York, 1969.

McMILLAN, P.   Khrushchev and the Arts: The Politics of Soviet Culture, 1962–1964. Cambridge, Mass., 1965.

McNEAL, R. H.   The Bolshevik Tradition: Lenin, Stalin, Khrushchev, Brezhnev. 2d edition. Englewood Cliffs, N.J., 1975.

————.   Lenin, Stalin, Khrushchev: Voices of Bolshevism. Englewood Cliffs, N.J., 1963.

MEDVEDEV, ROY.   A Question of Madness. New York, 1971.

————.   Let History Judge: The Origins and Consequences of Stalinism. New York, 1971, 1973.

MEDVEDEV, ZHORES.   The Medvedev Papers. New York, 1971.

MEISNER, B.   The Communist Party of the Soviet Union: Party Leadership. New York, 1956.

MELGUNOV, S. P.   The Bolshevik Seizure of Power. New York, 1972.

MEYER, A.   Leninism. Cambridge, Mass., 1957.

————.   Soviet Communism. New York, 1960.

MIHAILOV, M.   Moscow Summer. Trans. from Serbo-Croatian. New York, 1965.

MOORE, B.   Soviet Politics: The Dilemma of Power. Cambridge, Mass., 1950.

MORTON, H. and R. TÖKES, eds.   Soviet Politics and Society in the 1970's. New York, 1974.

MOSELY, P. E.   The Kremlin and World Politics. New York, 1961.

————, Ed. *The Soviet Union, 1922–1962: A Foreign Affairs Reader.* New York, 1963.

NETTL, J. *The Eastern Zone and Soviet Policy in Germany, 1945–1950.* New York, 1951.

————. *The Soviet Achievement.* London, 1967.

NORTH, R. *Moscow and the Chinese Communists.* 2d ed., Stanford, 1961.

NOVE, A. *The Soviet Economy.* 2d ed., New York, 1967.

————. *Was Stalin Really Necessary?* London, 1964.

NOVE, A. and J. NEWTH. *The Soviet Middle East.* London, 1967.

PAGE, S. *Lenin and World Revolution.* New York, 1959.

PAYNE, R. *The Life and Death of Lenin.* New York, 1964.

PETHYBRIDGE, R., ed. *The Development of the Communist Bloc.* Boston, 1965.

————. *A History of Postwar Russia.* New York, 1970.

PETROV, V., compiler. *"June 22, 1941," Soviet Historians and the German Invasion.* Columbia, S.C., 1968.

PIPES, R. *The Formation of the Soviet Union: Communism and Nationalism, 1917–1923.* Cambridge, Mass., 1954.

PISTRAK, L. *The Grand Tactician: Khrushchev's Rise to Power.* New York, 1961.

POSSONY, S. *Lenin: The Compulsive Revolutionary.* Chicago, 1964.

RABINOWITCH, A. *Prelude to Revolution: The July Uprising.* Bloomington, Ind., 1969.

RADKEY, O. H. *The Agrarian Foes of Bolshevism: Promise and Default of the Russian Socialist Revolutionaries, February to October 1917.* New York, 1958.

————. *The Election of the Russian Constituent Assembly of 1917.* Cambridge, Mass., 1950.

————. *The Sickle under the Hammer: the Russian Socialist Revolutionaries in the Early Months of Soviet Rule.* New York, 1963.

RAUCH, G. VON *A History of Soviet Russia.* 6th ed. New York, 1972.

REDDAWAY, P. *Uncensored Russia.* New York, 1972.

REED, J. *Ten Days That Shook the World.* New York, 1960.

RESHETAR, J. *A Concise History of the Communist Party of the Soviet Union.* New York, 1960.

————. *The Ukrainian Revolution, 1917–1920.* Princeton, 1952.

RIEBER, A. J. *Stalin and the French Communist Party, 1941–1947.* New York, 1962.

RIEBER, A. J. and R. NELSON. *A Study of the USSR and Communism: An Historical Approach.* Chicago, 1962.

RIGBY, T. H. *Communist Party Membership in the USSR, 1917–1967.* Princeton, 1968.

ROSENBERG, A. A. *A History of Bolshevism.* Garden City, N.Y., 1967.

ROSENBERG, W. G. *A. I. Denikin and the Anti-Bolshevik Movement in South Russia.* Amherst, Mass., 1961.

ROSTOW, W. W. *The Dynamics of Soviet Society.* New York, 1963.

ROTHBERG, A. *The Heirs of Stalin: Dissidence and the Soviet Regime, 1953–1970.* Ithaca, N.Y., 1972.

RUBINSTEIN, A. Z., ed. *The Foreign Policy of the Soviet Union.* New York, 1960.

SAKHAROV, A. D. *Progress, Coexistence and Intellectual Freedom.* Trans. and introd. by H. Salisbury. New York, 1968.

SALISBURY, H. *The 900 Days: The Siege of Leningrad.* New York, 1969.

SCHWARTZ, S.   *The Jews in the Soviet Union.* Syracuse, N.Y., 1951.

SCHUMAN, F.   *Government in the Soviet Union.* New York, 1961.

———.   *Russia Since 1917: Four Decades of Soviet Politics.* New York, 1957.

SCHWARTZ, H.   *Labor in the Soviet Union.* New York, 1952.

SCHWARTZ, M.   *The Foreign Policy of the USSR: Domestic Factors.* Encino, Cal., 1975.

SCHWARTZ, H.   *The Soviet Economy Since Stalin.* Philadelphia, 1965.

SCOTT, D.   *Russian Political Institutions.* New York, 1958.

SCOTT, J.   *Behind the Urals.* Boston, 1942.

SEATON, A.   *The Russo-German War, 1941–45.* New York, 1971.

SERGE, V.   *From Lenin to Stalin.* New York, 1973.

———.   *Year One of the Russian Revolution.* New York, 1972.

SETON-WATSON, H.   *The East European Revolution.* 3d ed. New York, 1956.

———.   *From Lenin to Khrushchev: The History of World Communism.* New York, 1951.

SHAPIRO, L.   *The Communist Party of the Soviet Union.* New York, 1960.

———.   *The Origins of the Communist Autocracy: Political Opposition in the Soviet State: First Phase, 1917–1922.* Cambridge, Mass., 1955.

SHULMAN, M.   *Beyond the Cold War.* New Haven, 1966.

———.   *Stalin's Foreign Policy Reappraised.* Cambridge, Mass., 1963.

SLONIM, H.   *Soviet Russian Literature: Writers and Problems.* New York, 1964.

SMITH, H.   *The Russians.* New York, 1975.

SMITH, E.   *The Young Stalin.* New York, 1967.

SMOLANSKY, O.   *The Soviet Union and the Arab East under Khrushchev.*

SOBEL, L.   *Russia's Rulers: The Khrushchev Period.* New York, 1971.

SOLZHENITSYN, A.   *The Gulag Archipelago.* 2 vols. New York, 1974–75.

———.   *Letter to the Soviet Leaders.* New York, 1974.

SONTAG, R. J. and J. BEDDIE, eds.   *Nazi-Soviet Relations, 1939–1941.* Washington, D.C., 1948.

SOUVARINE, B.   *Stalin, A Critical Survey of Bolshevism.* New York, 1939.

STALIN, J.   *Problems of Leninism.* Moscow, 1940.

———.   *Works.* Moscow, 1953–55. 13 vols.

STEENBERG, S.   *Vlasov.* New York, 1970.

STROYEN, W.   *Communist Russia and the Russian Orthodox Church, 1943–1962.* Washington, D.C., 1967.

STRUVE, G.   *Soviet Russian Literature, 1917–1945.* Norman, Okla., 1951.

SUKHANOV, N. N.   *The Russian Revolution of 1917.* 2 vols., New York, 1962.

SULZBERGER, C.   *The Coldest War: Russia's Game in China.* New York, 1974.

SWAYZE, H.   *Political Control of Literature in the USSR, 1946–1959.* Cambridge, Mass., 1962.

SWEARER, H. and M. RUSH.   *The Politics of Succession in the USSR: Materials on Khrushchev's Rise to Leadership.* Boston, 1964.

TATU, M.   *Power in the Kremlin: From Khrushchev to Kosygin.* New York, 1969.

TIMASHEFF, N.   *The Great Retreat.* New York, 1946.

———.   *Religion in Soviet Russia.* New York, 1942.

TOWSTER, J.   *Political Power in the USSR, 1917–1947.* New York, 1948.

TREADGOLD, D.   *Twentieth Century Russia.* 4th ed. Chicago, 1976.

TROTSKY, L.   *The History of the Russian Revolution.* 3 vols., New York, 1932–37.

———.   *The Revolution Betrayed.* New York, 1937.

———.   *Stalin: An Appraisal of the Man and His Influence.* New York, 1941.

TUCKER, R. C.   *The Soviet Political Mind.* New York, 1963.

———. *Stalin as Revolutionary, 1879–1929.* New York, 1973.

ULAM, A. *The Bolsheviks.* New York, 1965.

———. *Expansion and Coexistence: A History of Soviet Foreign Policy, 1917–1973.* 2d ed. New York, 1974.

———. *The New Face of Soviet Totalitarianism.* Cambridge, Mass., 1963.

———. *Stalin: The Man and His Era.* New York, 1973.

ULLMAN, R. H. *Intervention and the War. Anglo-Soviet Relations, 1917–1921.* Princeton, 1961.

VARNOCK, E. and H. FISHER, eds. *The Testimony of Kolchak and Other Siberian Materials and Documents.* Stanford, 1935.

VILLMOW, J. *The Soviet Union and Eastern Europe.* Englewood Cliffs, N.J., 1965.

VON LAUE, TH. *Why Lenin? Why Stalin?* London, 1966.

VUCINICH, A. S. *The Soviet Academy of Sciences.* Stanford, 1956.

VYSHINSKY, A. *The Law of the Soviet State.* New York, 1948.

WADE, R. *The Russian Search for Peace: February–October 1917.* Stanford, 1969.

WARTH, R. *Soviet Russia in World Politics.* New York, 1963.

WEINBERG, G. *Germany and the Soviet Union, 1939–1941.* Leiden, 1954.

WERTH, A. *Russia at War, 1941–45.* New York, 1964.

WHEELER-BENNETT, J. W. *The Forgotten Peace: Brest-Litovsk.* New York, 1939.

WOLIN, S. and R. SLUSSER, eds. *The Soviet Secret Police.* New York, 1957.

ZAGORIA, D. *The Sino-Soviet Conflict, 1955–1961.* Princeton, 1962.

ZALESKI, E. *Planning for Economic Growth in the Soviet Union, 1918–1932.* Chapel Hill, N.C., 1971.

ZHUKOV, G. E. *Marshal Zhukov's Greatest Battles.* Trans. from Russian. New York, 1969.

ZINNER, P. *Communist Strategy and Tactics in Czechoslovakia, 1918–1948.* New York, 1963.

Appendixes

Appendix A

Soviet Leaders

Chairmen of the Council of People's Commissars (Prime Ministers after 1946):

V. I. Lenin	1917–24	G. M. Malenkov	1953–55
A. I. Rykov	1924–30	N. A. Bulganin	1955–58
V. M. Molotov	1930–41	N. S. Khrushchev	1958–64
J. V. Stalin	1941–53	A. N. Kosygin	1964–

Full Members of Politburo (Presidium, 1952–66) of the Soviet Communist Party:

Lenin, V. I.	1919–24	Voznesenskii, N. A.	1947–49
Trotskii, L. D.	1919–26	Bulganin, N. A.	1948–58
Stalin, J. V.	1919–53	Kosygin, A. N.	1949–50,
Kamenev, L. B.	1919–25		1960–
Krestinskii, N. N.	1919–21	Andrianov, V. M.	1952–53
Zinoviev, G. E.	1921–26	Aristov, A. B.	1952–53,
Rykov, A. I.	1922–30		1957–61
Tomskii, M. P.	1922–30	Ignatiev, S. D.	1952–53
Bukharin, N. I.	1924–29	Korochenko, D. S.	1952–53
Molotov, V. M.	1926–57	Kuusinen, O. V.	1952–53,
Voroshilov, K. E.	1926–60		1957–64
Kalinin, M. I.	1926–46	Kuznetsov, V. V.	1952–53
Rudzutak, Ia. E.	1926–32	Malyshev, V. A.	1952–53
Kuibyshev, V. V.	1927–35	Melnikov, L. G.	1952–53
Kaganovich, L. M.	1930–57	Mikhailov, N. A.	1952–53
Kirov, S. M.	1930–34	Pervukhin, M. G.	1952–57
Kosior, S. V.	1930–38	Ponomarenko, P. K.	1952–53
Ordzhonikidze, G. K.	1930–37	Saburov, M. Z.	1952–57
Andreyev, A. A.	1932–52	Shvernik, N. M.	1952–53,
Chubar, V. Ia.	1935–38		1957–66
Mikoyan, A. I.	1935–66		1952–53,
Zhdanov, A. A.	1939–48	Suslov, M. A.	1955–
Khrushchev, N. S.	1939–64	Chesnokov, D. I.	1952–53
Beria, L. P.	1946–53	Shkiriatov, M. F.	1952–53
Malenkov, G. M.	1946–57	Kirichenko, A. I.	1955–60

Brezhnev, L. I.	1957–	Shelepin, A. N.	1964–75
Zhukov, G. K. June–Oct.	1957	Shelest, P. E.	1964–73
Furtseva, E. A.	1957–61	Mazurov, K. T.	1965–
Beliaev, N. I.	1957–60	Pelshe, A. Ia.	1966–
Ignatov, N. G.	1957–61	Grishin, V. V.	1971–
Kozlov, F. R.	1957–64	Kulakov, F. D.	1971–
Mukhitdinov, N. A.	1957–61	Kunaev, D. A.	1971–
Podgorny, N. V.	1960–	Shcherbitskii, V. V.	1971–
Polianskii, D. S.	1960–	Andropov, Iu. V.	1973–
Voronov, G. I.	1961–73	Gromyko, A. A.	1973–
Kirilenko, A. P.	1962–	Grechko, A. A.	1973–76

Appendix B

Area and Population of the Union Republics (January 1, 1973)

	Area (in 1,000 sq. km.)	*Population (in 1,000s)*	*Capital*	*Population (in 1,000s)*
Russian SFSR............	17,075.4	132,189	Moscow	7,410
Ukrainian SSR...........	603.7	48,237	Kiev	1,827
Belorussian SSR.........	207.6	9,202	Minsk	1,038
Uzbek SSR..............	447.4	12,896	Tashkent	1,504
Kazakh SSR.............	2,717.3	13,695	Alma-Ata	794
Georgian SSR...........	69.7	4,835	Tbilisi	946
Azerbaijani SSR.........	86.6	5,421	Baku	1,337
Lithuanian SSR.........	65.2	3,233	Vilnius	409
Moldavian SSR.........	33.7	3,722	Kishinev	415
Latvian SSR............	63.7	2,430	Riga	765
Kirghiz SSR............	198.5	3,145	Frunze	463
Tadshik SSR............	143.1	3,188	Dushanbe	411
Armenian SSR..........	29.8	2,667	Erevan	842
Turkmen SSR...........	488.1	2,360	Ashkhabad	272
Estonian SSR...........	45.1	1,405	Tallinn	386
USSR................	22,402.2	248,625	Moscow	

Appendix C

Largest Cities of the USSR (January 1, 1973)

1. Moscow..................	7,410,000	11. Minsk..................	1,038,000
2. Leningrad...............	4,133,000	12. Odessa..................	962,000
3. Kiev....................	1,827,000	13. Tbilisi.................	946,000
4. Tashkent...............	1,504,000	14. Cheliabinsk.............	928,000
5. Baku...................	1,337,000	15. Dnepropetrovsk.........	922,000
6. Kharkov................	1,307,000	16. Donetsk.................	919,000
7. Gorkii.................	1,238,000	17. Kazan..................	919,000
8. Novosibirsk.............	1,221,000	18. Omsk...................	905,000
9. Kuibyshev...............	1,117,000	19. Perm...................	901,000
10. Sverdlovsk..............	1,099,000	20. Volgograd...............	869,000

Appendix D

Soviet Production of Selected Industrial Items

	1913	1940	1958	1974
Pig iron..................	4.2	14.9	39.6	99.9 million tons
Steel.....................	4.3	18.3	54.9	136.0 "
Coal.....................	29.2	165.9	496.1	684.0 "
Petroleum................	10.3	31.1	113.2	459.0 "
Electric power............	2.0	48.3	235.4	975.0 billion kwh.
Automobiles (not including trucks or buses)..........	.45 (1910–15)	5.5	107.8	1,119.0 thousand vehicles

Index

Index

*This book has been set in 9 and 8 point
Primer, leaded 2 points. Part and chapter
numbers are 48 point Lydian. Part titles are
24 point Lydian and chapter titles are 18
point Lydian. The size of the type page is
27 by 46½ picas.*